# JUSTICE ADMINISTRATION
## Police, Courts, and Corrections Management

# JUSTICE ADMINISTRATION
## Police, Courts, and Corrections Management

*Fifth Edition*

**KENNETH J. PEAK**
*University of Nevada, Reno*

PEARSON
Prentice
Hall

Upper Saddle River, New Jersey 07458

**Library of Congress Cataloging-in-Publication Data**

Peak, Kenneth J.
  Justice administration : police, courts, and corrections management / Kenneth J. Peak.— 5th ed.
    p. cm.
  Includes bibliographical references and index.
  ISBN 0-13-220673-0
  1. Criminal justice, Administration of—United States. 2.  Law enforcement—United States.
3. Prison administration—United States.  I. Title.
    HV9950.P43 2007
    364.973—dc22                                                    2005034085

**Executive Editor:** Frank Mortimer, Jr.
**Associate Editor:** Sarah Holle
**Marketing Manager:** Adam Kloza
**Editorial Assistant:** Kelly Krug
**Production Editor:** Shelley Creager, TechBooks/GTS York, PA Campus
**Production Liaison:** Barbara Marttine Cappuccio
**Director of Manufacturing and Production:** Bruce Johnson
**Managing Editor:** Mary Carnis
**Manufacturing Manager:** Ilene Sanford
**Manufacturing Buyer:** Cathleen Petersen
**Senior Design Coordinator:** Mary Siener
**Cover Designer:** Vicki Kane
**Cover Image:** Getty Image, Photodisc.
**Composition:** TechBooks/GTS York, PA Campus
**Printing and Binding:** R. R. Donnelley & Sons

**Photo Credits:** Page 3, Tony Freeman/PhotoEdit; p. 22, Ryan McVay/Getty Images, Inc.-Photodisc; p. 63, AP World Wide Photos; pp. 83, 194, 358, Spencer Grant/PhotoEdit; p. 115, Simon Harding/Robert Harding World Imagery; p. 145, Mark Wilson/Getty Images, Inc.-Liaison; pp. 177, 425, Steve Gorton/Dorling Kindersley Media Library; p. 215, Philip Kamrass/The Image Works; p. 241, Mikael Karlsson/Arresting Images; p. 269, Olga Shalygin/AP World Wide Photos; p. 294, Marcel Loermans/Getty Images, Inc.-Stone Allstock; p. 329, Blue Water Photo/Index Stock Imagery, Inc; p. 391, Michael Newman/PhotoEdit; p. 459,  Nicole Bengiveno/New York Times Agency.

Pearson Education LTD.                     Pearson Education Australia PTY, Limited
Pearson Education Singapore, Pte. Ltd       Pearson Education North Asia Ltd
Pearson Education, Canada, Ltd             Pearson Educación de Mexico, S.A. de C.V.
Pearson Education–Japan                     Pearson Education Malaysia, Pte. Ltd

10  9  8  7  6  5
ISBN 0-13-220673-0

*To those administrators who strive to the greatest extent possible to be humble, moral, democratic, open to new ideas, and a little better than they were the day before. They understand that true leadership is a "first among equals" enterprise that entails much more than having a title and authority.*

# CONTENTS

## Chapter 5

## Police Issues and Practices                                           115

## Chapter 6

## Terrorism and Homeland Defense                                        145

## PART III

# THE COURTS                                                           175

### *Chapter* 7

### Court Organization and Operation                                    177

### *Chapter* 8

### Court Personnel Roles and Functions                                 194

*Chapter 11*

**Corrections Personnel Roles and Functions**                      **269**

*Chapter 12*

## Corrections Issues and Practices                                      294

# PART V

# ISSUES SPANNING THE JUSTICE SYSTEM: ADMINISTRATIVE CHALLENGES AND PRACTICES                                      327

*Chapter 13*

## Ethical Considerations                                      329

## *Chapter 14*

## **Rights of Criminal Justice Employees**    **358**

## *Chapter 15*

## **Special Challenges: Discipline, Labor Relations, and Liability**    **391**

# PREFACE

This fifth edition of *Justice Administration: Police, Courts, and Corrections Management* continues to be the sole book of its kind: a single author's examination of all facets of the criminal justice system as well as several related matters of interest to prospective and current administrators. The author has held several administrative and academic positions in a criminal justice career spanning more than 35 years; thus, this book's 17 chapters contain a palpable "real-world" flavor not found in most textbooks. (This edition has one less chapter than its predecessor, with materials from the previous edition's chapter on future developments being embedded into several other chapters; this was done to make the book's length more compatible with the number of weeks in an academic semester.)

More than 30 case studies are included throughout the text; these case studies are intended to allow the reader to experience some of the kinds of problems confronted daily by justice administrators; with a fundamental knowledge of the system and a reading of the appropriate chapters, readers should be in a position to arrive at several feasible solutions to each problem that is presented.

In addition to the chapters concerning police, courts, and corrections administration, the book also includes chapters on personnel and financial administration, rights of criminal justice employees, technologies, discipline and liability, and ethics. Articles from *Law Enforcement News* and other sources are interspersed throughout the book. Two appendices provide related Web sites and some writings of noted early philosophers. A new chapter has been added dealing with homeland defense and terrorism; in addition, new chapter sections in this edition include the "Ten Commandments" for police executives and discussions of courtroom civility and violence, the Prison Litigation Reform Act, inappropriate prison staff–inmate relationships, administering the death penalty, probation–police partnerships, computer crime and probation, workplace loyalty, drug courts, and new technologies (including those for use in dealing with terrorism as well as augmented reality and unmanned aerial vehicles).

A practice continued in this edition is the listing of key terms and concepts and chapter learning objectives, which appear at the beginning of each chapter.

Criminal justice is a people business. This book reflects that fact as it looks at human foibles and some of the problems of personnel and policy in justice administration. Thanks to many innovators in the field, a number of exciting and positive changes are occurring. The general goal of the book is to inform the reader of the primary people, practices, and terms that are utilized in justice administration.

I would like to add a brief explanation as to why a future developments component is included in several of the book's chapters. Justice administration exists in a dynamic world where society and its problems and challenges are constantly evolving. As a result, our lives will be drastically altered as the world continues to change. Our choice is either to ignore the future until it is on us or to try to anticipate what the future holds and gear our resources to cope with it. Not predicting the future would be akin to driving a car without looking out the windshield—and who can afford to drive into this new 21st century with their eyes fixed firmly on the rear-view mirror? Criminal justice administrators must anticipate what the future holds so they can bring appropriate resources and methods to bear on the problems ahead.

Finally, there may well be activities, policies, actions, and my own views with which the reader will disagree. This is not at all bad, because in the management of people and agencies there are no absolutes, only ideas and endeavors to make the system better. From its beginning (which includes an introduction by the Honorable Procter Hug, Jr.) through its final chapter, the reader is provided with a comprehensive and penetrating view of what is certainly one of the most difficult and challenging positions that one can occupy in America: the administration of a criminal justice agency. I solicit your input concerning any facet of this textbook; feel free to contact me if you have ideas for improving it.

## Acknowledgments

This edition, like its four predecessors, is the result of the professional assistance of several people. First, I continue to benefit by the guidance of the staff at Prentice Hall. This effort involved Frank Mortimer, Executive Editor, as well as Sarah Holle, Associate Editor. Copyediting was masterfully accomplished by Philip Koplin. I also wish to acknowledge the invaluable assistance of Mike Hooper, Commission on Police Officers Standards and Training, Sacramento, California, and Thomas M. Ryan, State University of New York Utica, Utica, New York, whose reviews of this edition resulted in many beneficial additions and modifications.

Ken Peak
peak_k@unr.edu

# ABOUT THE AUTHOR

Ken Peak is a full professor and former chairman of the Department of Criminal Justice, University of Nevada, Reno, where he was named "Teacher of the Year" by the university's Honor Society. He has served as chairman of the Police Section of the Academy of Criminal Justice Sciences, as well as president of the Western and Pacific Association of Criminal Justice Educators. He entered municipal policing in Kansas in 1970 and subsequently held positions as a nine-county criminal justice planner for southeast Kansas, director of a four-state Technical Assistance Institute for the Law Enforcement Assistance Administration, director of university police at Pittsburg State University, and assistant professor of criminal justice at Wichita State University. He has published 17 textbooks and two historical books on Kansas bootlegging and temperance. His other recent books include *Policing America: Methods, Issues, Challenges,* 5th ed.; *Women in Law Enforcement Careers* (with Vivian B. Lord); *Community Policing and Problem Solving: Strategies and Practices,* 4th ed. (with Ronald W. Glensor); and *Police Supervision,* 2nd. ed. (with Ronald W. Glensor and L. K. Gaines). He also has published more than 50 journal articles and chapters in edited books. His teaching interests include policing, administration, victimology, and comparative justice systems. He holds a doctorate from the University of Kansas.

# INTRODUCTION

*Judge Procter Hug, Jr.* *

Our criminal justice system has three major components: the police, the courts, and the correctional institutions. The police are responsible for protecting the public from criminal conduct; the courts are responsible for assuring that this is done in

---

*Procter Hug, Jr., graduated from Stanford Law School in 1958. After admission to the Nevada Bar, he went into private practice in the Reno area. He served as a member of the Board of Governors of the American Bar Association for 1977 and 1978, and was the Nevada State Delegate to the House of Delegates of the American Bar Association from 1972 to 1978. He was appointed a Ninth Circuit Judge by

conformance with the law and without violating constitutional rights; the correctional organizations are responsible for administering the punishment for criminal conduct and returning, where possible, violators to society as responsible citizens. Each component has its special administrative requirements, as this book well illustrates. It is important, as this book points out, that there is an important interrelationship of the administration of these organizations. The police have the responsibility of maintaining order, preserving the safety of the public, and responding to health and safety issues of individuals. Keeping this major mission in mind, police administrators must be aware of rulings of the courts that preserve the constitutional rights of all persons, including those suspected of criminal activity. It would be easy for police officers, who are on the front line protecting the public, to become understandably exasperated with having to comply with "technical" rules designed to protect the constitutional rights of all of us when they are sure that they have discovered or arrested the real criminal. Yet, administrators must assure that police conduct conforms to legal and constitutional requirements.

The courts, in evaluating the constitutionality of police conduct, must be aware of the difficult job the police are called on to do and the legitimate needs of these law enforcement officers in protecting the public. The administration of the court system should reflect this interrelated responsibility.

The correctional organizations, in administering punishment for criminal conduct, must be sure that it is humane and does not violate the rights of those being held in the system. Moreover, the administration of the correctional organization should do what it can to rehabilitate those who will be returned to society. Administrators of the police and the courts have responsibilities with regard to those returned to society through parole and probation.

This book, in reviewing the justice system as a whole, makes an important contribution to the administration of justice. It provides a basis of understanding for those who wish to enter employment in one of the areas of criminal justice and also helps those who are interested to determine which segment is attractive to them.

This book also provides a basis for thinking through the total effectiveness and fairness of our criminal justice system. It raises issues of the desirability and effectiveness of mandatory minimum sentences, sentencing guidelines, and the reasons such a high percentage of our population is in prison. It addresses the

---

President Jimmy Carter on September 15, 1977. Judge Hug assumed the position of Chief Judge of the Ninth Circuit on March 1, 1996. He stepped down as the Chief Judge on December 1, 2000, and resumed his duties as an active Article III Judge of the Ninth Circuit Court of Appeals. He has served as a member of the Board of Directors of the National Judicial College and the American Judicature Society, is a Life Member of the American Law Institute, and has served as a member of the Nevada Board of Regents of the University of Nevada and as Deputy Attorney General and General Counsel to the University of Nevada System. He was also a charter member and served on the Board of Directors of the National Association of College and University Attorneys. He was given the Distinguished Nevadan Award by the University of Nevada in 1982 and the Alumnus of the Year Award in 1988.

personnel policies governing employees of the justice system and improvements to be considered. It provides stimulus in evaluating the way we deal with drug crimes, prisoners with drug addictions, and the problem of drugs in prison.

The evaluation of our criminal justice system as a whole presented in this book provides a valuable resource, not only for understanding our criminal justice system as it currently exists, but also for evaluating its strengths and shortcomings and how it can be improved in the future.

# PART I

# JUSTICE ADMINISTRATION
## An Introduction

*This part, consisting of two chapters, sets the stage for the later analysis of criminal justice agencies and their issues, problems, functions, and challenges in Parts II through V. Chapter 1 examines the scope of justice administration and why we study it. Chapter 2 discusses organization and administration in general, looking at both how organizations are managed and how people are motivated. The introductory section of each chapter previews the specific chapter content.*

# Chapter 1

# The Study and Scope
of Justice Administration

## Key Terms and Concepts

| | |
|---|---|
| Administration | Due process |
| Conflict model | Managers |
| Consensus model | Social contract |
| Criminal justice network | Supervisors |
| Criminal justice nonsystem | System fragmentation |
| Criminal justice process | |

## Learning Objectives

As a result of reading this chapter, the student will:

- learn the concepts of *administration, manager,* and *supervisor*
- understand and be able to distinguish among criminal justice process, network, and nonsystem
- understand system fragmentation and how it affects the amount and type of crime
- be familiar with consensus and conflict theorists and their theories
- understand the two goals of the American criminal justice system
- be able to distinguish between extrinsic and intrinsic rewards and how they relate to the criminal justice system

> *[T]he ordinary administration of criminal and civil justice … contributes, more than any other circumstance, to impressing upon the minds of the people affection, esteem, and reverence towards the government.*
> —Alexander Hamilton, *The Federalist,* No. 17

> *We confide in our strength without boasting of it; we respect that of others without fearing it.*
> —Thomas Jefferson, 1793

## Why Study Justice Administration?

The new millennium began by putting many corporate administrators on the defensive or in a negative (even criminal) light. The lengthening list of disgraced and prosecuted chief executive officers (CEOs) brought a crisis of corporate leadership that affected all executives, as average citizens began paying attention to the litany of CEOs who failed in corporate governance, and indicated their disgust through actions that dramatically affected the stock markets. Administration has never been easy, and in the face of this public outrage against executives in the private sector, criminal justice administrators in the public sector must wonder whether they, too, will be pressured to put stricter controls in place and to bring greater accountability to their own organizations.

Many of us may find it difficult when we are young to imagine ourselves assuming a leadership role in later life. As one person quipped, we may even have difficulty envisioning ourselves serving as captain of our neighborhood block watch program. The fact is, however, that organizations increasingly seek people with a high level of education and experience as prospective administrators. The college experience, in addition to transmitting knowledge, is believed to make people more tolerant and secure and less susceptible to debilitating stress and anxiety than those who do not have this experience. We also assume that administration is a science that can be taught; it is not a talent that one must be born with. Unfortunately, however, administrative skills are often learned through on-the-job training; many of us who have worked for a boss with inadequate administrative skills can attest to the inadequacy of this training.

## *Purpose of the Book and Key Terms*

This book alone, as is true for any other single work on the subject of administration, cannot instantly transform the reader into a bona fide expert in organizational behavior and administrative techniques. It alone cannot prepare someone to accept the reins of administration, supervision, or leadership; formal education, training, and experience are also necessary for such undertakings.

Many good, basic books about administration exist; they discuss general aspects of leadership, the use of power and authority, and a number of specialized subjects that are beyond the reach of this book. Instead, here I simply consider some of the major theories, aspects, and issues of administration, laying the foundation for the reader's future study and experience.

Many textbooks have been written about *police* administration; a few have addressed administering courts and corrections agencies. Even fewer have analyzed justice administration from a *systems* perspective, considering all of the components of the justice system and their administration, issues, and practices. This book takes that perspective. Furthermore, most books on administration are immersed in "pure" administrative theory and concepts; in this way, the *practical* criminal justice perspective is often lost on many college and university students. Conversely, many books dwell on minute concepts, thereby obscuring the administrative principles involved. This book, which necessarily delves into some theory and specialized subject matter, focuses on the practical aspects of justice administration.

*Justice Administration* is not written as a guidebook for a major, sweeping reform of the U.S. justice system. Rather, its primary intent is to familiarize the reader with the methods and challenges of criminal justice administrators. It also challenges the reader, however, to consider what reform is desirable or even necessary and to be open-minded and visualize where changes might be implemented.

Although the terms *administration, manager,* and *supervisor* are often used synonymously, each is a unique concept that is related to the others. **Administration** encompasses both management and supervision; it is the process by which a group of people is organized and directed toward achieving the group's objective. The exact nature of the organization will vary among the different types and sizes of agencies, but the general principles and the form of administration are similar. Administration focuses on the overall organization, its mission, and its relationship with other organizations and groups external to it.

**Managers,** who are a part of administration, are most closely associated with the day-to-day operations of the various elements within the organization. **Supervisors** are involved in the direction of staff members in their daily activities, often on a one-to-one basis. Confusion may arise because a chief administrator may act in all three capacities. Perhaps the most useful and easiest description is to define top-level personnel as administrators, mid-level personnel as managers, and those who oversee the work as it is being done as supervisors.[1] In policing, for example, although we tend to think of the chief executive as the administrator, the bureau chiefs or commanders as managers, and the sergeants as supervisors, it is important to note that often all three of these roles are required of one administrator.

The terms *police* and *law enforcement* are generally used interchangeably. Many people in the police field believe, however, that the police do more than merely enforce laws; they prefer to use the term police.

## *Organization of the Book*

To understand the challenges that administrators of justice organizations face, we first need to place justice administration within the big picture. Thus, in Part I, Justice Administration: An Introduction, I discuss the organization, administration, and general nature of the U.S. justice system; the state of our country with respect to crime and government control; and the evolution of justice administration in all of its three components: police, courts, and corrections.

Parts II, III, and IV, which discuss contemporary police, courts, and corrections administration, respectively, follow the same organization: The first chapter of each part deals with the *organization and operation* of the component, followed in the next chapter by an examination of the component's *personnel roles and functions,* and in the third chapter, by a discussion of *issues and practices* (including future considerations). Each of these chapters concludes with several case studies, presenting the kinds of problems confronted daily by justice administrators. Several discussion questions follow each case study. With a fundamental knowledge of the system and a reading of the chapters in each part, readers should be able to engage in some critical analysis—even, it is hoped, some spirited discussions—and arrive at several feasible solutions to the problems presented.

Part V examines administrative problems and factors that influence the entire justice system, including the rights of criminal justice employees, financial administration, and technology for today and the future.

This initial chapter sets the stage for later discussions of the criminal justice system and its administration. I first consider whether the justice system comprises a "process," a "network," a "nonsystem," or a true "system." A discussion of the legal and historical bases for justice and administration follows (an examination of what some great thinkers have said about governance in general is provided at the end of the book, in Appendix II). The differences between public-sector and private-sector administration are reviewed next, and the chapter concludes with a discussion of policymaking in justice administration. After completing this chapter, the reader will have a better grasp of the structure, purpose, and foundation of our criminal justice system.

# A True *System* of Justice?

What do justice administrators—police, courts, and corrections officials— actually *administer*? Do they provide leadership over a system that has succeeded in accomplishing its mission? Do individuals within the system work amiably and communicate well with one another? Do they all share the same goals? Do their efforts result in crime reduction? In short, do they compose a *system*? I now turn to these questions, taking a fundamental yet expansive view of justice administration.

The U.S. criminal justice system attempts to decrease criminal behavior through a wide variety of uncoordinated and sometimes uncomplementary efforts. Each system component—police, courts, and corrections—has varying degrees of responsibility and discretion for dealing with crime. Each system component fails, however, to engage in any coordinated planning effort; hence, relations among and between these components are often characterized by friction, conflict, and deficient communication. Role conflicts also serve to ensure that planning and communication are stifled.

For example, one role of the police is to arrest suspected offenders. Police typically are not judged by the public on the quality (e.g., having probable cause) of arrests, but on their number. Prosecutors often complain that police provide case reports of poor quality. Prosecutors, for their part, are partially judged by their success in obtaining convictions; a public defender or defense attorney is judged by success in getting suspected offenders' charges dropped. The courts are very independent in their operation, largely sentencing offenders as they see fit. Corrections agencies are torn between the philosophies of punishment and rehabilitation, and in the view of many, wind up performing neither function with any large degree of success. These agencies are further burdened with overcrowded conditions, high caseloads, and antiquated facilities.[2] Unfortunately, this situation has existed for several decades and continues today.

This criticism of the justice system or process—that it is fragmented and rife with role conflicts and other problems—is a common refrain. Following are several views of the criminal justice system as it currently operates: the process, network, and nonsystem points of view. Following the discussion of those three viewpoints, I consider whether criminal justice truly represents a system.

## *A Criminal Justice* **Process?**

What is readily seen in the foregoing discussion is that our criminal justice system may not be a system at all. Given its current operation and fragmentation, it might be better described as a **criminal justice process.** As a process, it involves the decisions and actions taken by an institution, offender, victim, or society that influence the offender's movement into, through, or out of the justice system.[3] In its purest form, the criminal justice process occurs as shown in Figure 1.1. Note that the horizontal effects result from factors such as the amount of crime, the number of prosecutions, and the type of court disposition affecting the population in correctional facilities and rehabilitative programs. Vertical effects represent the primary system steps or procedures.[4]

At one end of this process are the police, who understandably may view their primary role as getting lawbreakers off the street. At the other end of the process are the corrections officials, who may see their role as being primary custodial in nature. Somewhere in between are the courts, which try to ensure a fair application of the law to each case coming to the bar.

As a process, the justice system cannot reduce crime by itself, nor can any of the component parts afford to be insensitive to the needs and problems of the other parts. In criminal justice planning jargon, "You can't rock one end of the boat." In other words, every action has a reaction, especially in the justice process. If, say, a bond issue for funds to provide 10 percent more police officers on the streets is passed in a community, the additional arrests made by those added police personnel will have a decided impact on the courts and corrections components. Obviously, although each component operates largely on its own, the actions and reactions of each with respect to crime will send ripples throughout the process.

Much of the failure to deal effectively with crime may be attributed to organizational and administrative fragmentation of the justice process. Fragmentation exists among the components of the process, within the individual components, among political jurisdictions, and among persons.

## *A Criminal Justice* **Network?**

Other observers contend that U.S. justice systems constitute a **criminal justice network.**[5] According to Steven Cox and John Wade, the justice system functions much like a television or radio network whose stations share many programs, but in which each station also presents programs that the network does not air on other stations. The network appears as a three-dimensional model in which the public, legislators, police, prosecutors, judges, and correctional officials interact with one another and with others who are outside the traditionally conceived criminal justice system.[6]

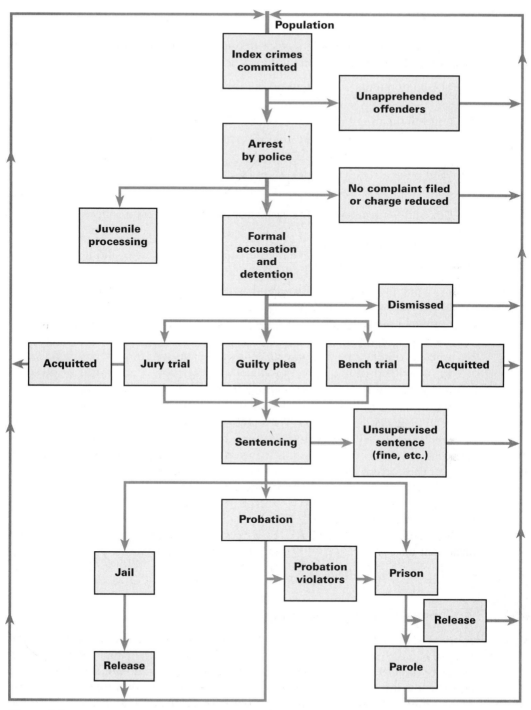

**Figure 1.1**

Criminal Justice Model. *Source:* Adapted from the President's Commission on Law Enforcement and Administration of Justice, *The Challenge of Crime in a Free Society* (Washington, D.C.: U.S. Government Printing Office, 1967), pp. 262–263.

Furthermore, the criminal justice network is said to be based on several key yet erroneous assumptions, including the following:

1. The components of the network cooperate and share similar goals.
2. The network operates according to a set of formal procedural rules to ensure uniform treatment of all persons, the outcome of which constitutes "justice."
3. Each person accused of a crime receives due process and is presumed innocent until proven guilty.
4. Each person receives a speedy, public trial before an impartial jury of his or her peers and is represented by competent legal counsel.[7]

Cox and Wade asserted that these key assumptions are erroneous for the following reasons:

1. The three components have incompatible goals and are continually competing with one another for budgetary dollars.
2. Evidence indicates that blacks and whites, male and female individuals, and middle-class and lower-class citizens receive differential treatment in the criminal justice network.
3. Some persons are prosecuted, some are not; some are involved in plea bargaining, others are not; some are convicted and sent to prison, whereas others convicted of the same type of offense are not. A great deal of the plea negotiation process remains largely invisible, such as "unofficial probation" with juveniles. In addition, Cox and Wade argued, considerable evidence points to the fact that criminal justice employees do not presume their clients or arrestees to be innocent.
4. Finally, these proponents of a "network" view of the justice process argued that the current backlog of cases does not ensure a speedy trial, even though a vast majority (at least 90 percent) of all arrestees plead guilty prior to trial.[8]

Adherents of this position, therefore, believe that our criminal justice system is probably not a just network in the eyes of the poor, minority groups, or individual victims. Citizens, they also assert, may not know what to expect from such a network. Some believe that the system does not work as a network at all and that this conception is not worth their support.[9]

## *A Criminal Justice* Nonsystem?

Many observers argue that the three components of the justice system actually comprise a **criminal justice nonsystem.** They maintain that the three segments of the U.S. system that deal with criminal behavior do not always function in harmony and that the system is neither efficient enough to create a credible fear of punishment nor fair enough to command respect for its values.

Indeed, these theorists are given considerable support by the President's Commission on Law Enforcement and the Administration of Justice (commonly known as the *Crime Commission*), which made the following comment:

The system of criminal justice used in America to deal with those crimes it cannot prevent and those criminals it cannot deter is not a monolithic, or even a consistent, system. It was not designed or built in one piece at one time. Its philosophic core is that a person may be punished by the Government, if, and only if, it has been proven by an impartial and deliberate process that he has violated a specific law. Around that core, layer upon layer of institutions and procedures, some carefully constructed and some improvised, some inspired by principle and some by expediency, have accumulated. Parts of the system—magistrates, courts, trial by jury, bail—are of great antiquity. Other parts—juvenile courts, probation and parole, professional policemen—are relatively new. Every village, town, county, city and State has its own criminal justice system, and there is a Federal one as well. All of them operate somewhat alike, no two of them operate precisely alike.[10]

Alfred Cohn and Roy Udolf stated that criminal justice "is not a system, and it has little to do with justice as that term is ordinarily understood."[11] Also in this school of thought are Burton Wright and Vernon Fox, who asserted that "the criminal justice system . . . is frequently criticized because it is not a coordinated structure—not really a system. In many ways this is true."[12]

These writers would probably agree that little has changed since 1971, when *Newsweek* stated in a special report entitled "Justice on Trial" that

America's system of criminal justice is too swamped to deliver more than the roughest justice—and too ragged really to be called a system. "What we have," says one former government hand, "is a non-system in which the police don't catch criminals, the courts don't try them, and the prisons don't reform them. The system, in a word, is in trouble. The trouble has been neglect. The paralysis of the civil courts, where it takes five years to get a judgment in a damage suit . . . the courts—badly managed, woefully undermanned and so inundated with cases that they have to run fast just to stand still."[13]

Unfortunately, in many jurisdictions, those words still ring true. Too often, today's justice administrators cannot be innovators or reformers, but rather simply "make do." As one law professor stated, "Oliver Wendell Holmes could not survive in our criminal court. How can you be an eminent jurist when you have to deal with this mess?"[14]

Those who hold that the justice system is in reality no system at all can also point to the fact that many practitioners in the field (police, judges, prosecutors, correctional workers, private attorneys) and academicians concede that the entire justice system is in crisis, even rapidly approaching a major breakdown. They can cite problems everywhere—high numbers of police calls for service and overcrowded court dockets and prison populations. In short, they contend that the system is in a state of dysfunction, largely as a result of its fragmentation and lack of cohesion.[15]

**System fragmentation** is largely believed to directly affect the amount and type of crime that exists. Contributing to this fragmentation are the wide discretionary powers possessed by actors in the justice system. For example, police officers (primarily those having the least experience, education, and training) have great discretion over whom they arrest and are effectively able to dictate policy as they go about performing their duties. Here again, the Crime Commission was moved to comment as follows, realizing that how the police officer moves around his or her territory depends largely on this discretion:

> Crime does not look the same on the street as it does in a legislative chamber. How much noise or profanity makes conduct "disorderly" within the meaning of the law? When must a quarrel be treated as a criminal assault: at the first threat, or at the first shove, or at the first blow, or after blood is drawn, or when a serious injury is inflicted? How suspicious must conduct be before there is "probable cause," the constitutional basis for an arrest? Every [officer], however sketchy or incomplete his education, is an interpreter of the law.[16]

Judicial officers also possess great discretionary latitude. State statutes require judges to provide deterrence, retribution, rehabilitation, and incapacitation—all in the same sentence. Well-publicized studies of the sentencing tendencies of judges—in which participants were given identical facts in cases and were to impose sentences based on the offender's violation of the law—have demonstrated considerable discretion and unevenness in the judges' sentences. The nonsystem advocates believe this to be further evidence that a basic inequality exists—an inequality in justice that is communicated to the offender.[17]

Finally, fragmentation also occurs in corrections—the part of the criminal justice process that the U.S. public sees the least of and knows the least about. Indeed, as the Crime Commission noted, the federal government, all 50 states, the District of Columbia, and most of the country's 3,047 counties now engage in correctional activities of some form or another. Each level of government acts independent of the others, and responsibility for the administration of corrections is divided within given jurisdictions as well.[18]

With this fragmentation comes polarity in identifying and establishing the primary goals of the system. The police, enforcing the laws, emphasize community protection; the courts weigh both sides of the issue—individual rights and community needs; and corrections facilities work with the individual. Each of these groups has its own perception of the offender, creating goal conflict; that is, the goal of the police and the prosecutor is to get the transgressor off the street, which is antithetical to the "caretaker" role of the corrections worker, who often wants to rehabilitate and return the offender to the community. The criminal justice process does not allow many alternative means of dealing with offenders. The nonsystem adherent believes that eventually the offender will become a mere statistic, more important on paper than as a human being.[19]

Because the justice process lacks sufficient program and procedural flexibility, these adherents argue, its workers either can circumvent policies, rules, and regulations or adhere to organizational practices they know are, at times, dysfunctional. (As evidence of the former, they point to instances of *informal* treatment of criminal cases; e.g., a police officer "bends" someone's constitutional rights in order to return stolen property to its rightful owner; or a juvenile probation officer, without a solid case but with strong suspicion, warns a youth that any further infractions will result in formal, court-involved proceedings.)

### *Or a True Criminal Justice* System?

That all of the foregoing perspectives on the justice system are grounded in truth is probably evident by now. In many ways, the police, courts, and corrections components work and interact to function like a process, a network, or even a nonsystem. However, the justice system may still constitute a true system. As Willa Dawson stated, "Administration of justice can be regarded as a system by most standards. It may be a poorly functioning system but it does meet the criteria nonetheless. The systems approach is still in its infancy."[20] J. W. La Patra added that "I do believe that a criminal justice system [CJS] does exist, but that it functions very poorly. The CJS is a loosely connected, nonharmonious, group of social entities."[21]

To be fair, however, perhaps this method of dealing with offenders is best after all; it may be that having a well-oiled machine—in which all activities are coordinated, goals and objectives are unified, and communication between participants is maximized, all serving to grind out "justice" in a highly efficacious manner—may not be what we truly want or need in a democracy.

I hope that I have not belabored the subject; however, it is important to establish early in this book the type of system and components that you, as a potential criminal justice administrator, may encounter. You can reconcile for yourself the differences of opinion described earlier. In this book, I adhere to the notion that even with all of its disunity and lack of fluidity, what criminal justice officials administer in the United States is a system. Nonetheless, it is good to look at its operation and shortcomings and, as stated earlier, confront the criminal justice system's problems and possible areas for improvement.

Now that we have a systemic view of what it is that criminal justice managers actually administer, it would be good to look briefly at how they go about doing it. I first consider the legal and historical bases that created the United States as a democracy regulated by a government and by a system of justice; I include the consensus–conflict continuum, with the social contract on one end and the maintenance of the status quo/repression on the other. Next, I distinguish between administration and work in the public and private sectors because the styles, incentives, and rewards of each are, by their very nature, quite different. This provides the foundation for the final point of discussion, a brief look at the policymaking process in criminal justice agencies.

## The Foundations of Justice and Administration: Legal and Historical Bases

Given that our system of justice is founded on a large, powerful system of government, the following questions must be addressed: From where is that power derived? How can governments presume to maintain a system of laws that effectively governs its people and, furthermore, a legal system that exists to punish persons who willfully suborn those laws? We now consider the answers to those questions.

## *The Consensus versus Conflict Debate*

U.S. society has innumerable lawbreakers. Most of them are easily handled by the police and do not challenge the legitimacy of the law while being arrested and incarcerated for violating it. Nor do they challenge the system of government that enacts the laws or the justice agencies that carry them out. The stability of our government for more than 200 years is a testimony to the existence of a fair degree of consensus as to its legitimacy.[22] Thomas Jefferson's statements in the Declaration of Independence are as true today as the day when he wrote them and are accepted as common sense:

> We hold these truths to be self-evident, that all men are created equal, that they are endowed by their Creator with certain inalienable Rights, that among these are Life, Liberty and the pursuit of Happiness—That to secure these rights, Governments are instituted among Men, deriving their just powers from the consent of the governed. That whenever any Form of Government becomes destructive of these ends, it is the Right of the People to alter or abolish it.

The principles of the Declaration are almost a paraphrase of John Locke's *Second Treatise on Civil Government,* which justifies the acts of government on the basis of Locke's theory of social contract. In the state of nature, people, according to Locke, were created by God to be free, equal, independent, and with inherent inalienable rights to life, liberty, and property. Each person had the right of self-protection against those who would infringe on these liberties. In Locke's view, although most people were good, some would be likely to prey on their fellows, who in turn would constantly have to be on guard against such evildoers. To avoid this brutish existence, people joined together, forming governments to which they surrendered their rights of self-protection. In return, they received governmental protection of their lives, property, and liberty. As with any contract, each side has benefits and considerations; people give up their rights to protect themselves and receive protection in return. Governments give protection and receive loyalty and obedience in return.[23]

Locke believed that the chief purpose of government was the protection of property. Properties would be joined together to form the commonwealth. Once the people unite into a commonwealth, they cannot withdraw from it, nor can their lands be removed from it. Property holders become members of that commonwealth only with their express consent to submit to the government of the commonwealth. This is Locke's famous theory of *tacit consent*: "Every Man . . . doth hereby give his *tacit Consent,* and is as far forth obliged to Obedience to the Laws of the Government."[24] Locke's theory essentially describes an association of landowners.[25]

Another theorist connected with the **social contract** theory is Thomas Hobbes, who argued that all people were essentially irrational and selfish. He maintained that people had just enough rationality to recognize their situation and to come together to form governments for self-protection, agreeing "amongst themselves to submit to some Man, or Assembly of men, voluntarily, on confidence to be protected by him against all others."[26] Therefore, they existed in a state of consensus with their governments.

Jean-Jacques Rousseau, a conflict theorist, differed substantively from both Hobbes and Locke, arguing that "Man is born free, but everywhere he is in chains."[27] Like Plato, Rousseau associated the loss of freedom and the creation of conflict in modern societies with the development of private property and the unequal distribution of resources. Rousseau described conflict between the ruling group and the other groups in society, whereas Locke described consensus within the ruling group and the need to use force and other means to ensure the compliance of the other groups.[28]

Thus, the primary difference between the consensus and conflict theorists with respect to their view of government vis-à-vis the governed concerns their evaluation of the legitimacy of the actions of ruling groups in contemporary societies. Locke saw those actions as consistent with natural law, describing societies as consensual, and arguing that any conflict was illegitimate and could be repressed by force and other means. Rousseau evaluated the actions of ruling groups as irrational and selfish, creating conflicts among the various groups in society.[29]

This debate is important because it plays out the competing views of humankind toward its ruling group; it also has relevance with respect to the kind of justice system (or process) we have. The systems model has been criticized for implying a greater level of organization and cooperation among the various agencies of justice than actually exists. The word *system* conjures an idea of machinelike precision in which wasted effort, redundancy, and conflicting actions are nearly nonexistent; our current justice system does not possess such a level of perfection. As mentioned earlier, conflicts among and within agencies are rife, goals are not shared by the system's three components, and the system may move in different directions. Therefore, the systems approach is part of the **consensus model** point of view, which assumes that all parts of the system work toward a common goal.[30] The **conflict model,** holding that agency interests tend to make actors within the system self-serving, provides the other approach. This view notes the pressures for success, promotion, and general accountability, which together result in fragmented efforts of the system as a whole, leading to a criminal justice nonsystem.[31]

This debate also has relevance for criminal justice administrators. Assume a consensus–conflict continuum, with social contract (the people totally allow government to use its means to protect them) on one end and class repression on the other. That our administrators *not* allow their agencies to "drift" too far to one end of the continuum or the other is of paramount importance. Americans cannot allow the compliance or conflict that would result at either end; the safer point is toward the middle of the continuum, where people are not totally dependent on their government for protection and maintain enough control to prevent totalitarianism.

## *Crime Control through Due Process*

Both the systems and nonsystems models of criminal justice provide a view of agency relationships. Another way to view American criminal justice is in terms of its goals. Two primary goals are (1) the need to enforce the law and maintain social order and (2) the need to protect people from injustice.[32] The first, often referred to as the crime control model, values the arrest and conviction of criminal offenders. The second, because of its emphasis on individual rights, is commonly known as the due process model. **Due process**—found in the Bill of Rights, particularly in the Fourteenth Amendment—is a central and necessary part of our system. It requires a careful and informed consideration of the facts of each individual case. Due process seeks to ensure that innocent people are not convicted of crimes.

The dual goals of crime control and due process are often suggested to be in constant and unavoidable opposition to each other. Many critics of criminal justice as it exists in the United States argue that our attempt to achieve "justice" for offenders too often occurs at the expense of due process. Other, more conservative observers believe that our system is too lenient with its clients, coddling offenders rather than protecting the innocent.

We are never going to be in a position to avoid ideological conflicts such as these. However, some observers, such as Frank Schmalleger, believe it is realistic to think of the U.S. system of justice as representative of *crime control through due process*.[33] This model of crime control is infused with the recognition of individual rights, which provides the conceptual framework for this book.

## Public-Sector versus Private-Sector Administration

That people derive positive personal experiences from their work has long been recognized.[34] Because work is a vital part of our lives and carries tremendous meaning in terms of our personal identity and happiness, the right match of person to job has long been recognized as a determinant of job satisfaction.[35] Factors such as job importance, accomplishment, challenge, teamwork, management fairness, and rewards become very important.

People in both the public (i.e., government) and private (e.g., retail business) sectors derive positive personal satisfactions from their work. The means by which they arrive at those positive feelings and are rewarded for their efforts, however, are often quite different. Basically, whereas private businesses and corporations can use a panoply of *extrinsic* (external) rewards to motivate and reward their employees, people working in the public sector must achieve job satisfaction primarily through *intrinsic* (internal) rewards.

Extrinsic rewards include perquisites such as financial compensation (salary and benefits package), a private office, a key to the executive washroom, bonuses, trips, a company car, awards (including designations such as the employee of the month or the insurance industry's "million-dollar roundtable"), an expense account, membership in country clubs and organizations, and a job title. The title assigned to a job can affect one's general perceptions of the job regardless of actual job content. For example, the role once known disparagingly as "grease monkey" in a gasoline service station has commonly become known as "lubrication technician," garbage collectors have become "sanitation engineers," and so on. Enhancement of job titles is done to add job satisfaction and extrinsic rewards to what may often be lackluster positions.

Corporations often devote tremendous sums of time and money to bestowing extrinsic rewards, incentives, and job titles to employees to enhance their job satisfaction. These rewards, of course, cannot and do not exist in the public sector anywhere near the extent that they do in the private sector.

As indicated earlier, public-sector workers must seek and obtain job satisfaction primarily from within—through intrinsic means. These workers, unable to become wealthy through their salaries and to be in a position that is filled with perks, need jobs that are gratifying and that intrinsically make them feel good about themselves and what they accomplish. Practitioners often characterize criminal justice work as intrinsically rewarding, providing a sense of worth in making the world a little better place in which to live. These employees also seek appreciation from their supervisors and co-workers and generally enjoy challenges.

To be successful, administrators should attempt to understand the personalities, needs, and motivations of their employees and attempt to meet those needs and provide motivation to the extent possible. The late Sam Walton, the multi-billionaire founder of Wal-Mart stores, provided a unique example of the attempt to do this. One night, Walton could not sleep, so he went to a nearby all-night bakery in Bentonville, Arkansas, bought four dozen doughnuts, and took them to a distribution center where he chatted with graveyard-shift Wal-Mart employees. From that chat, he discovered that two more shower stalls were needed at that location.[36] Walton obviously solicited—and valued—employee input and was concerned about their morale and working conditions. Although Walton was known to be unique in his business sense, these are elements of administration that can be applied by all public administrators.

## Policymaking in Justice Administration

The most complex and comprehensive approach to effecting planned change in criminal justice is by creating a *policy*. Policies vary in the complexity of the rule or guidelines being implemented and the amount of discretion given to those who apply them. For example, police officers are required to read *Miranda* warnings to suspects before they begin questioning them if the information might later be used in court against the defendant. This is an example where discretion is relatively constrained, although the Supreme Court has formulated specific exceptions to the rule. Sometimes policies are more complex, such as the "social" policy of President Lyndon Johnson's War on Poverty in the 1960s. Organizations, too, create policies specifying how they are going to accomplish their mission, expend their resources, and so on.[37]

Imagine the following scenario. Someone in criminal justice operations (e.g., a city or county manager or a municipal or criminal justice planner) is charged with formulating an omnibus policy with respect to crime reduction. He or she might begin by trying to list all related variables that contribute to the crime problem: poverty; employment; demographics of people residing within the jurisdiction; environmental conditions (such as housing density and conditions and slum areas); mortality, morbidity, and suicide rates; educational levels of the populace; and so on.

The administrator would request more specific information from each justice administrator within the jurisdiction to determine where problems might exist in the practitioners' view of the police, courts, and corrections subsystems. For example, a police executive would contribute information concerning calls for service, arrests, and crime data (including offender information and crime information—time of day, day of week, methods, locations, targets, and so on). The status of existing programs, such as community policing and crime prevention, would also be provided. From the courts, information would be sought concerning the sizes of civil and criminal court dockets and backlogs ("justice delayed is justice denied"). Included in this report would be input from the prosecutor's office concerning the quality and quantity of police reports and arrests, as well as data on case dismissals and conviction rates at trial. From corrections administrators would come the average officer caseload and recidivism and revocation rates. Budgetary information would certainly be solicited from all subsystems, as well as miscellaneous data regarding personnel levels, training levels, and so on. Finally, the administrator would attempt to formulate a crime policy, setting forth goals and objectives for addressing the jurisdiction's needs.

As an alternative, the policymaker could approach this task in a far less complex manner, simply setting, either explicitly or without conscious thought, the relatively simple goal of "keeping crime down." This goal might be compromised or complicated by other factors, such as a bullish economy. This administrator could in fact disregard most of the other variables discussed earlier as being beyond his or her current needs and interest and would not even attempt to consider them as immediately relevant. The criminal justice practitioners would not be pressed to attempt to provide information and critical analyses. If pressed for time (as is often the case in these real-life scenarios), the planner would readily admit that these variables were being ignored.[38]

Because executives and planners of the alternative approach expect to achieve their goals only partially, they anticipate repeating endlessly the sequence just described as conditions and aspirations change and as accuracy of prediction improves. Realistically, however, the first of these two approaches assumes intellectual capacities and sources of information that people often do not possess; furthermore, the time and money that can be allocated to a policy problem are limited. Public agencies are in effect usually too hamstrung to practice the first method; it is the second method that is followed. Curiously, however, the literature on decision making, planning, policy formulation, and public administration formalizes and preaches the first approach.[39] The second method is much neglected in this literature.

In the United States, probably no part of government has attempted a comprehensive analysis and overview of policy on crime (the first method just described). Thus, making crime policy is at best a rough process. Without a more comprehensive process, we cannot possibly understand, for example, how a variety of problems—education, housing, recreation, employment, race, and policing methods—might encourage or discourage juvenile delinquency. What we normally engage in is a comparative analysis of the results of similar past policy decisions. This explains why justice administrators often believe that outside experts or academics are not helpful to them—why it is safer to "fly by the seat of one's pants." Theorists often urge the administrator to go the long way to the solution of his or her problems, following the scientific method, when the administrator knows that the best available theory will not work. Theorists, for their part, do not realize that the administrator is often in fact practicing a systematic method.[40] So, what may appear to be mere muddling through is both highly praised as a sophisticated form of policymaking and decision making as well as soundly denounced as no method at all. What society needs to bear in mind is that justice administrators possess an intimate knowledge of past consequences of actions that outsiders do not. Although seemingly less effective and rational, this method, according to policymaking experts, has merit. Indeed, this method is commonly used for problem solving in which the means and ends are often impossible to separate, aspirations or objectives undergo constant development, and drastic simplification of the complexity of the real world is urgent if problems are to be solved in reasonable periods of time.[41]

## Summary

This chapter presented the foundation for the study of justice administration. It also established the legal existence of governments, laws, and the justice agencies that administer them. It demonstrated that the three components of the justice system are independent and fragmented and often work at odds with one another toward the accomplishment of the system's overall mission.

## Questions for Review

1. Do the three justice components (police, courts, and corrections) constitute a true system or are they more appropriately described as a process or a true nonsystem? Defend your response.
2. What are the legal and historical bases for a justice system and its administration in the United States? Why is the conflict-versus-consensus debate important?

3. What are some of the substantive ways in which public-sector and private-sector administration are similar? How are they dissimilar?

4. Which method, a rational process or just muddling through, appears to be used in criminal justice policymaking today? Which method is probably best, given real-world realities? Explain your response.

## Notes

1. For a more thorough explication of these terms and roles, particularly as applied in policing, see Richard N. Holden, *Modern Police Management* (Upper Saddle River, N.J.: Prentice Hall, 1986).
2. Michael E. O'Neill, Ronald F. Bykowski, and Robert S. Blair, *Criminal Justice Planning: A Practical Approach* (San Jose, Calif.: Justice Systems Development, 1976), p. 5.
3. Ibid., p. 12.
4. Ibid.
5. Steven M. Cox and John E. Wade, *The Criminal Justice Network: An Introduction,* 2nd ed. (Dubuque, Iowa: Wm. C. Brown, 1989), p. 1.
6. Ibid., p. 4.
7. Ibid., p. 12.
8. Ibid., pp. 13–14.
9. Philip H. Ennis, "Crime, Victims, and the Police," *Transaction* 4 (June 1967):36–44.
10. The President's Commission on Law Enforcement and the Administration of Justice, *The Challenge of Crime in a Free Society* (Washington, D.C.: U.S. Government Printing Office, 1967), p. 7.
11. Alfred Cohn and Roy Udolf, *The Criminal Justice System and Its Psychology* (New York: Van Nostrand Reinhold, 1979), p. 152.
12. Burton Wright and Vernon Fox, *Criminal Justice and the Social Sciences* (Philadelphia: W. B. Saunders, 1978).
13. "Justice on Trial: A Special Report," *Newsweek* (March 8, 1971):16.
14. Ibid., p. 18.
15. Alan R. Coffey and Edward Eldefonso, *Process and Impact of Justice* (Beverly Hills, Calif.: Glencoe Press, 1975), p. 32.
16. The President's Commission, *Challenge of Crime in a Free Society,* p. 5.
17. Coffey and Eldefonso, *Process and Impact of Justice,* p. 35.
18. Ibid., p. 39.
19. Ibid., p. 41.
20. Willa Dawson, "The Need for a System Approach to Criminal Justice," in Donald T. Shanahan (ed.), *The Administration of Justice System—An Introduction* (Boston: Holbrook, 1977), p. 141.
21. J. W. La Patra, *Analyzing the Criminal Justice System* (Lexington, Mass.: Lexington Books, 1978), p. 75.
22. Alexander B. Smith and Harriet Pollack, *Criminal Justice: An Overview* (New York: Holt, Rinehart and Winston, 1980), p. 9.
23. Ibid., p. 10.
24. Ibid., p. 366.

25. Thomas J. Bernard, *The Consensus-Conflict Debate: Form and Content in Social Theories* (New York: Columbia University Press, 1983), p. 78.

26. Thomas Hobbes, *Leviathan* (New York: E. P. Dutton, 1950), pp. 290-291.

27. Jean-Jacques Rousseau, "A Discourse on the Origin of Inequality," in G. D. H. Cole (ed.), *The Social Contract and Discourses* (New York: E. P. Dutton, 1946), p. 240.

28. Bernard, *Consensus-Conflict Debate,* pp. 83, 85.

29. Ibid., p. 86.

30. Frank Schmalleger, *Criminal Justice Today,* 8th ed. (Upper Saddle River, N.J.: Prentice Hall, 2005), p. 18.

31. One of the first publications to express the nonsystems approach was the American Bar Association, *New Perspective on Urban Crime* (Washington, D.C.: ABA Special Committee on Crime Prevention and Control, 1972).

32. Schmalleger, *Criminal Justice Today,* p. 24.

33. Ibid., p. 25.

34. Fernando Bartolome and Paul A. Lee Evans, "Professional Lives Versus Private Lives: Shifting Patterns of Managerial Commitment," *Organizational Dynamics* 7 (1982):2-29; Ronald C. Kessler and James A. McRae, Jr., "The Effect of Wives' Employment on the Mental Health of Married Men and Women," *American Sociological Review* **47** (1979):216-227.

35. Robert V. Presthus, *The Organizational Society* (New York: Alfred A. Knopf, 1962).

36. Joseph A. Petrick and George E. Manning, "How to Manage Morale," *Personnel Journal* 69 (October 1990):87.

37. Wayne N. Welsh and Philip W. Harris, *Criminal Justice Policy and Planning,* 2nd ed. (Cincinnati, Ohio: Lexis/Nexis/Anderson, 2004), p. 5.

38. This scenario is modeled on one set out by Harvard economist, Charles E. Lindblom, "The Science of 'Muddling Through,'" *Public Administration Review* **19** (Spring 1959):79-89.

39. Ibid., p. 80.

40. Ibid., p. 87.

41. Ibid., p. 88.

# Chapter 2

# Organization
# and Administration
## Principles and Practices

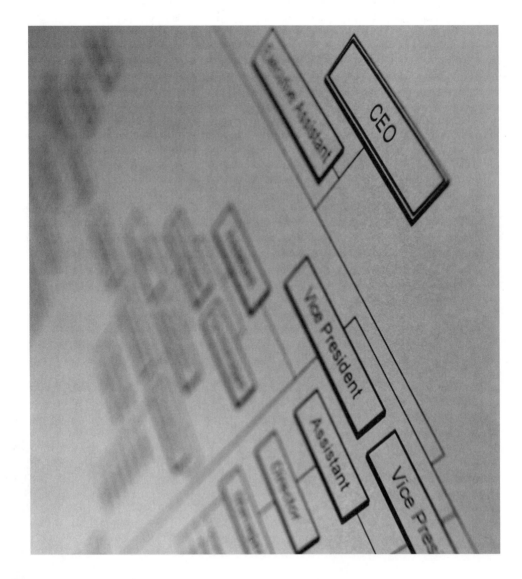

# Key Terms and Concepts

| | |
|---|---|
| Autocratic leaders | Maintenance or hygiene factors |
| Consciously coordinated | Management |
| Decoding | Medium |
| Democratic leader | Motivational factors |
| Empathy | Organization |
| Encoding | Reception |
| Feedback | Relatively identifiable boundary |
| Generation X/Y | Social entity |
| Grapevine | Transmission |
| Laissez-faire leader | Unity of command |
| Leadership | |

# Learning Objectives

As a result of reading this chapter, the student will:

- be familiar with the elements of organization
- know the different principles of organizational structure
- understand the term *management*
- be familiar with the different aspects of communication and their role in the criminal justice system
- understand the barriers to effective communication
- be familiar with and be able to distinguish among the different historical approaches to management
- know the different primary leadership theories
- be familiar with the types of leadership skills
- have an understanding of the different managerial theories
- know the kinds of challenges—cultural and work related—that are faced when persons of varying ages are in the same workplace

> *We are born in organizations, educated by organizations, and most of us spend much of our lives working for organizations. We spend much of our leisure time paying, playing, and praying in organizations. Most of us will die in an organization, and when the time comes for burial, the largest organization of all—the state—must grant official permission.*
>
> —Amitai Etzioni

# Introduction

It is no surprise that *Dilbert*—one of today's most popular cartoon strips and television programs—portrays downtrodden workers, inconsiderate bosses, and dysfunctional organizations. Scott Adams's cartoon "hero," a mouthless engineer with a perpetually bent necktie, is believed by many Americans to be representative of today's workers. They believe that the Dilbert principle—the most ineffective workers are systematically moved to the place where they can do the least damage—is alive and well. Although a sizable majority of U.S. workers routinely indicate that their workplace is a pleasant environment, more than 70 percent also experience stress at work because of red tape, unnecessary rules, poor communication with management, and other causes. Indeed, what gives Adams grist for the Dilbert mill is the way managers mishandle their employees and carry out downsizing.[1]

This chapter examines organizations and the employees within them and how they should be managed and motivated. The chapter offers a general discussion of organizations, focusing on their definition, theory and function, and structure. Included are several approaches to managing and communicating within organizations.

I review historical schools of thought concerning management and examine organizational leadership theories. I then focus on one of the most important aspects of leadership, personnel administration. After a discussion of several motivational techniques for employees based on findings by major theorists in the field, I conclude with a look at some of the unique challenges posed by younger (so-called Generation X/Y) employees.

# Defining Organizations

Like *supervision* and *management,* the word *organization* has a number of meanings and interpretations that have evolved over the years. We think of organizations as entities of two or more people who cooperate to accomplish an objective(s). In that sense, certainly, the concept of organization is not new. Undoubtedly, the first organizations were primitive hunting parties. Organization and a high degree of coordination were required to bring down huge animals, as revealed in fossils from as early as 40,000 years ago.[2]

An **organization** may be formally defined as "a consciously coordinated social entity, with a relative identifiable boundary, that functions on a relatively continuous basis to achieve a common goal or set of goals."[3] The term **consciously coordinated** implies management. **Social entity** refers to the fact that organizations are composed of people who interact with one another and with people in other organizations. **Relatively identifiable boundary** alludes to the organization's goals and the public served.[4] Using this definition, we can consider many types of formal groups as full-blown organizations. Four different types of formal organizations have been identified by asking the question "Who benefits?" Answers include (1) mutual benefit associations, such as police labor unions; (2) business concerns, such as General Motors; (3) service organizations, such as community mental health centers, where the client group is the prime beneficiary; and (4) commonweal organizations, such as the Department of Defense and criminal justice agencies, where the beneficiaries are the public at large.[5] The following analogy is designed to help the reader to understand organizations.

An organization corresponds to the bones that structure or give form to the body. Imagine that the hand is a single mass of bone rather than four separate fingers and a thumb made up of bones joined by cartilage to be flexible. The single mass of bones could not, because of its structure, play musical instruments, hold a pencil, or grip a baseball bat. A criminal justice organization is analogous. It must be structured properly if it is to be effective in fulfilling its many diverse goals.[6]

It is important to note that no two organizations are exactly alike. Nor is there one best way to run an organization.

# Organizational Theory and Function

## *Elements of an Organization*

Max Weber (1864–1920), known as the *father of sociology,* explored in depth the organizational structure as well as the dynamics related to bureaucracy. He argued that if a bureaucratic structure is to function efficiently, it must have the following elements:

1. *Rulification and routinization.* Organizations stress continuity. Rules save effort by eliminating the need for deriving a new solution for every problem. They also facilitate standard and equal treatment of similar situations.
2. *Division of labor.* This involves the performance of functions by various parts of an organization along with providing the necessary authority to carry out these functions.
3. *Hierarchy of authority.* Each lower office is under the control and supervision of a higher one.
4. *Expertise.* Specialized training is necessary. Only a person who has demonstrated adequate technical training is qualified to be a member of the administrative staff.
5. *Written rules.* Administrative acts, decisions, and rules are formulated and recorded in writing.[7]

Bureaucracies are often criticized on two grounds. First, they are said to be inflexible, inefficient, and unresponsive to changing needs and times. Second, they are said to stifle the individual freedom, spontaneity, and self-realization of their employees.[8] James Q. Wilson referred to this widespread discontent with modern organizations as the "bureaucracy problem," where the key issue is "getting the frontline worker … to do 'the right thing.'"[9] In short, then, bureaucracies themselves can create problems.

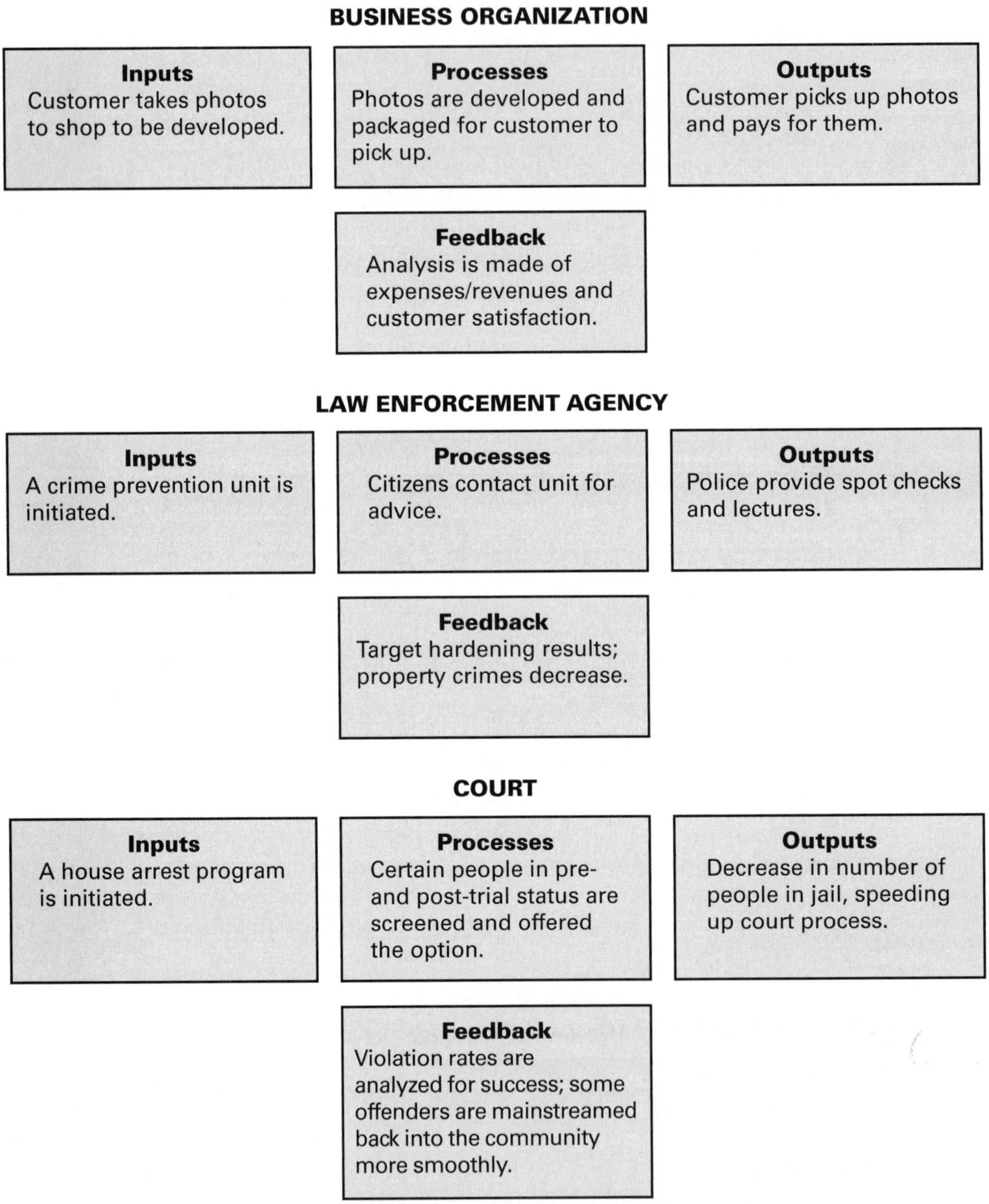

## BUSINESS ORGANIZATION

| **Inputs** | **Processes** | **Outputs** |
|---|---|---|
| Customer takes photos to shop to be developed. | Photos are developed and packaged for customer to pick up. | Customer picks up photos and pays for them. |

**Feedback**
Analysis is made of expenses/revenues and customer satisfaction.

## LAW ENFORCEMENT AGENCY

| **Inputs** | **Processes** | **Outputs** |
|---|---|---|
| A crime prevention unit is initiated. | Citizens contact unit for advice. | Police provide spot checks and lectures. |

**Feedback**
Target hardening results; property crimes decrease.

## COURT

| **Inputs** | **Processes** | **Outputs** |
|---|---|---|
| A house arrest program is initiated. | Certain people in pre- and post-trial status are screened and offered the option. | Decrease in number of people in jail, speeding up court process. |

**Feedback**
Violation rates are analyzed for success; some offenders are mainstreamed back into the community more smoothly.

**Figure 2.1**

The Organization as an Input–Output Model.

**PROBATION/PAROLE AGENCIES**

| **Inputs** | **Processes** | **Outputs** |
|---|---|---|
| Parole guidelines are changed to shorten length of incarceration and reduce overcrowding. | Qualified inmates are contacted by parole agency and given new parole dates. | A higher number of inmates are paroled into the community. |

**Feedback**
Parole officer's caseload and revocation rates might increase; less time to devote per case.

**CORRECTIONAL INSTITUTION**

| **Inputs** | **Processes** | **Outputs** |
|---|---|---|
| Person is incarcerated for felony offense(s). | Prison incapacitates and often provides counseling, GED or higher; job skills; other treatment or programming. | Person is released— generally supervised—to maintain a noncriminal lifestyle. |

**Feedback**
Does inmate recidivate (return to the institution for committing new crimes or for violating parole conditions)?

**Figure 2.1**

*(continued)*

## Organizational Inputs/Outputs

Another way to view organizations is as systems that take *inputs,* process them, and thus produce *outputs.* These outputs are then sold in the marketplace or given free to citizens in the form of a service. A police agency, for example, processes reports of criminal activity and, like other systems, attempts to satisfy the customer (crime victim). Figure 2.1 demonstrates the input/output model for the police and private business. There are other types of inputs by police agencies; for example, a robbery problem might result in an input of newly created robbery surveillance teams, the processing would be their stakeouts, and the output would be the number of subsequent arrests by the team. Feedback would occur in the form of conviction rates at trial.

# Organizational Structure

All organizations have an organizational structure or table of organization, be it written or unwritten, very basic or highly complex. An experienced manager uses this organizational chart or table as a blueprint for action. The size of the organization depends on the demand placed on it and the resources available to it. Growth precipitates the need for more personnel, greater division of labor, specialization, written rules, and other such elements.

In building the organizational structure, the following principles should be kept in mind:

1. *Principle of the objective.* Every part of every organization must be an expression of the purpose of the undertaking. You cannot organize in a vacuum; you must organize for something.
2. *Principle of specialization.* The activities of every member of any organized group should be confined, as far as possible, to the performance of a single function.
3. *Principle of authority.* In every organized group, the supreme authority must rest somewhere. There should be a clear line of authority to every person in the group.
4. *Principle of responsibility.* The responsibility of the superior for the acts of his or her subordinates is absolute.
5. *Principle of definition.* The content of each position, the duties involved, the authority and responsibility contemplated, and the relationships with other positions should be clearly defined in writing and published for all concerned.
6. *Principle of correspondence.* In every position, the responsibility and the authority to carry out the responsibility should correspond.
7. *Span of control.* No person should supervise more than six direct subordinates whose work interlocks.[10]

A related, major principle of hierarchy of authority is **unity of command,** which refers to placing one and only one superior officer in command or in control of every situation and employee. When a critical situation occurs, it is imperative that someone be responsible and in charge. The unity-of-command principle ensures, for example, that multiple and/or conflicting orders are not issued to the same police officers by several superior officers. For example, a patrol sergeant might arrive at a hostage situation, deploy personnel, and give all appropriate orders, only to have a shift lieutenant or captain come to the scene and countermand the sergeant's orders with his or her own orders. This type of situation would obviously be counterproductive for all concerned. All officers must know and follow the chain of command at such incidents. Every person in the organization should report to one and only one superior officer. When the unity-of-command principle is followed,

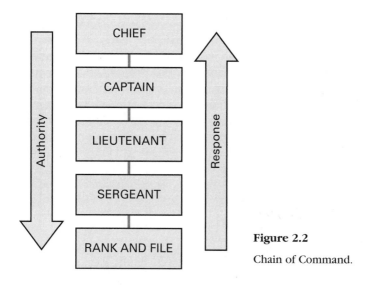

**Figure 2.2**

Chain of Command.

everyone involved is aware of the actions initiated by superiors and subordinates. A simple structure indicating the direct line of authority in a chain of command is shown in Figure 2.2.

An organization should be developed through careful evaluation of its responsibilities, otherwise the agency may become unable to respond efficiently to client needs. For example, the implementation of too many specialized units in a police department (e.g., community relations, crime analysis, media relations) may obligate too many personnel to these functions and result in too few patrol officers. Today, 56 to 90 percent of all sworn personnel are assigned to patrol.[11]

The classic pyramidal design is shown in Figure 2.3. The pyramidal structure has the following characteristics:

1. Nearly all contacts take the form of orders going *down* and reports of results going *up* the pyramid.
2. Each subordinate must receive instructions and orders from only one boss.
3. Important decisions are made at the top of the pyramid.
4. Superiors have a specific "span of control," supervising only a limited number of people.
5. Personnel at all levels except at the top and bottom have contact only with their boss above them and their subordinates below them.[12]

## Leading the Organization

Over 20 years ago Peter Drucker, often referred to as the *business guru*,[13] conducted a study of the Los Angeles Police Department; among Drucker's findings was: "You police are so concerned with doing things right that you fail to do the

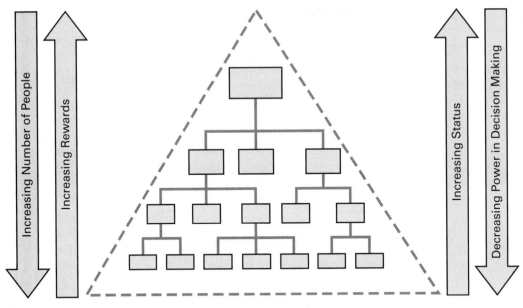

**Figure 2.3**

Organization pyramid. *Source:* Adapted from L. R. Sayles and G. Strauss, *Human Behavior Organizations* (Upper Saddle River, N.J.: Prentice Hall, 1966), p. 349.

right things." Drucker added that "Managers do things right; leaders do the right thing." In other words, administration cannot be so concerned with managing that they fail to lead.[14]

We now look at leaders and what they can do to motivate their subordinates.

## *What Is Leadership?*

Probably since the dawn of time, when cave dwellers clustered into hunting groups and some particularly dominant person assumed a leadership role over the party, administrators have received advice on how to do their jobs from those around them. Even today, manuals for leaders and upwardly mobile executives abound, offering quick studies in how to govern others. Although many have doubtless been profitable for their authors, most of these how-to primers on leading others enjoy only a brief, ephemeral existence.

To understand **leadership,** we must first define the term. This is an important and fairly complex undertaking, however. Perhaps the simplest definition is to say that leading is "getting things done through people." In general, it may be said that a manager operates in the status quo, but a leader takes risks. Managers are conformers, leaders are reformers. Managers control; leaders empower. Managers supervise; leaders coach. Managers are efficient; leaders are effective. Managers are position oriented; leaders are people-oriented. In sum, police administrators must be both skilled managers and effective leaders.[15]

Other definitions of leadership include the following:

- "The process of influencing the activities of an individual or a group in efforts toward goal achievement in a given situation."[16]
- "Working with and through individuals and groups to accomplish organizational goals."[17]
- "The activity of influencing people to strive willingly for group objectives."[18]
- "The exercise of influence."[19]

> Conversely, it has been said that the manager may be viewed as a team captain, parent, steward, battle commander, fountain of wisdom, poker player, group spokesperson, gatekeeper, minister, drill instructor, facilitator, initiator, mediator, navigator, candy-store keeper, linchpin, umbrella-holder and everything else between nurse and Attila-the-Hun.[20]

In criminal justice organizations, leaders take the macro view; their role might best be defined as "the process of influencing organizational members to use their energies willingly and appropriately to facilitate the achievement of the [agency's] goals."[21] I discuss leaders and mangers in greater length later in this chapter and in Chapter 4.

# Organizational Communication

## *Definition and Characteristics*

Communication is one of the most important dynamics of an organization. Indeed, a major role of today's administrators and other leaders is communication. Managers of all types of organizations spend an overwhelming amount of their time in the process of—and coping with problems in—communication.

Today we communicate via e-mail, facsimile machines, video camcorders, cellular telephones, satellite dishes, and on and on. We converse orally, in written letters and memos, through our body language, via television and radio programs, through newspapers and meetings. Even private thoughts—which take place four times faster than the spoken word—are communication. Every waking hour, our minds are full of ideas. Psychologists say that nearly 100,000 thoughts pass through our minds every day, conveyed by a multitude of media.[22] Communication becomes exceedingly important and sensitive in a criminal justice organization because of the nature of information that is processed by practitioners—particularly police officers, who often see people at their worst and when they are in the most embarrassing and compromising situations. To "communicate" what is known about these kinds of behaviors could be devastating to the parties concerned. A former Detroit police chief lamented several decades ago that "many police officers, without realizing they carry such authority, do pass on rumors. The average police officer doesn't stop to weigh what he says."[23] Certainly the same holds true today and extends to courts and corrections personnel, especially in view of the very high-tech communications equipment now in use.

Studies have long shown that communication is the primary problem in administration, and lack of communication is employees' primary complaint about their immediate supervisors.[24] Mark Twain said that "The difference between the right word and the almost right word is the difference between lightning and lightning bug."[25]

Managers are in the communications business. It has been said that,

> Of all skills needed to be an effective manager/leader/supervisor, skill in communicating is *the* most vital. In fact, research has shown that 93 percent of police work is one-on-one communication. Estimates vary, but all studies emphasize the importance of communications in everyday law enforcement operations.[26]

Several elements compose the communication process: encoding, transmission, medium, reception, decoding, and feedback.[27]

*Encoding.* To convey an experience or idea, we translate, or encode, that experience into symbols. We use words or other verbal behaviors or nonverbal behaviors such as gestures to convey the experience or idea.

*Transmission.* This element involves the translation of the encoded symbols into some behavior that another person can observe. The actual articulation (moving our lips, tongue, etc.) of the symbol into verbal or nonverbal observable behavior is transmission.

*Medium.* Communication must be conveyed through some channel or medium. Media for communication include sight, hearing, taste, touch, or smell. Some other media are television, telephone, paper and pencil, and radio. The choice of the medium is important. For example, a message that is transmitted via formal letter from the chief executive officer will carry more weight than if the same message is conveyed via a secretary's memo.

*Reception.* The stimuli, the verbal and nonverbal symbols, reach the senses of the receiver and are conveyed to the brain for interpretation.

*Decoding.* The individual who receives the stimuli develops some meaning for the verbal and nonverbal symbols and decodes the stimuli. These symbols are translated into some concept or experience for the receiver. Whether or not the receiver is familiar with the symbols or whether or not interference such as any noise or physiological problem occurs determines how closely the message that the receiver has decoded approximates the message that the sender has encoded.

*Feedback.* When the receiver decodes the transmitted symbols, he or she usually provides some response or feedback to the sender. If someone appears puzzled, we repeat the message or we encode the concept differently and transmit some different symbols to express the same concept. Feedback that we receive acts as a guide or steering device and lets us know whether the receiver has interpreted our symbols as we intended. Feedback is obviously a crucial element in guaranteeing that the proper meaning that the sender intended was in fact conveyed to the receiver.

## *Communication within Criminal Justice Organizations*

An organization's systems of communication are usually created by establishing formal areas of responsibility and explicit delegations of duties, including statements of the nature, content, and direction of the communications that are necessary for the group's performance. Most criminal justice administrators prefer a formal system, regardless of how cumbersome it may be, because they can control it and because it tends to create a record for future reference. Several human factors, however, affect the flow of communication. Employees typically communicate with those persons who can help them to achieve their aims; they avoid communicating with those who do not assist, or may retard, their accomplishing those goals; and they tend to avoid communicating with people who threaten them and make them feel anxious.[28] Other barriers to effective communication are discussed later.

Communication within a criminal justice organization may be downward, upward, or horizontal. There are five types of downward communication within a criminal justice organization:

1. *Job instruction.* Communication relating to the performance of a certain task

2. *Job rationale.* Communication relating a certain task to organizational tasks

3. *Procedures and practice.* Communication about organizational policies, procedures, rules, and regulations (discussed in Chapter 3)

4. *Feedback.* Communication appraising how an individual performs the assigned task

5. *Indoctrination.* Communication designed to motivate the employee[29]

Other reasons for communicating downward—implicit in this list—are opportunities for administrators to spell out objectives, to change attitudes and mold opinions, to prevent misunderstandings from lack of information, and to prepare employees for change.[30]

*Upward* communication in a criminal justice organization may be likened to a trout trying to swim upstream: With its many currents of resistance, it is a much harder task than to float downstream. Several deterrents restrict upward communication. The physical distance between superior and subordinate impedes upward communication. Communication is often difficult and infrequent when superiors are isolated and seldom seen or spoken to. In large criminal justice organizations, administrators may be located in headquarters that are removed from the operations personnel. The complexity of the organization may also cause prolonged delays of communication. For example, if a corrections officer or a patrol officer observes a problem that needs to be taken to the highest level, normally this information must first be taken to the sergeant, then to the lieutenant, captain, deputy warden or chief, and so on. At each level, these higher individuals will reflect on the problem, put their own interpretation on it (possibly including how the problem might affect them professionally or even personally), and possibly even dilute or distort the problem. Thus, delays in communication are inherent in a bureaucracy. Delays could mean that problems are not brought to the attention of the chief executive for a long time. The more levels the communication passes through, the more it is filtered and diluted in its accuracy.

There is also the danger that administrators have a "no news is good news" or "slay the messenger" attitude, thereby discouraging the reception of information. Unless the superior does in fact maintain an open-door atmosphere, subordinates are often reluctant to bring, or will temper, bad news, unfavorable opinions, and mistakes or failures to the superior.[31] Administrators may also believe that they know and understand what their subordinates want and think, and that complaints from subordinates are an indication of disloyalty.

For all of these reasons, administrators may fail to take action on undesirable conditions brought to their attention; this will cause subordinates to lose faith in their leaders. Many time-consuming problems could be minimized or eliminated if superiors would take the time to listen to their employees.

*Horizontal* communication thrives in an organization when formal communication channels are not open.[32] The disadvantage in horizontal communication is that it is much easier and more natural to achieve than vertical communication and therefore it often replaces vertical channels. The horizontal channels are usually of an informal nature and include the grapevine, discussed next. The advantage is that horizontal communication is essential if the subsystems within a criminal justice organization are to function in an effective and coordinated manner. Horizontal communication among peers may also provide emotional and social bonds that build morale and feelings of teamwork among employees.

## The Grapevine

In addition to the several barriers to effective communication just discussed, the so-called **grapevine**—termed as such because it zigzags back and forth across organizations—can also serve to hinder communication. Communication includes rumors, and probably *no* type of organization in our society has more grapevine "scuttlebutt" than police agencies. Departments even establish "rumor control" centers during major crisis situations. Compounding the usual barriers to communication is the fact that policing, prisons, and jails are 24-hour, 7-day operations, so that rumors are easily carried from one shift to the next.

The grapevine's most effective characteristics are that it is fast, it operates mostly at the place of work, and it supplements regular, formal communication. On the positive side, it can be a tool for management to get a feel for employees' attitudes, to spread useful information, and to help employees vent their frustrations. However, the grapevine can also carry untruths and be malicious. Without a doubt, the grapevine is a force for administrators to reckon with on a daily basis.

## *Oral and Written Communication*

Our society tends to place considerable confidence in the written word within complex organizations. It establishes a permanent record, but transmitting information in this way does not necessarily ensure that the message will be clear to the receiver. Often, in spite of the writer's best efforts, information is not conveyed clearly to the receiver. This may be due in large measure to shortcomings with the writer's skills. Nonetheless, criminal justice organizations seem to increasingly rely on written communication, as evidenced by the proliferation of written directives found in most agencies.

This tendency for organizations to promulgate written rules, policies, and procedures has been caused by three contemporary developments. First is the *requirement for administrative due process* in employee disciplinary matters, encouraged by federal court rulings, police officer bill of rights legislation, and labor contracts. Another development is *civil liability.* Lawsuits against local governments and their criminal justice agencies and administrators have become commonplace; written agency guidelines prohibiting certain acts provide a hedge against successful civil litigation.[33] Written communication is preferred as a medium for dealing with citizens or groups outside the criminal justice agency. This means of communication provides the greatest protection against the growing number of legal actions taken against agencies by activists, citizens, and interest groups.

Finally, a third stimulus is the *accreditation movement.* Agencies that are either pursuing accreditation or have become accredited must possess a wealth of written policies and procedures.[34]

In recent years, electronic mail (e-mail) has proliferated as a communication medium in criminal justice organizations. E-mail provides an easy-to-use and almost instantaneous communication with anyone possessing a personal computer—in upward, downward, or horizontal directions. For all its advantages, however, e-mail messages can lack security and can be ambiguous—not only with respect to content meaning, but also with regard to what they represent. Are such messages, in fact, mail, to be given the full weight of an office letter or memo, or should they be treated more as offhand comments?[35]

## *Other Barriers to Effective Communication*

In addition to the barriers just discussed, several other potential barriers to effective communication exist. Some people, for example, are not good listeners. Unfortunately, listening is one of the most neglected and the least understood of the communication arts.[36] We allow other things to obstruct our communication, including time constraints, inadequate or too great a volume of information, the tendency to say what we think others want to hear, failure to select the best word, prejudices, and strained sender–receiver relationships.[37] In addition, subordinates do not always have the same "big picture" viewpoint that superiors possess and also do not always communicate well with someone in a higher position who is perhaps more fluent and persuasive than they are.

## Cultural Empathy

It is important to note that at least 90 percent of communication is *nonverbal* in nature, involving posture, facial expressions, gestures, tone of voice ("it's not what you say, but how you say it"), and so on.[38] People learn to interpret these nonverbal messages by growing up in a particular culture, but not every culture interprets nonverbal cues in the same way.

For example, in some cultures the avoidance of eye contact by looking to the ground is meant to convey respect and humility. Making what to some people are exaggerated hand gestures may be a normal means of communication in some cultures, and social distance for conversation for some societies may be much closer than it is in the United States. Someone from Nigeria, for example, may stand less than 15 inches from someone while conversing, whereas about 2 feet is a comfortable conversation zone for Americans. These few examples demonstrate why criminal justice practitioners must possess cultural empathy and understand the cultural cues of citizens from other nations.

# Historical Approaches to Management

According to Ronald Lynch,[39] the history of **management** can be divided into three approaches and time periods: (1) scientific management (1900-1940), (2) human relations management (1930-1970), and (3) systems management (1965-present).

## Scientific Management

Frederick W. Taylor, who first emphasized time and motion studies, is known today as the *father of scientific management.* Spending his early years in the steel mills of Pennsylvania, Taylor became chief engineer and later discovered a new method of making steel; this allowed him to retire at age 45 to write and lecture. He became interested in methods for getting greater productivity from workers, and was hired in 1898 by Bethlehem Steel, where he measured the time it took workers to shovel and carry pig iron. Taylor recommended giving workers hourly breaks and going to a piecework system, among other adjustments. Worker productivity soared; the total number of shovelers needed dropped from about 600 to 140, and worker earnings increasing from $1.15 to $1.88 per day. The average cost of handling a long ton (2,240 pounds) dropped from $0.072 to $0.033.[40]

Taylor, who was highly criticized by unions for his management-oriented views, proved that administrators must know their employees. He published a book, *The Principles of Scientific Management,* in 1911. His views caught on, and soon emphasis was placed entirely on the formal administrative structure; terms such as *authority, chain of command, span of control,* and *division of labor* were coined.

PLANNING:  working out in broad outline what needs to be done and the methods for doing it to accomplish the purpose set for the enterprise

ORGANIZING:  the establishment of a formal structure of authority through which work subdivisions are arranged, defined, and coordinated for the defined objective

STAFFING:  the whole personnel function of bringing in and training the staff and maintaining favorable conditions of work

DIRECTING:  the continuous task of making decisions, embodying them in specific and general orders and instructions, and serving as the leader of the enterprise

COORDINATING:  the all-important duty of interrelating the various parts of the organization

REPORTING:  informing the executive and his or her assistants as to what is going on, through records, research, and inspection

BUDGETING:  all that is related to budgeting in the form of fiscal planning, accounting, and control

**Figure 2.4**

Gulick's POSDCORB. *Source:* Luther Gulick and Lyndall Urwick, *Papers on the Science of Administration* (New York: Institute of Public Administration, 1937).

In 1935, Luther Gulick formulated the theory of POSDCORB, an acronym for planning, organizing, staffing, directing, coordinating, reporting, and budgeting (Figure 2.4); this philosophy was emphasized in police management for many years. Gulick stressed the technical and engineering side of management, virtually ignoring the human side.

The application of scientific management to criminal justice agencies was heavily criticized. It viewed employees as passive instruments whose feelings were completely disregarded. In addition, employees were considered to be motivated by money alone.

## *Human Relations Management*

Beginning in 1930, people began to realize the negative effects of scientific management on the worker. A view arose in policing that management should instill pride and dignity in officers. The movement toward human relations management began with the famous studies conducted during the late 1920s through the mid-1930s by the Harvard Business School at the Hawthorne plant of the Western Electric Company.[41] These studies, which are discussed in more detail later in this chapter, found that worker productivity is more closely related to *social* capacity than to physical capacity, that noneconomic rewards play a prominent part in motivating and satisfying employees, and that employees do not react to management and its rewards as individuals but as members of groups.[42]

In the 1940s and 1950s, police departments began to recognize the strong effect of the informal structure on the organization; agencies began using techniques such as job enlargement and job enrichment to generate interest in policing as a career. Studies indicated that the supervisor who was "employee centered" was more effective than one who was "production centered." Democratic or participatory management began to appear in police agencies. The human relations approach had its limitations, however. With the emphasis placed on the employee, the role of the organizational structure became secondary; the primary goal seemed to many to be social rewards, with little attention given to task accomplishment. Many police managers saw this trend as unrealistic. Employees began to give less and expect more in return.[43]

### Systems Management

In the mid-1960s, features of the human relations and scientific management approaches were combined in the *systems management* approach. Designed to bring the individual and the organization together, it attempted to help managers use employees to reach desired production goals. The systems approach recognized that it was still necessary to have some hierarchical arrangement to bring about coordination, that authority and responsibility were essential, and that overall organization was required.

The systems management approach combined the work of Abraham Maslow,[44] who developed a hierarchy of needs; Douglas McGregor,[45] who stressed the general theory of human motivation; and Robert Blake and Jane Mouton,[46] who developed the "managerial grid," which emphasized two concerns—for task and for people—that managers must have. (These theories are discussed in greater detail later.) In effect, the systems management approach holds that to be effective, the manager must be interdependent with other individuals and groups and have the ability to recognize and deal with conflict and change. More than mere technical skills are required; managers require knowledge of several major resources: people, money, time, and equipment.[47] Team cooperation is required to achieve organizational goals.

Several theories of leadership also have evolved over the past several decades, the most common being trait theory, leadership styles, and situational approaches. Each is discussed briefly next.

## Primary Leadership Theories

### Trait Theory

*Trait theory* was popular until the 1950s. This theory was based on the contention that good leaders possessed certain character traits that poor leaders did not. Those who developed this theory, Stogdill and Goode, believed that a

| Traits | Skills |
|---|---|
| Adaptable to situations | Clever (intelligent) |
| Alert to social environment | Conceptually skilled |
| Ambitious and achievement oriented | Creative |
| Assertive | Diplomatic and tactful |
| Cooperative | Fluent in speaking |
| Decisive | Knowledgeable about group task |
| Dependable | Organized (administrative ability) |
| Dominant (desire to influence others) | Persuasive |
| Energetic (high activity level) | Socially skilled |
| Persistent | |
| Self-confident | |
| Tolerant of stress | |
| Willing to assume responsibility | |

**Figure 2.5**

Traits and skills commonly associated with leadership effectiveness. *Source:* Gary Yuki, *Leadership in Organizations* (Upper Saddle River, N.J.: Prentice Hall, 1981), pp. 70, 121–125.

leader could be identified through a two-step process. The first step involved studying leaders and comparing them to nonleaders to determine which traits only the leaders possessed. The second step sought people who possessed these traits to be promoted into managerial positions.[48]

A study of 468 administrators in 13 companies found certain traits in successful administrators. They were more intelligent and better educated; had a stronger need for power; preferred independent activity, intense thought, and some risk; enjoyed relationships with people; and disliked detail work more than their subordinates.[49] Figure 2.5 shows traits and skills commonly associated with leader effectiveness, according to Gary Yuki. Following this study, a review of the literature on trait theory revealed the traits most identified with leadership ability: intelligence, initiative, extroversion, sense of humor, enthusiasm, fairness, sympathy, and self-confidence.[50]

Trait theory has lost much of its support since the 1950s, partly because of the basic assumption of the theory that leadership cannot be taught. A more important reason, however, is simply the growth of new, more sophisticated approaches to the study of leadership. Quantifiable means to test trait theory were limited. What does it mean to say that a leader must be intelligent? By whose standards? As compared with persons within the organization or within society? How can traits such as sense of humor, enthusiasm, fairness, and the others listed earlier be measured or tested? The inability to measure these factors was the real flaw in and reason for the decline of this theory.

## *Style Theory*

A study at Michigan State University investigated how leaders motivated individuals or groups to achieve organizational goals. The study determined that leaders must have a sense of the task to be accomplished as well as the environment in which their subordinates work. Three principles of leadership behavior emerged from the Michigan study:

1. Leaders must give task direction to their followers.
2. Closeness of supervision directly affects employee production. High-producing units had less direct supervision; highly supervised units had lower production. Conclusion: Employees need some area of freedom to make choices. Given this, they produce at a higher rate.
3. Leaders must be employee oriented. It is the leader's responsibility to facilitate employees' accomplishment of goals.[51]

In the 1950s, Edwin Fleishman began studies of leadership at Ohio State University. After focusing on leader behavior rather than personality traits, he identified two dimensions of basic principles of leadership that could be taught: *initiating structure* and *consideration* (Figure 2.6).[52] Initiating structure referred to supervisory behavior that focused on the achievement of organizational goals, and consideration was directed toward a supervisor's openness toward subordinates' ideas and respect for their feelings as persons. High consideration and moderate initiating structure were assumed to yield higher job satisfaction and productivity than high initiating structure and low consideration.[53]

The major focus of style theory is the adoption of a single managerial style by a manager based on his or her position in regard to initiating structure and consideration. Three pure leadership styles were thought to be the basis for all managers: autocratic, democratic, and laissez-faire.

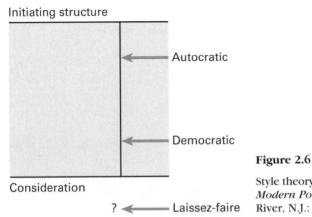

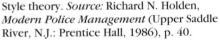

**Figure 2.6**

Style theory. *Source:* Richard N. Holden, *Modern Police Management* (Upper Saddle River, N.J.: Prentice Hall, 1986), p. 40.

**Autocratic leaders** are leader centered and have a high initiating structure. They are primarily authoritarian in nature and prefer to give orders rather than invite group participation. They have a tendency to be personal in their criticism. This style works best in emergency situations in which strict control and rapid decision making are needed. The problem with autocratic leadership is the organization's inability to function when the leader is absent. It also stifles individual development and initiative because subordinates are rarely allowed to make an independent decision.[54]

The **democratic leader** tends to focus on working within the group and strives to attain cooperation from group members by eliciting their ideas and support. Democratic managers tend to be viewed as consideration oriented and strive to attain mutual respect with subordinates. Democratic leaders operate within an atmosphere of trust and delegate much authority. This style is useful in organizations in which the course of action is uncertain and problems are relatively unstructured. It often taps the decision-making ability of subordinates. In emergency situations requiring a highly structured response, however, democratic leadership may prove too time-consuming and awkward to be effective. Thus, although the worker may appreciate the strengths of this style, its weaknesses must be recognized as well.[55]

The third leadership style, that of the **laissez-faire leader,** is a hands-off approach in which the leader is actually a nonleader. The organization in effect runs itself, with no input or control from the manager. This style has no positive aspects, as the entire organization is soon placed in jeopardy. In truth, this may not be a leadership style at all; instead, it may be an abdication of administrative duties.

## *Situational Leadership*

Situational leadership theory recognizes that the workplace is a complex setting subject to rapid changes. Therefore, it is unlikely that one way of managing these varying situations would be adequate. In this view, the best way to lead depends on the situation.

In 1977, Paul Hersey and Kenneth Blanchard[56] presented a model of situational leadership that has been used for training by many major corporations and the military. Their model emphasizes the leader's behavior in relationship to followers' behavior (see Figure 2.7). Situational leadership requires that the leader evaluate follower readiness in two ways; willingness (motivation) and ability (competence).

Situational leadership takes into account worker readiness; readiness is defined as the capacity to set high but attainable goals, the willingness to take responsibility, and the education and/or experience of the individual or the group. Figure 2.7 depicts the various levels of follower maturity, which are defined as follows:

R1. The followers are neither willing nor able to take responsibility for task accomplishment.

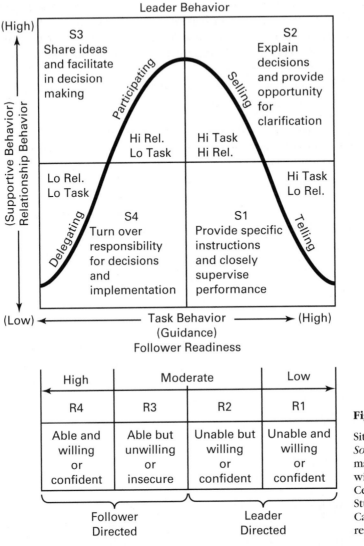

Leader Behavior

(High)

S3
Share ideas and facilitate in decision making

*Participating*

S2
Explain decisions and provide opportunity for clarification

*Selling*

Hi Rel.
Lo Task

Hi Task
Hi Rel.

Lo Rel.
Lo Task

Hi Task
Lo Rel.

*Delegating*

S4
Turn over responsibility for decisions and implementation

S1
Provide specific instructions and closely supervise performance

*Telling*

(Low) ← Task Behavior → (High)
(Guidance)

(Supportive Behavior)
Relationship Behavior

Follower Readiness

| High | Moderate | | Low |
|------|----------|--|-----|
| R4 | R3 | R2 | R1 |
| Able and willing or confident | Able but unwilling or insecure | Unable but willing or confident | Unable and willing or confident |

Follower Directed                Leader Directed

**Figure 2.7**

Situational leadership. *Source:* Copyrighted material. Reprinted with permission of Center for Leadership Studies, Escondido, Calif. 92025. All rights reserved.

R2. The followers are willing but are not able to take responsibility for task accomplishment.

R3. The followers are not willing but are able to take responsibility for task accomplishment.

R4. The followers are willing and able to take responsibility for task accomplishment.

Task behavior, shown in Figure 2.7, is essentially the extent to which a leader engages in one-way communication with subordinates; relationship behavior is the extent to which the leader engages in two-way communication (by providing positive reinforcement, emotional support, and so on).

There are four basic styles of leadership that are associated with task accomplishment; the definitions of these four styles of leadership are as follows:

S1. *Telling.* High task/low relationship style is characterized by one-way communication in which the leader defines the roles of followers and tells them what, how, when, and where to do various tasks.

S2. *Selling.* High task/high relationship behavior is provided by two-way communication and socioemotional support to get followers to voluntarily buy into decisions that have been made.

S3. *Participating.* High relationship/low task behavior indicates both leader and follower have the ability and knowledge to complete the task.

S4. *Delegating.* Low relationship/low task behavior gives followers the opportunity to "run their own show" with little supervision.

The bell-shaped curve in the style-of-leader portion of Figure 2.7 means that, as the readiness level of followers develops, the appropriate style of leadership moves correspondingly. For example, a police supervisor who has a subordinate whose maturity is in the R3 range (able but unwilling) would be most effective employing an S3 (participating) style of leadership.

Hersey and Blanchard asserted that leaders could reduce their close supervision and direction of individuals and increase delegation as followers' readiness to complete tasks increased. The difficulty of this style of leadership is its dependence on the ability of leaders to diagnose the ability of followers and then adjust their leadership style to the given situation. This is often easier said than done.

## The Managerial Grid

In 1964, Blake and Mouton developed their managerial grid from the studies done by Edwin Fleishman and others at Ohio State University. The Ohio team used two variables, focus on task (initiating structure) and focus on relationships (consideration), to develop a management quadrant describing leadership behavior. The managerial grid (Figure 2.8) includes five leadership styles based on concern for output (production) and concern for people. Using a specially developed testing instrument, researchers can assign a numerical score based on subjects' concern for each variable. Numerical indications such as 9,1; 9,9; 1,1; and 5,5 are then plotted on the grid using the scales on the horizontal and vertical axes. The grid is read like a map, right and up. Each axis is numbered 1 to 9, with 1 indicating the minimum effort or concern and 9 the maximum. The horizontal axis represents the concern for production and performance goals, and the vertical axis represents the concern for human relations or empathy.

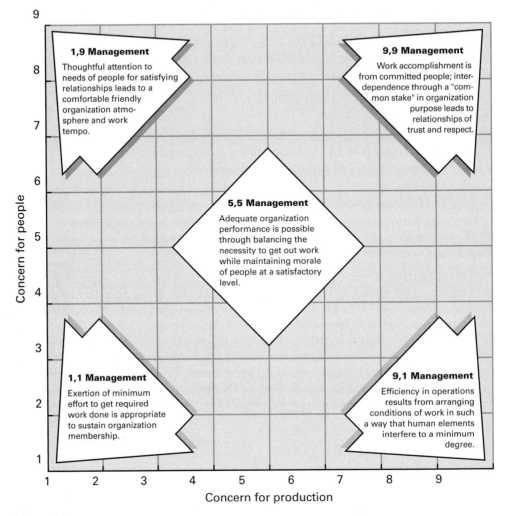

**Figure 2.8**

Management grid. *Source:* Reprinted by permission of *Harvard Business Review* [Nov.-Dec. 1964]. An exhibit from "Breakthrough in Organizational Development" by Robert R. Blake, Jane S. Mouton, Louis B. Barnes, and Larry E. Greiner. Copyright 1964 by the President and Fellows of Harvard College. All rights reserved.

The points of orientation are related to styles of management. The lower-left-hand corner of the grid shows the 1,1 style (representing a minimal concern for task or service and a minimal concern for people). The lower-right-hand corner of the grid identifies the 9,1 style. This type of leader would have a primary concern for the task or output and a minimal concern for people. Here, people are seen as tools of production. The upper-left-hand corner represents the 1,9 style, often referred to as "country club management," with minimum effort given to output or task. The upper right, 9,9, indicates high concern for both people and production—a "we're all in this together," common-stake approach of mutual respect and trust. In the center—a 5,5, "middle-of-the-road" style—the leader has a "give a little, be fair but firm" philosophy, providing a balance between output and people concerns.[57]

These five leadership styles can be summarized as follows[58]:

- Authority–compliance management (9,1)
- Country club management (1,9)
- Middle-of-the-road management (5,5)
- Impoverished management (1,1)
- Team management (9,9)

# Types of Leadership Skills

In 1975, Robert Katz identified three essential skills that leaders should possess: technical, human, and conceptual. Katz defined a *skill* as the capacity to translate knowledge into action in such a way that a task is accomplished successfully.[59] Each of these skills (when performed effectively) results in the achievement of objectives and goals, which is the primary task of management.

*Technical skills* are those a manager needs to ensure that specific tasks are performed correctly. They are based on proven knowledge, procedures, or techniques. A police detective, a court administrator, and a probation officer have all developed technical skills directly related to the work they perform. Katz wrote that a technical skill "involves specialized knowledge, analytical ability within that specialty, and facility in the use of the tools and techniques of the specific discipline."[60] This is the skill most easily trained for. A court administrator, for example, has to be knowledgeable in areas such as computer applications, budgeting, caseload management, space utilization, public relations, and personnel administration; a police detective must possess technical skills in interviewing, fingerprinting, and surveillance techniques.[61]

*Human skills* involve working with people, including being thoroughly familiar with what motivates employees and how to utilize group processes. Katz visualized human skills as including "the executive's ability to work effectively as a group member and to build cooperative effort within the team he leads."[62] Katz added that the human relations skill involves tolerance of ambiguity and empathy. *Tolerance of ambiguity* means that the manager is able to handle problems when insufficient information precludes making a totally informed decision. **Empathy** is the ability to put oneself in another's place. An awareness of human skills allows a manager to provide the necessary leadership and direction, ensuring that tasks are accomplished in a timely fashion and with the least expenditure of resources.[63]

*Conceptual skills,* Katz said, involve "coordinating and integrating all the activities and interests of the organization toward a common objective."[64] Katz considered such skills to include "an ability to translate knowledge into action." For example, in a criminal justice setting, a court decision concerning the admissibility of evidence would need to be examined in terms of how it affects detectives, other court cases, the forensic laboratory, the property room, and the work of the street officer.

Katz emphasized that these skills can be taught to actual and prospective administrators; thus, good administrators are not simply born but can be trained in the classroom. Furthermore, all three of these skills are present in varying degrees for each management level. As one moves up the hierarchy, conceptual skills become more important and technical skills less important. The common denominator for all levels of management is *human* skills. In today's litigious environment, it is inconceivable that a manager could neglect the human skills.

# Motivating Employees

One of the most fascinating subjects throughout history is how to motivate people. Some have sought to do so through justice (Plato), others through psychoanalysis (Freud), some through conditioning (Pavlov), some through incentives (Taylor), and still others through fear (any number of dictators and despots). From the Industrial Revolution until today, managers have been trying to get a full day's work from their subordinates. The controversy in the early 1990s caused by Japanese businessmen who stated that American workers were lazy certainly raised our collective ire; many U.S. businesspeople and managers would probably agree that better worker motivation is needed. As Donald Favreau and Joseph Gillespie stated, "Getting people to work, the way you want them to work, when you want them to work, is indeed a challenge."[65]

Many theories have attempted to explain motivation. Some of the best known are those resulting from the Hawthorne studies and those developed by Abraham Maslow, Douglas McGregor, and Frederick Herzberg, all of which are discussed here along with the expectancy and contingency theories.

## *The Hawthorne Studies*

As mentioned earlier, one of the most important studies of worker motivation and behavior, launching intense interest and research in those areas, was the Western Electric Company's study in the 1920s. In 1927, engineers at the Hawthorne plant of Western Electric near Chicago conducted an experiment with several groups of workers to determine the effect of illumination on production. The engineers found that when illumination was increased in stages, production increased. To verify their findings, they reduced illumination to its previous level; again, production increased. Confused by their findings, they contacted Elton Mayo and his colleague Fritz Roethlisberger from Harvard to investigate.[66] First, the researchers selected several experienced women assemblers for an experiment. Management removed the women from their formal group and isolated them in a room. The women were compensated on the basis of the output of their group. Next, researchers began a series of environmental changes, each discussed with the women in advance of its implementation. For example, breaks were introduced and light refreshments were served. The normal 6-day week was reduced to 5 days and the workday was cut by 1 hour. *Each* of these changes resulted in increased output.[67] To verify these findings, researchers returned the women to their original working conditions; breaks were eliminated, the 6-day workweek was reinstituted, and all other work conditions were reinstated. The results were that production again increased!

Mayo and his team then performed a second study at the Hawthorne plant. A new group of 14 workers—all men who worked in simple, repetitive telephone coil-winding duties—were given variations in rest periods and workweeks.[68] The men were also put on a reasonable piece rate—that is, the more they produced, the more money they would earn. The assumption was that the workers would strive to produce more because it was in their own economic interest to do so.

The workers soon split into two informal groups on their own, each group setting its own standards of output and conduct. The workers' output did not increase. Neither too little nor too much production was permitted, and peers exerted pressure to keep members in line. The values of the informal group appeared to be more powerful than the allure of bigger incomes:

1. Don't be a "rate buster" and produce too much work.
2. If you turn out too little work, you are a "chiseler."
3. Don't be a "squealer" to supervisors.
4. Don't be officious; if you aren't a supervisor, don't act like one.[69]

Taken together, the Hawthorne studies revealed that people work for a variety of reasons, not just for money and subsistence. They seek satisfaction for more than their physical needs at work and from their co-workers. For the first time, clear evidence was gathered to support workers' social and esteem needs. As a result, this collision between the human relations school, begun in the Hawthorne studies, and traditional organizational theory sent researchers and theorists off in new and different directions. At least three major, new areas of enquiry evolved: (1) what motivates workers (leading to the work of Maslow and Herzberg), (2) leadership (discussed earlier), and (3) organizations as behavioral systems.

## *Maslow's Hierarchy of Needs*

Abraham H. Maslow (1908–1970), founder of the humanistic school of psychology, conducted research on human behavior at the Air University, Maxwell Air Force Base, Alabama, during the 1940s. His approach to motivation was unique

## EXHIBIT 2.1
## Leadership's Bond of Trust

*By Lawrence B. Kokkelenberg*

The old military dogma, one also quite familiar to many areas of the private sector, was "I am the boss you are the subordinate, just do what I tell you to do. You don't have to trust me, in fact you don't even have to like me. Just follow orders." Many old adages support this paradigm: "Leadership is a lonely position." "A manager's job is to manage, not run a popularity contest." "If you are going to lead, then lead." "When I tell you to jump, just go up, I'll tell you when to come down."

This autocratic approach worked well for America for 200 years, but that was back in the days when life was simple. Back then if you did not work, you did not eat. Today if you don't work, you can make a pretty good living. We are not economically or financially bound by a job today as we were then. Back then, having a job was only a means to an end (providing for your family). Today, having a meaningful career is an important end in itself. Back then, we worked for someone; today we want to work with someone. (Today there are no "employees"; everyone is an "associate.") Back then, work came first, then family. For many workers today, family is first and work second. Back then there was [*sic*] little, if any, civil rights laws, today, everyone has rights.

Times have changed, people's values have changed. People today are more sophisticated and more mature than the workers of 50 years ago. In fact,

the entire culture has changed, and if leadership does not change its style then it is the leadership that is out of sync with the culture and the desires of the American work force. The new Generation X'ers will only serve to prove the above even further and more rapidly than the current generation.

More than ever before in the history of American management, values are critical. ... A leader's values color the entire organization or country. ... Values drive the behavior and therefore the culture of an organization. All organizations have values, whether they know it or not. Simply watch how people are treated in any organization and you'll see their informal values. Trust is one of those critical values.

Why is trust important? Because all good sustained relationships require trust. Think about this: Would you voluntarily follow anyone you did not trust? We learned this lesson in Vietnam about not trusting our military leaders. Look what happened to those individuals.

To be a leader, you must have followers. So the question to ask yourself is why in the world would anyone choose to voluntarily follow you. What traits or characteristics do you possess that would encourage people to say, "I'll go with you anywhere"? Here is the acid test. If you left your current department or agency and went to another, would you have people who would want to transfer with you, or would the remaining staff now have a party because you're gone?

Certainly one of the key characteristics of an effective leader is that followers trust him or her. Have you ever worked for someone you did not trust? What was the atmosphere like? How would you characterize your relationship with him or her? What were some of the qualities or traits of this boss? Contrast this with someone you did trust. What was this atmosphere like? How would you characterize this trusting relationship? What were some of the qualities or traits of this boss?

Leadership is not about position, title or rank; it is about developing, possessing or acquiring the necessary traits to encourage people to voluntarily follow us. We tend to trust those individuals who have integrity, solid values and a strong character ethic. We tend not to trust those individuals who are duplicitous, upholding the law for others while violating it themselves. How many officers speed on their way to and from work every day, and then write tickets for citizens who do the same? ...

If you want to be a trusted leader, work on your character and be trustworthy. Over time, establish yourself as an individual of great character and moral strength, walk the talk, have integrity, be honest and fair, do the right things and you will be a trusted leader.

*Source:* Reprinted with permission from *Law Enforcement News,* May 15, 2001, pp. 9, 10. John Jay College of Criminal Justice (CCNY), 555 West 57th St., New York, NY 10019.

in that the behavior patterns analyzed were those of motivated, happy, and production-oriented people—achievers, not underachievers. He studied biographies of historical and public figures, including Abraham Lincoln, Albert Einstein, and Eleanor Roosevelt; he also observed and interviewed some of his contemporaries—all of whom showed no psychological problems or signs of neurotic behavior.

Maslow hypothesized that if he could understand what made these people function, it would be possible to apply the same techniques to others, thus achieving a high state of motivation. His observations were coalesced into a *hierarchy of needs.*[70]

Maslow concluded that because human beings are part of the animal kingdom, their basic and primary needs or drives would be physiological: air, food, water, sex, and shelter. These needs are related to survival. Next in order of importance are needs related to safety or security: protection against danger, murder, criminal assault, threat, deprivation, and tyranny. At the middle of the hierarchy is belonging, or social needs: being accepted by one's peers and association with members of groups. At the next level on the hierarchy are the needs or drives related to ego: self-esteem, self-respect, power, prestige, recognition, and status. Located at the top of the hierarchy is self-realization or actualization: self-fulfillment, creativity, becoming all that one is capable of becoming.[71] Figure 2.9 depicts this hierarchy.

Unlike the lower needs, the higher needs are rarely satisfied. Maslow suggested that to prevent frustration, needs should be filled in sequential order. A

| Self-Realization Needs | Job-Related Satisfiers |
|---|---|
| Reaching Your Potential<br>Independence<br>Creativity<br>Self-Expression | Involvement in Planning<br>Your Work<br>Freedom to Make Decisions<br>Affecting Work<br>Creative Work to Perform<br>Opportunities for Growth<br>and Development |

| Esteem Needs | Job-Related Satisfiers |
|---|---|
| Responsibility<br>Self-Respect<br>Recognition<br>Sense of Accomplishment<br>Sense of Competence | Status Symbols<br>Merit Awards<br>Challenging Work<br>Sharing in Decisions<br>Opportunity for Advancement |

| Social Needs | Job-Related Satisfiers |
|---|---|
| Companionship<br>Acceptance<br>Love and Affection<br>Group Membership | Opportunities for Interaction<br>with Others<br>Team Spirit<br>Friendly Co-workers |

| Safety Needs | Job-Related Satisfiers |
|---|---|
| Security for Self and Possessions<br>Avoidance of Risks<br>Avoidance of Harm<br>Avoidance of Pain | Safe Working Conditions<br>Seniority<br>Fringe Benefits<br>Proper Supervision<br>Sound Company Policies, Programs,<br>and Practices |

| Physical Needs | Job-Related Satisfiers |
|---|---|
| Food<br>Clothing<br>Shelter<br>Comfort<br>Self-Preservation | Pleasant Working Conditions<br>Adequate Wage or Salary<br>Rest Periods<br>Labor-Saving Devices<br>Efficient Work Methods |

**Figure 2.9**

Maslow's hierarchy of human needs. *Source:* A. H. Maslow, *Motivation and Personality*, 2nd ed. (New York: Harper & Collins, 1970).

satisfied need is no longer a motivator. Maslow's research also indicated that once a person reaches a high state of motivation (i.e., esteem or self-realization levels), he or she will remain highly motivated, will have a positive attitude toward the organization, and will follow a "pitch in and help" philosophy.

## McGregor's Theory X/Theory Y

Douglas McGregor (1906–1967), who served as president of Antioch College and then on the faculty of the Massachusetts Institute of Technology, was one of the great advocates of humane and democratic management. At Antioch, McGregor tested his theories of democratic management. He noted that behind every managerial decision or action are assumptions about human behavior. He chose the simplest terms possible with which to express them, designating one set of assumptions as Theory X and the other Theory Y.[72]

*Theory X managers* hold traditional views of direction and control, such as the following:

- The average human being has an inherent dislike of work and will avoid it if possible. This assumption has deep roots, beginning with the punishment of Adam and Eve and their banishment into a world where they had to work for a living. Management's use of negative reinforcement and the emphasis on "a fair day's work" reflect an underlying belief that management must counter an inherent dislike for work.[73]

- Because of this human characteristic of dislike of work, most people must be coerced, controlled, directed, or threatened with punishment to get them to put forth adequate effort toward the achievement of organizational objectives. The dislike of work is so strong that even the promise of rewards is not generally enough to overcome it. People will accept the rewards and demand greater ones. Only the threat of punishment will work.[74]

- The average human being prefers to be directed, wishes to avoid responsibility, has relatively little ambition, and wants security above all. This assumption of the "mediocrity of the masses" is rarely expressed so bluntly. Although much lip service is paid to the "sanctity" of the worker and human beings in general, many managers reflect this assumption in practice and policy.

(*Note:* Theory X managers would be autocratic and classified as a 9,1 on the managerial grid.)

*Theory Y managers* take the opposite view of the worker:

- The expenditure of physical and mental effort in work is as natural as play or rest. The average human being does not inherently dislike work; it may even be a source of satisfaction, to be performed voluntarily.

- External control and the threat of punishment are not the only means for bringing about effort toward organizational objectives.

- Commitment to objectives is a function of the rewards associated with their achievement. The most significant of such rewards—satisfaction of ego and self-actualization needs—can be direct products of effort directed toward organizational objectives.

- Under proper conditions, the average human being learns not only to accept, but also to seek responsibility. Under this view, the avoidance of responsibility, lack of ambition, and the emphasis on security are general consequences of experience, not inherent human characteristics.
- The capacity to exercise a high degree of imagination, ingenuity, and creativity in the solution of organizational problems is widely, not narrowly, distributed in the population.
- Under the conditions of modern industrial life, the intellectual potentialities of the average human being are only partially utilized.

## Herzberg's Motivation–Hygiene Theory

During the 1950s, Frederick Herzberg conducted a series of studies in which he asked workers, primarily engineers, to describe the times when they felt particularly good and particularly bad about their jobs. The respondents identified several sources of satisfaction and dissatisfaction in their work. Then, from these findings, Herzberg isolated two vital factors found in all jobs: maintenance or hygiene factors and motivational factors.

**Maintenance or hygiene factors** are those elements in the work environment that meet an employee's hedonistic need to avoid pain. Hygiene factors include the necessities of any job (e.g., adequate pay, benefits, job security, decent working conditions, supervision, interpersonal relations). Hygiene factors do not satisfy or motivate; they set the stage for motivation. They are, however, a major source of dissatisfaction when they are inadequate.[75]

**Motivational factors** are those psychosocial factors that provide intrinsic satisfaction and serve as an incentive for people to invest more of their time, talent, energy, and expertise in productive behavior. Examples include achievement, recognition, responsibility, the work itself, advancement, and potential for growth. The absence of motivators does not necessarily produce job dissatisfaction.[76]

Although these needs are obviously related, they represent totally different dimensions of satisfaction.

## Expectancy and Contingency Theories

In the 1960s, *expectancy theory* was developed, holding that employees will do what their managers or organizations want them to do if the following are true:

1. The task appears to be possible (employees believe they possess the necessary competence).
2. The reward (outcome) offered is seen as desirable by the employees (intrinsic rewards come from the job itself; extrinsic rewards are supplied from others).
3. There is a perception in the mind of employees that performing the required behavior or task will bring the desired outcome.
4. There is a good chance that better performance will bring greater rewards.[77]

## Exhibit 2.2
## Real Leadership Is More Than Just a Walk in the Park

*By Lawrence D. Kokkelenberg*

"If you think you're a leader, but nobody is following you, then you are just out for a walk."

Bosses have subordinates, but true leaders have followers regardless of their rank or title. Historically, when individuals thought of leadership, they thought of rank. For rookies, it was the field training officer and for everyone else it was the level(s) above their rank. That perception, along with a top-down chain of command, caused a lot of people to believe that they cannot or should not do anything about reoccurring or organizational problems. Organizational problems were beyond their authority, even if they saw departmental problems and solutions; they simply waited for those above them to resolve it.

In many police academies we teach the recruits to have good independent judgment and decision-making out on the street. But when it comes to department or agency issues, we enforce a chain-of-command approach. Today, departments and agencies are telling their employees that you are a leader regardless of your position, title or rank; if you see a problem, solve it or bring it to your boss's attention. ...

Leadership begins with self-discipline or leadership of self. You must have self-confidence, self-worth, a sense of purpose and direction in your life, and established values that you choose to live by, before you can effectively have interdependence and work well with others.

Today many departments and agencies are adopting a cradle-to-grave approach to leadership. It begins with recruits at the academy and ends with senior law enforcement executives. There are essentially four levels of leadership and at each level different knowledge and skill sets are necessary. There is a different focus at each level, yet there is a common thread running through the entire program, and each level builds on the one before it.

1. At the core is personal leadership, which is leadership of self. Included here are ethics, developing values, self-confidence, and character development. Every recruit class and every academy should spend considerable time teaching and demonstrating ethics, value development, character development and the consequences that attend to the lack of these traits. Background checks are not sufficient. They only cull out the obvious and recent problem applicants. Avoiding the recruitment of felons is not the same as character development.

2. At the next level—FTO's, sergeants, lieutenants—the focus is on leadership of others, or interpersonal leadership. This level includes a wide variety of supervisory and management skills—most importantly, what it takes to lead others, what are the traits of effective leaders, and how to develop those traits. The recognition that leadership is a choice, not a position, is critical here.

3. Next comes the management level of leadership (shift commanders, bureau chiefs, etc.). At this level there is broader responsibility, yet not at the senior command level. Leadership entails an understanding of organizational psychology and organizational effectiveness, systems, structure and their impact on behavior. Managerial style, mission vision and values development and their impact on the department's performance are a part of this level's skills to be learned.

4. The fourth level is the organizational level, and is for senior law enforcement executives who deal more with a large-scale or big-picture perspective. Strategy development, systems design, process mapping, re-engineering, leading organizational change and the development of agency culture are a part of this level's skill set.

For decades, leadership development has been looked at as a single training program, not a progression; as an event, not a process. For years we have promoted individuals to leadership positions simply because they were in the right spot at the right time, or because they were friends with someone above them. For years some departments have promoted the wrong people simply because they needed the position filled (crisis hiring on the belief that anyone is better than no one).

Many police agencies are now paying the price for past and current management and leadership malpractice. Police reputations and citizen trust are low, we are having trouble attracting high quality candidates to the profession, citizen suspicions and complaints, police turnover and police prosecutions are all up—the list goes on. Lack of leadership certainly contributed to the current problems and it will be the new leadership that helps reestablish policing as the noble profession it is, and regains citizen and world respect.

*Source:* Reprinted with permission from *Law Enforcement News,* February 14, 2001, p. 9. John Jay College of Criminal Justice (CCNY), 555 West 57th St., New York, NY 10019.

Expectancy theory will work for an organization that specifies what behaviors it expects from people and what the rewards or outcomes will be for those who exhibit such behaviors. Rewards may be pay increases, time off, chances for advancement, a sense of achievement, or other benefits. Managers and organizations can find out what their employees want and see to it that they are provided with the rewards they seek. Walter Newsom[78] said that the reality of the expectancy theory can be summarized by the "nine C's": (1) capability (does a person have the capability to perform well?), (2) confidence (does a person believe that he or she can perform the job well?), (3) challenge (does a person have to work hard to perform the job well?), (4) criteria (does a person know the difference between good and poor performance?), (5) credibility (does a person believe the manager will deliver on promises?), (6) consistency (do subordinates believe that all employees receive similar preferred outcomes for good performance, and vice versa?), (7) compensation (do the outcomes associated with good performance reward the employee with money and other types of rewards?), (8) cost (what does it cost a person, in effort and outcomes forgone, to perform well?), and (9) communication (does the manager comunicate with the subordinate?).

Later, in the 1970s, Morse and Lorsch built on McGregor's and Herzberg's theories with their theory of motivation called *contingency theory*. This theory sought to determine the fit between the organization's characteristics and its tasks and the motivations of individuals. The basic components of the contingency theory are that (1) among people's needs is a central need to achieve a sense of competence, (2) the ways in which people fulfill this need will vary from person to person, (3) competence motivation is most likely to be fulfilled when there is a fit between task and organization, and (4) a sense of competence continues to motivate people even after competence is achieved. In essence, we all want to be competent in our work. Contingency theory contends that people performing highly structured and organized tasks perform better in Theory X organizations and that those who perform unstructured and uncertain tasks perform better under a Theory Y approach. This theory tells managers to tailor jobs to fit people or to give people the skills, knowledge, and attitudes they will need to become competent.[79]

# A Diversion: Managing Generation X/Y Employees

Although not a major theory, many articles and books[80] have been written about understanding and motivating those persons now filling the workplace who were born between 1965 and 1980, **Generation X/Y:** Generation X was born between 1965 and 1975, and Generation Y was born between 1976 and 1980.[81] The Gen Xers grew up very quickly amid rising crime rates and violence, as hostage crises and major disasters unfolded around them; their youthful years were met with a national fear of AIDS; and they entered the job market only to be confronted with new terms like "downsizing."[82] They have been termed "slackers," and maligned for being unreliable, not willing to work long hours, think in terms of "job," not "career," and have unrealistic expectations about raises and promotions.[83] The Y Generation, or Echo Boomers, are viewed by some as coddled and confident, technologically savvy, and with an attitude that says, "I'm here to make a difference."[84]

The American workplace has become a playing field of competing viewpoints and values, as four generations—Silents (mostly retired, born between 1925 and 1942), Baby Boomers (born between 1946 and 1964), Gen Xers, and Echo Boomers—share the same workspace and attempt to navigate unknown cultural territory.[85] Clearly, a major challenge and diversity issue in the workplace is age diversity. It is obviously important that leaders in organizations with employee age diversity understand the potential for clashes between seasoned and young employees over issues like work ethic, respect for authority, dress code, and work arrangements.

What can "seasoned" administrators do when there are Generation X and Y employees in the workplace? First, it is recommended that these leaders understand that the younger employee's preferred work environment is casual and friendly, technologically up to date, neat and orderly, collegial, and a place to learn and includes a high level of freedom. Furthermore, such leaders should avoid judging those whose work ethic is slightly different from theirs; accommodate individual needs whenever possible; forgive impatience (if individuals are anxious for raises and promotions); and, when possible, allow room for mistakes and for the youthful workers to fix the mistakes themselves and to learn from them.[86]

## Summary

Most young people entering the labor force would probably like to retain their individuality, feel free to express themselves, have a sense of being an important part of the team, and realize both extrinsic and intrinsic rewards from their work. The reality is, however, that a majority of people entering the job market will work within the structure of an organization that will not meet all of their personal needs.

We have seen that many organizations have a highly refined bureaucracy. Whether an organization will meet one's individual needs depends largely on its administrative philosophy. Therefore, the discussions in this chapter covered the structure and function of organizations and, just as important, how administrators and subordinates function within them. Also shown to be of major importance is the need for effective communication.

The point to be made above all else is that administrators must know their people. In addition to covering several prominent theories that have withstood the test of time, I pointed out some approaches that have not succeeded. One can learn much from a failed approach or even from a poor boss who failed to appreciate and understand subordinates and practiced improper or no motivational techniques.

## Questions for Review

1. Define *organization*. What is its function and structure?
2. What are the three historical approaches to management? Distinguish between the historical approaches to management and the more "enlightened," contemporary view.
3. What are some of the skills that strong leaders will commonly possess (use the Katz model) and some of the common weaknesses in leadership?
4. What are three major theories concerning the motivation of employees?
5. What does *communication* mean? What is its importance in organizations? Explain some of the major barriers to effective communication and why it can be particularly problematic in criminal justice agencies.

6. Objectively assess what kind of leader you would likely be (if helpful, use the management grid). Is it an effective style? What are some of the possible advantages and disadvantages of that style?

7. What kinds of challenges are posed by Generation X/Y employees working alongside employees of older generations, and what might the administrator know and do to prevent or to ameliorate problems?

# Notes

1. Steven Levy, "Working in Dilbert's World," *Newsweek* (August 12, 1996):52-57.
2. David A. Tansik and James F. Elliott, *Managing Police Organizations* (Monterey, Calif.: Duxbury Press, 1981), p. 1.
3. Stephen P. Robbins, *Organizational Theory: Structure, Design and Applications* (Upper Saddle River, N.J.: Prentice Hall, 1987).
4. Larry K. Gaines, John L. Worrall, Mittie D. Southerland, and John E. Angell, *Police Administration,* 2nd ed. (New York: McGraw-Hill, 2002), p. 8.
5. Peter W. Blau and W. Richard Scott, *Formal Organizations* (Scranton, Pa.: Chandler, 1962), p. 43.
6. Gaines et al., *Police Administration,* p. 12.
7. Max Weber, *The Theory of Social and Economic Organization,* trans. A. M. Henderson and Talcott Parsons (New York: Oxford University Press, 1947), pp. 329-330.
8. James Q. Wilson, *Varieties of Police Behavior* (Cambridge, Mass.: Harvard University Press), pp. 2-3.
9. Ibid., p. 3.
10. Adapted from Lyndall F. Urwick, *Notes on the Theory of Organization* (New York: American Management Association, 1952).
11. Gaines et al., *Police Administration,* p. 12.
12. Leonard R. Sayles and George Strauss, *Human Behavior in Organizations* (Upper Saddle River, N.J.: Prentice Hall, 1966), p. 349.
13. See, for example, Samuel C. Certo, *Principles of Modern Management: Functions and Systems,* 4th ed. (Boston: Allyn and Bacon, 1989), p. 103.
14. Quoted in Wayne W. Bennett and Karen M. Hess, *Management and Supervision in Law Enforcement,* 4th ed. (Belmont, Calif.: Wadsworth, 2004), p. 52.
15. Ibid., pp. 53-54.
16. Paul Hersey and Kenneth H. Blanchard, *Management of Organizational Behavior,* 3rd ed. (Upper Saddle River, N.J.: Prentice Hall, 1977), p. 12.
17. Ibid.
18. Quoted in Bennett and Hess, *Management and Supervision in Law Enforcement,* p. 52.
19. Ibid.
20. Roger D. Evered and James C. Selman, "Coaching and the Art of Management," *Organizational Dynamics* (Autumn 1989):16.
21. Charles R. Swanson, Leonard Territo, and Robert W. Taylor, *Police Administration: Structures, Processes, and Behavior,* 6th ed. (Upper Saddle River, N.J.: Prentice Hall, 2005), p. 272.

22. Charles R. Swanson, Leonard Territo, and Robert W. Taylor, *Police Administration,* 2nd ed. (New York: Macmillan, 1988), p. 86.

23. Louis A. Radelet, *The Police and the Community: Studies* (Beverly Hills, Calif.: Glencoe, 1973), p. 92.

24. Institute of Government, University of Georgia, *Interpersonal Communication: A Guide for Staff Development* (Athens, Ga.: Author, 1974), p. 15.

25. Quoted in Swanson, Territo, and Taylor, *Police Administration,* p. 308.

26. Bennett and Hess, *Management and Supervision in Law Enforcement,* p. 72.

27. See R. C. Huseman, ibid., pp. 21-27. Material for this section was also drawn from Swanson, Territo, and Taylor, *Police Administration,* pp. 309-311.

28. Swanson, Territo, and Taylor, *Police Administration,* pp. 312-313.

29. D. Katz and R. L. Kahn, *The Social Psychology of Organizations* (New York: John Wiley, 1966), p. 239. As cited in P. V. Lewis, *Organizational Communication: The Essence of Effective Management* (Columbus, Ohio: Grid, 1975), p. 36.

30. Lewis, *Organizational Communication,* p. 38.

31. Swanson, Territo, and Taylor, *Police Administration,* p. 315.

32. See R. K. Allen, *Organizational Management Through Communication* (New York: Harper & Row, 1977), pp. 77-79.

33. Swanson, Territo, and Taylor, *Police Administration,* p. 343.

34. Stephen W. Mastrofski, "Police Agency Accreditation: The Prospects of Reform," *American Journal of Police* **5**(3) (1986):45-81.

35. Alex Markels, "Managers Aren't Always Able to Get the Right Message Across with E-Mail." *The Wall Street Journal* (August 6, 1996), p. 2.

36. Robert L. Montgomery, "Are You a Good Listener?" *Nation's Business* (October 1981): 65-68.

37. Bennett and Hess, *Management and Supervision in Law Enforcement,* p. 82.

38. G. Weaver, "Law Enforcement in a Culturally Diverse Society," *FBI Law Enforcement Bulletin* (September 1992):1-10.

39. Ronald G. Lynch, *The Police Manager: Professional Leadership Skills,* 3rd ed. (New York: Random House, 1986), p. 4.

40. Certo, *Principles of Modern Management,* p. 35.

41. See Elton Mayo, *The Human Problems of an Industrial Civilization* (New York: Macmillan, 1933).

42. Paul M. Whisenand and Fred Ferguson, *The Managing of Police Organizations,* 3rd ed. (Upper Saddle River, N.J.: Prentice Hall, 1989), pp. 218-219.

43. Lynch, *Police Manager,* pp. 5-6.

44. Abraham H. Maslow, *Motivation and Personality* (New York: Harper & Row, 1954).

45. Douglas McGregor, *The Human Side of Enterprise* (New York: McGraw-Hill, 1960).

46. Robert R. Blake and Jane S. Mouton, *The Managerial Grid* (Houston, Tex: Gulf, 1964).

47. Lynch, *Police Manager,* pp. 7-8.

48. Richard Holden, *Modern Police Management,* 2nd ed. (Upper Saddle River, N.J.: Prentice Hall, 1994), p. 47.

49. Thomas A. Mahoney, Thomas H. Jerdee, and Alan N. Nash, "Predicting Managerial Effectiveness," *Personnel Psychology* (Summer 1960):147-163.

50. Joe Kelly, *Organizational Behavior: An Existential Systems Approach,* rev. ed. (Homewood, Ill.: Richard D. Irwin, 1974), p. 363.

51. Bennett and Hess, *Management and Supervision in Law Enforcement,* p. 57.

52. Edwin Fleishman, "Leadership Climate, Human Relations Training and Supervisory Behavior," *Personnel Psychology* **6** (1953):208–222.

53. Stephen M. Sales, "Supervisory Style and Productivity: Review and Theory," in Larry Cummings and William E. Scott (eds.), *Readings in Organizational Behavior and Human Performance* (Homewood, Ill.: Richard D. Irwin, 1969), p. 122.

54. Holden, *Modern Police Management,* pp. 39–40.

55. Ibid., pp. 41–42.

56. Paul Hersey and Kenneth H. Blanchard, *Management of Organizational Behavior* (Upper Saddle River, N.J.: Prentice Hall, 1977).

57. Donald F. Favreau and Joseph E. Gillespie, *Modern Police Administration* (Upper Saddle River, N.J.: Prentice Hall, 1978), p. 80.

58. Bennett and Hess, *Management and Supervision in Law Enforcement,* p. 40.

59. Robert L. Katz, "Skills of an Effective Administrator," *Harvard Business Review* **52** (1975):23.

60. Ibid., p. 23.

61. Dan L. Costley and Ralph Todd, *Human Relations in Organizations* (St. Paul, Minn.: West, 1978).

62. Ibid., p. 24.

63. James M. Higgins, *Human Relations: Concepts and Skills* (New York: Random House, 1982).

64. Ibid., p. 27.

65. Favreau and Gillespie, *Modern Police Administration,* p. 85.

66. Warren Richard Plunkett, *Supervision: The Direction of People at Work* (Dubuque, Iowa: Wm. C. Brown, 1983), p. 121.

67. Elton Mayo, *The Social Problems of an Industrial Civilization* (Boston: Division of Research, Graduate School of Business Administration, Harvard University, 1945), pp. 68–86.

68. Favreau and Gillespie, *Modern Police Administration,* pp. 100–101.

69. Frederick J. Roethlisberger and William J. Dickson, *Management and the Worker* (Cambridge, Mass.: Harvard University Press, 1939), p. 522.

70. Favreau and Gillespie, *Modern Police Administration,* p. 87.

71. Ibid.

72. Ibid., p. 88.

73. Ibid., p. 89.

74. Ibid.

75. Harry W. More and W. Fred Wegener, *Behavioral Police Management* (New York: Macmillan, 1992), pp. 163–164.

76. Frederick Herzberg, "One More Time: How Do You Motivate Employees," in Walter E. Netemeyer (ed.), *Classics of Organizational Behavior* (Oak Park, Ill.: Moore, 1978).

77. Randall S. Schuler, *Personnel and Human Resources Management* (St. Paul, Minn.: West, 1981), pp. 41–43.

78. Walter B. Newsom, "Motivate, Now!" *Personnel Journal* (February 1990):51–55.

79. Plunkett, *Supervision,* pp. 131–132.

80. See, for example, Douglas Coupland, *Generation X: Tales for an Accelerated Culture* (New York: St. Martin's, 1992); Carolyn A. Martin and Bruce Tulgan, *Managing Generation Y* (Amherst, Mass.: HRD Press, 2001).

81. Stephen's Generation X Site, http://www.users.metro2000.net/~stabbott/genx.htm (accessed September 7, 2005).

82. Dan King, "Defining a Generation: Tips for Uniting Our Multi-Generational Workforce," http://www.careerfirm.com/generations.htm (accessed February 3, 2005).

83. Claire Raines, "Generation X Managing Generation X," http://www.generationsatwork.com/articles/genx.htm (accessed February 3, 2005).

84. Ibid., p. 2.

85. King, "Defining a Generation," p. 1.

86. Raines, "Managing Generation X," p. 2.

# PART II

# THE POLICE

*This part consists of four chapters. Chapter 3 examines the organization and operation of police departments. Chapter 4 covers personnel roles and functions, and Chapter 5 discusses police issues and practices. Chapter 6 examines the functions of law enforcement administrators in relation to terrorism and homeland defense. The introductory section of each chapter previews the specific chapter content, and case studies in police administration appear at the end of each chapter.*

# Chapter 3

# Police Organization and Operation

## Key Terms and Concepts

| | |
|---|---|
| Administrative intensity | Organizational change |
| Centralization | Organizational structure |
| COPPS | Policies |
| Division of labor | Procedures |
| Formalization | Rules and regulations |
| Functional differentiation | S.A.R.A. |
| Military model | Spatial differentiation |
| Occupational differentiation | Specialization |
| Organization | Vertical differentiation |

## Learning Objectives

As a result of reading this chapter, the student will:

- understand why police agencies are arranged into organizations
- understand the division of labor in an organization
- be familiar with the seven elements of police organizational structure
- know how the military model can both help and hinder policing
- understand community policing and its problem-solving S.A.R.A. process
- know the importance of police supervisors, chief executives, and mid-level managers in effecting change
- comprehend the purposes of policies, procedures, rules, and regulations in police organizations

> *Good order is the foundation of all things.*
> —Edmund Burke

> *From harmony, from heavenly harmony/ This universal frame began.*
> —John Dryden, "A Song for "St. Cecilia's Day"

## Introduction

To perform smoothly (at least as smoothly as society, resources, politics, and other influences permit), police agencies must be organized to enhance the accomplishment of their basic mission and goals. This chapter examines the elements of contemporary police organization and what is needed organizationally to effect the transition to a community policing and problem-solving operation.

First I consider how law enforcement agencies constitute, and operate as, bona fide organizations, including the need for specialization in larger agencies. I then review the seven elements of police organizational structure; included are examples of basic as well as more specialized organizational structures for police agencies. After an overview of policies, procedures, rules, and regulations that provide guidelines for organizations, I examine what is now the dominant concept in police philosophy and operations: community-oriented policing and problem solving, or COPPS; this approach has caused many changes in the organization and administration of police agencies. I define the term and discuss the problem-solving process. Following that, I examine what must occur for police organizations to change, including the roles of chief executives, mid-level managers, and first-line supervisors.

The chapter concludes with two case studies.

# Police Agencies as Organizations

## *The Grouping of Activities*

An **organization** is an artificial structure created to coordinate either people or groups and resources to achieve a mission or goal.[1] Certainly police agencies fit this definition. First, the organization of these agencies includes a number of specialized units (e.g., patrol, traffic, investigation, records). The role of chief executives, mid-managers, and first-line supervisors is to ensure that these units work together to reach a common goal; allowing each unit to work independently would lead to fragmentation, conflict, and competition and would subvert the entire organization's goals and purposes. Second, police agencies consist of people who interact within the organization and with external organizations.

Through mission statements, policies and procedures (discussed later), and management style, among other factors, police administrators attempt to ensure that the organization meets its overall goals of investigating and suppressing crime and that the organization works amiably with similar organizations. As the organization becomes larger, the need for people to cooperate to achieve the organizational goals increases. The formal organizational charts discussed later in this chapter assist in this endeavor by spelling out areas of responsibility and lines of communication and by defining the chain of command.

Police administrators modify or design the structure of their organization to fulfill their mission. An organizational structure reflects the formal organization of task and authority relationships determined to be best suited to accomplishing the police mission (organizational structures are discussed and shown later in this chapter).

## *The Division of Labor*

The larger an agency, the greater is the need for specialization and the more vertical (taller) its organizational chart becomes. Some 2,300 years ago, Plato observed that "each thing becomes ... easier when one man, exempt from other tasks, does one thing."[2]

**Specialization,** or the **division of labor,** is one of the basic features of traditional organizational theory.[3] Specialization produces different groups of functional responsibilities, and the jobs allocated to meet these different responsibilities are held by people who are considered to be especially well qualified to perform those jobs. Thus, specialization is crucial to effectiveness and efficiency in large organizations.[4]

Specialization makes the organization more complex, however, by complicating communication, increasing the units from which cooperation must be obtained, and creating conflict among different units. Specialization creates an increased need for coordination because it adds to the hierarchy, which can lead to narrowly defined jobs that stifle the creativity and energy of their incumbents. Police administrators are aware of these potential shortcomings of specialization and attempt through various means to inspire their employees to the extent possible. For example, personnel can be rotated to various jobs and given additional responsibilities that challenge them. In addition, in a medium-sized department, for example, serving a community of 100,000 or more, a police officer with 10 years of police experience can have had the responsibilities of dog handler, motorcycle officer, detective, and/or traffic officer while being a member of special weapons or hostage negotiation teams.

In sum, the advantages to specialization in large police departments include the following:

- *Placement of responsibility.* The responsibility for the performance of given tasks can be placed on specific units or individuals. For example, the traffic division investigates all accidents and the patrol division handles all calls for service.
- *Development of expertise.* Those who have specialized responsibilities receive specialized training. Homicide investigators can be sent to forensic pathology classes; special weapons and tactics teams train regularly to deal with terrorists or hostage situations.
- *Group esprit de corps.* Groups of specially trained persons share a camaraderie and depend on one another for success; this leads to cohesion and high morale.
- *Increased efficiency and effectiveness.* Specialized units have a high degree of proficiency in job task responsibility. For example, a specially trained financial crimes unit normally is more successful with complex fraud cases than is a general detective division.[5]

## Elements of Police Organizational Structure

According to Mintzberg, an **organizational structure** can be defined simply as the sum total of the ways in which it divides its labor into distinct tasks and then achieves coordination among them.[6] This definition translates into measures that are relatively easy to compute.

Supported in part by a grant from the National Institute of Justice, Edward R. Maguire, Heunhee Shin, Zihong Zhao, and Kimberly D. Hassell accomplished an excellent analysis of organizations and structural change in large police agencies. Essentially, they determined that there are seven specific elements of law enforcement organizational structure; the first four are types of structural "differentiation" or methods of dividing labor. They are (1) functional, (2) occupational, (3) spatial, and (4) vertical differentiation, and (5) centralization, (6) formalization, and (7) administrative intensity.[7]

1. **Functional differentiation** is the degree to which tasks are broken down into functionally distinct units. A police agency with a homicide unit, an accident reconstruction unit, and a juvenile division is more functionally differentiated than one that only employs patrol officers. Law enforcement organizations became more functionally differentiated throughout the twentieth century, adding new bureaus, divisions, and specialized units to perform separate functions as the need arose.[8]

2. **Occupational differentiation** measures distinctions within the staff (job titles) and the extent to which an organization relies on specially trained workers from distinct occupational groups. Civilianization has increased in policing, and today civilian police employees represent a separate occupational group.[9]

3. **Spatial differentiation** is the extent to which an organization is spread geographically. A police agency with a headquarters and several precinct stations is more spatially differentiated than a department that operates out of a single police facility. Police agencies with a single patrol beat and a single facility are the least spatially differentiated. Those agencies that carve the jurisdiction into a large number of small beats, with functioning ministations scattered throughout the jurisdiction and district stations in different areas of the community, are the most spatially differentiated.[10]

4. **Vertical differentiation** focuses on the hierarchical nature of an organization's command structure, including its (a) segmentation, (b) concentration, and (c) height. Organizations with elaborate chains of command are more vertically differentiated than those with "flatter" command structures. *Segmentation* is the number of command levels in an organization, from the lowest ranking to the highest. Some agencies maintain "status" ranks that carry greater prestige and/or pay but no supervisory or command authority other than in very limited circumstances. Examples are master police officers and corporals in some agencies, who are given supervisory authority on rare occasion, such as when a sergeant is unavailable. Other rank structures are a mix of functional and hierarchical differentiation; for example, sometimes detectives may receive greater pay and prestige than other officers but have no greater supervisory or command authority. *Concentration* is the percentage of personnel located at various levels, and *height* is the social distance between the lowest- and highest-ranking employees in the organization. Police agencies in which patrol officers can drop in routinely to chat with

the chief of police or sheriff are less vertically differentiated than those in which there is significant social distance between the chief and the lowest-ranking employees.[11]

5. **Centralization** is the extent to which the decision-making capacity within an organization is concentrated in a single individual or a small select group. Organizations in which lower-ranking employees are given the autonomy to make decisions are less centralized than those in which senior administrators make most decisions.

6. **Formalization** is the extent to which employees are governed by specific rules and policies. Some factors in law enforcement, including liability issues and accreditation, are likely to encourage increases in formalization.

7. **Administrative intensity** refers to the proportion of organizational resources committed to administration. Organizations with high levels of administrative intensity are often thought of as being more bureaucratic.[12]

# Examples of Police Organization

## *The Basic Organizational Structure*

As noted, an organizational structure helps departments carry out the many complex responsibilities of policing. It should be noted, however, that organizational structures vary from one jurisdiction to another and are fluid in nature. The highly decentralized nature and the different sizes of police departments in the United States, as well as turnover in the chief executive officer (chief of police or sheriff) position, cause these structures to change. It is possible, however, to make certain general statements about all agencies to characterize a "typical" police organization.

The police traditionally organize along military lines with a rank structure that normally includes the patrol officer, sergeant, lieutenant, captain, and chief. Many departments, particularly larger ones, employ additional ranks, such as corporal, major, and deputy chief, but there is a legitimate concern that these departments will become top heavy. The military rank hierarchy allows the organization to designate authority and responsibility at each level and to maintain a chain of command. The military model also allows the organization to emphasize supervisor–subordinate relationships and to maintain discipline and control. The quasi-military style of policing is discussed later.

Every police agency, regardless of size, has a basic plan of organization. In addition, every such agency, no matter how large or small, has an organizational structure. A visitor to the police station or sheriff's office may even see this organizational structure displayed prominently on a wall. Even if it is not on paper, such a structure exists. A basic organizational structure for a small agency is shown in Figure 3.1.

Operational or line elements involve policing functions in the field and may be subdivided into primary and secondary line elements. The patrol function—often

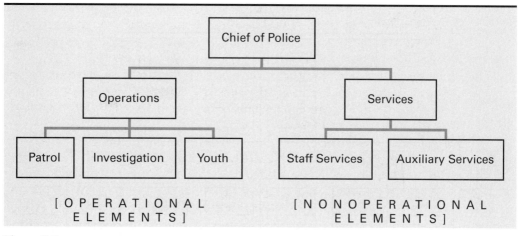

**Figure 3.1**

Basic police organizational structure.

called the "backbone" of policing—is the primary line element because it is the major law enforcement responsibility within the police organization. Most small police agencies, in fact, can be described as patrol agencies with the patrol forces responsible for all line activities. Such agencies provide routine patrol, conduct criminal and traffic investigations, and make arrests. These agencies are basically generalists. In a community that has only one policing employee—a city marshal, for example—he or she obviously must perform all the functions just listed. This agency's organizational chart is a simple horizontal one with little or no specialization.

Investigative and youth activities are the secondary operational elements. These functions would not be needed if the police were totally successful in their patrol and crime prevention efforts—an obviously impossible goal. Time and area restrictions on the patrol officers, as well as the need for specialized training and experience, require some augmenting of the patrol activity.

The nonoperational functions and activities can become quite numerous, especially in a large community. These functions fall within two broad categories: *staff services* (also known as administrative) and *auxiliary* (or technical) *services*. The staff services are usually people oriented and include recruitment, training, promotion, planning and research, community relations, and public information services. Auxiliary services involve the types of functions that a non-police person rarely sees, including jail management, property and evidence handling, crime laboratory services, communications (dispatch), and records and identification. Many career opportunities exist for persons interested in police-related work who cannot or do not want to be a field officer.

Consider the organizational structure for a larger police organization, that of the Portland, Oregon, Police Bureau (PPB) (see Figure 3.2) Portland has a

# Portland Police Bureau
## Organizational Chart

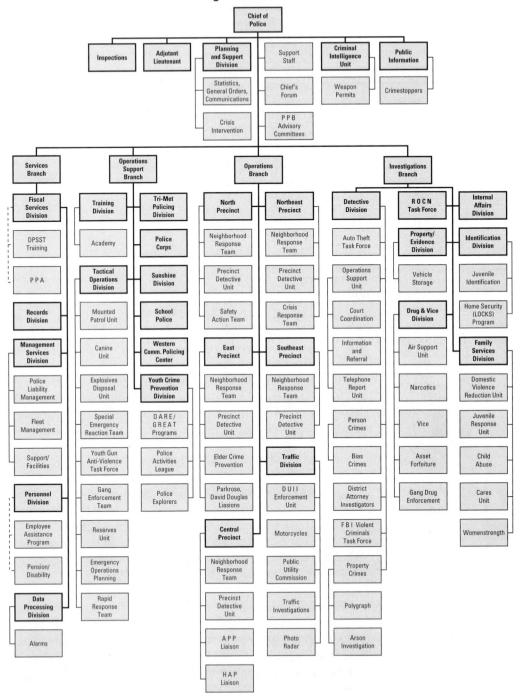

## Figure 3.2

Portland police bureau organizational chart. Reprinted with permission.

population of about 560,000, but the metropolitan area (consisting of five counties) has about 2 million people.[13] The PPB has about 1,350 total personnel, 1,000 of whom are sworn.[14] Like all organizations, especially those that are medium or large in size, some of the PPB functions are unique to that organization.[15]

Portland's and other cities' organizational structures are designed to fulfill five functions: apportioning the workload among members and units according to a logical plan; ensuring that lines of authority and responsibility are as definite and direct as possible; specifying a unity of command throughout, so there is no question as to which orders should be followed; placing responsibility and authority, and if responsibility is delegated, holding the delegator responsible; and coordinating the efforts of members so that all will work harmoniously to accomplish the mission.[16] In sum, this structure establishes the chain of command and determines lines of communication and responsibility.

## Commentary on the Quasi-Military Style of Policing

Police experts have long written about the quasi-military style of policing.[17] Egon Bittner, for example, felt that the adoption of the **military model** by the police—wearing uniforms, using rank designations, adopting hierarchical command structure, acquiring legal authority (use of weapons and force)—was a reaction to the political influences over the police in the late nineteenth century that contributed to corruption[18] (e.g., payoffs for underenforcement of laws, political activity to "get out the vote").

Proponents of the militaristic style of policing uphold the model's tradition, its imposition of control and commanding authority with strict discipline,[19] respect for chain of command and rigid rank differences, "elite warrior" self-image, and centralized command. Critics of the model, however, note that it is excessively rigid, controlled by micromanaging bureaucrats, autocratic, secretive, intellectually and creatively constraining, and highly resistant to any initiative that will allow employee participation in the decision-making processes. In other words, it is said to often discourage creativity; cultivate the "us-versus-them" and "war on crime" mentalities;[20] eschew scientific or academic approaches in favor of an "applied" focus; rely heavily on tradition, or the "we've always done it this way" approach, causing a commitment to outmoded methods of operation; and have a distinct tendency to mismatch talent with job positions.

With today's emphasis on community-oriented policing and problem solving (COPPS, discussed later), many COPPS advocates believe that the quasi-military model is incompatible with this philosophy. As one police chief executive put it,

> Whereas community policing requires a policing approach that demonstrates openness, a service orientation, innovative/creative thinking, and problem solving, these characteristics are not likely to be developed in a militaristic managerial model. This is a style which at worst will tend to give rise to an operational police culture which is action oriented, cynical, suspicious, reactive and, most importantly in the context of community policing, insular and isolated from the general community.[21]

Some types of situations, such as critical incidents, will likely compel the retention of command and control in police training and tactical application. But in nonemergency situations involving a focus on crime and disorder, problem-solving policing requires personal and intellectual reasoning skills, skills that must be trained if a COPPS culture is to be developed.

# Organizational Guidelines: Policies, Procedures, Rules, and Regulations

Policies, procedures, rules, and regulations are important for defining role expectations for all police officers. The officers are granted an unusually strong power in a democratic society; because they possess such extraordinary powers, police officers pose a potential threat to individual freedom. Thus, because police agencies are service oriented in nature, they must work within well-defined, specific guidelines designed to ensure that all officers conform to behavior that will enhance public protection.[22]

Related to this need for policies, procedures, rules, and regulations is the fact that police officers possess a broad spectrum of discretionary authority in performing their duties. This fact, coupled with the danger posed by their work and the opportunities to settle problems informally, work against having narrow, inflexible job requirements.

Thus, the task for the organization's chief executive is to find the middle ground between unlimited discretion and total standardization. The police role is much too ambiguous to become totally standardized, but it is also much too serious and important to be left completely to the total discretion of the patrol officer. As Gary Sheehan and Gary Cordner put it, the idea is for chief executives to "harness, but not choke, their employees."[23]

Organizational policies are more general than procedures, rules, or regulations. **Policies** are basically guides to the organization's philosophy and mission and help to interpret those elements to the officers.[24] Policies should be committed to writing, then modified according to the changing times and circumstances of the department and community.

**Procedures** are more specific than policies; they serve as guides to action. A procedure is "more specific than a policy but less restrictive than a rule or regulation. It describes a method of operation while still allowing some flexibility within limits."[25]

Many organizations are awash in procedures. Police organizations have procedures that cover investigation, patrol, booking, radio communications, filing, roll-call, arrest, sick leave, evidence handling, promotion, and others. Such procedures are not totally inflexible, but they do describe in rather detailed terms the preferred methods for carrying out policy.

Some procedures are mandated by the U.S. Supreme Court. A good example is the Court's 1985 decision in *Tennessee v. Garner*. This decision resulted in a new policy concerning the use of deadly force. Officers are allowed to use deadly force only when a "suspect threatens the officer with a weapon or there is probable cause to believe that [the suspect] has committed a crime involving the infliction or threatened infliction of serious physical harm."[26]

Some police executives have attempted to run their departments via flurries of memos containing new procedures. This path is often fraught with difficulty. An abundance of standardized procedures can stifle initiative and imagination, as well as complicate jobs.[27] On the positive side, procedures can decrease the time wasted in figuring out how to accomplish tasks and thereby increase productivity. As they do with policies, chief executives must seek the middle ground in drafting procedures and remember that it is next to impossible to have procedures that cover all possible exigencies.

**Rules and regulations** are specific managerial guidelines that leave little or no latitude for individual discretion; they require action (or in some cases, inaction). Some require officers to wear their hats when outside their patrol vehicle, check the patrol vehicle's oil and emergency lights before going on patrol, not consume alcoholic beverages within 4 hours of going on duty, and arrive in court 30 minutes before sessions open or at roll call 15 minutes before scheduled duty time. Rules and regulations are not always popular, especially if perceived as unfair or unrelated to the job. Nonetheless, they contribute to the total police mission of community service.

Rules and regulations should obviously be kept to a minimum because of their coercive nature. If they become too numerous, they can hinder action and give the message that management believes that it cannot trust the rank and file to act responsibly on their own. Once again, the middle range is the best. As Thomas Reddin, former Los Angeles police chief, stated,

> Certainly we must have rules, regulations and procedures, and they should be followed. But they are no substitutes for initiative and intelligence. The more a [person] is given an opportunity to make decisions and, in the process, to learn, the more rules and regulations will be followed.[28]

Next I discuss COPPS, including some evaluation and research efforts.

# Community-Oriented Policing and Problem Solving

## *Rationale and Definition*

Community-oriented policing and problem solving—**COPPS**—has emerged as the dominant strategy of policing. It is an approach to crime detection and prevention that provides police officers and supervisors with new tools for addressing recurrent problems that plague communities and consume a majority of police agency time and resources. The California Department of Justice provided the following definition for COPPS:

> Community-oriented policing and problem solving is a philosophy, management style, and organizational strategy that promotes proactive problem solving and

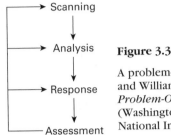

**Figure 3.3**

A problem-solving process. *Source:* John E. Eck and William Spelman, *Problem-Solving: Problem-Oriented Policing in Newport News* (Washington, D.C.: U.S. Department of Justice, National Institute of Justice, 1987), p. 43.

police–community partnerships to address the causes of crime and fear as well as other community issues.[29]

Two principal and interrelated components emerge from this definition: community engagement (partnerships) and problem solving. With its focus on collaborative problem solving, COPPS seeks to improve the quality of policing.

The S.A.R.A. process discussed next provides the police with the tools necessary to accomplish these tasks.

## *The S.A.R.A. Process*

**S.A.R.A.** (*S*canning, *A*nalysis, *R*esponse, *A*ssessment). Figure 3.3 provides officers with a logical step-by-step framework in which to identify, analyze, respond to, and evaluate crime, fear of crime, and neighborhood disorder. This approach, with its emphasis on in-depth analysis and collaboration, replaces officers' short-term, reactive responses with a process vested in longer-term outcomes.

### *Scanning: Problem Identification*
Scanning involves problem identification. It initiates the problem-solving process by conducting a preliminary inquiry to determine whether a problem really exists and whether further analysis is needed. A problem may be defined as a cluster of two or more similar or related incidents that are of substantive concern to the community and to the police. If the incidents to which the police respond do not fall within the definition of a problem, then the problem-solving process is not applicable.

Numerous resources are available to the police for identifying problems, including calls for service data—especially repeat calls, crime analysis information, police reports, and officers' experiences. Scanning helps the officer to determine whether a problem really exists before moving on to more in-depth analysis.

### *Analysis: Determining the Extent of the Problem*
Analysis is the heart of the problem-solving process. It is the most difficult and important step in the S.A.R.A. process. Without analysis, long-term solutions are unlikely and the problem will persist.

**Figure 3.4**

Problem analysis traingle. *Source:* Bureau of Justice Assistance, U.S. Department of Justice, *Comprehensive Gang Initiative: Operations Manual for Implementing Local Gang Prevention and Control Programs* (Draft, October 1993), pp. 3–10.

Here, officers gather as much information as possible from a variety of sources. A complete and thorough analysis consists in officers identifying the seriousness of the problem, all persons affected, and the underlying causes. Officers should also assess the effectiveness of current responses.

Many tools are available to assist with analysis. Crime analysis may be useful in collecting, collating, analyzing, and disseminating data relating to crime, incidents not requiring a report, criminal offenders, victims, and locations. Mapping and geographic information systems (GIS) can identify patterns of crime and "hotspots." Police offense reports can also be analyzed for suspect characteristics, victim characteristics, and information about high-crime areas and addresses. Computer-aided dispatch (CAD) is also a reliable source of information, as it collects data on all incidents and specific locations from which an unusual number of incidents require a police response.

Generally, three elements are needed for a problem to occur: an *offender,* a *victim*, and a *location*. The problem analysis triangle, shown in Figure 3.4, helps officers to visualize the problem and understand the relationship among the three elements. The three elements must be present for a crime or harmful event to occur; removing one or more of these elements will remove the problem. Strategies for removing one of these elements are only limited by an officer's ability to develop responses and the available resources.

### Response: Formulating Tailor-Made Strategies

Once a problem has been clearly defined, officers may seek the most effective responses. Developing long-term solutions to problems is of paramount importance with COPPS; however, officers cannot ignore the fact that more serious situations may require immediate action. For example, in the case of an open-air drug market involving rival gang violence, police may initially increase the number of patrols in the area to arrest offenders, gain control of public space, and secure the safety of residents and officers. Once this is accomplished, long-term responses, which include the collaborative efforts of officers, residents, and other agencies, may be considered.

Administrators must bear in mind that responses to substantive problems rarely involve a single agency or tactic or a quick fix. Arrest is often viewed as the only response to a problem even though it is rarely sufficient to provide more permanent resolutions. More appropriate responses often involve the police and public and other appropriate actors, including businesses, private and social service organizations, and other government agencies.

Patrol officers have many options to use to respond to problems, but they should not expect to eliminate every problem they take on. With some social problems, such as gangs and homelessness, elimination is impractical and improbable.

Another important prevention tool for COPPS is crime prevention through environmental design (CPTED). CPTED teaches officers how building space, architectural design, lighting, and other such features of the environment contribute to criminal opportunities. Both situational crime prevention and CPTED provide officers with tools necessary to employ comprehensive prevention strategies.

### Assessment: Evaluating Overall Effectiveness

The final stage of the S.A.R.A. process is assessment. Here, officers evaluate the effectiveness of their actions and may use the results to revise their responses, collect more data, or even redefine the problem. A COPPS initiative that is not reinforced by an evaluation process may have difficulty establishing whether it succeeded and thus should continue to receive resources. Therefore, rigorous evaluation is an essential component of the COPPS initiative. Evaluations provide knowledge; key decision makers in the jurisdiction need a gauge of the strategy's impact and cost effectiveness.

## Desired Organizational Elements under COPPS

Part of the analysis of police organizations by Maguire et al. included the extent to which those organizations changed during the 1990s, when COPPS was in full bloom. To accomplish its goals, COPPS relies on some form of structural innovation for its implementation efforts: reducing levels of vertical and functional differentiation (officers being "uniformed generalists," responsible for developing customized responses to a wide variety of situations), increasing levels of occupational differentiation (greater use of civilians in police agencies, thereby freeing up officers from desks and onto the streets) and spatial differentiation (using more ministations and precincts to extend officers into their communities) and decreasing formalization (less reliance on and enforcement of formal written rules, policies, and procedures), centralization (shared decision making), and administrative intensity (smaller administrative components and less bureaucracy, concentrating employees on the streets and not at desks).[30]

Maguire et al. determined that large municipal organizations in the United States experienced significant decreases in centralization and administrative intensity, together with significant increases in occupational differentiation. These changes are consistent with the structural reform agendas of community policing (which call for law enforcement administrators to decrease the levels of centralization and administrative intensity within their organizations). On the other hand, the "flattening" of the police hierarchy did not occur, and segmentation, or the number of command levels, did not change significantly during the 1990s.[31] Height experienced a significant increase, and there was no change in formalization. With regard to spatial differentiation, although there was a significant increase in the number of police stations, there was also a significant increase in the use of ministations.[32]

Overall, Maguire et al., found room for optimism for community policing reformers, with police agencies being less centralized, employing a greater proportion of civilian employees, and having leaner administrative components. Spatially, they have more ministations and police stations, but their beat coverage has remained about the same. Police organizations are capable of experiencing change in many dimensions: in culture, leadership, management, programs, and operations, although many of these changes were not reflected in their analysis.[33]

Most community policing reformers felt it was essential for law enforcement agencies to move from the traditional organizational structures to accommodate COPPS' philosophy and operations. Although policing has only been in the community policing era a relatively short period of time, by now much has been written about how agencies modified their structures, as well as their implementation and evaluation of COPPS. There are also countless examples of the resulting successes they have realized through COPPS in dealing with crime and disorder.[34] The reader is encouraged to explore some of those resources to better understand the current era of policing and the importance of organizational structure and change, which I discuss next.

# Effecting Change in Organizations

As can be seen, bringing about change in policing is not always simple. It can and does occur, however. As we will see, several key individuals—starting with the first-line supervisor—must carve out the path.

## *Change Begins with the Supervisor*

**Organizational change** begins or ends with an agency's first-line supervisors; the link between street officers and the organization is their sergeant. Indeed, the quality of an officer's daily life is often dependent on the supervisor. There is, however, some cause for supervisors' reluctance to change.

A difficult hurdle that supervisors must overcome is the idea that giving line officers the opportunity to be creative and take risks does not diminish the role or authority of the supervisor. Risk taking and innovation require mutual trust between supervisors and line officers. The supervisor's role changes from being a "controller," primarily concerned with rules, to being a "facilitator" and "coach" for officers engaged in COPPS work. Supervisors must also be well skilled in problem solving, especially in the analysis of problems and evaluation of efforts. Conducting workload analysis and finding the time for officers to solve problems and engage the community are important aspects of supervision. A supervisor must also be prepared to intercede and remove any roadblocks to officers' problem-solving efforts. A supervisor should assist officers with managing their beats and time utilized for COPPS activities. In addition, supervisors should not contribute to the COPPS initiative becoming a mere public relations campaign; the emphasis is always on results.[35]

To gain time for officers to engage in COPPS functions, departments should review their patrol plan to determine whether units are fielded in proportion to workload. Delaying response time to calls for service can also provide more time for officers. Response time research has determined that rapid responses are not needed for most calls. Furthermore, dispatchers can set citizens' expectations of when an officer will arrive. Slower police responses to nonemergency calls has been found to be satisfactory to citizens if dispatchers tell them an officer might not arrive at their home right away. Managers have also garnered more time for officers by having nonsworn employees handle noncrime incidents.[36]

## *The Chief Executive and Mid-Level Manager*

Major change in philosophy and practices is required within a police organization before a major shift such as COPPS can be made. The police organization needs a viable change agent; the person at the top is responsible for setting both the policy and tone of the organization. The chief executive must be both visible and credible and create a climate conducive to change. Employees must be involved in the change process. Gauging the pace and degree of change is also necessary. It is essential, however, that chief executives communicate the idea that COPPS is department-wide in scope and encourage and guide all officers to engage in problem solving.

Mid-level managers also play a crucial role in the implementation of a COPPS philosophy. They must not view COPPS as a threat to their power. Middle managers are essential to the process of innovation, much of which can originate only at their level.[37] As George Kelling and William Bratton observed,

> Ample evidence exists that when a clear vision of the business of the organization is put forward, when mid-managers are included in planning, when their legitimate self-interests are acknowledged, and when they are properly trained, mid-managers can be the leading edge of innovation and creativity.[38]

Mid-level managers and first-line supervisors are discussed in greater detail in Chapter 4.

# CASE STUDIES

The following two case studies will help the reader understand and apply some of this chapter's materials in a real-world context.

## Malfunction Junction

Junction City, a rapidly growing community of 150,000 residents, is an agriculturally based area located in the center of the state, about 20 miles from the ocean. The city gains a population of 10,000 to 20,000 visitors a day during the summer months, when ocean recreation is a popular activity. Owing to local growth in the meat-packing industry, the city's demographics are changing rapidly, especially its Hispanic population. The downtown area of the city has slowly deteriorated over the last few years, resulting in increased crime and disorder. A property tax cap has resulted in reduced revenues to local jurisdictions, and the recent recession has also taken a substantial toll on the city's budget; the result has been significant reductions in staffing. The police department now has 100 sworn and 35 nonsworn personnel, and has experienced its share of budget cuts and reduced staffing levels. The chief of police of 10 years' duration retired recently, leaving in his wake an agency that is still very traditional in nature and growing in its number of desk-bound administrative personnel and degree of rank structure (corporal, sergeant, lieutenant, captain, deputy chief, commander, and chief). The morale of the department is poor due to the increases in workload due to tourism and agricultural expansion. You have been hired as the new chief. As a result of the current situation, the city manager and council are calling for an emergency meeting with you to discuss the future of the department. They explain that at a recent council retreat, they heard a consultant's presentation on the implementation and operation of community policing and problem solving, and now seek your views on this strategy, its potential for Junction City, and how you might approach its implementation (*Note:* They emphasize that you are to explain how you might reorganize the agency from its current, traditional status, with only one police facility and its administration- and rank-laden status).

### Questions for Discussion

1. In your meeting, how will you respond concerning whether community policing is the panacea for the city's woes?
2. Do you envision any problems with "traditional-thinking" officers and supervisors still working in the organization? If so, how will you handle their concerns?
3. Using the seven elements of police organizational structure described in this chapter, where does it appear that you would need to reorganize the agency, especially to accommodate COPPS?

4. Would you anticipate that the officers' workload would be reduced or increased under the COPPS strategy?

5. What types of information would you use to evaluate the progress of your community policing initiative?

# Sins and the City

Officers assigned to your district have been responding to a number of noise complaints, reckless driving, and fight calls in the area of 7500 Commercial Row. This area contains a number of restaurants, bars, and several strip malls that attract juveniles and young adults. Within the last week, there have also been three gang-related drive-by shootings and seven gas drive-offs. A majority of the underaged adults are attracted to the area by a dance club located in one of the strip mall centers and two all-night fast-food restaurants. All three locations attract large crowds that loiter and drink alcohol in their parking lots. The owners of the shopping centers and restaurants have also complained about thousands of dollars in vandalism by the loitering youths.

## Question for Discussion

1. How would you use the S.A.R.A. process (scanning, analysis, response, and assessment) to address this problem?

# Summary

This chapter explored the importance and elements of police organizational structure, including the division of labor and the policies, procedures, rules, and regulations that accompany them. Emphasis was placed on the organizational needs of the increasingly implemented concept of community-oriented policing and problem solving. It was clearly demonstrated that this shift in philosophy and strategies has brought with it the need for a new and accommodating organizational structure and issues of how to evaluate this initiatives to see what works.

# Questions for Review

1. What are the distinctions among policy, procedure, and rules and regulations? Why are they necessary in law enforcement agencies? What are their relationship and role vis-à-vis police discretion?

2. What aspects of law enforcement agencies make them bureaucracies? Can such a form of organization ever be eliminated?

3. What is the basic police organizational structure? How have contemporary police organizations changed from the more traditional, bureaucratic form?

4. What are some of the major recent research findings concerning policing? How have they affected the field?

5. What role do innovation and values play in police organizations?

6. What is meant by *community-oriented policing and problem solving?* How does this concept differ from past policing methods? How can its outcomes be evaluated? Under this strategy, what important roles are played by chief executives, mid-level managers, and first-line supervisors?

## Notes

1. Wayne W. Bennett and Karen M. Hess, *Management and Supervision in Law Enforcement,* 4th ed. (Belmont, Calif.: Wadsworth, 2004), p. 2.

2. *The Republic of Plato,* trans. Allen Bloom (New York: Basic Books, 1968), p. 7.

3. Luther Gulick and L. Urwick (eds.), *Papers on the Science of Administration* (New York: Augustus M. Kelley, 1969).

4. Charles R. Swanson, Leonard Territo, and Robert W. Taylor, *Police Administration: Structures, Processes, and Behavior,* 6th ed. (Upper Saddle River, N.J.: Prentice Hall, 2005), pp. 232–233.

5. Ibid., p. 233.

6. Henry Mintzberg, *The Structure of Organizations* (Upper Saddle River, N.J.: Prentice-Hall, 1979), p. 253.

7. Edward R. Maguire, Heunhee Shin, Zihong Zhao, and Kimberly D. Hassell, "Structural Change in Large Police Agencies During the 1990s," *Policing: An International Journal of Police Strategies & Management* **26**(2) (2003):251–275.

8. Ibid., p. 255.

9. Ibid., p. 259.

10. Ibid., p. 261.

11. Ibid., pp. 266–267.

12. Ibid., pp. 268–270.

13. Portland, Oregon, population statistics from http://www.oregoncitylink.com/portland/demographics.htm (accessed November 8, 2004).

14. Information from http://www.portlandonline.com/index.cfm?c=29708 (accessed September 7, 2005).

15. In the Portland Police Bureau (PPB) organizational structure shown in Figure 3.2, DPSST is the Department of Public Safety Standards and Training, to which the PPB loans officers; PPA is the Portland Police Association, or the bureau's collective bargaining agent; the Management Services Division manages the bureau's facilities, liability, and loss control; the Sunshine Division includes personnel who work to provide food, clothing, and toys to needy families; the HAP liaisons and Safety Action Team include officers assigned to the Housing Authority of Portland; Douglas and Parkrose liaisons are officers working in school districts; APP liaison is a private association of businesses that fund one officer position for downtown; the Public Utility Commission includes grant-funded positions for conducting traffic enforcement along interstate corridors; ROCN is the Regional Organized Crime and Narcotics task force; and WomenStrength is a program that teaches women self-defense tactics.

16. President's Commission on Law Enforcement and Administration of Justice, *Task Force Report: The Police* (Washington, D.C.: U.S. Government Printing Office, 1967), p. 46.

17. See, for example, Egon Bittner, "The Quasi-Military Organization of the Police," in Victor Kappeler (ed.), *Police and Society: Touchstone Readings,* 2nd ed. (Long Grove, Ill.: Waveland, 2003), pp. 170–181.

18. Ibid.

19. Thomas J. Cowper, "The Myth of the 'Military Model' of Leadership in Law Enforcement," in Quint C. Thurman and Jihong Zhao (eds.), *Contemporary Policing: Controversies, Challenges, and Solutions* (Los Angeles: Roxbury, 2004), pp. 113–125.

20. Samuel Walker and Charles M. Katz, *The Police in America,* 5th ed. (Columbus, Ohio: McGraw-Hill, 2005).

21. John Murray, "Developing the 'Right' Police for Community Policing," *Platypus Magazine* 74 (March 2002), 7–13.

22. Robert Sheehan and Gary W. Cordner, *Introduction to Police Administration,* 2nd ed. (Cincinnati, Ohio: Anderson, 1989), pp. 446–447.

23. Ibid., p. 449.

24. Ibid.

25. O. W. Wilson and Roy C. McLaren, *Police Administration,* 3rd ed. (New York: McGraw-Hill, 1972), p. 79.

26. 471 U.S. 1 (1985).

27. Raymond O. Loen, *Manage More by Doing Less* (New York: McGraw-Hill, 1971), pp. 86–89.

28. Thomas Reddin, "Are You Oriented to Hold Them? A Searching Look at Police Management," *The Police Chief* (March 1966):17.

29. California Department of Justice, *COPPS: Community-Oriented Policing and Problem Solving. Office of the Attorney General, Crime Violence Prevention Center* (Sacramento, Calif.: Author, 1995).

30. Maguire, et al., "Structural Change in Large Police Agencies During the 1990s," pp. 254–255.

31. Ibid., p. 270.

32. Ibid., p. 271.

33. Ibid., p. 272.

34. For a fundamental view of community-oriented policing and problem solving, see, for example, Herman Goldstein, *Problem-Oriented Policing* (New York: McGraw-Hill, 1990); Kenneth J. Peak and Ronald W. Glensor, *Community Policing and Problem Solving: Strategies and Practices,* 4th ed. (Upper Saddle River, N.J.: Prentice Hall, 2004; and Robert Trojanowicz and Bonnie Bucqueroux, *Community Policing: A Contemporary Perspective* (Cincinnati, Ohio: Anderson, 1990). Also note that each year the U.S. Department of Justice, National Institute of Justice, publishes the Best Practices in Problem-Oriented Policing: Winners of the Herman Goldstein Award for Excellence in Problem-Oriented Policing.

35. Police Executive Research Forum. *Supervising Problem-Solving* (Washington, D.C.: Author, 1990).

36. John Eck and William Spelman. "A Problem-Oriented Approach to Police Service Delivery," in Dennis Jay Kenney (ed.), *Police and Policing: Contemporary Issues* (New York: Praeger, 1989), pp. 95–111.

37. John Eck and William Spelman, *Solving Problems: Problem Oriented Policing in Newport News. Research in Brief* (Washington, D.C.: U.S. Department of Justice, National Institute of Justice, 1987).

38. George L. Kelling and William J. Bratton, *Implementing Community Policing: The Administrative Problem* (Washington, D.C.: Police Executive Research Forum, 1992), p. 11.

# Chapter 4

# Police Personnel Roles and Functions

# Key Terms and Concepts

Captain

Chief executive officer (CEO)

Chief of police

Dissemination

Disturbance handler

Entrepreneur

Figurehead role

First-line supervisor

*Jordan v. The City of New London*

Leadership role

Liaison role

Lieutenant

Middle managers

Mintzberg model for CEOs

Monitoring/inspecting

Negotiator

Resource allocator

Sheriff

Spokesperson

# Learning Objectives

After reading this chapter, the student will:

- be able to describe each of Mintzberg's three main roles of the chief executive officer (CEO)
- know the steps taken by an assessment center to obtain the most capable chief executive and the skills the executive must possess
- understand the duties and qualifications for the office of chief of police
- know the duties performed by the sheriff's office
- be familiar with the criteria used to evaluate CEOs
- know the tasks performed by middle managers (captains and lieutenants)
- be familiar with the criteria for a first-line supervisor (patrol sergeant) position, as well as its roles and tasks
- understand the tasks of patrol officers and be able to name the 12 qualities imperative for entry-level officers
- know why a city and two federal courts ruled that a person who is too intelligent would not be good for police work, and the policy implications of that ruling
- know the roles and functions performed by all leadership personnel in COPPS

*The police are the public and the public are the police.*

—Robert Peel

# Introduction

Some of the most important and challenging positions in our society are those of a police administrator, manager, or supervisor. This chapter examines the roles and functions of law enforcement chief executives (chiefs of police and county sheriffs), middle managers (typically captains and lieutenants), first-line supervisors (sergeants), and patrol officers.

First I examine in general terms the roles of law enforcement chief executives, adapting Mintzberg's model of chief executive officers (CEOs). Next I review some general aspects of law enforcement leadership, including the assessment center process that can and is often used to hire chief executives; the "Ten Commandments" of good police leadership; and some of the critical components of the law enforcement organization that must be managed. Then I explore more specifically the functions of chiefs of police and sheriffs. Next I consider the roles and functions of middle managers (captains and lieutenants), supervisors (sergeants), and patrol officers (including the traits that executives should look for when trying to hire quality personnel, and whether, as recent federal court decisions have suggested, one can be too smart for police work). Finally, I look at the roles of each of these four levels under the community-oriented policing and problem-solving strategy.

The chapter concludes with two case studies.

# Roles of the Police Executive: The Mintzberg Model for CEOs

A police chief executive fills many roles. Henry Mintzberg[1] described a set of behaviors and tasks of chief executive officers in any organization. Following is an adaptation of the **Mintgberg model for CEOs** used to examine the three main roles of the **chief executive officer (CEO)** (the chief of police or sheriff): the interpersonal, the informational, and the decision-maker roles.

## *The Interpersonal Role*

The *interpersonal* role has three components: (1) the figurehead, (2) leadership, and (3) liaison duties.

In the **figurehead role**, the CEO performs various ceremonial functions. He or she rides in parades and attends civic events, speaks to school and university classes and civic organizations, meets visiting officials and dignitaries, attends academy graduations and swearing-in ceremonies and certain weddings and funerals, and visits injured officers. Like a city's mayor, whose public responsibilities include cutting ribbons and kissing babies, the police CEO performs these duties simply because of his or her title and position within the organization. Although chiefs or sheriffs are not expected to attend the grand opening of every retail or commercial business and other such events to which they are invited, they are certainly obligated from a professional standpoint to attend many civic functions and ceremonies.

The **leadership role** requires the CEO to motivate and coordinate workers while resolving various goals and needs within the department and the community. A chief or sheriff may have to urge the governing board to enact a code or ordinance that, whether or not popular, is in the best interest of the jurisdiction. For example, a chief in a western state recently led a drive to pass an ordinance that prohibited parking by university students in residential neighborhoods surrounding the campus. This was a highly unpopular undertaking, but the chief was prompted because of the complaints about hardships suffered by the area residents. The CEO also may provide leadership by taking stands on bond issues (seeking funds to hire more officers or build new buildings, for example) and by advising the governing body on the effects of proposed ordinances.

The **liaison role** is undertaken when the CEO of a police organization interacts with other organizations and coordinates work assignments. It is not uncommon for executives from a geographical area—the police chief, sheriff, ranking officer of the local highway patrol office, district attorney, campus police chief, and so on—to meet informally each month to discuss common problems and strategies. The chief executive also serves as liaison to regional law enforcement councils, narcotics units, crime labs, dispatching centers, and so on. He or she also meets with representatives of the courts, juvenile system, and other criminal justice agencies.

## The Informational Role ~spokesperson, inspector~

Another role identified by Mintzberg's model is the *informational* one. In this capacity, the CEO engages in tasks relating to (1) monitoring/inspecting, (2) dissemination, and (3) spokesperson duties.

In the **monitoring/inspecting** function, the CEO constantly reviews the department's operations to ensure that it is operating smoothly (or as smoothly as police operations can be expected to be). This function is often referred to as "roaming the ship"; many CEOs who isolated themselves from their personnel and the daily operations of the agency can speak from sad experience of the need to be involved and present. Many police executives use daily staff meetings to acquire information about their jurisdictions, especially criminal and other activities during the previous 24 hours.

**Dissemination** tasks involve distributing information to members of the department via memoranda, special orders, general orders, and policies and procedures as described in Chapter 3. The **spokesperson** function is related to the dissemination task but is focused more on providing information to the news media. This is a difficult task for the chief executive; news organizations, especially the television and print media, are competitive businesses that seek to obtain the most complete news in the shortest amount of time, which often translates into wider viewership and therefore greater advertising revenues for them. From one perspective, the media must appreciate that a criminal investigation can be seriously compromised by premature or excessive coverage. From the other perspective, the public has a legitimate right to know what is occurring in the community, especially matters relating to crime. Therefore, the prudent police executive attempts to have an open and professional relationship with the media in which each side knows and understands its responsibilities. The prudent chief executive also remembers the power of the media and does not alienate them; as an old saying goes, "Never argue with someone who buys his ink by the barrel." Unfortunately, many police executives (a good number who involuntarily left office) can speak of the results of failing to develop an appropriate relationship with the media.

An example of the good–bad relationship that often exists between the police and the media is the Washington, D.C.-area sniper investigation of late 2002. Although Montgomery County, Maryland, Police Chief Charles Moose was at times very frustrated by leaks of confidential information to the media, he also used the media to communicate with the snipers, who eventually were captured after the suspects' photographs and a vehicle description were broadcast. (This case is discussed more thoroughly in Chapter 6.)

## The Decision-Maker Role   entrepreneur, negotiator )

In the decision-maker role, the CEO of a police organization serves as (1) an entrepreneur, (2) a disturbance handler, (3) a resource allocator, and (4) a negotiator.

In the capacity of **entrepreneur,** the CEO must sell ideas to the members of the governing board or the department—perhaps helping them to understand a new computer or communications system, the implementation of a policing strategy, or different work methods, all of which are intended to improve the organization. Sometimes roles blend, as when several police executives band together (in their entrepreneurial and liaison functions) to lobby the state attorney general and the legislature for new crime-fighting laws.

As a **disturbance handler,** the executive's tasks range from resolving minor disputes between staff members to dealing with major events such as riots, continued muggings in a local park, or the cleanup of the downtown area. Sometimes the executive must solve intradepartmental disputes, which can reach major proportions. For example, the chief executive must intervene when friction develops between different units, as when the patrol commanders' instruction to street officers to increase arrests for public drunkenness causes a strain on the resources of the jail division's commander.

*never enough money*

As a **resource allocator,** the CEO must clearly understand the agency's budget and its budgetary priorities. The resource allocator must consider requests for funds from various groups. Personnel, for example, will ask for higher salaries, additional officers, and better equipment. Citizens may complain about speeding motorists in a specific area, which would require the allocation of additional resources to that neighborhood. In the resource-allocator role, the CEO must be able to prioritize requests and to defend his or her choices.

As a **negotiator,** the police manager resolves employee grievances and, through an appointed representative at the bargaining table, tries to represent the best interests of both the city and labor during collective bargaining. In this role, the CEO must consider rank and file's request for raises and increased benefits as part of budget administration. If funds available to the jurisdiction are limited, the CEO must negotiate with the collective bargaining unit to reach an agreement. At times, contract negotiations reach an impasse or deadlock.

I will elaborate on some of these chief executive functions later in the chapter; furthermore, labor relations—including unionism and collective bargaining—are discussed more fully in Chapter 15.

# Law Enforcement Executives, Generally

Prior to examining the role and functions of contemporary police executives, I first consider how such persons are selected for these positions. Given the responsibilities placed on those who occupy such positions, the means employed to test applicants for or to promote individuals into them becomes important.

## *Obtaining the Best: The Assessment Center*

To obtain the most capable people for chief executive positions (and also for middle-management and even supervisory positions) in policing, the assessment center method has surfaced as an efficacious means of hiring and promoting personnel. (*Note:* Sheriffs are normally elected, not hired or promoted into their position; thus, the assessment center is of little use for that position.) The assessment center method is now increasingly utilized for selecting people for all management or supervisory ranks. The assessment center process may include interviews; psychological tests; in-basket exercises; management tasks; group discussions; role-playing exercises such as simulations of interviews with subordinates, the public, and news media; fact-finding exercises; oral presentation exercises; and written communications exercises.[2]

The first step is to identify behaviors important to the successful performance of the position. Job descriptions listing responsibilities and skills should exist for all executive, mid-management, and supervisory positions (such as chief, captain, lieutenant, sergeant, and so on). Then each candidate's abilities and skill levels should be evaluated using several of the techniques mentioned.

Individual and group role playing provides a hands-on exercise during the selection process. Candidates may be required to perform in simulated police–community problems (they conduct a "meeting" to hear concerns of local minority groups), to react to a major incident (explaining what they would do and in what order in a simulated shooting or riot situation), to hold a news briefing, or to participate in other such exercises. They may be given an in-basket situation in which they receive an abundance of paperwork, policies, and problems to be prioritized and dealt with in a prescribed amount of time. Writing abilities may also be evaluated: Candidates may be given 30 minutes to develop a use-of-force policy for a hypothetical or real police agency. This type of exercise not only illustrates candidates' written communications skills and understanding of the technical side of police work, but also shows how they think cognitively and build a case.

During each exercise, several assessors or raters analyze each candidate's performance and record some type of evaluation; when the assessment center process ends, each rater submits his or her individual rating information to the person making the hiring or promotional decision. Typically selected because they have held the position for which candidates are now vying, assessors must not only know the types of problems and duties incumbent in the position, but also should be keen observers of human behavior.

Assessment centers are logistically more difficult to conduct as well as more labor-intensive and costly than traditional interviewing procedures, but they are well worth the extra investment. Monies invested at the early stages of a hiring or promotional process can help avoid selecting the wrong person and can prevent untold problems for years to come. Good executives, mid-managers, and supervisors make fewer mistakes and are probably sued less often.

## Skills of Good Managers

To expand on the discussion of leadership skills in Chapter 2, note the basic management skills the police executive must develop. First is *technical skill,* which involves specialized knowledge, analytical ability, and facility in the use of tools and techniques of the specific discipline. This is the skill most easily trained for. Examples in policing include budgeting, computer use, and fundamental knowledge of some specialized equipment, such as radar or breathalyzer machines.

Second is the *human skill,* which is the executive's ability to work effectively as a group member and build cooperation; this includes being sensitive to the needs and feelings of others, tolerating ambiguity, and being able to empathize with different views and cultures.

Finally, *conceptual skills* involve coordinating and integrating all the activities and interests of the organization into a common objective: in other words, being able to translate knowledge into action.[3]

These skills can be taught, just as other skills can, which proves that good administrators are not simply born, but can be trained in the classroom and by practicing the skills on the job.

## The "Ten Commandments"

Following is an adaptation of the "Ten Commandments" of being a police executive—rules of personal and professional conduct that are vital to one's success—developed by Jurkanin et al.[4]

1. Practice what you preach: You must lead by example, remembering that actions speak louder than words. The chief executive must be a person of morality, integrity, and honor.
2. A day's pay for a day-and-a-half of work: The chief must put in long hours to accomplish all that needs to be done, at the expense of personal freedoms. Staff meetings, phone conversations, luncheon meetings, press conferences,

interviews, report reading, and labor negotiations all take place during the day, leaving the evenings for letter and report writing, budget review, reading professional journals, attending governing board meetings, and meeting with civic, church, or other groups.

3. Maintain and promote integrity: See the First Commandment.

4. Develop a positive image: The chief executive is also responsible for the morale of the employees; although law enforcement can be filled with bad news, disappointment, and failures, the chief must work to accentuate the positive. Positive recognition of employees' contributions and valiant actions are one way to do so, with awards ceremonies, memorandums, and so forth.

5. Remain committed: The chief's goals, mission, and values must be committed to their implementation; this might mean taking risks, which can have its dangers. Failure must be faced immediately, and one must learn from mistakes. The chief executive can normally weather the storm by taking responsibility and being responsive.

6. Be respectful: Be prepared to stand up for employees who have performed admirably, while being fair, firm, concerned, and sincere. When possible, criticize in private, praise in public. Remember that there will always be some people who will vigorously oppose your views. Do not compromise yourself to try to obtain everyone's support.

7. Accept assistance from others: This will build a teamwork approach, although the chief remains the final authority in the agency. Two (or more) heads are always better than one. The chief also needs a confidante with whom to share thoughts, ideas, and concerns.

8. Be eager for knowledge: Stay abreast of technology, current events, topics that impact the community, and current management, leadership, and administration trends and issues. Be familiar with the history of the agency and community so as to avoid repeating past mistakes. Know the financial aspects of the jurisdiction. Employ both formal (workshops) and informal (networking with other executives) means of training and education. Encourage employees to do likewise.

9. Maintain a healthy lifestyle: One who is physically fit is better able to perform and react to demands of the position. Obviously, wise choices in diet, exercise, annual checkups, and avoidance of all things harmful to one's health are keys to healthy living.

10. Set personal goals: Having reached the helm, one should still review short-, medium-, and long-term objectives and skills that need development, to assist with establishing a future direction for oneself as well as for the organization. Along with career goals, personal goals should also be examined.

## *Managing the Organization's Critical Components*

Successful law enforcement administration demands that chief executives successfully manage several critical components of the organization.

Human resource planning includes recruitment, training, development, evaluation, and discipline of personnel. The quality of personnel and their management is the most important factor that affects the services provided by the organization.

Remember that the two types of law enforcement executives are those that have been sued and those that are going to be sued. The level of hierarchical responsibility, the high public profile, the oversight of potentially risky activities, an increasingly litigious society, and a civil justice system with a focus on individual rights place the modern law enforcement executive squarely in the path of litigation (see Chapter 15).[5] Finally, it is also critical that contemporary law enforcement executives also be well grounded in the political (see later discussion), labor-relations (Chapter 15), financial (see Chapter 16), and technological (Chapter 17) aspects of the role.

# Chiefs of Police

What do law enforcement executives do? In contrast to Mintzberg's rather sophisticated model described earlier, Ronald Lynch stated the primary tasks of these executives in simple terms:

> They listen, talk, write, confer, think, decide—about [personnel], money, materials, methods, facilities—in order to plan, organize, direct, coordinate, and control their research service, production, public relations, employee relations, and all other activities so that they may more effectively serve the citizens to whom they are responsible.[6]

Next I look at what the city officials and community expect of police chiefs, as well as how individuals ascend to this position.

## *Expectations of Government and Community*

The **chief of police** (also known as the *commissioner* or *superintendent*) is generally considered to be one of the most influential and prestigious persons in local government. Indeed, people in this position often amass considerable power and influence in their jurisdiction. Mayors, city managers and administrators, members of the agency, labor organizations, citizens, special-interest groups, and the media all have differing role expectations of the chief of police that often conflict.

The mayor or city manager likely wants the chief of police to promote departmental efficiency, reduce crime, improve service, and so on. Others appreciate the chief who simply keeps morale high and citizens' complaints low.

The mayor also expects the chief to communicate with city management about police-related issues and to be part of the city management team; to communicate city management's policies to police personnel; to establish agency policies, goals, and objectives and put them in writing; to develop an administrative system of managing people, equipment, and the budget in a professional and businesslike manner; to set a good example, both personally and professionally;

to administer disciplinary action consistently and fairly when required; and to select personnel whose performance will ably and professionally adhere to the organization's objectives.

Members of the agency also have expectations of the chief executive: to be their advocate, supporting them when necessary and representing the agency's interests when dealing with judges and prosecutors who may be indifferent or hostile. Citizens tend to expect the chief of police to provide efficient and cost-effective police services while keeping crime and tax rates down (often an area of built-in conflict) and preventing corruption and illegal use of force. Special-interest groups expect the chief to advocate policy positions that they favor. For example, Mothers Against Drunk Driving (MADD) would desire strong anti-DUI measures by the police. Finally, the media expect the chief to cooperate fully with their efforts to obtain fast and complete crime information.

## *Qualifications*

Qualifications for the position of police chief vary widely, depending on the size of the agency and the region of the country. Small agencies, especially those in rural areas, may not have any minimum educational requirement for the job. In the early 1970s, the National Advisory Commission on Criminal Justice Standards and Goals surveyed police chiefs and their superiors to determine the essential qualities for the job.

Education was found to be an important consideration; today, many agencies require a college education plus several years of progressively responsible police management experience. A survey by the Police Executive Research Forum of 358 police chiefs in jurisdictions of 50,000 or more residents found that chiefs were generally highly educated—87 percent held a bachelor's degree and 47 percent had a master's—and were more likely to be chosen from outside the agencies they headed, but they spent less than 5 years in the position.[7]

Police chief executives also need several types of important management skills. The National Advisory Commission asked police chiefs and their superiors to rate, on a scale of 1 to 10, the importance of 14 desirable management skills. The ability to motivate and control personnel and to relate to the community was considered most important. A survey today would probably yield similar results.[8]

Many cities finding themselves in need of a police chief have to consider whether it would be better to promote someone from within the ranks or hire from outside (perhaps using the assessment center process described earlier). Although it is perhaps more economical and certainly less trouble to select a police chief from within the organization as opposed to arranging an assessment center, both methods have advantages and disadvantages. One study of police chiefs promoted from within or hired from outside indicated only one significant difference in qualification: educational attainment. The outsiders were more highly educated. No differences were found with respect to other aspects of their background, attitudes, salary, tenure in current position or in policing, the size of agency or community, and current budget.[9] Some states, however, have made it nearly impossible for an outsider to come in. California has mandated that the chief be a graduate of its own Peace Officers Standards and Training (POST) academy; New Jersey and New York also encourage "homegrown" chiefs.[10]

## *Job Protection, Termination, and the Political Arena*

Traditionally, the job tenure of police chiefs has been short. A federal study in the mid-1970s found that the average length in office by chiefs of police was 5.4 years.[11] Another PERF study in the mid-1980s found the average to be practically unchanged, 5.5 years. That figure has not varied much in recent times.[12] This short tenure of police chiefs has several negative consequences. It prevents long-range planning, results in frequent new policies and administrative styles, and prohibits the development of the chief's political power base and local influence.

Police chiefs would of course prefer to possess some type of job protection against their arbitrary and unjustified removal from office by an elected or political officeholder.[13] In fact, some police chiefs have resigned and reverted back to their former position as assistant or deputy chief, simply to have some job protection until retirement.

In some states, statutory protections against such actions exist, or special boards or commissions have been created for the sole purpose of establishing recruitment, selection, and retention policies for chiefs of police. Other states require written notice of the basis for the proposed termination, a hearing on the charges, and a finding of cause before the dismissal can be effected. Still, police chiefs across the country are looking for job protections in local civil service codes, municipal ordinances, and such individual employment contracts as they can negotiate.[14]

Losing a job as police chief is not difficult to do. Although some, of course, lose their positions because of their shortcomings, others leave their post as a result of situations and conflicts outside their control. These conflicts have been termed *political arenas* and can be divided into three types based on their duration, intensity, and pervasiveness: (1) confrontation, (2) shaky alliance, and (3) a politicized organization.[15]

The first type of political arena, *confrontation,* occurs when the situational conflict is intense but brief and confined. Obvious examples are when a police chief is terminated in the aftermath of a major incident (e.g., a scandal or acts of racial profiling by officers). The second arena is the *shaky alliance,* in which conflict is less intense but still pervasive. An example involves a former Los Angeles police chief, Willie Williams—Daryl Gates's successor and the first outsider appointed as chief in that city in more than 40 years. Williams had to deal with both external pressures (the impact of the 1991 Rodney King incident on the public) and internal pressures (the resentful feelings from his own officers). This was a shaky alliance, and Williams's contract was not renewed.

The third type of political arena, a *politicized organization,* features pervasive but muted conflict that is tolerable for a time. This kind of conflict is commonplace in American policing, and in this situation, the chief's survival depends on external support. Examples would be a riot resulting from allegations of police brutality or a lengthy, unsuccessful, and possibly botched homicide investigation. For example, in the 1997 JonBenet Ramsey investigation, the Boulder, Colorado, chief of police had little support from the media, divided political support within the city council, and little support from his officers (he received a 2 to 1 vote of no confidence by the troops) and was forced to step down by an acting city manager.

The advent of community policing has also presented some risks for police chiefs; that element is discussed later in the section concerning the chief executive.

# The Sheriff

The position of **sheriff** has a long tradition, rooted in the time of the Norman conquest of England (in 1066), and it played an important part in the early law enforcement activities of colonial America. Unfortunately, because of television and movie depictions, many people today view the county sheriff as a bumbling, cruel, overweight, or corrupt individual wearing a cowboy hat and sunglasses while talking with a Southern drawl (see, e.g., movies such as *Smoky and the Bandit, Mississippi Burning, The Dukes of Hazzard, Walking Tall,* and many others).

This image is both unfair and highly inaccurate. Next, we examine the real role of today's county sheriffs.

## *Role and Functions*

Because of the diversity of sheriff's offices throughout the country, it is difficult to describe a "typical" sheriff's department; those offices run the gamut from the traditional, highly political, limited-service office to the modern, fairly nonpolitical, full-service police organization. It is possible, however, to list functions commonly associated with the sheriff's office:

1. Serving and/or implementing civil processes (divorce papers, liens, evictions, garnishments and attachments, and other civil duties, such as extradition and transportation of prisoners)
2. Collecting certain taxes and conducting real estate sales (usually for nonpayment of taxes) for the county
3. Performing routine order-maintenance duties by enforcing state statutes and county ordinances, arresting offenders, and performing traffic and criminal investigations
4. Serving as bailiff of the courts
5. Maintaining and operating the county correctional institutions[16]

Sheriffs, therefore, have a unique role in that they typically serve all three components of the justice system: (1) law enforcement (with patrol, traffic, and investigative functions), (2) the courts (as civil process servers and bailiffs), and (3) corrections (in the county jails). In many urban areas, civil process duties consume more time and resources than those involving law enforcement.[17]

Sheriffs are elected in all but two states (Rhode Island and Hawaii) thus, they tend to be aligned with a political party. As elected officials, sheriffs are important political figures and, in many rural areas, represent the most powerful political force in the county. As a result, sheriffs are far more independent than appointed municipal police chiefs, who can be removed from office by the mayors or city managers who appoint them. However, because they are elected, sheriffs receive considerable media scrutiny and are subject to state accountability processes.

Because of this electoral system, it is possible that the only qualification for getting into the office is the ability to get votes. In some areas of the country, the sheriff's term of office is limited to one 2-year term at a time (a sheriff cannot succeed himself or herself); thus, the office has been known to be rotated between the sheriff and undersheriff. In most counties, however, the sheriff has a 4-year term of office and can be reelected.

The sheriff enjoys no tenure guarantee, although one study found that sheriffs (averaging 6.7 years in office) had longer tenure in office than chiefs of police (5.4 years). This politicization of the office of sheriff can result in high turnover rates of personnel who do not have civil service protection. The uncertainty as to tenure is not conducive to long-range (strategic) planning. Largely as a result of the political nature of the office, sheriffs tend to be older, less likely to have been promoted through the ranks of the agency, and less likely to be college graduates and to have specialized training than police chiefs. Research has also found that sheriffs in small agencies have more difficulty with organizational problems (field activities, budget management) and that sheriffs in large agencies find dealing with local officials and planning and evaluation to be more troublesome.[18]

## Middle Managers: Captains and Lieutenants

Few police administration books contain information about the **middle managers** of a police department, the captains and lieutenants. This is unfortunate because they are too numerous and too powerful within police organizations to ignore. Opinions vary toward these mid-management personnel, however, as I discuss later.

Leonhard Fuld, one of the early progressive police administration researchers, said in 1909 that the **captain** is one of the most important officers in the organization. Fuld believed that the position had two broad duties—policing and administration. The captain was held responsible for preserving the public peace and protecting life and property within the precinct. Fuld defined the captain's administrative duties as being of three kinds: clerical, janitorial, and supervisory.[19]

Although every ranking officer in the police department exercises some managerial skills and duties, here we are concerned with the managers to whom first-line supervisors report, for they generally are unit commanders. In a mid-sized or large police agency, a patrol shift or watch may be commanded by a captain, who will have several lieutenants reporting to him or her. The lieutenants may assist the captain in running the shift, but when there is a shortage of sergeants as a result of vacations or retirements, the lieutenant may assume the duties of a first-line supervisor. In some respects, the lieutenant's position in some departments is a training ground for future unit commanders (captain rank or higher).

Perhaps the best way to understand what these shift commanders do is to examine the tasks they perform in a medium-sized police department. First, I examine the tasks generally performed by the captain, using the Lexington, Kentucky, Police Department as an example. The 15 most critical or important tasks performed by captains are as follows[20]:

1. Issuing assignments to individuals and units within the section
2. Receiving assignments for section/unit
3. Reviewing incoming written complaints and reports
4. Preparing routine reports
5. Reviewing final disposition of assignments
6. Ensuring that subordinates comply with general and special orders
7. Monitoring crime and other activity statistics
8. Evaluating the work of individuals and units within the section
9. Maintaining sector facilities
10. Discussing concerns and problems with people
11. Attending various staff meetings
12. Maintaining working contacts and responding to inquiries from other sections of the division
13. Reviewing and approving overtime in section/unit
14. Monitoring section/unit operations to evaluate performance
15. Fielding and responding to complaints against subordinates

A review of these tasks shows that captains have more administrative responsibilities than lieutenants or sergeants, with 9 of the 15 tasks being administrative in nature. Captains spend a substantial amount of time coordinating their units' activities with those of other units and overseeing the operation of their units. As an officer progresses up the chain of command, his or her responsibilities become more administrative. At the same time, captains also have supervisory responsibilities (tasks 1, 3, 5, 6, 8, and 15). Whereas a sergeant or lieutenant may be supervising individual officers, a captain is more concerned with individual tasks, unit activities, and the overall performance of the officers under his or her command.

Every commander and administrator in the department, including the police chief, possesses administrative and supervisory responsibilities to some extent. As can be seen from the previous list, the unit commander functions to some extent like a police chief. The unit commander has many of the same responsibilities as the chief, but on a smaller scale. The chief performs these functions for the total department, while the unit commander is concerned only with one unit.

Next, we examine the tasks generally performed by the **lieutenant,** again using the Lexington Police Department as an example. The 15 most important responsibilities for lieutenants include the following (this list is based on the frequency with which they are performed and their urgency)[21]:

1. Assisting in supervising or directing the activities of the unit
2. Performing the duties of a police officer
3. Ensuring that departmental and governmental policies are followed
4. Preparing duty roster
5. Reviewing the work of individuals or groups in the section
6. Responding to field calls requiring an on-scene commander
7. Holding roll call
8. Preparing various reports
9. Reviewing various reports
10. Coordinating the activities of subordinates on major investigations
11. Meeting with superiors concerning unit operations
12. Maintaining time sheets
13. Notifying captain/bureau commander of significant calls
14. Answering inquiries from other sections/units, divisions, and outside agencies
15. Serving as captain/bureau commander in absence of same

Notice that some of the tasks performed by the lieutenants are purely administrative in nature (tasks 4, 7, 8, and 12). These are administrative activities that occur in every operational unit in the police department. The lieutenants in Lexington also perform supervisory functions (tasks 1, 3, 5, 6, and 9). These functions include overseeing officers and sergeants to ensure that different tasks are completed. Here, direct supervision generally focuses on the most critical tasks or those tasks that when performed incorrectly can result in dire consequences. Tasks 11 and 13 through 15 are managerial in nature. These responsibilities are generally vested with a unit commander, but many lieutenants perform them, especially in the absence of the captain. Finally, lieutenants perform the duties of a police officer (task 2). With their supervisory and managerial responsibilities, they engage in a limited amount of police work. The list shows that lieutenants are involved in a wide range of supervisory, managerial, and police duties.

One potential problem of police organizations is that they may become top-heavy, with too many administrative, management, and supervisory personnel in general, or too many who are working in offices and not on the streets. Such structures can hinder the accomplishment of goals and objectives. Too often, middle managers become glorified paper pushers, especially in the present climate that requires myriad reports, budgets, grants, and so on.

The agency should determine what administrative, management, and supervisory functions are essential, and how many captains, lieutenants, and sergeants are needed to perform them. Some communities, such as Kansas City, Missouri, have eliminated the rank of lieutenant; they found that this move had no negative consequences.[22]

# First-Line Supervisors: The Patrol Sergeant

## Seeking the Gold Badge

Sometime during the career of a patrol officer (provided that he or she acquires the minimal years of experience), the opportunity for career advancement is presented—the chance to wear the sergeant's "gold badge." This is a difficult position to occupy because at this middle level, **first-line supervisors** are caught between upper management and the rank-and-file officers.

This initial promotional opportunity to attain the rank of sergeant is normally quite attractive. It is not uncommon for 60 to 65 percent or more of those who are eligible to take the test for promotion; thus, competition for the sergeant openings in most departments is quite keen.

Becoming a sergeant often involves an assessment center process, discussed earlier, and departmental and civil service procedures that are intended to guarantee legitimacy and impartiality in the process. Officers are often told it is best to rotate into different assignments before testing for sergeant, to gain exposure to a variety of police functions and supervisors. The promotional system, then, favors well-rounded officers; furthermore, being skilled at test taking is often of tremendous assistance, so even if one fails the first or several tests, going through the testing process can be invaluable. As with the chief executives' hiring process, an assessment center, which includes critical-incident, problem solving, in-basket, disciplinary problems, role-playing exercises and/or other components, will provide candidates with valuable training and testing experience. Other factors that might come into play as part of the promotional process include education and training, years of experience, supervisory ratings, psychological evaluations, and departmental commendations.

## Assuming the Position: General Roles and Functions

Administrative personnel know that a good patrol officer is not automatically a good supervisor. Because supervisors are promoted from within the ranks, they are often placed in charge of their friends and peers. Longstanding relationships are put under stress when a new sergeant suddenly has official authority over former equals. Leniency or preferential treatment often is expected of new sergeants by their former peers.

When new supervisors attempt to correct deficient behavior, their previous performance may be recalled as a means of challenging the reasonableness or legitimacy of their supervisory action. Supervisors with any skeletons in their closets can expect to hear those skeletons rattling as they begin to use their new-found authority. This places a great deal of pressure on the supervisor. A new supervisor therefore must go through a transitional phase to learn how to exercise command and get cooperation from subordinates.

The new supervisor is no longer responsible solely for her or his behavior but is responsible for the behavior of several other employees. The step from officer to supervisor is a big one and calls for a new set of skills and knowledge largely separate from those learned at lower levels in the organization.

Supervision is not only challenging in policing, but also in corrections, where supervisors must follow federal and state laws and court decisions that concern the custody, care, and treatment of inmates. Their subordinates, however, expect them to be understanding, to protect them from prison management's potentially unreasonable expectations and arbitrary decisions, and to represent their interests.

The supervisor's role, put simply, is to get his or her subordinates to do their very best. This task involves a host of actions, including communicating, motivating, leading, team building, training, appraising, counseling, and disciplining. Getting them to do their very best includes figuring out each subordinate's strengths and weaknesses, defining good and bad performance, measuring performance, providing feedback, and making sure that subordinates' efforts coincide with the organization's mission, values, goals, and objectives.

Supervising a group of subordinates is made more difficult because of the so-called "human element." People are complex and sometimes unpredictable. Rules and principles for communicating and leading and other supervisory tasks are rarely hard and fast because different people react differently. What works for a supervisor in one situation may not work for that supervisor in another situation, much less for some other supervisor. Thus, supervisors have to learn to read subordinates and diagnose situations before choosing how to respond. Supervisors have to become students of human behavior and of such behavioral science disciplines as psychology and sociology.

Effective supervision is also difficult because the job is dynamic, not static. Even without any turnover of personnel, one's subordinates change over time as they age, grow, mature, and experience satisfaction and dissatisfaction in their personal and work lives. In addition, turnover is common as a result of retirements, promotions, and transfers to other units within the department. When new subordinates come under the supervisor's wing, the supervisor must learn the best way to handle these new subordinates and also be attuned to the new officers' effects on other subordinates and on the work group as a whole.

It is not only one's subordinates who change; the organization and its environment change over time. The organization's rules and expectations may change. The public may make new demands. Societal values evolve and change. Effective supervision over the long haul requires continuous monitoring and adaptation. The department expects the supervisor to keep up with such changes to better supervise subordinates. Subordinates, on the other hand, expect the supervisor to help them to interpret and adapt successfully to this changing environment. Table 4.1 shows the expectations that both managers and rank-and-file officers have of first-line supervisors.

**TABLE 4.1**    Management's and Officers' Expectations of Supervisors

*MANAGEMENT'S EXPECTATIONS*

- Interpret departmental policies, procedures, and rules, and ensure that officers follow them
- Initiate disciplinary action when officers fail to follow policies
- Ensure that officers' paperwork and reports are accurate and filed on a timely basis
- Train officers when they are deficient or unskilled
- Complete performance evaluations
- Ensure that officers treat citizens respectfully, professionally, and impartially
- Ensure that officers' equipment and appearance are in order
- Backup officers and review their performance when officers answer calls for service
- Take charge of high-risk or potential critical-incident situations
- Make assignments to ensure that the objectives of the unit are met

*OFFICERS' EXPECTATIONS*

- Interpret departmental policies, procedures, and rules to meet the needs of the officers
- Handle disciplinary actions informally rather than taking direct action, especially regarding minor infractions
- Advocate for officers when they request vacation or time off
- Support them when there is a conflict with citizens
- Provide them support and backup at high-risk calls
- Assist them in getting better assignments and shifts
- Emphasize law enforcement activities over other activities such as providing services, community policing activities, or mundane assignments such as traffic control
- Understand that officers need to take breaks and sometimes attend to personal needs while on duty

### *Basic Tasks*

The following nine tasks are most important for police supervisors; they are listed with the most important first[23]:

1. Supervises subordinate officers in the performance of their duties
2. Disseminates information to subordinates
3. Ensures that general and special orders are followed
4. Reviews and approves various reports
5. Listens to problems voiced by officers
6. Answers calls
7. Keeps superiors apprised of ongoing situations
8. Provides direct supervision for potential high-risk calls or situations
9. Interprets policies and informs subordinates

# EXHIBIT 4.1
## Good, Better, Best
### What Makes Some Sergeants a Cut Above the Rest?

What is it that separates an excellent sergeant from one who is merely good? The ability to devise creative solutions that take into account life's moral ambiguities is a key ingredient and a more prudent use of sick leave doesn't hurt.

Those were the surprising findings of a National Institute of Justice study that attempted to tease out those differences by examining the work habits and backgrounds of a small sample of Baltimore's first-line supervisors.

In the report, "Identifying Characteristics of Exemplary Baltimore Police Department First Line Supervisors," researchers from Johns Hopkins University and the College of Notre Dame of Maryland used a focus group of commanders, police officers and supervisors to develop a set of characteristics that could be used by peers to identify sergeants they considered exemplary, and those who were less so.

Participants in the study were asked to think about supervisors they had known since 1985 and name the one they felt best met the criteria for leadership identified by a focus group of commanders, officers and sergeants. They were also asked to choose a second-best, and explain what it was that placed those supervisors in the second ranking.

Among the traits identified as vital by the focus group were character and integrity; knowledge of the job; management skills; communication skills; interpersonal skills; ability to develop entry-level officers; problem-solving and critical thinking skills; effectiveness as role model and as disciplinarian, and the ability to be proactive. ...

Where the groups differed significantly, however, was on tests given by researchers which rated moral reasoning; their tendency to select friends, relatives and authority figures in their lives as examples of moral excellence, as compared to the well-known historical or religious figures selected by the controls, and their use of non-line of duty sick days.

Those three factors were cited by the study as being the most distinguishing characteristics between the two groups.

"The most important difference was the moral reasoning," said Phyllis P. McDonald, director of research for Johns Hopkins University's School of Professional Studies in Business and Education, who was the NIJ program manager for the study. "They could solve police-related moral issues far better than their peers. They came up with more solutions, they were more complete and they were just better quality solutions." ...

"They are better at problem solving and their sick leave pattern is different because they may have a higher investment in the job," she told Law Enforcement News. ...

"It's the kind of person who thinks about it 24-hours a day, and gathers information, interrelates with subordinates, that kind of thing," she said.

Another factor that separated the exemplary from the less so was the

*(continued)*

confidence that their supervisors had in them. When lieutenants were asked whom they would choose in a crisis situation, McDonald said, most often it was the exemplary sergeant.

"We know they're better at decision-making, organizing, handling issues,

somehow," she said. "Those three areas are significant."

*Source:* Reprinted with permission from *Law Enforcement News,* March 15/31, 2003, pp. 1, 6. John Jay College of Criminal Justice (CCNY), 555 West 57th St., New York, NY 10019.

Tasks 1 and 8 on this list are global supervisory tasks that incorporate both direction and control. Tasks 2 and 9 are aspects of the directing function, whereas tasks 3 through 5 are elements of control. Thus, six of these top nine sergeant's tasks involve directing and controlling. The remaining three tasks provide interesting glimpses into some of the other duties and responsibilities performed by police supervisors: listening to subordinates' problems, notifying superiors of problems, and directly assisting subordinates in performing their work. Police supervisors provide an important communications link in the hierarchy between workers and management, as well as a sounding board for problems and grievances. They also get involved in performing street police work from time to time.

Supervisory tasks can range from the mundane (such as typing and filing reports, operating dictation equipment) to the challenging (assigning priorities to investigations, training personnel in forced entry procedures and barricaded-person situations). Tasks may be administrative (preparing monthly activity reports, scheduling vacation leave), operational (securing major crime scenes, assisting stranded motorists), general (maintaining inventory of equipment, training subordinates), or specialized (conducting stakeouts, training animals for use in specialized units).

## Types of Supervisors

Robin S. Engel[24] studied police supervisors and found four distinct types: traditional, innovative, supportive, and active. Each of these types can be found in any police department. A particular supervisor's style is largely dependent on his or her experiences on the job, his or her training, and the department's organizational climate.

The first type, *traditional,* is law enforcement oriented. Traditional supervisors expect their subordinates to produce high levels of measurable activities, such as traffic citations and arrests. They expect officers to respond to calls for service efficiently, place a great deal of emphasis on reports and other paperwork, and provide officers with a substantial amount of instruction and oversight. To a great extent, traditional supervisors are task oriented. They tend to place greater emphasis on punishment than rewards and often believe that they do not have a great deal of power in the department. These supervisors see their primary role as controlling subordinates. Traditional supervisors often have morale and motivation problems with their subordinates.

The second type is the *innovative* supervisor, who is most closely associated with community policing. To some extent, innovative supervisors are the opposite of traditional supervisors. Innovative supervisors generally do not place a great deal of emphasis on citations or arrests. They also depend more on developing relationships with subordinates as opposed to using power to control or motivate. Innovative supervisors usually are good mentors, and they tend to coach rather than order. They are open to new ideas and innovations. Their ultimate goal is to develop officers who can solve problems and have good relations with citizens. Innovative supervisors sometimes have problems with officers who are task oriented or who emphasize enforcement and neglect community relations.

The third type of supervisor is the *supportive* supervisor, who, like the innovate supervisor, is concerned with developing good relations with subordinates. The primary difference is that the supportive supervisor is concerned with protecting officers from what are viewed as unfair management practices. They see themselves as a buffer between management and officers. They attempt to develop strong work teams and motivate officers by inspiring them. Their shortcoming is that they tend to see themselves as "one of the boys," and they sometimes neglect emphasizing departmental goals and responsibilities.

The final category of supervisors according to Engel is the *active* supervisor, who tends to work in the field. Active supervisors sometimes are police officers with stripes or rank. They often take charge of field situations rather than supervise them, although they are active supervisors in most situations. They are able to develop good relations with subordinates because they are perceived as being hard working and competent. Their shortcoming is that by being overly involved in some field situations, they do not give their subordinates the opportunity to develop.

Engel[25] found that the four types of supervision were fairly evenly distributed in the departments. The most effective supervisor was the active supervisor. Subordinates working for active supervisors performed better in a number of areas, including problem solving and community policing. This led Engel to conclude that active supervisors were able to develop a more productive work unit because of their leading by example. It seems that working supervisors inspire subordinates to work and be productive.

Engel did identify one issue with active police supervisors: a higher incidence of use of force relative to the other types. Because active supervisors are very involved in the provision of police services, efforts should be made to ensure that they follow policies as well as that subordinates adhere to policies and procedures. Supervisors must not only be well trained and selected carefully, but they too must receive a measure of supervision from their superior.

If the supervisor fails to make sure that employees perform correctly, the unit will not be successful, causing difficulties for the manager, the lieutenant, or the captain.

A police department is really nothing more than the sum total of all its units, and one problem unit can adversely affect other units and detract from the department's total effectiveness. This is particularly true for police organizations because there is substantial interdependence among the various units in a police department. For example, if patrol officers do a poor job of writing reports when they respond to crimes, the workload of detectives who later complete the case's follow-up investigation will increase.

# The Patrol Officer

Countless books and articles have been written about, and other chapters in this book deal in part with, the beat officer. Here, I briefly discuss the nature of this position. Included is a review of a recent court decision and its policy implications, concerning an applicant's denial of police employment for scoring too high on a pre-employment examination.

## Basic Tasks

Many people believe that the police officer has the most difficult job in the United States. When broken down into fundamental terms, the police perform four basic functions: (1) enforcing the laws, (2) performing services (such as maintaining or assisting animal control units, reporting burned-out street lights or stolen traffic lights and signs, delivering death messages, checking the welfare of people in their homes, delivering blood), (3) preventing crime (patrolling, providing the public with information on locks and lighting to reduce the opportunity for crime), and (4) protecting the innocent (by investigating crimes, police are systematically removing innocent people from consideration as crime suspects).[26]

Because police officers are solitary workers, spending much of their time on the job unsupervised, and because those officers who are hired today will become the supervisors of the future, police administrators must attempt to attract the best individuals possible. A major problem of police administration today involves personnel recruitment.

## What Traits Make a Good Officer?

Although it may be difficult for the average police administrator to articulate what qualities he or she looks for when recruiting, training, and generally creating a "good" officer, some psychological characteristics can be identified. According to psychologist Lawrence Wrightsman,[27] it is important that good officers be *incorruptible*, of high moral character. They should be *well adjusted,* able to carry out the hazardous and stressful tasks of policing without "cracking up," and thick-skinned enough to operate without defensiveness. They also should be *people oriented* and able to respond to situations without becoming overly emotional, impulsive, or aggressive; they need to exercise restraint. They also need *cognitive skills* to assist in their investigative work.

Chief Dennis Nowicki[28] compiled 12 qualities that he believes are imperative for entry-level police officers:

1. *Enthusiasm.* Believes in what he or she is doing and goes about with a vigor that is almost contagious

2. *Good communications skills.* Highly developed speaking and listening skills; ability to interact equally well with people from all socioeconomic levels

3. *Good judgment.* Wisdom and analytical ability to make good decisions based on an understanding of the problem

4. *Sense of humor.* Ability to laugh and smile, to help officers cope with the regular exposure to human pain and suffering

5. *Creativity.* Ability to use creative techniques by placing themselves in the mind of the criminal and legally accomplishing arrests

6. *Self-motivation.* Making things happen, proactively solving difficult cases, creating their own luck

7. *Knowing the job and the system.* Understanding the role of a police officer, the intricacies of the justice system, what the administration requires, and using both formal and informal channels to be effective

8. *Ego.* Believing they are good officers, having self-confidence that enables solving difficult crimes

9. *Courage.* Ability to meet physical and psychological challenges, thinking clearly during times of high stress, admitting when they are wrong, standing up for what is difficult and right

10. *Understanding discretion.* Enforcing the spirit of the law, not the letter of the law; not being hardnosed, hardheaded, or hard-hearted; giving people a break and showing empathy

11. *Tenacity.* Staying focused; seeing challenges, not obstacles; not viewing failure as a setback, but as an experience

12. *Thirst for knowledge.* Staying current of new laws and court decisions, always learning (from the classroom but also via informal discussions with other officers)

## Can People Be Too Smart for Police Work?

Robert Jordan applied to become a police officer in New London, Connecticut; as part of the application process, Jordan was required to take a written examination to measure cognitive ability, on which he received a score of 33.

The city would only consider applicants who scored between 20 and 27 (based on the view that hiring overqualified applicants leads to subsequent job dissatisfaction and turnover), so Jordan was denied employment for scoring too high. Jordan brought an action in the U.S. District Court for the District of Connecticut,[29] arguing that his denial of a job opportunity was a violation of the equal protection clause of the constitutions of both the United States and Connecticut. The District Court held there was no such violation, that Jordan was neither a member of a protected class nor had a right to be employed as a police officer, and that governments have legitimate goals of fostering employment longevity and reducing turnover. The court also noted that the range provided by the test manufacturer was based on "a body of literature conclud[ing] that hiring overqualified applicants leads to subsequent job dissatisfaction and turnover."[30] Jordan's appeal to the Second Circuit Court of Appeals resulted in the same holding and outcome.[31]

In light of **Jordan v. The City of New London,** and to shed light on the practical impact of intelligence on policing, Tom Hughes surveyed 65 mid-level managers (e.g., lieutenants) attending the Southern Police Institute in Louisville, Kentucky. The major findings of this survey were as follows[32]:

- Only about one third (36.1 percent) felt that highly intelligent officers frequently left their agencies for other law enforcement jobs or non–law enforcement jobs
- With regard to their conduct on the street, intelligent officers cause fewer problems for supervisors (66.2 percent)
- Highly intelligent officers get sued less often (59.4 percent)
- Highly intelligent officers seem to get into less trouble (92.2 percent)

## Policy Implications

Although the impact of *Jordan* is uncertain (the court's opinion was not published in the federal reporter system, and was written with the admonition that it "may not be cited as precedential authority in this or any other court"),[33] the case does appear to have some potential practical and legal implications.

First, *Jordan* involves employment law, an area that has proven fertile for suits against the police. If other jurisdictions should follow the decision, in addition to possibly providing a reason to sue in the future for individuals who were not hired—as Robert Jordan did—this decision also promotes a negative image of individuals who do desire and select policing, and creates three concerns for police managers:

1. Such a policy may communicate to the public the idea that the best and brightest are not present in the occupation; this would also seem to be damaging to those departments seeking to implement community-oriented policing and problem solving (COPPS, discussed in Chapter 3), which seeks the best and brightest.

2. The morale of officers already in the field may be negatively affected by the image projected by the decision.
3. Although the decision may not be cited as authority, it could provide persuasive authority that could be used by future courts that address this issue.

Test makers appear to believe in the logic that intelligent persons will flee from the policing field due to frustration and boredom. In view of the Southern Police Institute survey, however, it would seem that further study is needed to determine the relationship between intelligence and attrition, lest *Jordan* continue to create or reinforce negative stereotypes of policing.[34]

Chapter 14 deals further with employment law and legislation.

### *Strategies for Hiring the Best*

Notwithstanding the *Jordan* decision, police agencies must still strive to recruit and hire the best personnel possible. In the early 1990s, many police departments were under intense pressure to select and hire more officers using federal and state grant funds. As has always been the case in policing, however, this haste did not serve those agencies well: By the late 1990s, many departments were faced with problems surrounding officer misconduct, and discovered they had hired officers with criminal records for offenses such as drug possession and domestic violence.[35] Therefore, agencies continue to be challenged in their attempts to look for the "right person" for the job. There are three important strategies departments can utilize in selection and hiring:

1. Have an organizational culture that supports a good selection process; clear, nonarbitrary rules allow those officers with excellent qualities to remain so. In organizations that do not reward hard work and honesty, good employees will be disillusioned and either adapt or leave.
2. A validated, job-related selection process is needed to hire the best candidates. Although psychological tests (the most frequently used test is the Minnesota Multiphasic Personality Inventory, or MMPI), and background investigations can screen out applicants who have serious psychological, drug, criminal history, and other problems, further steps are needed to identify the most qualified candidates. Assessment centers (discussed earlier) are the best way to do this because they are job related, valid, and do not have an adverse impact on protected groups.
3. A robust training and evaluation system is needed to support the selection process. Agencies must train their recruits well, teach them the correct skills, and evaluate them early and often.[36]

## Roles and Functions of Police Personnel under COPPS

Earlier in this chapter I examined the basic roles of chief executives, middle managers, and first-line supervisors. Next, I briefly examine their roles under COPPS.

## The Chief Executive

The advent of community policing has brought new challenges for police chiefs, calling for new skills and attitudes and even an ability to be an entrepreneur.[37] First, the police chief executive is ultimately responsible for all the facets of COPPS, from implementation to training to evaluation. Therefore, what is needed are chief executives who are "risk takers and boat rockers within a culture where daily exposure to life-or-death situations makes officers natural conservators of the status quo."[38] For them, "standing still is not only insufficient ... it is going backwards."[39] Therefore, police executives must be *viable change agents*. The chief executive must be both visible and credible and must create a climate conducive to change.

In sum, the chief executive's roles and responsibilities during the change to COPPS include the following:

- Articulating a clear vision to the organization
- Understanding and accepting the depth of change and time required to implement COPPS
- Assembling a management team that is committed to translating the new vision into action
- Being committed to removing bureaucratic obstacles whenever possible

## Middle Managers

COPPS's emphasis on problem solving necessitates that middle managers (captains and lieutenants) draw on their familiarity with the bureaucracy to secure, maintain, and use authority to empower subordinates, helping officers to actively and creatively confront and resolve issues, and sometimes using unconventional approaches on a trial-and-error basis.

Middle managers must *build on the strengths* of their subordinates, capitalizing on their training and competence.[40] They must "cheerlead," encouraging supervisors and patrol officers to actually solve the problems they are confronting.[41] The lieutenants are the "gatekeepers" and must develop the system, resources, and support mechanisms to ensure that the officers/detectives and supervisors can achieve the best results. The officers and supervisors cannot perform without the necessary equipment, resources, and reinforcement.[42]

In sum, the roles and responsibilities of middle managers during the change to COPPS include the following:

- Assuming responsibility for strategic planning
- Eliminating red tape and bottlenecks that impede the work of officers and supervisors
- Conducting regular meetings with subordinates to discuss plans, activities, and results
- Assessing COPPS efforts in a continuous manner

## *First-Line Supervisors*

Perhaps the most challenging aspect of changing the culture of a police agency lies in changing first-line supervisors. Supervisors must be convinced that COPPS makes good sense in today's environment.

The roles and responsibilities of first-line supervisors during a change to COPPS include the following:

- Understanding and practicing problem solving
- Managing time, staff, and resources
- Encouraging teamwork
- Helping officers to mobilize stakeholders
- Tracking and managing officers' problem solving
- Providing officers with ongoing feedback and support

## *Rank-and-File Officers*

All experts on the subject of police innovation and change emphasize the importance of empowering and using the input from the street officers. The patrol officer becomes a *problem solver*. There is an emphasis on practical intelligence—the ability to quickly analyze key elements of a situation and identify possible courses of action to reach logical conclusions. In order to formulate a response, the officer must define the problem and address the motivations of the offenders.[43]

Under COPPS, the patrol officer is expected to recognize when old methods are inadequate and new and different solutions are needed. The officer is expected to display many of the skills demanded in higher level personnel, such as detectives, including being creative, flexible, and innovative; working independently; and maintaining self-discipline. Communication skills are also vital. The officer must possess the ability to work cooperatively with others to solve problems and to listen.[44]

# CASE STUDIES

The following two case studies deal with CEO functions and disciplinary problems and assist the reader in understanding and applying administrative challenges in a real-world context.

## The Chief Executive's Busy Days

You have been the Park City police chief for 6 months, overseeing an agency of 60 sworn officers in a community of 80,000 people; your city abuts another, larger city, with a population of 160,000. These populations are deceptive, however, soaring during the summertime, because your area is a tourist-based gaming destination. Today is July 3, and at 8:00 a.m. you briefly attend a staff meeting of detectives, led by a deputy chief of operations, to learn the latest information concerning a highly publicized kidnapping. In the afternoon, you plan to deliver a news release concerning the case status. Then you will give the graduation speech at the area police academy, which is followed by your attending a meeting of the Tri-County Regional Major Case Squad, where you will discuss the latest intelligence information concerning a ring of circulating slot machine cheaters in your jurisdiction. You then learn from Communications that one of your motorcycle officers has gone down, and you speed to the hospital emergency room to wish him well. You then meet with your events staff and other city officials to finalize security and traffic plans for tomorrow's huge fireworks display because last year's event resulted in huge numbers of alcohol-related traffic and fighting arrests. You are also scheduled to ride in a car in the holiday parade. At day's end, you make final preparations for your July 5 presentation to the City Council concerning the need for a modern, 800-megahertz communications system, which you hope to convince the council to purchase. You also will be attending a special ceremony at a city park that honors area law enforcement officers who have been killed in the line of duty.

### Questions for Discussion

1. Using Mintzberg's model for CEOs, classify each of the functions mentioned in the case study into the interpersonal, informational, and decision-maker roles.
2. More specifically, which of this chief executive's tasks or activities would fall within the figurehead, leadership, liaison, monitoring/inspecting, dissemination, spokesperson, entrepreneur, disturbance-handler, resource-allocator, and negotiator functions? Explain.

# Intruding Ima and the Falsified Report

An 8-year employee of your police agency, Officer Ima Goodenough, is a patrol officer who often serves as field training officer. Goodenough is generally capable and experienced in both the patrol and detective divisions. She takes pride in being of the "old school" and has evolved a clique of approximately 10 people with whom she gets along, while mostly shunning other officers. As an officer of the old school, she typically handles calls for service without requesting cover units or backup. She has had six complaints of brutality lodged against her during the last 3 years. For Ima and her peers, officers who call for backup are "wimps." She has recently been involved in two high-speed pursuits during which her vehicle was damaged when she attempted to run the offender off the road. Ima will notify a supervisor only when dealing with a major situation. She is borderline insubordinate when dealing with new supervisors. She believes that, generally speaking, the administration exists only to "screw around with us." You, her shift commander, have been fed up with her deteriorating attitude and reckless performance for some time and have been wondering whether you will soon have occasion to take some form of disciplinary action against her. You have also learned that Ima has a reputation among her supervisors as being a "hot dog." Some of her past and present supervisors have even commented that she is a "walking time bomb" who is unpredictable and could "blow" at any time.

One day while bored on patrol, Ima decides to go outside her jurisdiction, responding to a shooting call that is just across the city limit and in the county. She radios the dispatcher that she is out "assisting," then walks into the home where paramedics are frantically working on a man with a head wound lying on the floor. Nearby on the floor is a large, foreign-made revolver; Ima holds and waves the revolver in the air, examining it. A paramedic yells at her, "Hey! Put that down, this may be an attempted homicide case!" Ima puts the revolver back on the floor. Meanwhile, you have been attempting to contact Ima via radio to get her back into her jurisdiction. Later, when the sheriff's office complains to you about her actions at their crime scene, you require that she write a report of her actions. She completes a report describing her observations at the scene but denies touching or picking up anything. Looking at Ima's personnel file, you determine that her performance evaluations for the past 8 years are "standard"— average to above average. She has never received a suspension from duty for her actions. Although verbally expressing their unhappiness with her for many years, Ima's supervisors have not expressed that disdain in writing.

## Questions for Discussion

1. What are the primary issues involved in this situation?
2. Do you believe that there are sufficient grounds for bringing disciplinary action against Goodenough? If so, what would be the specific charges? What is the appropriate punishment?

3. Do you believe that this is a good opportunity, and do grounds exist, for termination?

4. Does the fact that her supervisors have rated her as standard have any bearing on this matter or create difficulties in bringing a case for termination? If so, how?

## Summary

This chapter has shown the kinds of traits and duties that accompany today's law enforcement executive. Clearly, these individuals occupy positions of tremendous responsibility. Police executives, managers, and supervisors must decide what the best leadership method is, both inside and outside their organizations. They must be concerned with their agency's performance and standing with the community, governing board, and rank and file. Their abilities will be challenged in additional ways if the COPPS strategy is being contemplated or is already underway.

## Questions for Review

1. What are some of a police executive's primary roles? (Use the three major categories of the Mintzberg model of chief executive officers in developing your response.)

2. What are some elements of the police chief's and sheriff's positions that make them attractive and unattractive? Do you think that contemporary qualifications for the positions are adequate? How do chiefs and sheriffs differ in role and background?

3. How is the performance of chiefs and sheriffs evaluated? Are there other, better criteria that could be used? What personal traits are most important for persons occupying or seeking these offices?

4. What are the "Ten Commandments" of good executive leadership?

5. How do the role and function of sergeants differ from those of upper or middle management?

6. What are the three types of political arena conflicts that can cause police chiefs to lose their jobs?

7. What are the primary responsibilities of executive, management, and supervisory personnel under COPPS?

## Notes

1. Henry Mintzberg, "The Manager's Job: Folklore and Fact," *Harvard Business Review* **53** (July/August 1975):49–61.

2. For a comprehensive look at the assessment center process, and tips for how to participate as a candidate, see John L. Coleman, *Police Assessment Testing: An Assessment Center Handbook for Law Enforcement Personnel* (Springfield, Ill.: Charles C Thomas, 2002).

3. Robert Katz, "Skills of an Effective Administrator," *Harvard Business Review* (January/February 1955):33–41.

4. Thomas J. Jurkanin, Larry T. Hoover, Jerry L. Dowling, and Janice Ahmad, *Enduring, Surviving, and Thriving as a Law Enforcement Executive* (Springfield, Ill.: Charles C Thomas, 2001), pp. 12–29.

5. Ibid., pp. 64–65; also see, for example, Isidore Silver, *Police Civil Liability* (available through the LexisNexis Bookstore (http://www.lexisnexis.com/bookstore/catalog), a resource for law enforcement officers at all levels, with looseleaf supplements that are updated twice per year; Kenneth J. Peak, *Policing America: Methods, Issues, Challenges,* 5th ed. (Upper Saddle River, NJ: Prentice Hall, 2006), Chapter 11.

6. Ronald G. Lynch, *The Police Manager,* 3rd ed. (New York: Random House, 1986), p. 1.

7. "Survey Says Big-City Chiefs Are Better-Educated Outsiders," *Law Enforcement News*, April 30, 1998, p. 7.

8. Ibid.

9. Janice K. Penegor and Ken Peak, "Police Chief Acquisitions: A Comparison of Internal and External Selections," *American Journal of Police* **11** (1992):17–32.

10. Richard B. Weinblatt, "The Shifting Landscape of Chiefs' Jobs," *Law and Order* (October 1999):50.

11. National Advisory Commission on Criminal Justice Standards and Goals, *Police Chief Executive* (Washington, D.C.: U.S. Government Printing Office, 1976), p. 7.

12. Weinblatt, "The Shifting Landscape of Chiefs' Jobs," p. 51.

13. For an excellent compilation of articles concerning the chief's role, see William Geller (ed.), *Police Leadership in America: Crisis and Opportunity* (New York: Praeger, 1985).

14. Janet Ferris, "Present and Potential Legal Job Protections Available to Heads of Agencies," *Florida Police Chief* **14** (1994):43–45.

15. Henry Mintzberg, *Power In and Around Organizations* (Upper Saddle River, N.J.: Prentice Hall, 1983).

16. Ibid., pp. 50–53.

17. Charles R. Swanson, Leonard Territo, and Robert W. Taylor, *Police Administration: Structures, Processes, and Behavior,* 6th ed. (Upper Saddle River, N.J.: Prentice Hall, 2005), pp. 129–130.

18. Colin Hayes, "The Office of Sheriff in the United States," *The Prison Journal* **74** (2001):50–54.

19. Leonhard F. Fuld, *Police Administration* (New York: G. P. Putnam's Sons, 1909), pp. 59–60.

20. See Kenneth J. Peak, Larry K. Gaines, and Ronald W. Glensor, *Police Supervision and Management: In an Era of Community Policing,* 2nd ed. (Upper Saddle River, N.J.: Prentice Hall, 2004), Chapter 2, generally.

21. Ibid.

22. Richard N. Holden, *Modern Police Management,* 2nd ed. (Upper Saddle River, N.J.: Prentice Hall, 1994), pp. 294–295.

23. Peak, Gaines, and Glensor, *Police Supervision and Management,* Chapter 2, generally.

24. Robin S. Engel, "Patrol Officer Supervision in the Community Policing Era," *Journal of Criminal Justice* **30** (2002):51–64.

25. Robin S. Engel, "Supervisory Styles of Patrol Sergeants and Lieutenants," *Journal of Criminal Justice* **29** (2001):341–355.

26. Kenneth J. Peak, *Policing America: Methods, Issues, Functions*, 4th ed. (Upper Saddle River, N.J.: Prentice Hall, 2003), pp. 57–58.

27. Lawrence S. Wrightsman, *Psychology and the Legal System* (Monterey, Calif.: Brooks/Cole, 1987), pp. 85–86.

28. Adapted from Dennis Nowicki, "Twelve Traits of Highly Effective Police Officers," *Law and Order* (October 1999):45–46.

29. *Jordan v. City of New London* (1999), Civil No. 3:97CV1012 (PCD) U.S. District Court, District of Connecticut.

30. Ibid., p. 5.

31. United States Circuit Court of Appeals, Second Circuit, Summary Order No. 99-9188, August 23, 2000.

32. Tom "Tad" Hughes, "*Jordan v. City of New London,* Police Hiring, and IQ: 'When all the answers they don't amount to much,'" *Policing: An International Journal of Police Strategies & Management* **26**(2) (2003):309–310.

33. *Jordan v. City of New London* (1999).

34. Ibid.

35. Beth A. Sanders, "Maybe There's No Such Thing as a 'Good Cop': Organizational Challenges in Selecting Quality Officers," *Policing: An International Journal of Police Strategies & Management* **26**(2) (2003):313.

36. Ibid., pp. 322–323.

37. See, for example, Kenneth J. Peak and Ronald W. Glensor, *Community Policing and Problem Solving: Strategies and Practices,* 4th ed. (Upper Saddle River, N.J.: Prentice Hall, 2004).

38. Mike Tharp and Dorian Friedman, "New Cops on the Block," *U.S. News and World Report* (August 2, 1993):23.

39. John Eck, quoted in Tharp and Friedman, "New Cops on the Block," p. 24.

40. William A. Geller and Guy Swanger, *Managing Innovation in Policing: The Untapped Potential of the Middle Manager* (Washington, D.C.: Police Executive Research Forum, 1995), p. 105.

41. Ibid., p. 109.

42. Ibid., p. 112.

43. Ibid., p. 116.

44. Ibid., pp. 119–120.

# Chapter 5

# Police Issues
# and Practices

## Key Terms and Concepts

| | |
|---|---|
| DWBB | Typology of abuse of authority |
| Customs and Border Protection (CBP) | Undocumented aliens |
| Futures Working Group | Use-of-force continuum |
| High-Intensity Drug Trafficking Area | Vehicular pursuits |
| OTM | |

## Learning Objectives

After reading this chapter, the student will:

- know the types of abuse of authority, and what administrators and supervisors must do to manage the use of force
- understand why police vehicle pursuits must be supervised, and the means by which this can be accomplished
- see how the porous nature of our national borders provide opportunities for would-be terrorists and criminals
- have an understanding of the ramifications of racial profiling and some supervisory challenges that come with adherence to laws
- determine how far women and minorities have come, and how far they have to go before law enforcement agencies can begin to achieve higher levels of diversity
- understand some of the future issues facing police organizations

> *In utrumque paratus / Seu versare dolos seu certae occumbere morti.*
>
> *[Prepared for either event, to set his traps or to meet with certain death.]*
>
> —Virgil, 70–19 B.C.E.

## Introduction

Other chapters of this book include some of the pressing issues and contemporary practices of law enforcement executives, specifically, issues relating to police organization, operations, and personnel; later chapters will examine issues of homeland defense against terrorism, the application of technology, and the future.

This chapter looks at other, equally challenging issues. It has been said, tongue in cheek, that in the earlier days of policing, "a size 3 hat and a size 43 jacket" were the only qualifications for entering and doing the work of policing. Given the kinds of topics that are discussed in this chapter, this description could not be further from the truth today. In several regards, the police have increasingly been placed under the microscope with regard to how they deal with the public, exercise their force prerogative, guard our borders from uninvited intruders, and offer employment opportunity to all qualified Americans.

The chapter begins with an examination of how law enforcement executives must manage the use of force, including a typology of the abuse of authority and how use-of-force incidents should be reported and examined; also incorporated is a discussion of policy and supervisory aspects of vehicle pursuits. Following that, I look at the serious problem of border security, including a rather frightening view of the number of illegal aliens who come into our country each day, the havoc they wreak with respect to crime all across the nation, and the dangers they pose of terrorism. Next is another "hot button" issue: racial profiling, and what is being done by administrators to track, identify, and, it is hoped, eliminate it. I then turn to the subject of women and minorities in law enforcement ranks, including the chief executive position, and what needs to be done to achieve greater diversity. The chapter concludes with a consideration of future issues for policing, followed by four case studies.

# Managing the Use of Force

## *Power to Be Used Judiciously*

The 1991 Rodney King case and others similar to it raise the question in the public mind as to how often such incidents occur that are not videotaped. They also show how wide the rift between the police and public can be and demonstrate how critical effective police administration is in this country.

Unfortunately, the King incident was not the only one to receive national attention. After the King incident, Amadou Diallo, a 22-year-old, unarmed West African street vendor, was shot 19 times by four New York police officers who mistook him for a serial rapist. Abner Louima, a Haitian emigre, was beaten and sodomized by four Brooklyn, New York, police officers. Such celebrated cases are comparatively rare; most instances of police brutality involve relatively minor abuse: discourtesy, name calling, racial or ethnic slurs, or a shove that leaves no injury.[1] Still, these incidents raise the collective ire of all Americans, result in public demonstrations and protests, foster calls for the firing of police executives, and even provoke widespread rioting. If any good can come from such unfortunate incidents, perhaps it is educational in nature: that the public and police leadership realize that they must be aware of the potential for the use of excessive force by officers.

Americans and their judicial system bestow a tremendous amount of authority on their police officers. The police are the only element of our society (except for the military, under certain circumstances) who are allowed to use force against its citizens, up to and including that which is lethal in nature. The quid pro quo, however, is that the police are given this power and authority with the expectation that they will use it judiciously, only when necessary and as a last resort. A serious problem arises, however, when officers deploy this force improperly.

Regardless of the type of force used, police officers must use it in a legally acceptable manner. The U.S. Supreme Court ruled that the use of force at arrest must be

> Objectively reasonable in view of all the facts and circumstances of each particular case, including the severity of the crime at issue, whether the suspect poses an immediate threat to the safety of the officers or others, and whether he is actively resisting arrest or attempting to evade arrest by flight.[2]

However, determining what constitutes "objectively reasonable" is not an easy task.

Police officers are allowed to use only that force necessary to effect an arrest. Thus, the amount of force that a police officer uses is dependent on the amount of resistance demonstrated by the person being arrested. This concept is taught to police officers in training academies through a **use-of-force continuum,** which includes actions ranging from verbal commands to deadly force. Figure 5.1 shows the use-of-force continuum.

The use-of-force continuum attempts to illustrate how officers respond to suspects' actions. For example, if a suspect attempts to physically assault an officer using his or her fists, an officer possibly is justified in using a police baton, pepper spray, or some other less-than-lethal means to ward off the attack and subdue the suspect. On the other hand, if the suspect is brandishing a knife, the officer may be justified in using a firearm. In addition to using force that is necessary to effect the arrest, the officer must also respect the suspect's life. In 1985, the U.S. Supreme Court ruled that the shooting of any unarmed, nonviolent fleeing felony suspect violated the Fourth Amendment to the Constitution.[3] As a result, almost all major urban police departments enacted restrictive policies regarding deadly force.

## A Typology of Abuse of Authority

The use-of-force continuum shows the range of force that officers can employ. David Carter[4] looked at officers' conduct and provided a **typology of abuse of authority** which includes (1) physical abuse/excessive force, (2) verbal/psychological abuse, and (3) legal abuse/violations of civil rights.

### Physical Abuse and Excessive Force

As noted earlier, police use of physical force often results in substantial public scrutiny. Local incidents may not receive national media coverage, but they often have the same dramatic, chilling effect in a community. All police officers are judged by the actions of one or a few officers, and history has shown that such incidents can also result in rioting by citizens.

The application of deadly force can be a form of excessive force. When a police officer deliberately kills someone, a determination is made as to whether

| LEVELS OF RESISTANCE | LEVELS OF CONTROL OR FORCE |
|---|---|
| **Suspect's Actions** | **Officer's Response** |
| Psychological Intimidation<br>Nonverbal clues that indicate a subject's attitude, appearance, physical readiness | Officer presence<br>Verbal direction |
| Verbal Noncompliance<br>Verbal responses indicating unwillingness attitude | Officer presence<br>Verbal direction<br>Telling suspect what you want him or her to do |
| Passive Resistance<br>Physical actions that do not prevent officer's attempt to control, dead weight, active passiveness | Officer presence<br>Verbal direction<br>Soft empty-hand techniques<br>Wrist locks, pressure point control |
| Defensive Resistance<br>Physical actions that prevent officer's control without attempting to harm the officer | Officer presence<br>Verbal direction<br>Soft empty-hand techniques<br>Strikes with hands, feet, knee, elbow in response to defensive resistance; this level of control should only be used after lesser force has proved ineffective in controlling the suspect and applied only to nonvital areas. |
| Active Aggression<br>Physical assault on the officer | Officer presence<br>Verbal direction<br>Soft empty-hand techniques<br>Hard empty-hand techniques<br>Soft and hard intermediate weapons. Soft shall include radial arm locks, arm bars, etc. Hard shall include strikes with baton to nonvital areas. |
| Aggravated Active Aggression | Any of the above and lethal force |
| Deadly force encounters | Firearms, strikes to the head and other vital areas with impact weapons. |

**Figure 5.1**

Use-of-force continuum for law enforcement.

the homicide was justified to prevent imminent death or serious bodily injury to the officer or another person.

### *Verbal and Psychological Abuse*

Police officers sometimes abuse citizens by berating or belittling them. They antagonize citizens knowing that as police officers they are wrapped in the shroud of authority and that citizens must take the abuse. One of the most common methods used by police officers to verbally abuse citizens is through the use of profanity. Research indicates that profanity is used for a variety of reasons: as a source of power to control others,[5] as a weapon to degrade or insult others,[6] as a method of alienating others,[7] as a method of labeling others,[8] and as a way of defying authority.[9] Unfortunately, profanity has become a part of the police culture and many officers' everyday speech. When profanity is used liberally in the work setting, it increases the likelihood that it will be used inappropriately.

Profane language tends to polarize a situation. A citizen will either passively submit or respond aggressively—in either case, the citizen will distrust and dislike the police. When police officers use profanity, especially in an aggressive manner, the focus shifts from the problem to the officer's language, and when it is used aggressively, profanity can easily create greater physical risks to the officer. Furthermore, even if the officer intended to resolve the situation, it may no longer be possible because of the harm caused by the language. Because it can incite situations, profanity also increases the potential for liability and citizens' complaints; therefore, it also heightens the possibility of the officer's facing administrative action.[10]

For all of these reasons, profanity by the police toward citizens is not justified, wise, or advised. Supervisors should discourage its use and review every instance when an officer uses it with a citizen.

### *Legal Abuse and Violations of Civil Rights*

Legal abuse and civil rights violations consist of police actions that violate citizens' constitutional or statutory rights. This abuse usually involves false arrest, false imprisonment, and harassment. For example, a police officer may knowingly make an unlawful search, charge the suspect with a crime, and then lie about the nature of the search. Another example occurs when police officers hassle a criminal to gain information or hassle a business owner to obtain some monetary gain.

Supervisors and managers play a key role in preventing legal abuse and violations of citizens' civil rights. Supervisors frequently back up officers when responding to calls and observe situations that lead to an arrest. They should ensure that officers' decisions to arrest are based on probable cause, not some lesser standard. They should also review arrest reports and question officers when arrests are not observed to ensure that the arrests meet the probable cause standard.

Officers should provide the same level of services to all citizens, and they should use consistent decision-making criteria when deciding to make an arrest regardless of race, gender, or social standing.

## *Reporting and Examining Use-of-Force Occurrences*

To identify and monitor officers' use of force, law enforcement agencies need a comprehensive data-collection strategy. At a minimum, departments should utilize use-of-force reports completed by officers involved in forceful incidents. Traditionally, agencies required reports when officers used force that was likely to cause death or serious bodily harm (e.g., firing a weapon); in recent years, however, a growing number of agencies have begun documenting *all* instances involving force, regardless of the potential for deadly force or injuries.[11]

Administrators should implement supervisors' "control-of-persons" reports, requiring supervisors to go to the scene of all incidents when officers use force, to interview the officers, suspects, and witnesses and record their responses. Supervisors should also take photographs of any injuries or record complaints of injuries. These forms can also call for demographics, level and type of force, resistance, weapons, and other information (some agencies go further, wanting information on suspects' race, ethnicity, health status, nature of treatment, impairment, and observed behavior). This kind of information should be supplemented by a detailed narrative explaining each of the parties' perspectives, allowing the supervisor to write a sequential account of all relevant actions: the original call or observation, officer and suspect behaviors, why suspects resisted, and levels and types of resistance. Similarly, officers' actions, including levels of force and how it was used, are documented. It is crucial that supervisors capture the stories provided by the parties and not set out to justify the officers' actions or argue with the suspects.[12]

Regardless of the data-collection method used, it is important that officers receive proper training on when and how reports should be completed. Second, the nature and level of both police force and citizen resistance need to be measured; from a legal and policy perspective, the nature or degree of citizen resistance is a critical factor in determining whether the officer used legitimate and justifiable level(s) of force. Finally, the report on the use of force should account for multiple uses of both force and resistance. The best way to examine the force used by the officer is to understand the sequence of events and multiple stages of citizen resistance and officer force applied, not only the highest level used.[13]

# Vehicular Pursuits

## *A High-Stakes Operation*

**Vehicular pursuits** are also related to police use of force and pose great concern to police leadership. Civil litigation arising out of collisions involving police pursuits reveals it to be a high-stakes undertaking with serious and sometimes tragic results. Several hundred people are killed each year during police pursuits[14]; many of the resulting deaths and injuries involve innocent third parties or stem from minor traffic violations. The U.S. Supreme Court, as discussed in the next section, has strengthened most progressive chase policies, but the Court has also conferred a responsibility that must be borne by the police. The responsibility for seeing that proper policies and procedures exist rests squarely with the chief executive officer of the agency.

Pursuits place the police in a delicate balancing act. On one hand is the need to show that flight from the law is no way to freedom. If a police agency completely bans high-speed pursuits, its credibility with both law-abiding citizens and law violators may suffer; public knowledge that the agency has a no-pursuit policy may encourage people to flee, decreasing the probability of apprehension.[15] Still, according to one author, because of safety and liability concerns, "A growing number of agencies have the position that if the bad guy puts the pedal to the metal, it's a 'freebie.' They will not pursue him."[16]

On the other hand, the high-speed chase threatens everyone within range of the pursuit, including suspects, their passengers, and other drivers or bystanders. One police trainer tells officers to ask themselves a simple question to determine whether to continue a pursuit: "Is this person a threat to the public safety other than the fact the police are chasing him?" If the officer cannot objectively answer "yes," the pursuit should be terminated.[17]

## The Supreme Court's View

In May 1990, two Sacramento County, California, deputies responded to a fight call. At the scene, they observed a motorcycle with two riders approaching their vehicle at high speed; turning on their red lights, the deputies ordered the driver to stop. The motorcycle operator began to elude the officers, who initiated a pursuit reaching speeds of more than 100 miles per hour over about 1.3 miles. The pursuit ended when the motorcycle crashed; the deputies' vehicle could not stop in time and struck the bike's passenger, killing him; his family brought suit, claiming the pursuit violated the crash victim's due process rights under the Fourteenth Amendment.

In May 1998, the U.S. Supreme Court, in *County of Sacramento v. Lewis*,[18] ruled that the proper standard to be employed in these cases is whether the officer's conduct during the pursuit was conscience shocking; it further determined that high-speed chases with no intent to harm suspects do not give rise to liability under the Fourteenth Amendment.[19] The Court left unanswered many important questions, such as whether an innocent third party can file a claim against the police for damages, or whether a municipality can be held liable for its failure to train officers in pursuit issues.

## Leadership Rejoinder

The following incidents demonstrate the dangerous nature of police pursuits:

- In Omaha, Nebraska, a 70-mile per hour pursuit through a residential neighborhood of a motorcyclist for expired license plates ended when the motorcyclist ran a stop sign, crashing into another vehicle and killing the female passenger on the motorcycle.
- A sheriff's deputy in Florida intentionally rammed a vehicle during a pursuit for an outstanding misdemeanor warrant, causing a collision and killing a backseat passenger.

• A police officer pursuing a shoplifter in Mobile, Alabama, crashed into a mall security vehicle, seriously injuring the guard.

These and other tragic stories are all too common; again, the onus is on law enforcement executives to develop pursuit policies that consider input from line personnel, supervisors and managers, and attorneys versed in civil liability and remain vigilant in seeing that they are enforced. Pursuit policies provide general guidelines for the officer and supervisor. The courts will evaluate these policy issues when considering whether an agency or its officers or supervisors should be held culpable for damages or injuries resulting from pursuits.

The membership at the International Association of Chiefs of Police (IACP) Annual Conference in 1996 adopted a resolution and model pursuit policy to serve as a guideline for police executives. The resolution and policy, based on recommendations from the National Commission on Law Enforcement Driving Safety, were provided to the IACP's Highway Safety Committee. The resolution and policy, as shown in Figure 5.2, are purposely generic in nature so that agencies can individualize them to their specific needs.

The responsibility falls to the field supervisor to see that proper methods are employed by patrol officers during pursuits, whether the pursuit involves simply a primary pursuing officer and a backup or a more elaborate scenario.

Two rather elaborate methods of pursuit termination may be used. The first is *boxing:* Three police vehicles are positioned during the chase at the front, rear, and side of the suspect vehicle; the three police vehicles slow in unison, causing the offender to slow and eventually stop. This technique can result in damage to any or all of the vehicles involved. The second termination tactic, a *precision immobilization technique,* involves a police vehicle making contact with a suspect vehicle. The officer gently pushes one of the rear quarter panels of the suspect vehicle to displace its forward motion, causing it to spin. This technique also involves considerable risk to the officer and suspect.[20] Both of these methods, as well as other tactics employed during pursuits, are potentially perilous and require extensive officer training to obtain proficiency.

Oversight of pursuits enables a third, neutral party, the supervisor, to guard against what has been termed a *pursuit fixation,* wherein pursuing officers act recklessly.[21] Supervisors need to set the rules on what will be tolerated and what level of performance is expected during a pursuit. They must clearly establish that once the pursuit team is in place, other officers not directly involved should drive parallel to the pursuit, obeying all traffic laws.[22]

Supervisors depend on other officers to give them the information needed to make the decisions demanded by the courts. The supervisor needs to know the speed and direction of the fleeing suspect vehicle; the offense, suspected offense, or status (i.e., warrants) of the suspect; the number of police units involved in the pursuit; and the suspect's actions (is he or she close to putting others in danger with his or her driving?).[23] Supervisors serve as the "safety officer" of the pursuit—a role they may not wish to take because they do not want

Following are selected portions of the Sample Vehicular Pursuit Policy that was approved at the 103rd Annual Conference of the International Association of Chiefs of Police in Phoenix, Arizona, on September 30, 1996. Note the responsibilities of the supervisor as they pertain to communications, coordination, participation, and possible termination as they relate to the pursuit:

I. *Purpose*
 The purpose of this policy is to establish guidelines for making decisions with regard to pursuits.
II. *Policy*
 Vehicular pursuit of fleeing suspects can present a danger to the lives of the public, officers, and suspects involved in the pursuit. It is the responsibility of the agency to assist officers in the safe performance of their duties. To fulfill these obligations, it shall be the policy of this law enforcement agency to regulate the manner in which vehicular pursuits are undertaken and performed.
III. *Procedures*
 A. Initiation of Pursuit
  1. The decision to initiate pursuit must be based on the pursuing officer's conclusion that the immediate danger to the officer and the public created by the pursuit is less than the immediate or potential danger to the public should the suspect remain at large.
  2. Any law enforcement officer in an authorized emergency vehicle may initiate a vehicular pursuit when the suspect exhibits the intention to avoid apprehension by refusing to stop when properly directed to do so. Pursuit may also be justified if the officer reasonably believes that the suspect, if allowed to flee, would present a danger to human life or cause serious injury.
  3. In deciding whether to initiate pursuit, the officer shall take into consideration:
   a. Road, weather, and environmental conditions.
   b. Population density and vehicular and pedestrian traffic.
   c. The relative performance capabilities of the pursuit vehicle and the vehicle being pursued.
   d. The seriousness of the offense.
   e. The presence of other persons in the police vehicle.
   Upon engaging in a pursuit, the officer shall notify communications of the location, direction, and speed of the pursuit, the description of the pursued vehicle, and the initial purpose of the stop. When engaged in pursuit, officers shall not drive with reckless disregard for the safety of other road users.
 B. Supervisory Responsibilities
  1. When made aware of a vehicular pursuit, the appropriate supervisor shall monitor incoming information, coordinate and direct activities as needed to ensure that proper procedures are used, and have the discretion to terminate the pursuit.
  2. Where possible a supervisory officer shall respond to the location where a vehicle has been stopped following a pursuit.

**Figure 5.2**

IACP model vehicular pursuit policy. *Source:* International Association of Chiefs of Police "Sample Vehicle Pursuit Police," *Police Chief* (January 1997), p. 20.

to be unpopular with their officers, but one that is far better than attending an officer's funeral or visiting one in the hospital.

It is obvious the liabilities associated with police pursuits should be a primary concern of every police chief executive officer. The courts have awarded numerous six- and seven-figure settlements to plaintiffs seeking redress for injuries, damages, or deaths resulting from police pursuits. The development of pursuit policies and officer and supervisor training can help to protect agencies against liability suits.

It is the responsibility of command personnel and supervisors to ensure that officers thoroughly understand and comply with pursuit policies. In addition to the policy issues and supervisory information identified earlier, other factors considered by the courts to evaluate pursuit liability involve the following:

- *The reason for the pursuit.* Does it justify the actions taken by the officer?
- *Driving conditions.* Any factor that could hinder an officer's ability to safely conduct a pursuit should be considered sufficient reason to terminate.
- *The use of police warning devices.* Typically, lights and siren are required by state statutes.
- *Excessive speed.* This often depends on conditions of the environment. For example, a 30-mile-per hour pursuit in a school zone may be considered excessive and dangerous.
- *Demonstrations of due regard in officers' actions.* Officers who choose the course of safety will create the least danger to all parties affected and maintain the highest degree of protection from liability.
- *The use of deadly force.* There are few instances in which officers can justify driving tactics that result in the death of a fleeing driver; such situations include roadblocks, boxing in, and ramming.
- *Departmental policies and state law.* These must be obeyed; to do otherwise greatly increases the potential liability of both the officer and department.
- *Appropriate supervision and training.* In the absence of such measures, the department will be subject to a finding of negligence, and liability will attach.[24]

Police pursuits represent an ongoing, hazardous problem. Therefore, efforts must continue to develop electromagnetic field devices that officers can place on the roadway and use to interrupt the electronic ignition systems in suspect vehicles and terminate pursuits. In the meantime, tire deflation devices, which can end chases by slowly deflating one or more tires of a suspect's vehicle, have been welcomed by the police.[25]

# Border and Heartland Troubles

## *A Daily Deluge of Humanity*

Law enforcement organizations have been dealing with illegal immigrants for decades. Recently, however, the issue of immigration has taken on far more potentially dangerous dimensions than ever. Contemporary criminal justice administrators must have familiarity with the rapidly growing issue of **undocu-mented aliens** in the United States.

Ironically, despite all the current emphasis on homeland security (see Chapter 6), entering the United States illegally is frightfully easy, and this problem is not only a major one at our borders; Those who enter illegally are rapidly making their presence known through crimes and other activities in the less-populated areas of the Midwest and other regions as well.

Every day, more than 4,000 illegal aliens come across the busiest gateway into the United States—the 375-mile border between Arizona and Mexico. No searches of these border crossers will be performed for weapons, no photo-ID checks. Before long, many of them will obtain fake identification papers, including bogus Social Security numbers, to conceal their true identities and unlawful presence.[26]

One study of the problem estimates that 3 million illegal aliens flooded into the United States in 2004.[27] Of greater concern, perhaps, is that a small but growing number of these people come from countries other than Mexico; in fact, about 56,000 such persons (described officially as "Other Than Mexican," or **OTM**–other Latin Americans, but also intruders from Afghanistan, Bulgaria, Russia, China, Egypt, Iran, and Iraq) were arrested along the southwest border in a recent 1-year period, and about 190,000 of these OTMs melted into the U.S. population.[28] The problem is largely one of this country's making. The government does not want to address the problem as long as the cheap labor keeps down the cost of many goods and services. But many feel this is a short-sighted bargain; beyond the terrorism risks, there is a painful impact on the nation's citizens who are at the bottom of the ladder, whose pay is being held down by the presence of the illegals. The newly formed **Customs and Border Protection (CBP)** organization (discussed in Chapter 6), even with nearly 10,000 agents along the 1,251 miles of southern border, is no match for the onslaught.[29]

## *Crimes Wrought by Undocumented Aliens*

Were people illegally entering the United States merely seeking a better lifestyle than that in their home country, law enforcement's role would be fairly straight-forward: apprehending and deporting the uninvited guests. But there is more to their presence than looking for better-paying jobs. First is the importation, distribution, and clandestine manufacturing of drugs—most notably methampheta-mine. This problem is particularly severe—even termed *explosive*—in the midwestern states. An initiative by the federal Office of National Drug Control Policy, the **High-Intensity Drug Trafficking Area** program, has been attempting since 1996 to address this problem, which it recognizes is often run by Mexican organizations in rural areas firmly rooted in an agricultural industry that employs thousands of Mexican Americans and Mexican nationals (e.g., meat-packing plants).[30]

Another related, growing problem involving illegal aliens is that of "boosting"— the stealing of merchandise from retail stores—involving gangs of highly skilled, well-organized professionals from South America, and estimated to amount to about $10 billion every year in the United States. Most began as pickpockets in places like Colombia, Chile, Ecuador, and Peru before being brought here to ply their trade; the best of them move on to cargo thefts and jewelry heists. There may be as many as 1,000 of these teams operating every day, and about the only place they are ever "captured" is on the videotape in store security cameras. One or two people occupy the attention of the sales staff while the others do the stealing.[31]

### New Technologies: Drones and Databases

A pilot program that uses two unmanned aerial vehicles (UAVs, discussed more thoroughly in Chapter 17), or drones, to monitor illegal activity along the Arizona–Mexico border was begun in July 2004. The UAVs use thermal and night-vision equipment to spot illegal immigrants and can detect movement from 15 miles of altitude, read a license plate, and even detect weapons. In 39 days of surveillance of the border, the UAVs led to the apprehension of 248 illegal immigrants and the seizure of 518 pounds of marijuana. The vehicles are waist high, weigh about 1,000 pounds, have a 35-foot wingspan, fly faster than 100 miles per hour, and can stay aloft for 20 hours at a time.[32]

In early 2004 a new program was initiated entitled US-VISIT, or U.S. Visitor and Immigrant Status Indicator Technology, under which 24 million foreigners are expected to be checked annually at the nation's airports. The program allows customs agents to check passengers instantly against terrorist watch lists and a national database; the database is only available to law enforcement authorities on a need-to-know basis. Foreigners arriving at U.S. airports also have their fingerprints checked by pressing their index fingers onto an inkless scanner, and then have their photograph taken as they make their way through customs. The only exceptions are visitors from 27 countries—mostly European nations, as well as Canadians and Mexicans—coming into the country for a short time and not venturing far from the border.[33]

## Challenges with Racial Profiling

### A Hot Button Issue

A contemporary hot button issue in which police find themselves open to criticism and even disciplinary action involves *racial profiling* (also known as *bias-based policing*). This issue has driven a deep wedge between the police and minorities, many of whom claim to be victims of this practice. Indeed, a New Jersey state police superintendent was fired by that state's governor in March

EXHIBIT 5.1
## The Issue That Won't Go Away
**Nationwide, Profiling Concerns Still Rankle**

Police departments in Massachusetts may use up to $500 in community policing funds to counter the findings of a study by Northeastern University which found wide discrepancies in stops of black and white drivers in some cities.

State Public Safety Secretary Edward A. Flynn approved the request by 29 police chiefs, who claimed that the study's findings maligned their departments.

"Nothing is more critical than the credibility of the police in the minority community," Flynn said in a statement. "The use of community policing dollars for this purpose builds trust and openness between the community and law enforcement."

The study was ordered four years ago by the state Legislature. Researchers from the university's Institute on Race and Justice examined more than 1.3 million traffic tickets that were issued between April 2001 and June 2003.

Among the jurisdictions where it found disparities was Milton, a heavily Irish community south of Boston, where minorities received 58 percent of tickets during the period studied, despite making up only about 16 percent of drivers. ...

In other jurisdictions around the nation:

- Under a bill passed in March by the Georgia Legislature, police throughout the state would have to document the race and gender of every motorist pulled over by police, as well as provide information on why the car was stopped and whether a search was conducted. The legislation was opposed by both the Georgia State Patrol and the state chief's association on the grounds that it would cost too much to implement.

- Twenty-two of 23 Arkansas police and sheriff's departments contacted by The Arkansas Democrat-Gazette were found to be in compliance with a state law enacted on Jan. 1 by adopting a policy prohibiting racial profiling.

- A California-based firm was hired in February to collect traffic stop information from the Mount Prospect, Ill., Police Department and distribute it to state and federal authorities. The village ended a three-year federal probe last year by agreeing to collect a broader range of data. That task, said Chief Richard Eddington, would be too complex and time-consuming for the agency's staff and equipment.

- A $40,000 study commissioned by Reno, Nev., officials concluded in March that police did not arrest a disproportionate number of minorities during last year's Hot August Nights classic-car event. The police department has been harshly criticized for years by community members who claim that blacks are singled out at the event.

- New figures released in March in Houston's second annual Racial Profiling Statistical Report showed a slight improvement in the discrepancy between arrests and searches of whites and those of minorities. Blacks were 2.4 times more likely than whites to be searched in 2003, down from 3.0 times more likely the previous year. Hispanics were 1.8 times more likely than whites to be searched last year, down from 1.9 in 2002.

*Source*: Reprinted with permission from *Law Enforcement News*, June 2004, p. 11. John Jay College of Criminal Justice (CCNY), 555 West 57th St., New York, NY 10019.

1999 for statements concerning racial profiling that were perceived as racially insensitive.

Many people remain convinced that the justice system unfairly draws minorities into its web, and that police methods are at the forefront of this practice. Racial profiling—also known as accusing someone of "Driving While Black or Brown" **(DWBB)**—occurs when a police officer, acting on a personal bias, stops a vehicle simply because the driver is of a certain race.[34]

Anecdotal evidence of racial profiling has been accumulating for years, and now many people and groups (such as the American Civil Liberties Union) believe that all "pretext" traffic stops are wrong because the chance that racism and racial profiling will creep into such stops is very high.

For their part, many police executives defend such tactics as an effective way to focus their limited resources on likely lawbreakers; they argue that profiling is based not on *prejudice* but on *probabilities*—the statistical reality that young minority men are disproportionately likely to commit crimes. As explained by Bernard Parks, an African American and former police chief of Los Angeles,

> We have an issue of violent crime against jewelry salespeople. The predominant suspects are Colombians. We don't find Mexican-Americans, or blacks, or other immigrants. It's a collection of several hundred Colombians who commit this crime. If you see six in a car in front of the Jewelry Mart, and they're waiting and watching people with briefcases, should we play the percentages and follow them? It's common sense.[35]

Still, it is difficult for the police to combat the public's perception that traffic stops of minorities simply on the basis of race is widespread and prejudicial in nature.

## *Need for Data*

The best defense and advice for police administrators may be summarized in two words: *collect data*.[36] Collecting traffic stop data helps chiefs and commanders to determine whether officers are stopping or searching a disproportionate number of minorities and enables them to act on this information in a timely fashion.[37] In 1999, Connecticut was the first state to require all of its municipal police agencies and the state police to collect race data for every police-initiated traffic stop.[38] By mid-2001, at least 34 states had either enacted laws that included data collection or were considering data-collection legislation, and Congress has enacted federal racial profiling legislation. It is anticipated that eventually all states will require the tracking of race data for all contacts. Technology such as mobile data computers and wireless handheld devices is being adapted for this purpose.[39]

## Leadership Challenges

Law enforcement executives know that often, with the implementation of their new policies, many are simply "papered on": A memorandum is read at roll call, perhaps with a video, and copies of the new policy and procedure are distributed to officers' mailboxes (to be added to their personally signed-for handbook, which often collects dust on a shelf). Soon the policy fades from memory, unless reprised in mandatory annual training. With regard to racial profiling, however, the custom of ignoring policy is very unwise. This will continue to be a sensitive issue for the foreseeable future, especially now that racial profiling has been widely exposed; some citizens are going to feel aggrieved and be quicker to allege that "You only stopped me because I'm ____."

Because the legislatures of many states have compelled officers to comply with legal and organizational requirements of new laws concerning racial profiling (the most egregious for them being the collection of traffic-stop data), Michael E. Beurger, a former police officer-turned-academic, cautions supervisors to be prepared for a range of countermeasures designed to minimize the officers' discomfort. Work slowdowns, defiance, "going underground," balancing" or "ghosting," and behaviors summed up as "badmouthing" are all harbingers of future problems[40]:

- *Work slowdowns.* Faced with the possibility of being put in legal jeopardy, officers might cease doing proactive work and merely respond to complaints. Buerger emphasizes, however, that in the long run, "cops are cops ... as soon as the ruffled feathers are outweighed by the affront of criminal arrogance, officers will get the bad guys while still remaining in compliance with the law."

- *Defiance.* Several courses of action are available to officers who wish to defy the law. The most overt act is to leave the race section of the traffic stop data form blank, or record all persons stopped as being "other" (or some race or ethnicity that does not constitute the makeup of the city or county involved).

- *Going underground.* This response involves officers trying to evade scrutiny for racial profiling by making their suspicion stops "off the record." Unrecorded stops are dangerous for officers, of course; in the extreme case, if the officer is shot, no one knows where he or she is. Also, in an age of video cameras and cellular telephones and the heightened public awareness of the racial profiling issue, this is a thin veil of protection at best.

- *Balancing.* Here officer who has stopped a black person unfairly stops unoffending white motorists to protect himself or herself from the statistical microscope. It involves a lot of extra, unproductive work to "make the numbers come out right." Ghosting is the falsifying of patrol logs to also make the numbers look appropriate.
- *Badmouthing.* This is a generic term for any number of ways that officers may voice their displeasure about the law and their new duties. Officers who nurture a real grudge can create difficulties for an agency by mounting a balancing campaign as a political gesture.[41]

Now that racial profiling has been validated by a number of states and court cases, citizens will probably be less tolerant of the intrusion into their lives and more likely to complain about being stopped. When a citizen wishes to complain about being stopped or searched on the basis of race alone, the supervisor is often the first person to be contacted. Supervisors will need to develop a sense of when the complaining citizen has a legitimate grievance as well as the ability to distinguish unusual patterns in an officer's activity. The supervisor will be placed in a familiar spot—the middle—with the public and its expectation of equitable treatment on the one hand and officers' morale and expectation of their supervisor's understanding and equitable treatment on the other.

# Bringing Down the Walls: Women and Minorities Wearing the Badge

Over the last 30 years, the proportion of women police officers has grown steadily. During the 1970s, some formal barriers to hiring women were eliminated, such as height requirements; in addition, subjective physical agility tests and oral interviews were modified.[42] Some job discrimination suits further expanded women's opportunities.

## *Women as Officers and Chief Executives*

Women represent about 14.5 percent of the sworn personnel in municipal agencies, 13.5 percent of sworn personnel in county agencies, and 8.2 percent in small agencies. State agencies as a whole have a much lower percentage of female officers than either local or federal law enforcement agencies, 6.8 percent.[43] Women account for 14.8 percent of all federal officers, which is a bit higher than local agencies.[44]

Although this representation of women officers is low compared to their overall proportion in the total population, it becomes even more evident in the leadership ranks, where women number only 1 percent of the police chiefs in the United States.[45] The number of women serving as chiefs has expanded considerably, however, since Penny Harrington took over as chief in Portland

## Exhibit 5.2
## Gender Bender

While April Norman's gender never made her unusual as a member of the Eugene, Ore, Police Department, it certainly made her one of a kind at the Lewiston, Idaho, Police Department, where her law-enforcement career began nearly 30 years ago.

Norman, 50, retired from the Eugene department in March. She got her start in law enforcement as the only woman on the Lewiston force and, according to newspaper accounts at the time, the first female officer in the state. During her four years as a cop in Lewiston, Norman can remember being assigned less hazardous duty than her male co-workers. And when a case involved the accidental hanging of a child, Norman's supervisor at the time made her leave the scene.

"They were kind of proud of having the first woman," she told The Lewiston Morning Tribune. "I felt like their token. They weren't really interested in getting other women into the department."

And apparently they are still not. To this day, according to The Lewiston Morning Tribune, the 46-member Lewiston force still has just one female officer.

When Norman was hired, the headline in the local paper read: "Holy Handcuffs Batman, Lewiston has a Lady Cop!"

After four years of being treated with kid gloves, Norman left for Eugene, where she was one of several female officers, including one detective. Today the Eugene department has about 25 women in sworn positions, including captains, lieutenants and sergeants. The department's bomb squad is led by a female sergeant.

Among the cases Norman worked on was an extortion scheme by a man who posed as a doctor seeking a wife. Another was a rape investigation on the University of Oregon campus. Norman's final assignment was as a resource officer for North Eugene High School and the elementary and middle schools that feed it.

*Source:* Reprinted with permission from *Law Enforcement News*, June 2004, p. 7. John Jay College of Criminal Justice (CCNY), 555 West 57th St., New York, NY 10019.

(becoming the first woman chief in a large agency) in 1985 and Elizabeth (Betsy) Watson assumed the helm in Houston (becoming the first in a city of more than 1 million population) in 1990. As examples, in early 2004, newly appointed women were serving as chiefs of police in San Francisco, Boston, Detroit, and Milwaukee, providing further evidence that today's "mayors are looking for sophisticated CEOs who can oversee large budgets, negotiate thorny management problems, and set sound department-wide policy."[46]

A recent survey[47] identified 157 women serving as chiefs of police and 25 who were sheriffs; 96 of these chiefs participated in a survey intended to establish a demographic profile of the women. Forty-eight (49 percent) of these chief executives were in charge of municipal police departments, whereas 40 (42 percent) led college and university police departments. Only 7 of the respondents led agencies with more than 100 sworn officers (5 being municipal, 1 a campus police agency, and 1 a tribal agency). Conversely, 23 (25.8 percent) were in agencies with 10 or fewer officers. These women CEOs reflect the increasing levels of education achieved by today's chiefs, with three fourths having either a bachelor's or a master's degree. About one third had a partner who was also in policing.[48]

Certainly, a large enough proportion of women have now been employed in policing long enough to be considered for promotion. A number of researchers question the commitment of police agencies and their male administrators in promoting women and have made recommendations for changing the evaluation and promotional process.[49]

## *Key Issues*

Peter Horne identified several key issues that need to be addressed[50]:

1. *Recruitment.* Unfocused, random recruiting is unlikely to attract diversity. Literature such as flyers, posters, and brochures should feature female officers working in all areas of policing. Furthermore, agencies should go anywhere (local colleges, women's groups, female community leaders, gyms, martial arts schools) and use all types of media to attract qualified applicants.[51]

2. *Pre-employment physical testing.* Historically, women have been screened out disproportionately in the pre-employment screening physical testing used by many agencies. Tests that include such components as scaling a 6-foot wall, bench pressing one's own weight, and throwing medicine balls are likely to have an adverse impact on female applicants, so agencies should examine their physical tests to determine the reasons women are disproportionately screened out. In addition, agencies should permit all candidates to practice for the pre-employment physical exam.

3. *Academy training.* Recruits must be trained in sexually integrated academy classes to ensure full integration between female and male officers. Female instructors are especially important during academy training because they are positive role models and help female rookies to develop skills and confidence. Involving female instructors in firearms and physical/self-defense training will send a message that trained, veteran female officers can effectively handle the physical aspects of policing.

4. *Field training.* Field training officers (FTOs) play a crucial role in transforming the academy graduate into a competent field officer. FTOs should be both supportive of female rookies and effective evaluators of their competence. Women should also serve as FTOs.

5. *Assignments.* Agencies should routinely review the daily assignments of all probationary officers to assure they have equal opportunity to become

effective patrol officers. If women are removed from patrol early in their careers (for any reason), they will miss vital field patrol experience. The majority of supervisory positions exist in the patrol division, and departments generally believe that field supervisors must have adequate field experience to be effective and respected by subordinates.

6. *Promotions.* The so-called glass ceiling continues to restrict women's progress through the ranks. Performance evaluations and the overall promotional system utilized by agencies should be scrutinized for gender bias. For example, studies show that the more subjective the promotion process, the less likely women are to pass it. To provide more objectivity (in terms of ability to measure aptitude), the process may include more hands-on (practical, applied) tasks and the selection of board members of both genders.

7. *Harassment and discrimination.* Where they exist, sexual discrimination and harassment exact a human cost from the women involved—including a negative impact on their performance and careers (and, probably, a negative impact on the recruitment of other women into policing). A Police Foundation study found that "most women officers have experienced both sex discrimination and harassment on the job."[52] Departments need to have policies in place concerning sexual harassment and gender discrimination—and they need to enforce them.

8. *Mentoring.* The employee's experience as he or she transitions into the organization can be a deciding factor in whether the employee remains with the organization. Formal mentoring programs—which can begin even before the rookie enters the academy—have helped some agencies raise their retention rates for women; such programs can include having a veteran employee provide new hires with information concerning what to expect at the academy and beyond during field training and the probationary period.

9. *Career and family.* Police work can create a considerable amount of conflict between one's work life and one's family life. Police agencies should have a leave policy covering pregnancy and maternity leave. Light- or limited-duty assignments (e.g., desk, communications, records) can be made available to female officers when reassignment is necessary. Other issues include the availability of quality child care and shift rotation (which can more heavily burden single parents) and uniforms, body armor, and firearms that fit women.

As the community-oriented policing and problem-solving (COPPS, examined in Chapter 3) concept continues to expand, female officers can play an increasingly vital role. Experts also maintain that the verbal skills many women possess often have a calming effect that defuses potentially explosive situations.

Still, this clearly remains an area in which law enforcement must change. For women to serve effectively as police officers, executives must see the value of utilizing and vigorously recruiting, hiring, and retaining them. A basic task for the chief executive is to consider how departmental policies impact female officers with respect to selection, training, promotion, sexual harassment, and family leave. Most important, executives must set a tone of welcoming women into the department.

### Minorities as Law Enforcement Officers

The recruitment of minority officers also remains a difficult task. Probably the most difficult barrier has to do with the image that police officers have in the minority communities. Unfortunately, police officers have been seen as symbols of oppression and have been charged with using excessive brutality; they are often seen as an army of occupation.

Black police officers face problems similar to those of women who attempt to enter and prosper in police work. Until more black officers are promoted and can affect police policy and serve as role models, they are likely to be treated unequally and have difficulty being promoted—a classic catch-22 situation. Blacks considering a police career may be encouraged by a survey of black officers, which found that most thought their jobs were satisfying and offered opportunities for advancement.[53]

## The High Cost of Hunting Missing Persons in an Age of Media Superfluity

The May 2005 "kidnapping" of Jennifer Wilbanks—who actually was a runaway bride in Duluth, Georgia—triggered a massive search effort and media frenzy before she surfaced in New Mexico. This incident cost $60,000 for approximately 60 officers as well as the food and fuel required for the search. Similarly, in 2004 a Wisconsin student faked her own kidnapping, prompting a $97,000 mobilization of personnel (she pleaded guilty to obstructing officers), and in that same year a runaway bride in Ohio sparked a search involving bloodhounds and helicopters; she was charged with "inducing panic."[54]

Such occurrences place law enforcement administrators in a quandary in this age of 24-hour cable news, in which merciless media coverage forces agencies to devote large amounts of resources to solve crimes that are actually hoaxes. Prosecutors and police must also decide whether to seek restitution and/or to file charges against these runaway adults. Furthermore, while these faked crimes are being investigated, other actual crimes are not.[55]

Though the press certainly aids in many investigations, raising public awareness and generating crucial tips, it often hinders them as well. In response to these kinds of hoaxes, law enforcement administrators have had to become more sophisticated at managing the media, while anticipating which scenarios are likely to entice reporters. Chiefs of police and sheriffs have also become more adept at tracking the flow of information—or misinformation—circulated by news reports.[56]

# Future Considerations

## *Forecasts and Strategies*

To build a stronger partnership between all facets of law enforcement and the FBI, the **Futures Working Group** was formed in April 2002 and represents a partnership between the FBI and the Society of Police Futurists International (SPFI), which was founded in 1991 and is now located at Sam Houston State University, Huntsville, Texas. The goals of the partnership include the development of forecasts and strategies to maximize the effectiveness of all law enforcement entities as they strive to maintain peace and security.[57]

Defining solutions to the problems facing future law enforcement services is difficult at best. Factors such as locale, political environment, and economics will determine how an organization and its employees will view and react to the future. Additionally, for some law enforcement leaders the future is the next fiscal year, whereas for others it is a 3- to 5-year span of time toward which they have set into motion a strategic planning process. For still others, the future is next Friday and surviving without a crisis until their next day off. Any discussion of the future must include the short term as well as the long term and must give attention to operational issues, administrative issues, the community, and the basic philosophy of policing.[58]

## *COPPS and Other Trends*

Chapter 3 examined the current era of policing, COPPS; following are some futuristic issues that remain to be addressed with this program and other issues.

Several other issues for the future must be addressed if COPPS is to survive and thrive, including whether police chief executives will change the culture of their agencies, implement the concept, decentralize their department (pushing decision making downward), invest in the necessary technology for locating "hot spots," and develop the necessary mechanisms to support COPPS. These challenges also include recruitment, selection, training, performance appraisals, and reward and promotional systems.

Some futurists see COPPS undergoing a metamorphosis in the near future, including the following changes:

- Ethics will be woven into everything law enforcement agencies do: the hiring process, field training officer programs, and decision-making processes. There will be increased emphasis on accountability and integrity within police agencies as policing is elevated to a higher standing, reaching more toward being a true profession, with the majority of officers being required to possess a college degree.

- Formal awards ceremonies will concentrate as much or more on achievements in improving citizens' quality of life than on numbers of felony arrests or other high-risk activities.
- The rigid paramilitary style currently in effect will become obsolete, replaced by work teams consisting of line officers, community members, and business and corporate representatives.
- Neighborhoods will more actively participate in the identification, location, and capture of criminals.[59]

# CASE STUDIES

The first three case studies involve the role of police sergeant, racial profiling, and personnel problems, respectively; the fourth requires some thought about the future of policing. They all enable the reader to examine some of the issues and problems that are presented in this chapter.

## Racial Profiling? Or Good Police Work?

Officer James and Sergeant Drummond are on surveillance in a strip mall. A detective received an anonymous tip that a credit union might be robbed at 3:00 p.m. The detective also related to the patrol division that the person providing the tip is a known drug addict and not at all reliable, but given that there has been a string of credit union robberies during the last 2 months, Drummond decides to surveil the area with Officer James. The predominant suspects in the credit union robberies are Asians, and the officers have stopped and talked with several Asian people in the area, taking their names and other identifying information. At approximately 2:45 p.m., Drummond and James are notified by Communications that a security officer reported hearing a gunshot in the parking lot of a nearby grocery store where he is working. Because they are nearby and there might be a connection to the credit union robberies, Drummond and James decide to take the call. On arriving at the scene, the security officer meets the two officers and informs them that he "might have" heard a small-caliber pistol shot in the parking lot; he also believes that a young black man who walked into the grocery store a few minutes ago might be carrying a gun under his coat. About 10 minutes later, a 30-year-old black man comes walking out of the store. The officers draw their guns and order him down to the asphalt and then order him to crawl to their vehicle. At that time, an Asian woman carrying a child approaches the officers, yelling at them that the man is her husband and demanding to know what they are doing to him. The officers order her to her car, whereupon she faints on the asphalt while suffering an epileptic seizure. The black man, seeing his wife and child on the ground, now becomes very agitated; as a result, the officers use considerable force to subdue and handcuff him. He is arrested for resisting arrest and a host of other offenses; later he sues for violation of his civil rights.

### Questions for Discussion

1. Did the officers have just cause to be engaged in the initial (credit union) surveillance? To question Asian people in the area? Defend your answer.
2. Did the officers violate the black man's civil rights? Why or why not? If yes, would you support (as the chief of police) some form of disciplinary action against them?

3. Should the woman be entitled to collect damages? Why or why not?

4. In which (if any) aspects of this scenario do you believe the officers are guilty of engaging in racial profiling? Explain your answer.

5. Assume that this case led to a public outcry for a citizen review board to examine questionable police activities and recommend disciplinary and policy actions. Would you support the creation of such a board? Why or why not?

# "Racin' Ray's Wild Day"

Members of the Pineville County Sheriff's Department have been involved in several vehicle pursuits within the last year. One such incident resulted in the death of a 14-year-old juvenile who crashed during a pursuit while he was joyriding in his parents' car. This tragedy sparked a massive public outcry and criticism of the police department for using excessive force. A lawsuit is pending against the department and individual officers involved in the pursuit. You, the sheriff, immediately changed and tightened the department's policy regarding pursuits, now requiring that a supervisor cancel any pursuit that does not involve a violent felony crime or other circumstances that would justify the danger and potential liability. All officers have been trained in the new policy. A separate policy prohibits the firing of warning shots unless "circumstances warrant." It is now about 9:00 p.m. and Deputy Raymond "Racin' Ray" Ripley is patrolling in an industrial park in his sector. Deputy Ripley, having graduated from the police academy and field training about 6 months ago, engages in vehicle and foot pursuits at every opportunity; also, unbeknown to the sheriff and other supervisors, he occasionally goes home and picks up his pet German Shepherd dog for use in late-night building checks; he also has a TASER stun device in the trunk of his patrol car (he has not been trained in or authorized to use either of these less-lethal tools). He was providing extra patrol as a result of reports of vandalism and theft of building materials in that area of the county. He believes that after 8:00 p.m., no one should have any reason to be in "his" patrol sector. A parked vehicle attracts his attention because private vehicles are not normally parked in the area at this time. As Ripley approaches the vehicle with his cruiser's lights off and spotlight on, he notices the brake lights on the vehicle flash on and off. Ripley immediately gets out of his vehicle for a better view and calls dispatch for backup assistance in the event that there is a burglary or theft in progress. At this point, the vehicle takes off at a high rate of speed, in Ripley's direction. The deputy, now out of his vehicle, opens the door and lets his dog out of the car as well; seeing the vehicle coming at him from about 30 yards away, Ripley fires a warning shot into the ground. When it is about 15 yards away, the vehicle veers away from him and then leaves at a high rate of speed. As the escaping vehicle passes by, Ripley yells for the driver to halt, then takes out his TASER and fires, striking the side of the vehicle. Ripley then takes off in pursuit of the vehicle, and radios Dispatch concerning his observations and of his present pursuit. The shift commander—a patrol lieutenant—hears this radio transmission (as do you, the sheriff, while at home monitoring calls on a police scanner).

## Questions for Discussion

1. What are the central issues involved?
2. Is the deputy in compliance with the use-of-force policy? Defend your answer.
3. Should the lieutenant "shut down" Ripley's pursuit? Explain.
4. Should the deputy have fired warning shots under these circumstances? Why or why not?
5. Assume that the people who were in the parked vehicle lodge a complaint because of Ripley's actions with the dog, the warning shot, and the TASER; what kinds of policies and procedures normally cover Ripley's actions? Would your Internal Affairs Unit find that the deputy was at fault with any of them? Which of the deputy's actions do you as sheriff feel should result in disciplinary action against Ripley? Why or why not?
6. Are additional policies needed? Explain your answers.

# Adapting to the Responsibilities of the Role

Sgt. Tom Gresham is newly promoted and assigned to patrol on the graveyard shift; he knows each officer on his shift, and several are close friends. Sgt. Gresham was an excellent patrol officer and prided himself on his reputation and ability to get along with his peers. He also believed this trait would benefit him as a supervisor. From the beginning, Sgt. Gresham believed that he could get more productivity from his officers by relating to them at their level. He made an effort to socialize after work and took pride in giving his team the liberty of referring to him by his first name. Sgt. Gresham also believed that it was a supervisor's job to not get in the way of "good" police work. In his view, his team responded tremendously, generating the highest number of arrest and citation statistics in the entire department. Unfortunately, his shift was also generating the highest number of citizen complaints for abusive language and improper use of force, but few complaints were sustained by Internal Affairs. It was Gresham's opinion that complaints are the product of good, aggressive police work. He had quickly developed the reputation among subordinates as being "a cop's cop."

One Monday morning, Sgt. Gresham is surprised when called in to see you, his patrol captain. The Internal Affairs lieutenant is also present. You show Gresham a number of use-of-force complaints against his team over the last week while Sgt. Gresham was on vacation. Despite your efforts to describe the gravity of the situation, Gresham fails to grasp the seriousness of the complaints and how his supervisory style may have contributed to them.

### Questions for Discussion

**1.** What do you believe are some of Sgt. Gresham's problems as a new supervisor?

**2.** As his captain, what advice would you give to Gresham?

**3.** What corrective action must Sgt. Gresham take immediately with his team of officers?

## Gotham City Looks Beyond the Horizon

Gotham City has a number of new department heads, with varying levels of experience. Furthermore, recent crime, budget, and other crises have underscored the need for the city's departments to work more collaboratively and address problems of the future. Accordingly, the city manager is convening a strategic (long-term, 3- to 5-year) planning workshop in 1 week to bring all department heads together, to orient them concerning the city council's long-term priorities, and to discuss and address problems. You, the chief of police, must attend and represent the police department.

### Questions for Discussion

**1.** What kind of information do you need?

**2.** Where will this information be found, and by whom?

**3.** What are the factors that will affect the future of your city in its changing environment?

**4.** What kinds of future challenges would those factors pose for the police in your community?

## Summary

This chapter examined a number of issues that have challenged and will continue to challenge law enforcement administrators for years to come. Indeed, some of the issues have long been simmering in the public mind, whereas others have only recently come to the forefront of the public's attention.

Perhaps just as important as having administrators today who understand and deal with these problems are the subordinates of tomorrow; those who will wear the mantle of leadership in the future must likewise attempt to grasp the means of addressing these issues.

## Questions for Review

**1.** What are some of the problems involving police use of force?

**2.** What types of issues are involved in Carter's typology of abuse of police authority?

3. What are the various steps and methods employed in the use-of-force continuum?

4. What are the primary problems with protecting our borders? What is law enforcement doing—and what might be done to a greater extent—to staunch the flow of illegal aliens into our country? What ideas do you have that were not mentioned in the chapter?

5. What is racial profiling, and what can police leadership do to address it? What are the unique challenges that are brought to bear on supervisors in this regard?

6. What is the problem with police vehicle pursuits, and what has the U.S. Supreme Court stated about them? What policy and practical responsibilities do law enforcement administrators and patrol supervisors have in regard to pursuits?

7. What are some of the issues facing police in the future?

## Notes

1. Samuel Walker, *Police Accountability: The Role of Citizen Oversight* (Belmont, Calif.: Wadsworth, 2001), p. 141.
2. *Graham v. Connor,* 490 U.S. 386 (1989), p. 397.
3. *Tennessee v. Garner,* 471 U.S. 1, 105 S.Ct. 1694, 85 L.Ed.2d 1 (1985).
4. David Carter, "Theoretical Dimensions in the Abuse of Authority," in T. Barker and D. Carter (eds.), *Police Deviance* (Cincinnati, Ohio: Anderson, 1994), pp. 269–290.
5. G. W. Selnow, "Sex Differences in Uses and Perceptions of Profanity," *Sex Roles* **12** (1985):303–312.
6. D. L. Paletz and W. F. Harris, "Four-Letter Threats to Authority," *Journal of Politics* **37** (1975):955–979.
7. Selnow, "Sex Differences in Uses and Perceptions of Profanity," p. 306.
8. D. W. Warshay and L. H. Warshay, *Obscenity and Male Hegemony*. Paper presented at the annual meeting of International Sociological Association, Detroit, Michigan, 1978.
9. Paletz and Harris, "Four-Letter Threats to Authority," p. 955.
10. Ibid.
11. William Terrill, Geoffrey P. Alpert, Roger G. Dunham, and Michael R. Smith, "A Management Tool for Evaluating Police Use of Force: An Application of the Force Factor," *Police Quarterly* **6**(2) (June 2003):150–171.
12. Ibid., p. 152.
13. Ibid., pp. 153–154.
14. National Highway Traffic Safety Administration, *National Highway Traffic Safety Administration Statistics* (Washington, D.C.: Author, 1995).
15. C. B. Eisenberg, "Pursuit Management," *Law and Order* (March 1999):73–77.
16. A. Belotto, "Supervisors Govern Pursuits," *Law and Order* (January 1999):86.
17. G. T. Williams, "When Do We Keep Pursuing? Justifying High-Speed Pursuits," *The Police Chief* (March 1997):24–27.
18. 118 S.Ct. 1708.

19. Ibid. at p. 1720.

20. Eisenberg, "Pursuit Management," p. 77.

21. E. M. Sweeney, "Vehicular Pursuit: A Serious—and Ongoing—Problem," *The Police Chief* (January 1997):16-21.

22. Belotto, "Supervisors Govern Pursuits," p. 86.

23. Williams, "When Do We Keep Pursuing?" p. 27.

24. D. N. Falcone, M. T. Charles, and E. Wells, "A Study of Pursuits in Illinois," *The Police Chief* (March 1994):59-64.

25. Ibid.

26. Donald L. Barnett and James B. Steele, "Who Left the Door Open?" *Time* (September 20, 2004), pp. 51-66.

27. Ibid.

28. Ibid., p. 52.

29. Ibid., p. 53.

30. "Midwest HIDTA," http://www.ncjrs.org/ondcppubs/publications/enforce/hidta2001/midw-fs.html (accessed November 5, 2004).

31. CBSNEWS.com, "Boosting for Billions," http://www.cbsnews.com/stories/2004/02/20/20/60minutes/main601396.shtml (accessed November 5, 2004).

32. Amanda Lee Myers, "Officials Say Border Drones Producing Positive Results," Associated Press, *Reno Gazette Journal*, August 34, 2004, p. 4C.

33. "U.S. Airports Boost Security," Associated Press, *Reno Gazette Journal*, January 6, 2004, p. 2A.

34. R. Neubauer, quoted in Keith W. Strandberg, "Racial Profiling," *Law Enforcement Technology* (June 1999):62.

35. Quoted in Randall Kennedy, "Suspect Policy," *The New Republic* (September 13, 1999):30-35.

36. See, for example, Aether Systems, Mobile Government Division, "Special Report II: Overcoming the Perception of Racial Profiling," *Law and Order* (April 2001):94-101; J. A. Oliver, "Lessons Learned: Collecting Data on Officer Traffic Stops," *The Police Chief* (July 2001):23-29.

37. R. L. Garrett, "Changing Behavior Begins with Data," *Law Enforcement Technology* (April 2001):103.

38. S. M. Cox, "Racial Profiling: Refuting Concerns About Collecting Race Data on Traffic Stops," *Law and Order* (October 2001):61-65.

39. Aether Systems, "Special Report II," pp. 94-101.

40. Michael E. Buerger, "Supervisory Challenges Arising From Racial Profiling Legislation," *Police Quarterly* **5**(3) (September 2002):380-408.

41. Ibid., pp. 390-394.

42. Barbara Raffel Price, "Sexual Integration in American Law Enforcement," in William C. Heffernan and Timothy Stroup (eds.), *Police Ethics: Hard Choices in Law Enforcement,* (New York: John Jay Press, 1985), pp. 205-214.

43. National Center for Women & Policing, *Equality Denied: The Status of Women in Policing* (Washington, D.C.: Feminist Majority Foundation, 2001), p. 5.

44. U.S. Department of Justice, Bureau of Justice Statistics, "Federal Law Enforcement Officers, 2002," http://www.ojp.usdoj.gov/bjs/abstract/fleo02.htm (accessed January 21, 2004).

45. Dorothy Moses Schulz, "Women Police Chiefs: A Statistical Profile," *Police Quarterly* **6**(3) (September 2003):330-345.

46. Peg Tyre, "Ms. Top Cop," *Newsweek* (April 12, 2004), p. 49.

47. Schulz, "Women Police Chiefs, p. 333.

48. Ibid.

49. Ibid.

50. Peter Horne, "Policewomen: 2000 A.D. Redux," *Law and Order* (November 1999), p. 53.

51. For information about successful recruiting efforts as well as the diverse kinds of assignments women now occupy in law enforcement, see Vivian B. Lord and Kenneth J. Peak, *Women in Law Enforcement Careers: A Guide for Preparing and Succeeding* (Upper Saddle River, N.J.: Prentice Hall, 2005).

52. Quoted in Horne, "Policewomen," p. 59.

53. Lena Williams, "Police Officers Tell of Strains of Living as a 'Black in Blue,'" *The New York Times*, February 14, 1988, pp. 1, 26.

54. Arian Campo-Flores and Julie Scelfo, "Chasing Jennifer," *Newsweek* (May 16, 2005), pp. 34–35.

55. Ibid., p. 35.

56. Ibid.

57. "Focus on the Future: A Look Forward," *FBI Law Enforcement Bulletin* (January 2004):1.

58. Greenberg, "Future Issues in Policing," p. 315.

59. Dave Pettinari, "Are We There Yet? The Future of Policing/Sheriffing in Pueblo—Or in Anywhere, America," http://www.sierratimes.com/cgi-bin/ikonboard//topic.cgi.forum= 21& topic=11 (accessed September 19, 2005).

# Chapter 6

# Terrorism and Homeland Defense

## Key Terms and Concepts

Bureau of Customs and Border Protection

Bureau of Immigration and Customs Enforcement (ICE)

Critical incident management

Department of Homeland Security (DHS)

Directorates

Emergency Operations Center (EOC)

First responders

Incident Command System (ICS)

National Incident Management System (NIMS)

Posse Comitatus Act

Terrorism

Transportation and Security Administration (TSA)

## Learning Objectives

After reading this chapter, the student will:

- know the definition of terrorism and its categories and types (including nuclear, biological, agricultural, and cyberspace)
- understand the key elements of the National Incident Management System, the five components of the Incident Command System, and what is included in an Emergency Operations Center
- have a basic understanding of why administrative preplanning is important for dealing with acts of terrorism, what an action plan should include, and the kinds of technologies needed
- understand how interagency cooperation and command and control are key to the successful investigation of a terrorist attack or other critical incident
- be knowledgeable about mutual aid agreements and their importance for addressing crises
- know the basic law enforcement responses to terrorism

> *You gain strength, courage, and confidence by every experience in which you really stop to look fear in the face. You are able to say to yourself, "I lived through this horror. I can take the next thing that comes along." … You must do the thing you think you cannot do.*
> —Eleanor Roosevelt

## Introduction

The response to the devastation wrought by Hurricane Katrina along the Gulf Coast in late August 2005 demonstrated the need for planning and leadership prior to, during, and following times of crisis. In the wake of the hurricane, boundless finger pointing and laying of blame occurred concerning the delayed arrival of help to the suffering people of the region, particularly New Orleans. Politicians, the Federal Emergency Management Agency, and state, city, county, and military officials of the affected areas all tried to avoid culpability for the inadequate preparation and response. Even national polls varied widely in terms of which agency or individual Americans felt should bear the brunt of fury over the poor response. (And, indeed, much was made of the fact that the city of New Orleans had seemed to ignore years of warnings by many expert prognosticators and the U.S. Army Corps of Engineers that an implementable evacuation plan and infrastructural funding were needed to prevent such a disaster.) Clearly, if nothing else, Hurricane Katrina left no doubt of the importance not only of having a plan, but also of properly executing it in the eventuality of such a catastrophe.

Furthermore, historians and law enforcement administrators of the future will maintain that terrorist acts of the early twenty-first century changed forever the nature of policing and security efforts in the United States. Words are almost inadequate to describe how the events of September 11, 2001, modified and heightened the fears and concerns of all Americans with regard to domestic security and the methods and technologies necessary for safeguarding the general public.

As this chapter will demonstrate, it certainly behooves today's law enforcement executives at all levels of government to be prepared for all manner of terrorist attack. Command and control during the initial stages of such incidents and thereafter will often determine the ultimate outcomes and the safety of those involved.[1] On-scene leaders must also know the resources that are available to them from federal, state, and local agencies; they must also be cognizant of the protocols for working within established interagency cooperative procedures, as set forth in mutual aid agreements, all of which are discussed in this chapter. In sum, police administrators must ensure that the incident commanders or officers in charge with the responsibility for command and control during such attacks are operating on a well-laid foundation. This chapter provides an overview of the kind of foundation needed, as well as other resources that agencies are using to see that a sound action plan exists.

I begin with a discussion of the types and categories of terrorism that are known today (others could certainly materialize in the future). Next is an overview of the National Incident Management System that has been developed to assist public agencies to address major incidents. Included are brief discussions of an emergency response checklist, tactical concerns, and technical needs. Then I give an example of critical incident management involving a case that received wide national attention in 2002: the sniper case in the District of Columbia area. Next I discuss what one writer terms the "five major pieces of business" that remain for this country to be safe again from terrorism. Two case studies provided at chapter's end provide opportunities to apply the measures promulgated in the chapter and to get a better understanding of critical incident management.

# Types and Categories of Terrorism

## *Definitions*

Title 22, Section 265f(d), of the U.S. Code states the following: "Terrorism means premeditated, politically motivated violence perpetrated against non-combatant targets by subnational groups or clandestine agents, usually intended to influence an audience."[2] The FBI defines *terrorism* as "The unlawful use of force against persons or property to intimidate or coerce a government, the civilian population, or any segment thereof, in furtherance of political or social objectives."[3]

## *Categories*

The FBI divides the current international terrorist threat into three categories:

1. *Foreign sponsors of international terrorism.* At least six countries—Iran, Syria, Sudan, Libya, Cuba, and North Korea—have been designated as such sponsors and view terrorism as a tool of foreign policy. They fund, organize, network, and provide other support to formal terrorist groups and extremists.

2. *Formalized terrorist groups.* Autonomous organizations (such as bin Laden's al Qaeda, Afghanistan's Taliban, Iranian-backed Hezbollah, Egyptian Al-Gama'a Al-Islamiyya, and Palestinian Hamas) have their own infrastructures, personnel, finances, and training facilities. Examples of this type are the al Qaeda terrorists who attacked the World Trade Center towers and the Pentagon in 2001.

3. *Loosely affiliated international radical extremists.* Examples are the persons who bombed the World Trade Center in 1993. They do not represent a particular nation but may pose the most urgent threat to the United States because they remain relatively unknown to law enforcement agencies.[4] Terrorist attacks in the United States are also caused by *domestic* terrorists. An example is the April 1995 bombing of the Murrah Federal Office Building in Oklahoma City by Timothy McVeigh, killing 168 people and injured more than 500.[5] (McVeigh was executed in June 2001).

## *Nuclear, Biological, and Environmental Terrorism*

**Terrorism** can take many forms, and does not always involve bombs and guns. For example, in February 2002 a reporter interviewing Homeland Security Secretary Tom Ridge asked him to state what, of all things he had to worry about, including hijacked airliners, anthrax in the mail, smallpox, and so on, he worried about most. The secretary reportedly cupped his hands prayerfully, pressed his fingertips to his lips, and said, "Nuclear."[6]

All kinds of related scenarios come to the imagination: a homemade *nuclear* explosive device detonating inside a truck passing through one of the tunnels into Manhattan, or a hijacker dive-bombing a jetliner into an atomic research center. These kinds of threats are divided into broad categories. The less likely but far more devastating is an actual nuclear explosion—a great hole blown in the heart of New York or Washington, followed by a toxic cloud of radiation. The second category is a *radiological attack,* contaminating a public area with radioactive material by packing it with conventional explosives in a "dirty bomb" by dispersing it into the air or water or by sabotaging a nuclear facility.[7]

Nothing is really new about these perils; all September 11 did was turn a theoretical possibility into a reality. Indeed, if there is a weapon of mass destruction (WMD) to be used against the United States, a radiological type is likely the one we will see, packed with spent fuel from a nuclear reactor or with cobalt-60, which is readily available in hospitals for use in radiation therapy and in food processing.[8]

A terrorist who creates even a small-scale nuclear explosion will take us to a whole different territory from the dread of September 11; it is the event that preoccupies those who think about WMDs for a living. And, they believe, it is not a question of if, but when it will happen: It is the when and how that robs them of sleep.[9]

Regarding *biological* threats, the late-2001 use of anthrax in the United States left no doubt about peoples' vulnerability to biological weapons and the intention of some people to develop and use them. Smallpox, botulism, and plague also constitute major threats, and many experts feel that it is only a matter of time before biological weapons get into the wrong hands and are used like explosives in the past.[10]

All of this brings to mind the scenario of the movie *Andromeda Strain:* a toxic agent being genetically engineered in large quantities and sprayed into the population, that agent then reproducing itself and killing many people. The person who controls this toxin could then sell it to terrorists. One has to wonder why international terrorists have not already done so. This form of terrorism can wipe out an entire civilization. All that is required is a toxin that can be cultured and put into a spray form that can be weaponized and disseminated into the population. Fortunately, they *are* extremely difficult for all but specially trained individuals to make in large quantities and in the correct dose; they are tricky to transport, in that live organisms are delicate; and they must be dispersed in a proper molecular size to infect the lungs of the target. Like chemical weapons, they are also dependent on the wind and the weather, and are difficult to control.[11]

Finally, concerning *environmental* terrorism, the Earth Liberation Front (ELF) and a sister organization, the Animal Liberation Front, have been responsible for the majority of terrorist acts committed in the United States for several years. These "ecoterrorists" have burned greenhouses, tree farms, logging sites, ski resorts, and new housing developments. The groups' members have eluded capture, have no centralized organization or leadership, and are so secretive as to be described as "ghosts" who are more difficult to infiltrate than organized crime.[12]

## *Other Threats: Cyberterrorism and Agriculture Shock*

In addition to the aforementioned "conventional" forms of terrorism, law enforcement administrators must educate, train, and prepare themselves for other forms of attack from would-be terrorists as well: those from cyberspace and on agriculture. With respect to *cyberterrorism,* there are unsettling signs that terrorist groups such as al Qaeda are acquiring the desire and skill to use the Internet as a direct instrument of bloodshed. U.S. analysts now believe that by disabling or taking command of the floodgates in a dam, for example, or of substations handling 300,000 volts of electric power, an intruder could use virtual tools to destroy real-world lives and property. Regarded until recently as remote, the risks of cyberterrorism now command urgent White House attention.[13]

Because the digital controls of much of America's critical infrastructure were not designed with public access in mind, they typically lack even rudimentary security. Still, the U.S. intelligence community has not reached a consensus on the scale or imminence of this threat. Clearly, however, this is an area where much greater attention must be given: A computer seized at an al-Qaeda office contained models of a dam, made with structural architecture and engineering software, that enabled the planners to simulate its catastrophic failure.[14]

Terrorist attack with *agricultural* products is nearly as troublesome. Consider the 2001 outbreak of foot-and-mouth disease in Britain; 4 million cattle were culled to contain the disease. This outbreak was unintentional, but it can be seen as an expensive warning. Although smallpox and anthrax receive the bulk of our attention when we begin to assess the risk of bioterrorism, a deliberate attack on agriculture could disrupt trade and cripple agricultural industries.

This threat is now receiving attention. Funding in the United States has increased since September 11, and federal publications are detailing the problems that need to be addressed. Perhaps the best line of defense is rapid detection; in many agriculture settings, surveillance systems usually involve a farmer or local government employee noticing something unusual. However, the clinical symptoms of some diseases appear days after infection. With animals kept closely confined, entire farms can rapidly become infected. Early detection of crop pathogens is also vital. Crop diseases can go unnoticed for a long time, during which they are continually spreading. The U.S. Department of Agriculture is now attempting to improve this situation. Training modules are being developed for first responders, such as farmers and crop consultants who are likely to be the first to notice a problem.[15]

Of course, there is a much more serious related threat that would strike at the health of our nation: poisoning our *food supply*. The aforementioned foot-and-mouth disease seems a perfect conduit for a terrorist attack. The virus is endemic in much of the world and thus easy to obtain. Terrorists could contaminate 20 or 30 large livestock farms or ranches across the United States, allowing the disease to spread widely before veterinarians found it. Grain storage and transportation networks in the United States are also easily accessed; unprotected grain silos dot the countryside, and railway cars filled with grain sit for long periods on railway sidings. The public hysteria would be unimaginable if grain silos and railway cars were laced with contaminants and the poison had spread throughout the food network.[16]

# Law Enforcement Responses

## General Approaches and Posse Comitatus

Police have several possible means of addressing terrorism. On a broad level, there are four major aspects involved in dealing with terrorist organizations:

1. Gathering raw intelligence on the organization's structure, its members, and its plans (or potential) for the use of violence.
2. Determining what measures can be taken to counter or thwart terrorist activities.
3. Assessing how the damage caused by terrorists can be minimized through rapid response and containment of the damage.
4. Apprehending and convicting individual terrorists and dismantling their organizations.[17]

Another means of addressing terrorism, specifically that of a *domestic* nature, and perhaps the most fruitful, is military support of law enforcement. The **Posse Comitatus Act** of 1878 prohibits using the military to execute the laws domestically, the military may be called on, however, to provide personnel and equipment for certain special support activities, such as domestic terrorist events involving weapons of mass destruction.[18]

## The Department of Homeland Security

To combat terrorism, in the aftermath of September 11, a U.S. **Department of Homeland Security** (DHS) was formed, with five **directorates.** DHS was created by H.R. 5005, the Homeland Security Act of 2002; this legislation put 180,000 new federal employees to work and committed $14 billion in new monies for safeguarding the nation, of which $5.6 billion was to develop vaccines to protect against biological or chemical threats, $4 billion was for **first responders** (ensuring that local police, firefighters, and medical personnel received necessary training and equipment), and about $1 billion went for science and technology projects to counter the use of biological weapons and assess vulnerabilities.[19]

The primary enforcement arm of DHS is a newly established **Bureau of Immigration and Customs Enforcement (ICE).** The mission of ICE includes a vast array of investigative authority, from terrorist financing, money laundering, and illegal arms dealing to immigration fraud and migrant smuggling. With a workforce of 14,000, ICE and its investigative and intelligence resources make it equipped to address the complex criminal enterprises that threaten the United States.[20]

**EXHIBIT 6.1**
**Seeking a Master Plan to Fight Terrorism**

(Following are among the key law enforcement-related recommendations from the *9/11 Commission Report*. References are to page numbers in the authorized edition published by W. W. Norton & Company. The report is also available on the commission's Web site, at www.9-11commission.gov.)

Vigorous efforts to track terrorist financing must remain front and center in U.S. counterterrorism efforts. The government has recognized that information about terrorist money helps us to understand their networks, search them out, and disrupt their operations. (382)

Targeting travel is at least as powerful a weapon against terrorists as targeting their money. The United States should combine terrorist travel intelligence, operations, and law enforcement in a strategy to intercept terrorists, find terrorist travel facilitators, and constrain terrorist mobility. (385)

The U.S. border security system should be integrated into a larger network of screening points that includes our transportation system and access to vital facilities, such as nuclear reactors. The President should direct the Department of Homeland Security to lead the effort to design a comprehensive screening system, addressing common problems and setting common standards with systemwide goals in mind. (387)

The Department of Homeland Security, properly supported by the Congress, should complete, as quickly as possible, a biometric entry-exit screen-

ing system, including a single system for speeding qualified travelers. It should be integrated with the system that provides benefits to foreigners seeking to stay in the United States. Linking biometric passports to good data systems and decisionmaking is a fundamental goal. No one can hide his or her debt by acquiring a credit card with a slightly different name. Yet today, a terrorist can defeat the link to electronic records by tossing away an old passport and slightly altering the name in the new one. (389)

Secure identification should begin in the United States. The federal government should set standards for the issuance of birth certificates and sources of identification, such as drivers' licenses. Fraud in identification documents is no longer just a problem of theft. At many entry points to vulnerable facilities, including gates for boarding aircraft, sources of identification are the last opportunity to ensure that people are who they say they are and to check whether they are terrorists. (390)

Hard choices must be made in allocating limited resources. The U.S. government should identify and evaluate the transportation assets that need to be protected, set risk-based priorities for defending them, select the most practical and cost-effective ways of doing so, and then develop a plan, budget, and funding to implement the effort. The plan should assign roles and missions to the relevant authorities (federal, state, regional and local) and to private stakeholders. (391)

The TSA [Transportation Security Administration] and the Congress must give priority attention to improving the ability of screening checkpoints to detect explosives on passengers. (393)

Emergency response agencies nationwide should adopt the Incident Command System (ICS). When multiple agencies or multiple jurisdictions are involved, they should adopt a unified command. Both are proven frameworks for emergency response. In the future, the Department of Homeland Security should consider making funding contingent on aggressive and realistic training in accordance with ICS and unified command procedures. (397)

We recommend the establishment of a National Counterterrorism Center (NCTC), built on the foundation of the existing Terrorist Threat Integration Center (TTIC). Breaking the older mold of national government organizations, this NCTC should be a center for joint operational planning and joint intelligence. (403)

A specialized and integrated national security workforce should be established at the FBI consisting of agents, analysts, linguists and surveillance specialists who are recruited, trained, rewarded and retained to ensure the development of an institutional culture imbued with a deep expertise in intelligence and national security. (426)

*Source:* Reprinted with permission from *Law Enforcement News,* September 2004, p. 8. John Jay College of Criminal Justice (CCNY), 555 West 57th St., New York, NY 10019.

## Five Directorates

DHS's 23 federal agencies compose five major divisions, or **directorates**[21]:

1. Border and Transportation Security
2. Emergency Preparedness and Response
3. Chemical, Biological, Radiological, and Nuclear Countermeasures
4. Information Analysis and Infrastructure Protection
5. Management

Besides these five directorates, discussed in what follows, other critical agencies have been folded into DHS or are newly created, including agencies within the U.S. Coast Guard, the U.S. Secret Service, and the Bureau of Citizenship and Immigration Services. Figure 6.1 shows the DHS organizational structure and includes all of its key components.

Next I discuss the five directorates of DHS.

1. *Border and Transportation Security (BTS)*

   Under the BTS is the **Bureau of Customs and Border Protection,**[22] a new federal program initiated in early 2004 and under which 24 million foreigners are expected to be checked annually at the nation's airports, as discussed in Chapter 8. Its organizational structure is shown in Figure 6.2.

   The new **Transportation and Security Administration (TSA)** assumed responsibility for aviation security in November 2001. TSA protects

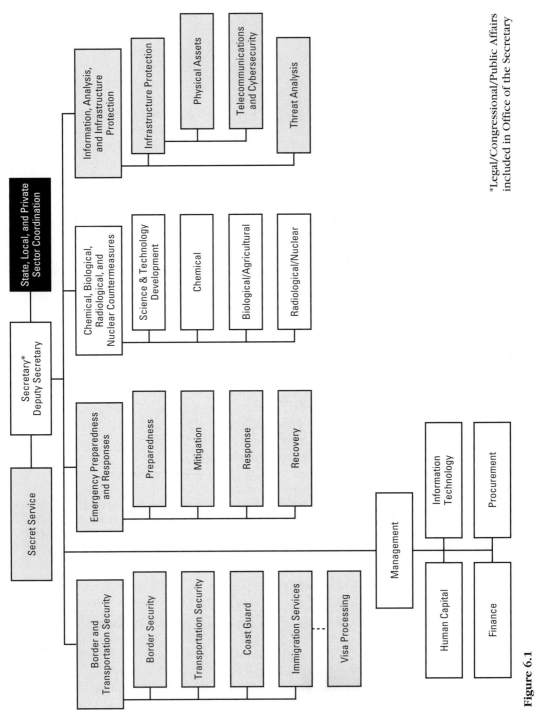

**Figure 6.1**

The organizational structure of the Department of Homeland Security. *Source:* Department of Homeland Security.

*Legal/Congressional/Public Affairs included in Office of the Secretary

**Law Enforcement Levels and Functions**

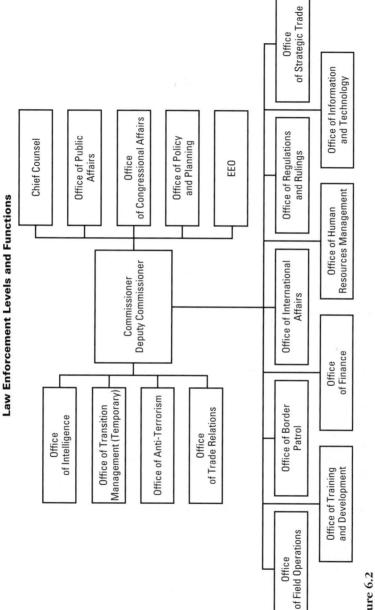

**Figure 6.2**

The organizational structure of the Bureau of Customs and Border Protection. EEO, Equal Employment Opportunity. *Source:* Bureau of Customs and Border Protection.

the nation's transportation systems to ensure freedom of movement for people and commerce. Although its Web site provides relatively scant information and is guarded for security purposes, it states that its annual budget request is about $5 billion.

TSA initially supervised the federal *Air Marshal Service,* which provides about 5,000 specially trained, armed agents who are deployed worldwide on anti-hijacking missions. However, under a reorganization in December 2003, the air marshals were moved from TSA to the Bureau of Immigration and Customs Enforcement. ✓new agency did not exist prior 9/11

2. *Emergency Preparedness and Response*

   This directorate ensures that the nation is prepared for, and able to recover from, terrorist attacks and natural disasters. It builds on the very successful history of the Federal Emergency Management Agency (FEMA), and continues FEMA's efforts to reduce the loss of life and property through preparedness, prevention, response, and recovery. The directorate develops and manages a national system to design curriculums, set standards, evaluate, and reward performance in training efforts. It focuses on risk mitigation by promoting disaster-resistant communities, leads the DHS response to any sort of biological or radiological attack, and coordinates the involvement of National Guard and other federal efforts.[23]

3. *Chemical, Biological, Radiological, and Nuclear Countermeasures*

   This directorate is the primary research and development (R&D) arm of DHS, organizing the vast scientific and technological resources of the nation to mitigate the effects of terrorism. It unifies and coordinates the federal efforts to develop scientific and technological countermeasures and sponsors R&D to invent new vaccines, antidotes, and therapies against biological and chemical warfare agents. Included in its mandate are constant examinations of the nation's vulnerabilities, its security systems, and threats and weaknesses.[24]

4. *Information Analysis and Infrastructure Protection (IAIP)*

   IAIP merges under one roof the ability to identify and assess a broad range of intelligence information from other agencies (the CIA, FBI, and so forth) concerning threats to the homeland. When necessary, it issues timely warnings and encourages citizens to take appropriate preventive protective action. It coordinates the federal government's lines of communication with state and local public safety agencies, and protects our critical infrastructure (e.g., food and water; health, safety, and emergency services; transportation, finance, and postal system); included is a high priority placed on protecting our cyber infrastructure.[25]

5. *Management*

   This directorate is responsible for budget, appropriations, accounting and finance, procurement, human resources, information technology systems, facilities, property, equipment, and other resources relating to the responsibilities of DHS. Key to the success of DHS is the success of its 180,000 employees, and this directorate ensures that the employees have the necessary resources, means of communication, and clear responsibilities that are needed.[26]

# Establishing Command and Control: The National Incident Management System

In Homeland Security Presidential Directive—5, *Management of Domestic Incidents,* President George W. Bush directed the former secretary of the U.S. Department of Homeland Security, Tom Ridge, to develop and administer a **National Incident Management System** (NIMS). This system is to provide a consistent nationwide approach for federal, state, and local governments to work effectively together to prepare for, prevent, respond to, and recover from domestic incidents. This directive requires all federal departments and agencies to adopt the NIMS and to use it, and to make its adoption and use by state and local agencies a condition for federal preparedness assistance beginning in fiscal year 2005. The directive also required Secretary Ridge to develop a national response plan to provide operational direction for federal support to state and local incident managers.[27]

The NIMS is a lengthy document that cannot be duplicated here in its entirety; therefore, the following discussion is limited to some of its primary components:

I.  Command and Management
    A. *The Incident Command System*
       The **Incident Command System** (ICS) was created to coordinate response personnel from more than one agency or teams from more than one jurisdiction, and has been adopted to help local police agencies respond to terrorist incidents. A key strength of ICS is its unified command component, which is composed of four sections: operations, planning, logistics, and finance. Under ICS, all agencies go to the same location and establish a unified command post.[28] The most critical period of time for controlling a crisis is those initial moments when **first responders** arrive at the scene. They must quickly contain the situation, analyze the extent of the crisis, request additional resources and special teams if needed, and communicate available information and intelligence to higher headquarters. Their initial actions provide a vital link to the total police response, and will often determine its outcome.

Next I briefly discuss the five major functions of ICS—command, operations, planning, logistics, and finance/administration—as shown in Figure 6.3.

1. *Command.* The command staff is responsible for overall management of the incident. When an incident occurs within a single jurisdiction, without any overlap, a single incident commander should be designated with overall incident management responsibility to develop the objectives on which an actual action plan will be based. The unified command (UC) concept is used in multijurisdictional or multiagency in-

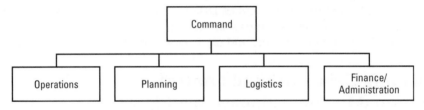

**Figure 6.3**

Five major functions of the National Incident Command System. *Source:* U.S. Department of Homeland Security, *National Incident Command System* (Washington, D.C.: Author, March 1, 2004), p. 13.

cidents to provide guidelines for agencies with different legal, geographic, and functional responsibilities to coordinate, plan, and interact effectively. The composition of the UC will depend on the location(s) and type of incident.

2. *Operations.* The operations section is responsible for all activities focused on reduction of immediate hazard, saving lives and property, establishing control of the situation, and restoring normal operations. Resources for this section might include specially trained, single-agency personnel and equipment, and even special task forces and strike teams.

3. *Planning.* The planning section collects, evaluates, and disseminates incident situation information and intelligence to the incident commander or unified command, prepares status reports, displays situation information, and maintains status of resources assigned to the incident.

4. *Logistics.* The logistics section is responsible for all support requirements needed to facilitate effective incident management: facilities, transportation, supplies, equipment maintenance and fuel, food services, communications and technology support, and emergency medical services.

5. *Finance/Administration.* This section is not required at all incidents, but will be involved where incident management activities require finance and other administrative support services—compensation/claims, determining costs, procurement, and so on. Law enforcement executives also need to create budget line-item codes and emergency purchase orders before such an event, so they will be readily available and accessible.

B. *ICS Initial Duties and Responsibilities*
The following checklist provides the necessary information for quickly assessing the personnel, equipment, and other resources needed during the initial stages of any critical incident:

1. What is the exact nature and size of the incident?
2. What are the location's characteristics and its surroundings?

3. Are dangers to persons and property present, such as armed suspects, fire, or hazardous materials?
4. Are there any unusual circumstances, such as snipers, explosives, or broken utilities present?
5. Is there a need to evacuate, and are antilooting measures required?
6. Is traffic control needed?
7. Is an inner perimeter needed to control the immediate scene?
8. Are additional personnel for inner and outer perimeter, evacuation, rescue, special weapons and tactics (SWAT, discussed later), negotiators, or other specialists needed?
9. Will a command post (CP) and staging area for additional personnel and emergency support be needed?
10. What emergency equipment and personnel is needed, and what safe routes are available for their response to the staging area?
11. What other equipment, supplies, and facilities will be needed?
12. Are there any dead or injured persons who require medical assistance or transport to the hospital?
13. What other needs are there (food and drink for long-term incidents, tactical units, rescue operations, bomb squad, K-9, tow trucks, and so on)?[29]

In connection with these issues, former Oklahoma Governor Frank Keating wrote about his experiences with, and local responses to, the attack on the Murrah Federal Office Building in Oklahoma City. Keating emphasized that the first responders to a terrorist attack will be people from the *local* area—often not even trained public employees, but mere bystanders—and certainly not trained federal or state emergency personnel (who may take hours or even days to arrive at the scene). For that reason, it is important to remember that the local first responders are the front line in meeting the terrorist threat, and they must therefore be adequately trained and equipped for the job.

Furthermore, Keating believed that, because the initial responders are local, the urge to federalize people should be resisted because it makes no sense when the mission remains largely local: "Opening the federal umbrella ... makes sense when the mission is largely federal in nature—for example, a combat environment or an overseas deployment—but not when the mission remains largely local."[30] [During task force investigations involving federal, state, and local agencies, such as the bombing in Oklahoma and the sniper case in the Washington, D.C., area, discussed later, U.S. Code Title 28, Section 566(c), authorizes local officers to be federally deputized to participate in federal investigative efforts, including serving search warrants and making arrests.[31]]

C. *Multiagency Coordination Systems.* These define the operating characteristics, interactive management components, and organizational structure of supporting incident management entities through mutual-aid agreements and other assistance arrangements (mutual aid arrangements are discussed later).

A multiagency coordination system is a combination of facilities, equipment, personnel, procedures, and communications integrated into a common system to coordinate and support domestic incident management activities. Multiagency coordination systems may contain **emergency operations centers** (EOCs), which represent the physical location at which the coordination of information and resources to support incident management activities normally takes place.

An incident command post (ICP), located at or in the immediate vicinity of an incident site, although primarily focused on the tactical on-scene response, may perform an EOC-like function in smaller-scale incidents or during the initial phase of the response to larger, more complex events. For complex incidents, EOCs may be staffed by personnel representing multiple jurisdictions and functional disciplines (e.g., a bioterrorism incident would likely include a mix of law enforcement, emergency management, public health, and medical personnel).

EOCs may be permanent organizations and facilities or established to meet temporary, short-term needs. The physical size, staffing, and equipping of an EOC will depend on the size of the jurisdiction, resources available, and anticipated incident management workload. Core functions such as coordination, communications, dispatch and tracking, and information management should be included. When incidents cross jurisdictional boundaries or involve complex incident management situations, a multiagency coordination entity (e.g., an emergency management agency) may be used to facilitate incident management and policy coordination.

D. *Public Information Systems.* These refer to processes, procedures, and systems for communicating timely and accurate information to the public during crisis or emergency situations. Governor Keating maintained that the answer to the question, "How much do we tell the public?" is a simple one: You tell them everything that does not need to be safeguarded for valid reasons of security. The agency chief executives and incident commanders should conduct regular media briefings "on everything from body counts to alerts involving the composite drawings of the suspects." Openness and candor are essential, and keeping the public informed will render good results. Keating added that government does not merit the trust of the public it serves "if it is overly secretive."[32] He also felt that teamwork between personnel of different agencies is also key before and after an incident, especially in those circumstances where there are many radio frequencies and institutional policies in play (the ICS, discussed earlier, can be of assistance here).[33]

II. Preparedness
   A. *Planning.* Plans describe how personnel, equipment, and other resources are used to support incident management and incident response activities.

They provide mechanisms and systems for setting priorities, integrating multiple entities and functions, and ensuring that communications and other systems are available.

B. *Training.* Training includes standard courses on multiagency incident command and management, organizational structure, and operational procedures, as well as the use of supporting technologies.

C. *Exercises.* Incident management organizations and personnel must participate in realistic exercises, including those of multijurisdictional nature, to improve integration and interoperability and optimize resource utilization during incident operations.

D. *Personnel qualification and certification.* Qualification and certification activities are undertaken to identify and publish national standards and to measure performance against the standards to ensure that incident management and emergency responder personnel are qualified and certified to perform NIMS-related functions. In this same vein, it is also important for administrative personnel to remember that "experts are called experts for a reason," and a terrorist attack or other critical incident might involve local funeral directors, dentists, physicians, biochemists, bomb experts, crane operators, and many others. Such people work for years to acquire their knowledge and skills, and administrators of agencies involved in responding to a terrorist attack should use these people and allow them to do their jobs.[34]

E. *Equipment acquisition and certification.* Incident organizations and personnel at all levels rely on various types of equipment to perform their missions; the acquisition of equipment that will perform to certain standards, and that will operate with similar equipment used by other jurisdictions, is critical.

F. *Mutual aid.* Interagency mutual aid agreements are essential for responding to attacks and disasters. Mutual aid agreements provide a coalition of reinforcements from neighboring agencies for jurisdictions. These joint-powers agreements allow for the sharing of resources among participating agencies and the establishment of clear policies concerning command and control when an attack or a disaster occurs. Mutual aid agreements are commonly used to share personnel and equipment in a major tactical situation. Few agencies have the capability of handling a major tactical incident alone and must rely on the assistance of larger, neighboring metropolitan agencies, county sheriff's departments, or state agencies and federal agencies for assistance.[35]

G. *Publications management.* This refers to forms, developing publication materials—including establishing naming and numbering protocols—and revising documents when necessary.

H. *Supporting technologies.* Technology and technological systems provide supporting capabilities essential to implementing and refining the NIMS. These include voice and data communications systems, information management systems (i.e., record keeping and resource tracking), data display systems, and any specialized technologies that facilitate ongoing operations.

## Emergency Response Checklist

Recently the U.S. Department of Justice and the Federal Emergency Management Agency issued an *Emergency Response to Terrorism Job Aid* checklist detailing the actions that are to be taken by law enforcement and rescue agencies in the event of terrorist attack. This manual's section on law enforcement's activities when responding to terrorism are delineated in Exhibit 6.2.

It is often difficult to predict how long it will take to bring a major occurrence under control (the catastrophic terrorist attack on New York City's World Trade Center not only resulted in heavy loss of life but also necessitated about 1 year to clean up the debris; rebuilding the site required several more years). Natural disasters present another problem. Whereas tornados and earthquakes may occur in only minutes, the cleanup and restoration of damaged bridges, freeways, and

---

**EXHIBIT 6.2**
**Law Enforcement's Emergency Response to Terrorism**

**If First on Scene:**

- Isolate/secure the scene, establish control zone
- Establish command
- Stage incoming units

**If Command Has Been Established:**

- Report to command post
- Evaluate scene safety/security (ongoing criminal activity, secondary devices, additional threats)
- Gather witness statements and document institute notifications (FBI, explosive ordnance squad, private security, and so forth)
- Request additional resources

- Secure outer perimeter
- Control traffic
- Use appropriate self-protective measures
- Initiate public safety measures (evacuations as necessary)
- Assist with control/isolation of patients
- Preserve evidence
- Participate in a unified command system with fire, medical, hospital, and public works agencies

*Source:* Adapted from U.S. Department of Justice, Federal Emergency Management Agency, *Emergency Response to Terrorism: Self-Study* (Washington, D.C.: Author, June 1999).

buildings can take months or even years. De Jong[36] recommended that executives and incident commander adhere to the principles of containment, communication, coordination, and control when responding to critical incidents:

*Containment.* Containment ensures that a crisis does not escalate beyond police control or resources. Containment also keeps innocent people from entering areas of danger and allows police to isolate a suspect for apprehension in a tactical situation.

*Communication.* Communicating the status of a crisis to dispatch for higher headquarters and other responding personnel is a first priority for the on-scene commander and may be accomplished by dealing with the foregoing questions. For more prolonged operations, an emergency operations center and/or command post should be established.

*Coordination.* The coordination of ongoing logistical needs also becomes a priority for the on-scene commander. This can involve requests for additional personnel, equipment, and specialized units such as SWAT, hostage negotiators, hazardous materials team, and so on.

*Control.* At this stage, personnel and equipment are deployed to the incident. The three previous elements should be implemented before any response is attempted.

## Tactical Concerns

Tactical problems present many unique concerns and dangers for the incident commander's consideration. FBI training for managing confrontational situations adopts De Jong's[37] principles into a four-phase framework for organization and deploying personnel and resources to tactical incidents:

*Preconfrontation/preparation phase.* Training should address individual officers' tactical skills, team skills (such as hostage negotiators, SWAT, and command post staff), and systems skills (agency's capabilities to manage a command post). Multiagency exercises provide one method for training and testing an agency's preparation and capabilities.

*Contingency planning.* The focus is on identifying any potential problems, logistical requirements, strategies and tactics, communications needs, and command and control requirements for any potential tactical situation.

*Immediate-response phase.* Control of the scene and isolating the threat is paramount in any response to a tactical situation. An initial assessment of the situation may be provided by dealing with the foregoing questions. Establishing an inner and an outer perimeter will help to isolate the suspect and keep all nonessential personnel a safe distance from danger.

*Deliberate/specific planning phase.* During this phase, strategies for responding to the incident are developed. These may include maintaining negotiations, emergency or deliberate assault, or arranging surrender. Tactical response plans are carefully briefed by all tactical personnel and coordinated with all other responses before initiation.

*Resolution phase.* Resolution entails maintaining control, negotiations, and intelligence during an incident. The goal of this phase is to end the incident without injury to anyone involved. Assault tactics should consider all available intelligence information. A direct assault is often the last resort and consideration.

As noted, this framework will guide incident commanders during the first few minutes of their arrival at scenes requiring tactical operations; the type of situation will dictate further measures that need to be taken.[38]

With respect to biological agents, the role of the police will vary depending on whether they are the first responder. In either event, they must become knowledgeable about bioweapons and how to react to ascertain if the agent is transmittable, as well as the appropriate agencies to get involved. Then, if a biological or chemical agent is deployed overtly and therefore discovered quickly, the police will respond immediately; if covert (and, say, the hospitals do not begin to see cases until many days after the agent is released), the police will be responsible for conducting a later investigation. If hundreds of people are showing up at hospitals, then the police will also have to maintain order.[39]

## Technology Needs

Of particular concern among the law enforcement community is the gap between technologies available to the police and those used by persons and groups planning terrorist acts. Recently the National Institute of Justice conducted a survey of law enforcement technology needs for combating terrorism, interviewing 198 individuals representing 138 agencies from 50 states. The interviewees were queried about their needs in such areas as intelligence gathering; surveillance; command, control, and communication (C3); site hardening; detecting, disabling, and containing explosive devices; and defending against weapons of mass destruction [i.e., nuclear, biological, chemical (NBC) devices] and cyberterrorism.[40]

By far the most pressing technology needs concerned ready access to current intelligence, a national terrorism intelligence database accessible to all state and local law enforcement agencies. Improved means of detecting and analyzing explosive devices was also a major need, as were better NBC protective gear (such as masks, suits, and gloves); C3 was another area of greatest need.

## Interagency Cooperation, Command and Control: The Washington, D.C.-Area Sniper Investigation

Many of the concepts and recommendations described here involving terrorism and **critical incident management** were involved in the Washington, D.C.-area sniper case. For 23 days in October 2002, a two-person sniper team terrorized the Washington, D.C., and central Virginia regions. This case would ultimately involve 14 shootings and 10 deaths, and its investigation included more than 20 local, 2 state, and at least 10 federal law enforcement agencies. It was clearly one of the largest and most complex multijurisdictional investigations ever, and was said to have had "the feel of a fast-paced hockey game with life or death consequences, sweeping into town with the intensity of a tornado and leaving a community both traumatized and relieved 23 days later."[41]

Many lessons were learned from this case, which captured the attention of millions of people in the United States, Europe, and beyond. It required those local agencies affected by shootings to engage simultaneously in emergency management, case management, and incident management. The emergency management component comprised the on-scene response to the shootings; the case management component included the criminal investigation; and the incident management component consisted of coordinating the resources of dozens of agencies, reducing public fears and working with the media. The ultimate goal, of course, was to solve the case; at the same time, agency resources were used to manage crime scenes, close roads, calm the community, and construct a well-supported task force of thousands of law enforcement officials and officers.

Four significant factors emerged as crucial from this case:

1. *Careful planning and preparation.* Pre-event planning can be critical to mobilizing resources when they are needed. As much as possible, agencies should develop plans and policies before an incident, including mutual aid agreements (discussed earlier) with other agencies likely to provide resources and assistance during a crisis. Agencies should determine ahead of time how they will manage crime scenes, implement roadblocks, and interview suspects. Agency officials need to think about issues such as officer overtime, line-of-duty injuries, and use-of-force policies and how they apply to officers on loan from other agencies. They should not only develop response plans, but also practice them, conducting exercises and including those agencies with which they would likely partner.

2. *Defining roles and responsibilities.* During complex investigations, law enforcement personnel of all ranks need to understand their roles and responsibilities. The unique demands of these types of cases can pressure individuals to modify traditional roles or to develop new ones (e.g., many investigators in the sniper case were upset with executives and managers who became involved in investigative responsibilities). In addition, the involvement of federal investigators can cause anxiety among local and state officials who may not want to cede control of the investigation.

3. *Managing information efficiently.* Reliable information flow is crucial to the success of such a major investigation. The ability to collect, analyze, and disseminate tips, leads, intelligence, and criminal histories can mean the difference between a quick apprehension and a prolonged, frustrating effort. A system is needed that will allow the agencies involved to exchange and analyze information.

4. *Maintaining effective communication.* The importance of maintaining effective communication cannot be overstated in such a case. Officials in such investigations need to communicate daily on a tactical and a strategic level and strive for continuous information exchanges and feedback. Agencies need a mechanism for providing a daily briefing to staff and must also communicate with residents, government leaders, and the media.[42]

In sum, police executives in such cases must manage the chaos and provide the leadership needed to reduce fear, support police personnel, and coordinate complex operational and logistical efforts. A number of important decisions must be made: Who is in charge? If the investigation crosses jurisdictional lines or involves several levels of government, the answer may not be self-evident. Determining who is in charge of the investigation will also influence where the task force will be located. In the sniper case, the task force was located in Montgomery County, Maryland, because it was the site of the first shooting. The Sniper Task Force leadership rested with three individuals—Montgomery County Police Chief Charles Moose (his agency had legal authority to investigate the murders), FBI Special Agent in Charge Gary Bald, and Alcohol, Tobacco, and Firearms Special Agent in Charge Michael Bouchard (whose agencies initially dedicated the most resources to the investigation). A shared leadership role was the most logical arrangement.[43]

Another major challenge is establishing the command center quickly and in the correct location. (The decision in the sniper case to headquarter the task force in Montgomery County was relatively straightforward, but in other cases the decision may not be so easy.) Some of the factors that could influence task force location or leadership include the following[44]:

- the agency with the first shooting, or most shootings
- the agency with the highest profile
- the agency with the most or best evidence
- the agency with the most experience in such investigations or a pre-existing command center
- the jurisdiction that will prosecute the case
- the extent of federal involvement and the location of federal resources (some local agencies may simply lack the resources or the expertise to fully conduct a complex, high-profile, multijurisdictional investigation)

Regarding the latter element, the request for federal or other outside assistance, an important element concerns the *timing* of such requests by the law enforcement executive. If the request comes too late, chiefs or sheriffs may look like they cannot succeed. If they ask too early, they look like they do not have faith in the skills of their own people to handle the case. It is a delicate balancing act.[45]

Police leaders should also see that the task force is structured so that it has the ability to:

- apprehend the offender(s)
- manage the resources (e.g., officers/investigators, materials, facilities)

- work with the public
- communicate with government leaders

The effectiveness of the task force will depend on another very important factor: pre-existing relationships of the agencies involved. Federal, state, and local agencies will generally work well alongside one another, but the extent of their collaboration and the level of success they achieve will often depend on their prior relationships and partnerships. Indeed, in the sniper case, of all the keys to success, the one mentioned after the fact and most strongly emphasized by every law enforcement executive was the importance of pre-existing relationships.[46]

Executives should also strive during such investigations to keep their patrol officers informed of all pertinent and current information about the investigation and provided with a list of questions to ask when talking to residents or conducting field interviews. Patrol officers must also continue to provide routine patrol during the task force investigation.[47]

Evidence response and collection protocols should also be developed prior to the event, specifying who can enter crime scenes and collect evidence, the types of evidence that can be collected, and the procedures for analysis.[48]

In sum, although the Washington, D.C.-area sniper case certainly was not without challenges, conflicts, and errors, it was a highly successful effort by the many agencies and officers involved. The lessons learned from this case will serve as an important blueprint for those law enforcement executives who will be similarly challenged in the future.[49]

## Unfinished Business with Regard to Vulnerability to Terrorism

Today many people feel this nation has not faced up to the realities of our changed world. Indeed, Harlan Ullman argued that there are "five major pieces of business" that remain for this country to be safe from terrorism[50]:

1. The first piece of unfinished business, and the most serious, relates to the fact that the September 11 attacks were directed against America's openness, freedom, and complete accessibility. As security becomes more important, its needs inherently conflict with freedom. The basis of our political system is the target. How we deal with this potential weakness and vulnerability may prove the most difficult challenge the nation has faced since the Civil War.

2. The second piece is the inherent vulnerability to disruption of the U.S. infrastructure; that is, our networks for commerce, communications, banking, power, food, emergency services, and the like. There are no means for protecting all or even much of this infrastructure for an extended period.

3. The country's national security organization was designed for an era that no longer exists—the Cold War. The Commission on National Security Strategy,

co-chaired by two former U.S. senators (Gary Hart and Warren Rudman), called this structure "dysfunctional"; they both went on to serve on another commission, which reported in 2002 that America was "still unprepared ... and still in danger."

4. The chief danger to the United States emanates from the "crescent of crisis," the region of the Middle East and Persian Gulf where conflict and extremism abound. As long as the causes that breed this extremism exist, then the United States will be at great risk.

5. There is a need to construct a strategic framework to replace that of the Cold War. The United States has not yet been able to weave together NATO, the European Union, Russia, China, and other key states in a partnership to deal with these new dangers.

What can be done? Ullman argued that in the process of protecting ourselves, we must not do grave damage to our freedom, and must remain within the framework of the Constitution and our laws. Next, the National Security Act of 1947 must be revised to restructure the country's organization in line with the twenty-first century, not the Cold War. The old structure was vertical, with responsibilities neatly divided among federal agencies; this system worked well when our only threat was the Soviet Union. Today, a horizontal governmental structure is needed, cutting across many government agencies and branches. For example, law enforcement and intelligence are no longer separable when it comes to terror and extremism.[51]

Furthermore, many more employees will be needed in the area of homeland security as this matter becomes a higher priority. Good people must be attracted into this service, with good incentives. Without addressing these domestic deficits, the nation cannot be more secure.[52]

Finally, Ullman argued that a new strategic framework is essential. A starting point is preventing the use and spread of weapons of mass destruction, nuclear weapons in particular, and reducing them to the lowest possible number.[53] We must also acknowledge our own limitations. Little can be done, for instance, about terrorists' rising capacity for violence.

Past policies are inadequate. The advantage in this war has shifted to the terrorists, who have become more powerful and tolerant of risk, and often have a great willingness to die for their cause. As a result, the terrorists have a lot of leverage to hurt us. Their capacity to exploit this leverage depends on their ability to understand the complex systems that we depend on so critically, and our defense depends on that same understanding.[54]

# CASE STUDIES

The following case studies afford the reader an opportunity to apply the measures promulgated in this chapter's discussion of the National Incident Management System to hypothetical examples.

> General Instructions: Consider for each case study the kinds of advance planning that should be done; the five major functions of ICS (command, operations, planning, logistics, and finance/administration); the initial duties and responsibilities of law enforcement and other response personnel; technology and equipment needs; and public information responsibilities. For some or all, you must also consider what multiagency coordination must be accomplished—particularly those activities that should occur in the emergency operations center and/or incident command post.

## "The River Ran Through It"

Early one morning a man backs his small fishing boat, containing a duffel bag, two fishing rods, and a picnic basket, down the boat ramp and into the water on a remote side of a river that runs through your city. He cranks the boat's motor and begins trolling toward the river's dam, about 2 miles upriver. After a slow, 30-minute ride, the phony fisherman approaches the dam's spillway. He then removes four interconnected backpacks from the duffel bag and lowers them into the water. The boat is maneuvered so the backpacks come to rest along the sloping spillway. A button on a control device is depressed, and a large explosion is heard for miles. A very destructive terrorist act has been put in motion. A fireball is seen as the underwater explosion blasts a massive hole in the earthen wall. A huge avalanche of water carves a widening chasm in the wall of the dam, and the dam's 10 billion cubic meters of water begins to barrel through the river valley. Within minutes of the explosion, the first call of the dam break reaches you, the city's police chief; a frantic scramble ensues as media and emergency rescue teams begin to alert everyone living downstream. Reports are also quickly coming in about people drowning near the dam. Panic is beginning to set in as nearby residents frantically try to escape to higher ground. A major hydroelectric plant has been damaged, and reports are beginning to come in concerning telephone and power outages. Several miles of roads have been wiped out.

## "Spills That Can Kill"

A. You are the sheriff of Miller County, which has about 200,000 residents. The county seat is Metro City, with a population of 70,000, located in the center of the county. Three smaller incorporated cities border Metro City. Union Rails, Incorporated, has informed you that it plans to increase the number of trains going daily through the county, and that several of those trains will be carrying hazardous industrial materials. Each rail car containing such materials will be appropriately marked, and bills of lading identifying the cargo and its hazard will be available. The railroad is requesting a meeting with local officials to discuss the area's hazardous materials (HAZMAT) response capabilities in the event of an accident. Your agency has no such plan. The board of county commissioners directs you to provide them with recommendations concerning the impact on the cities of transporting HAZMAT materials through the urban area. You must also determine what the jurisdictions need to do to prepare for the increase in rail traffic.

1. Which governmental agencies in the area would need to be involved in developing this plan, and what should they be addressing?
2. What types of mutual aid agreements and personnel training should be provided?
3. What other action plans should be developed?

B. In this scenario, assume the worst case: An explosion occurs at the rail yard in your city, and soon there is a huge hazardous-materials cloud rising. What is your response?

## Summary

This chapter has examined the organizational and administrative responsibilities for laying the groundwork for responding to terrorist attacks and other critical incidents. Serious concerns about terrorism by all Americans will not be dispelled in the foreseeable future. The ongoing conflict between Israel and the Palestinians, the spread of radical Islamic fundamentalism, the antigovernment narcoterrorists in several South American countries, and the existence of our own homegrown terrorist groups strongly suggest that North Americans will face the threat of terrorism for some time to come[55] and that municipal and county law enforcement agencies will be our first line of defense. Within the 50 states, there are 3,000 counties and 18,000 cities that must be protected. The job of getting law enforcement, emergency services, public-health agencies, and private enterprises coordinated and working together at local, state, and federal levels is a daunting task.[56] Indeed, as Ullman put it, there remains much "unfinished business" to address to reduce this nation's vulnerability to terrorism.

In sum, it simply will not do for federal, state, or local law enforcement executives to await the occurrence of an attack before developing plans for coping with it; the cost in human lives and property is potentially too great to be left to "make it up as we go along" methods or on-the-job training. It behooves all police personnel to know and understand their own agency and existing multiagency, regional protocol and procedures, as well as mutual aid agreements, for addressing these situations. Anything less would be a disservice to themselves and to the public they serve.

# Items for Review

1. Define terrorism and the kinds of categories and types that are described in this chapter.

2. Outline the structure and function of the Department of Homeland Defense and its five directorates.

3. Describe the National Incident Management System; include in your description the five major functions of the Incident Command System; the initial duties and responsibilities of law enforcement and other response personnel; technology and equipment needs; public information responsibilities; and the activities that occur in an emergency operations center and/or incident command post.

4. Explain what is meant by a mutual aid agreement and why interagency cooperation is so important in the investigation of a major attack or incident.

5. Explain the four major factors that emerged as crucial from the Washington, D.C.-area sniper case.

6. List the major components of the Emergency Response Checklist.

7. Explain what should be the law enforcement administrator's philosophy and practice with regard to *public information* during a critical incident, and why.

8. Explain Ullman's "five pieces of unfinished" business with regard to the country's vulnerability to terrorism.

# Notes

1. N. Kaiser, "The Tactical Incident: A Total Police Response," *FBI Law Enforcement Bulletin* (August 1990):14–18.

2. C. Jylland-Halverson, R. Stoner, and S. Till, "Terrorism: The Hostage Negotiator's Ultimate Challenge," *Law Enforcement Trainer* (January/February 2000):14–43.

3. Quoted in M. K. Rehm, and W. R. Rehm, "Terrorism Preparedness Calls for Proactive Approach," *The Police Chief* (December 2000):38–43.

4. J. F. Lewis, Jr., "Fighting Terrorism in the 21st Century," *FBI Law Enforcement Bulletin* (March 1999):3.

5. Ibid.

6. Bill Keller, "Nuclear Nightmares," *New York Times Magazine* (May 26, 2002):22, 24–29.

7. Ibid.

8. Ibid.

9. Ibid.

10. K. Strandberg, "Bioterrorism: A Real or Imagined Threat?" *Law Enforcement Technology* (June 2001):88–97.

11. D. Rogers, "A Nation Tested: What Is the Terrorist Threat We Face and How Can We Train for It?" *Law Enforcement Technology* (November 2001):16–21.

12. D. Westneat, "Terrorists Go Green," *U.S. News and World Report* (June 4, 2001):28.

13. Barton Gellman, "The Cyber-Terror Threat," *The Washington Post*, July 14, 2002, p. 3A.

14. Ibid.

15. Virginia Gewin, Agriculture Shock, *Nature* (January 9, 2003):106–108.

16. Thomas Homer-Dixon, "The Rise of Complex Terrorism," *Foreign Policy* **128** (January/February 2002):52–62.

17. E. J. Tully and E. L. Willoughby, "Terrorism: The Role of Local and State Police Agencies," http://www.neiassociates.org/state-local.htm (accessed 31 July 2002).

18. D. G. Bolgiano, "Military Support of Domestic Law Enforcement Operations: Working Within Posse Comitatus," *FBI Law Enforcement Bulletin* (December 2001):16–24.

19. White House news release, http://www.whitehouse.gov/news/releases/2003/10/20031001-4.html (accessed January 4, 2004).

20. Department of Homeland Security, Bureau of Immigration and Customs Enforcement, http://uscis.gov/graphics/publicaffairs/statements/032003—ICE.htm (accessed January 4, 2004).

21. DHS Organization, "Securing Our Borders," http://www.dhs.gov/dhspublic/interapp/editorial/editorial—0089.xml (accessed January 4, 2004).

22. U.S. Customs and Border Protection, "About CBP Spotlight," http://www.customs.ustreas.gov/xp/cgov/toolbox/about/ (accessed January 4, 2004).

23. DHS Organization: Emergency Preparedness and Response, "Preparing America," http://www.dhs.gov/dhspublic/interapp/editorial/editorial—0093.xml (accessed January 4, 2004).

24. DHS Organization: Research & Technology, http://www.dhs.gov/dhspublic/theme—home5.jsp (accessed September 19, 2005).

25. DHS Organization: Information Analysis & Infrastructure Protection, "Synthesizing and Disseminating Information," http://www.dhs.gov.dhspublic/interapp/editorial/editorial—0094.xml (accessed January 4, 2004).

26. DHS Organization: Management, "Building a Team of Professionals," http://www.dhs.gov/dhspublic/interapp/editorial/editorial—0096.xml (accessed January 4, 2004).

27. U.S. Department of Homeland Security, *National Incident Management System* (Washington, D.C.: Author, March 2004), pp. viii, ix.

28. J. Buntin, "Disaster Master," *Governing* (December 2001):34–38.

29. N. F. Iannone and M. P. Iannone, *Supervision of Police Personnel,* 6th ed. (Upper Saddle River, NJ: Prentice Hall, 2001).

30. Frank Keating, "Catastrophic Terrorism: Local Response to a National Threat," *Journal of Homeland Security* (August 2001); available at http://www.homelandsecurity.org/journal/Articles/Keating.htm (accessed November 1, 2004).

31. Gerard R. Murphy and Chuck Wexler, *Managing a Multi-jurisdictional Case: Lessons Learned from the Sniper Investigation* (Washington, D.C.: Police Executive Research Forum, October 2004), p. 39.

32. Keating, "Catastrophic Terrorism."

33. Ibid.

34. Ibid.

35. Buntin, "Disaster Master," p. 38.

36. D. DeJong, "Civil Disorder: Preparing for the Worst," *FBI Law Enforcement Bulletin* (March 1994):1–7.

37. Ibid.

38. U.S. Department of Justice, Federal Bureau of Investigation, National Domestic Preparedness Office (2001), http://www.fas.org/irp/agency/doj/fbi/ndpo/ (accessed January 5, 2004).

39. Strandberg, "Bioterrorism," p. 90.

40. U.S. Department of Justice, National Institute of Justice Research in Brief, *Inventory of State and Local Law Enforcement Technology Needs to Combat Terrorism* (Washington, D.C.: Author, January 1999).

41. Murphy and Wexler, *Managing a Multi-jurisdictional Case,* p. 113.

42. Ibid., pp. 15-17.

43. Ibid., p. 20.

44. Ibid., p. 21.

45. Ibid., p. 28.

46. Ibid., p. 25.

47. Ibid., pp. 87-88.

48. Ibid., p. 88.

49. Ibid., pp. 117-118.

50. Harlan Ullman, "Defusing Dangers to U.S. Security," *The World and I* (January 2003), pp. 38-43.

51. Ibid.

52. Ibid.

53. Ibid.

54. Ibid.

55. Tully and Willoughby, "Terrorism."

56. J. Meisler, "The New Frontier of Homeland Security," *Government Technology's Tech Trends 2002: Combined Effort* (August 2002):26-30.

# PART III

# THE COURTS

*This part consists of three chapters. Chapter 7 examines court organization and operation, Chapter 8 covers personnel roles and functions, and Chapter 9 discusses court issues and practices. The introductory section of each chapter previews the specific chapter content. Case studies in court administration appear at the end of each chapter.*

# Chapter 7

# Court Organization and Operation

## Key Terms and Concepts

| | |
|---|---|
| Adversarial system | Litigation |
| Alternative dispute resolution | Mediation |
| Arbitration | Policy |
| Functional organization | |

## Learning Objectives

As a result of reading this chapter, the student will:

- have an understanding of how courts differ from bureaucracies
- be familiar with court organization
- know the four components of court unification
- understand the importance of court decor and decorum
- be familiar with the ramifications of the adversarial system
- have an understanding of policymaking and the influence of courts on it
- understand why the legal system has become overwhelmed
- know the importance of Alternative Dispute Resolution (ADR) and why it is considered the wave of the future
- be familiar with the components of arbitration and mediation
- know the importance of citizen groups in the courtroom

> *The place of justice is a hallowed place.*
>
> — Francis Bacon
>
> *Courts and camps are the only places to learn the world in.*
> — Earl of Chesterfield

## Introduction

Courts have existed in some form for thousands of years. Indeed, the ancient trial court of Israel, and the most common tribunal throughout its biblical history, was the "court at the gate," where elders of each clan resolved controversies within the kin group. In the fourth century B.C.E., courts in Athens, Greece, dealt with all premeditated homicides and heard cases. The court system has survived the dark eras of the Inquisition and the Star Chamber (which, in England during the 1500s and 1600s, without a jury, enforced unpopular political policies and meted out severe punishment, including whipping, branding, and mutilation). The U.S. court system developed rapidly after the American Revolution and led to the establishment of law and justice on the western frontier.

This chapter opens with some quantitative information concerning the number of federal courts and cases disposed of per annum. Next, I go inside the courts, considering their special nature in our country, as well as typical courtroom decor and decorum. Then, I discuss how the courts attempt to get at truth within the controversial adversary system of justice. The nature of courts as organizations is examined next, including some court organizational structures and whether the courts represent bureaucracies in the usual sense. Then, I discuss the role of courts as policymaking bodies, followed by a review of a relatively new and promising concept, alternative dispute resolution, which addresses the overcrowded court dockets. Then, I examine both historical and current arguments and recommendations for reforming court organizations. The chapter concludes with a case study concerning court administration.

# By the Numbers: Court Statistics

There are 208 statewide general (meaning they can hear all types of cases) and limited (restricted types of cases) jurisdiction court systems in the United States. About 9,065 full-time judges serve in the 71 statewide trial court systems of general jurisdiction alone. There are also about 327 drug courts in 43 states; all but 17 states have family courts with jurisdiction over domestic and marital matters.[1]

It is impossible to gauge with any certainty the number of criminal cases begun, terminated, and pending in all of these courts, particularly at the local level. It is reported, however, that the U.S. Supreme Court disposes of about 8,400 cases annually,[2] with the U.S. district courts' 680 judges disposing of about 70,000 cases, of which 19,000 (or 27 percent) are drug related.[3] Furthermore, each year there are nearly 1 million felony convictions in state courts, more than one third of which are drug related.[4]  *$\frac{1}{3}$ of cases are drug related*

# Inside the Courts: Decor, Decorum, Citizens

## *Hallowed Places*

Practically everything one sees and hears in an American courtroom is intended to convey the sense that the courtroom is a hallowed place in our society. Alexis de Tocqueville, in his study of the United States more than a century ago, observed the extent to which our legal system permeates our lives:

> Scarcely any political question arises in the United States that is not resolved, sooner or later, into a judicial question. Hence all parties are obliged to borrow, in their daily controversies, the ideas, and even the language, peculiar to judicial proceedings. [T]he spirit of the law, which is produced in the schools and courts

of justice, gradually penetrates beyond their walls into the bosom of society, where it descends to the lowest classes, so that at last the whole people contract the habits and the tastes of the judicial magistrate.[5]

The physical trappings and demeanor one finds in the courts convey this sense of importance. On their first visit, citizens often are struck by the court's high ceilings, ornate marble walls, and comparatively expensive furnishings.

A formalized level of decorum is accorded this institution. All people must rise when the judge enters the courtroom; permission must be granted before a person can approach the elevated bench; and a general air of deference is granted the judge. A vitriolic utterance that could lawfully be directed to the president of the United States could result in the utterer's being jailed for contempt of court when directed to a judge.

The design of the courtroom, although generally dignified in nature, also provides a safe, functional space that is conducive to efficient and effective court proceedings. The formal arrangement of the participants and furnishings reflects society's view of the appropriate relationships between the defendant and judicial authority. The courtroom must accommodate judges, court reporters, clerks, bailiffs, witnesses, plaintiffs, defendants, attorneys, juries, and spectators, as well as police officers, social workers, probation officers, guardians ad litem, interpreters, and the press. Space must also be allotted for evidence, exhibits, recording equipment, and computers.

Judges and court staff now may require high-technology audiovisual equipment and computer terminals to access automated information systems. Chapter 17 discusses the kinds of technologies that are now commonly used in the nation's courtrooms.

## *Justice in the Eye of the Beholder*

Whether or not justice is done in the courtrooms depends on the interests or viewpoints of the affected or interested parties. A victim may not agree with a jury's verdict; a "winner" in a civil case may not believe that he or she received an adequate sum of money for the suffering or damages involved. Thus, because "justice" is not always agreed on, the courts must *appear* to do justice. The court's responsibility is to provide a fair hearing, with rights accorded to all parties to speak or not to speak, to have the assistance of counsel, to cross-examine the other side, to produce witnesses and relevant documents, and to argue their viewpoint. This process, embodied in the due process clause, must appear to result in justice.[6]

Certainly, many people today are put off with accounts of what they perceive as coddling of offenders and the ravages of the "law's delay," discussed thoroughly in Chapter 8. People tell their neighbors of long waits at the courthouse to take care of business or of having been summoned for jury service. They hear victims and witnesses talk of having been treated badly at the hands of the justice system. Being summoned for and serving jury duty is for many people, however, an enjoyable and educational experience, one they feel is their civic duty (which it is, from a legal standpoint).

Several citizen's groups interested in reforming the system have engaged in court-watching efforts; such groups include Mothers Against Drunk Drivers, the League of Women Voters, and the National Council of Jewish Women.

## *Seeking Truth in an Adversarial Atmosphere*

Ralph Waldo Emerson stated that "every violation of truth ... is a stab at the health of human society."[7] Certainly, most people would agree that the traditional, primary purpose of our courts is to provide a forum for seeking and—through the adversarial process—obtaining the truth. Indeed, the U.S. Supreme Court declared in 1966 in *Tehan v. United States ex rel. Shott*[8] that "the basic purpose of a trial is the determination of truth."

Today, however, increasing numbers of Americans have the impression that truth is being compromised and even violated with regularity in the trial, plea bargaining, and appellate apparatus of our justice system, thereby "stabbing at the health of human society."

High on their list of impediments is the **adversarial system** itself—perhaps reaching its apex in the O. J. Simpson trial, which included jury nullification (acquitting a defendant because the jury disagrees with a law or the evidence), lawyer grandstanding, improper and racist police procedures, and a general circus atmosphere allowed by the judge and engaged in by the media. Although many people would argue that such a system is vital to a free democratic society, under this system the courtroom becomes a battleground where participants often have little regard for guilt or innocence; rather, concern centers on whether the state is able to prove guilt beyond a reasonable doubt. To many people, this philosophy flies in the face of what courts were intended to accomplish. In the adversary system, the desire to win can become overpowering. As one state supreme court justice put it, prosecutors "are proud of the notches on their gun."[9] Defense counsel enjoy winning equally. The attention can shift from the goal of finding truth to being effective game players.

Should this system be modified or replaced? That is an important and difficult question. As one law professor observed, "Lawyers are simply not appropriate to correct the defects of our adversary system. Their hearts will never be in it; it is unfair to both their clients and themselves to require them to serve two masters."[10]

It would appear, however, that the adversarial system is here to stay. Indeed, several safeguards have been put in place to enable this system to reach the truth. First, evidence is tested under this approach through cross-examination of witnesses. Second, power is lodged with several different people; each courtroom actor is granted limited powers to counteract those of the others. If, for example, the judge is biased or unfair, the jury can disregard the judge and reach a fair verdict. If the judge believes the jury has acted improperly, he or she can set aside the jury's verdict and order a new trial. Furthermore, both the prosecuting and defense attorneys have certain rights and authority under each state's constitution. This series of checks and balances is aimed at curbing misuse of the criminal courts.

# Courts as Organizations

## *A Nonbureaucratic Work Group*

In the view of many academics, the courts have erroneously been characterized as bureaucracies.[11] Bureaucracies have separate divisions tied together by a distinctive authoritarian structure or hierarchy. They also have well-defined organizational rules governing the disposition of particular tasks, including individually defined, specialized ones.[12] These characteristics do not apply to courts.

Here I examine how courts differ from the typical organization and how court administration is made more complex because of this uniquely informal structure and organization. Indeed, courts are relatively autonomous single work units that do not function in a bureaucratic manner. A trial court is an entity that does not report to a single authority figure in a chain of command. It often ignores formal rules in favor of shared decision making among judges, prosecutors, and defense attorneys.[13]

Rather than being bureaucracies, trial courts are informal work groups in which interaction among members occurs on a continuing basis. Court participants have discretion in carrying out their tasks; they are interdependent but also have the ability to modify formal rules and procedures so that participants can complete their assignments successfully. A professional bond exists because most of the participants are lawyers. A bureaucratic management style generally would be inappropriate for the courts. In fact, the more a judge insists on being treated with great deference, the more that work group's cohesion diminishes. More important, participants' roles are interchangeable: Defense attorneys may become prosecutors or judges, and vice versa.[14]

Formal authority is modified in trial courts in many ways. For example, whereas the judge has the authority to make the major decisions—setting bail, determining guilt, and imposing sentence—he or she often relies on input from others. In addition, because they know more about cases coming to court, the judges' subordinates (prosecutors and defense attorneys) can influence his or her decisions by selective information flow.[15]

For these informal work groups to be effective, group norms must be enforced. Group members who comply with the norms of behavior are rewarded; those who do not are subject to sanctions. Defense attorneys who do not file unnecessary motions or avoid pushing for "unreasonable" plea bargains may be rewarded, such as being allowed more time to read the police reports of their cases. Similarly, prosecutors may receive more time to talk with witnesses or defense counsel. Conversely, sanctions for defense attorneys who violate group norms may include less access to case information, not being appointed to represent indigents in future cases, or harsher sentences imposed on their clients. Furthermore, prosecutors may not receive requested continuances (most requests for continuances come from the district attorney's office).[16] In sum, it is important to remember that the courtroom work group is a social organization, with people interacting, with cooperation between the actors, and with a commonly understood set of practices.[17]

## *Organizational Structure*

Chapter 3 discussed organizational structures, both in general and as concerns police agencies. Courts are organized in similar fashion, providing a more **functional organization** by spelling out areas of responsibility and lines of communication and defining the chain of command.

Figure 7.1 shows an organizational structure for a county district court serving a population of 300,000. Note the variety of functions and programs that exist in addition to the basic court role of hearing trials and rendering dispositions.

Court organization can be quite complicated and technical. Even lawyers who regularly use the courts sometimes find the details of court organization confusing. Terms that refer to the court system include many shorthand phrases that are confusing to the outsider.[18]

Three concepts—jurisdiction, trial versus appellate courts, and the dual court system—underlie court organization.

1. *Jurisdiction.* Court structure is largely determined by the types of cases a court may hear and decide. Jurisdiction is the power of a court to decide a dispute. It has three subcomponents:

   * *Geographical.* Courts are authorized to hear and decide disputes within a specified geographical area; thus, a New York court normally has no jurisdiction to try a person accused of committing a crime in New Jersey.

   * *Subject matter.* Trial courts of *limited* jurisdiction hear a restricted category of cases, typically misdemeanors and civil suits involving small sums of money. Trial courts of *general* jurisdiction are empowered to hear all other types of cases within their jurisdiction.

   * *Hierarchical.* This term refers to different court functions and responsibilities. *Original* jurisdiction means that a court has the authority to try a case and decide it; *appellate* jurisdiction means a court can review cases that have already been decided by another court.

2. *Trial and appellate courts.* Virtually all cases, whether civil or criminal, begin in the trial court. The losing party in the trial court generally has the right to request an appellate court review of the case. The appellate court's primary function is to ensure that the trial court correctly interpreted and applied the law. It reexamines old rules, devises new ones, and interprets unclear language of past court decisions or statutes. Appellate and trial courts are organized and operate quite differently because their roles are different.

3. *Dual court system.* The United States has both a single, national court system and a separate court systems in each of the 50 states, plus the District of Columbia and the U.S. territories. This effectively means there are more than 50 different court systems. Although they may be similar in structure, their operations are anything but identical; each court system has its own structure

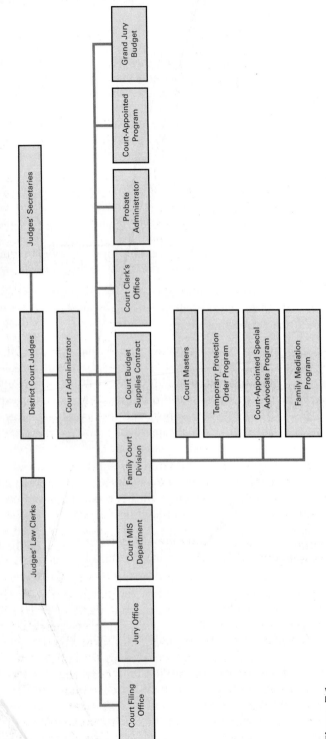

**Figure 7.1**

Organizational structure for a district court serving a population of 300,000.
(MIS = Management Information Systems).

and law enforcement and correctional systems; there will be variations in how the law is interpreted and applied and how offenders are sentenced. This dual court system contributes a considerable amount of complexity to the criminal justice system, causing confusion in such areas as the constitutional prohibition against double jeopardy.[19]

# The Influence of Courts in Policymaking

The judicial branch has the responsibility to determine the legislative intent of the law and to provide public forums—the courts—for resolving disputes. This is accomplished by determining the facts and their legal significance in each case. If the court determines the legal significance of the facts by applying an existing rule of law, it is engaging in pure dispute resolution.[20] On the other hand, "if to resolve the dispute the court must create a new rule or modify an old one, that is law creation."[21]

Determining what the law says and providing a public forum involve the courts in policymaking. **Policy** can be defined as choosing among alternative choices of action, particularly in the allocation of limited resources "where the chosen action affects the behavior and well-being of others who are subject to the policymaker's authority."[22] The policy decisions of the courts affect virtually all of us in our daily living. In recent decades, the courts have been asked to deal with issues that previously were within the purview of the legislative and judicial branches. Because many of the Constitution's limitations on government are couched in vague language, the judicial branch must eventually deal with potentially volatile social issues, such as those involving prisons, abortion, and schools.[23]

U.S. Supreme Court decisions have dramatically changed race relations, resulted in the overhaul of juvenile courts, increased the rights of the accused, prohibited prayer and segregation in public schools, legalized abortion, and allowed for destruction of the U.S. flag. State and federal courts have together overturned minimum residency requirements for welfare recipients, equalized school expenditures, and prevented road and highway construction from damaging the environment. They have eliminated the requirement of a high school diploma for a firefighter's job and ordered increased property taxes to desegregate public schools. The only governmental area that has not witnessed judicial policymaking since the Civil War is foreign affairs. Cases in which courts make policy determinations usually involve government, the Fourteenth Amendment, and the need for equity—the remedy most often used against governmental violations of law. Recent policymaking decisions by the judicial branch have not been based on the Constitution, but rather on federal statutes concerning the rights of the disadvantaged and consumers and the environment.[24]

Perhaps nowhere have the nation's courts had more of an impact than in the prisons—from which nearly 60,000 prisoner petitions are filed each year in the U.S. district courts.[25] Among these accomplishments of judicial intervention have been extending recognized constitutional rights of free speech, religion, and due process to prisoners; abolishing the South's plantation model of prisons; accelerating the professionalization of U.S. correctional managers; encouraging a new generation of correctional administrators more amenable to reform; reinforcing the adoption of national standards for prisons; and promoting increased accountability and efficiency of prisons. The only failure of judicial intervention has been its inability to prevent the explosion in prison populations and costs.[26]

The courts have become particularly involved in administrative policy because of public interest–group litigation. For example, legislation was enacted allowing citizen lawsuits when certain federal regulatory agencies, such as the Environmental Protection Agency (EPA), failed to perform certain duties as required by statute. Thus a citizens' environmental group was allowed to sue the EPA.

It may appear that the courts are overbroad in their review of issues. However, it should be remembered that judges "cannot impose their views . . . until someone brings a case to court, often as a last resort after complaints to unresponsive legislators and executives."[27] Plaintiffs must be truly aggrieved or have *standing*. The independence of the judicial branch, particularly at the federal court level, at which judges enjoy lifetime appointments, allows the courts to champion the causes of the underclasses: those with fewer financial resources or votes (by virtue of, say, being a minority group) or without a positive public profile.[28] It is also important to note that the judiciary is the "least dangerous branch," having no enforcement powers. Moreover, the decisions of the courts can be overturned by legislative action. Even decisions based on the Constitution can be overruled by subsequent constitutional amendment. Thus, the judicial branch depends on a perception of legitimacy surrounding its decisions.[29]

## Decreasing Litigation: Alternative Dispute Resolution

This chapter began with a statistical overview of the nation's courts and their annual caseloads. Although these lawsuits—both criminal and civil—have arguably resulted in better safety and quality of life in the United States, the fact remains that the weight of this **litigation** has imposed a tremendous workload on the nation's courts.

Several methods are now being proposed to reduce the number of lawsuits in this country. One is to limit punitive damages, with only the judge being allowed to levy them. Another is to force losers to pay the winners' legal fees. The process of discovery also warrants examination. This process involves exchange of information between prosecutors and defense attorneys, to ensure that the adversary system does not give one side an unfair advantage over the other. Many knowledgeable people believe that the process of discovery wastes much time and could be revamped.[30]

Another proposal that is already in relatively widespread use is **alternative dispute resolution** (ADR). Realizing that the exploding backlog of both criminal and civil cases pushes business cases to the back of the queue, many private corporations are attempting to avoid courts and lawyers by using alternative means of resolving their legal conflicts. Some corporations have even opted out of litigation altogether; about 600 top corporations have signed pledges with other companies to consider negotiation and other forms of ADR prior to suing other corporate signers.[31]

ADR is appropriate when new law is not being created. ADR can provide the parties with a forum to reach a resolution that may benefit both sides. Litigation is adversarial; ADR can resolve disputes in a collaborative manner that allows parties' relationship to be maintained. Furthermore, ADR proceedings are normally confidential, with only the final agreement being made public. ADR is also much more expedient and less costly than a trial.[32]

## *ADR Options: Arbitration and Mediation*

The two most common forms of ADR used today are arbitration and mediation. **Arbitration** is similar to a trial, though less formal. An arbitrator is selected or appointed to a case; civil court rules generally apply. Parties are usually represented by counsel. The arbitrator listens to testimony by witnesses for both sides; then, after hearing closing remarks by counsel, the arbitrator renders a verdict. Arbitration may be mandatory and binding, meaning that the parties abandon their right to go to court once they agree to arbitrate. The arbitration award is usually appealable. Types of disputes commonly resolved through arbitration include collective bargaining agreements, construction and trademark disputes, sales contracts, warranties, and leases.[33]

**Mediation** is considerably less formal and more "friendly" than arbitration. Parties agree to negotiate with the aid of an impartial person who facilitates the settlement negotiations. A mediation session includes the mediator and both parties; each side presents his or her position and identifies the issues and areas of dispute. The mediator works with the parties until a settlement is reached or the negotiations become deadlocked; in the latter case, the matter may be continued in court. Mediation is not binding or adversarial; instead, mediation encourages the parties to resolve the dispute among themselves. Mediation is commonly used when the parties in dispute have a continuing relationship, as in landlord-tenant disputes, long-term employment/labor disputes, and disputes between businesses.[34]

The leading ADR firm is Judicial Arbitration & Mediation Services, Inc. (JAMS), based in Orange, California, and started in 1979. It employs a panel of about 200 former judges. Washington-based Endispute, Inc., and the Philadelphia-based Judicate, Inc., are rapidly growing in the field as well. These private arbitration and mediation firms charge $300 to $350 per hour, a huge savings from the $300 an hour that a battery of lawyers might each charge litigants.[35]

Given the increasing number of lawsuits in this country, it appears that ADR is the wave of the future; as one law professor noted, "In the future, instead of walking into a building called a courthouse, you might walk into the Dispute Resolution Center."[36]

# Attempts at Reforming Court Organization

The current status of state court systems—both courts of last resort and intermediate courts of appeals—is shown in Figures 7.2 and 7.3. It will be seen that there is widespread variation in terms of these courts' names and the number of judges for each.

Historically, court reform has centered on implementing a unified court system. Indeed, since the beginning of the 1900s, the organization of U.S. courts has been a primary concern of court reformers who believe the multiplicity of courts is inefficient.

A unified court system would, first and foremost, shift judicial control to centralized management. The loose network of independent judges and courts would be replaced by a hierarchy with authority concentrated in the state capital.

Other perceived benefits of court unification would include the following four general principles[37]:

1. *Simplified court structure.* Court reformers stress the need for a simple, uniform court structure for the entire state. In particular, the multiplicity of minor and specialized courts, which often have overlapping jurisdiction,

| | |
|---|---|
| **Supreme Court** | Alabama (9), Alaska (5), Arizona (5), Arkansas (7), California (7), Connecticut (7), Delaware (5), Florida (7), Georgia (7), Hawaii (5), Idaho (5), Illinois (7), Indiana (5), Iowa (9), Kansas (7), Kentucky (7), Louisiana (8), Michigan (7), Minnesota (9), Mississippi (9), Missouri (7), Montana (7), Nebraska (7), Nevada (5), New Hampshire (5), New Jersey (7), New Mexico (5), North Carolina (7), North Dakota (5), Ohio (7), Oklahoma (9),[a] Oregon (7), Pennsylvania (7), Rhode Island (5), South Carolina (5), South Dakota (5), Tennessee (5), Texas (9),[a] Utah (5), Vermont (5), Virginia (7), Washington (9), Wisconsin (7), Wyoming (5) |
| **Court of Appeals** | District of Columbia (9), Maryland (7), New York (7) |
| **Supreme Judicial Court** | Maine (7), Massachusetts (7) |
| **Court of Criminal Appeals** | Oklahoma (3),[a] Texas (9)[a] |
| **Supreme Court of Appeals** | West Virginia (5) |

[a]Two courts of last resort in these states.

**Figure 7.2**

Courts of last resort in U.S. states.

| | |
|---|---|
| **Appeals Court** | Massachusetts (14) |
| **Appellate Court** | Connecticut (9), Illinois (42) |
| **Appellate Division of Superior Court** | New Jersey (28) |
| **Appellate Divisions of Superior Court** | New York (48) |
| **Appellate Terms of Supreme Court** | New York (15) |
| **Commonwealth Court** | Pennsylvania (9) |
| **Court of Appeals** | Alaska (3), Arizona (21), Arkansas (6), Colorado (16), Georgia (9), Idaho (30), Indiana (5), Iowa (6), Kansas (10), Kentucky (14), Michigan (24), Minnesota (16), Missouri (32), Nebraska (6), New Mexico (10), North Carolina (12), North Dakota (3)[b], Ohio (65), Oklahoma (12)[a], Oregon (10), South Carolina (6), Tennessee (12)[a], Utah (7), Virginia (10), Washington (23), Wisconsin (15) |
| **Court of Appeal** | California (88), Louisiana (55), Texas (80) |
| **Court of Civil Appeals** | Alabama (3) |
| **Court of Criminal Appeals** | Alabama (5), Tennessee (9) |
| **Court of Special Appeals** | Maryland (13) |
| **District Court of Appeals** | Florida (57) |
| **Intermediate Court of Appeals** | Hawaii (3) |
| **Superior Court** | Pennsylvania (15) |

[a]Civil only
[b]Temporary

**Figure 7.3**

Intermediate courts of appeal.

would be consolidated; therefore, variations among counties would be eliminated. There would be a three-tier system: a state supreme court at the top, an intermediate court of appeal, and a single trial court.

Looking at a system that has become unified on a statewide basis is instructive. Kansas, which unified its court system in 1977, has a supreme court (with seven justices and appellate and original jurisdiction); an intermediate court of appeals (seven justices who hear appeals from district courts); a district court (70 district, 64 associate district, and 76 district magistrate judges; general original jurisdiction in all civil and criminal matters, hearing appeals from lower courts); and municipal courts (384 judges who handle city ordinance violation, with no jury trials).[38] This is actually about as simple as court unification can be.

Witness the Kansas court system *prior to* unification: a supreme court; 29 district courts (no intermediate court of appeals); 93 county courts, handling civil cases, felony preliminaries, misdemeanors, and jury trials; 8 city courts hearing civil matters, felony preliminaries, misdemeanors, and jury trials;

5 magistrate courts hearing civil cases, felony preliminaries, and misdemeanors; 109 probate courts; 109 juvenile courts; 4 common pleas courts handling civil cases, felony preliminaries, and misdemeanors; and 384 municipal courts, hearing city ordinance violations, including traffic violations, resulting in less than 1-year imprisonment.[39] Note the several different titles and types of courts, with similar yet different roles and jurisdiction. Imagine the confusion, redundancy, and fragmentation that existed.

2. *Centralized administration.* Reformers envision the state supreme court working with state and county court administrators and providing leadership for the state court system.

3. *Centralized rule making.* Reformers argue that the state supreme court should have the power to adopt uniform rules that would be followed by all courts in the state, including procedures for meting out discipline against attorneys and setting time standards for disposing of cases. This change would shift control from the legislatures to judges and lawyers.

4. *Centralized budgeting.* With unification would come centralized budgeting by the state judicial administrator, who would report to the state supreme court. A single budget would be prepared for the entire state judiciary and sent to the state legislature. The governor's power to recommend a judicial budget would be eliminated. Lower courts would be dependent on the supreme court for their monies.

Although judicial reformers have achieved considerable success in these regards, with many states substantially unifying their court systems, they believe there is still much that needs to be accomplished. For example, statewide financing has not fared well. In many states, the county still finances the major trial courts to a significant degree.

Why have these reform proposals been slow to progress? One concern is that the concept of a unified court system does not allow for a desirable diversity; the standard blueprint of court organization fails to consider, for example, important differences in the working environment of courts in densely populated cities as opposed to those in sparsely inhabited rural areas. Today court reform concentrates more on improving the quality of justice meted out by American courts and less on providing a neater organizational chart. The general public has little interest in seeing the courts' organizational structures changed. The emerging agenda of court reform includes topics such as reducing trial court delay (discussed in Chapter 9) and creating alternative dispute resolution (discussed earlier).[40]

# CASE STUDY

The following case study, concerning an embattled court system and personnel issues, will help the reader consider real-world court problems.

## Chief Judge Cortez's Embattled Court

You have just been hired as the new court administrator for a medium-sized court with approximately 90 employees. Once on the job, you discover that you have been preceded by two heavy-handed court administrators who together lasted less than 1 year on the job because of their inability to handle employee conflicts and to achieve a minimal level of productivity. They were more or less forced to resign because of a lack of employee cooperation and increasing talk of unionization. There is general turmoil and distrust throughout the organization. Employees do not trust each other, and as a group, they do not trust management. The courthouse runs on gossip and inertia. There is very little official communication throughout the organization. Prior court administrators made no attempt to solicit employee opinions or ideas. The judges are all aware of the problem, but they have formed no clear consensus as to how to respond to it. In fact, there is turmoil and conflict among the judges themselves. They engage in "turf protection" with operating funds and the court's cases and often take sides in office squabbles. As a result, they are unable to come to any clear consensus or to provide the court administrator with any guidance. The chief judge, Dolores Cortez, has served in that capacity for 10 years and is known to be exceedingly fair, compassionate, and competent; however, she is approaching retirement (in 6 months) and appears unwilling to take a firm stand on, or a strong interest in, addressing intraoffice disputes and difficulties. In fact, she is not altogether convinced that there is a problem. Furthermore, in past years she has been quite reluctant to intervene in arguments between individual judges.

### Questions for Discussion

1. As the "new kid on the block," how would you respond to this organizational problem? What is the first issue you would address, and how would you address it? What additional problems require your attention?

2. As court administrator, how would you respond to the inability of the judges to develop a consensus? How could the decision-making process be improved?

3. What techniques could be employed to improve communication through the organization, lessen tension and strife, and generally create a more harmonious work environment?

4. What would be your general approach to Judge Cortez? To her successor?

# Summary

This chapter reviewed the distinctive nature of the courts and their organization. U.S. courts, which have thus far resisted attempts to be bureaucratized, have comparatively little formalized, hierarchical structure or chain of command, but are composed of informal work groups and are largely autonomous.

Several areas of concern were highlighted as well. One increasing concern has to do with the burgeoning caseloads of the courts; alternative dispute resolution was proposed as a means of helping in this area of court operation. Another problem presented in this chapter is the need for court reform; many notable authorities believe changes are necessary to improve court efficiency. It is clear that until a number of political impediments are overcome, widespread court reform is unlikely.

# Questions for Review

1. How do the courts differ from the police or other traditional bureaucracies in their organization? How and why do courts eschew the usual characteristics found in a bureaucracy?
2. In what ways are courts unique in terms of their decor and decorum?
3. In what ways does alternative dispute resolution hold promise for reducing the current avalanche of lawsuits?
4. What are some perceived benefits of unifying the state court systems? How would a unified state court system be organized?
5. What are some hindrances to court reform?
6. Why is the adversarial system of justice believed to impede the determination of truth in the courtroom? What are some safeguards that argue for continuation of this system?

# Notes

1. U.S. Department of Justice, Bureau of Justice Statistics, "Court Organization Statistics," http://www.ojp.usdoj.gov/bjs/courts.htm (accessed September 21, 2005).
2. U.S. Department of Justice, Bureau of Justice Statistics, *Sourcebook of Criminal Justice Statistics 2003* (Washington, D.C.: U.S. Government Printing Office, 2004), p. 465.
3. Ibid., p. 405.
4. Ibid., p. 449.
5. Alexis de Tocqueville, *Democracy in America*, Vol. 1, trans. H. Reeve (New York: D. Appleton, 1904), pp. 283–284.
6. H. Ted Rubin, *The Courts: Fulcrum of the Justice System* (Santa Monica, Calif.: Goodyear, 1976), p. 3.
7. Stephen Whicher and R. Spiller (eds.), *The Early Lectures of Ralph Waldo Emerson* (Philadelphia: University of Pennsylvania Press, 1953), p. 112.

8. 382 U.S. 406 (1966), 416.
9. Thomas L. Steffen, "Truth as Second Fiddle: Reevaluating the Place of Truth in the Adversarial Trial Ensemble," *Utah Law Review* 4 (1988):821.
10. W. Alschuler, "The Preservation of a Client's Confidences: One Value Among Many or a Categorical Imperative?" *University of Colorado Law Review* **52** (1981):349.
11. Edward J. Clynch and David W. Neubauer, "Trial Courts as Organizations: A Critique and Synthesis," in Stan Stojkovic, John Klofas, and David Kalinich (eds.), *The Administration and Management of Criminal Justice Organizations: A Book of Readings,* 3rd ed. (Prospect Heights, Ill.: Waveland Press, 1999), pp. 69–88.
12. Peter M. Blau and Marshall W. Meyer, *Bureaucracy in Modern Society* (New York: Random House, 1971), Chapter 2.
13. Clynch and Neubauer, "Trial Courts as Organizations," p. 43.
14. Ibid., pp. 46–48.
15. Ibid., pp. 49–50.
16. Ibid., pp. 51–52.
17. David W. Neubauer, *America's Courts and the Criminal Justice System,* 8th ed. (Upper Saddle River, N.J.: Prentice Hall, 2005), p. 113.
18. Ibid., p. 59.
19. Adapted from Neubauer, *America's Courts and the Criminal Justice System,* pp. 59–61.
20. Howard Abadinsky, *Law and Justice: An Introduction to the American Legal System,* 4th ed. (Chicago: Nelson-Hall, 1999), p. 33.
21. Richard A. Posner, *The Federal Courts: Crisis and Reform* (Cambridge, Mass.: Harvard University Press, 1985), p. 3.
22. Harold J. Spaeth, *Supreme Court Policy Making: Explanation and Prediction* (San Francisco: W. H. Freeman, 1979), p. 19.
23. Abadinsky, *Law and Justice,* p. 174.
24. Ibid., p. 170.
25. U.S. Department of Justice, *Sourcebook of Criminal Justice Statistics 2000,* p. 467.
26. Malcolm M. Feeley and Edward L. Rubin, *Judicial Policy Making and the Modern State: How the Courts Reformed America's Prisons* (New York: Cambridge University Press, 1998).
27. Stephen L. Wasby, *The Supreme Court in the Federal System,* 3rd ed. (Chicago: Nelson-Hall, 1989), p. 5.
28. Abadinsky, *Law and Justice,* p. 171.
29. Ibid., p. 166.
30. Bob Cohn, "The Lawsuit Cha-Cha," *Newsweek* (August 26, 1991):59.
31. Michele Galen, Alice Cuneo, and David Greising, "Guilty!" *Business Week* (April 13, 1992):63.
32. American Bar Association, *Dispute Resolution: A 60-Minute Primer* (Washington, D.C.: Author, 1994), pp. 1–2.
33. Ibid., p. 3.
34. Ibid., p. 4.
35. Quoted in American Bar Association, *Dispute Resolution.*
36. Ibid., p. 64.
37. Neubauer, *America's Courts and the Criminal Justice System,* pp. 88–89.
38. William E. Hewitt, Geoff Gallas, and Barry Mahoney, *Courts That Succeed* (Williamsburg, Va.: National Center for State Courts, 1990), p. vii.
39. Ibid., p. vii.
40. Neubauer, *America's Courts and the Criminal Justice System,* p. 92.

# Chapter 8

# Court Personnel Roles and Functions

# Key Terms and Concepts

Court administration

Court clerk

Court Executive Development
  Program (CEDP)

Court management

Courtroom civility

Executive appointment

Judicial administration

Merit selection

Nonpartisan elections

Partisan elections

# Learning Objectives

As a result of reading this chapter, the student will:

- be able to define and understand judicial administration and court administration
- have an understanding of partisan elections, nonpartisan elections, merit selection, and appointment of judges
- understand the importance of maintaining civility in the courtroom
- know the benefits and problems encountered by judges, including the problems faced by newly appointed judges
- be familiar with the three phases of the court development program
- understand the duties of judges as court managers
- know the importance of court clerks
- understand the six major duties of court administrators
- know the five strategies that judges follow in determining the quality of work by administrators
- understand the components of jury administration

> *Four things belong to a Judge:*
>
> *To hear courteously,*
>
> *To answer wisely,*
>
> *To consider soberly, and*
>
> *To decide impartially.*
>
> —Socrates

# Introduction

Chapter 6 looked at the "hallowed" nature of the courts, and how the courts and judges—with gavels, flowing robes, ornate surroundings, and other aspects of decor and decorum that are accorded their office—are enveloped by a mystique of importance and authority. This chapter expands that discussion, focusing more on judges and other key personnel who are involved in court administration.

The administration of the judicial process is probably the least understood area of justice administration, and possibly all of criminal justice. This lack of understanding is compounded by the fact that, very often, even judges and court administrators are not formally trained in their roles. Furthermore, few judges would probably "like to spend all day or most of the day handling union grievances or making sure that employees know what their benefits are."[1] Opportunities to receive training and education are expanding, however, and this chapter addresses some of the means by which that can be accomplished.

I begin by defining and distinguishing the terms *judicial administration* and *court administration* and then consider judges: how they ascend to the bench, benefits and problems of the position, and some thoughts on good judging and courtroom civility. Then I specifically examine their role as the ultimate judicial administrator. The historically important role of court clerks is then reviewed, including the unique role played by those clerks in rural communities. Next, I examine the relatively new position of the specially trained court administrator, including training and duties, judges' evaluation criteria, and conflict among judicial administrators. Then I give an overview of the problems court administrators might confront with composing and maintaining juries, especially during sequestration and notorious trials.

The chapter concludes with a case study.

## Defining Judicial Administration

The purpose of judicial independence is to mitigate arbitrariness in judging. But what is the purpose of **judicial administration?** That is more difficult to define. Consequently, as Russell Wheeler noted, "many court administrators today find themselves under the inevitable strain of not knowing for certain what their purpose is."[2]

Most works on judicial administration point to Roscoe Pound as the founder of the study of judicial administration because of his 1906 essay, "The Causes of Popular Dissatisfaction with Administration of Justice." However, one should properly regard as just as much a founding document a major essay by Woodrow Wilson written 19 years earlier (in 1887), entitled "The Study of Administration." Wilson stressed that the vocation of administration was a noble calling, and not a task for which every person was competent.[3] He emphasized that policy and administration are two different matters and, with great foresight, wrote that judges were responsible for judging and "establishing fundamental court policy," and that a third task was for a "trained executive officer, working under the chief judge or presiding judge, [to] relieve judges generally [of] the function of handling the numerous business and administrative affairs of the courts."[4] Courts have *not* always regarded administration as a noble calling, but they have always defended the distinction Wilson drew between policy and administration.[5]

Wilson's essay certainly gives intellectual respectability to the field of administration. However, it also poses two troubling problems. First, although it may be accurate in the abstract to state that a wall exists between administration and policy, almost every administrator and policymaker knows, as Wheeler phrased it, that "the wall is full of many gaps and is easily scaled."[6] Policy decisions inevitably intertwine with administrative decisions. Second, trying to honor this policy–administration dichotomy would leave the administrator adrift when confronted with inevitable policy decisions. For example, today's court administrator must often set policy for dealing with such issues as celebrity cases, evidence, case scheduling, and the use of cameras in the courtroom—the kinds of issues discussed here and in Chapter 9.

The difficulty of defining judicial administration became obvious during the 1970s, when it nevertheless became an attractive vocation. Various people and commissions tried to define it but seemed capable only of listing the duties of the office. For example, the National Advisory Commission on Criminal Justice Standards and Goals stated in 1973 that "the basic purpose of court administration is to relieve judges of some administrative chores and to help them perform those they retain."[7] Furthermore, in 1974, the American Bar Association specified a variety of functions for the court administrator to perform "under the authority of the judicial council and the supervision of the chief justice."[8]

The problem of definition continued into the 1980s; one law professor who had conducted a large amount of research in the field believed in 1986 that the safest approach was "not ... to attempt a definition" but simply "to accept that it is a sub-branch of administration—more precisely of public administration."[9]

To assist in this dilemma and provide more clarity, a good working definition of judicial administration was advanced by Russell Wheeler and Howard Whitcomb; this definition allows an analysis from a variety of perspectives: "The direction of and influences on the activities of those who are expected to contribute to just and efficient case processing—except legal doctrinal considerations, insofar as they dispose of the particular factual and legal claims presented in a case."[10] This definition also separates the judicial and nonjudicial functions of the court and implies that a *set* of people share a role norm and that judicial administration constitutes *all* of the factors that direct and influence those people.[11]

Notably, however, the term **court administration** might be conceived of loosely as the specific activities of those persons who are organizationally responsible for manipulating these various judicial administration directions and influences.[12] This term is more commonly used in this chapter because I focus on the development of the role and functions of the *individual trial court administrator*. This will become clearer as the chapter unfolds and the judge's and court administrator's relationship is discussed.

# The Jurists

## *Those Who Would Be Judges: Methods of Selection*

To a large extent, the quality of justice Americans receive depends on the quality of the judges who dispense it. Many factors have a bearing on the quality of judicial personnel: salary, length of term, prestige, independence, and personal satisfaction with the job. The most important factor considered by court reformers is judicial selection.[13]

A variety of methods are used to select judges: partisan elections, nonpartisan elections, merit selection, or appointment. Figure 8.1 depicts regional patterns in the methods of judicial selection. It shows that partisan elections are concentrated in the South, nonpartisan elections in the West and upper Midwest, legislative elections and executive appointments in the East, and merit selection west of the Mississippi River. How selection is conducted determines who becomes a judge.[14]

| Partisan Election | Nonpartisan Election | Merit | Appointment |
| --- | --- | --- | --- |
| Alabama | California | Alaska | Maine (G) |
| Arkansas | Florida | Arizona | New Hampshire (G) |
| Illinois | Georgia | Colorado | New Jersey (G) |
| Indiana | Idaho | Connecticut | Rhode Island (G) |
| Louisiana | Kentucky | Delaware | South Carolina (L) |
| Mississippi | Michigan | District of Columbia | Virginia (L) |
| Missouri* | Minnesota | Hawaii | |
| New York | Montana | Iowa | |
| North Carolina | Nevada | Kansas | |
| Pennsylvania | North Dakota | Maryland | |
| Tennessee | Ohio | Massachusetts | |
| Texas | Oklahoma | Nebraska | |
| West Virginia | Oregon | New Mexico | |
| | South Dakota | Utah | |
| | Washington | Vermont | |
| | Wisconsin | Wyoming | |

L = Legislative appointment; g = Gubernatorial appointment
*Partisan election in nonmetropolitan circuits.

**Figure 8.1**

Initial selection of state judges (trial courts of general jurisdiction). *Source:* American Judicature Society, *Judicial Selection in the United States: A Compendium of Provisions,* 2nd ed. (Chicago: American Judicature Society, 1993).

Following is a discussion of the primary methods of judicial selection (only three states use the **executive appointment** method, whereby a vacancy is filled by the governor). In some states, judges are selected using **partisan elections** (the nominee's party is listed on the ballot). In other states, judges are selected using **nonpartisan elections** (no party affiliations are listed on the ballot). Nevertheless, even in these elections, partisan influences are often present: Judicial candidates are endorsed or nominated by parties, receive party support during campaigns, and are identified with party labels. In either case, although campaigns for judgeships are normally low key and low visibility, in recent years some contests—particularly for state supreme court seats—have been contentious and costly election battles, involving millions of dollars.

The general lack of information about judges and the low levels of voter interest, however, give incumbent judges important advantages in running for reelection. The prestigious title of "judge" is often listed on the ballot in front of the judge's name or on political signs and billboards. Few sitting judges are even opposed for reelection.[15]

**Merit selection** has been favored by court reformers wanting to "remove the courts from politics!" They point to three problems with popular elections of judges: (1) Elections fail to encourage the ablest lawyers to seek judicial posts and discourage qualified persons who want to avoid the rigors (if not the ordeal) of a campaign; (2) elections may provide an incentive for judges to decide cases in a popular manner; and (3) the elective system is a contest in which the electorate is likely to be uninformed about the merits of the candidates. To solve these problems, reformers advocate merit selection, also known as the Missouri Bar Plan. Thirty-four states and the District of Columbia use the merit system, and a number of other states have considered it. Merit selection involves the creation of a nominating commission whenever a vacancy occurs for any reason; the commission is composed of lawyers and laypersons; this group suggests a list of qualified nominees (usually three) to the governor, who chooses one person as judge. After serving a period on the bench, the new judge stands uncontested before the voters. The sole question on the ballot is, "Should Judge X be retained in office?" If the incumbent wins a majority of the votes, then he or she earns a full term of office, and each subsequent term is secured through another uncontested "retention ballot." Most judges are returned to office by a healthy margin.[16]

The question is often raised as to which method is best for choosing judges. A key criterion is whether one system produces better judges than the others. In short, methods of judicial selection are not related to judges' personal characteristics. No evidence exists that one selection system produces better judges than another system.[17]

## Benefits and Problems

Judges enjoy several distinct benefits of office, including life terms for federal positions and in some states. Ascending to the bench can be the capstone of a successful legal career for a lawyer, even though a judge's salary can be less than that of a lawyer in private practice. Judges certainly warrant a high degree of respect and prestige as well; from arrest to final disposition, the accused face judges at every juncture involving important decisions about their future: bail, pretrial motions, evidence presentation, trial, punishment.

Although it would seem that judges are the primary decision makers in the court, such is not always the case. Judges often accept recommendations from others who are more familiar with the case—for example, bail recommendations from prosecutors, plea agreements struck by prosecuting and defense counsels, and sentence recommendations from the probation officer. These kinds of input are frequently accepted by judges in the kind of informal courtroom network that exists. Although judges run the court, if they deviate from the consensus of the courtroom work group, they may be sanctioned: Attorneys can make court dockets go awry by requesting continuances or by not having witnesses appear on time.

Other problems can await a new jurist-elect or appointee. Judges who are new to the bench commonly face three general problems:

1. *Mastering the breadth of law they must know and apply.* New judges would be wise, at least early in their career, to depend on other court staff, lawyers who appear before them, and experienced judges for invaluable information on procedural and substantive aspects of the law and local court procedures. Through informal discussions and formal meetings, judges learn how to deal with common problems. Judicial training schools and seminars have also been developed to ease the transition into the judiciary. For example, the National Judicial College (NJC), located on the campus of the University of Reno, Nevada, is a full-time institution offering nearly 70 educational sessions per year—including a number that are offered on the Web as well as in 10 cities across the country—for more than 3,300 state judges, including judges from around the world (see Exhibit 8.1).

---

**EXHIBIT 8.1**
**Judges Must Train to Take the Bench**

At the National Judicial College (NJC) in Reno, Nevada, classroom bells—not gavels and bailiffs—rule the day. And the underlying message rings loud: Wearing a black robe alone does not a judge make. In times when the legal profession and the courts are coming under increased scrutiny and public criticism, the weight of judicial robes can be heavy.

At the judicial college, the goal is not only to coach lawyers on how to be judges, but to teach veteran judges how to be better arbiters of justice. For many lawyers, the move to the other side of the bench is an awesome transition. "Judges aren't born judges," said U.S. Supreme Court Justice Sandra Day O'Connor, who attended the NJC on her election as an

Arizona Superior Court judge in 1974. She recalled her anxieties the first time she assumed the bench: "It was frightening, really. There was so much to think about and to learn." Justice Anthony M. Kennedy, who is on the judicial college's faculty, described the college as

> an institutional reminder of the very basic proposition that an independent judiciary is essential in any society that is going to be based on the rule of law. Judicial independence cannot exist unless you have skilled, dedicated, and principled judges. This leads to so many different areas—judicial demeanor, how to control a courtroom, basic rules of civility, how to control attorneys. These are difficult skills for judges to learn. They're not something judges innately have. Judges have to acquire these skills.

Founded in 1963, the college put on its first course the following year in Boulder, Colorado. It is the only full-time institution in the country that provides judicial training primarily for state judges. It is affiliated with the American Bar Association, which pays about 10 percent of the college's annual budget. Other money comes from an endowment fund, donations, and program tuition and fees. Regular curriculum includes courses on courtroom technology; dealing with jurors; courtroom disruptions; domestic violence; managing complex cases; death penalty issues; traffic cases; ethics; mediation; family law; forensic, medical, and scientific evidence; and opinion writing.

As legal issues become increasingly complex and courts become overloaded with cases, judicial training becomes more critical. As stated by Joseph R. Weisberger, chief justice of the Rhode Island Supreme Court and an NJC instructor for 30 years, "It is the judiciary that transforms constitutional rights and liberties from a piece of parchment and printed words into living, breathing reality."

*Sources*: The National Judicial College 2005 Course Catalog; information also taken from Sandra Chereb, Associated Press, "Judges Must Train to Take the Bench," *Reno Gazette-Journal*, May 28, 1996, pp. 1B, 5B. Used with permission.

2. *Administering the court and the docket while supervising court staff.* One of the most frustrating aspects of being a judge is the heavy caseload and corresponding administrative problems. Instead of having time to reflect on challenging legal questions or to consider the proper sentence for a convicted felon, trial judges must move cases. They can seldom act like a judge in the "grand tradition." As Abraham Blumberg noted several years ago, the working judge must be politician, administrator, bureaucrat, and lawyer in order to cope with the crushing calendar of cases.[18] Judges are required to be competent administrators, a fact of judicial life that comes as a surprise to many new judges. One survey of 30 federal judges found that 23 (77 percent) acknowledged having major administrative difficulties on first assuming the bench. Half complained of heavy caseloads, stating that their judgeship had accumulated backlogs and that other adverse conditions compounded the problem. A federal judge maintained that it takes about 4 years to "get a full feel of a docket."[19]

The NJC offers several courses that can assist judges in better administering their courts. The following 1-week courses are available:

- Court Management for Judges and Court Administrators (covering topics such as managing human resources, conflict resolution, team building, budgeting, data collection, public relations)
- Management Skills for Presiding Judges
- Judges as Change Agents: Problem Solving Courts

The National Center for State Courts in Williamsburg, Virginia, also has a program designed specifically for management and leadership in the courts: the Institute for Court Management's **Court Executive Development Program (CEDP).**[20]

3. *Coping with the psychological discomfort that accompanies the new position.* Most trial judges experience psychological discomfort on assuming the bench. Seventy-seven percent of new federal judges acknowledged having psychological problems in at least one of five areas: maintaining a judicial bearing both on and off the bench, the loneliness of the judicial office, sentencing criminals, forgetting the adversary role, and local pressure. One aspect of the judicial role is that of assuming a proper mien, or "learning to act like a judge." One judge remembers his first day in court: "I'll never forget going into my courtroom for the first time with the robes and all, and the crier tells everyone to rise. You sit down and realize that it's all different, that everyone is looking at you and you're supposed to do something."[21] Like police officers and probation and parole workers, judges complain that they "can't go to the places you used to. You always have to be careful about what you talk about. When you go to a party, you have to be careful not to drink too much so you won't make a fool of yourself."[22] And the position can be a lonely one:

> "After you become a … judge some people tend to avoid you. For instance, you lose all your lawyer friends and generally have to begin to make new friends. I guess the lawyers are afraid that they will some day have a case before you and it would be awkward for them if they were on too close terms with you.[23]

Judges frequently describe sentencing criminals as the most difficult aspect of their job: "This is the hardest part of being a judge. You see so many pathetic people and you're never sure of what is a right or a fair sentence."[24]

## Good Judging and Courtroom Civility

What traits make for "good judging?" Obviously, judges should treat each case and all parties before them in court with absolute impartiality and dignity while providing leadership as the steward of their organization in all of the **court management** areas described in the following section. In addition to those official duties, however, other issues and suggestions have been put forth.

Hostility toward lawyers carried over from England, and the clerk was the intermediary between the litigants and the justice of the peace. During the late seventeenth century, American courts became more structured and formalized. Books were available that imposed English court practices in the colonies, and clerks, judges, and attorneys were provided proper forms that had to be used. In fact, some of the forms used by clerks 200 years ago are similar to those in use today.[40]

Clerks have traditionally competed with judges for control over local judicial administration. In fact, one study found that the majority (58.9 percent) of elected clerks perceived themselves as colleagues and equal with the judges.[41] Court clerks have not as a rule been identified with effective management, however:

> Generally they are conservative in nature and reflect the attitudes and culture of the community. Their parochial backgrounds, coupled with their conservative orientation, in part accounts for this resistance to change. This resistance often compels judicial systems to retain archaic procedures and managerial techniques.[42]

## *The Forgotten Majority: Clerks in Rural Courts*

Much of the United States is rural in nature. Nearly four fifths of its courts exist in rural counties. A *rural court* is any trial court of general jurisdiction having fewer than two full-time judges authorized.[43] An enormous difference in court administration exists between urban courts and rural courts.

The small scale of rural courts affects the type of person who serves as clerk. Urban courts pay high salaries to obtain specially trained and educated court administrators, but rural clerks often have less training and education and receive lower salaries.[44]

Although ultimately accountable for caseflow management, the clerk actually has little power to control the calendar. In most rural courts, lawyers actually review the proposed calendar before it is final. Clerks in rural courts are challenged by conditions such as a single court reporter who is responsible for courtroom work in a large area, the lack of a local crime laboratory, the need to bring expert witnesses from outside, and the limited availability of the trial judge, often only a few days each month.

Other duties of rural court clerks include keeping tradition by maintaining records concerning the land grants of the town ancestors and the naturalization of the people who broke the sod and of births, deaths, marriages, and divorces in the community.

# Trained Court Administrators

## *Development and Training*

One of the most recent and innovative approaches to solving the courts' management problems has been the creation of the position of court administrator. This relatively new criminal justice position began to develop in earnest during the 1960s; since that time, the number of practicing trial court administrators has increased tenfold and continues to expand. Actually, this concept has its roots in early England, where, historically, judges have abstained from any involvement in court administration. This fact has not been lost on contemporary court administrators and proponents of this occupation: "It seems to be a very valuable characteristic of the English system that the judges expect to *judge* when they are in the courthouse ... it does not allow time for administrative distractions."[45]

The development of the position of court administrator has been sporadic. In the early 1960s, probably only 30 people in the United States worked as court administrators. By 1970, there were fewer than 50 such specially trained employees.[46] Estimates differ concerning the expansion of the administrator's role during the 1980s. One expert maintained that by 1982 between 2,000 and 3,000 people were in the ranks of court managers;[47] another argued that there were only about 500.[48] At any rate, most agree that more than twice as many of these positions were created between 1970 and 1980 than in the preceding six decades.[49]

By the 1980s every state had established a statewide court administrator, normally reporting to the state supreme court or the chief justice of the state supreme court. The three primary functions of state court administrators are preparing annual reports summarizing caseload data, preparing budgets, and troubleshooting.[50]

Today, few, if any, metropolitan areas are without full-time court administrators[51] (the court organization chart shown in Chapter 7 demonstrates the breadth of responsibilities held by court administrators). An underlying premise and justification for this role is that by having a trained person performing the tasks of court management, judges are left free to do what they do best: decide cases. Indeed, since the first trial court administrative positions began to appear, "there was little doubt or confusion about their exact purpose."[52] (As will be seen later, however, there has been doubt and confusion concerning their proper role and functions.)

As court reformers have called for better-trained specialists (as opposed to political appointees) for administering court processes, the qualifications for this position have come under debate. The creation of the Institute for Court Management in 1970 was a landmark in the training for this role, legitimizing its standing in the legal profession. Many judges, however, still believe that a law degree is essential, whereas others prefer a background in business administration. There will probably never be total agreement concerning the skills and background necessary for this position, but the kind of specialized training that is offered by the institute and a few graduate programs in judicial administration across the country would seem ideal.

Court administrators are trained specifically to provide the courts with the expertise and talent they have historically lacked. This point was powerfully made by Bernadine Meyer:

> Management—like law—is a profession today. Few judges or lawyers with severe chest pains would attempt to treat themselves. Congested dockets and long delays

are symptoms that court systems need the help of professionals. Those professionals are managers. If court administration is to be effective, judicial recognition that managerial skill and knowledge are necessary to efficient performance is vital.[53]

## *General Duties*

Trial court administrators generally perform six major duties:

1. *Reports.* Administrators have primary responsibility for the preparation and submission to the judges of periodic reports on the activities and state of business of the court.
2. *Personnel administration.* Court administrators serve as personnel officers for the court's nonjudicial personnel.
3. *Research and evaluation.* This function is to improve court business methods.
4. *Equipment management.* Administrators are engaged in procurement, allocation, inventory control, and replacement of furniture and equipment.
5. *Preparation of court budget.*
6. *Training coordination.* Court administrators provide training for nonjudicial personnel.[54]

Other duties that are assumed by the trained court administrator include jury management, case flow or calendar management, public information, and management of automated data processing.[55]

# How Judges Evaluate Administrators

Like other administrative mortals, judges and court administrators often see their world through rose-colored glasses. As one Arizona judge observed,

> Judges and court administrators are not likely to view themselves in a negative light. As part of an organization that creates a certain amount of respect and awe for itself, it is not surprising that the [judge] and the court administrator may believe that they are better than they actually are. As a result, their top members frequently believe that the awe displayed toward them is intrinsic to their person, and not to the office.[56]

This view of the world can be an impediment to objective assessment and clear decision making. Still, the judge needs to be able to determine whether his or her court administrator is performing competently and effectively.

According to John Greacen,[57] judges follow several basic strategies in determining the quality of work performed by their administrators:

1. *The judge looks for indications of good management.* A well-managed organization will have a number of plans and procedures in place, including personnel policies, recruitment and selection procedures, an orientation program for new employees, performance evaluation procedures, a discipline

and grievance process, case management policies, financial controls, and other administrative policies (such as for facilities and records management).

2. *The judge should be getting regular information.* Critically important reports and data on the court's performance, plans, activities, and accomplishments should be provided to the judge on a routine basis. The judge should be notified of the number of case filings, terminations, and pending cases; financial information; staff performance; long- and short-range plans; and other statistical data.

3. *Judges should be watching carefully.* Judges observe a lot of the staff's activities. They alone can make an assessment of their administrator's strengths and weaknesses. How does the administrator respond to problems and crises? Does he or she show initiative?

4. *Judges must often ask others about the performance of the administrator.* This includes soliciting input from lawyers, other judges, and other court staff members.

# Jury Administration

The jury system has been in the forefront of the public's mind in recent years, primarily as a result of the jury nullification concept (the right of juries to nullify or refuse to apply law in criminal cases despite facts that leave no reasonable doubt that the law was violated).[58] Here, however, I focus on the responsibilities of the court administrator in ensuring that a jury is properly composed and sustained during trials. Elements of the jury system that involve court administration include jury selection, sequestration, comfort, and notorious cases.

Regarding jury selection, the court administrator is responsible for compilation of a master jury list; this is a large pool of potential jurors compiled from voter registration, driver's license, or utility customer or telephone customer lists to produce a representative cross section of the community. From that master list, a randomly selected smaller venire (or jury pool) is drawn; a summons is mailed out to citizens, asking them to appear at the courthouse for jury duty. There, they will be asked questions and either retained or removed as jury members.

Here is where juror comfort enters in. Unfortunately, many jurors experience great frustration in the process, being made to wait long hours, possibly in uncomfortable physical surroundings, while receiving minimal compensation and generally being inconvenienced. Courts in all states now have a juror call-in system, enabling jurors to dial a phone number to learn whether their attendance is needed on a particular day; in addition, many jurisdictions have reduced the number of days a juror remains in the pool.

Some trials involving extensive media coverage require jury sequestration—jurors remain in virtual quarantine, sometimes for many weeks, and are compelled to live in a hotel together. This can be a trying experience for jurors and certainly poses great logistical problems for court administrators. The court administrator must also consider security issues (protecting the jury from outside interference and providing for conjugal visits, room searches, transportation, and so on) as well as jurors' personal needs (such as entertainment and medical supplies).[59]

The existence of notorious cases—those involving celebrities or particularly egregious crimes—has always been a part of, and caused problems in, courtrooms: the trials of O. J. Simpson, Susan Smith, Mike Tyson, William Kennedy Smith, Oliver North, Marion Barry, Bernhard Goetz, John Gotti, Manuel Noriega, and the police officers who were tried for assaulting Rodney King were clearly "notorious."[60] Court administrators and other court staff members must deal with media requests; courtroom and courthouse logistics for handling crowds, the media, and security; and the management of the court's docket of other cases. A notorious trial may also require that a larger courtroom be used and many attorneys accommodated.[61] A number of other issues must be considered: Are identification and press passes and entry screening devices needed? Do purses, briefcases, and other such items need to be searched? Perhaps the most important task in managing notorious cases is communication with the media, often by setting aside a certain time when reporters may discuss the case.[62]

# CASE STUDY

The following case study will help the reader to consider some of this chapter's materials, specifically concerns about court budgeting and operations.

## The Court Administrator and the Prudent Police Chief

You are the court administrator in a system that has the following procedure for handling traffic matters:

1. All persons who are given a traffic citation are to appear in court at 9:00 A.M. on either Monday or Wednesday within 2 weeks of their citation date. They are given a specific date to appear.

2. Persons cited are not required to appear, either at the return date or at trial; they have the option of staying home and simply forfeiting their bond, which has been posted in advance of their initial appearance.

3. At the initial appearance, the arresting agency is represented by a court officer who has previously filed copies of all the citations with the clerk of the court.

4. The clerk, prior to the return date on the citation, prepares a file for each citation.

5. The clerk calls each case, and those persons appearing are requested by the court to enter a plea; if the plea is "not guilty," the matter is set for trial at a future date.

6. One case is scheduled per hour. On the trial date, the prosecutor and arresting officer are required to appear, ready for trial.

7. Statistics show that 75 percent of those persons pleading not guilty in this jurisdiction fail to appear for trial.

The chief of police in the court's jurisdiction is concerned about overtime for officers. He communicates with you, the court administrator, about this concern and explains that all police officers who appear in court for trial are entitled to the minimum 2 hours of overtime when they are not appearing during their regular shift. He views this as a tremendous and unnecessary expense to the city, in view of the fact that most of the officers are not needed because the defendants do not appear. He recognizes that defendants have a right to post bond under the law and simply forfeit it at the initial appearance or on the trial date. He is interested, however, in devising some system to save the city the tremendous cost for all the officers' overtime. He explains that other municipalities are faced with similar problems.

# Questions for Discussion

1. What kind of a system would you propose to address the problem, and how would you go about accomplishing this end? In creating a modified system, you are to work within the existing law, with no changes in statutes or ordinances.

2. After you have completed designing a system and explaining how you would go about obtaining the cooperation of the judges, prosecutors, clerk's office, and other law enforcement agencies as well as that of the defense bar, discuss any proposed changes in the law you think might improve the system further.

3. How would you go about accomplishing other *significant* changes for improvement in the procedures and operation of this system? Consider the creation of an ongoing mechanism or committee that would propose, discuss, adopt, and carry out changes for the benefit of the system as a whole.

# Summary

Today, the functions of judges and court administrators are quite different from those seen in earlier times, and involve policymaking as well. It is clear that, as one New York judge put it,

> The "grand tradition" judge, the aloof brooding charismatic figure in the Old Testament tradition, is hardly a real figure. The reality is the working judge who must be politician, administrator, bureaucrat, and lawyer in order to cope with a crushing calendar of cases.[63]

In addition, the nonlawyers who help judges to run the courts, judicial administrators, now possess a basic body of practical knowledge, a rudimentary theoretical perspective, and a concern for professional ethics.

It was also shown that several obstacles still exist in the total acceptance of court administration as an integral part of the judiciary. Court administration in many ways is still a developing field. Still, it has come far from its roots and is evolving into a bona fide element of the American justice system.

# Questions for Review

1. Why is the term *judicial administration* multifaceted? What would be a good working definition for this term? For *court administration*?

2. How might judges and court administrators receive training for their roles?

3. How have court clerks traditionally assumed and performed the role of court administrator? What are some of the unique problems of being a court clerk in a rural area?

4. Why is civility so important for the appearance of justice and propriety in our courts?

5. What criteria may be employed by judges to evaluate the effectiveness of their administrators?

6. What are the court administrator's duties in general? What issues must the court administrator address in composing or sequestering a jury? For notorious cases?

# Notes

1. Robert C. Harrall, "In Defense of Court Managers: The Critics Misconceive Our Role," *Court Management Journal* **14** (1982):52.

2. Russell Wheeler, *Judicial Administration: Its Relation to Judicial Independence* (Williamsburg, Va.: National Center for State Courts, 1988), p. 19.

3. Woodrow Wilson, "The Study of Administration," *Political Science Quarterly* **2** (1887):197; reprinted in *Political Science Quarterly* **56** (1941):481.

4. Quoted in Paul Nejelski and Russell Wheeler, Wingspread Conference on Contemporary and Future Issues in the Field of Court Management 4 (1980).

5. Wheeler, *Judicial Administration,* p. 21.

6. Ibid., p. 22.

7. National Advisory Commission on Criminal Justice Standards and Goals, *Courts* (Washington, D.C.: U.S. Government Printing Office, 1973), p. 171.

8. American Bar Association, *Standards on Court Organization, Standard 1.41* (1974).

9. Ian R. Scott, "Procedural Law and Judicial Administration," *Justice System Journal* **12** (1987):67–68.

10. Russell R. Wheeler and Howard R. Whitcomb, *Judicial Administration: Text and Readings* (Upper Saddle River, N.J.: Prentice Hall, 1977), p. 8.

11. Ibid.

12. Ibid., p. 9.

13. David W. Neubauer, *America's Courts and the Criminal Justice System,* 8th ed. (Belmont, Calif.: Wadsworth, 2005), p. 180.

14. Barbara Luck Graham, "Do Judicial Selection Systems Matter? A Study of Black Representation on State Courts," *American Politics Quarterly* **18** (1990):316–336.

15. Neubauer, *America's Courts and the Criminal Justice System,* pp. 176–178.

16. Ibid., p. 178.

17. Craig Emmert and Henry Glick, "The Selection of State Supreme Court Justices," *American Politics Quarterly* **16** (1988):445–465.

18. Abraham Blumberg, *Criminal Justice* (Chicago: Quadrangle Books, 1967).

19. Wheeler and Whitcomb, *Judicial Administration,* p. 370

20. National Center for State Courts Web page, http://www.ncsconline.org. (accessed September 16, 2005).

21. Wheeler and Whitcomb, *Judicial Administration,* p. 372.

22. Ibid.

23. Ibid.

24. Ibid., p. 373.

25. William A. Batlitch, "Reflections on the Art and Craft of Judging," *The Judges Journal* **43**(4) (Fall 2003):7-8.

26. Charles E. Patterson, "The Good Judge: A Trial Lawyer's Perspective," *The Judges Journal* **43**(4) (Fall 2003):14-15.

27. See, for example, Allen K. Harris, "The Professionalism Crisis—The 'Z' Words and Other Rambo Tactics: The Conference of Chief Justices' Solution," 53 S.C. L. Rev. 549, 589 (2002).

28. In re First City Bancorp of Tex., Inc., 282 F.3d 864 (5th Cir. 2002).

29. *People v. Williamson,* 172 Cal. App. 3d 737, 749 (1985).

30. *Landry v. State,* 620 So. 2d 1099, 1102-03 (Fla. Dist. Ct. App. 1993).

31. *Gaddy v. Cirbo,* 293 P.2d (Colo. 1956), at 962.

32. Marla N. Greenstein, "The Craft of Ethics," *The Judges Journal* **43**(4) (Fall 2003):17-18.

33. Ty Tasker, "Sticks and Stones: Judicial Handling of Invective in Advocacy," *The Judges Journal* **43**(4) (Fall 2003):17-18.

34. Roscoe Pound, "Principles and Outlines of a Modern Unified Court Organization," *Journal of the American Judicature Society* **23** (April 1940):229.

35. See, for example, the Missouri Constitution, Article V, Sec. 15, paragraph 3.

36. Forest Hanna, "Delineating the Role of the Presiding Judge," *State Court Journal* **10** (Spring 1986):17-22.

37. David W. Neubauer, *America's Courts and the Criminal Justice System,* 7th ed. (Belmont, Calif.: Wadsworth), 2002, p. 117.

38. Robert A. Wenke, "The Administrator in the Court," *Court Management Journal* **14** (1982):17-18, 29.

39. Marc Gertz, "Influence in the Court Systems: The Clerk as Interface," *Justice System Journal* **2** (1977):30-37.

40. Robert B. Revere, "The Court Clerk in Early American History," *Court Management Journal* **10** (1978):12-13.

41. G. Larry Mays and William Taggart, "Court Clerks, Court Administrators, and Judges: Conflict in Managing the Courts," *Journal of Criminal Justice* **14** (1986):1-7.

42. Larry Berkson, "Delay and Congestion in State Systems: An Overview," in Larry Berkson, Steven Hays, and Susan Carbon (eds.), *Managing the State Courts: Text and Readings* (St. Paul, Minn.: West, 1977), p. 164.

43. Kathryn L. Fahnestock and Maurice D. Geiger, "Rural Courts: The Neglected Majority," *Court Management Journal* **14** (1982):4-10.

44. Ibid., pp. 6, 8.

45. Ernest C. Friesen and I. R. Scott, *English Criminal Justice* (Birmingham, England: University of Birmingham Institute of Judicial Administration, 1977), p. 12.

46. Harvey E. Solomon, "The Training of Court Managers," in Charles R. Swanson and Susette M. Talarico (eds.), *Court Administration: Issues and Responses* (Athens, Ga.: University of Georgia, 1987), pp. 15-20.

47. Ernest C. Friesen, "Court Managers: Magnificently Successful or Merely Surviving?" *Court Management Journal* **14** (1982):21.

48. Solomon, "The Training of Court Managers," p. 16.

49. Harrall, "In Defense of Court Managers," p. 51.

50. Neubauer, *America's Courts and the Criminal Justice System,* p. 117.

51. Ibid.

52. Geoffrey A. Mort and Michael D. Hall, "The Trial Court Administrator: Court Executive or Administrative Aide?" *Court Management Journal* **12** (1980):12-16, 30.

53. Bernadine Meyer, "Court Administration: The Newest Profession," *Duquesne Law Review* **10** (Winter 1971):220-235.

54. Mort and Hall, "The Trial Court Administrator," p. 15.

55. Ibid.

56. James Duke Cameron, Isaiah M. Zimmerman, and Mary Susan Downing, "The Chief Justice and the Court Administrator: The Evolving Relationship," 113 *Federal Rules Decisions* 443 (1987).

57. Greacen, "Has Your Court Administrator Retired?," p. 18.

58. Darryl Brown, "Jury Nullification Within the Rule of Law," *Minnesota Law Review* **81** (1997):1149-1200.

59. Timothy R. Murphy, Genevra Kay Loveland, and G. Thomas Munsterman, *A Manual for Managing Notorious Cases* (Washington, D.C.: National Center for State Courts, 1992), pp. 4-6. See also Timothy R. Murphy, Paul L. Hannaford, and Kay Genevra, *Managing Notorious Trials* (Williamsburg, Va.: National Center for State Courts, 1998).

60. Murphy, Loveland, and Munsterman, *A Manual for Managing Notorious Cases,* pp. 53, 73.

61. Ibid., p. 23.

62. Ibid., pp. 27-30.

63. Blumberg, *Criminal Justice*, p. 120.

# Chapter 9

# Court Issues
# and Practices

## Key Terms and Concepts

Case delay

Crime control model

Courthouse violence

Due process model

Exclusionary rule

Gender bias

Individual calendar system

Jury science

Master calendar system

Nontargeted violence

Plea bargaining

Problem-solving courts

Targeted violence

Threat assessment

Trying juveniles as adults

## Learning Objectives

As a result of reading this chapter, the student will:

- understand the differences between the due process and crime control models
- have a firm grasp of the growing movement for problem-solving courts
- be knowledgeable about courthouse violence, both actual and potential, and what must be done to assess and deal with threats to court actors
- be familiar with the problems and consequences of, and solutions to, trial delays
- understand the two systems used in scheduling cases
- be familiar with such issues as gender bias, juveniles being tried as adults, the exclusionary rule, the use of cameras in the courtroom, and plea bargaining
- have an understanding of some of the issues facing the courts in the future

*Justice is such a fine thing that we cannot pay too dearly for it.*
—Alain Rene LeSage

# Introduction

In reality, many of the topics discussed previously, primarily in Chapter 7—such as reforming court organization and unification, use of the adversary system, and alternative dispute resolution—could have been included in this chapter. They are challenging areas. This chapter, however, examines additional contemporary issues and practices.

It is helpful for court administrators to view court issues and practices through the lenses of the crime control and due process models of criminal justice; these models represent what might be termed the "hard-line" and the "soft-line" approaches toward offenders and how the justice system should deal with them. Therefore, the chapter begins with an overview of those opposing models. Then, because history has shown that our courts—like the rest of our society—can be mean and brutish places, I review courthouse violence, its basic forms, and how to perform a threat assessment. Next I discuss how problem-solving courts are expanding and using their authority and innovative techniques to forge new responses to chronic social, human, and legal problems. Then I examine the dilemma of delay (including its consequences, suggested solutions, and two systems of scheduling cases), and then review the issues of gender bias, juveniles being tried as adults, the exclusionary rule, use of cameras during trial, and plea bargaining from the courts' point of view.

After a brief discussion of jury science, the chapter concludes with a consideration of future issues in the courts and three case studies.

# Justice from the Due Process and Crime Control Perspectives

As noted earlier, several of the issues and practices discussed later in this chapter will be viewed in terms of the crime control and due process models of criminal justice. The main points of these two philosophies are presented here.

In 1968, Herbert Packer[1] presented these two now-classic, competing models, which describe how criminal cases are processed. The **due process model** holds that defendants should be presumed innocent, that the courts' first priority is protecting suspects' rights, and that granting too much freedom to law enforcement officials will result in the loss of freedom and civil liberties for all Americans. Therefore, each court case must involve formal fact finding to uncover mistakes by the police and prosecutors. This view also stresses that crime is not a result of individual moral failure, but is the result of social influences (such as unemployment, racial discrimination, and other factors that disadvantage the poor); thus, courts that do not follow this philosophy are fundamentally unfair to these defendants. Furthermore, rehabilitation will prevent further crime.

Standing in contrast is the **crime control model,** which views crime as a breakdown of individual responsibility and places the highest importance on repressing criminal conduct, thus protecting society. Those persons who are charged are presumed guilty, and the courts should not hinder effective enforcement of the laws; rather, legal loopholes should be eliminated and offenders swiftly punished. The police and prosecutors should have a high degree of discretion. Punishment will deter crime, so there must be speed and finality in the courts to ensure crime suppression.

# Courthouse Violence

- A man charged with the stabbing death of an 8-year-old boy in Virginia calmly rises from his seat during a pretrial hearing and attacks his attorney, knocking him unconscious.

- A young Ohio man sitting in the back of a courtroom shouts "You dead" and lunges at a teenager seated nearby; within seconds, the entire courtroom erupts into a wild brawl involving more than a dozen spectators and officers.
- A Pennsylvania courthouse is evacuated for 3 hours after a bomb threat is called into its switchboard.
- A courthouse janitor in Nebraska is shot to death at work by a man with whom he had scuffled earlier in the day; the man then walks through the courthouse, shooting at the doors of other offices before police arrive.[2]

These are but a few of many such incidents of **courthouse violence** that have occurred across the nation in recent years.  Today, mirroring the rest of society, our courts have become dangerous venues.

## *Types of Courthouse Violence*

There are two types of violence that can occur in courthouses.

- **Nontargeted violence** involves an individual who has no specific pre-existing intention of engaging in violence but who, either during, at the conclusion of, or sometime shortly after the court proceeding, becomes incensed and defiant at some procedure or outcome and acts out in the courtroom or public corridors. If this person also has a weapon, it might be used against the source of the grievance—a judge, attorney, witness, court employee, defendant or plaintiff, or bystander. If there are no judicial security screening devices or patrols on the premises, the person may proceed to attack people within the courthouse.
- **Targeted violence** involves an individual who expressly intends to engage in courthouse violence. These persons often simmer and stew for long periods of time, so there is often some delay in responding to real or perceived affronts and insults. During this time, these people may or may not make threats and often create plans to circumvent security measures. The deliberate focus is on the individuals or the judiciary itself.[3]

Of the two groups, the nontargeting group has been responsible for most of the violent incidents in our nation's courthouses. With proper security precautions, many of these acts can be prevented or thwarted. This is a daunting task, however. Each year nearly 100 million cases are filed in the nation's 18,000 lower courts (61 million cases) and its 2,000 major trial courts (31 million cases),[4] which are presided over by more than 11,000 judges and quasi-judicial officers (e.g., masters, magistrates).[5] Because each filed case is potentially contentious, violence is also a potential outcome.

Other disturbing behaviors can affect the courts' functions as well. For example, judges can be sent inappropriate communications containing threatening activity. Bombings of state and local government buildings have occurred as well (207 such incidents occurred between the early and mid-1990s).[6] Concerns about such acts of violence have spurred the implementation of enhanced security measures in many of our nation's courthouses, most of which have focused on the courts' physical environment, to detect weapons. Duress alarms and video surveillance cameras have been installed and separate prisoner, court staff, and public areas created. These measures, however, have failed to address a number of critical issues, such as how to prevent violent eruptions in courtrooms, how to identify those courts that are most susceptible to violent acts, and how to protect individuals who may be targeted for assault. Sheriff's personnel, who are most often charged with court security, must be well equipped to handle threats against judges and other judicial staff, particularly outside the courthouse. Sufficient resources are not available to provide these court actors with around-the-clock protection.[7]

## *Making a Threat Assessment*

A good beginning point for enhancing courthouse security is the **threat assessment** approach. A good threat assessment involves three principles:

1. Targeted violence is the end result of an understandable and often discernible process of thinking and acting. Acts of targeted violence are neither impulsive nor spontaneous. Ideas about mounting an attack usually develop over time; the subject engages in planning the attack, and might collect information about the target, the setting, or other related attacks. This suggests that many incidents of targeted violence may be preventable.

2. One must distinguish between making an expressed threat and posing a threat. Many people who make threats do not pose a serious risk of harm to a target; they may make idle threats for a variety of reasons. On the other hand, many who pose a serious risk of harm will not issue direct threats prior to an attack. Although all threats should be taken seriously, they are not the most reliable indicator of risk.

3. The risk for violence is the product of an interaction among the potential attacker, his or her current situation, the target, and the setting. One might reasonably examine the development and evolution of ideas concerning the attack, preparatory behaviors, and how the individual has dealt with what he or she felt to be unbearable stress in the past. Consideration of the subject's current situation may include an assessment of what stressful events are occurring in the subject's life, how he or she is responding, and how others in the subject's environment are responding to his or her stress and potential risk. Things to be considered include the subject's degree of familiarity with the target's work and lifestyle patterns, the target's vulnerability, and the target's sophistication about the need for caution.[8]

Clearly, at a minimum, all courts should employ certain security procedures, such as the following: On arrival at a courthouse, persons are required to pass through the security control point located at the front door (this control point is equipped much like a security control point at airports) and to pass purses, briefcases, or anything else they may be carrying through an x-ray machine.

They are also required to place any metal objects in the trays provided and then pass through the magnetometer (a device that indicates the presence of metal objects). If they are carrying anything that can be construed as a weapon, they can take it back to their vehicle or leave it with the security officer and pick the item up when they leave the court (and, of course, are subject to arrest if found to be carrying a weapon that is illegal to carry or possess by law). If they continue to set off the magnetometer after all items are removed, the security officer will pass a hand-wand around their person to determine what is continuing to set off the alarm.

# Problem-Solving Courts

## *"Therapeutic Justice," Not "McJustice"*

The decade of the 1990s served as a significant launching pad for court reform across the United States as judges and other court actors experimented with new ways to deliver justice: drug courts (discussed later) expanded into every state, and new domestic violence, mental health, and community courts began targeting different kinds of problems in different places, all with a desire to improve the results for victims, litigants, defendants, and communities.

Although **problem-solving courts** are still very much a work in progress, they share some common elements: They use their authority to forge new responses to chronic social, human, and legal problems, such as family dysfunction, addiction, delinquency, and domestic violence, that have proven resistant to conventional solutions.[9] Community courts, like those in New York, target misdemeanor "quality-of-life" crimes (e.g., prostitution, shoplifting, and low-level drug possession) and have offenders pay back the community by performing service functions. Similar stories can be told about the genesis and spread of domestic violence courts, mental health courts, and others.[10]

What has prompted such experiments? Several social and historical forces set the stage for these efforts:

- Breakdown and loss of respect among social and community institutions (such as families and organized religion) that have traditionally addressed social problems.
- A surge in the nation's incarcerated population, which forced policymakers to rethink their approach to crime.
- Trends emphasizing the accountability of public institutions, along with technological innovations (discussed in Chapter 17) that have improved analysis of court outcomes.
- Advances in the quality and availability of therapeutic interventions, particularly drug treatment programs.
- Shifts in public policies and priorities, such as the "broken windows" theory that says society must address low-level crimes to prevent more serious crimes later.

Perhaps the most important forces are rising caseloads and increasing frustration with the standard approach to case processing.[11]

With declining public confidence in the criminal justice system, judges bemoaning that their courts have become places of "McJustice" (a reference to the fast-food industry) and "plea bargaining mills," and attorneys taking a closer look at the roles they play and the outcomes they achieve, there have been calls for this new "therapeutic jurisprudence."[12]

Critics worry that defendants may be coerced into participating in these courts, and that judges have greater license to make rulings based on their personal views rather than on the law. Although these might be legitimate concerns, problem-solving courts continue to multiply. Indeed, the Conference of Chief Justices and the Conference of State Court Administrators passed a joint resolution to encourage the broad integration, in the future, "of the principles and methods employed in problem solving courts into the administration of justice."[13]

Problem-solving courts help to achieve tangible outcomes for victims, offenders, and society; they rely on the active use of judicial authority to change the behavior of litigants, with judges staying involved with each case long after adjudication. Although the verdict is still out on these courts, the results have been impressive; for example, drug court participants are more likely to complete mandated substance abuse treatment than those who seek help on a voluntary basis, and are less likely to recidivate as well.[14] Furthermore, studies have found that these first-generation courts reduced probation violation and dismissal rates in domestic violence cases, improved public safety (and confidence) in justice in communities harmed by crime, and are well worth pursuing.[15]

# In the Spotlight: Drug Courts

Drug courts are now proliferating: By the end of 2004, there were 1,212 drug courts operating in all 50 states and the District of Columbia; another 476 drug court programs were in the planning process. Drug court participants undergo long-term treatment and counseling, sanctions, incentives, and frequent court appearances. Successful completion of the program results in dismissal of charges, reduced or set-aside sentences, lesser penalties, or a combination of these. Most important, graduating participants gain the necessary tools to rebuild their lives. The drug court model includes the following key components:

- Incorporating drug testing into case processing
- Creating a nonadversarial relationship between the defendant and the court
- Identifying defendants in need of treatment and referring them to treatment as soon as possible after arrest
- Providing access to a continuum of treatment and rehabilitation services
- Monitoring abstinence through frequent, mandatory drug testing[16]

In addition to providing tremendous cost savings (incarceration of drug-using offenders costs between $20,000 and $50,000 per year versus $2,500 to $4,500 annually for a drug court offender), studies report drug court participants having a recidivism rate of 16.4 percent at 1 year after graduation and 27.5 percent at 2 years after graduation; this compares with recidivism rates of 43.5 percent and 58.6 percent, respectively, for drug offenders who were imprisoned. Drug court participants, whose drug use is substantially reduced while they are participating in the program, cite three reasons for their success: close supervision and encouragement by judges, intensive treatment, and on-going monitoring.[17]

# The Dilemma of Delay

## *"Justice Delayed..."*

There is no consensus as to how long is too long with respect to bringing a criminal case to trial, and the test is a balancing one with regard to the prosecutor's and defense attorney's conduct.[18] Still, a point at which Packer's models begin to diverge involves **case delay.** The crime control model inherently calls for swift justice to protect society by incarcerating offenders, whereas due process advocates call for a more thoughtful and careful approach.

The principle that "justice delayed is justice denied" says much about the long-standing goal of processing court cases with due dispatch. Charles Dickens condemned the practice of slow litigation in nineteenth-century England, and Shakespeare mentioned "the law's delay" in *Hamlet*. Delay in processing cases is one of the most long-standing problems of U.S. courts. The public often hears of cases that have languished on court dockets for years. This can only erode public confidence in the judicial process.[19] The overload in our bloated court system has been building for years, with the most immediate source of pressure for the courts being the intensifying drug war; with increasing drug arrests, backlogs are growing.

Case backlog and trial delay affect many of our country's courts. The magnitude of the backlog and the length of the delay vary greatly, however, depending on the court involved. It is best to view delay not as a problem but as a symptom of a problem.[20] Generally, the term *delay* suggests abnormal or unacceptable time lapses in the processing of cases. Yet some time is needed to prepare a case. What is a concern is *unnecessary* delay. However, there seems to be no agreed-on definition of what unnecessary delay is.

## *The Consequences*

The consequences of delay can be severe. It can jeopardize the values and guarantees inherent in our justice system. Delay deprives defendants of their Sixth Amendment right to a speedy trial. Lengthy pretrial incarceration pressures can cause a defendant to plead guilty.[21] In contrast, delay can strengthen a defendant's bargaining position; prosecutors are more apt to accept pleas to a lesser charge when dockets are crowded. Delays cause pretrial detainees to clog the jails, police officers to appear in court on numerous occasions, and attorneys to expend unproductive time appearing on the same case.

One contributing factor to court delay is the lack of incentive to process cases speedily. Although at least 10 states require cases to be dismissed and defendants to be released if they are denied a speedy trial,[22] the U.S. Supreme Court has refused to give the rather vague concept of a "speedy trial" any precise time frame.[23] The problem with time frames, however, is twofold: First, more complex cases legitimately take a long time to prepare; and second, these time limits may be waived due to congested court dockets. In sum, there is no legally binding mechanism that works.

## Suggested Solutions

The best-known legislation addressing the problem is the Speedy Trial Act of 1974, amended in 1979. It provides firm time limits: 30 days from the point of arrest to indictment and 70 days from indictment to trial. Thus, federal prosecutors have a total of 100 days from the time of arrest until trial. This speedy trial law has proven effective over the years.

Unfortunately, however, laws that attempt to speed up trials at the state level have had less success than this federal law because most state laws fail to provide the courts with adequate and effective enforcement mechanisms. As a result, the time limits specified by speedy trial laws are seldom followed in practice.[24]

A number of proposals have emerged to alleviate state and local courts' logjams, ranging from judicial jury selection and limits on criminal appeals to six-person juries. The latter was actually suggested more than two decades ago as a means of relieving congestion of court calendars and reducing court costs for jurors.[25] Thirty-three states have specifically authorized juries of fewer than 12, but most allow smaller juries only in misdemeanor cases. In federal courts, defendants are entitled to a 12-person jury unless the parties agree in writing to a smaller one.[26]

Some reformers suggest that the courts' greatest need is for better management and efficiency. In considering how the courts could function better, however, we need to bear in mind that justice must be served. Where justice ends and expediency begins can be a difficult distinction to comprehend. Courthouse officials are to both "do justice" and move cases.

One experiment that seems to have great promise toward unclogging courts and reducing delay was launched in Detroit, Michigan's largest district court. Known as "pre-exam waiver hearings," the program allows defendants facing drug, gun, or auto theft charges (which compose more than half of all criminal cases) to waive their preliminary examinations 1 week earlier than normal. This program has thus far unclogged the courts, kept police and witnesses from showing up in court for proceedings that never occurred, and saved the court more than a half million dollars annually. The program causes police and prosecutorial personnel to present their reports much more quickly; the jails save money by reducing the time defendants spend behind bars, and police save tens of thousands of dollars in overtime pay because officers do not have to attend waived hearings.[27]

## Case Scheduling: Two Systems

A key part of addressing case delay concerns the ability of the court administrator to set a date for trial. Scheduling trials is problematic because of forces outside the administrator's control: slow or inaccurate mail delivery, which can result in notices of court appearances arriving after the scheduled hearing; an illegible address that prevents a key witness or defendant from ever being contacted about a hearing or trial; or a jailer's inadvertent failure to include a defendant on a list for transportation. If just one key person fails to appear, the matter must be rescheduled. Furthermore, judges have limited ability to control the actions of personnel from law enforcement, probation, or the court reporter's offices, all of whom have scheduling problems of their own.[28]

The two primary methods by which cases are scheduled by the courts are the individual calendar and the master calendar.

### Individual Calendar System

The simplest procedure for scheduling cases is the **individual calendar system.** A case is assigned to a single judge, who oversees all aspects of it from arraignment to pretrial motions and trial. The primary advantage is continuity; all parties to the case know that a single judge is responsible for its conclusion. There are other important advantages as well. Judge shopping (where attorneys try to get their client's case on a particular judge's docket) is minimal, and administrative responsibility for each case is fixed. In addition, it is easier to pinpoint delays because one can easily compare judges' dockets to determine where cases are moving along and where they are not.

This system, however, is often affected by major differences in "case stacking" because judges work at different speeds. In addition, if a judge draws a difficult case, others must wait. Because most cases will be pleaded, however, case stacking is not normally a major problem unless a judge schedules too many cases for adjudication on a given day. Conversely, if a judge stacks too few cases for hearing or adjudication each day, delay will also result. If all cases settle, the judge has dead time, with a large backlog and nothing to do for the rest of the day.

### Master Calendar System

The **master calendar system** is a more recent development. Here, judges oversee (usually on a rotating basis) given stages of a case: preliminary hearings, arraignments, motions, bargaining, or trials. A judge is assigned a case from a central or master pool; once he or she has completed that phase of it, the case is returned to the pool. The primary advantage with this system is that judges who are good in one particular aspect of litigation (such as preliminary hearings) can be assigned to the job they do best. The disadvantage is that it is more difficult to pinpoint the location of or responsibility for delays. Judges also have less incentive to keep their docket current because when they dispose of one case, another appears. In addition, the distribution of work can be quite uneven. If, for example, three judges are responsible for preliminary hearings and one is much slower than the others, an unequal shifting of the workload will ensue; in other words, the two harder-working judges will be penalized by having to work more cases.

### *Which System Is Best?*

Each of the calendar systems has advantages and disadvantages, and a debate has developed over which is best. The answer probably depends on the nature of the court. Small courts, such as the U.S. district courts, use the individual calendar system more successfully. Largely because of their complex dockets, however, metropolitan and state courts almost uniformly use the master calendar system. Research indicates that courts using the master calendar experience the greatest difficulty. Typical problems include the following: (1) Some judges refuse to take their fair share of cases; (2) the administrative burden on the chief judge is often great; and (3) as a result of these two factors, a significant backlog of cases may develop. In those courts where the master calendar system was discontinued in favor of the individual system, major reductions in delay were realized.[29]

# A Blockbuster Supreme Court Decision on Federal Sentencing Guidelines

What was termed a blockbuster U.S. Supreme Court decision was rendered in January 2005 concerning the federal courts and the Sentencing Reform Act of 1984.[30] The Act created the U.S. Sentencing Commission to establish sentencing policies and guidelines for the federal criminal justice system. The Act also required federal courts to use the sentencing guidelines when determining the appropriate sentence for a crime, using an elaborate point system where points are assigned to various levels of offenses and the defendant's history. The purpose was to ensure that similarly situated defendants were treated more or less alike rather than depend on the judge to which he or she happened to be assigned.[31]

The Supreme Court's decision came in *U.S. v. Booker*.[32] The defendant, Booker, was found guilty by a jury of possessing at least 50 grams of crack cocaine, based on evidence that he actually had 92.5 grams. Under those facts, the Guidelines required a possible 210- to 262-month sentence. Although the jury never heard any such evidence, the judge, finding by a preponderance of the evidence that Booker possessed the much larger amount of cocaine, rendered a sentence that was almost 10 years longer than what the Guidelines prescribed.[33]

By a 5 to 4 vote, the U.S. Supreme Court found that the U.S. Sentencing Guidelines violated the Sixth Amendment by allowing judicial, rather than jury, factfinding to form the basis for the sentencing; in other words, letting in these judge-made facts is unconstitutional. The Guidelines also allowed judges to make such determinations with a lesser standard of proof than that of the jury's "beyond a reasonable doubt" and to rely on hearsay evidence that would not be admissible at trial.[34]

The Court did not discard the Guidelines entirely. The Guidelines, the Court said, are to be merely advisory. Thus, the Guidelines are a resource a judge can look at, but may choose to ignore. Although courts still must "consider" the Guidelines, they need not follow them. In addition, sentences for federal crimes will become subject to appellate review for "unreasonableness," allowing appeals courts to clamp down on particular sentences that seem far too harsh. The Court also conceded that Congress might come up with a better remedy; Congress now has the opportunity to carefully and deliberately develop a more effective and just federal sentencing system.[35]

# Other Issues

### *Gender Bias*

Another concern for judges who administer the courts concerns accusations of **gender bias.** As we have become a more diverse society, so have problems increased in this regard. Indeed, at least 36 states have created task forces to investigate gender bias in the legal system.[36] These task forces consistently found problems in gender bias in four areas of the legal system: domestic violence, sexual assault, divorce, and behavior toward female workers.

Domestic violence is the area in which the state task forces found gender bias to be the most common. Some members of the courtroom work group believe that domestic violence is a private matter and should not be dealt with in the court system. As an example, a New York woman was assaulted by her husband who used a telephone to hit her; from the bench the judge said, "What's wrong with that? You've got to keep them in line once in a while."[37]

Sexual assault is another area that is still problematic. Sexual assault is under-reported because women think they will not be believed and will be blamed or have their sexual history thrown open to scrutiny. Divorce cases were found by the task forces to disadvantage women in terms of alimony, division of property, and child support (the outcomes were biased against men, however, in child custody awards).[38]

With respect to court workers, female lawyers (who now constitute from one third to one half of all law students and more than 10 percent of the nation's judges) and court employees report offensive and intolerable actions toward women participants in the legal system. Judges and attorneys address female lawyers in a demeaning manner, using terms such as "sweetie," "little lady lawyer," "pretty eyes," and "dear." Sexist remarks or jokes are also heard.[39] Gender bias can also affect hiring and promotions. Many female lawyers perceive that it is harder to get hired, and once hired they are paid less and have fewer opportunities for promotion.

Sometimes "black robe disease"—overstepping the bounds of propriety due to ignorance or arrogance—is more of a problem of machismo. For example, a 22-year-old Michigan coed was awaiting sentencing by a 54-year-old judge for a DUI charge; the judge asked her to meet him at a bar on a Saturday night to discuss her case.[40] Other cases concerning judicial ethics are discussed in Chapter 13.

Although it is difficult to estimate the true extent of gender bias, it is important to recognize and deal with it whenever it occurs. Perceptions of gender bias are a serious matter because they affect litigants' view of the fairness of the justice system.

## *Should Juveniles Be Tried as Adults?*

During the mid-1990s, the nation's focus on crime began to shift from drugs to juvenile crime, particularly violent crime. Beginning in the mid-1980s, a juvenile crime wave that would be like none other was predicted to be on the horizon; a "superpredator" form of juvenile offender was anticipated to prey on society in large numbers, bolstered by the realization that the juvenile population would increase from 27 million to 39 million by 2000. That prediction, however, never came to pass.[41]

Numerous states are responding to public perceptions that violent juvenile crime is a growing menace, however, by making it easier to transfer juveniles from the relatively "protective shroud" of juvenile court to the jurisdiction of adult courts, thus **trying juveniles as adults.** The philosophy and treatment of juveniles is quite different in the latter, where the process is adversarial instead of amicable and punitive rather than treatment oriented.

States are also lowering the age and increasing the list of crimes for which juveniles can be transferred. The state of Georgia, for example, enacted a mandatory transfer for juveniles 13 years and older who have been charged with specified serious offenses (if convicted, a 13-year-old may face a minimum 10-year prison sentence). Today, at least 24 states have laws sending violent juveniles to adult courts.[42]

Concerns regarding due process include the worry that this approach carries the possibility of juveniles being incarcerated with adult offenders and possibly being raped or assaulted by the older inmates. Advocates of restorative justice emphasize that juveniles are the prime example of where efforts at reconciliation are likely to yield more positive results than punitive measures.[43]

Should juveniles be prosecuted as adults? If so, under what conditions should they be sentenced and incarcerated? Should potential and traditional rehabilitative philosophies and functions of the juvenile court be taken into account? These questions must be addressed, not only in light of the hardened nature of today's violent juvenile offenders, but also in terms of what the future holds for juvenile violence.

## Should the Exclusionary Rule Be Banned?

The **exclusionary rule** quickly became controversial for both crime control and due process advocates when it was adopted in 1961 by the U.S. Supreme Court in *Mapp v. Ohio*.[44] The view of the crime control model—as expressed by President Ronald Reagan in 1981—was, and is, that the rule "rests on the absurd proposition that a law enforcement error, no matter how technical, can be used to justify throwing an entire case out of court. The plain consequence is a grievous miscarriage of justice: the criminal goes free."[45]

To many legal experts who are inclined toward the due process model, however, illegal conduct by the police cannot be ignored. They believe that a court that admits tainted evidence tolerates the unconstitutional conduct that produced it and demonstrates an "insufficient commitment to the guarantee against unreasonable search and seizure."[46]

Although the exclusionary rule remains controversial, the nature of the debate has changed. Initially, critics called for complete abolition of the rule; now, they suggest modifications. Former Chief Justice Warren Burger urged an "egregious violation standard," whereby the police could be liable to civil suits when believed to be in error. Others support an exception for reasonable mistakes by the police. In fact, the U.S. Supreme Court recognized an "honest mistake" or "good faith" exception to the rule only in extremely narrow and limited circumstances.[47] Furthermore, the Rehnquist Court includes six justices who have publicly criticized *Mapp*. This majority, however, has not been able to fashion a means of replacing *Mapp* while prohibiting truly bad-faith searches by the police. As a result, predicting the future of the exclusionary rule is difficult at best.

Should the exclusionary rule be abolished outright? Modified? Kept in its present form? These are compelling questions that our society and its courts may continue to ponder for many years to come.

## Should Cameras Be Banned?

As the trial of actor Robert Blake (charged with murdering his wife, Bonny Lee Bakley) was being prepared in 2002, the controversy over whether cameras should be allowed in court—with a well-known actor playing himself in a real-life courtroom drama—was rekindled. The widely televised trial of O. J. Simpson clearly caused rethinking about whether cameras should be allowed in courtrooms.

Perceptions that Simpson's lawyers played to the cameras apparently had an impact in several highly publicized cases that followed: A judge refused to allow broadcasts in the trial of Susan Smith, a South Carolina woman accused of drowning her two young sons in 1995,[48] and a California judge barred cameras in the trial of Richard Allen Davis, who kidnapped and killed Polly Klaas in 1993.

By the late 1990s, however, despite the Simpson trial backlash, opposition cooled; a study found that four of every five television requests were approved by judges in California in 1998 and 1999.[49] Indeed, a judge allowed coverage of the trial of four police officers accused (and acquitted) of murdering Amadou Diallo in New York City in 2000.

The Blake trial once again brought to center stage all of the concerns that have been lodged against the practice of televising high-publicity trials. Opponents of cameras in court—including due process advocates—complain that televising trials distorts the process by encouraging participants to play to the cameras, and that by covering only sensational trials and presenting only dramatic moments of testimony, the trial process is not portrayed accurately.[50] They argue that in celebrity cases even the witnesses "exaggerate things to give themselves a bigger role."[51] Supporters of the concept, conversely, maintain that televising trials has an educational value, providing the public with a first-hand view of how court proceedings operate. Indeed, studies have found that viewers of a television trial of moderate interest became more knowledgeable about the judicial process.[52]

The question of publicizing high-profile cases is not a new one. Cameras or recording devices were forbidden in the courthouse following the excessive press coverage of the trial of German immigrant Bruno Hauptman, who was accused of kidnapping and murdering the son of famous aviator Charles Lindbergh in the 1930s. This case is the reason that television stations began to hire artists to provide sketches of courtroom participants.

Restrictions on cameras in the courtroom are changing, however. The Supreme Court unanimously held that electronic media and still-photographic coverage of public judicial proceedings does not violate a defendant's right to a fair trial; states are therefore free to set their own guidelines. Only two states prohibit all forms of electronic coverage of criminal trial proceedings, whereas 35 states allow electronic coverage of criminal trials.[53] The remaining states are as yet undecided on the issue.

To prevent disruption of the proceedings and to prohibit camera operators from moving about the courtroom while the trial is in session, states include limitations on this electronic coverage. Furthermore, some states require the consent of the parties, meaning either side can veto coverage of the proceedings. In others, the news media need only receive permission from the trial judge to broadcast the proceedings.[54]

The lingering question is whether cameras are an asset or a liability in the courtroom. To answer, one must determine whether their value as a tool of education and publicity overcomes the potential liabilities.

## *Does Plea Bargaining Belong?*

Some people within the court system believe the institution of **plea bargaining** reduces the courthouse to something akin to a Turkish bazaar, where people barter over the price of copper jugs.[55] They see it as justice on the cheap. Others believe that plea bargaining works to make the job of the judge, prosecutor, and defense attorney much easier. Primary opposition to plea bargaining involves ideological preferences. No matter on which side of the issue one stands, however, it is ironic that both police and civil libertarians oppose plea bargaining, but for different reasons.

Police and others in the crime control camp view plea bargaining as undesirable because defendants can avoid conviction for crimes they actually committed while pleading to and receiving a sentence for lesser offenses. The police see victims at their worst and are highly upset when, for example, an accused rapist is allowed to plead guilty to a lesser charge because a prosecutor believes that evidence is lacking for a rape conviction. These advocates of crime control would much prefer to see the defendant convicted for the crime charged.

Similarly, civil libertarians and supporters of the due process model oppose plea bargaining because when agreeing to plead to a crime(s), the accused forfeits a long list of due process protections afforded under the Bill of Rights: the presumption of innocence; the government's burden of proof; and the rights to face one's accuser, to testify and present witnesses in one's defense, to have an attorney, to appeal, and so on. Another concern is that an innocent defendant might be forced to enter a plea of guilty.

A bargained agreement on reduced charges may be the product of initial overcharging and/or of evidence problems that surface later. Furthermore, defendants who gain the most from plea bargaining are the less serious, marginal offenders in cases lacking in evidence. By contrast, defendants in serious cases who have prior criminal histories do not benefit. In short, plea bargaining appears to reflect a rational rather than a coercive process.

Overall, does plea bargaining sacrifice the rights of the defendant? Or does justice suffer by giving too much benefit to guilty persons? These are the fundamental questions that have swirled around this concept since its inception.

## Jury Science

Another issue that is entering today's courtrooms relates to various services provided under the general designation of **jury science.** Although scientific jury selection—hiring a private consulting firm to sample a geographical area and determine what constitutes a jury of one's peers—has been around for many years, methods used and services provided by many firms today to assist trial attorneys *are* relatively new in their development. Many private firms provide consultation with jury selection and focus on the thought processes of jurors to also make the jury more predictable. Using what they market as "proven scientific techniques,"[56] such firms analyze litigation issues and advise clients and attorneys on every facet of case development, providing such services as field work, focus groups, jury simulations, witness preparation, mock trials, and courtroom observation. They will also prepare courtroom graphics, animations, and estimates of the probability of damages based on jury research.

# Future Considerations

## *Shifts in Philosophy and Practice*

Futurists have been considering needed changes in the courts as their caseloads expand, society demands greater assistance from the courts in addressing its social ills, and technology continues to advance. Clement Bezold offered some interesting court-related speculations for the early twenty-first century[57]:

1. Private businesses offering adjudication, arbitration, and mediation will increasingly compete with public courts to resolve disputes more quickly and fairly.
2. The vast majority of judicial decision making (in areas such as small claims, traffic courts, and status offenses) will be by nonlawyer, citizen judges.
3. Court programs will become increasingly decentralized and closer to client groups.
4. Court organizational structures will become more informal, with less reliance on hierarchical, bureaucratic structures, and with shared leadership.

Certainly not to be overlooked in the courts' future are the impacts of high technology on their internal operations, some of which are discussed in Chapter 17. Future court actors may wear headsets that allow them to listen to the audio-taped evidence; the judge might turn on "white noise," allowing only the judge, defendants, and lawyers to hear conversations, thus allowing all to remain seated during bench conferences; and everyone in the courtroom might view documentary evidence on computers, with terminals shared by jurors and the public and press.[58]

The two hottest issues in court technology today are electronic filing of documents with the court (where there has been a lack of involvement of users in the design and development of the system) and the integration of criminal justice information systems.[59]

## *Trends and Expectations*

Several critical trends will shape the courts in the next decade, including the following[60]:

- Increasing demand for culturally appropriate court and justice services, including interpreters (because immigration patterns will result in continued growth in Latino, Middle Eastern, and Asian populations).
- An increasing number of diverse expectations for the courts' role in society (complex social and economic problems increase the debate about the role of the judicial branch relative to the other two branches of government, and new types of cases will result in increasing service demands on courts).
- Alterations in family composition (declining numbers of traditional families will result in courts having to redefine and deal with different kinds of disputes).

- More demand for acceptance of alternative lifestyles (increases in the number of single-member, unrelated-adult, and single-parent families, as well as collections of elderly people and same-sex relationships, will bring about new areas of law and greater demand for nontraditional family–oriented programs).
- Increasing manipulation of public opinion about crime and the courts using mass media (the increasingly competitive nature of the media business will lead to increased awareness—often distorted—of the court system, more special-interest group demands on the courts, difficulty ensuring fair trials in some unusual or sensational cases, and a need to develop better ways to inform the press and the public.)
- Rapidly emerging information and networking technology (creating a need for increased court participation in designing data-collection and analysis standards, maintaining information network software, making information available to better manage cases, increasing public access to records, changing evidence rules, and changing the method for the compilation, manipulation, and storage of records).

# CASE STUDIES

The following case studies help the reader to consider some of this chapter's subject matter, specifically concerns about courthouse violence and case delay/scheduling.

## Carol's Construct for Court Chaos

Carol Smith, a divorced mother of one, employed as an assistant manager at a large discount center, was denied custody of her 10-year-old son following a bitter divorce (in which her husband accused her of neglect and inattentive behavior toward the child). In July, she filed several actions against the county and other parties, alleging violations of her civil rights. When those petitions were denied, she petitioned the state's supreme court, writing a letter about her case that stated in part that "This county's courts and social services do not have a bit of compassion for anyone, and cared nothing about protecting my rights or administering due process to me. I should not have to be paying all of these lawyer's fees and losing so much sleep about getting my son back. No one should have to turn to such actions as the World Trade Center to get some proper attention, but that is the only thing some people will listen to." Smith later told some former co-workers at a grocery store that if the supreme court would not hear her case, she would go to the state capital "and shoot up the place." Then, when the supreme court did decline to review her case, she became very distraught. A number of her neighbors were very alarmed at her behavior, as she kept ranting about her violent intentions. One day she left her home and went to the state capital, where she went to the supreme court building. While there, she called a relative back at her home and stated that she had "found her purpose in life," that she "planned to shoot the top judge," and had bought a gun. The relative contacted the police, who arrested her for making terroristic threats against the judge's life.

Looking at this case from a threat perspective:

1. What potential motives for the behavior first brought her to official attention?
2. What events represented significant losses to her, which she found quite stressful?
3. What elements of the case point to her having a reasonable level of cognitive ability that would allow her to formulate and execute a plan if she chose to do so?
4. What communications and arrangements did she make that indicated she planned to carry out her threat?
5. What events might have increased or decreased the likelihood of an attack?
6. Taken together, which of the events can be seen as suggesting that she was on a pathway toward a violent attack?

# An Unmanageable
# Case-Management Quandary*

You are court administrator for a court with 50 employees. This court, which used to dispose of about 700 cases per month, now hears an average of 100 criminal and 400 civil cases per month. Case filings have doubled in the last 7 years. The present "hybrid" combination of the individual and master case-management systems has evolved over a long period of time through tradition and expediency. A growing caseload and increasing difficulties in avoiding a backlog, however, have prompted the judges to rethink their present system. Criminal cases that used to reach final disposition in a month now require 2 to 3 months. The situation shows no signs of improving in the foreseeable future. Again, the court has a mixed calendar system. Two judges are assigned to hear criminal cases and motions for a 1-month period, whereas the remaining four judges hear all manner of civil matters on a random basis on the filing of the civil complaint. The judges are responsible for the management of these cases until final disposition. At the end of the 1-month period, the two judges hearing criminal cases return to the civil division and two other judges rotate onto the criminal bench; any pending criminal cases or motions are then heard by these two incoming criminal judges. One of the judges hears all juvenile-related matters in addition to any assignment in the criminal and civil divisions. The court collects statistics on the number of court filings and motions filed in each division on a month-to-month basis.

## Questions for Discussion

1. In a general way, discuss both the merits and difficulties posed by this case-management approach. What is your response to the general advantages and disadvantages of both the individual and the master calendar systems?
2. What specific problems could arise in the criminal division? Why?
3. What specific problems could be created by the permanent assignment of a judge to the juvenile division? What advantages?
4. What comments would you make with regard to the court's statistical report? Are other data needed for management purposes? If so, what kind?

# A Court Futures Forum

Assume that your jurisdiction is planning a new, week-long, futures-oriented program, "Leadership Forum for 2010," which will bring professionals together from the business and governmental sectors. Topics to be discussed at the

---

*Contributed by Dennis Metrick, Management Analyst, Court Services Department, Administrative Office of the Courts, Phoenix, Arizona.

forum include a wide array of area issues, challenges, methods, and concerns. Assume further that you are a court administrator. After applying and being selected to attend this program, you are advised that you are to make a 60-minute presentation concerning your profession generally as well as the future challenges facing your local court's organization.

### Questions for Discussion

1. Using some of the materials discussed in the chapters of this book dealing with court organization and administration, how would you briefly explain to this group your role as a chief executive of your court?

2. What would be some of the important *current* themes and issues that you would take to the forum concerning a court administrator's job to indicate its complexities and challenges?

3. How would you describe the changing nature of the court administrator's role and the *future* issues and challenges of this position?

## Summary

This chapter discussed several challenges involving the courts, generated from both internal and external sources, for today and for the future.

It is obvious that contemporary and future court issues and operations carry tremendous challenges for administrators. Those who serve as court leaders must be innovative, open to new ideas, accountable, well trained, and educated for the challenges that lie ahead. Certainly, legislators and policymakers must also become more aware of the difficulties confronting the courts and be prepared to provide additional resources for meeting the increasing caseloads, issues, and problems of the future.

## Questions for Review

1. Give examples of problem-solving courts; how are they different in philosophy and function from traditional courts?

2. What are the differences between courthouse violence that is targeted and nontargeted, and how can a threat assessment help to determine whether someone poses a serious risk to court safety?

3. What are the possible consequences of and solutions for combating delay in the courts?

4. What are the two primary methods of case scheduling employed by the courts? What are advantages and disadvantages of each?

5. Should juveniles be tried as adults? Why or why not?

6. Should the exclusionary rule be banned? Why or why not?

7. Give some examples of gender bias in the courts. What might judges and administrators do to address the problem?

8. Should plea bargaining and courtroom cameras be kept or barred from our legal system? Why or why not?

9. What are the services provided and methods used in the field of jury science?

10. What are some of the future issues facing the courts?


# Notes

1. Herbert L. Packer, *The Limits of the Criminal Sanction* (Stanford, Calif.: Stanford University Press, 1968).

2. Don Hardenbergh and Neil Alan Weiner, "Preface," in Don Hardenbergh and Neil Alan Weiner (eds.), *The Annals of the American Academy of Political and Social Science, Vol. 576: Courthouse Violence: Protecting the Judicial Workplace* (Thousand Oaks, Calif.: American Academy of Political and Social Science, July 2001), p. 9.

3. Ibid., p. 10.

4. David W. Neubauer, *America's Courts and the Criminal Justice System,* 8th ed. (Belmont, Calif.: Wadsworth, 2005), p. 423.

5. Ibid., p. 82.

6. Bryan Vossekuil, Randy Borum, Robert Fein, and Marisa Reddy, "Preventing Targeted Violence Against Judicial Officials and Courts," in Hardenbergh and Weiner (eds.), *The Annals of the American Academy of Political and Social Science, Vol. 576: Courthouse Violence*, pp. 78–90.

7. Ibid.

8. Ibid.

9. Greg Berman and John Feinblatt, "Problem-Solving Courts: A Brief Primer," *Law & Policy* **23**(2) (April 2001):125–140.

10. Ibid., p. 127.

11. Ibid., p. 128.

12. Ibid., pp. 129–130.

13. Conference of Chief Justices and the Conference of State Court Administrators, "CCJ Resolution 22 COSCA Resolution in Support of Problem-Solving Courts," *Journal of the Center for Families, Children and the Courts* **2** (2000):2–3.

14. Berman and Feinblatt, "Problem-Solving Courts," p. 133.

15. Ibid., p. 138.

16. U.S. Department of Justice, National Criminal Justice Reference Service, "In the Spotlight: Drug Courts," http://www.ncjrs.org/spotlight/drug_courts/summary.html (accessed February 17, 2005).

17. U.S. Department of Justice, National Criminal Justice Reference Service, "Drug Court Resources: Facts and Figures," http://www.ncjrs.org/drug_courts/facts.html (accessed February 17, 2005).

18. *Barker v. Wingo,* 407 U.S.514 (1972).

19. Neubauer, *America's Courts and the Criminal Justice System,* pp. 127–128.

20. Ibid., p. 126.

21. Ibid., p. 128.

22. See *Barker v. Wingo,* 407 U.S. 514 (1972).

23. Ibid., p. 522.

24. Neubauer, *America's Courts and the Criminal Justice System,* p. 130.

25. National Advisory Commission on Criminal Justice Standards and Goals, *Courts* (Washington, D.C.: U.S. Government Printing Office, 1973), p. 12.

26. Neubauer, *America's Courts and the Criminal Justice System,* p. 352.

27. Jim Dyer, "Court Reform Unclogs Docket," *The Detroit News,* June 11, 1998, p. C1.

28. Steven Flanders, *Case Management and Court Management in the United States District Courts* (Washington, D.C.: Federal Judicial Center, 1977).

29. David W. Neubauer, Maria Lipetz, Mary Luskin, and John Paul Ryan, *Managing the Pace of Justice: An Evaluation of LEAA's Court Delay Reduction Programs* (Washington, D.C.: U.S. Government Printing Office, 1981).

30. 18 U.S.C. Secs. 3551–3626 and 28 U.S. C. Secs. 991–998 (October 12, 1984).

31. Mark Allenbaugh, "The Supreme Court's New Blockbuster U.S. Sentencing Guidelines Decision," http://writ.news.findlaw.com/allenbaugh/20050114.html (accessed January 17, 2005).

32. *U.S. v. Booker,* 543 U.S.125 S.Ct. 738 (2005).

33. FindLaw Legal News, "*United States v. Booker,*" http://caselaw.lp.findlaw.com/scripts/printer_friendly.pl?page=us/000/04-104.html (accessed January 17, 2005).

34. Allenbaugh, "The Supreme Court's New Blockbuster U.S. Sentencing Guidelines Decision," p. 2.

35. Ibid.

36. Craig Hemmens, Kristin Strom, and Elicia Schlegel, *Gender Bias in the Courts: A Review of the Literature.* Paper presented at the Academy of Criminal Justice Sciences, Louisville, Kentucky, March 1997.

37. Gail Diane Cox, "Judges Behaving Badly (Again)," *The National Law Journal* **21** (May 3, 1999):1–5.

38. Neubauer, *America's Courts and the Criminal Justice System,* p. 204.

39. Hemmens, Strom, and Schlegel, "Gender Bias in the Courts."

40. Cox, "Judges Behaving Badly (Again)," pp. 1–5.

41. Kevin Johnson and Gary Fields, "Juvenile Crime 'Wave' May Be Just a Ripple," *USA Today,* December 13, 1996, p. 3.

42. Neubauer, *America's Courts and the Criminal Justice System,* p. 510.

43. Ibid.

44. 367 U.S. 643.

45. Quoted in Neubauer, *America's Courts and the Criminal Justice System,* p. 310.

46. Yale Kamisar, "Is the Exclusionary Rule an 'Illogical' or 'Unnatural' Interpretation of the Fourth Amendment?" *Judicature* **78** (1994):83–84.

47. See, for example, *U.S. v. Leon,* 486 U.S. 897 (1984), and *Illinois v. Krull,* 480 U.S. 340 (1987).

48. Jesse Holland, "Susan Smith Judge Bars TV Cameras from Murder Trial," *Times-Picayune,* June 25, 1995, p. 1A.

49. Zanto Peabody, "Blake Case Revives Issue of Cameras in Court," *Los Angeles Times,* May 27, 2002, p. 1A.

50. Paul Thaler, *The Watchful Eye: American Justice in the Age of the Television Trial* (Westport, Conn.: Praeger, 1994).

51. Peabody, "Blake Case Revives Issue of Cameras in Court," p. 1A.

52. S. L. Alexander, "Cameras in the Courtroom A Case Study," *Judicature* **74** (1991):307–313; Paul Raymond, "The Impact of a Televised Trial on Individuals' Information and Attitudes," *Judicature* **57** (1992):204–209.

53. Alexander, "Cameras in the Courtroom."

54. Neubauer, *America's Courts and the Criminal Justice System,* p. 376.

55. Alvin Rubin, "How We Can Improve Judicial Treatment of Individual Cases Without Sacrificing Individual Rights: The Problems of the Criminal Law," *Federal Rules of Decisions* **70** (1976):176.

56. For example, for the kinds of services provided, see Trial Practices, Inc., http://www.trialpractice.com/intro.htm (accessed February 3, 2005).

57. Adapted from Clement Bezold, "On Futures Thinking and the Courts," *The Court Manager* **6** (Summer 1991):4–11.

58. S. L. Alexander, "A Reality Check on Court/Media Relations," *Judicature* **84** (November–December 2000):146–149.

59. Lawrence P. Webster, "How Technology Can Help Court Leaders Address the Justice Needs of a Multicultural Society in the Twenty-first Century," *The Court Manager* **15** (2000):45–49.

60. Adapted from John A. Martin and Brenda J. Wagenknecht-Ivey, "Courts 2010: Critical Trends Shaping the Courts in the Next Decade," *The Court Manager* **15**(1) (2000):6–16.

# PART IV

# CORRECTIONS

*This part includes three chapters about corrections administration. Chapter 10 examines corrections organization and operation, including prisons, jails, and probation and parole agencies. Chapter 11 covers personnel roles and functions, and Chapter 12 reviews corrections issues and practices. Specific chapter content is previewed in the introductory section of each chapter. Case studies appear at the end of each chapter.*

# Chapter 10

# Corrections Organization and Operation

# Key Terms and Concepts

Central office

Custodial organization

Customer model

Due deference doctrine

Employer model

Frivolous lawsuits

Hands-off doctrine

New-generation jail

Parole

Personnel model

Prison director

Prison industries

Prison Litigation Reform Act

Probation

Rehabilitation

Treatment organization

Warden

# Learning Objectives

After reading this chapter, the student will:

- be familiar with the general features of a correctional organization
- have an idea of the personnel and divisions found in the central office and their functions
- be familiar with prison organization and the different responsibilities of the prison warden
- have an understanding of the different factors affecting prison and jail populations
- have an understanding of inmates' rights
- understand the "hands-off" doctrine
- know the rationale, provisions, and impact of the Prison Litigation Reform Act
- know how the "new-generation" jail differs from the traditional model
- know the systems theory of probation, and the six categories of probation systems, including their resources, activities, and outcomes
- know the three services of parole agencies and the two models used for administering them
- know the advantages of the independent and consolidated models of parole
- be familiar with the intermediate-sanctions concept

> *The founders of a new colony ... recognized it among their earliest practical necessities to allot a portion of the virgin soil as a cemetery, and another portion as the site of a prison.*
>
> —Nathaniel Hawthorne
>
> *Even I/Regained my freedom with a sigh.*
>
> —Lord Byron

# Introduction

The administration of prisons, jails, and probation and parole functions in our society is largely unknown and misunderstood. Indeed, most of what the public "knows" about the inner workings of these organizations is obtained through Hollywood's eyes and depictions—*Shawshank Redemption, The Green Mile, Escape from Alcatraz,* and *Cool Hand Luke* are a few examples of such popular depictions that are frequently shown on television.

These and other portrayals of prison and jail life typically show the administrators and their staff being cruel, bigoted, corrupt, and morally base. In addition, prison literature of the past such as Jack Henry Abbott's *In the Belly of the Beast,* Eldridge Cleaver's *Soul on Ice,* George Jackson's *Soledad Brother,* and Malcolm Braly's *On the Yard,* among others, have presented similar views. This chapter presents a more contemporary and realistic view.

The beginning of the next section shows that corrections is now a boom industry in terms of both expenditures and employment; I look at some reasons for the increases in corrections populations. Then I focus on correctional agencies as organizations, including a view of the statewide central offices overseeing prison systems and their related functions, as well as a typical individual prison organization and administration. Then I review inmate rights and civil rights litigation (including the new Prison Litigation Reform Act, enacted to decrease frivolous prisoners' petitions). I also look at the organization of local jails, and then examine probation and parole agencies as organizations. The chapter ends with two case studies.

# Correctional Organizations

## *Inmates, Employment, Expenditures*

Even with the recent, widely reported decline in crime in the United States, corrections can still be regarded as a boom industry. The number of people under some form of correctional supervision has been increasing, and today about 6.9 million people are in prison or jail or on probation or parole[1]—3.1 percent of all adult U.S. residents, or about 1 in every 32 adults.[2] Figure 10.1 depicts this increase.

In order of frequency, about 4,800,000 individuals are on probation, 2,130,000 are in prison, 775,000 are on parole, and 713,000 are in local jails awaiting trial or serving a sentence.[3] Correctional administrators are also responsible for holding about 3,400 persons on death rows; 37 states and the federal government have capital punishment statutes.[4]

There are about 717,000 correctional employees in the United States; most (about 450,000) are state employees and 228,000 are local.[5] The custody and treatment of criminals make corrections an expensive undertaking. It now costs nearly $50 billion per year for corrections activities in the United States, compared with $65 billion for the police functions and $32 billion for courts.[6]

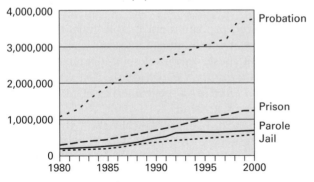

Adult correctional populations, 1980–2000

**Figure 10.1**

Adult correctional populations, 1980 to 2000. *Source:* Bureau of Justice Statistics Correctional Surveys (The Annual Probation Survey, National Prisoner Statistics, Survey of Jails, and The Annual Parole Survey) as presented in *Correctional Populations in the United States, 1997* and *Prisoners in 2000* (Washington, D.C.: Bureau of Justice Statistics, 2002), p. 1.

## Why the Increase in Corrections Populations?

Several factors affect prison and jail populations, which now total about 2.13 million men and women.[7] First is the nation's drug problem. Data show that the number of persons admitted to state prisons for drug offenses has for several years exceeded the number entering for violent or property crimes. Other commonly cited factors include truth-in-sentencing laws, violence on television and in the movies, and a general deterioration of morals and of the family. In sum, the nation has become more punitive in nature.

Truth in sentencing for prison inmates began in 1984 in Washington State. The concept, which involves restriction or elimination of parole eligibility and good-time credits, quickly spread to other states after a determination in 1996 that prisoners were serving on average about 44 percent of their court sentence. To assure that offenders serve larger portions of their sentence, Congress authorized funding for additional state prisons and jails if states met eligibility criteria for truth-in-sentencing programs.[8] To qualify, states must require violent offenders to serve at least 85 percent of their prison sentence. By 1998, 27 states and the District of Columbia qualified; 14 states have abolished early parole board release for all offenders.[9]

A philosophical shift about the purpose of incarceration also contributed to prison crowding. In response to the apparent failure of **rehabilitation** policies, the now-prevailing philosophy sees prisons as places to incarcerate and punish inmates in an effort to deter crime. This philosophy has resulted in get-tough sentencing practices (including mandatory sentencing laws), which contribute to rising prison populations. Legislators have essentially removed the word *rehabilitation* from the penal code while focusing on fixed sentences. This shift from rehabilitating inmates to "just desserts" is based on the view that offenders make "free will" decisions to commit crimes and, therefore, no longer deserve compassion and "correction." U.S. citizens, however, may be leaning more toward rehabilitative efforts. One survey found that about 48 percent of Americans believed that it is more important to try to rehabilitate people who are in prison than merely to punish them (14.6 percent).[10]

Robert Martinson's well-publicized finding that "almost nothing works" in correctional treatment programs served to ignite a firestorm of debate that has lasted nearly two decades.[11] Although Martinson's methodology was brought into serious question and he later attempted to recant his findings, his assessment clearly had a major impact. Legislators and corrections administrators became unwilling to fund treatment programs from dwindling budgets, whereas academics and policymakers claimed that the medical model of correctional treatment programs failed to accomplish its goals. Paul Louis and Jerry Sparger noted that "perhaps the most lasting effect of the 'nothing works' philosophy is the spread of cynicism and hopelessness" among prison administrators and staff members.[12]

An even greater widening between the rehabilitation and just-deserts approaches occurred in the 1980s. Ted Palmer[13] identified these modified positions as the "skeptical" and "sanguine" camps. The skeptics believed that relatively few prison programs work and that successful ones account for only negligible reductions in recidivism. Furthermore, they believed that rehabilitation programs had not been given an adequate chance in correctional settings because they were either poorly designed or badly implemented. The sanguine perspective is that although the existing rehabilitation programs have not been very effective to date, evidence indicates that many programs provide positive treatment for selected portions of the offender population. A reassessment of Martinson's "nothing works" statement by Palmer and others has given new hope for rehabilitation. Palmer rejected Martinson's indictment of correctional treatment modalities and demonstrated that many of the programs initially reviewed by Martinson were actually quite successful.[14] Other research has supported Palmer's position.[15] Still, the rehabilitative philosophy is not expected to see a resurgence in the foreseeable future.

Some observers, however, also believe that the just-deserts logic is defeated by a combination of demography and justice system inefficiency. Each year, a new crop of youths in their upper teens constitutes the majority of those arrested for serious crimes. As these offenders are arrested and removed from the crime scene, a new crop replaces them: "The justice system is eating its young. It imprisons them, paroles them, and rearrests them with no rehabilitation in between," according to Dale Secrest.[16]

Still, large-scale, long-term imprisonment unquestionably keeps truly serious offenders behind bars, preventing them from committing more crimes.

## *General Mission and Features*

Correctional organizations are complex, hybrid organizations that utilize two distinct yet related management subsystems to achieve their goals: One is concerned primarily with managing correctional employees, and the other is concerned primarily with delivering correctional services to a designated offender population. The correctional organization, therefore, employs one group of people—correctional personnel—to work with and control another group—offenders.

The mission of corrections agencies has changed little over time. It is as follows: to protect the citizens from crime by safely and securely handling criminal offenders while providing offenders some opportunities for self-improvement and increasing the chance that they will become productive and law-abiding citizens.[17]

An interesting feature of the correctional organization is that *every* correctional employee who exercises legal authority over offenders is a supervisor, even if the person is the lowest-ranking member in the agency or institution. Another feature of the correctional organization is that—as with the police—everything a correctional supervisor does may have civil or criminal ramifications, both for himself or herself and for the agency or institution. Therefore, the legal and ethical responsibility for the correctional (and police) supervisor is greater than it is for supervisors in other types of organizations.

Finally, two different philosophies exist as to what a correctional organization should be: (1) a **custodial organization,** which emphasizes the caretaker functions of controlling and observing inmates, and (2) a **treatment organization,** which emphasizes rehabilitation of inmates. These different philosophies contain potential conflict for correctional personnel.

## Prisons as Organizations

As noted earlier in this chapter, the mission of most prisons is to provide a safe and secure environment for staff and inmates, as well as programs for offenders that can assist them after release.[18] This section describes how prisons are organized to accomplish this mission. First, I look at the larger picture—the typical organization of the central office within the state government that oversees *all* prisons within its jurisdiction, and then I look at the characteristic organization of an individual prison.

### Statewide Central Offices

The state's central organization that oversees its prison system is often called the **central office.** Some of the personnel and functions that are typically found in a central office are discussed in the following subsections.

#### Office of the Director

Each state normally has a central department of corrections that is headed by a secretary (or someone with a similar title); in turn, the secretary appoints a person to direct the operation of all of the prisons in the state. The **prison director** sets policy for all wardens to follow in terms of how the institutions should be managed and inmates treated (with regard to both custody and treatment). In addition to the director, the staff within the office of the director includes public or media affairs coordinators, legislative liaisons, legal advisers, and internal affairs representatives.

As one of the largest state agencies, a tremendous demand for public information is made on correctional agencies. If a policy issue or a major incident is involved, the media will contact the director for a response. The office of public affairs also oversees the preparation of standards reports, such as an annual review of the department and its status or information regarding a high-profile program or project. In addition, because state correctional agencies use a large percentage of the state budget, the legislature is always interested in its operations. Therefore, there is usually an office of legislative affairs, which responds to legislative requests and tries to build support for resources and programs.[19]

Legal divisions, typically composed of four to six attorneys, often report to the director as well. The work of the legal division includes responding to inmate lawsuits, reviewing policy for its legal impact, and offering general advice regarding the implementation of programs in terms of past legal decisions. These attorneys will predict how the courts are likely to respond to a new program in light of legal precedents.

Finally, the director's office usually has an inspector or internal affairs division. Ethics in government is a major priority; corrections staff may be enticed to bring contraband into a prison or may be physically abusive to inmates. Whenever there is a complaint of staff misconduct by anyone, the allegation needs to be investigated.

## Administration Division

Two major areas of the administrative division of a corrections central office are budget development/auditing and new prison construction. The administrative division collects information from all of the state's prisons, other divisions, and the governor's office to create a budget that represents ongoing operations and desired programs and growth. Once approved by the governor's office, this division begins to explain the budget to the legislative budget committee, which reviews the request and makes a recommendation for funding to the full legislative body. After a budget is approved, this division maintains accountability of funds and oversees design and construction of new and renovated facilities.[20]

## Correctional Programs Division

A central office will usually have a division that oversees the operation of correctional programs, such as security, education, religious services, mental health, and unit management. It is clear that

> Offenders enter prison with a variety of deficits. Some are socially or morally inept; others are intellectually or vocationally handicapped; some have emotional hangups that stem from ... psychological problems; still others have a mixture of varying proportions of some or even all of these.[21]

Having to deal with inmates suffering from such serious and varied problems is a daunting task for correctional organizations. Prison culture makes the environment inhospitable to programs designed to rehabilitate or reform.

A major contemporary problem among persons entering prison is drug addiction. Drug-addicted offenders are subjected to one of three types of treatment programming, which attempts to address the problem: punitive (largely involving withdrawal and punishment), medical (consisting of detoxification,

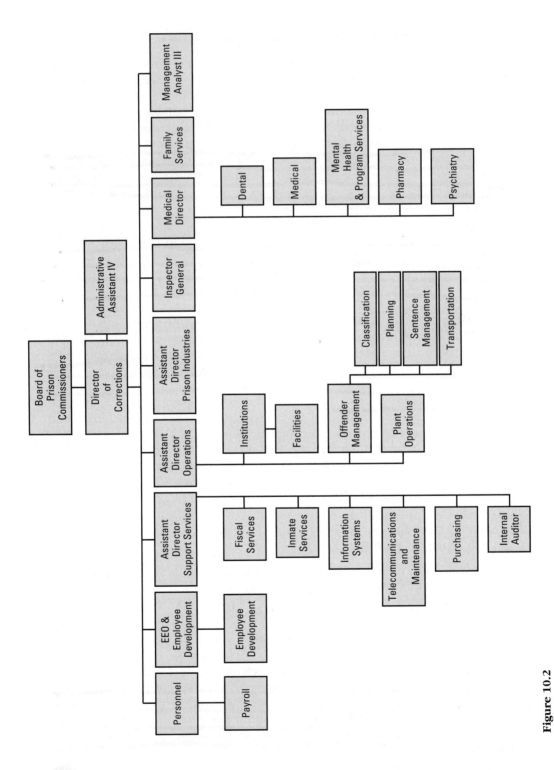

**Figure 10.2**

Organizational structure for a correctional central office.
(EEO = Equal Employment Opportunity).

rebuilding physical health, counseling, and social services), and the communal approach (using group encounters and seminars conducted by former addicts who serve as positive role models).[22] Chapter 12 discusses what prison administrators are doing to interdict drugs coming into prisons and the kinds of treatment programs that are maintained in them.

### *Medical or Health Care Division*

One of the most complicated and expensive functions within a prison is health care. As a result, this division develops policy, performs quality assurance, and looks for ways to make health care more efficient for inmates and less expensive for the prison. One of the best outcomes for a corrections health care program involved HIV/AIDS. A widespread epidemic of HIV/AIDS cases was initially feared in prisons (through homosexual acts and prior drug use), but such an outbreak never happened: Today, the overall rate of confirmed AIDS among the nation's prison population is 0.6 percent, and has been growing at a much slower rate than that of the overall prison population.[23]

### *Human Resource Management Division*

The usual personnel functions of recruitment, hiring, training, evaluations, and retirement are accomplished in the human resource management division. Affirmative action and labor relations (discussed in Chapter 15) may also be included. Workplace diversity is important for corrections agencies, particularly with the growing number of African American and Hispanic inmates (4,848 black male inmates per 100,000 male blacks in the United States and 1,668 Hispanic male inmates per 100,000 male Hispanic, as compared with 705 white inmates per 100,000 male whites).[24] Most states have a unionized workforce, and negotiating and managing labor issues are time consuming. Therefore, this division has staff with expertise in labor relations.

Figure 10.2 shows the organizational structure of a central office in a state of 3 million people.

## Prison Organization and Administration

Over time, prison organizational structures (Figure 10.3) have changed considerably to respond to external needs. Until the beginning of the twentieth century, prisons were administered by state boards of charities, boards composed of citizens, boards of inspectors, state prison commissions, or individual prison keepers. Most prisons were individual provinces; wardens, who were given absolute control over their domain, were appointed by governors through a system of political patronage. Individuals were attracted to the position of **warden** because it carried many fringe benefits, such as a lavish residence, unlimited inmate servants, food and supplies from institutional farms and warehouses, furnishings, and a personal automobile. Now most wardens or superintendents are civil service employees who have earned their position through seniority and merit.[25]

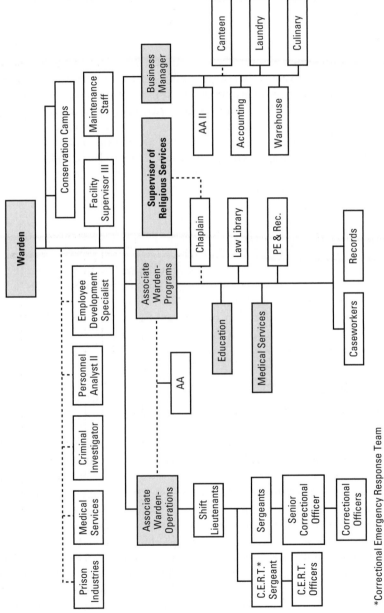

*Correctional Emergency Response Team

**Figure 10.3**

Organizational structure for a maximum security prison.
(AA = Administrative Aide; PE & Rec. = Physical Education and Recreation).

Attached to the warden's office are (possibly by some other title) an institutional services inspector and the institutional investigator who deals with inmate complaints against staff. As mentioned in the earlier section about the central office, prisons also need personnel who deal with labor contracts and the media and who collect and provide this information to the central office. A computer services manager maintains the management information systems.

Also reporting to the warden are deputy or associate wardens, each of whom supervises a department within the prison. The deputy warden for operations will normally oversee correctional security, unit management, the inmate disciplinary committee, and recreation. The deputy warden for special services will typically be responsible for the library, mental health services, drug and alcohol recovery services, education, prison job assignments, religious services, and prison industries. The deputy warden for administration will manage the business office, prison maintenance, laundry, food service, medical services, prison farms, and the issuance of clothing.[26]

I now discuss correctional security, unit management, education, and penal industries in greater detail:

- The correctional security department is normally the largest department in a prison, with 50 to 70 percent of all staff. It supervises all of the security activities within a prison, including any special housing units, inmate transportation, and the inmate disciplinary process. Security staff wears military-style uniforms; a captain normally runs each 8-hour shift, and lieutenants often are responsible for an area of the prison; sergeants oversee the rank-and-file correctional staff.

- The unit management concept was originated by the federal prison system in the 1970s and now is used in nearly every state to control prisons by providing a "small, self-contained, inmate living and staff office area that operates semi-autonomously within the larger institution."[27] The purpose of unit management is twofold: to decentralize the administration of the prison and to enhance communication among staff and between staff and inmates. Unit management breaks the prison into more manageable sections based on housing assignments; assignment of staff to a particular unit; and staff authority to make decisions, manage the unit, and deal directly with inmates. Units are usually composed of 200 to 300 inmates; staff are not only assigned to units, but their offices are also located in the housing area, making them more accessible to inmates and better able to monitor inmate activities and behavior. Directly reporting to the unit manager are "case managers," or social workers, who develop the program of work and rehabilitation for each inmate and write progress reports for parole authorities, classification, or transfer to another prison. Correctional counselors also work with inmates in the units on daily issues, such as finding a prison job, working with their prison finances, and creating a visiting and telephone list.[28]

- Education departments operate the academic teaching, vocational training, library services, and sometimes recreation programs for inmates. An education

**Figure 10.4**

Organizational structure for a prison industry. *Source:* Richard
P. Seiter, *Correctional Administration: Integrating Theory and Practice*
© 2002. Reprinted by permission of Pearson Education, Inc., Upper
Saddle River, N.J.

department is managed in similar fashion to a conventional elementary or high
school, with certified teachers for all subjects that are required by the state
department of education or are part of the General Education Degree (GED)
test. Vocational training can include carpentry, landscaping or horticulture,
food service, and office skills.

• **Prison industries** are legislatively chartered as separate government corporations and report directly to the warden because there is often a requirement that the industry be self-supporting or operate from funds generated
from the sale of products. Generally, no tax dollars are used to run the programs, and there is strict accountability of funds. A typical prison industry
organizational structure is presented in Figure 10.4. Correctional administrators report that joint ventures provide meaningful, productive employment
that helps to reduce inmate idleness and supplies companies with a readily
available and dependable source of labor, as well as the partial return to
society of inmate earnings to pay state and federal taxes, offset incarceration
costs, contribute to the support of inmates' families, and compensate victims. Different types of business relationships have been developed. In the
**personnel model,** prisoners are employed by the state division of correctional industries, which in turn charges the companies a fixed rate for their
labor. In the **employer model,** the company employs the inmates, and
private companies own and operate their prison-based businesses, with prison
officials providing the space in which the companies operate as well as a qualified labor pool from which the companies hire employees. In the **customer
model,** the company contracts with the prison to provide a finished product
at an agreed-on price. The correctional institution owns and operates the business that employs the inmates. To be sure, these joint ventures provide challenges and problems: absenteeism and rapid turnover of employees, limited

opportunities for training, and logistical concerns. Still, many inmates partici-pate in these programs, show up for their jobs on time, work hard during their shifts, and have been hired by companies after their release.[29]

# Inmate Litigation

## *Rights of Inmates*

Incarceration in prisons and jails entails stringent restrictions on freedom of movement and the loss of numerous privileges; however, inmates enjoy sev-eral important constitutional rights. The legal standing of prison inmates has changed tremendously since 1871 when the Virginia Supreme Court told Woody Ruffin, a convicted murderer, that he was a "slave of the state" with no rights that need be recognized.[30]

The demise of the **hands-off doctrine,** by which courts deferred to the expertise of correctional administrators in the operation of their institutions, began in the mid-1960s; in *Cooper v. Pate,*[31] the U.S. Supreme Court held that state inmates could bring lawsuits against prison authorities under Title 42, Section 1983, of the Civil Rights Act. This decision began a new era for inmates and represented the beginning of what has been an explosion in inmate litigation. During the 1971–1972 Supreme Court term, following the deadly prison riot at Attica, New York, additional court decisions expanded prisoners' rights and remedies. One of the major decisions was *Wolff v. McDonnell* (1974),[32] in which the U.S. Supreme Court stated that "there is no Iron Curtain drawn between the Constitution and the prisons of this country." Previous to *Wolff,* inmates had no universally recognized due process rights during disciplinary hearings; the widespread discretion given to correctional administrators was open to potential abuse. In *Wolff,* the Court gave inmates facing severe disciplinary action certain due process protections, including advance written notice of the charges, the right to a fair and impartial hearing, the right to present evidence and call witnesses in their behalf, the use of counsel, and a written statement of the decision reached and reasons for it.

## *A Resurgence of the Hands-off Doctrine?*

The turning point in this expansion of inmates' rights was the 1979 case of *Bell v. Wolfish,* termed the "cornerstone of the future edifice of correctional law."[33] This case involved, among other issues, double-bunking in the Metropolitan Correctional Center in New York City. The Court seemed to revert to the original hands-off, **due deference doctrine,** declaring in a 6–3 decision that jail manage-ment should be left to corrections personnel. In other words, the Court said that deference should be extended to persons with expertise in correctional matters, and administrative decisions should not be invalidated by the Court unless extreme circumstances required it. From this point to the present, federal courts have generally deferred to the expertise of prison administrators in cases involving day-to-day operations (court activism concerning overcrowding notwithstanding).

## *Increases in Litigation and Frivolous Lawsuits prior to the New Millennium*

The volume of inmate litigation increased significantly following the *Cooper v. Pate* decision in 1964. In 1966, 218 petitions were filed, and the number increased to 16,741 in 1981.[34] In 1980, inmates in state and federal correctional institutions filed 23,287 petitions alleging both civil and criminal violations and seeking compensatory damages, injunctions, and property claims.[35] By 1990, the number of such petitions had swollen to nearly 43,000, and more than 64,000 petitions were filed in 1996.[36]

Prisoners sued primarily because they were either unwilling to accept their conviction or wished to harass their keepers.[37] Inmate litigants tend to fall into one of two categories. First are those who file a single suit during their entire period of incarceration (usually requiring the assistance of others to do it); one study found that 71 percent of all litigants filed only one action but accounted for about half of all litigation.[38] The other group is composed of inmates who make law a prison career—the so-called "jailhouse lawyers."[39]

Whereas in past decades the media brought to light many abuses inside prisons, in the 1980s and 1990s media attention began turning in another direction: reports of trivial and **frivolous lawsuits** filed by inmates. Following are some examples:

- A death row inmate sued corrections officials for taking away his Gameboy electronic game
- A prisoner sued 66 defendants alleging that unidentified physicians implanted mind control devices in his head
- A prisoner sued demanding L.A. Gear or Reebok "Pumps" instead of Converse
- An inmate claimed his rights were violated because he was forced to send packages via UPS rather than U.S. mail
- An inmate sued for $100 million alleging he was told that he would be earning $29.40 within three months, but only made $21
- An inmate sued because he was served chunky instead of smooth peanut butter
- An inmate claimed it was cruel and unusual punishment that he was forced to listen to his unit manager's country and western music
- An inmate claimed $1 million in damages because his ice cream melted (the judge ruled that the "right to eat ice cream ... was clearly not within the contemplation" of our nation's forefathers).[40]

Such examples of litigation caused an uproar over frivolous civil rights lawsuits brought by inmates. Furthermore, the expense of defending against such lawsuits, coupled with the fact that the United States has the world's largest and costliest prison system,[41] combined to foster public resentment against prisons and prisoners.

## *The Prison Litigation Reform Act*

By the late 1980s the courts were displaying more tolerance for minor violations of prisoners' constitutional rights, as exemplified by the following three cases:

1. *Turner v. Safley* (1987),[42] in which the U.S. Supreme Court stated that "when a prison regulation impinges on inmates' constitutional rights, the regulation is valid if it is reasonably related to legitimate penological interests."
2. *Wilson v. Seiter* (1991),[43] which stated that when an inmate claims that the conditions of his or her confinement violate the Eighth Amendment, he or she must show a culpable state of mind on the part of prison officials.
3. *Sandin v. Conner* (1995),[44] which emphasized the Supreme Court's desire to give "deference and flexibility to state officials trying to maintain a volatile environment." This decision made it "more difficult to bring constitutional suits challenging prison management."[45]

Then, in April 1996, the **Prison Litigation Reform Act** of 1995 (PLRA) was enacted.[46] The PLRA has been praised by proponents as necessary "to provide for appropriate remedies for prison condition lawsuits, to discourage frivolous and abusive prison lawsuits, and for other purposes."[47]

The PLRA has four main parts[48]:

- *Exhausting of administrative remedies.* Before inmates may file a lawsuit, they must first try to resolve their complaint through the prison's grievance procedure, which usually includes giving a written description of their complaint to a prison official; if the prison requires additional steps, such as appealing to the warden, then the inmate must also follow those steps.
- *Filing fees.* All prisoners must pay court filing fees in full. If they do not have the money up front, they can pay the fee over time through monthly installments from their prison commissary account. A complex statutory formula requires the indigent prisoner to pay an initial fee of 20 percent of the greater of the prisoner's average balance or the average deposits to the account for the preceding 6 months.
- *Three-strikes provision.* Each lawsuit or appeal that an inmate files that is dismissed for being frivolous, malicious, or not stating a proper claim counts as a "strike." After an inmate receives three strikes, he or she cannot file another lawsuit *in forma pauperis*—that is, he or she cannot file another lawsuit unless he or she pays the entire court filing fee up front (an exception is if the inmate is at risk of suffering serious physical injury in the immediate future, described in the next point). An appeal of a dismissed action that is dismissed is a separate strike, and even dismissals that occurred prior to the effective date of the PLRA count as strikes.
- *Physical injury requirement.* An inmate cannot file a lawsuit for mental or emotional injury unless he or she can also show physical injury. (The courts differ in their evaluation of what constitutes sufficient harm to qualify as physical injury).

Did the PLRA achieve its goal of decreasing frivolous lawsuits by inmates? According to the U.S. Department of Justice's Bureau of Justice Statistics, the PLRA appears to have resulted in a decrease in the number of civil rights petitions filed by state and federal prison inmates. Between 1995 (the year before implementation) and 2000, the number of civil rights petitions filed in U.S. district courts decreased from 41,679 to 25,504 (or 39 percent); furthermore, the filing rate, as number of civil rights petitions filed per 1,000 inmates, fell from 37 to 19. Time will tell whether this downward trend will continue and whether the PLRA is solely responsible if it does, but early indications are positive that the kinds of frivolous petitions as those shown earlier are going away.[49]

# Jails as Organizations

Across the United States, approximately 3,316 jails are locally administered.[50] Their organization and hierarchical levels are determined by several factors: size, budget, level of crowding, local views toward punishment and treatment, and even the levels of training and education of the jail administrator. An organizational structure for a jail serving a population of about 250,000 is suggested in Figure 10.5.

The administration of jails is frequently one of the major tasks of county sheriffs. Several writers have concluded that sheriff and police personnel primarily see themselves as law enforcers first and view the responsibility of organizing and operating the jail as an unwelcome task.[51] Therefore, their approach is often said to be at odds with advanced corrections philosophy and trends.

## *The "New-Generation" Jail*

As noted previously, in the past the federal courts have at times abandoned their traditional hands-off philosophy toward prison and jail administration, largely in response to the deplorable conditions and inappropriate treatment of inmates. The courts became more willing to hear inmate allegations of constitutional violations ranging from inadequate heating, lighting, and ventilation to the censorship of mail. One of every five cases filed in federal courts was on behalf of prisoners,[52] and 20 percent of all jails were a party in a pending lawsuit.[53]

In response to this deluge of lawsuits and to improve conditions, many local jurisdictions constructed new jail facilities. The court-ordered pressures to improve jail conditions afforded an opportunity for administrators to explore new ideas and designs. The term **new-generation jail** was coined to characterize a style of architecture and inmate management totally new and unique to local detention facilities, and it represented a new era in correctional thought.[54] The concept was endorsed by the American Correctional Association and the Advisory Board of the National Institute of Corrections. W. Walter Menninger, director of law and psychiatry at the Menninger Foundation in Topeka, Kansas, observed that

> Careful studies of these new generation facilities have found significant benefits for inmates, staff and society at large. There are fewer untoward incidents and assaults,

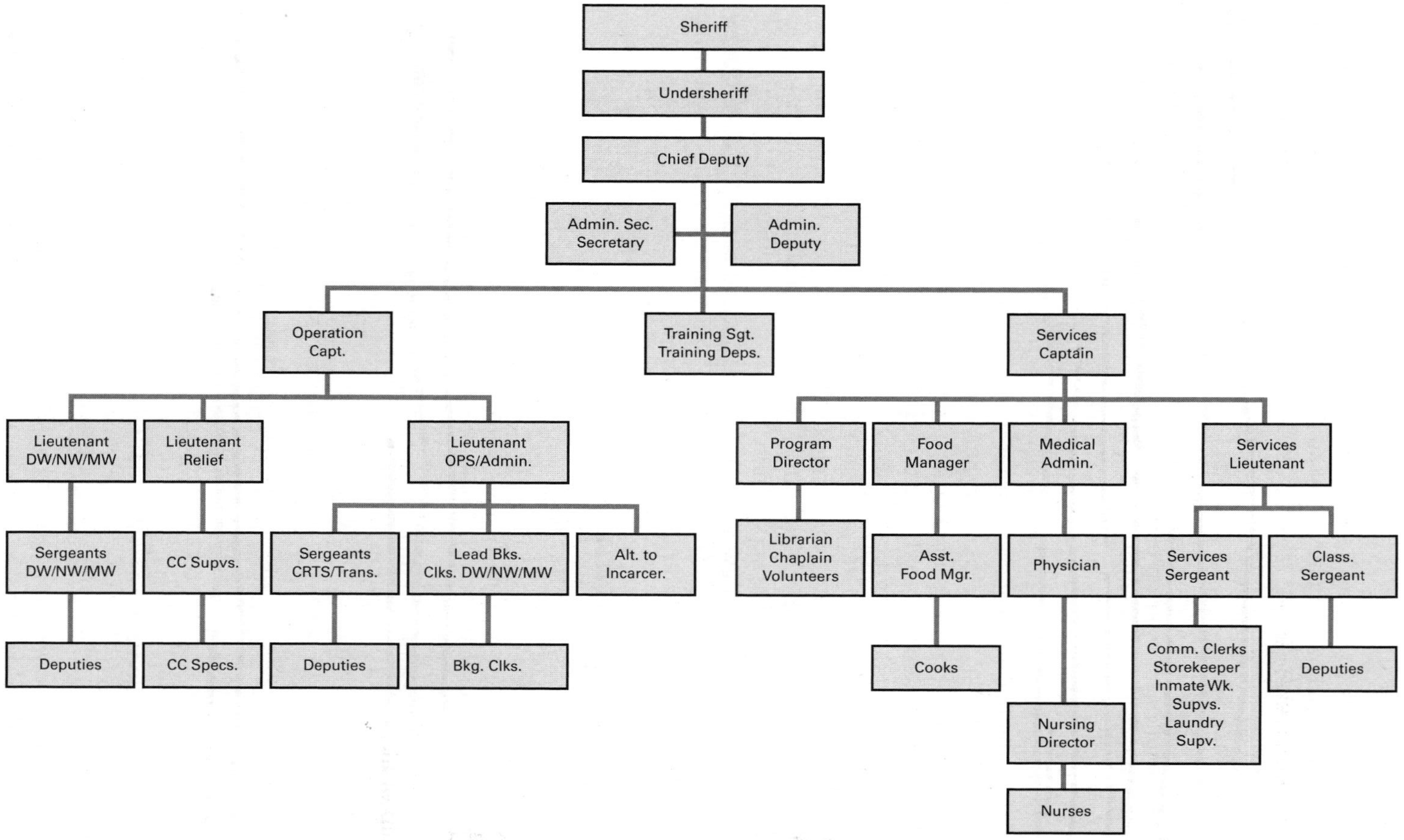

**Figure 10.5**

Organizational structure for a jail serving a county of 250,000 population.
(DW = day watch; NW = night watch; MW = mid-watch; CC = conservation camps; CRTS/Trans. = Courts Transportation; OPS/Admin. = Operations/Administration; Comm. Clerks = Commissary clerks).

[a] greater level of personal safety for both staff and inmates, greater staff satisfaction, more orderly and relaxed inmate housing areas, [and] a better maintained physical plant. Finally, these facilities are cost effective to construct and to operate.[55]

There are several reasons for the fact that new-generation jails are not expanding in number, however. First, new jails are not typically built until old jails either wear out or become too small. Second, there is often a public perception that such facilities are "soft on crime." Finally, these facilities simply do not have the *appearance* of being a jail.[56] To the extent possible, symbols of incarceration were to be removed in these new jails, which were to have no bars in the living units; windows were to be provided in every prisoner's room; and padded carpets, movable furniture, and colorful wall coverings were to be used to reduce the facility's institutional atmosphere. Inmates were to be divided into small groups of approximately 40 to 50 for housing purposes. Officers were to interact with inmates rather than remain inside an office or behind a desk. The interior features of the facility were designed to reduce the "trauma" of incarceration.[57]

The most important features of many of these facilities were one cell per inmate; direct staff supervision; and "functional inmate living units," which were to locate all "sleeping, food, and hygiene facilities ... in one self-contained, multi-level space."[58] A corrections officer was to be assigned to each unit to ensure direct and continuous supervision.

The first facility of the new generation style opened in the 1970s in Contra Costa County, California. This facility quickly became a success and was deemed cost effective to build and safer for inmates and staff.

## *Making Jails Productive*

The 1984 Justice Assistance Act removed some of the long-standing restrictions on interstate commerce of prisoner-made goods. By 1987, private sector work programs were under way in 14 state correctional institutions and two county jails.[59] Today, many inmates in U.S. jails are involved in productive work. Some simply work to earn privileges, and others earn wages applied to their custodial costs and compensation to crime victims. Some hone new job skills, improving their chances for success following release. At one end of the continuum is the trusty (an inmate requiring a low security level) who mows the grass in front of the jail and thereby earns privileges; at the other end are jail inmates working for private industry for real dollars.[60]

Some jails have undertaken training programs for their inmates, following the recommendations of the American Jail Association. For example, one state-of-the-art facility in the West trains inmates to operate a plastic sign–engraving machine and has plans to teach dog grooming at the local animal control center. The engraving equipment, as well as the facility's 24 computers for inmate use, cost taxpayers nothing; they were purchased through commissary funds (monies acquired from sales of canned goods, cigarettes, coffee, and other such items). This jail's inmates can also earn a GED, and the facility is considering programs in auto detailing, food service, book mending, mailing service, painting, printing, carpet installation, and upholstering.

# Probation and Parole Agencies as Organizations

Community corrections originated in the years following World War II, when returning veterans encountered adjustment problems as they attempted to reenter civilian life.[61] It has also been stated that community corrections is "the last bastion of discretion in the criminal justice system."[62] Community corrections is typically viewed as a humane, logical, and effective approach for working with and changing criminal offenders.[63]

## *Probation Systems*

### *Types of Systems*

Figure 10.6 depicts an organizational structure for a regional probation and parole organization. **Probation** is the most frequently used sanction of all; it costs offenders their privacy and self-determination and usually includes some element of the other sanctions: jail time, fines, restitution, or community service.[64] Probation in the United States is administered by more than 2,000 different agencies. Its organization is a patchwork that defies simple explanation. In about three fourths of the states, adult probation is part of the executive branch of state government.[65] By contrast, more than half of the agencies providing juvenile probation services are administered in juvenile courts on the local level.[66]

According to Howard Abadinsky, the administration of probation systems can be separated into six categories[67]:

1. *Juvenile.* Separate probation services for juveniles are administered on a county, municipal, or state level.
2. *Municipal.* Independent probation units are administered by the lower courts under state laws and guidelines.
3. *County.* Under laws and guidelines established by the state, a county operates its own probation agency.
4. *State.* One agency administers a central probation system, which provides services throughout the state.
5. *State combined.* Probation and parole services are administered on a statewide basis by one agency.
6. *Federal.* Probation is administered as an arm of the federal courts.

This patchwork nature of probation systems has raised two central organizational issues concerning the administration of probation services: Should probation be part of the judicial or the executive branch of government? Does the lack of uniformity in administering probation make justice less equitable statewide?[68] These important and lingering issues were first considered nearly 40 years ago by the President's Commission.[69]

Abadinsky argued that probation administered by the judiciary on a county level promotes diversity:

> Innovative programming can be implemented more easily in a county agency since it has a shorter line of bureaucratic control than would a statewide agency. A

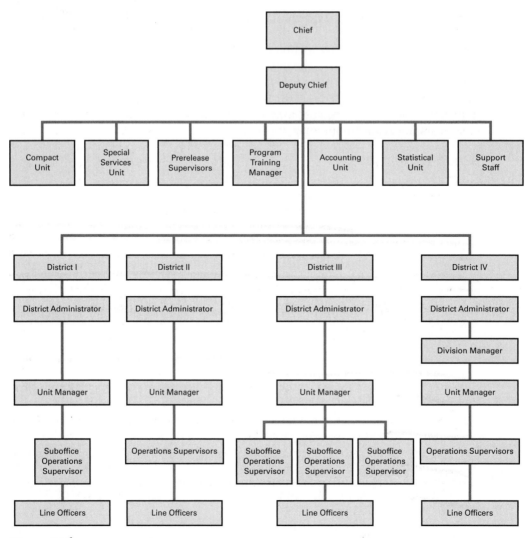

**Figure 10.6**

Organizational structure for a regional adult probation and parole agency.

county agency can more easily adapt to change, and the successful programs of one agency can more easily be adopted by other probation departments ... and unsuccessful programs avoided. Although the judiciary is nominally responsible for administering probation, the day-to-day operations are in the hands of a professional administrator—the chief probation officer.[70]

One problem with the county-level administration of probation services, however, is that of reduced oversight of operations. The officer/client ratios may differ from one county to another, which would probably not occur if services were monitored by a statewide agency whose personnel could easily be shifted from one county to another to equalize caseloads.

### Systems Theory

As with the administration of police, court, or prison organizations, the probation department administrator's goals may affect the services provided to the client, which in turn may have an impact on the client's request for services. This systematic interaction between an organization's resources and structure and the community has been referred to as its "socio-technical environment,"[71] meaning that the principles of the system are organized to execute the basic production technologies of the organization.

Each probation administrator needs to recognize that the organization is a system of inputs, processes, and outputs (discussed in Chapter 2). For probation, inputs are clients coming into the office for counseling and supervision (the processes); outputs are the probationer's obtaining employment, acquiring a skill, observing a curfew, and so on. This understanding of probation, using systems theory, provides a means of learning how probation departments function and interact with their environment and of examining the resources, activities, and outcomes in a way that can identify the goals, describe the day-to-day activities, and link the department's activities to resources and outcomes.

According to systems theory, probation may be conceptualized as a network of interwoven resources, activities, and outcomes.[72] According to Hardyman, resources include the probation department's funding level, goals, policies and procedures, organizational structure, and caseload; the probation staff's characteristics; the services available to probationers; and the rates of unemployment, poverty, and crime in the county. Activities are supervision techniques, rewards, leadership style, contacts, and direct and indirect services provided by the probation department. Outcomes according to systems theory are the number of probationers who were arrested, incarcerated, and/or cited for a technical violation during the follow-up period, as well as the needs of probationers that were considered.[73]

## Parole Systems

### Models for Providing Services

The administration of **parole** is much less complex than probation because parole services are administered centrally on a statewide basis.[74] (It should also be noted that in about 20 states, probation officers also serve as parole officers; thus, much of the information presented in the previous section applies to parole as well.) One state agency administers the parole function on a statewide basis, except that in a number of states, parolees from a local jail come under the supervision of a county probation and parole department.[75]

A parole agency can provide three basic services: parole release, parole supervision, and executive clemency. In a number of states that have abolished parole release (such as California), parole officers continue to supervise offenders released by the prison on good time (reduction of sentence through good behavior).

The National Advisory Commission on Criminal Justice Standards and Goals delineated two basic models for administering parole services:

1. *The independent model.* A parole board is responsible for making release (parole) determinations as well as supervising persons released on parole (or good time). It is independent of any other state agency and reports directly to the governor.
2. *The consolidated model.* The parole board is a semiautonomous agency within a large department that also administers correctional institutions. Supervision of persons released on parole (or good time) is under the direction of the commissioner of corrections, not the parole board.[76]

Both models sometimes combine probation services with parole services in a single statewide agency.

The President's Commission summarized the advantages of the independent model[77]:

1. The parole board is in the best position to promote the idea of parole and to generate public support and acceptance of it. Because the board is accountable for parole failures, it should be responsible for supervising parolees.
2. The parole board that is in direct control of administering parole services can evaluate and adjust the system more effectively.
3. Supervision by the parole board and its officers properly divorces parole release and parolees from the correctional institution.
4. An independent parole board in charge of its own services is in the best position to present its own budget request to the legislature.

The advantages of including both parole services and institutions in a consolidated department of corrections were summarized by the President's Commission as follows[78]:

1. The correctional process is a continuum; all staff, both institutional and parole, should be under a single administration rather than be divided, which avoids competition for public funds and friction in policies.
2. A consolidated correctional department has consistent administration, including staff selection and supervision.
3. Parole boards are ineffective in performing administrative functions; their major focus should be on case decision, not on day-to-day field operations.
4. Community-based programs that fall between institutions and parole, such as work release, can best be handled by a single centralized administration.

Clearly, the trend in this country, beginning in the late 1960s, has been in the direction of consolidation.

# CASE STUDIES

The following two case studies will help the reader to apply some of this chapter's materials to real-world issues of prison organization and operations (case studies concerning jails and probation are presented in Chapters 11 and 12).

## As Bad as It Can Get

You are the deputy warden for operations in a comparatively small (500 inmates) maximum-security prison for adults. As is typical, you oversee correctional security, unit management, the inmate disciplinary committee, and recreation. One Wednesday at about 2:00 a.m., an inmate who is a minority group member with a history of mental health problems and violent behavior begins destroying his cell and injures himself by ramming into the walls. The supervisor in charge collects a group of four correctional officers with the intention of removing the inmate from his cell and isolating, medicating, and checking him for injuries. The group of four—all fairly new on the job, untrained in cell extraction or self-defense, and without any specialized extraction equipment—prepares to enter the cell. When the officers open the cell door, the inmate charges at them, knocking down two of the officers. They finally wrestle the inmate to the floor, although he is still struggling. One officer attempts to subdue him by wrapping his arm around the inmate's neck, pressing on his carotid artery. Finally the inmate quiets down and is restrained and removed to another, larger cell. After 15 minutes, however, the inmate has failed to regain consciousness. A medical staff person rushes to the cell, sees the inmate in an unconscious state, and then has him taken to a local hospital. After the inmate has remained in a comatose condition for 2 months and has been classified as brain dead, the family opts to remove the life-support system that has sustained him.

### Questions for Discussion

1. What, if any, inmate rights are involved in this case?
2. Which, if any, of the inmate's rights were violated?
3. To what extent does the prison system's central office become involved? What kinds of policies need to be developed to cover any similar occurrences in the future?
4. As deputy warden, what disciplinary action would you consider against the officers? Was there intent present?
5. What policy needs and problems exist with regard to new policies? Facilities for mentally ill inmates? Officer training? Equipment?
6. Assume that about 1 month prior to this incident, a minority woman was fired from a high-profile position by the warden for incompetence, and thus this incident adds more fuel to the flames. What would be your or the warden's responses to claims by minority groups that your institution has obviously been shown to be racist?

# When Politics Trumps Policy

For 2 years, you have been director of a prison system for adults in a medium-sized state. As a result of revenue shortfalls for several years, it has been a constant struggle to keep a full labor force in your state's 10 prisons and to lure professional staff members to work and live in the more rural areas where they are located. During the last 6 months, however, you have managed to assemble a fine staff of wardens and other subordinates in the prisons and have implemented a number of policies that provide for educational, vocational, and treatment opportunities, which have been gaining national attention for their effectiveness. Recidivism has been reduced to 30 percent, and your policies are beginning to be accepted by staff and citizens alike. Running a "Take Back the Streets" anticrime campaign, a politically inexperienced person (formerly a popular college quarterback at a state university) was recently elected governor. The new governor has just sent you a letter stating in effect that your institution is not the "Ritz" and demanding that all "frivolous, mamby-pamby programs teaching the ABCs and where cons learn how to hammer nails" be ceased immediately. He asks for your written response, a plan for tightening security, and the implementation of tougher inmate programs within 1 month.

## Questions for Discussion

1. How would you respond? Would you just capitulate and rescind some or all of these programs? Explain your answer.

2. Is there any room to negotiate with the governor? As a tradeoff, would you offer to put in place some programs that are known to be tough on inmates? If so, what kind?

3. Before dismantling your policies and programs, would you attempt to see how much internal and external support you have for them? If yes, whom would you contact, and how?

4. How might you go about demonstrating how successful your policies have been?

## Summary

This chapter presented an overview of corrections as a "boom" industry; it discussed correctional, prison, and jail organization and administration; inmate rights and litigation; and probation and parole. The chapter also demonstrated how the times have changed with respect to the manner in which corrections is organized and administered, and provided a glimpse into some of the kinds of issues and problems that challenge administrators, all of which are furthered examined in later chapters.

# Chapter 1

38. Jim Thomas, "Repackaging the [
*Journal of Criminal and Civil C*

39. Ibid., p. 50.

40. Jennifer A. Puplava, "Peanut Bu
law.indiana.edu/ilj.v73/no1/pup.

41. Francis X. Cline, "Prisons Run C
28, 1993, p. B7.

42. 107 S. Ct. 2254 (1987), at 2254.

43. 111 S. Ct. 2321 (1991).

44. 115 S. Ct. 2321 (1995), at 2293.

45. Linda Greenhouse, "High Court
June 20, 1995, p. A11.

46. Public Law No. 104-134, 110 Sta
U.S.C., 28 U.S.C., and 42 U.S.C.]

47. See 141 *Congressional Record*
Dole's statement in his introdu
provided other examples of the
to cure: "insufficient storage loc
the failure of prison officials to
employee."

48. American Civil Liberties Union,
aclu.org/Prisons/Prisons.cfm?ID=

49. U.S. Department of Justice, Bur
*District Courts, 2000, with Tr*
2002), p. 1.

50. U.S. Department of Justice, *B*
*Inmates at Midyear 1998* (Was
pp. 1, 7.

51. For example, see James M. Moyn
*opment and Growth* (Chicago:
Miller, and Paul B. Wice, *Partici*
*the Performance* (Upper Saddle

52. J. Moore, "Prison Litigation and t
**8** (1981):1.

53. National Sheriffs' Association, *Th*
Author, 1982), p. 55.

54. Linda L. Zupan, *Jails: Reform a*
Anderson, 1991), p. 71.

55. Quoted in William R. Nelson ar
Library Information Specialists, 1

56. Matt Leone, personal communica

57. Zupan, *Jails*, p. 67.

58. R. Wener and R. Olson, *User B*
*tional Centers: Final Report* (Wa

59. U.S. Department of Justice, *Natic*
*Productive* (Washington, D.C.: A

60. Ibid., p. 16.

61. Belinda McCarthy and Bernard M
*Parole: Theory and Practice,* 7th

# Questions for Review

1. What is the typical organization of a "central office" that oversees a state's prison system? An individual prison?

2. What are some of the major administrative positions within a prison system?

3. What factors contribute to the increase in the prison population in the United States?

4. What is a new-generation jail, and how might it help to reduce the effects of overcrowding and increase the quality of life in institutions?

5. What constitutional rights do inmates possess? What is the current doctrine concerning court oversight of prison administration?

6. What are the major rationales and provisions of the Prison Litigation Reform Act?

7. In what major ways do jails differ from prisons in their organization and administration?

8. What are the various types of probation system administered in the United States? Describe each.

9. Should probation services be placed within the judicial or the executive branch of government? Defend your answer.

10. What are the two basic models of parole administration?

# Notes

1. U.S. Department of Justice, Bureau of Justice Statistics, "Prison Statistics," http://www.ojp.usdoj.gov/bjs/prison.htm; "Probation and Parole Statistics," http://www.ojp.usdoj.gov/bjs/pandp.htm (accessed September 21, 2005).

2. U.S. Department of Justice, Bureau of Justice Statistics Web page, "The number of adults in the correctional population has been increasing," http://www.ojp.usdoj.gov/bjs/correct.htm (accessed June 24, 2002).

3. U.S. Department of Justice Bureau of Justice Statistics, "Key Crime & Justice Facts at a Glance," http://www.ojp.usdoj.gov/bjs/glance.htm#corpop (accessed September 21, 2005).

4. U.S. Department of Justice, Bureau of Justice Statistics Web page, "Capital Punishment Statistics," http://www.ojp.usdoj.gov/bjs/cp.htm (accessed September 21, 2005).

5. U.S. Department of Justice, Bureau of Justice Statistics, *Justice Expenditure and Employment in the United States, 2001* (Washington, D.C.: Author, 2004), p. 6.

6. U.S. Department of Justice, Bureau of Justice Statistics, http://www.ojp.usdoj.gov/bjs/glance/tables/exptyptab.htm (accessed September 21, 2005).

7. U.S. Department of Justice, Bureau of Justice Statistics, "Corrections Statistics," http://www.ojp.usdoj.gov/bjs/correct.htm (accessed September 21, 2005).

8. See the Violent Offender Incarceration and Truth-in-Sentencing Incentive Grants program, Public Law 103–322, 108 Stat. 1796 (1994).

9. U.S. Department of Justice, *Bureau of Justice Statistics Special Report, Truth in Sentencing in State Prisons* (Washington, D.C.: Author, 1999), pp. 1–3.

10. Kathleen Maguire and Anr
    *1997* (Washington, D.C.: U

11. T. Paul Louis and Jerry R. Sp
    and Jack E. Dison (eds.), *A
    (Newbury Park, Calif.: Sage

12. Ibid., p. 149.

13. Ted Palmer, "The 'Effecti
    (1983):3–10.

14. Ibid.

15. See D. A. Andrews, "Progra
    the CAVIC Research," in R
    *Treatment* (Toronto, Cana
    *tracting with Conduct Pro*

16. Quoted in Andrews, "Prog

17. Richard P. Seiter, *Correcti*
    Saddle River, N.J.: Prentice

18. Ibid., p. 192.

19. Ibid., p. 189.

20. Ibid., pp. 190–191.

21. Robert Levinson, "Try So
    *Imprisonment* (Beverly H

22. Louis and Sparger, "Treatm

23. U.S. Department of Justic
    Jails," http://www.ojp.usd

24. U.S. Department of Justic
    http://www.ojp.usdoj.gov

25. James A. Inciardi, *Crimin*
    p. 454.

26. Ibid., p. 194.

27. United States Bureau of Pri
    1977), p. 6.

28. Seiter, *Correctional Admi*

29. U.S. Department of Justic
    *Joint Ventures with the*
    Office, 1995), pp. 2–3.

30. *Ruffin v. Commonwealth*

31. 378 U.S. 546 (1964).

32. 418 U.S. 539 (1974).

33. 441 U.S. 520 (1979); quo
    and Prisoners' Rights L
    *Correctional Theory and*

34. A. E. D. Howard, "The S
    *Review* 375 (1982): 375–

35. Timothy J. Flanagan and K
    *1991* (Washington, D.C.: U

36. Ibid. Also see Kathleen M
    *tice Statistics 1995* (Wash

37. Jim Thomas, Kathy Harr
    Litigation," *Criminology*

62. Todd R. Clear, "Punishment and Control in Community Supervision," in Hartjen and Rhine (eds.), *Correctional Theory and Practice*, pp. 31–42.

63. See the President's Commission on Law Enforcement and Administration of Justice, *Task Force Report: Corrections* (Washington, D.C.: U.S. Government Printing Office, 1967), p. 7.

64. Barry J. Nidorf, "Community Corrections: Turning the Crowding Crisis into Opportunities," *Corrections Today* (October 1989):82–88.

65. Abadinsky, *Probation and Parole,* p. 104.

66. Ibid., p. 57.

67. Ibid., pp. 104–105.

68. Ibid., pp. 106–107.

69. See President's Commission, *Task Force Report,* pp. 35–37.

70. Abadinsky, *Probation and Parole,* p. 107.

71. Eric Trist, "On Socio-Technical Systems," in Kenneth Benne and Robert Chin (eds.), *The Planning of Change,* 2nd ed. (New York: Holt, Rinehart and Winston, 1969), pp. 269–281.

72. Daniel Katz and Robert I. Kahn, *The Social Psychology of Organizations* (New York: John Wiley, 1966).

73. Patricia L. Hardyman, "Management Styles in Probation: Policy Implications Derived from Systems Theory," in Hartjen and Rhine (eds.), *Correctional Theory and Practice*, p. 68.

74. Abadinsky, *Probation and Parole,* p. 223.

75. Ibid.

76. National Advisory Commission on Criminal Justice Standards and Goals, *Corrections* (Washington, D.C.: U.S. Government Printing Office, 1973), pp. 396–397.

77. President's Commission, *Task Force Report,* p. 71.

78. Ibid.

# Chapter 11

# Corrections Personnel Roles and Functions

# Key Terms and Concepts

Correctional officer (CO) typology

Death penalty

Detention as a career path

Inappropriate staff–inmate
  relationships

Jail personnel

Middle managers

New old penology

NIC Executive Training Program for
  New Wardens

Probation management styles

Stress and burnout

Supervisors

Warden

# Learning Objectives

As a result of reading this chapter, the student will:

- know the general duties of prison wardens, prison corrections officers, jail employees, and probation and parole officers
- be familiar with the principles of good prison leadership and the training needs of new wardens for them to be successful
- know the basic responsibilities of prison wardens in carrying out executions
- have an understanding of the responsibilities of middle managers and supervisors
- know the duties and eight types of correctional officers
- understand how jails are different from prisons
- be familiar with the causes and effects of job stress and burnout in correctional facilities
- be familiar with probation administrators' management styles

> *The mood and temper of the public in regard to the treatment of crime and criminals is one of the most unfailing tests of the civilization of any country.*
>
> —Winston Churchill

# Introduction

This chapter focuses on personnel within correctional institutions and probation and parole agencies. Presented first is a profile of prison wardens (the role of the *director* of a state prison system was discussed in Chapter 10), needs of and methods for preparing new wardens for the position, and recommendations for administering prisons. I then discuss the death penalty and correctional middle managers and supervisors; next I examine in greater detail the front-line personnel in prisons: correctional officers (COs). This section includes a typology of the eight types of COs in terms of their overall orientation toward, and how they select and view, their occupation. Then, I consider the "cousins" of prisons, the local jails: their purpose and environment, how jail personnel select their type of work and facility, female detention personnel, and problems in selecting people who want detention as a career path. Next I give a brief discussion of stress and burnout in corrections, and then shift to the functions of probation and parole functions (as well as a controversy over the arming of these officers); also included in this section is an overview of probation administrators' management styles. The chapter concludes with three case studies.

Two basic principles constitute the philosophy of corrections administrators: First, whatever the reasons a person is incarcerated, he or she is not to suffer pains beyond the deprivation of liberty—confinement itself is the punishment. Second, regardless of the crime, the prisoner must be treated humanely and in accordance with his or her behavior; even the most heinous offender is to be treated with respect and dignity and given privileges if institutional behavior warrants it.[1] My analysis of institutional management is predicated on these two principles.

# Prisons

## *The Warden: A Profile*

A state director of prisons once stated in the author's justice administration class that the job of prison **warden** is the most difficult in all of corrections[2]; this assessment is probably true because the warden must take the director's general policies and put them into effect throughout the prison while being responsible for the smooth day-to-day operation of the institution. These correctional executives also oversee the fastest-growing agencies in state government; administer increasingly visible operations; and are held accountable by politicians, auditors, the press, organized labor, and numerous other stakeholders.[3] Wardens work within a field that has become more demanding, consumes an increasing share of public funds, and involves responsibility for the lives and safety of others.

Of course, both staff and inmates are sensitive to the warden's granting of what each side perceives to be a strengthened position for the other side. For example, if a policy is enacted that gives the staff more power over inmates, the inmates will be unhappy, perhaps even rebellious; conversely, if a policy is put into practice that the staff thinks affords too much additional freedom to inmates, the staff will feel sold out. Furthermore, the prison director, typically appointed by and serving at the pleasure of the state's governor, can exert on the warden all manner of political influences at any point in time.

A national survey by Kim et al.[4] of 641 male and female prison wardens at adult state prisons provided the following demographic and ideological information: Regional differences account for a great degree of gender difference; in fact, the South employs 21,862 female corrections officers, fully half of the female correctional population in the United States. Of the prison wardens, 85.9 percent were men, and 14.1 percent were women. The mean age of all wardens was 47 years, with that for men being about 47.6 years and that for women, 44.9 years. The majority (81.3 percent) were white, with 70.8 percent being white men; African American men made up 11.8 percent. White women made up 10.4 percent, and 3.0 percent were African American women. A large proportion of the respondents had experience working as correctional officers (57.6 percent) or treatment officers (62.6 percent). Almost half of the male wardens (49.1 percent) had some military experience, whereas only 7.5 percent of the women had military backgrounds. Almost half of the wardens had a graduate degree, a law degree, or some graduate work; female wardens were more likely to have done such postbaccalaureate work (61.1 percent, compared with 47.8 percent of the men).

Regarding the goals of imprisonment, male wardens ranked their four preferred goals as follows: incapacitation, deterrence, rehabilitation, and retribution. Female wardens, however, ranked them thus: incapacitation, rehabilitation, deterrence, and retribution. A greater proportion of female wardens (89.9 percent) than male wardens (83.3 percent) strongly or very strongly agreed that rehabilitation programs had an important place in their institutions. A majority of the wardens thought that the following prison amenities should be reduced or eliminated in prisons: martial arts instruction, conjugal visitation, cosmetic surgery and dentistry, condom distribution, disability benefits, sexually oriented reading material, and nonregulation clothing. Male wardens were more likely than female wardens to support the reduction of college education, copy privileges, condom distribution, full-time recreation director, musical instruments, and special diets. In contrast, female wardens were more likely to support reduction of organ transplants, weight lifting, boxing, and tobacco smoking. Generally, data support the findings that females wardens seem more likely to reduce amenities that can potentially promote violence in prison and more interested than male wardens in health conditions of inmates.

Overall, Kim et al. concluded that although the differences between male and female wardens are somewhat noticeable, the roles of corrections administrators are becoming more gender neutral.[5]

## Preparing New Wardens for Success

The explosive growth of the nation's incarcerated population, discussed in Chapter 10, has increased the need for competent correctional administrators to ensure public safety, see that staff and inmates are safe, and spend tax dollars effectively. They must also understand and appreciate the importance of culture (the sum total of the organization's history, staff, inmates, community, and past leadership) as they begin their tenure at an institution. Today's correctional administrator must excel in more than just correctional operations and not rely on the all-powerful, autocratic working style and a strong paramilitary organization of decades past.[6]

New wardens who were surveyed by McCampbell indicated they would have been better prepared for these challenges had they had job experience or skills in business administration/fiscal management; personnel and labor relations; legislative issues; and media and public relations.[7] Unfortunately, however, a large majority (90 percent) of new wardens also reported in this survey that they did not receive any special training or orientation for their new responsibilities prior to, or just after, they received their assignment. Since 1994 there has been a training program for new wardens, as well as related publications and other resources, available from the National Institute of Corrections (NIC). Participants in this **NIC Executive Training Program for New Wardens** stated that the best advice they received on assuming the role included the following[8]:

- Do not let it go to your head; keep the job in perspective.
- Have faith in yourself.
- Do not shut out your family; maintain balance in your life.
- Be fair and consistent with inmates and staff.
- Remember that your every statement is subject to scrutiny.
- Do not beat yourself up over small things; you will have enough big stuff to worry about.

## *Principles of Good Prison Leadership*

Throughout the nineteenth century and the early part of the twentieth century, studies of prisons generally focused on the administrators rather than on the inmates. Beginning in the 1940s, however, an ideological shift from studying prison administration to studying inmates occurred. The central reason for the shift seems to have been that these institutions were poorly managed or were what prison researcher John J. DiIulio Jr. referred to as "ineffective prisons."[9] Many writers expressed grave doubts about the efficacy of correctional administrators and expressed the idea that prison managers could do nothing to improve conditions behind bars.

It is not surprising that when contemporary researchers attempt to relate prison management practices to the quality of life behind bars, the results are normally quite negative: Prisons that are managed in a tight, authoritarian fashion are plagued with disorder and inadequate programs; those that are managed in a loose, participative fashion are equally troubled; and those with a mixture of these two styles are not any better.[10]

In a 3-year study of prison management in Texas, Michigan, and California, however, DiIulio found that levels of disorder (rates of individual and collective violence and other forms of misconduct), amenities (availability of clean cells, decent food, etc.), and service (availability of work opportunities and educational programs) did not vary with any of the following factors: a higher socioeconomic class of inmates, higher per capita spending, lower levels of crowding, lower inmate-to-staff ratios, greater officer training, more modern plant and equipment, and more routine use of repressive measures. DiIulio concluded that "all roads, it seemed, led to the conclusion that the quality of prison life depended mainly on the quality of prison management."[11]

DiIulio also found that prisons managed by a stable team of like-minded executives, structured in a paramilitary, security-driven, bureaucratic fashion had better order, amenities, and service than those managed in other ways, *even when* the former institutions were more crowded, spent less per capita, and had higher inmate/staff ratios: "The only findings of this study that, to me at least, seem indispensable, is that … *prison management matters*" (emphasis in original).[12]

Studies analyzing the causes of major prison riots found that they were the result of a breakdown in security procedures—the daily routine of numbering, counting, frisking, locking, contraband control, and cell searches—that are the heart of administration in most prisons.[13] Problems in areas such as crowding, underfunding, festering inmate–staff relations, and racial animosities may make a riot more *likely,* but poor security management will make riots *inevitable*.[14]

DiIulio offered six general principles of good prison leadership[15]:

1. Successful leaders focus, and inspire their subordinates to focus, on results rather than process, on performance rather than procedures, on ends rather than means. In short, managers are judged on results, not on excuses.

2. Professional staff members—doctors, psychiatrists, accountants, nurses, and other nonuniformed staff—receive some basic prison training and come to think of themselves as correctional officers first.

3. Leaders of successful institutions follow the "management by walking around" (MBWA) principle. These managers are not strangers to the cellblocks and are always on the scene when trouble erupts.

4. Successful leaders make close alliances with key politicians, judges, journalists, reformers, and other outsiders.

5. Successful leaders rarely innovate, but the innovations they implement are far-reaching and the reasons for them are explained to staff and inmates well in advance. Line staff are notoriously sensitive to what administrators do "for inmates" versus "what they do for us." Thus, leaders must be careful not to upset the balance and erode staff loyalty.

6. Successful leaders are in office long enough to understand and, as necessary, modify the organization's internal operations and external relations. DiIulio used the terms *flies, fatalists, foot soldiers,* and *founders.* The flies come and go unnoticed and are inconsequential. Fatalists also serve brief terms, always complaining about the futility of incarceration and the hopelessness of correctional reform. The foot soldiers serve long terms, often inheriting their job from a fly or fatalist and make consequential improvements whenever they can. Founders either create an agency or reorganize it in a major and positive way.

To summarize, to "old" penologists, prison administrators were admirable public servants, inmates were to be restricted, and any form of self-government was eschewed. To "new" penologists, prison administrators are loathsome and evil, inmates are responsible victims, and complete self-government is the ideal. DiIulio called for a **new old penology,** or a shift of attention from the society of captives to the government of keepers. He asserted that tight administrative control is more conducive than loose administrative control to decent prison conditions. This approach, he added, will "push administrators back to the bar of attention," treating them at least as well as their charges.[16]

## Administering the Death Penalty

One of the major responsibilities of prison administrators, in 37 states and in federal prisons, is to carry out the **death penalty.** By law, the warden or a representative presides over the execution.

To minimize the possibility of error, executions are carried out by highly trained teams. The mechanics of the process have been broken down into several discrete tasks and are practiced repeatedly. During the actual death watch—the 24-hour period that ends with the prisoner's execution—a member of the execution team is with the prisoner at all times. During the last 5 or 6 hours, two officers are assigned to guard the prisoner. The prisoner then showers, dons a fresh set of clothes, and is placed in an empty, tomb-like death cell. The warden reads the court order, or death warrant. Meanwhile, official witnesses—normally 6 to 12 citizens—are prepared for their role. The steps that are taken from this point to perform the execution depend on the method of execution that is used.[17]

Lethal injection is the predominant method of execution and is employed in 36 states and in federal prisons; 9 states authorize electrocution; 4 states, lethal gas; 3 states, hanging; and 3 states, firing squad (17 states authorize more than one method).[18]

Approximately 3,400 prisoners are now under sentence of death in the United States; 56 percent are white, 42 percent are black, and 2 percent are of other races; 47 (about 1.4 percent) are women.[19]

Recently the U.S. Supreme Court rendered two significant decisions concerning the death penalty: In *Roper v. Simmons* (March 2005), the Supreme Court abolished the death penalty for convicted murderers who were less than 18 years of age when they committed their crimes; this decision ended a practice used in 19 states and affected about 70 death-row inmates who were juveniles when they committed murder. In *Atkins v. Virginia* (June 2002), the Court held that the execution of mentally retarded persons—which was permissible in 20 states—constituted cruel and unusual punishment.[20]

## Achieving Racial Balance

The rapid growth of the inmate population, an increased level of oversight by the federal courts, increased demands from the public, and a change in the demographic composition of the inmate population (more African American and Hispanic prisoners) all have presented wardens with a new set of challenges.

As a result, half of all maximum-security wardens now have a policy on racially integrating male inmates within prison cells to try to achieve racial balance. Similarly, about 40 percent of these wardens do not allow their inmates to object to their cell assignments.[21]

## *Middle Managers and Supervisors*

Chapter 4 examined in detail the roles of *police* supervisors and managers. It would be repetitious to dwell at length here on those roles and functions because most of them apply to *corrections* supervisors and managers as well. The reader is encouraged to review those roles and functions in Chapter 4.

Clearly, **supervisors** have one of the most demanding positions in correctional institutions. They must direct work activities, assign tasks, provide employee feedback, and serve as technical experts for the staff reporting to them. They serve as boss, adviser, counselor, mentor, coach, trainer, and motivator.

**Middle managers,** although not on the front lines, are also in challenging and important positions. They are responsible for organizing their departments, planning and developing goals and objectives, overseeing the efficient use of resources, and developing effective communication networks throughout the organization.

## *"Thy Brother's Keeper": Correctional Officers*

Subordinate to the institutional administrator, middle managers, and supervisors is the correctional staff itself—those who, in the words of Gordon Hawkins, are "the other prisoners."[22] Their role is particularly important, given that they provide the front-line supervision and control of inmates and constitute the level from which correctional administrators may be chosen.

Most applicants for positions as correctional officers may have had little knowledge of the job when they applied. A job description for the position might read something like this:

> [They] must prevent rape among two hundred convicts enraged by their powerlessness and sexual deprivation ... prevent violence among the convicts ... shake down all cells for contraband ... know what is going on in the convicts' heads and report it to their supervisors ... account for all material entering or leaving each cellblock ... maintain sanitation in each cell ... give individual attention to all ... convicts ... [and] prevent the suicide or running amok of the raped, the depressed, and the terrified ... and look out for their own physical and psychological survival.[23]

In most assignments, correctional officers experience stimulus overload, are assailed with the sounds of "doors clanging, inmates talking or shouting, radios and televisions playing, and food trays banging ... [and odors] representing an institutional blend of food, urine, paint, disinfectant, and sweat."[24]

Correctional officers are not allowed to provide informal counseling or to aid in the rehabilitative effort. Due process rights for prisoners have made corrections jobs even more difficult.[25] Therein lies what Hawkins and Alpert referred to as "the big bitch" of correctional officers: They are losing power and influence while inmates are gaining them as they are accorded more due process rights.[26] This frustration can be vented in physical ways. Although certainly not frequent today, beatings and even sexual attacks by some officers have been documented.[27]

## A Typology: Eight Types of Correctional Officers

Correctional officers play an influential role in the lives of many inmates because of their direct and prolonged interaction. They are also responsible for creating and maintaining a humane environment in prisons and jails.

Mary Ann Farkas[28] categorized correctional officers (COs) into five types—rule enforcer, hard liner, people worker, synthetic officer, and loner—based on their orientation toward rule enforcement, extent of mutual obligations with colleagues, orientation toward negotiation or exchange with inmates, and their desire to incorporate human service activities into their approach. Farkas added three residual types that were identified by respondents in her study: officer friendly, lax officer, and wishy-washy. These eight types in this **correctional officer typology** are discussed next.

**Rule enforcers,** about 43 percent of correctional officers, are the most common type in Farkas's sample. Rule enforcers are characterized as rule bound and inflexible in discipline and have an esprit de corps with others sharing their enforcement philosophy. They are more likely than other correctional officers to be younger than 25 years old and to have a baccalaureate degree; they tend to have less work experience and to work the evening or night shifts. They typically work on posts involving direct inmate contact, such as the regular housing units and in maximum-security or segregation units. They are more likely to have entered corrections for extrinsic reasons, including job security, benefits, and job availability. They possess a militaristic approach toward inmates, expecting deference to their authority and obedience to their orders. Rule enforcers are not willing to negotiate or use exchange as a strategy to gain inmate compliance.[29]

The **hard liners** are actually a subtype and an extreme version of the rule enforcers. They are hard, aggressive, power hungry, and inflexible with rules and possess little interpersonal skill. These officers are also more likely to be men, with a high school education or GED, and between the ages of 26 to 36 years. They also tend to work later shifts and in maximum-security or segregation units, and they endorse militaristic values and distinction and deference to rank and chain of command. At times, they may become abusive and aggressive toward inmates and perceive acting tough as the way a CO is supposed to act to maintain control and order.[30]

**People workers** (22 percent of COs) are characterized as "professionals trying to be social, responsible, and trying their very best." They have a more comfortable style with inmates, are more flexible in rule enforcement and disciplinary measures, use their own informal reward and punishment system, and believe that the way to gain inmate compliance is through interpersonal communication and personalized relations. They regard an overreliance on conduct reports as an indication of one's inability to resolve difficult situations. They often discuss issues privately with inmates instead of embarrassing them in front of peers. They are concerned with conflict resolution, relying on verbal skills in defusing situations, enjoy the challenge of working with inmates, and actually prefer the posts with more inmate contact.[31]

The **synthetic officers** (14 percent) are essentially a synthesis of the rule enforcer and the people worker types. They are typically older (37 years and older), more experienced officers who work in regular inmate housing units on the day shift. Synthetic officers try to modify the formalized policies and procedures to emphasize organizational directives and interpersonal skills. They follow rules and regulations closely, yet they try to consider the circumstances. They are careful not to deviate too far from procedure, however, which might cause sanctions for themselves. Strict enforcement of rules and flexibility in enforcement are juggled in their interactions with inmates.[32]

**Loners** (8 percent) are also similar to rule enforcers but differ in the motivation behind their policy of strict enforcement. Loners closely follow rules and regulations because they fear criticism of their performance. Female and black officers are more likely to be represented in this type. Loners are likely to be between the ages of 26 and 36 years and less experienced COs and to work on solitary posts. Loners believe their job performance is more closely watched because of their female and/or minority status, as well as the need to constantly prove themselves. They do not feel accepted by other officers, nor do they identify with them. They are wary of inmates. There is a basic mistrust, even fear of working with inmates.[33]

The three residual types—the lax officer, officer friendly, and wishy-washy—are officers who reject the official values and goals of the formal organization. Their rule enforcement is erratic, inconsistent, or nonexistent.

The **lax officers** are described as passive, apathetic, or timid. They are generally veteran male COs who are weary of arguments with inmates and writing conduct reports. They are just "doing their time," wanting to get through the day with a minimum of effort. **Officer-friendly** types are subtypes of people workers, wanting to be liked by all inmates and easily manipulated by inmates to give lots of "second chances." They negotiate with inmates to maintain order and gain compliance by overlooking minor violations or doing favors. They typically have little loyalty or affinity to other officers. **Wishy-washy** types are unpredictable, moody, and inconsistent. They communicate and help inmates at one time, then are distant and rule oriented at another. They are likely to be accused of favoritism and mistrusted by inmates because they do not follow through on promises.

To summarize, age and seniority are associated with officer types. Rule enforcers and hard liners tend to be younger, less experienced COs, whereas older, more experienced officers belong to the people worker or synthetic officer categories. Generally, as officers mature, they become more interested in service delivery.

Although one might assume that more educated officers are inclined toward rehabilitation and are less punitive or aggressive toward inmates, Farkas found that rule enforcers were more likely to hold baccalaureate or master's degrees; she suggested that education may not be a strong indicator of human service attitudes.[34] Considerable evidence suggests that higher education may lead to lower job satisfaction. One observer noted that "except for the somewhat disappointing finding that [correctional officers] with more education are less satisfied with their jobs, the overall picture shows that education is not related to any attitudinal variable examined thus far."[35] Other studies have determined that as officers' educational levels increased, so did their desire to become administrators, the less likely they were to feel a sense of accomplishment working as correctional officers or to want to make a career of corrections, the more likely they were to express dissatisfaction with the pace of career advancement, the more interest they had in counseling,[36] but the less willing they were to engage in rehabilitation activities.[37]

Shift and work assignment also affect one's orientation—the more custodial types of officers work later shifts because they are newer officers and are more likely to work on units with more difficult inmates (such as maximum-security, segregation, or units for inmates with behavioral problems). Finally, the reason for becoming a CO is related to officer type: People workers are attracted to intrinsic factors of correctional work because of its interesting and challenging aspects. Rule enforcers and hard liners become officers for extrinsic reasons: job security and benefits of state employment and job availability.

These CO typologies are actually modes of accommodation or adaptation to the organizational factors of the correctional institutions, including overcrowded conditions, more troublesome inmates, and a more litigious environment.[38]

# Inappropriate Relationships with Inmates

Despite formal policing prohibiting familiarity between offenders and prison staff employees, infractions occur that range from "serious" (e.g., love affairs) to "unserious" (e.g., giving or receiving candy or soft drinks to/from an inmate). Contemporary prisons are no longer sex segregated, and female security officers work in male institutions. This situation allows for different types of **inappropriate staff–inmate relationships** to occur. Worley et al.[39] found three types of "turners"—offenders identified as developing inappropriate relationships with staff members:

1. *Heart breakers.* They seek to form an emotional bond with the staff members, which can even lead to marriage; they generally act alone, and may spend several months courting a staff member.
2. *Exploiters.* They use an employee as a means for obtaining contraband or fun and excitement; they usually act with the help of other inmates, are very manipulative, and likely to use a "lever" (intimidation) on prison employees.

3. *Hell-raisers.* These inmates engage in a unique kind of psychological warfare, and simply want to cause trouble and create hell for the prison system. They often have long histories of personal involvement, and form relationships as a way to create problems or disruptions. They thrive on putting staff members into situations where their jobs are compromised, and enjoy the notoriety that follows their relationship being exposed. They focus on staff members (e.g., secretaries; trustees have even become involved with staff members' spouses), and not security officers.

Worley et al. point out that such behaviors are not the norm in penal environments; nevertheless, prison administrators must understand that offenders are very persistent in initiating interactions with employees for a variety of reasons.[40]

# Jail Personnel

## *Jail Purpose and Environment*

As noted in Chapter 10, about 713,000 persons are incarcerated in 3,316 local jails in the United States, either awaiting trial or serving a sentence.[41] Furthermore, about 229,000 people are employed in local jails.[42] The jail is the point of entry into the criminal justice system. Whereas prisons hold persons who have committed felonies and have been sentenced to at least 1 year in prison, jails hold persons who are arrested and booked for criminal activity or are waiting for a court appearance if they cannot arrange bail, as well as those who are serving sentences of up to 1 year for misdemeanors. Jails also temporarily hold felons whose convictions are on appeal or who are awaiting transfer to a state prison.

Perhaps one of the most neglected areas in criminal justice research concerns individuals who are employed in local jails; what limited studies have been performed generally focus on the conditions of confinement. **Jail personnel,** however, often must work in an environment that is unstable, uncertain, and unsafe. Therefore, it would be beneficial for jail administrators to become knowledgeable about why people choose to work in local jails, as well as jail employee job satisfaction and turnover.

## *Choosing Jail Work and Type of Facility*

Studies have fairly consistently shown that both male and female workers utilize a standard set of priorities in choosing the work they prefer: salary, autonomy, prestige, and location.[43] Although individual motivation will vary, certainly these factors, along with job security, will come into play when someone considers a jail career. Furthermore, research indicates that, given a choice, men and women apparently prefer predominantly male occupations, as they are generally better paying, more prestigious, carry more authority, and offer more opportunities for advancement than their female-dominated counterparts.[44]

One study of correctional officers in a southwestern state found that 83 percent of the COs expressed a preference for working in men's prisons because men are perceived as being easier to manage and more respectful (particularly of female officers).[45] Officers' overall view was that women are more prone than men to irrational outbursts.[46]

Correctional officers also see the women's facility as something less than a "real prison." Women's prisons typically have a much smaller inmate population than men's, with only one officer assigned to a dormitory, so officers are isolated from one another for the majority of their shifts. This situation differs markedly from men's prisons, where officers are almost never assigned alone; the strong team structure and the sense of being a member of a team that are thus present in men's prisons are primary reasons for both male and female correctional officers preferring to work with male inmates.[47]

## Female Jail Employees

The primary stimulus for the employment of female officers in local jails has been the need to comply with federal guidelines on hiring, various court orders to implement hiring quotas to increase female representation, or to rewrite entrance exams and requirements to encourage the employment of women.[48]

Several administrative factors have also driven the need for more female employees. First, jails must house both male and female inmates, and women are needed to supervise the female residents. Second, female officers are needed to conduct searches of female visitors. Third, a rapid expansion of the jail workforce has increased demand and opened job opportunities for qualified female applicants.[49]

Despite this increased female presence in jail work, the role of a female jail employee or deputy is different from that in other workplaces, in that violence is prevalent in the work environment and it is perceived to be a highly sex-typed male job requiring dominance, authoritativeness, and aggressiveness. Studies have shown that, quite often, female deputies believe that they are judged as members of a gender class rather than as individuals—that male workers don't see them as equals.[50]

One of the most pervasive themes expressed by nearly every female officer in each of the jails studied was the perception that female staff members possess more effective communication skills than do male staff and that female officers rely more on their verbal skills. Male officers are more confrontational than are female officers. Men working in jails are more willing than female officers to employ threats, intimidation, and physical coercion in order-maintenance tasks.[51] It has also been determined that female jail deputies are more likely than male deputies to develop friendly relationships with inmates to get inmates to follow the rules—often through the strategic use of humor.[52]

According to Nancy Jurik, perhaps the most demoralizing realization for women employed in jails is that their opportunities for advancement are limited.

Women in corrections routinely experience exclusion, discrimination, and hostility from male supervisors and co-workers. Supervisors who are biased against women working as corrections officers use performance evaluations to discourage them and keep them in subordinate positions.[53]

## Detention as a Career Path

Because no single jail administrator is responsible for statewide jail management, detention officers may manage their jails according to vastly different perceptions and philosophies concerning their staffing and operation. Most jails are supervised by a sheriff's office, where career advancement may be quite limited. When jails are separate units of local government with their own director, they tend to attract more qualified administrators with greater career commitments. A separate, jail-related career path for correctional workers in jail administration is currently needed.

As mentioned earlier, many local jail facilities hire people first as detention officers, who, after attending their basic academy training, may work for 3 to 5 years in detention; eventually, wanting to do "real police work," they transfer to the patrol division as soon as a vacancy becomes available and after attaining a sufficient amount of seniority within their law enforcement agency. This situation often results in tremendously high turnover rates in the jail, as well as large numbers of less experienced detention personnel and low job satisfaction on the part of jail employees. In addition, many good officers resign, being unwilling to serve a period of several years working in detention.

Jail administrators finding themselves in this situation—having difficulty in recruiting people into detention, and then experiencing high employee attrition and low job satisfaction in detention—would do well to take one of two approaches: (1) attempt to create two separate career paths—one in patrol and one in detention. Those who begin on one path can choose to remain in it, be promoted within it, and, it is hoped, even retire from it. Of course, the detention program of the agency must be made attractive enough for one to pursue **detention as a career path.** (2) The administrative, middle management, and supervisory personnel can attempt to convince newly hired personnel to look at the "big picture": that only about 20 percent of their 20-year career will be spent working in detention, with the remaining 80 percent spent as a road deputy.

## Employee Training

Jail administrators and employees need to be thoroughly trained in all aspects of their job. Jail workers have been criticized for being untrained and apathetic, although most are highly effective and dedicated. One observer wrote that

> Personnel is still the number one problem of jails. Start paying decent salaries and developing decent training and you can start to attract bright young people to jobs in jails. If you don't do this, you'll continue to see the issue of personnel as the number one problem for the next 100 years.[54]

Training should be provided on the booking process, inmate management and security, general liability issues, policies related to AIDS, problems of inmates addicted to alcohol and other drugs, communication and security technology, and issues concerning suicide, mental health problems, and medication.

# Correctional Officer Stress and Burnout

As the prison population continues to blossom, the conditions within correctional facilities will remain stressful for staff members. A listing of potential stressors for officers, which can lead to **stress and burnout** (i.e., the depletion of an individual's physical and mental resources), includes role ambiguity and conflict, workload, understaffing, overcrowding, lack of participation in decision making, inmate contact, and job danger. Such stressors can lead to the following health-related problems for officers: cardiac difficulties, substance abuse, hypertension problems, and an increase in sick leave.[55]

Although studies have been inconsistent as to whether correctional officers' gender and educational level are significantly related to stress, studies have indicated that one's job title and workstation can lead to higher stress levels. Specifically, officers in entry-level positions experience lower levels of stress than do officers with other titles; it may be that new officers are more optimistic regarding their ability to be of service to society and helping a troubled population, but this enthusiasm wanes as they mature in the job.[56]

Interestingly, however, the workstation where officers were assigned (e.g., living areas, the "yard," recreational area, cafeteria) did *not* result in differing levels of stress or burnout. Therefore, one implication for corrections administrators is that regularly scheduled rotations of shift and workstation may help reduce the potential for burnout.[57]

# Probation and Parole Officers

## *Primary Duties*

Probation and parole officers must possess important skills similar to those at a prison caseworker, such as good interpersonal communication, decision making, and writing skills. They operate very independently, with less supervision than most prison staff. These officers are trained in the techniques for supervising offenders and then assigned a case load. Probation and parole officers supervise inmates at the two ends of the sentencing continuum (incarceration being in the middle). Probation officers supervise offenders with a suspended sentence, monitoring their behavior in the community and their compliance with the conditions of their probation and suspended prison sentence. Parole officers supervise inmates who have been conditionally released from prison and returned to their community. These officers report violations of the conditions of offenders' release to the body that authorized their community placement and placed conditions on their behavior (the court for probation, and the parole board for parole).[58]

## To Arm or Not to Arm?

Whether probation and parole officers should be armed continues to be an oft-debated topic in corrections. The debate revolves around whether a probation or parole officer can effectively perform traditional duties while armed. Traditionalists believe that carrying a firearm contributes to an atmosphere of distrust between the client and the officer; enforcement-oriented officers, conversely, view a firearm as an additional tool to protect themselves from the risk associated with violent, serious, or high-risk offenders.[59]

Officers must make home and employment visits in the neighborhoods in which offenders live; some of these areas are not safe, and officers must often inform offenders that they will be recommending their revocation, which could result in imprisonment. Most probation and parole agencies believe that if officers carry weapons they are perceived differently than as counselors or advisors who guide offenders into treatment and self-help programs. Over the last two decades there has been a move from casework to surveillance by officers, however; the caseloads include more dangerous offenders.

There is no standard policy for these agencies regarding weapons, and officers themselves are not in agreement about being armed. Some states classify probation and parole officers as peace officers and grant them the authority to carry a firearm both on and off duty.[60] Some authors believe that officers should not be required to carry a firearm if they are opposed to arming, and that providing an option allows for a better officer/assignment match.[61] In sum, it would seem the administrator's decision concerning arming should be placed on the need, officer safety, and local laws and policies.

# Probation Management Styles

Patricia Hardyman's study of probation administrators focused on their **probation management styles**—this style being the fundamental determinant of the nature of the probation organization—and was instructive in its description of the impact of this style on the department's operation. Few departments, even those with hierarchical organizational structure, had a pure management style; administrators vacillated among a variety of styles, including laissez-faire, democratic, and authoritarian. The degree to which administrators included the probation officers in the decision-making process and communicated with officers varied. The authoritarian administrator created emotional and physical distance between the officers and themselves. Surprisingly, the most common management style used by probation administrators was laissez-faire.[62]

Hardyman found that many probation administrators simply did not participate in the day-to-day activities and supervision strategies of the staff. They remained remote but made final decisions on critical policies and procedures.[63] Hardyman also found that few probation administrators across the country operated with the democratic style. Those who did, of course, listened more to the concerns and suggestions of the line supervisors and officers. The administrator still made final decisions, but information was generally sought from the line staff and their opinions were considered. Officers working under this style had a greater sense that their opinions mattered and that the administrator valued their input. An additional benefit of the democratic style was that the administrators had power by virtue of both their position and their charisma, which inspired teamwork and task accomplishment.[64]

# CASE STUDIES

The following three case studies deal with corrections personnel roles and functions and will help the reader to consider some of the chapter information concerning employee behaviors. The first case study shows the kinds of problems faced by a middle manager in a prison and the ways in which he or she spends time during a tour of duty; the second and third case studies involve jail and parole scenarios, respectively.

## The Wright Way

Lieutenant Bea Wright has been in her current position in the state prison for 1 year and is shift supervisor on swing (evening) shift, with 20 officers on her shift. There is also a recreation and development lieutenant, who oversees the yard, commissary, and other high-participation activities during the shift. Wright begins at 4:00 p.m. by holding a roll call for officers, briefing them on the activities of the day, any unusual inmate problems or tensions in progress, and special functions (such as Bible study groups) that will be happening during the evening. Soon after roll call, Wright has the staff conduct the very important evening count—important because inmates have not been counted since morning. At about 5:00 p.m., Wright determines that there are only four correctional officers in the dining room with 1,000 inmates, so she contacts other units (such as education, library, recreation) to have them send available staff to the dining hall for support. After dinner, Wright finds a memo from the warden, asking her to recommend ways of improving procedures for having violent inmates in the Special Housing Unit (SHU) taken to the recreation area in the evening. Wright asks two of her top COs who work in the SHU to provide her with some preliminary information concerning the system in place and any recommendations they might have. While walking the yard, Wright observes what appears to be an unusual amount of clustering and whispering by inmates, by race; she asks a sergeant to quietly survey the COs to determine whether there have also been unusual periods of loud music or large amounts of long-term foodstuffs purchased in the commissary (together, these activities by inmates might indicate that a race war is brewing or an escape plan being developed). Furthermore, as she is on the way to her office an inmate stops her, saying that a group of inmates is pressuring him to arrange to have drugs brought into the prison and he fears for his safety. Wright arranges for him to be called out of the general population the next day under the guise of being transported to a prison law library, at which time he can privately meet with an investigator and thus not draw suspicion to himself for talking to the staff. At about 9:00 p.m., Anderson, a CO, comes to her office to report that he overheard another CO, Jones, making disparaging remarks to other staff members concerning Anderson's desire to go to graduate school and to become a warden some day. Anderson acknowledges that he does not get along with Jones, is tired of his "sniping," and asks Wright to intercede. She also knows that Jones has been argumentative with other staff members and inmates of late and makes a mental note to visit with him later in the shift to see if he is having personal problems.

## Questions for Discussion

1. Does it appear that Lt. Wright, although fairly new in her position, has a firm grasp of her role and performs well in it?
2. In what ways is it shown that Wright seeks input from her subordinates?
3. How does she delegate and empower her subordinates?
4. Is there any indication that Wright is interested in her correctional officers' training and professional development?
5. In which instances does Wright engage in mediation? MBWA (management by walking around)?

# The Wraung Way*

Randall Wraung has been a shift supervisor at the Granite County Detention Facility for the last 3 years. He was promoted to sergeant, performed patrol duties, and had about 10 years' experience with the sheriff's office. Wraung enjoys taking new hires under what he terms his "unofficial tutelage," priding himself in the fact that he knows every aspect of the jail's operation.

Wraung is supervising a newly hired deputy, Tom Sharpe, who is a graduate of the local university's criminal justice program and, like all new hires, is initially assigned to detention. Sharpe finds Wraung to be an interesting and outspoken person. In their conversations about work in the jail, Wraung decides to give Tom some insights.

"I have some good advice for you, kid, and for anyone else going into this job." Wraung continues, "First, try to get out of the jail and into a patrol car as soon as you possibly can. Office politics are extremely bad in here, where you're surrounded and watched by brass all the time. Plus, you can't use any of your university education or academy training 'inside,' so you'll want to get out on a beat as soon as possible.

"Second, I find that you have to be realistic about your chances for having any positive influence with the scum who come through here. Oh, I've worked with lots of people who thought they could change the world in here. Me? Well, I'm a realist. Let's face it. We get the people everyone else has given up on, so what can we be expected to do? I tell visitors that 'We get the cream of the crap here,' and I mean it. Don't set your expectations very high, and you won't be

---

*Contributed by Ted Heim, Professor Emeritus, Washburn University, Topeka, Kansas.

disappointed. I have always been able to keep a good perspective. Hell, the top brass around here and the politicians over at the courthouse give us plenty to laugh at. All you need to do when you're down is look at some of the orders these clowns put out and some of the things our glorious leaders tell the public about treatment, efficiency, blah, blah, blah. I personally don't believe stuff like boot camp and the jail's educational and industry programs even belong here.

"The job tends to get you down if you let it. I have found that you have to find a relief from all the frustrations you experience and the problems created by some of the SOBs who come through here. About once a week, the gang and I hold 'choir practice' at a bar down the street. After about five or six beers, this place and the world look a helluva lot better. People who don't work in corrections can't understand the need to let off a little steam once in a while. Gladly, I am half way to being able to just retire and walk away from this place."

## Questions for Discussion

1. Assume that you are Wraung's lieutenant and, while standing in the hallway, you overhear this conversation. What would be your immediate reaction to Wraung's expression of his views of the job and the inmates? To Sharpe? What long-term actions would you take with Wraung and/or Sharpe?

2. If you were Wraung's supervisor, would you feel compelled to look into, leave alone, or halt the "choir practices"?

3. Assume that you are Sharpe; of all the points made by Wraung, are there any with which you agree? Disagree? Why or why not? Is there any value whatever to listening to such candor from someone like Wraung?

4. Is Wraung the sort of employee who should be supervising others? Dealing at all with the public?

5. Do you believe such cynicism is common in corrections? In criminal justice, generally? In most other occupations? Explain your answer.

## "Cheerless Chuck" and the Parole Officer's Orientation Day

"So, you're the new parole officer with a criminal justice degree from the university? Well, I hope you last longer than the last recruit I had. She meant well, but I guess her idealistic ideas about the job of parole officer couldn't handle the realities of the work. In a way, I understand what she went through. Same thing happened to me 12 years ago when I started this job. There I was, fresh out of college with a brand new diploma with *Social Work* written on it. I figured that piece of paper made me a social worker, and I better get right to work fixing society. It didn't take me long to realize that the real world was different from what I had learned in college. It was like I had been trained as a sailor, and I was about to set out on a voyage, but I couldn't take the time to steer the ship because I was so busy bailing water. The crises we deal with here make it darned difficult to do the work we all see needs to be done. Years ago, when I first started with the parole department, things were a lot better than they are now. Caseloads were lower, fewer people were getting parole who didn't deserve it, and the rest of the criminal justice system was in a lot better shape, which made our jobs a lot easier to do.

"Think about it. We vote in politicians who promise the public that they are going to 'get tough' on crime and the first thing they do is allot more money for law enforcement stuff: beat cops, car computers, helicopters, and so on. These things are great, but all they do is add more people into a system that is already overloaded. No one gets elected by promising to build more courts or add jail and prison space, or probation and parole officers. Eventually these added police officers arrest more people than the system can handle. The courts back up, which in turn messes up the prisons and the jails. The inmates stuck in these crowded places get tired of living like sardines, so they sue the prisons and jails. Remember, the Constitution prohibits cruel and unusual punishment. A lot of times inmates' complaints are legitimate, and they win. The judge orders the prison to lower its population to a reasonable level, which forces the parole board to consider more inmates for early release. They come knocking on our doors, hoping we can get them out of the mess that politics and budgets have created. Nobody mentions giving the parole department more officers, or a bigger budget for added administrative help. No, the bucks go to the flashy, visible things like cops and cars.

"Meanwhile, in the last 10 years, our average caseload for a parole officer has increased 75 percent. We have more people who need supervision, and we are doing it on a budget that has not kept pace with the remainder of the criminal justice system. This wouldn't be so bad if the system was at least adding things to other areas, like the jail or the courts. The problem here is that we depend on the jail to hold our parolees who have violated their conditions. We catch some of them using booze or drugs, and we are supposed to bring them in to the county jail to wait for a hearing to decide if they are going back to prison or back on the street. But the jail has its own set of problems. A couple of years ago the U.S. district court slapped a population cap on our jail. If it goes over that population, the jail will not accept our violators. So we send them home. If they get into more serious trouble, we call it a new crime, the police arrest them, and the jail has to take them. Then they have to sit and wait for the court to catch up, since the courts are not in much better shape than the jail. I guess the job would be easier if the prisons were doing their jobs, too. I can't really blame them, since the prisons are funded in much the same way that parole is. We are not 'glamorous' places to send your tax dollars, but if the prisons were getting more money, they might be able to improve the quality of inmate they send to us. Maybe a little more vocational training and substance abuse counseling, so they could stay off the booze and drugs. Possibly then fewer of these parolees would wind up back behind bars a few years later.

"The worst part about the job is the caseload. We presently have so many on parole that I am lucky if I can get a phone call to each of them once a week, and maybe a home visit once a month. You can't tell me that a phone call and a home visit are really keeping these guys from committing crimes. The sad part about it is that with the proper budget and staff, we could really make a difference. We spend so much time bailing water out of the boat, we don't realize that there is no one steering, and we are just drifting in circles.

"By the way, my name is Charlie Matthews, but everyone calls me Chuck. I'm a supervisor here as well as the designated new-employee orientation specialist and all-round public relations person. I hope I've not depressed you too much on your first day, but now is a good time to drop your idealism and get to work 'bailing.' What're your views and ideas?"

## Questions for Discussion

1. Should Chuck be retained as orientation coordinator? Why or why not?
2. How would changes in politics affect the parole system directly and indirectly?
3. How does an old criminal justice planning adage that "you can't rock one end of the boat" seem to be applicable to what Chuck says about law enforcement getting so much new political funding?
4. What kinds of administrative problems and practices might be responsible for this agency's situation?
5. Why do crowded jails and prisons make the job of parole officers more difficult?
6. How could practices of the jails and prisons change the success of the parole system?
7. Based on Chuck's assessment of the local situation, where do you believe the greatest misconceptions about courts and corrections exist?

## Summary

This chapter examined those criminal justice employees who work in correctional institutions and probation and parole agencies, with particular emphasis placed on administrators. Certainly, as noted in Chapter 10, substantial pressures are now placed on these administrators by the external and internal environments. They must maintain a secure environment while attempting to offer some degree of treatment to their clients, who should not leave incarceration or the probation/parole experience in a much worse condition than when they entered. At the same time, another increasingly difficult challenge is that these administrators must constantly strive to maintain a competent, dedicated workforce that will also uphold the primary tenets of incarceration: providing a secure environment while also ensuring that inmates are treated with respect and dignity.

# Questions for Review

1. What is meant by the term *new old penology*?

2. According to DiIulio, what are some major principles of successful prison administration?

3. What are some of the major problems encountered by prison or jail employees?

4. What factors contribute to their stress and burnout, and what can their administrators do toward alleviating those problems?

5. What are the eight types of correctional officers? How do age, length of service, type of assignment, and education affect where one fits in this typology?

6. In the case study involving Lt. Wright, what are some of the major elements and problems of the role that are made evident?

7. What are the three types of inmates who engage in inappropriate activities with correctional staff members?

8. What are the functions of middle managers and supervisors in jails and prisons (see Chapter 3 if necessary)?

9. Describe the prison warden and his or her role. What kinds of training and education are necessary for a new warden to succeed?

10. Why is there often a detention-or-patrol tension or dichotomy for new jail hires? What can jail administrators do to try to convince employees that they should consider a career in the detention field?

# Notes

1. John J. DiIulio Jr., *Governing Prisons: A Comparative Study of Correctional Management* (New York: Free Press, 1987), p. 167.

2. Personal communication, Ron Angelone, Director, Nevada Department of Prisons, April 27, 1992.

3. F. T. Cullen, E. J. Latessa, R. Kopache, L. X. Lombardo, and V. S. Burton Jr., "Prison Wardens' Job Satisfaction," *The Prison Journal* 73 (1993):141–161.

4. Ahn-Shik Kim, Michael DeValve, Elizabeth Quinn DeValve, and W. Wesley Johnson, "Female Wardens: Results from a National Survey of State Correctional Executives," *The Prison Journal* 83(4) (December 2003):406–425.

5. Ibid.

6. Susan W. McCampbell, "Making Successful New Wardens," *Corrections Today* 64(6) (October 2002):130–134. Also see the National Institutional of Corrections Web site, http://nicic.org.

7. Ibid.

8. Ibid.

9. John J. DiIulio Jr., "Well Governed Prisons are Possible," in George F. Cole, Marc C. Gertz, and Amy Bunger (eds.), *The Criminal Justice System: Politics and Policies,* 8th ed. (Belmont, Calif.: Wadsworth, 2002) pp. 411–420.

10. Ibid., p. 449.

11. DiIulio, *Governing Prisons,* p. 256.

12. Ibid.

13. Bert Useem, *States of Siege: U.S. Prison Riots, 1971-1986* (New York: Oxford University Press, 1988).

14. DiIulio, "Well Governed Prisons Are Possible," p. 413.

15. John J. DiIulio Jr., *No Escape: The Future of American Corrections* (New York: Basic Books, 1991), Chapter 1.

16. DiIulio, "Well Governed Prisons Are Possible," p. 456.

17. See Robert Johnson, *Death Work: A Study of the Modern Execution Process,* 2nd ed. (Belmont, Calif.: West/Wadsworth, 1998); Robert Johnson, "This Man Has Expired," *Commonweal* (January 13, 1989):9-15.

18. Timothy Bonczar and Tracy L. Snell, *Bureau of Justice Statistics Bulletin: Capital Punishment, 2003* (Washington, D.C.: U.S. Department of Justice, Office of Justice Programs, November 2004), pp. 1, 4.

19. Ibid.

20. *Roper v. Simmons,* No. 03-633 (2005); *Atkins v. Virginia,* 536 U.S. 304 (2002).

21. Barbara Sims, "Surveying the Correctional Environment: A Review of the Literature," *Corrections Management Quarterly* **5**(2) (Spring 2001):1-12.

22. Gordon Hawkins, *The Prison* (Chicago: University of Chicago Press, 1976).

23. Adapted from Carl Weiss and David James Friar, *Terror in the Prisons* (Indianapolis, Ind.: Bobbs-Merrill, 1974), p. 209.

24. Ben M. Crouch, *The Keepers: Prison Guards and Contemporary Corrections* (Springfield, Ill.: Charles C Thomas, 1980), p. 73.

25. Hawkins and Alpert, *American Prison Systems,* p. 340.

26. Ibid., p. 345.

27. See Lee H. Bowker, *Prison Victimization* (New York: Elsevier, 1980), Chapter 7.

28. Mary Ann Farkas, "A Typology of Correctional Officers," *International Journal of Offender Therapy and Comparative Criminology* **44** (2000):431-449.

29. Ibid., pp. 438-439.

30. Ibid., pp. 439-440.

31. Ibid., pp. 440-441.

32. Ibid., p. 442.

33. Ibid., pp. 442-443.

34. Ibid.

35. Susan Philliber, "Thy Brother's Keeper: A Review of the Literature on Correctional Officers," *Justice Quarterly* **4** (1987):9-37.

36. Robert Rogers, "The Effects of Educational Level on Correctional Officer Job Satisfaction," *Journal of Criminal Justice* **19** (1991):123-137.

37. David Robinson, Frank J. Porporino, and Linda Simourd, "The Influence of Educational Attainment on the Attitudes and Job Performance of Correctional Officers," *Crime and Delinquency* **43** (1997):60-77.

38. Ibid., pp. 445-446.

39. Robert Worley, James W. Marquart, and Janet L. Mullings, "Prison Guard Predators: An Analysis of Inmates Who Established Inappropriate Relationships with Prison Staff, 1995-1998," *Deviant Behavior: An Interdisciplinary Journal* **24** (2003): 175-194.

40. Ibid., p. 93.

41. U.S. Department of Justice, Bureau of Justice Statistics Web page, "Key Crime & Justice Facts at a Glance" http://www.ojp.usdoj.gov/bjs/glance.htm#corpop (accessed September 21, 2005).

42. U.S. Department of Justice, Bureau of Justice Statistics, *Justice Expenditure and Employment in the United States, 1999* (Washington, D.C.: Author, February 2002), p. 6.

43. See, for example, Christine Bose and Peter Rossi, "Gender and Jobs: Prestige Standings of Occupations as Affected by Gender," *American Sociological Review* **48** (1983): 316–330; Christopher Jencks, L. Perman, and Lee Rainwater, "What Is a Good Job? A New Measure of Labor Market Success," *American Journal of Sociology* **93** (1988): 1322–1357; D. Kaufman and M. Fetters, "Work Motivation and Job Values Among Professional Men and Women: A New Accounting," *Journal of Vocational Behavior* **16** (1980):251–262.

44. Christine L. Williams, *Still a Man's World: Men Who Do "Women's" Work* (Berkeley, Calif.: University of California Press, 1995).

45. Dana M. Britton, "Cat Fights and Gang Fights: Preference for Work in a Male-Dominated Organization," *The Sociological Quarterly* **40** (1999):455–474.

46. Ibid., p. 462.

47. Ibid., pp. 465–466.

48. Mark R. Pogrebin and Eric D. Poole, "Women Deputies and Jail Work," *Journal of Contemporary Criminal Justice* **14** (May 1998):117–134.

49. Ibid., pp. 117–118.

50. Ibid., p. 120.

51. Ibid.

52. Ibid., p. 125.

53. Nancy C. Jurik, "An Officer and a Lady: Organizational Barriers to Women Working as Correctional Officers in Men's Prisons," *Social Problems* **32** (1985):375–388.

54. Quoted in Advisory Commission on Intergovernmental Relations, *Jails: Intergovernmental Dimensions of a Local Problem* (Washington, D.C.: Author, 1984), p. 1.

55. Robert D. Morgan, Richard A. Van Haveren, and Christy A. Pearson, "Correctional Officer Burnout: Further Analyses," *Criminal Justice and Behavior* **29**(2)(April 2002):144–160.

56. Ibid.

57. Ibid.

58. Richard P. Seiter, *Correctional Administration: Integrating Theory and Practice* (Upper Saddle River, N.J.: Prentice Hall, 2002), pp. 387–388.

59. Shawn E. Small and Sam Torres, "Arming Probation Officers: Enhancing Public Confidence and Officer Safety," *Federal Probation* **65**(3) (2001):24–28.

60. Seiter, *Correctional Administration,* p. 387.

61. Small and Torres, "Arming Probation Officers," p. 27.

62. Patricia L. Hardyman, "Management Styles in Probation: Policy Implications Derived from Systems Theory," in Clayton A. Hartjen and Edward E. Rhine (eds.), *Correctional Theory and Practice* (Chicago: Nelson-Hall, 1992), pp. 61–81.

63. Ibid.

64. Ibid., p. 71.

# Chapter 12

# Corrections Issues and Practices

# Key Terms and Concepts

| | |
|---|---|
| Boot camps | Intermediate sanctions |
| Day reporting | Pennsylvania plan |
| Drug interdiction | Prison Rape Elimination Act of 2003 |
| Electronic monitoring | Privatization |
| House arrest | Sexual coercion |
| Inmate suicide | Shock incarceration |
| Intensive supervision | Shock probation/parole |

# Learning Objectives

After reading this chapter, the student will:

- be familiar with victimization in correctional institutions
- be familiar with shock incarceration programs
- be aware of issues concerning various inmate groups, inmate suicide, the sexually coerced, inmate, and the mentally ill, female, and minority populations
- have an understanding of the Pennsylvania Plan
- be familiar with the treatment of drug problems in prisons
- understand the pros and cons of privatization in correctional operations and programs
- be familiar with alternatives to incarceration that are intermediate sanctions
- understand the unique challenges of supervising computer offenders on probation
- know some of the advantages of partnerships between probation and police officers
- understand some of the issues facing corrections in the future

> *I never saw a man who looked / With such a wistful eye / Upon that little tent of blue / Which prisoners call the sky.*
>
> —Oscar Wilde
>
> *Boredom is beautiful.*
>
> —Former Nevada prison warden

# Introduction

The preceding two chapters addressed some of the organizational and personnel issues and functions related to correctional institutions (i.e., prisons and jails) and community corrections (probation and parole). This chapter discusses additional issues for correctional administrators regarding their operations.

First, I briefly examine some substantive (e.g., overcrowding and problems involving the inmate population) and administrative (budgeting, human resource management, planning, and projecting for the future) issues. Then, I discuss selected issues in the institutional setting that concern certain offender populations: the sexually coerced inmate, inmate suicides, and the aging, juvenile, female, mentally ill, and minority inmates. Next is a review of drug use, interdiction, and treatment in prisons, followed by an overview of the privatization of prisons. The subject of intermediate sanctions—punishments that are more severe than mere probation, but less than prison—is addressed next, including intensive probation/parole, house arrest, electronic monitoring, shock probation and parole, shock incarceration, and day reporting.

Then I review a unique program in which a crisis of youth violence is addressed by a partnership between probation and police officers, and then discuss some legal and supervisory challenges that involve computer offenders. The chapter concludes with a consideration of future issues in corrections and three case studies.

# Issues Facing Correctional Administrators

These are not times for weak-spirited corrections leaders and managers. Today's correctional environment differs from that of the past in several ways. First, political and judicial involvement in correctional policy and practice are strong influences. Second, correctional agencies now use a large percentage of the public budget of the federal, state, and local governments. Finally, because of the extensive media coverage of high-profile crimes and sentencing practices, citizens have developed a strong interest in and opinion of criminals' treatment.[1]

To be successful, correctional administrators must be some of the best in government service because many practical issues confront them. Those issues may be divided into two broad categories: substantive and administrative. I discuss both next.

## *Substantive Correctional Issues*

Substantive issues involve matters and knowledge that are specific to the practice and profession of corrections, including factors such as dealing with increasingly overcrowded prisons and managing prisoners who are serving extremely long terms.

Managers of community-based correctional operations must consider what is often referred to as a new narrative for community supervision, one that deals more with supervision and public safety than with assistance and counseling for offenders.[2] Both prison and community correctional staff must deal with offenders who are now younger, more violent, and more likely to be associated with gangs.

Increases in the number of prisoners in state and federal institutions (see Chapter 10) present several issues for administrators: the prediction of which offender categories will grow and by how much, the development of management policy for the expected increase (e.g., added bed space or diversion of offenders?), public and political support for the approach, and the implementation of plans for managing the increase in offenders.

Each year, the average length of prison confinement increases as Congress and state legislatures adopt three-strikes laws for repeat offenders and extend the number of crimes for which offenders must serve a "natural life" (their life span) sentence. Long sentences present administrators with several formidable problems because of the diversity of the prison population and the severity of offenses that result in these lengthy sentences. Not only must correctional administrators determine the appropriate design and construction of prisons to house these inmates, but they must also look at how these longer sentences affect traditional approaches for inmate discipline and rewards to promote safe environments for staff and other inmates.[3]

Proponents of longer sentences argue that such sentences maximize the correctional goals of incapacitation and deterrence; they suggest that these longer sentences effectively reduce crime and therefore justify the significant increase in the number of inmates.[4] Opponents, however, argue that this increase in prison terms creates collateral issues and unintended social consequences, such as the recruitment by seasoned offenders of younger individuals to replace those criminals arrested and incarcerated, and the deterioration of the family that results from removing the parent-age male offender from the home.[5]

For most of the 1990s, community supervision (probation and parole) underwent a transition from helping and counseling offenders to risk management and surveillance.[6] This new focus has been accompanied by additional allocations of resources for incarceration, rather than for probation and parole. In this view, crime is seen as a social phenomenon. Offenders are addressed not as individuals, but as aggregate populations.[7] Therefore, community corrections and prison administrators must confront a basic and critical issue: managing an offender population that has changed dramatically during the last 25 years. In sum, as Richard Seiter observed,[8]

> As a group, today's offenders are more prone to gang involvement and violence, are younger and more impulsive, are serving longer sentences, and have little hope or belief that they will successfully return to the community as law abiding citizens. Many more offenders are dealing with medical and mental health issues. Last, juvenile offenders increasingly act like adults in their sophistication and types of crimes.

## Administrative Correctional Issues

The kinds of administrative issues that must be confronted by today's corrections leaders include areas such as *budgeting, human resource management, planning,* and *projecting for the future*. As budgets have grown, demanding a larger share of governmental resources, political scrutiny has increased. Today, the budgets for correctional agencies are more than $57 billion.[9] Of these expenditures, 93 percent are for state and local governments combined; the federal government spends the rest.[10]

The challenge for correctional administrators is twofold. First, they must convince elected officials that maintaining at least the same level of funding is essential and this probably will need to increase as the number of offenders increases each year (as shown in Chapter 9). Second, as the private sector becomes involved in operating correctional programs, competition develops, and public correctional administrators must ensure that their budgets are not out of line with the operating expenses of the private sector companies.[11]

Another complex administrative issue involves human resource management problems and challenges that result from rapid expansion, such as recruitment, training and staff development, professionalizing staff, and labor relations. In periods of rapid growth, correctional agencies must add line staff, train them, and prepare them to take over challenging duties. Furthermore, each new prison or community-based agency needs supervisors, managers, and administrators. Rapid growth requires rapid development of staff, who must be prepared to advance in the organization and take over added responsibilities (corrections personnel are discussed thoroughly in Chapter 10). The human resources issues also include dealing with labor organizations, discussed in Chapter 15.

A third administrative issue involves planning for the future. Corrections agencies have had nearly two centuries of slow change; now they must prepare for more rapid change rather than dwell on the routine. Correctional administrators must constantly respond to changing circumstances in the internal and external environments. The external environment includes interest groups outside the correctional organization, such as the media, political supervisors, the legislature, other criminal justice and social service agencies, and a variety of interest groups that include victims and offender families. The philosophy of correctional issues will evolve into public policy from the input of this external arena.[12]

Today's correctional administrator must be more sophisticated than in the past and have a broad base of leadership skills, as well as the following qualities: be well grounded experientially and academically in correctional operations and theory, in management skills and techniques, and in major public policy development and political skills. Many have the first two; few have all three.[13]

Many correctional administrators bemoan the fact that they spend more time on issues external to the organization than on dealing with their agency's central mission. They regularly deal with interest groups that either support or disagree with the agencies' policies. They often give media interviews to explain a policy or describe a situation or incident. They respond almost daily to their executive branch leaders or to members of the legislature.[14]

Corrections administrators must be both proactive as well as reactive. Proactive responses usually result from a challenge to an established policy or the administrator's interest in changing a policy. The administrator must be involved with education and coalition building. Reactive responses often result from a serious incident, such as a prison escape, a serious crime committed by a parolee, a disturbance or riot, or a union picket or walkout (collective bargaining in corrections is discussed in Chapter 15). Both types of issues require considerable time, and both require considerable patience, excellent communication skills, and a foundation of trust and confidence in the administrator by others.[15]

# Issues Concerning Inmate Populations

Not only must correctional administrators deal with issues such as institutional population and design, budgets, politics, and the Eighth Amendment (which prohibits cruel and unusual punishment), they must also cope with problems relating to the types of inmates who are under their supervision. Next, I discuss some administrative problems as they involve inmates who are sexually victimized, aging, juvenile, female, mentally ill, and/or members of a minority group.

## *Sexual Coercion in Correctional Institutions*

Inmate **sexual coercion** is not a subject that correctional administrators care to discuss; nevertheless, it remains an issue—one that has been termed "the plague that persists"[16]—and must be addressed.

 continu

### *The Extent of Victimization*

People serving terms in correctional institutions do not leave their sexuality at the front gate, and long ago researchers began studying and publishing their results about this issue. One scholar, Paul Tappan, even maintained that from a biological point of view, homosexuality is normal behavior in correctional institutions.[17] Homosexuality is a universal concomitant of sex-segregated living and a perennial issue in camps, boarding schools, single-sex colleges, training schools, and, of course, correctional facilities.[18]

Persons entering prisons and jails express their sexuality in many forms, some of which are innocuous and others violent. If placed on a continuum, solitary or mutual masturbation or the manufacturing of a sexual object would be at one end (the author recalls during a prison tour a correctional officer describing inmates' creation of a so-called "Fifi bag," constructed from a rolled-up magazine, a towel, and lubrication jelly, for use as a sexual apparatus), consensual homosexual behavior in the middle, and gang rapes at the other end.

The true extent of prison sexual assault is unknown; it is likely to be underreported for fear of reprisals and not wanting to be labeled a "snitch" or one who is weak.[19] One study, however, estimated that in 1 year, approximately 359,000 men and 5,000 women were sexually assaulted while in U.S. prisons.[20] Another study of sexual coercion rates in seven prisons for men found that 21 percent of the inmates had experienced pressured or forced sexual contact and 7 percent had been raped.[21]

Factors that appear to increase sexual coercion rates include large population size (more than 1,000 inmates), understaffed workforces, racial conflict, barracks-type housing, inadequate security (often with low-paid, undermotivated staff who fail to complete assigned rounds), and a high percentage of inmates incarcerated for crimes against persons.[22] Furthermore, inmates who are young, physically small or weak, suffering from mental illness, known to be "snitches," not gang affiliated, or convicted of sexual crimes are at increased risk of sexual victimization.[23]

### Administrators' Roles

Prison administrators are often incredulous as to how rapes can be occurring in their institutions, especially if their facility has a reputation for good management and few problems with violent inmates. These officials obviously play a major role in the prevention, intervention, and prosecution of sexual assaults. Identifying and segregating targets from perpetrators is a prevention tactic (but incidents still occur even in protective custody). Facilities may need to increase surveillance in vulnerable areas: transportation vans, holding tanks, shower rooms, stairways, and storage areas. Administrators may also need to install more security cameras. Finally, it is suggested that new inmates be informed of the potential for being sexually assaulted while incarcerated and be told about prevention and what medical, legal, and psychological help is available if they are targeted.[24]

### New Legislation

In September 2003, President Bush signed into law the **Prison Rape Elimination Act of 2003** (P.L. 108-79). This legislation requires the Bureau of Justice Statistics to develop a new national data collection effort on the incidence and prevalence of sexual assault within correctional facilities. There are also to be public hearings on the prisons with the highest and lowest rates, and a commission will develop national standards for preventing prison rape.[25]

### Averting Inmate Suicides

Another longstanding problem that has not declined is **inmate suicide.** Among prison inmates, the suicide rate is about 1.5 times that of the general population, or 14 per 100,000; among jail inmates, that rate increases to about 9 times that of the general population. People who are newly arrested and brought to local jails have the highest suicide rate—about 250 times that of the population as a whole.[26] Prison inmates typically have the lowest suicide rate because, for the most part, prisons have better mental health resources and monitoring ability. However, risk factors increase for prison inmates if they are held in a special housing unit, have received a long sentence, or have been convicted of a violent crime.[27]

Jails, conversely, often have few mental health resources, and inmates who are fresh off the street may undergo withdrawal from drugs and alcohol when first incarcerated. Jail inmates are also more susceptible to suicidal tendencies if the have recently experienced negative life events, such as a spouse's instigating a divorce action, other family members indicating they want no further contact with the prisoner, or receiving new charges while in jail. Being bullied by other inmates increases the risk for both prison and jail inmates.[28]

There are suicide-prevention strategies that prison administrators and psychiatrists can employ. Certain tools, such as the "strong cloth safety smock," can be used for inmates who are acutely suicidal. Most (80 to 90 percent) of inmates commit suicide by hanging themselves with bed clothes or sheets; the smock cannot be ripped or torn to form a noose. Bedding can also be made with the same material. Another resource is the "cutdown tool," which is a specialized knife built to hook onto cloth and used by staff to cut through fibers very quickly to prevent death by suicide, but which cannot be used by inmates as a weapon.[29]

For adult inmates, true suicide prevention begins at the point of arrest, however; the police still play a critical role in observing and communicating important information about the arrestee's behavior to staff working in lockup facilities, where the risk of suicide is especially high.[30]

Suicide by juveniles in confinement has received little attention when compared with adult inmates. In 2004, the National Center on Institutions and Alternatives conducted the first national survey on juvenile suicides in confinement. The study identified 110 such suicides between 1995 and 1999, with 41.8 percent occurring in training schools/secure facilities, 36.7 percent in detention centers, 15.2 percent in residential treatment centers, and 6.3 percent in reception/diagnostic centers. Almost half (48.1 percent) occurred in state-run facilities; 68.4 percent of the victims were white, 79.7 percent were young men, and the average age of victims was 15.7 years; furthermore, 87.9 percent had a prior substance abuse history, 74.3 percent had a history of mental illness, 71.4 percent had a history of suicidal behavior, 74.7 percent were assigned to single-occupancy rooms, and 98.7 percent were by hanging. None were under the influence of drugs or alcohol at the time of the suicide. Preventive measures in juvenile facilities include written procedures, intake screening, staff training, and close observation.[31]

## *The Aging Offender*

About 20 percent of the inmates in state and federal prisons are age 55 years or older.[32] As the United States in general, the prison population is "graying" at a rapid rate.

Administrators and staff are facing a number of challenges with the growing population of older inmates in local, state, and federal correctional facilities. The effects of longer sentences, truth-in-sentencing laws, "three-strikes" legislation, and the war on drugs have resulted in more people going to prison and staying there longer, also resulting in older inmates (defined as having reached age 50).[33]

The bottom line for correctional administrators is the need to take a systems approach to planning and implementing programs and services for these inmates. First, it is eminently practical to take a wellness approach to managing older inmates. Providing prevention programs as well as chronic and acute medical services for older inmates will keep them healthy and functioning independently; this, in turn, will save money and resources over time. For example, testing and treatment of high cholesterol can delay a debilitating stroke or heart attack; this is cheaper than providing 24-hour per day care for a bedridden inmate. Second, greater consideration should be given to compassionate release legislation, which exists in less than half of the states. Finally, this systems approach should also include incorporating specialists (such as persons from the field of aging) from outside the prison to provide expertise in programming for older people.[34]

Another consideration would be the parole of inmates who are infirm and no longer pose a threat to themselves or others; this can help to ease the crowding problem. There are also the issues of housing accommodations and assignments. Older inmates cannot climb into upper bunks and often do not wish to share a cell with younger inmates, who have different habits (e.g., smoking) and preferences in music, television, and so on.

## Juvenile Offenders Sentenced as Adults

With an increasing percentage of violent crimes being committed by youths, one of the outcomes of the just-deserts perspective toward crime has been the movement to treat serious juvenile offenders as adults. The waiver of juveniles to adult courts has increased. About 104,000 juveniles are in detention in the United States, 4,100 in adult state prisons; furthermore, 35,000 (34 percent) of them are incarcerated for committing a violent offense.[35]

The criminal processing of juveniles as adults creates many issues for correctional administrators. The crux of the problem concerns housing and programming: Should violent juvenile offenders be kept separate from older offenders? Should the institutions provide programs and activities designed to meet their needs as youths? If so, then in effect a new system is created, one that must be operated with almost separate resources and programs. Few adult correctional agencies have educational, vocational, and life-skills programs that meet the needs of young offenders.

Similarly, most states do not have enough juveniles in their adult system to make the development of such programs cost effective. Meanwhile, problems involved in inmate movement, meal service, and medical care and other service and delivery programs make total separation of juveniles an almost impossible task.[36]

Adult correctional administrators must now face philosophical, political, and operational issues as they try to deal with the onslaught of these youthful offenders.

## Female Offenders

Like the aged and juveniles in prison, the number of female prisoners is also increasing. There are 101,000 women in state prisons.[37] About 53,600 (53 percent) have minor children.[38]

In addition to the sexual abuse problems facing female inmates, a foremost issue for correctional administrators is how to provide the same quantity and quality of programs and service for female prisoners as are provided for male prisoners, including maintaining similar staff–inmate ratios; providing work, education, parent–child, and recreational program opportunities; providing comparable health care; and ensuring a satisfactory number of minimum-security spaces for women eligible for such placement.[39]

Most states have only one or two female prisons. This causes problems for families and children in terms of visiting (the majority of female inmates are mothers, many of whom harbor feelings of guilt and isolation)[40] and less separation of inmates by security classification. Many prisons have established parenting programs, which include training in improving parenting skills and finding ways to be parental figures while in prison.

Because female prisons have a different culture than that of male prisons (women expect and need a different style of communication with each other and with staff), correctional administrators must understand and be sensitive to this culture and the different needs and problems of female offenders.[41]

## Mentally Ill Offenders

Since the deinstitutionalization movement of the 1970s, the number of criminal offenders and inmates suffering from mental illness has been increasing. It is estimated that 137,000 inmates held in 1,500 state correctional facilities are receiving therapy and/or counseling; about 10 percent of them are also taking psychotropic medications.[42]

In prison, these individuals pose a dual dilemma for administrators. They are often violent and may be serving a long period of incarceration. Therefore, they require a high security level and are housed with other offenders who have committed equally serious offenses who are serving equally long sentences. The presence of potentially violent, mentally ill prisoners in high-security and probably overcrowded institutions is a dangerous situation.[43]

Mental illness must be treated while inmates are incarcerated. The key to dealing with treatment involves partnerships between the state and local correctional agencies and state and local mental health services agencies. Local mental health agencies can be used to provide counseling and support to probationers. Many states have also developed excellent programs for inmates with mental health problems. The challenge for correctional administrators is to maintain a viable program to treat and control a difficult group of offenders. The treatment of this group requires resources, trained staff, and appropriate facilities.[44]

## Minority Inmates

Race and corrections remains perhaps one of the most controversial topics today, owing largely to the disproportionately high number of minorities in the criminal justice and correctional systems. An estimated 22 percent of male blacks ages 35 to 44 have been confined in federal or state prison, compared to 10 percent of male Hispanics and 3.5 percent of male whites.[45]

Many people believe that systemic racism confronts the minority offender who enters the judicial process;[46] studies show, however, that although racism may exist at some points in the justice system, systemwide discrimination does not exist.[47]

Minorities are disproportionately involved in crime, especially violent crime, both as the perpetrators and as the victims. Crime is linked with poverty, drug use, and blocked opportunity for legitimate approaches to economic success. Therefore, it appears that the disproportionate number of minorities under correctional supervision has more to do with social factors influencing crime and social class than with racism. Even so, the high numbers of minorities in correctional systems cause problems for administrators, who must strive for effective affirmative action programs to have a workforce that mirrors, to the extent possible, the inmate population. This not only enhances the potential for positive communications between staff and offenders, but also reduces the perception by offenders that the system is racist and that they have a "right" to misbehave.

## Segregating Inmates

Can prison administrators segregate inmates by race? In February 2005 the U.S. Supreme Court said only in rare circumstances, limiting the broad discretion wardens enjoy in other contexts. Although the court stopped short of overturning a California policy that places newly arrived inmates with a cellmate of the same race or ethnicity for the first 60 days, five justices voted to send the case back to a lower court to assess whether the policy is necessary to prevent violence.

The central question in the case was which legal standard should be used by the court in arriving at its decision. One series of Supreme Court decisions says that the "strict scrutiny" test applies to government racial classifications, such as affirmative action policies. (The appellant, inmate Garrison S. Johnson, who is black, was double-celled several times with inmates of the same race on arrival at state prisons, and argued that the prison policy should have to meet this higher legal standard, serve a "compelling interest," and be "narrowly tailored" to achieve that goal.) The appellee, conversely, argued that the court should defer to the judgment of prison administrators, and that prison rules need only be rationally connected to a legitimate government interest. The high court agreed with Johnson, saying that here, prisons must meet the more demanding strict scrutiny test, and that judicial review of racial classifications is necessary to guard against invidious discrimination.[48]

# Drug Use in Prisons: Interdiction and Treatment

More than half of all adult arrestees test positive for drug use at the time of their apprehension; their drug use prior to incarceration is typically chronic. More than three fourths (78 percent) of state and federal prisoners have used drugs at some time.[49]

Furthermore, offenders still manage to obtain illicit drugs during their incarceration, threatening the safety of inmates and staff while undermining the authority of correctional administrators, contradicting rehabilitative goals, and reducing public confidence.[50]

Next I discuss Pennsylvania's drug interdiction plan to prevent illicit drugs from coming into the state's prisons. Then I look at what can be done to treat offenders' substance abuse problems inside the institution.

## The Pennsylvania Plan

The state of Pennsylvania was compelled to acknowledge that drug use was pervasive in several of its prisons. Six inmates had died from overdoses in a 2-year period, and assaults on corrections officers and inmates had increased. To combat the problem, the state first adopted a zero-tolerance drug policy, the so-called **Pennsylvania plan:** Inmates caught with drugs were to be criminally prosecuted, and those testing positive (using hair testing) were to serve disciplinary custody time. Highly sensitive drug detection equipment was employed to detect drugs that visitors might try to smuggle into the prison, to inspect packages arriving in the mail, and to detect drugs that correctional staff might try to bring in. New policies were issued for inmate movement and visitation, and a new phone system was installed to randomly monitor inmates' calls.[51]

The results were impressive. The state's 24 prisons became 99 percent drug free. The number of drug finds during cell searches dropped 41 percent; assaults on staff decreased 57 percent; inmate-on-inmate assaults declined 70 percent; and weapons seized during searches dropped from 220 to 76. Marijuana use dropped from 6.5 percent before interdiction to 0.3 percent, and there were significant declines in the use of other types of drugs. Pennsylvania now believes that the foundation has been laid for inmates to abstain from drug use during service of their sentences—a necessary first step toward long-term abstinence and becoming a better citizen for their families and communities.[52]

## Treating the Problem in Prisons

During the last several years, a number of aggressive federal and state initiatives have been undertaken to expand substance treatment within correctional settings. These initiatives have been fueled by the high rates of substance abuse among offenders and the view that intensive, prison-based treatment efforts can significantly reduce postprison substance use and recidivism.[53]

Several barriers remain for correctional administrators in implementing substance treatment programs, however. First, institutions tend to use limited criteria (such as any lifetime drug use, possession, drug sales, trafficking) to determine the need for treatment, leading to a large portion of the treatment population who have not severely abused substances; conversely, many inmates who legitimately need treatment may be excluded for reasons unrelated to their substance abuse problems (gang affiliation or the commission of a sexual or violent offense). Treatment staff should be involved in the selection of candidates to ensure the appropriateness of the program population.[54]

Second, it is difficult to locate and recruit qualified and experienced staff in the remote areas where prisons are often located. In addition, counselors who are well suited for community-based treatment programs will not necessarily be effective in the prison setting. They often resist the rigid custody regulations that are common in institutional settings. For these reasons, limited human resources and high turnover rates for drug abuse treatment counselors make staffing an ongoing problem for prison administrators.[55]

Possible solutions to this staffing problem include offering sufficient wages and other amenities to induce counselors to move to and stay with the prison; recruiting and training "lifers" as inmate counselors and mentors; and professionalizing treatment positions for correctional officers. With the use of counselors, certification and financial incentives would help toward retaining staff, as well as enhance their professional development for the treatment setting.[56]

# The Move toward Privatization

## *Emergence of the Concept*

Perhaps the most controversial approach to reducing the cost of corrections has been the **privatization** of correctional operations and programs. Private vendors not only supply health care services, educational and vocational training, and an array of other services to public institutions,[57] but they also construct and/or manage prisons and detention facilities. The largest and most prominent of the private corporations attempting to operate correctional institutions is Corrections Corporation of America (CCA), formed in 1983.[58]

## *Arguments For and Against*

Proponents for privatization of prisons and jails believe that it will be able to offer a greater diversity of programs and facilities and increase the ability to handle special inmate populations or offer special rehabilitative or training programs.[59] The strongest argument for the concept, however, is the belief that private industry can respond more quickly than governmental bureaucracies and in a more cost-effective manner to the current pressure for more prison space because they are not bound by state civil service rules or by employee unions. Proponents maintain that a private prison will charge the state less per day to hold each inmate than the publicly operated facility will by reducing building and labor costs and using economies of scale. They also argue that the profit motive creates an inherent efficiency.[60] Finally, one study in Florida found that inmates released from private prisons had lower recidivism rates (10 percent) than those released from public institutions (19 percent), and that those released from private prisons who reoffended committed less serious subsequent offenses than did their public prison counterparts.[61]

Those who have studied the operation of private prisons since they were initiated have identified 10 key issues that should be part of any deliberations regarding the use of private prisons[62]:

1. *Propriety.* Can the punishment of offenders be delegated to nonpublic agencies?

2. *Cost and efficiency.* Are private prisons operated less expensively than public prisons?

3. *Quality.* Does the profit motive diminish the drive for delivery of quality services and programs to inmates?

4. *Quantity.* Does the involvement of the private sector to make a profit encourage the expansion of imprisonment beyond what is in the public interest?

5. *Flexibility.* Does the private sector's not having to follow bureaucratic governmental policies for purchasing and personnel management increase efficiency?

6. *Security.* Does an emphasis on profits and cost cutting undermine security for inmates, staff, and community?

7. *Liability.* What impact does contracting with a private firm have on governmental liability for violation of inmates' constitutional rights?

8. *Accountability and monitoring.* How will private contractors be monitored to fulfill requirements and be held responsible if they do not?

9. *Corruption.* Without restraints found in government to reduce the likelihood of corruption, will there be an increase in corrupt activities by personnel in private prisons?

10. *Dependence.* Will the public sector become dependent on the private sector contract, and if so, how will it affect decision making?

At this time, there are no firm conclusions about the cost efficiency and overall superiority of private prisons versus public prisons. The most important element for correctional administrators considering contracting with the private sector is to be extremely specific in the Request for Proposal (RFP) regarding minimal levels of programs and to build in procedures to monitor and hold the private sector accountable for meeting these levels.

## Alternatives to Incarceration: Intermediate Sanctions

The United States is not soft on crime, but because prisons are not in a position to effect great change,[63] the search for solutions must include correctional programs in the community. The demand for prison space has created a reaction throughout corrections.[64] With the cost of prison construction now exceeding a quarter of a million dollars per cell in maximum-security institutions, cost-saving alternatives are becoming more attractive if not essential.

A real alternative to incarceration needs to have three elements to be effective: It must incapacitate offenders enough so that it is possible to interfere with their lives and activities to make committing a new offense extremely difficult; it must be unpleasant enough to deter offenders from wanting to commit new crimes; and it has to provide real and credible protection for the community.[65]

The aforementioned realities of prison construction and overcrowding have led to a search for intermediate punishments.[66] This in turn has brought about the emergence of a new generation of programs, making community-based corrections, according to Barry Nidorf, a "strong, full partner in the fight against crime and a leader in confronting the crowding crisis."[67] Economic reality dictates that cost-effective measures be developed, and this is motivating the development of **intermediate sanctions.**[68]

A survey by the Bureau of Justice Statistics found that, of all persons being supervised outside a jail facility, 24 percent were engaged in community service and 17.8 percent were involved in electronic monitoring; fewer than 1 percent were undergoing home detention only.[69] Table 12.1 shows the number of persons under jail supervision by program type.

## *Intensive Probation or Parole*

**Intensive supervision** has become the most popular program in probation and parole. Early versions were based on the premise that increased client contact would enhance rehabilitation while affording greater client control. Current programs are simply a means of easing the burden of prison overcrowding.[70]

Intensive supervision can be classified into two types: those stressing diversion, and those stressing enhancement. A diversion program is commonly known as a "front door" program because its goal is to limit the number of generally low-risk offenders who enter prison. Enhancement programs generally select already sentenced probationers and parolees and subject them to closer supervision in the community than they receive under regular probation or parole.[71]

As of 1990, jurisdictions in all 50 states had instituted *intensive supervision probation* (ISP). Persons placed on ISP are supposed to be those offenders who, in the absence of intensive supervision, would have been sentenced to imprisonment. In parole, intensive supervision is viewed as risk management—allowing for a high-risk inmate to be paroled but under the most restrictive of circumstances. In either case, intensive supervision is a response to overcrowding; although ISP is invariably more costly than regular supervision, the costs "are compared not with the costs of normal supervision but rather with the costs of incarceration."[72]

ISP is demanding for probationers and parolees and does not represent freedom; in fact, it may stress and isolate repeat offenders more than imprisonment does. Given the option of serving prison terms or participating in ISPs, many offenders have chosen prison.[73] Many offenders may prefer to serve a short prison term rather than spend five times as long in an ISP. Consider the alternatives now facing offenders in one western state:

*ISP.* The offender serves 2 years under this alternative. During that time, a probation officer visits the offender two or three times per week and

**TABLE 12.1** Persons under Jail Supervision by Confinement Status and Type of Program, United States, 1995–2003

| CONFINEMENT STATUS AND TYPE OF PROGRAM | PERSONS UNDER JAIL SUPERVISION | | | | | | | | |
|---|---|---|---|---|---|---|---|---|---|
| | 1995 | 1996 | 1997 | 1998 | 1999 | 2000 | 2001 | 2002 | 2003 |
| **Total** | 541,913 | 591,469 | 637,319 | 664,847 | 687,973 | 687,033 | 702,044 | 737,912 | 762,672 |
| **Held in jail** | 507,044 | 518,492 | 567,079 | 592,462 | 605,943 | 621,149 | 631,240 | 665,475 | 691,301 |
| **Supervised outside a jail facility**[a] | 34,869 | 72,977 | 70,239 | 72,385 | 82,030 | 65,884 | 70,804 | 72,437 | 71,371 |
| Electronic monitoring | 6,788 | 7,480 | 8,699 | 10,827 | 10,280 | 10,782 | 10,017 | 9,706 | 12,678 |
| Home detention[b] | 1,376 | 907 | 1,164 | 370 | 518 | 332 | 539 | 1,037 | 594 |
| Day reporting | 1,283 | 3,298 | 2,768 | 3,089 | 5,080 | 3,969 | 3,522 | 5,010 | 7,965 |
| Community service | 10,253 | 17,410 | 15,918 | 17,518 | 20,139 | 13,592 | 17,561 | 13,918 | 17,102 |
| Weekender programs | 1,909 | 16,336 | 17,656 | 17,249 | 16,089 | 14,523 | 14,381 | 17,955 | 12,111 |
| Other pretrial supervision | 3,229 | 2,135 | 7,368 | 6,048 | 10,092 | 6,279 | 6,632 | 8,702 | 11,452 |
| Other work programs[c] | 9,144 | 14,469 | 6,631 | 7,089 | 7,780 | 8,011 | 5,204 | 5,190 | 4,498 |
| Treatment programs[d] | NA | 10,425 | 6,693 | 5,702 | 8,500 | 5,714 | 5,219 | 1,256 | 1,891 |
| Other | 887 | 517 | 3,342 | 4,493 | 3,602 | 2,682 | 7,729 | 9,663 | 3,080 |

[a]Excludes persons supervised by a probation or parole agency.
[b]Includes only those without electronic monitoring.
[c]Includes persons in work release programs, work gangs/crews, and other work alternative programs.
[d]Includes persons under drug, alcohol, mental health, and other medical treatment.

*Source:* U.S. Department of Justice, Bureau of Justice Statistics, *Prison and Jail Inmates at Midyear 2003* (Bulletin NCJ 203947) (Washington, D.C.: Author, 2004), p. 7.

phones on the other days. The offender is subject to unannounced searches of his or her home for drugs and has his or her urine tested regularly for alcohol and drugs. The offender must strictly abide by other conditions as set by the court: not carrying a weapon, not socializing with certain persons, performing community service, and being employed or participating in training or education. In addition, he or she will be strongly encouraged to attend counseling and/or other treatment, particularly if he or she is a drug offender.

*Prison.* The alternative is a sentence of 2 to 4 years of which the offender will serve only about 3 to 6 months. During this term, the offender is not required to work or to participate in any training or treatment but may do so voluntarily. Once released, the offender is placed on a 2-year routine parole supervision and must visit his or her parole officer about once a month.[74]

Although evidence of the effectiveness of this program is lacking, it has been deemed a public relations success.[75] Intensive supervision is usually accomplished by severely reducing caseload size per probation or parole officer, leading to increased contact between officers and clients or their significant others (such as spouse or parents), and it is hoped that this increased contact will improve service delivery and control and thus reduce recidivism.[76]

## House Arrest

Since the late 1980s, **house arrest** has become increasingly common. With house arrest, offenders receive a "sentence" of detention in their own homes, and their compliance is often monitored electronically. The primary motivation for using this intermediate sanction is a financial one: the conservation of scarce resources. It is also hoped, of course, that house arrest is more effective at preventing recidivism than traditional probation alone or incarceration.

Many people apparently feel that house arrest is not effective or punitive enough for offenders. Indeed, one study reported that nearly half (44 percent) of the public feels that house arrest is not very effective or not effective at all.[77]

Does house arrest work? Looking at a sample of 528 adult felony offenders who had been released from house arrest, Jeffrey Ulner[78] found that the sentence combination associated with the least likelihood of rearrest was house arrest/probation. The combinations of house arrest/work release and house arrest/incarceration were also significantly associated with decreased chances of rearrest compared to traditional probation. Furthermore, whenever any other sentence option was paired with house arrest, that sentence combination significantly reduced chances and severity of rearrest.[79] Clearly, house arrest works when used in tandem with other forms of sentencing options.

What is it about house arrest that might explain its success? It puts the offender in touch with opportunities and resources for rehabilitative services (such as substance abuse or sex offender counseling, anger management classes, and so on), which supports the contention that for intermediate sanctions of any type to reduce recidivism, they must include a rehabilitative emphasis.[80]

## *Electronic Monitoring*

**Electronic monitoring** is another form of intermediate sanction, and is often used in conjunction with house arrest; it applies to offenders whose crimes are less serious than those requiring long-term incarceration but are more serious than those committed by persons serving standard probation. Two basic types of electronic monitoring devices are available: active and passive.

The former are continuous signaling devices attached to the offender that constantly monitor his or her presence at a particular location. A receiver–dialer apparatus is attached to the offender's telephone and detects signals from the transmitter. A central computer accepts reports from the receiver–dialer over telephone lines, compares them with the offender's curfew schedule, and alerts corrections officials to unauthorized absences.[81] Simpler, continuous signaling systems that do not use a telephone consist of only two basic components: a transmitter and a portable receiver. The transmitter, which is strapped to the offender's ankle or wrist or worn around the neck, emits a radio signal that travels about one city block. By driving past the offender's residence, place of employment, or wherever he or she is supposed to be, the officer can verify his or her presence with the handheld portable receiver.[82]

The passive type of electronic monitoring involves the use of programmed contact devices that contact the offender periodically to verify his or her presence. Various manufacturing companies use a different method to assure that the offender is the person responding to the call and is in fact at the monitored location as required. One system uses voice verification technology. Another system uses satellite technology. The subject wears an ankle bracelet and carries or wears a portable tracking device about the size of a small lunchbox, weighing 3.5 pounds. A Global Positioning System satellite constellation is able to establish an offender's whereabouts within 150 feet of his or her location 24 hours a day.[83]

With home detention programs, which are often implemented for repeat drunk-driving and other types of offenders, a computer dials the client's home telephone number on random days; the client answers and, by placing an electronic bracelet attached to his or her wrist to the telephone, sends a code to the computer. The computer then asks several verifying questions of the client, and a report is sent to the office.

## *Shock Probation/Parole*

Shock probation is another less costly intermediate alternative to incarceration that is supported by many correctional administrators. This form of corrections combines a brief exposure to incarceration with subsequent release. It allows sentencing judges to reconsider the original sentence to prison and, upon motion, to recall the inmate after a few months in prison and place him or her on probation, under conditions deemed appropriate. The idea is that the "shock" of a short stay in prison will give the offender a taste of institutional life and will make such an indelible impression that he or she will be deterred from future crime and will avoid the negative effects of lengthy confinement.[84]

In many states, each candidate for **shock probation/parole** must obtain a community sponsor who will be responsible for the applicant's actions while in the community. The sponsor serves as an adjunct to and a resource for the probation officer. Specific activities for the sponsor can include providing transportation to work, checking on compliance with curfew and other restrictions, assisting with housing and employment problems, and maintaining contact with the probation officer. The offender may also be required to perform community service, usually physical labor.[85]

## Boot Camps/Shock Incarceration

Correctional **boot camps,** also called **shock incarceration,** were first implemented as an intermediate sanction in 1983.[86] The early version of these programs placed offenders in a quasi-military program of 3 to 6 months' duration similar to a military basic training program. The goal was to reduce recidivism, prison and jail populations, and operating costs. Offenders generally served a short institutional sentence and then were put through a rigorous regimen of drills, strenuous workouts, marching, and hard physical labor. To be eligible, inmates generally had to be young, nonviolent offenders.

Unfortunately, early evaluations of boot camps generally found that participants did no better than other offenders without this experience.[87] Only boot camps that were carefully designed, targeted the right offenders, and provided rehabilitative services and aftercare were deemed likely to save the state money and reduce recidivism.[88] As a result of these findings, the number of boot camps declined; by the year 2000, only 51 prison boot camps remained.[89] Boot camps have evolved over time, however, and are now in their third generation. The first-generation camps were those just discussed, with military discipline and physical training being stressed. Second-generation camps emphasized rehabilitation by adding such components as alcohol and drug treatment and social skills training (some even including postrelease electronic monitoring, house arrest, and random urine tests). Recently, in the third generation, some boot camps have substituted an emphasis on educational and vocational skills for the military components.[90]

A recent U.S. Department of Justice report, co-authored by Attorney General John Ashcroft, stated that correctional administrators and planners might learn from boot camps' failures to reduce recidivism or prison populations by considering the following[91]:

1. Building reintegration into the community into an inmate's program may improve the likelihood he or she will not recidivate.
2. Programs that offer substantial reductions in time served to boot camp "graduates" and that choose for participation inmates with longer sentences are the most successful in reducing prison populations.
3. Chances of reducing recidivism increase when boot camps last longer and offer more intensive treatment and postrelease supervision.

### Exhibit 12.1
### When the Prison Doors Reopen

One year after a consortium of federal agencies launched a multimillion-dollar national effort called Going Home to rehabilitate and re-introduce convicts back into their communities, jurisdictions in Wisconsin, Georgia and Mississippi, among others, created their own local versions of the program in 2004:

- With help of a $300,000 federal grant, Macon, Ga., officials formed a steering committee, including members of the law enforcement community, corrections, education and clergy, to create a re-entry program. Its target population will come from the Macon Transitional Center, a state-run facility where former inmates live after being released from prison.

- A new program aimed at reducing recidivism was unveiled in Racine, Wis. The initiative will focus on high-risk offenders before they are released. The Community Re-entry Program will cost $91,000.

- Augusta, Ga., implemented a faith-based component to its re-entry

program, which calls for churchgoers to essentially adopt a newly released convict and bring the individual to church services with them.

As a way of recouping some of the money spent on incarceration, officials in a number of jurisdictions have implemented room-and-board fees. Last year, the Macomb County, Mich., Sheriff's Department collected $1.5 million from 22,000 people that had spent time in its jail. In 2004:

- An Oklahoma law took effect in August that requires anyone locked up in either a county or municipal jail to pay for the costs of incarceration, including booking, receiving and processing out, housing, food, clothing, medical and dental care and psychiatric services. The services could add up to as much as $3,000. The daily cost is estimated to be $30 to $35 a day.

*Source:* Reprinted with permission from *Law Enforcement News,* December 2004, p. 11. John Jay College of Criminal Justice (CCNY), 555 West 57th St., New York, NY 10019.

## Day Reporting Centers

Another intermediate sanction that has gained recent popularity among correctional administrators and policymakers is the **day reporting** center. Such centers originated in Great Britain as a response to less serious but chronic offenders who lacked basic skills and were often dependent on drugs or alcohol. The British experience led several U.S. states to begin setting up day reporting centers in the mid-1980s. The purposes of day reporting centers are to heighten control and surveillance of offenders placed on community supervision, increase offender access to treatment programs, give officials more proportional and certain sanctions, and reduce prison or jail crowding. Offenders report to the centers frequently (usually once or twice a day), and treatment services (job training and placement, counseling, and education) are usually provided on-site either by the agency running the program or by other human services agencies.[92]

One study of the effect of day reporting centers on recidivism found no significant reduction in the rate of rearrest. The author pointed out, however, that regardless of effect on recidivism, the center "empowers the individual offender by offering him or her literacy courses, GED preparation, substance abuse counseling, and anger management courses."[93]

# Reinventing Probation: Partnering with the Police

## *A Crisis in Boston*

Each year thousands of men and women are made subject to probation orders, community service orders, drug treatment, and testing orders. And each year new ideas emerge on how best to supervise the recipients of such interventions.[94] Knowing what can work with probation supervision is key to its long-term success.

Probation is both a sentence and a status. As a sentence, it is by far the most popular option in use with offenders. As a status, it can mean for the offender certain conditions, including avoiding subsequent arrest, reporting to a probation officer, not leaving the state without permission, paying restitution, and obtaining counseling, among others.[95]

Notwithstanding these conditions, however, many probation officers—like police officers—realize that they see the same offenders in the court corridor week after week, from a "revolving door" vantage point. What can be done to enhance the success of probation and to make probationers comply with the conditions of their sentence? One promising approach was recently launched in Boston, where youth violence had reached crisis proportions.

A few probation officers in Boston began asking judges to include curfews and area restrictions in the conditions of probation. Then the officers departed from the traditional model of probation by leaving their desks; one- or two-person probation teams were matched with a similar team from the police gang unit as part of Operation Night Light. They typically met at gang unit headquarters to prepare for the evening's work. The probation officers had identified 10 to 15 probationers that they wanted to see that evening, concentrating on those thought to be "active" on the street. Using an unmarked car and in street clothes, the team made home visits to determine whether the probationer was abiding by his or her curfew, and frequently stopped and parked at corners where youths congregate, while generally tightening supervision and using stricter enforcement. These activities soon caused word to spread on the street that there was a new mode of operation in probation—and a new level of jeopardy for those who ignored their probationary obligations. These increased enforcement efforts were also bolstered by a commitment to provide services to youth who needed help, with employment being at the top of the list; getting kids jobs kept them busy and therefore unavailable for gang activities while providing spending money and teaching them responsibility, punctuality, and other lessons.[96]

Both the probation and police agencies sustained benefits from their partnership. Probation officers were able to enter the most crime-ridden areas of the city into the late evening because the police provide a high degree of security for them. The police, for their part, had a new tool available to them to help get the offenders off the streets. For both sides came the ability to exchange valuable information and the heightened ability to apprehend probation violators.

Were these efforts by probation–police teams, involving 7,000 contacts with probationers over 10 years, successful? The results were indeed impressive; most important was the dramatic drop in the numbers of homicides, with 16 homicides being committed by juveniles during the latter 6 years of the program, compared to 58 being committed during its initial 6 years. Operation Night Light is also felt to be responsible for the reduced levels of gang-related violence as well as increased compliance with terms of probation. In addition, court personnel also believed that probationary sentences have more credibility because of the stricter enforcement that the program provides.[97]

## *Before Replication is Attempted . . .*

Can this strategy be replicated and successful in other jurisdictions, with juvenile or even adult offenders? Possibly, but only, according to Ronald Corbett Jr.,[98] if correctional administrators and policymakers remember the following:

- *Principles travel, programs don't.* People, places, conditions, and resources will vary from place to place; what works in one jurisdiction may not work in another, so one should custom tailor the general approach to local realities; "steal ideas, not programs."

- *It takes a crisis.* A hard truth is that often it takes a crisis to jumpstart reform efforts; without a shared sense of urgency, the mandate for change can be very weak and uncertain; "you cannot instigate a crisis, but you can reveal one."

- *Look for natural leaders.* Wherever reform is occurring, "there is a monomaniac with a mission;" major results require extraordinary leaders; the best ideas are never self-executing, and uninspired management can undermine the best models, whereas real leadership can breathe life into the most rudimentary ideas.

- *Start small.* Overreaching squanders resources, divides attention, strains logistics, and makes retreat difficult.

- *Take stock of existing relationships.* The best working relationships do not come easily; they are built around "a lot of coffee cups, in the back rooms of station houses, in drafty church basements, in courthouse corridors, and at the scenes of shootings; it takes a while to learn who you can rely on, whose back you are willing to cover," and agencies must have a sufficient number of allies for reform.

# Computer Crime and the Probation Officer

## *Legal Provisions*

The computer has become the tool of choice for a new generation of offenders. This requires probation offices, like law enforcement agencies, to be staffed with computer-literate employees.

First, today's probation officers must understand the statutes pertaining to e-mail and other forms of stored electronic communication. Federal law, specifically 18 U.S.C. Secs. 2701 through 2771, provides for both criminal and civil penalties for anyone who accesses without authorization a facility through which electronic communication services are provided and "thereby obtains, alters, or prevents authorized access to wire or electronic communication while in storage." Probation officers supervising offenders must not access any unopened e-mail or similar electronic communication in storage without specific authorization of the court or consent of the offender.[99]

Furthermore, any offender with a computer, particularly one with a modem, can be considered a publisher within the meaning of the Privacy Protection Act (PPA). The PPA provides for civil penalties for anyone who seizes, without a subpoena, work products or documents that are intended for dissemination to the public. The following are general exceptions to this provision: information that is contraband or fruits or instrumentalities of the crime (e.g., child pornography, illegally copied software); information that is evidence of crime committed by the subject (e.g., diary confession to a particular offense); and to prevent death or serious injury.[100]

## *Supervising the Computer Offender*

Although it may be that the best condition of probation for the computer offender is for him or her to have no computer at all, there are three areas of concern regarding such a broad restriction: first, the term "computer" is becoming increasingly difficult to define; it can also include a cell phone, palm pilot organizer, and pager. What is allowed and not allowed? Second, as a result of this problem with terminology, judges may not wish to prohibit all access to computers, so specific conditions pertaining to the Internet, bulletin board systems, and chat rooms may be more appropriate. Finally, a no-computer condition placed on an offender typically includes the phrase "unless authorized by the probation officer." Such wording provides the probation officer the authority to either completely restrict or give authorization in certain circumstances.[101]

For these reasons, the officer should remember that issuing a blanket denial for computer use may not always pass court scrutiny. To address the problem and to avoid later difficulties, a probation officer must be qualified to conduct an educated assessment of a computer offender before he or she makes recommendation about computer restrictions. Furthermore, seizing a computer takes very specific skills and knowledge. Evidence can be lost by merely turning on the system without the proper procedures in place. The offender may have "hot keys" that when struck activate programs that destroy data.[102]

# Corrections and the Future

## *The Changing Nature of "Justice," Treatment, and Custody*

The movement today is toward restorative justice, which seeks to restore at least some of the tangible losses experienced by the victim through negotiated restitution arrangements, as well as the offender's sense of personal accountability for the harm caused by his or her actions. Programs based on restorative justice can be expected to proliferate in the future, especially as victims continue to demand greater representation in the justice process.[103]

Treatment for offenders is also a continuing part of the corrections process. Offender treatment today is more likely to be offered on a *voluntary* basis, rather than as an inducement for early release. Treatment now takes on a more pragmatic orientation. In contrast to counseling, group therapy, and other forms of treatment, the emphasis today (and likely for the foreseeable future) is placed on developing productive employment skills.[104]

The physical features of correctional institutions are also beginning to change, especially in local jails, where some of the most antiquated facilities are being razed or modernized, small jails are being consolidated through regionalization, and new architectural and management styles are reflecting the principles of direct supervision ("new generation") jailing. Both prisons and jails are also becoming more electronically sophisticated; locks and keys are giving way to computers, video cameras, "smart cards," and even satellite surveillance. As corrections administrators are expected to do more with less, methods of tracking inmate movements and purchases through electronic scanning devices are also expanding, as are user fees for services ranging from health care to transportation and even food and lodging.[105]

## *Changing Personnel and Populations*

The times are changing with respect to corrections personnel in the areas of recruitment and retention, decision making, and treatment of their charges. Indeed, surveys have identified institutional crowding, staff and funding shortages, and resulting workload increases as the key problems that corrections is anticipated to face in the immediate future.[106]

The ability of corrections administrators to recruit and retain the quality of personnel needed during this new century will largely depend on how well they can accommodate diversity, decentralized decision making, and ongoing career development. Greater consideration by government of privatization (discussed earlier) as an attempt to save money may also affect corrections practices as well as how corrections personnel approach their work: The "threat" of privatization may compel public employees to believe their job security is endangered, thus stimulating them to provide better services at lower cost in the public sector.[107]

The expanding use of computers is also having a substantial impact throughout the corrections field, performing what were previously time-consuming and labor-intensive tasks. Corrections will also be especially challenged to meet the needs of its changing population, including increasing numbers of female offenders as well as those who have AIDS or are physically impaired, very young, or elderly. Nor is there expected to be any decline in the number of correctional clients suffering from drug or alcohol addictions or mental disorders.

Correctional administrators of the future must try to harness and direct the change process. According to Alvin Cohn, the progressive correctional manager is proactive, views the organization as a system, and plans for and attempts to control its future.[108]

# CASE STUDIES

The following case studies will help the reader to consider some of the challenges facing today's correctional administrators and provide opportunities to consider the application of chapter materials.

## "Double, Double, Toil and Trouble"

There seems to be trouble brewing in a nearby medium-level adult prison. Inmate informers have noted several conditions that point to the fact that a riot may be imminent: Inmates are stocking up on long-term items (e.g., canned goods) in the commissary and banding together more throughout the institution by racial groupings; furthermore, inmates tend to be seen standing in or near doorways, as if preparing for a quick exit. Over the last several months the inmates have become increasingly unhappy with their conditions of confinement—not only lodging the usual complaints about bland food, but also with the increasing numbers of assaults and gang attacks—and many are either very young, nonviolent offenders, or very old and frail. For their part, the staff have also become increasingly unhappy, particularly with their low salaries and benefits, perceived unsafe working conditions and attacks on officers, institutional overcrowding, the number of sexual attacks that seem to be occurring with inmates, and a trend toward greater amounts of drugs and other forms of contraband found in the cellblocks. They demand that the prison administration ask the courts to give more consideration to house arrest and other intermediate sanctions as well as the legislature to consider privatization of the prison.

As the state's prison system director, the governor's office has asked that you prepare an immediate position paper for the chief executive setting forth a plan for dealing with this prison's current situation.

1. What are the critical issues that should be dealt with immediately?
2. How would you proceed to defuse the potential for a riot?
3. What would be your response to the suggestions for prison privatization and the use of intermediate sanctions?
4. What if anything might be done to address the concerns of the inmates? The staff?

## "Out-of-Town Brown" and the Besieged Probation Supervisor

Joan Casey is a career probation officer. She majored in criminal justice as an undergraduate, holds memberships in several national correctional organizations, attends training conferences, and does a lot of reading on her own time to stay current in the field. Casey began working for the Collier County Probation Department soon after she graduated from college and was promoted to a supervisory position, where she supervises an adult probation unit consisting of eight seasoned probation officers. The unit is responsible for investigating approximately 80 offenders a month and preparing presentence investigation (PSI) reports on them. Collier County Probation Department has made the front page of the local newspapers twice in the last month. Both times it was a nightmare for the chief probation officer, Jack Brown, and the entire agency. "Northside Stalker Gets Probation!" screamed the first headline, and then, just a week later, "Collier County Soft on Crime!" Brown called a management team meeting: "Better PSIs," he said, "or heads are gonna roll!" Everybody got the point. This week Brown is on annual leave and Casey is the designated officer in charge. One of Casey's probation officers has recommended intermediate sanctions for a 23-year-old man who murdered his stepfather with a knife after suffering many years of physical and mental abuse. The young man had no prior record, and had been an incest victim since he was 5 years old; he is considered an otherwise nonviolent person, a low recidivism risk. Casey is aware of the probation officer's recommendation and agrees with it. However, Casey receives a call from a well-known, veteran local television anchor—a strong crusader in the local war against crime. He knows the young man will be sentenced tomorrow.

## Questions for Discussion

1. What should Casey's response be to the reporter (other than hanging up or telling him to call back) concerning the agency's recommendation?
2. If Casey elects to discuss her officer's recommendation for some form of intermediate sanction, how can she justify such sanctions in general, and in this case specifically?
3. Do you feel the probation officer's recommendation is correct based on these facts? Why or why not?
4. Which form of intermediate sanction would appear to hold the most promise for the offender in this case?

## A Corrections Futures Forum

Assume that your jurisdiction is planning a new, week-long, futures-oriented program, "Leadership Forum for 2010," which will bring professionals together from the business and governmental sectors. Topics to be discussed at the forum include a wide array of area issues, challenges, methods, and concerns. Assume further that you are a prison or probation/parole administrator. After applying and being selected to attend this program, you are advised that you are to make a 60-minute presentation concerning your profession generally, as well as the future challenges facing your local corrections organization.

## Questions for Discussion

1. Using some of the materials discussed in the chapters of this book dealing with corrections organization and administration, how would you briefly explain to this group your role as a chief executive of your agency?

2. What would be some of the important *current* themes and issues that you would take to the forum concerning a corrections administrator's job to indicate its complexities and challenges?

3. How would you describe the changing nature of the corrections administrator's role and the *future* issues and challenges of this position?

# Summary

This chapter has examined several major contemporary and future issues confronting correctional administrators. It is clear that many, if not all of these issues do not lend themselves to easy or quick resolutions and will continue to pose challenges to correctional administrators for many years. Included in this discussion were several new forms of diversion termed intermediate sanctions.

Corrections agencies bear the brunt of the combined effects of increased crime, tough mandatory sentencing laws leading to an increased incarceration of offenders, a get-tough public and justice system attitude toward crime that permeates the country, and overcrowded prisons and large probation and parole caseloads. As a result, and as this chapter has shown, they must develop new ways to deal with offenders.

# Questions for Review

1. What are some primary substantive and administrative issues facing corrections administrators?

2. What are correctional administrators' roles in preventing and dealing with sexual coercion?

3. How can prison administrators interdict and treat the drug problem?

4. What are some challenges confronting correctional administrators with respect to special populations: the sexually coerced, aging, juvenile, females, the mentally ill, and minority inmates?

5. What are some advantages and disadvantages of privatization?

6. Why are intermediate sanctions being used so widely?

7. What do *intensive supervision* and *electronic monitoring* mean?

8. How can shock probation further the goals of corrections? Boot camps/shock incarceration? What successes and problems have been found with these practices?

9. In what ways, and for what types of crime problems, might community corrections personnel partner with the police?
10. What are some of the challenges involved with probation supervision of the computer offender?
11. What are some of the future issues challenging corrections administrators?

# Notes

1. Richard P. Seiter, *Correctional Administration: Integrating Theory and Practice* (Upper Saddle River, N.J.: Prentice Hall, 2002), p. 18.
2. Edward E. Rhine, "Probation and Parole Supervision: In Need of a New Narrative," *Corrections Management Quarterly* **1** (1997):71-75.
3. Timothy J. Flanagan, "Correctional Policy and the Long-Term Prisoner, in Timothy Flanagan (ed.), *Long-Term Imprisonment: Policy, Science, and Correctional Practice* (Newbury Park, Calif.: Sage, 1995), p. 249.
4. Edwin W. Zedlewski, "Why Prisons Matter: A Utilitarian Review," *Corrections Management Quarterly* **1** (1997):15-24.
5. Todd R. Clear, "Ten Unintended Consequences of the Growth of Imprisonment," *Corrections Management Quarterly* **1** (1997):25-31.
6. J. Simon and M. M. Freely, "True Crime: The New Penology and Public Discourse on Crime," in T. G. Bloomberg and S. Cohen (eds.), *Punishment and Social Control* (New York: Aldine De Gruyter, 1995).
7. Rhine, "Probation and Parole Supervision," pp. 71-75.
8. Richard P. Seiter, "Offenders and Issues Force Managerial Change," *Corrections Management Quarterly* **1** (1997):iv.
9. U.S. Department of Justice, Bureau of Justice Statistics, "Key Facts at a Glance," http://www.ojp.usdoj.gov/bjs/glance/tables/exptyptab.htm (accessed September 21, 2005).
10. U.S. Department of Justice, Bureau of Justice Statistics, "Justice Expenditure and Employment Statistics," http://www.ojp.usdoj.gov/bjs/eande.htm (accessed September 21, 2005).
11. Seiter, *Correctional Administration,* p. 22.
12. Ibid., p. 25.
13. Chase Riveland, "The Correctional Leader and Public Policy Skills," *Correctional Management Quarterly* **1** (1997):24.
14. Seiter, *Correctional Administration,* p. 25.
15. Ibid.
16. Robert W. Dumond, "Inmate Sexual Assault: The Plague That Persists," *The Prison Journal* **80** (December 2000):407-414; see also Human Rights Watch, *No Escape: Male Rape in U.S. Prisons* (New York: Author, 2001).
17. Paul W. Tappan, *Crime, Justice, and Correction* (New York: McGraw-Hill, 1960), pp. 678-679.
18. Ibid., p. 678.
19. Ibid.
20. S. Donaldson, "Rape of Incarcerated Americans: A Preliminary Statistical Look," http://www.sspr.org/docs/stats/html (accessed June 22, 2000).

21. Cindy Struckman-Johnson and David Struckman-Johnson, "Sexual Coercion Rates in Seven Midwestern Prison Facilities for Men," *The Prison Journal* **80** (December 2000):379-390. See also Christopher Hensley, Robert W. Dumond, Richard Tewksbury, and Doris A. Dumond, "Possible Solutions for Preventing Inmate Sexual Assault: Examining Wardens' Beliefs," *American Journal of Criminal Justice* **27**(1) (2002):19-33.

22. Ibid.

23. Dumond, "Inmate Sexual Assault," p. 408.

24. Leanne Fiftal Alarid, "Sexual Assault and Coercion Among Incarcerated Women Prisoners: Excerpts from Prison Letters," *The Prison Journal* **80** (December 2000):391-406.

25. U.S. Department of Justice, *Bureau of Justice Statistics Status Report, Data Collections for the Prison Rape Elimination Act of 2003* (Washington, D.C.: Author, 2004), pp. 1-2.

26. Eve Bender, "Averting Prison Suicides Requires Special Strategies," *Psychiatric News* **39**(24) (December 17, 2004), pp. 1-2; http://pn.psychiatryonline.org/cgi/content/full/39/24/15 (accessed February 4, 2005).

27. Ibid., pp. 2-3.

28. Ibid.

29. Ibid., p. 4.

30. Ibid.

31. Lindsay M. Hayes, *Juvenile Suicide in Confinement: A National Survey* (Baltimore: National Center on Institutions and Alternatives, 2004), pp. ix-xi, 38.

32. U.S. Department of Justice, Bureau of Justice Statistics, *Prevalence of Imprisonment in the U.S. Population*, 1974-2001 (Washington, D.C.: Author, 2003), p. 1.

33. Joann Brown Morton, "Implications for Corrections of an Aging Prison Population," *Corrections Management Quarterly* **5**(1) (2001):78, 80.

34. Ibid., pp. 85, 87.

35. Kathleen Maguire and Ann L. Pastore (eds.), "Sourcebook of Criminal Justice Statistics," http://www.albany.edu/sourcebook/ (accessed September 21, 2005), pp. 487, 507.

36. Seiter, *Correctional Administration*, pp. 419-420.

37. Maguire and Pastore, "Sourcebook of Criminal Justice Statistics," p. 508.

38. Ibid., p. 521.

39. Ibid., p. 420.

40. See Kathleen O'Shea, *Women on the Row: Revelations from Both Sides of the Bars* (Ithaca, N.Y.: Firebrand Books, 2000).

41. Seiter, *Correctional Administration*, p. 420-421.

42. Maguire and Pastore, "Sourcebook of Criminal Justice Statistics," pp. 543-544.

43. Ibid., pp. 422-425.

44. Ibid.

45. U.S. Department of Justice, *Prevalence of Imprisonment*, p. 1.

46. See, for example, Coramae Richey Mann, "Racism in the Criminal Justice System: Two Sides of a Controversy," *Criminal Justice Research Bulletin* (Huntsville, Tex.: Sam Houston State University, 1987), 3.

47. See William Wilbanks, *The Myth of a Racist Criminal Justice System* (Belmont, Calif.: Wadsworth, 1987); Joan Petersilia, "Racial Disparities in the Criminal Justice System: Executive Summary of Rand Institute Study, 1983," in Daniel Georges-Abeyle (ed.), *The Criminal Justice System and Blacks* (New York: Clark Boardman Company, 1984), pp. 225-258.

48. *Johnson v. California*, 03-636 (2005).

49. U.S. Department of Justice, Bureau of Justice Statistics, "More Than Three-Quarters of Prisoners Had Abused Drugs in the Past," News Release, January 5, 1999, http://www.ojp.usdoj.gov/bjs/pub/press/satsfp97.pr (accessed July 2, 2002).

50. Thomas E. Feucht and Andrew Keyser, *Reducing Drug Use in Prisons: Pennsylvania's Approach* (Washington, D.C.: National Institute of Justice Journal, October 1999), p. 11.

51. Ibid., pp. 11–12.

52. Ibid., pp. 14–15.

53. David Farabee, Michael Prendergast, Jerome Cartier, Harry Wexler, Kevin Knight, and M. Douglas Anglin, "Barriers to Implementing Effective Correctional Drug Treatment Programs," *The Prison Journal* **79** (June 1999):150–162.

54. Ibid., p. 152.

55. Ibid., p. 153.

56. Ibid., pp. 154–155.

57. Camille Camp and George Camp, "Correctional Privatization in Perspective," *The Prison Journal* **65** (1985):14–31.

58. Craig Becker and Mary Dru Stanley, "The Downside of Private Prisons," *The Nation* (June 15, 1985), p. 729.

59. Robert B. Levinson, "Okeechobee: An Evaluation of Privatization in Corrections," *The Prison Journal* **65** (1985):75–94; J. Mullen, "Corrections and the Private Sector," *The Prison Journal* **65** (1985):1–13.

60. Ted Gest, "Prisons for Profit: A Growing Business," *U.S. News and World Report* (July 2, 1984):45–46.

61. Kaduce Lonn Lanza, Karen F. Parker, and Charles W. Thomas, "A Comparative Recidivism Analysis of Releasees from Private and Public Prisons," *Crime and Delinquency* **45** (1999):28–47.

62. Charles Logan, *Private Prisons: Cons and Pros* (New York: Oxford University Press, 1990).

63. John P. Conrad, "The Redefinition of Probation: Drastic Proposals to Solve an Urgent Problem," in Patrick McAnany, Doug Thomson, and David Fogel (eds.), *Probation and Justice: Reconsideration of Mission* (Cambridge, Mass.: Oelgeschlager, Gunn, and Hain, 1984), p. 258.

64. Peter J. Benekos, "Beyond Reintegration: Community Corrections in a Retributive Era," *Federal Probation* **54** (March 1990):53.

65. Ibid.

66. Belinda R. McCarthy, *Intermediate Punishments: Intensive Supervision, Home Confinement, and Electronic Surveillance* (Monsey, N.Y.: Criminal Justice Press, 1987), p. 3.

67. Barry J. Nidorf, "Community Corrections: Turning the Crowding Crisis into Opportunities," *Corrections Today* (October 1989):85.

68. Benekos, "Beyond Reintegration," p. 54.

69. U.S. Department of Justice, Bureau of Justice Statistics, *Prison and Jail Inmates at Midyear 2003* (Washington, D.C.: Author, 2004), p. 490.

70. Howard Abadinsky, *Probation and Parole: Theory and Practice,* 7th ed. (Upper Saddle River, N.J.: Prentice Hall, 2000), p. 410.

71. Joan Petersilia and Susan Turner, *Evaluating Intensive Supervision Probation/Parole: Results of a Nationwide Experiment* (Washington, D.C.: National Institute of Justice, 1993).

72. Lawrence A. Bennett, "Practice in Search of a Theory: The Case of Intensive Supervision—An Extension of an Old Practice," *American Journal of Criminal Justice* **12** (1988):293–310.

73. Ibid., p. 293.

74. This information was compiled from ISP brochures and information from the Oregon Department of Correction by Joan Petersilia.

75. Todd R. Clear and Patricia R. Hardyman, "The New Intensive Supervision Movement," *Crime and Delinquency* **36** (January 1990):42-60.

76. Ibid., p. 44.

77. Barbara A. Sims, "Questions of Corrections: Public Attitudes Toward Prison and Community-Based Programs," *Corrections Management Quarterly* **1**(1) (1997):54.

78. Jeffery T. Ulmer, "Intermediate Sanctions: A Comparative Analysis of the Probability and Severity of Recidivism," *Sociological Inquiry* **71**(2) (Spring 2001):164-193.

79. Ibid., p. 184.

80. Ibid., p. 185.

81. Annesley K. Schmidt, "Electronic Monitors: Realistically, What Can Be Expected?" *Federal Probation* **59** (June 1991):47-53.

82. Abadinsky, *Probation and Parole,* p. 428.

83. David Brauer, "Satellite 'Big Brother' Tracks Ex-Inmates," *Chicago Tribune,* December 18, 1998, p. 31.

84. Jeanne B. Stinchcomb and Vernon B. Fox, *Introduction to Corrections*, 5th ed. (Upper Saddle River, N.J.: Prentice Hall, 1999), p. 165.

85. Abadinsky, *Probation and Parole,* p. 434.

86. Gaylene Styve Armstrong, Angela R. Gover, and Doris Layton MacKenzie, "The Development and Diversity of Correctional Boot Camps," in Rosemary L. Gido and Ted Alleman (eds.), *Turnstile Justice: Issues in American Corrections* (Upper Saddle River, N.J.: Prentice Hall, 2002), pp. 115-130.

87. Doris Layton MacKenzie, "Boot Camp Prisons and Recidivism in Eight States," *Criminology* **33**(3) (1995):327-358.

88. Doris Layton MacKenzie and Alex Piquero, "The Impact of Shock Incarceration Programs on Prison Crowding," *Crime and Delinquency* **40**(2) (April 1994):222-249.

89. John Ashcroft, Deborah J. Daniels, and Sarah V. Hart, *Correctional Boot Camps: Lessons from a Decade of Research* (Washington, D.C.: U.S. Department of Justice, Office of Justice Programs, June 2003), p. 2.

90. Ibid.

91. Ibid., p. 9.

92. Dale G. Parent, "Day Reporting Centers: An Evolving Intermediate Sanction," *Federal Probation* **60** (December 1996):51-54.

93. Liz Marie Marciniak, "The Addition of Day Reporting to Intensive Supervision Probation: A Comparison of Recidivism Rates," *Federal Probation* **64** (June 2000):34-39.

94. Stephen Farrall, "'J' Accuse: Probation Evaluation-Research Epistemologies (Part One: The Critique)," *Criminal Justice* (London) **3**(2) (2003):161-179.

95. Ronald P. Corbett, Jr., "Reinventing Probation and Reducing Youth Violence," in Gary S. Katzmann (ed.), *Securing our Children's Future: New Approaches to Juvenile Justice and Youth Violence* (Washington, D.C.: Brookings Institution Press, 2002), pp. 175-199.

96. Ibid., pp. 179-182.

97. Ibid., p. 184.

98. Ibid., pp. 194-195.

99. Arthur L. Bowker and Gregory B. Thompson, "Computer Crime in the 21st Century and Its Effect on the Probation Officer," *Federal Probation* **65**(2) (2001):18-24.

100. Ibid., p. 22.

101. Ibid., p. 19.

102. Ibid., p. 20.

103. Stinchcomb and Fox, *Introduction to Corrections,* pp. 652–653.

104. Ibid., p. 654.

105. Ibid.

106. U.S. Department of Justice, National Institute of Justice, *NIJ Survey of Wardens and State Commissioners of Corrections* (Washington, D.C.: Author, 1995), p. 2

107. Stinchcomb and Fox, *Introduction to Corrections,* p. 659.

108. Alvin W. Cohn, "The Failure of Correctional Management: Recycling the Middle Manager," *Federal Probation* **59**(2) (June 1995):10.

# PART V

# ISSUES SPANNING THE JUSTICE SYSTEM
## Administrative Challenges and Practices

*The five chapters in this part focus on administrative problems or methods spanning the entire justice system. Chapter 13 examines ethical considerations that relate to police, courts, and corrections administration. The rights of criminal justice employees are reviewed in Chapter 14, and Chapter 15 discusses several challenges involving human resources (employee discipline, labor relations, and liability). Chapter 16 discusses financial administration, and Chapter 17 reviews the latest technological hardware and software now in use in criminal justice agencies. With the exception of Chapter 17, case studies are provided in each chapter.*

# Chapter 13

# Ethical Considerations

# Key Terms and Concepts

| | |
|---|---|
| Absolute ethics | Gratuities |
| Deontological ethics | Loyalty |
| Ethics | Relative ethics |

# Learning Objectives

As a result of reading this chapter, the student will:

- be able to distinguish between absolute and relative ethics
- be familiar with the utilitarian approach to ethics
- have an understanding of ethics among criminal justice employees
- be familiar with how employees play a role in the ethics of the court system
- understand why loyalty to one's agency superiors is problematic
- know the different tests for the justice system recruit

> *Everything secret degenerates, even the administration of Justice; nothing is safe that shows it cannot bear discussion and publicity.*
>
> —Lord Acton

# Introduction

At its root, criminal justice administration is about people and activities; in the end, the primary responsibilities of administrators involve monitoring subordinates' activities to ensure that they act correctly relative to their tasks and responsibilities and that these duties and responsibilities are conducted in an acceptable and effective manner.

Therefore, this chapter is essentially concerned with what constitutes "correct" behavior in the administration of criminal justice. Individuals and organizations have standards of conduct. To understand organizations, it becomes important to comprehend these standards and their etiology.

The chapter opens with a glimpse into the kinds of ethical situations criminal justice employees experience, providing three scenarios that are based on actual cases. Then I discuss ethics in general, reviewing philosophical foundations and types of ethics.

Next I examine ethics in policing. Because of their contact with and criticisms by the public and the unique kinds of vices, crimes, and temptations to which they are directly exposed, the police are given much more attention than are the personnel in the courts or corrections, who are discussed next. Although justice administrators are mentioned throughout, the chapter then looks at some specific challenges that they face, guidelines they must issue, some ethical tests for justice professionals, and a consideration of the value of organizational loyalty.

I conclude with seven case studies that the reader will find of interest in attempting to understand and resolve ethical quandaries.

*[handwritten: thwart  Obstruct, Frustrate  delete]*

## Food for Thought: Some Ethical Dilemmas

To frame the concept of ethics, I begin this chapter with three true scenarios:

*Police.* Seeing a vehicle weaving across the center line of the highway, Officer A stops the car, approaches the driver's door, and immediately detects a strong odor of alcohol. The motorist is removed from the car and joins Officer A and a backup, Officer B, on the roadside. Officer A decides to use a portable breath test device to confirm his suspicions of DUI, and he gives a sterile plastic mouthpiece to the driver to blow into. The driver attempts to thwart the test by appearing (but failing) to blow into the mouthpiece. Irritated by this attempt, Officer A yanks the mouthpiece away, throws it on the ground, and arrests the driver for DUI. At trial, the driver claimed the mouthpiece was flawed (blocked) so he was unable to blow through it; Officer A testifies under oath that it had not been blocked and as "evidence," he takes a mouthpiece out of his pocket, stating it was the mouthpiece he had used for the test that night. Officer B, sitting in the room, hears this testimony and knows differently, having seen Officer A impatiently throw the mouthpiece on the ground.[1]

*Courts.* For several weeks, a wealthy divorcee receives menacing telephone calls that demand dates and sexual favors. The caller's voice is electronically disguised. The suspect also begins stalking the woman. After working some clues and tailing a suspect, a federal agent finally makes contact with a suspect, determining that he is the chief judge of the state's supreme court. Upon confronting him, the agent is told by the judge to "forget about it, or you'll be checking passports in a remote embassy."[2]

*Corrections.* A corrections officer in a minimum-security facility for young offenders is working the night shift when a youth is admitted. The youth is frightened because this is his first time in custody, and the officer places him in isolation because the youth told the staff he is feeling suicidal. Over the next several days, the officer develops a friendship with the youth. Looking through the youth's file, the officer learns that the boy does not wish to remain male; rather, he wants to be female. One day while doing a routine cell search, the officer observes the youth stuffing women's panties into his pillowcase. With a terrified and pleading look, the youth explains he prefers them to boxer shorts and begs the officer not to mention this to other staff or youths in the facility. The officer ponders what to do; surely the boy would be seriously harangued if others knew of the panties, and it does not seem to be a "big deal"; on the other hand, if the officer does not report the event and the boy's choice of underwear is revealed later, the officer knows he will lose credibility with other staff and the administration.[3]

Each of these reality-based scenarios poses an ethical dilemma for the criminal justice employee involved. In each case, the officer or agent had to determine the best course of action. In making this determination, the employee had to draw on his or her ethical foundation and training and even the organization's subculture.

These scenarios should be kept in mind as this chapter examines ethics and many related dilemmas.

---

### EXHIBIT 13.1
### WHO POLICES THE POLICE?
#### Overcoming the "Rat" Stigma in Internal-Affairs Assignments

In the image fueled by countless television police dramas, internal affairs divisions are peopled by self-hating cops whose incompetence on the street has led them to become veritable traitors with few if any friends on the force.

While this perspective is somewhat at odds with reality, assignment to an IA unit still carries enough of a stigma that selecting such personnel is among the most critical, even problematic, decisions made by police executives. In some major-city departments, however, serving as an internal affairs investigator is increasingly viewed as a necessary stepping stone to career advancement and often provides benefits not usually available to those in other areas of policing.

With some 80 percent of the law enforcement agencies in the United States staffed by 25 or fewer sworn officers, there is no generalization about the workings of internal affairs divisions— or perceptions held about them—that would be valid, say policing experts. In small departments, their functions may tend to be limited, while in big departments, such as New York City and Los Angeles, their quality, structure and content can vary widely. Thus, issues such as how to attract top investigators to the unit, how long they remain there, and the message that the assignment conveys to others in the agency are all things with which law enforcement officials must grapple, say observers. ...

Two views have prevailed. One is that assignment to IA is a part of a career track, while the other suggests that those assigned to IA will subsequently require protection because of potential enemies. ...

In 1995, ... the New York City Police Department, Mayor Rudolph Giuliani and then–Commissioner William J. Bratton unveiled a number of reforms aimed at improving recruitment, training and overall supervision within the Internal Affairs Bureau. The strategies included making assignment to the unit a two-year hitch which would then provide investigators with entry into the Detective Bureau, the

Organized Crime Control Bureau or other coveted divisions.

That approach exemplifies what Edwin J. Delattre, dean of the School of Education at Boston University and author of "Character and Cops," cites as a "very old truth about human nature"— namely, that virtue has the best chance of succeeding when it is also advantageous: ... "Much of the time all of us have mixed motives for our actions, usually more mixed than even the most honest and self-knowledgeable of us fully recognize. Accordingly, the disposition to do 'right when there is no one to make [us] do it but [ourselves]' may be strengthened by awareness that we are not making some permanent sacrifice in behaving rightly."

The majority of departments that have paid attention to the NYPD's strategy have acknowledged that an effective way to draw the best people into IA—both by assignment and volunteering—is by having "good places for them to land and choices of assignment in homicide, organized crime or investigative units after" IAB, said Delattre. ...

*Source:* Reprinted with permission from *Law Enforcement News,* March 31, 2000, pp. 1, 6. John Jay College of Criminal Justice (CCNY), 555 West 57th St., New York, NY 10019.

# Ethics

## *Philosophical Foundations*

The term **ethics** is rooted in the ancient Greek idea of *character.* Ethics involves doing what is right or correct and is generally used to refer to how people should behave in a professional capacity. Many people would argue, however, that no difference should exist between one's professional and personal behavior. Ethical rules of conduct should apply to everything a person does.

A central problem with understanding ethics is the question of "whose ethics" or "which right." This becomes evident when one examines controversial issues such as the death penalty, abortion, use of deadly force, and gun control. How individuals view a particular controversy largely depends on their values, character, or ethics. Both sides on controversies such as these believe they are morally right. These issues demonstrate that to understand behavior, the most basic values must be examined and understood.

Another area for examination is that of **deontological ethics,** which does not consider consequences but instead examines one's duty to act. The word *deontology* comes from two Greek roots, *deos,* meaning duty, and *logos,* meaning study. Thus, deontology means the study of duty. When police officers observe a violation of law, they have a duty to act. Officers frequently use this as an excuse when they issue traffic citations that appear to have little utility and do not produce any great benefit for the rest of society. For example, when an officer writes a traffic citation for a prohibited left turn made at two o'clock in the morning when no traffic is around, the officer is fulfilling a departmental duty to enforce the law. From a utilitarian standpoint (where we judge an action by its consequences), however, little if any good was served. Here, duty and not good consequences was the primary motivator.

Immanuel Kant, an eighteenth-century philosopher, expanded the ethics of duty by including the idea of "good will." People's actions must be guided by good intent. In the previous example, the officer who wrote the traffic citation for an improper left turn would be acting unethically if the ticket was a response to a quota or some irrelevant motive. On the other hand, if the citation was issued because the officer truly believed that it would result in some good, it would have been an ethical action.

Some people have expanded this argument even further. Richard Kania[4] argued that police officers should be allowed to freely accept gratuities because such actions would constitute the building blocks of positive social relationships between the police and the public. In this case, duty is used to justify what under normal circumstances would be considered unethical. Conversely, if officers take gratuities for self-gratification rather than to form positive community relationships, then the action would be considered unethical by many.

## Types of Ethics

Ethics usually involves standards of fair and honest conduct; what we call conscience, the ability to recognize right from wrong; and actions that are good and proper. There are absolute ethics and relative ethics. **Absolute ethics** has only two sides, something is either good or bad, black or white. Some examples in police ethics would be unethical behaviors such as bribery, extortion, excessive force, and perjury, which nearly everyone would agree are unacceptable behaviors by the police.

**Relative ethics** is more complicated and can have a multitude of sides with varying shades of gray. What is considered ethical behavior by one person may be deemed highly unethical by someone else. Not all ethical issues are clear-cut, however, and communities *do* seem willing at times to tolerate extralegal behavior if there is a greater public good, especially in dealing with problems such as gangs and the homeless. This willingness on the part of the community can be conveyed to the police. Ethical relativism can be said to form an essential part of the community policing movement, discussed more fully later.

A community's acceptance of relative ethics as part of criminal justice may send the wrong message: that there are few boundaries placed on justice system employee behaviors and that, at times, "anything goes" in their fight against crime. As John Kleinig[5] pointed out, giving false testimony to ensure that a public menace is "put away" or the illegal wiretapping of an organized crime figure's telephone might sometimes be viewed as "necessary" and "justified," though illegal. Another example is that many police believe they are compelled to skirt along the edges of the law—or even violate it—in order to arrest drug traffickers. The ethical problem here is that even if the action could be justified as morally proper, it remains illegal. For many persons, however, the protection of society overrides other concerns.

This viewpoint—the "principle of double effect"—holds that when one commits an act to achieve a good end and an inevitable but intended effect is negative, then the act might be justified. A longstanding debate has raged about balancing the rights of individuals against the community's interest in calm and order.

These special areas of ethics can become problematic and controversial when police officers use deadly force or lie and deceive others in their work. Police could justify a whole range of activities that others may deem unethical simply because the consequences resulted in the greatest good for the greatest number—the *utilitarian* approach. If the ends justified the means, perjury would be ethical when committed to prevent a serial killer from being set free to prey on society. In our democratic society, however, the means are just as important, if not more important, than the desired end.

The community—and criminal justice administrators—cannot tolerate completely unethical behavior, but they may seemingly tolerate extralegal behavior if there's a greater public good, especially with regard to gang members and the homeless.

It is no less important today than in the past for criminal justice employees to appreciate and come to grips with ethical considerations. Indeed, ethical issues in policing have been affected by three critical factors[6]: (1) the growing level of temptation stemming from the illicit drug trade; (2) the potentially compromising nature of the organizational culture—a culture that can exalt loyalty over integrity, with a "code of silence" that protects unethical employees; and (3) the challenges posed by decentralization (flattening the organization and pushing decision making downward) through the advent of community oriented policing and problem solving (COPPS, discussed later).

# Ethics in Policing

## *A Primer: The Oral Interview*

During oral interviews for a position in policing, applicants are often placed in a hypothetical situation that tests their ethical beliefs and character. For example, they are asked to assume the role of a police officer who is checking on foot an office supplies retail store that was found to have an unlocked door during early morning hours. On leaving the building, the officer observes another officer, Smith, removing a $100 writing pen from a display case and placing it in his uniform pocket. What should the officer do?

This kind of question commonly befuddles the applicant: "Should I rat on my fellow officer? Overlook the matter? Merely tell Smith never to do that again?" Unfortunately, applicants may do a lot of "how am I *supposed* to respond" soul searching and second-guessing with these kinds of questions.

Bear in mind that criminal justice agencies do not wish to hire someone who possesses ethical shortcomings; it is simply too potentially dangerous and expensive, from both a litigation and a morality standpoint, to take the chance of bringing someone into an agency who is corrupt. That is the reason for such questioning and a thorough background investigation of applicants.

Before responding to a scenario like the one concerning Officer Smith, the applicant should consider the following issues: Is this likely to be the first time that Smith has stolen something? Don't the police arrest and jail people for this same kind of behavior?

In short, police administrators should *never* want an applicant to respond that it is acceptable for an officer to steal. Furthermore, it would be incorrect for an applicant to believe that police do not want an officer to "rat out" another officer. Applicants should never acknowledge that stealing or other such activities are to be overlooked.

## A "Slippery Slope"? Lying and Deception

In many cases, no clear line separates acceptable behavior from behavior that is unacceptable. The two are separated by an expansive "gray" area that comes under relative ethics. Some observers have referred to such illegal behavior as a "slippery slope": People tread on solid or legal ground but at some point slip beyond the acceptable into illegal or unacceptable behavior.

Criminal justice employees lie or deceive for different purposes and under varying circumstances. In some cases, their misrepresentations are accepted as an integral part of a criminal investigation, whereas in other cases, they are viewed as violations of law. David Carter and Thomas Barker[7] examined police lying and perjury and developed a taxonomy that centered on a distinction between accepted lying and deviant lying. *Accepted lying* includes police activities intended to apprehend or entrap suspects. This type of lying is generally considered to be trickery. *Deviant lying*, on the other hand, refers to occasions when officers commit perjury to convict suspects or are deceptive about some activity that is illegal or unacceptable to the department or public in general.

### Accepted Lying

Deception has long been practiced by the police to ensnare violators and suspects. For many years, it was the principal method used by detectives and police officers to secure confessions and convictions. It is allowed by the law, and to a great extent, it is expected by the public. Gary Marx[8] identified three methods police use to trick a suspect: (1) performing the illegal action as part of a larger, socially acceptable, and legal goal; (2) disguising the illegal action so that the suspect does not know it is illegal; and (3) morally weakening the suspect so that the suspect voluntarily becomes involved.

The courts have long accepted deception as an investigative tool. For example, in *Illinois v. Perkins,*[9] the U.S. Supreme Court ruled that police undercover agents are not required to administer the *Miranda* warning to incarcerated inmates when investigating crimes. Lying, although acceptable by the courts and the public in certain circumstances, does result in an ethical dilemma. It is a dirty means to accomplish a good end; the police use untruths to gain the truth relative to some event.

### Deviant Lying

In their taxonomy of lying, Barker and Carter[10] identified two types of deviant lying: lying that serves legitimate purposes and lying that conceals or promotes crimes or illegitimate ends.

Lying that serves legitimate goals occurs when officers lie to secure a conviction, obtain a search warrant, or conceal omissions during an investigation. Barker[11] found that police officers believe that almost one fourth of their agency would commit perjury to secure a conviction or to obtain a search warrant. Lying becomes an effective, routine way to sidestep legal impediments. When left unchecked by supervisors, managers, and administrators, lying can become organizationally accepted as an effective means to nullify legal entanglements and remove obstacles that stand in the way of convictions. Examples include using the services of nonexistent confidential informants to secure search warrants, concealing that an interrogator went too far, coercing a confession, or perjuring oneself to gain a conviction.

Lying to conceal or promote criminality is the most distressing form of deception. Examples range from when the police lie to conceal their use of excessive force when arresting a suspect to obscuring the commission of a criminal act.

### Gratuities  — Given Free of charge

**Gratuities** are commonly accepted by police officers as a part of their job. Restaurants frequently give officers free or half-price meals and drinks, and other businesses routinely give officers discounts for services or merchandise. Many police officers and departments accept these gratuities as a part of the job. Other departments prohibit such gifts and discounts but seldom attempt to enforce any relevant policy or regulation. Finally, some departments attempt to ensure that officers do not accept free or discounted services or merchandise and routinely enforce policies or regulations against such behavior.

There are two basic arguments *against* police acceptance of gratuities. First is the slippery slope argument, discussed earlier, which proposes that gratuities are the first step in police corruption. This argument holds that once gratuities are received, police officers' ethics are subverted and they are open to additional breaches of their integrity. In addition, officers who accept minor gifts or gratuities are then obligated to provide the donors with some special service or accommodation. Furthermore, some propose that receiving a gratuity is wrong because officers are receiving rewards for services that, as a result of their employment, they are obligated to provide. That is, officers have no legitimate right to accept compensation in the form of a gratuity. If the police ever hope to be accepted as members of a full-fledged profession, then they must address whether the acceptance of gratuities is professional behavior.

subvert—to corrupt
       under
                      integrity—honesty.

---

### EXHIBIT 13.2
### Ethics Campaign Focuses on Stupid Mistakes

Cops are a lot better at jumping into gun battles than they are at preventing their partners from "doing something stupid," particularly when involved in an emotionally-charged situation, says Deputy Chief Keith Bushey of the San Bernardino County, Calif., Sheriff's Department, who is spearheading a nationwide police ethics campaign aimed at keeping officers from making critical errors in judgment.

Members of the sheriff's department participated in a production in July that had all the trappings of a Hollywood movie. Playing themselves, they acted out a number of scenarios in front of the cameras in which they stopped a fellow officer from crossing an ethical line.

In one, a handcuffed suspect with a black eye is laying across the trunk of a sheriff's cruiser. An officer, his eye blackened as well, has his arm drawn back, ready to strike. His partner is holding him back. In another scenario, a deputy is making sexual advances on a female police explorer. And in the third, an officer is stopping his partner from conducting a dangerous pursuit in a patrol vehicle.

The photos will be turned into posters and, if adopted by the International Association of Chiefs of Police, will be displayed at the organization's annual conference and made available for sale to law enforcement agencies across the country.

"We have to realize there are a lot of things that are essentially destructive behavior that cops do," Bushey told Law Enforcement News. "Sometimes it's excessive force, sometimes it's sexual harassment … getting close to a female explorer scout, sometimes it's foolish driving. There are all kinds of things and we have to be one another's safety devices, we have to be one another's keepers." …

Bushey called ethics the No. 1 priority of police and deputies across the country.

"Sometimes it requires tremendous courage to tell a partner, especially a senior partner, that he or she is doing something foolish, or even physically intervene to keep somebody from doing something foolish," he said. "It requires courage, loyalty, common sense, the whole nine yards."

*Source:* Reprinted with permission from *Law Enforcement News,* September 15/31, 2003, p. 1. John Jay College of Criminal Justice (CCNY), 555 West 57th St., New York, NY 10019.

---

Police officers who solicit and receive free gifts were categorized by the Knapp Commission in New York City into "grass-eaters" and "meat-eaters."[12] *Grass-eaters* are officers who freely accept gratuities and sometimes solicit minor payments and gifts. *Meat-eaters,* on the other hand, spend a significant portion of the workday aggressively seeking out situations that could be exploited for financial gain. These officers were corrupt and were involved in thefts, drugs, gambling, prostitution, and other criminal activities.

At least in some cases, it seems that taking gratuities may be a first step toward corruption. Gratuities do indeed provide a slippery slope from which officers can easily slide into corruption. The problem is that many officers fail to understand when and where to draw the line. Once a police department decides on a policy, it should ensure that all officers are familiar with that policy. Supervisors and managers must fully understand the department's policy regarding gratuities and emphatically enforce it; once a department draws the line distinguishing what is acceptable, it is responsible for ensuring that the rules are followed.

In a different light, one writer[13] argues that retail store and restaurant owners often feel an indebtedness toward the police, and gratuities provide an avenue of repayment. Thus, gratuities result in social cohesion between the police and businessowners, and the acceptance of gratuities does not necessarily lead to the solicitation of additional gratuities and gifts or corruption.

Figure 13.1 is an example of a policy developed by a sheriff's office concerning gratuities.

## Greed and Temptation

Fundamentally, the expecting and accepting of larger gratuities (setting aside for a moment the debate about whether police officers should receive free coffee or meals) and bribes or "shakedowns" are about greed. This greed is perhaps viewed by the individual officer as an entitlement because of what is perceived as an overall corrupt society, a low-paying job, the kind of work that has to be

---

1. Without the express permission of the Sheriff, members shall not solicit or accept any gift, gratuity, loan, present, or fee where there is any direct or indirect connection between this solicitation or acceptance of such gift and their employment by this office.
2. Members shall not accept, either directly or indirectly, any gift, gratuity, loan, fee or thing of value, the acceptance of which might tend to improperly influence their actions, or that of any other member, in any matter of police business, or which might tend to cast an adverse reflection on the Sheriff's Office.
3. Any unauthorized gift, gratuity, loan, fee, reward or other thing falling into any of these categories coming into the possession of any member shall be forwarded to the member's commander, together with a written report explaining the circumstances connected therewith. The commander will decide the disposition of the gift.

—Washoe County (Nevada) Sheriff's Office

**Figure 13.1**

Washoe County, Nevada, Sheriff's Office gratuity policy.

done, and so on. Mature people, however, simply do not use their position for self-indulgence. Consider the following account, related by Albert A. Seedman,[14] who served from patrol officer to chief of detectives in the New York City Police Department:

> Just before Christmas [in New York City] in 1947, [Captain Ray McGuire and Officer Albert Seedman] helped lug into the office dozens of cartons of toys that had been recovered from a hijacking case. There were dolls, teddy bears, and stuffed animals of all kinds. McGuire, busy overseeing the operation, saw that it was close to three o'clock. He said, "I was going to stop at Macy's to pick up some toys for my girls." One of the detectives mentioned he had to do the same at Macy's. McGuire handed him a twenty-dollar bill. "Pick up a pair of dolls for me, will ya?" If there were two dolls in that office, there were two thousand. Yet I doubt it ever occurred to McGuire that a pair would never be missed. Or that the owner would be delighted to make them a gift.

The habit of not even considering greedy behavior, of not speculating about ways to profit from office, prevents such conduct from even occurring to most officers.[15]

[The author recalls one rainy, cold midwestern night when he was dispatched with two other officers to a robbery scene. An elderly couple had been beaten, robbed, and tied to chairs in their home as a young man ransacked it, took a large amount of cash, and fled. During the offender's flight, he dropped much of the money, some of which was flowing down the curb and into the storm sewer by the time the officers arrived. In pouring rain, the three officers hurriedly collected all the cash that could be retrieved in the yard, flowing down the curb, and—while on their bellies in the deluge—from out of the storm sewer. As with Seedman's story, it never even occurred to the officers to divert any of the couple's funds to their pockets; all that could be located was returned to them. Such accounts, of course, are legion among the police but seldom appear on the front page.]   *large group of/MEMBERS*

Edward Tully[16] underscored the vast amount of temptation that confronts today's police officers and what police leaders must do toward combating it:

> Socrates, Mother Teresa, or other revered individuals in our society never had to face the constant stream of ethical problems of a busy cop on the beat. One of the roles of [police leaders] is to create an environment that will help the officer resist the temptations that may lead to misconduct, corruption, or abuse of power. The executive cannot construct a work environment that will completely insulate the officers from the forces which lead to misconduct. The ultimate responsibility for an officer's ethical and moral welfare rests squarely with the officer.

Most citizens have no way of comprehending the amount of temptation that confronts today's police officers. They frequently find themselves alone inside retail businesses after normal business hours, clearing the building after finding an open door or window. A swing or graveyard shift officer could easily obtain considerable plunder during these occasions, acquiring everything from clothing to tires for his personal vehicle. At the other end of the spectrum is the potential for huge payoffs from drug traffickers or other big-money offenders who will gladly pay the officer to look away from their crimes. Some officers, of course, find this temptation impossible to overcome.

## Community Policing

Community-oriented policing and problem solving (COPPS, examined in Chapter 3) is characterized by more frequent and closer contacts with the public, resulting, in the minds of many observers, in less accountability and, by extension, more opportunities for corruption. Is there a relationship between unethical behavior and COPPS? Should this be a major concern? Probably not. First, only a small fraction of police officers have violated their oath of office throughout history, which includes a long tradition of using discretionary authority. Second, working more closely with the public also serves to heighten the officers' visibility and trust with the citizenry. COPPS is founded on trust and community interaction. But that is not to say that there should not be scrutiny and accountability.

A case study at the end of the chapter concerns ethics and community policing.

## Training, Supervision, Values

Another key element of ethics in policing is the recruitment and training of police personnel. Like people in other occupations, new officers may learn early how to steal at a burglary scene or from the body of a dead person, or they may learn how to commit perjury in court, how to cover misdeeds of their peers, how to shake people down, or how to beat people up. Or they may be fortunate enough to work in an agency in which none of these actions is ever suggested to them.

Formal training programs in ethics can help to ensure that officers understand their department's code of ethics, elevate the importance of ethics throughout the agency, and underscore top management's support. It is imperative that police administrators see that applicants are thoroughly tested, trained, and exposed to an anticorruption environment by proper role modeling.

No supervision of police officers, no matter how thorough and conscientious, can keep bad cops from doing bad things. There are simply too many police officers and too few supervisors. If there is not enough supervision, then the bad cop will not be afraid. As Marcus Aurelius said, "A man should be upright, not be kept upright." There must be leadership at every level. Line officers are sincere and hard working; their leaders need to ensure that core values are part of the department's operations and become the basis of subordinates' behavior.

The organization's culture is also important in this regard. The police culture often exalts loyalty over integrity. Given the stress usually generated more from within the organization than from outside and the nature of life-and-death decisions they must make daily, even the best officers who simply want to catch criminals may become frustrated and vulnerable to bending the rules for what they view as the greater good of society.

EXHIBIT 13.3
**LAPD Takes Next Step in Developing Monitoring System for 10,000 Officers**

...The Los Angeles Police Department has hired a small information systems consulting firm to develop a monitoring system for its 10,000 officers.

...The program will use data-mining techniques to provide a broad statistical overview of an officer's long-term performance, as well as zoom in on specifics to provide detailed breakdowns of an officer's daily activity. Development of such a system is a requirement of a consent decree entered into with the Justice Department....

Officers who use force against suspects far more than average, for example, would fall into a red category; those who are less aggressive would be placed in the yellow or green category....

The system is fair and accurate because the firm spent a considerable amount of time studying how law enforcement agencies function....

[The system] will also help departments identify good performers....

*Source:* Reprinted with permission from *Law Enforcement News*, July/August 2001, p. 5. John Jay College of Criminal Justice (CCNY), 555 West 57th St., New York, NY 10019.

Police agencies must also attempt to shape standards of professional behavior. Many begin to do so by articulating their values, such as "We believe in the sanctity of life" and "We believe that providing superior service to the citizens is our primary responsibility." Other rules try to guide officer behavior, such as not lying or drinking in excess in a public place.

## Ethics in the Courts

### *The Evolution of Standards of Conduct*

The first call during the twentieth century for formalized standards of conduct in the legal profession came in 1906, with Roscoe Pound's speech "The Causes of Popular Dissatisfaction with the Administration of Justice." The American Bar Association (ABA) quickly responded by formulating and approving the Canons of Professional Ethics in 1908 governing lawyers. No separate rules were provided for judges, however.

The first Canons of Judicial Ethics probably grew out of baseball's 1919 scandal in which the World Series was "thrown" to the Chicago White Sox by the Cincinnati Reds. Baseball officials turned to the judiciary for leadership and hired U.S. District Court Judge Kenesaw Mountain Landis as baseball commissioner—a position for which Landis was paid $42,500, compared to his $7,500 earnings per year as a judge. This affair prompted the 1921 ABA convention to pass a resolution of censure against the judge and appoint a committee to propose standards of judicial ethics.[17]

In 1924, the ABA approved the Canons of Judicial Ethics under the leadership of Chief Justice William Howard Taft, and in 1972, the ABA approved a new Model Code of Judicial Conduct; in 1990, the same body adopted a revised Model Code. Nearly all states and the District of Columbia have promulgated standards based on the code. In 1974, the United States Judicial Conference adopted a Code of Conduct for Federal Judges, and Congress has over the years enacted legislation regulating judicial conduct, including the Ethics Reform Act of 1989.

## *The Judge*

Ideally, our judges are flawless. They do not allow emotion or personal biases to creep into their work, treat all cases and individual litigants with an even hand, and employ "justice tempered with mercy." The perfect judge would be like the one described by the eminent Italian legal philosopher Pierro Calamandrei:

> The good judge takes equal pains with every case no matter how humble; he knows that important cases and unimportant cases do not exist, for injustice is not one of those poisons which ... when taken in small doses may produce a salutary effect. Injustice is a dangerous poison even in doses of homeopathic proportions.[18]

Not all judges, of course, can attain this lofty status. Recognizing this fact, nearly 800 years ago King John of England met with his barons on the field of Runnymede and, in the Magna Carta, promised that henceforth he would not "make men justices . . . unless they are such as know the law of the realm and are minded to observe it rightly."[19]

The subject of judicial ethics seemed to arouse little interest until relatively recently. Indeed, from 1890 to 1904, an era of trusts and political corruption, only a few articles were published on the subject of judicial ethics. In contrast, since 1975, more than 900 articles have appeared in magazines and newspapers under the topic of judges and judicial ethics.

Judges can become engaged in improper conduct or overstep their bounds in many ways: abuse of judicial power (against attorneys or litigants); inappropriate sanctions and dispositions (including showing favoritism or bias); not meeting the standards of impartiality and competence (discourteous behavior, gender bias and harassment, incompetence); conflict of interest (bias; conflicting financial interests or business, social, or family relationships); and personal conduct (criminal or sexual misconduct, prejudice, statements of opinion).[20]

Following are examples of some true-to-life ethical dilemmas involving the courts:[21]

1. A judge convinces jailers to release his son on a nonbondable offense.
2. A judge is indicted on charges that he used his office for a racketeering enterprise.

3. Two judges attend the governor's $500 per person inaugural ball.

4. A judge's alleged intemperate treatment of lawyers in the courtroom was spurred by a lawyer's earlier complaints against the judge.

5. A judge is accused of acting with bias in giving a convicted murderer a less severe sentence because the victims were homosexual.

6. A judge whose car bears the bumper sticker "I am a pro-life Democrat" acquits six pro-life demonstrators of trespassing at an abortion clinic on the ground of necessity to protect human life.

These incidents certainly do little to bolster public confidence in the justice system. People expect more from judges, who are "the most highly visible symbol of justice."[22] The quality of the judges determines the quality of justice.

Many judges recoil at the need for a code of judicial conduct or an independent commission to investigate complaints. They dislike being considered suspect and put under regulation. No one likes to be watched, but judges must heed Thomas Jefferson's admonition that everyone in public life should be answerable to someone.[23]

Unfortunately, codes of ethical conduct have not served to eradicate the problems or allay concerns about judges' behavior. Indeed, as three professors of law put it, "The public and the bar appear at times to be more interested in judicial ethics and accountability than the judges are."[24] One judge, who teaches judicial ethics at the National Judicial College in Reno, stated that most judges attending the college admit never having read the Code of Judicial Conduct before seeking judicial office.[25] Some judges also dismiss the need for a judicial conduct code because they believe that it governs aberrant behavior, which, they also believe, is rare among the judiciary. According to the American Judicature Society, however, during one year, 25 judges were suspended from office and more than 80 judges resigned or retired either before or after formal charges were filed against them; 120 judges also received private censure, admonition, or reprimand.[26]

The Code of Judicial Conduct strives to strike a balance between allowing judges to participate in social and public discourse and prohibiting conduct that would threaten a judge's independence. The essence of judicial independence is that judges' minds, according to John Adams, "should not be distracted with jarring interests; they should not be dependent upon any man, or body of men."[27]

Living by the code is challenging; the key to judicial ethics is to identify the troublesome issues and to sharpen one's sensitivity to them, that is, to create an "ethical alarm system" that responds.[28] Perhaps the most important tenet in the code and the one that is most difficult to apply is that judges should avoid the appearance of impropriety.

By adhering to ethical principles, judges can maintain their independence and follow the ancient charge Moses gave to his judges in Deuteronomy:

> Hear the causes between your brethren, and judge righteously. Ye shall not respect persons in judgment; but ye shall hear the small as well as the great; ye shall not be afraid of the face of man; for the judgment is God's; and for the cause that is too hard for you, bring it unto me, and I will hear it.[29]

## Lawyers for the Defense

Defense attorneys, too, must be legally and morally bound to ethical principles as agents of the courts. Elliot Cohen[30] suggested the following moral principles for defense attorneys:

1. Treat others as ends in themselves and not as mere means to winning cases.
2. Treat clients and other professional relations in a similar fashion.
3. Do not deliberately engage in behavior apt to deceive the court as to truth.
4. Be willing, if necessary, to make reasonable personal sacrifices of time, money, and popularity for what you believe to be a morally good cause.
5. Do not give money to, or accept money from, clients for wrongful purposes or in wrongful amounts.
6. Avoid harming others in the course of representing your client.
7. Be loyal to your client and do not betray his or her confidence.

## Prosecutors

Prosecutors can also improve their ethical behavior. Contrary, perhaps, to what is popularly believed, it was decided over a half century ago that the primary duty of a prosecutor is "not that he shall win a case, but that justice shall be done."[31]

Instances of prosecutorial misconduct were reported as early as 1897[32] and are still reported today. One of the leading examples of unethical conduct by a prosecutor was *Miller v. Pate*,[33] in which the prosecutor concealed from the jury in a murder trial the fact that a pair of undershorts with red stains on it were stained not by blood but by paint.

If similar (though not so egregious) kinds of misconduct occur today, one must question why. According to Cohen,[34] the answer is simple: Misconduct works. Oral advocacy is important in the courtroom and can have a powerful effect. Another significant reason for such conduct is the harmless error doctrine, in which an appellate court can affirm a conviction despite the presence of serious misconduct during the trial. Only when appellate courts take a stricter, more consistent approach to this problem will it end.[35]

## Other Court Employees

Other court employees have ethical responsibilities as well. Primarily known as "confidential employees," these are justice system functionaries who have a special role in the court system and work closely with a judge or judges. These individuals have a special responsibility to maintain the confidentiality of the court system and thus have a high standard of trust. For example, an appellate court judge's secretary is asked by a good friend who is a lawyer whether the judge will be writing the opinion in a certain case. The lawyer may be wishing to attempt to influence the judge through his secretary, renegotiate with an opposing party, or engage in some other improper activity designed to alter the case outcome.[36] Bailiffs, court administrators, court reporters, courtroom clerks, and law clerks all fit into this category. The judge's secretary, of course, must use his or her own ethical standard in deciding whether to answer the lawyer's question.

It would be improper for a bailiff who is accompanying jurors back from a break in a criminal trial to mention that the judge "sure seems annoyed at the defense attorney" or for a law clerk to tell an attorney friend that the judge she works for prefers reading short bench memos.[37]

# Ethics in Corrections

Corrections personnel confront many of the same ethical dilemmas as police personnel. Thus, prison and jail administrators, like their counterparts in the police realm, would do well to understand their occupational subculture and its effect on ethical decision making.

The strength of the corrections subculture correlates with the security level of a correctional facility and is strongest in maximum-security institutions. Powerful forces within the correctional system have a stronger influence over the behavior of correctional officers than the administrators of the institution, legislative decrees, or agency policies.[38] Indeed, it has been known for several decades that the exposure to external danger in the workplace creates a remarkable increase in group solidarity.[39]

Some of the job-related stressors for corrections officers are similar to those the police face: the ever-present potential for physical danger, hostility directed at officers by inmates and even by the public, unreasonable role demands, a tedious and unrewarding work environment, and dependence on one another to effectively and safely work in their environment.[40] For these reasons, several norms of corrections work have been identified: always go to the aid of an officer in distress; do not "rat"; never make another officer look bad in front of inmates; always support an officer in a dispute with an inmate; always support officer sanctions against inmates; and do not wear a "white hat" (participate in behavior that suggests sympathy or identification with inmates).[41]

Security issues and the way in which individual correctional officers have to rely on each other for their safety make loyalty to one another a key norm. The proscription against ratting out a colleague is strong. In one documented instance, two officers in the Corcoran, California, state prison blew the whistle on what they considered to be unethical conduct by their colleagues: Officers were alleged to have staged a gladiator-style fight among inmates from different groups in a small exercise yard. The two officers claimed that their colleagues would even place bets on the outcome of the fights, and when the fights got out of hand, the officers would fire shots at the inmates. Since the institution had opened in 1988, eight inmates had been shot dead by officers and numerous others had been wounded. The two officers who reported these activities were labeled by colleagues as "rats" and "no-goods" and had their lives threatened; even though they were transferred to other institutions, the labels traveled with them. Four correctional officers were indicted for their alleged involvement in these activities, and were all acquitted in a state prosecution in 2001.[42]

In another case, a female corrections officer at a medium-security institution reported some of her colleagues for sleeping on the night shift. She had first approached them and expressed concern for her safety when they were asleep and told them that if they did not refrain from sleeping, she would have to report them to the superintendent. They continued sleeping, and she reported them. The consequences were severe: Graffiti was written about her on the walls, she received harassing phone calls and letters, her car was vandalized, and some bricks were thrown through the windows of her home.[43]

It would be unfair to suggest that the kind of behavior depicted here reflects the behavior of corrections officers in all places and at all times. The case studies do demonstrate, however, the power and loyalty of the group, and correctional administrators must be cognizant of that power. It is also noteworthy that the corrections subculture, like its police counterpart, provides several positive qualities, particularly in crisis situations, including mutual support and protection, which is essential to the emotional and psychological health of officers involved; there is always the "family" to support you.

# Guiding Decision Making

One of the primary purposes of ethics is to guide decision making.[44] Ethics provides more comprehensive guidelines than law and operational procedures and answers questions that might otherwise go unanswered. When in doubt, justice administrators and employees should be able to consider the ethical consequences of their actions or potential actions to determine how they should proceed. To assist, guidelines must be in place to assist employees in making operational decisions. Criminal justice leaders obviously play a key role in ethics. Not only must they enforce and uphold ethical standards, they must also set an example and see that employees are instructed in the ethical conduct of police business.

Some experts in police ethics lay problems involving employees' ethics, and their lapses in good conduct squarely at the feet of their leaders; for example, Edward Tully[45] stated the following:

> Show me a[n] agency with a serious problem of officer misconduct and I will show you a department staffed with too many sergeants not doing their job. [Leaders must] recognize the vital and influential role sergeants play within an organization. They should be selected with care, given as much supervisory training as possible, and included in the decision making process. Sergeants are the custodians of the culture, the leaders and informal disciplinarians of the department, and the individual most officers look to for advice.

Stephen Vicchio[46] added another caveat. Even in communities where all seems to be going well with respect to ethical behavior, trouble may be lurking beneath the surface:

> In departments where corruption appears to be low and citizen complaints are minimal, we assume that the officers are people of integrity. Sometimes this is a faulty assumption, particularly if the motivation to do the right thing comes from fear of punishment.

Most efforts to control justice system employee behavior are rooted in statutes and departmental orders and policies. These written directives spell out inappropriate behavior and, in some cases, behavior or actions that are expected in specific situations. Written directives cannot address every contingency, however, and employees must often use their discretion. These discretionary decisions should be guided by ethics and values. When there is an ethics or policy failure, the resulting behavior is generally considered to be illegal or inappropriate.

## Some Ethics Tests for the Justice Professional

Following are some tests to help guide the criminal justice employee to decide what is and is not ethical behavior:[47]

- *Test of common sense.* Does the act make sense or would someone look askance at it?
- *Test of publicity.* Would you be willing to see what you did highlighted on the front page of the local newspaper?
- *Test of one's best self.* Will the act fit the concept of oneself at one's best?
- *Test of one's most admired personality.* What would one's parents or minister do in this situation?
- *Test of hurting someone else.* Will it cause pain for someone?
- *Test of foresight.* What is the long-term likely result?

Other questions that the officer might ask are, Is it worth my job and career? Is my decision legal?

Another tool is that of "the Bell, the Book, and the Candle": Do bells or warning buzzers go off as I consider my choice of actions? Does it violate any laws or codes in the statute or ordinance books? Will my decision withstand the light of day or spotlight of publicity (the candle)?[48]

In sum, all we can do is seek to make the best decisions we can and be a good person and a good justice system employee, one who is consistent and fair. We need to apply the law, the policy, the guidelines, or whatever it is we dispense in our occupation without bias or fear and to the best of our ability, being mindful along the way that others around us may have lost their moral compass and attempt to drag us down with them. To paraphrase Franklin Delano Roosevelt, "Be the best you can, wherever you are, with what you have."

## Is Workplace Loyalty Always Good?

*Loyalty*

*If you work for someone, in heaven's name, work for him!*
*Speak well of him and stand by the institution he represents.*
*Remember, an ounce of loyalty is worth a pound of cleverness.*

*If you must growl, condemn, and eternally find fault, resign your position. And when you are on the outside, damn to your heart's content; but as long as you are part of the institution do not condemn it. If you do, the first high wind that comes along will blow you away, and probably you will never know why.*

—Author unknown

This quote certainly leaves no doubt that, at least in its author's mind, **loyalty** to the organization, and to one's superior, is highly desired. But is such unequivocal loyalty always a good thing, especially in criminal justice organizations? Certainly one would think that justice-system administrators would view loyalty as a very positive attribute for their employees. There are some, however, who have serious doubts about whether loyalty is indeed an asset.

Sam S. Souryal and Deanna L Diamond, for example, believed that criminal justice employees often suffer from a "personal loyalty syndrome," which holds them responsible to an altogether different set of loyalty expectations. They are often compelled to offer unwavering personal loyalty to their superiors and, as a result, can violate constitutional provisions, legal requirements, or the public good. Therefore, in extreme cases, practitioners may find themselves justifying untruth, impeding justice, supporting cover-ups, and lying under oath.[49]

Souryal and Diamond argued that there are several paradoxes with the expectation and practice of personal loyalty to superiors in criminal justice agencies:

- Despite the emotional support for the practice, there is no mention of it in agency rules and regulations. If loyalty is such a great virtue, why are agency rules and regulations silent about it?
- Superiors usually make demands for loyalty when the agency is under attack, not when the agency is stable and business is conducted "as usual."
- Personal loyalty to superiors ignores the fact that some superiors are not worthy of loyalty; hundreds of supervisors and administrators are fired or disciplined each year for violating agency rules.
- Loyalty is a one-way street (superiors need not return the loyalty).[50]

In sum, there are three types of loyalty for justice practitioners to follow, and to think about before offering their loyalties unconditionally; ranked from most important to least important, they are as follows:

First is *integrated* loyalty, the highest and most virtuous level of loyalty at the workplace. It is genuine concern by each worker to the values and ideals of the profession, honoring the ideals of accountability, rationality, fairness, and good will. This is the cornerstone of all workplace loyalties and pursued before any institutional loyalty.

Second is *institutional* loyalty; it is the obligation of each agency member, including subordinates and superiors, to support the agency's mission. Examples include the obligation of police, court, and probation and parole officers to be loyal to agency policies, rules, and regulations. It is the most supportive and durable, and should be positioned ahead of loyalty to superiors.

Finally, there is *personal* loyalty, the lowest level of loyalty in the workplace, because it is mechanical in nature. Examples include the obligation of deputy sheriffs to be loyal to their sheriff. It is the most volatile and temporal, and may never replace institutional loyalty.[51]

In the final analysis, criminal justice administrators need to educate themselves in the exercise of workplace loyalties—both in terms of its being an asset and a detriment—as it relates to ethics, public service, and the public good. They must act in good faith, and at a minimum be certain that the loyalties of their subordinates are legally and morally justified.

# CASE STUDIES

Following are seven case studies.[52] Some are hypothetical, whereas others are based on real-life situations. They pose ethically relative (shades-of-gray) dilemmas for command, supervisory, and officer-level personnel.

True ethical dilemmas have no clear or obvious solutions. Often, all choices are no-win in nature. Consider the questions posed at the end of each case study.

## Case Study 13.1

Assume that the police have multiple leads that implicate Smith as a pedophile, but they have failed in every attempt to obtain a warrant to search Smith's car and home where evidence might be present. Officer Jones feels frustrated and, early one morning, takes his baton and breaks a rear taillight on Smith's car. The next day he stops Smith for operating his vehicle with a broken taillight; he impounds and inventories the vehicle and finds evidence leading to Smith's conviction on 25 counts of child molestation and possession of pornography. Jones receives accolades for the apprehension.

### Queries

Do Officer Jones's "ends" justify the "means"? What if he believes he is justified in "taking bad guys off the streets"? What if he argues that he is correct in this approach because he was molested as a child? What constitutional issues are involved?

## Case Study 13.2

Officer Rogers has commenced a problem-solving project in a comparatively affluent neighborhood that is plagued with transients and prostitutes. One of his first activities in scanning the problem is to conduct a rather cursory, door-to-door survey of residents to learn what they know about these problems. At one residence, Miss Larue, recently divorced, seductively dressed in a nightgown, and slightly intoxicated, says she is a cousin of the chief's and asks the officer to come in to talk and have lunch.

### Queries

What should Rogers do? Assume further that Rogers's supervisor, Sgt. Tracy Zane, is driving by and witnesses this conversation and sees the officer enter the home. What should Zane do?

# Case Study 13.3

There have been problems between rival gang members in one section of the city. Officer Blackwood works with both sides to alleviate the tension and tries hard to develop programs and rapport and to gain gang members' respect. Eventually, the problem calms down. Soon Blackwood begins observing carloads of young men, many of whom are underage, driving around and blatantly drinking. When she confronts them, they tell Blackwood that she should "be cool" about their "harmless" drinking activities because they're cooperating with her and are no longer shooting at each other. They obviously want to take advantage of their new rapport with Blackwood.

## Queries

How should Blackwood respond? At what point do/should the police sacrifice their ethical and legal expectations in attempting to develop rapport and calm in the neighborhood?

# Case Study 13.4

Officer Burns is known to have extreme difficulty relating to persons of color and others who are socially different from himself. The officer never received any sensitivity or diversity training at the academy or within the department. His supervisor fails to understand the weight of the problem and has little patience with Burns. So, to correct the matter, the supervisor decides to assign Burns to a minority section of town so he will improve his ability to relate to diverse groups. Within a week, Burns responds to a disturbance at a housing project where residents are partying noisily. Burns immediately begins yelling at the residents to quiet down; they fail to respond, so Burns draws his baton and begins poking residents and ordering them to comply with his directions. The crowd immediately turns against Burns, who then has to radio for backup assistance. After the other officers arrive, a fight ensues between them and the residents, and several members of both sides are injured and numerous arrests are made.

## Queries

How could the supervisor have dealt better with Burns's lack of sensitivity? What should the supervisor/administration do with Burns? Are there any liability or negligence issues present in this situation?

# Case Study 13.5

A municipal court judge borrows money from court employees, publicly endorses and campaigns for a candidate for judicial office, conducts personal business from chambers (displaying and selling antiques), directs other court employees to perform personal errands for him during court hours, suggests to persons appearing before him to contribute to certain charities in lieu of paying fines, and uses court employees to perform translating services at his mother's nursery business.

### Queries

Which, if any, of these activities would be unethical? Why? Taken together, would they warrant the judge's being disciplined? Removed from office? (See the outcome at the end of the case studies.)

## Case Study 13.6

Dale has worked in the county jail for 7 years. He is a dedicated, competent employee, one who is well respected by colleagues and administrators alike. But personal problems have arisen in his life: His wife of 10 years is filing for divorce, and his young daughter has serious behavioral problems. On this particular day, Dale reports for work tired and irritable after dealing with problems at home. One 18-year-old inmate quickly begins to get on his nerves. Small and "yappy," the boy never stops whining, carrying on for several hours with his high-pitched, increasingly maddening talk. Finally, after telling the boy to "shut up or else" several times, Dale loses control and slaps him hard on the face, leaving a welt and a small cut; the blow was loud enough to be heard by other inmates. For the first time, Dale has lost his temper and taken out his frustrations on an inmate. Another officer is sent to cover his post, and Dale goes to the superintendent's office. He recounts the incident, concluding with "I did it, I hit him hard and I deserve to be fired. Or would you let me resign? I'm very sorry it happened this way."

### Queries

As the superintendent, what would you do? Fire Dale? Allow him to resign? Take some other course of action? How much weight, if any, should legitimately be given to his personal problems? To what extent, if any, would your decision be guided by the institution's subculture?

## Case Study 13.7

You have been employed for 2 months as a corrections officer at a detention center with about 15 young offenders, most of whom have psychological problems. You are beginning to fit in well and to be invited to other staff members' social functions. During today's lunchtime, you are in the dining room and notice eight of the youths sitting at one table. One of them is an immature 18-year-old whose table manners are disgusting. Today, he decides to pour mounds of ketchup over his meal, swirling it around his plate, and then slurping it into his mouth. He then eats with his mouth open and spits the food across the table when he is talking. You, the other officers, and even other inmates are sickened by his behavior. A fellow officer, Tom, gets up and tugs the boy away from the table by his shirt collar. The officer sets the boy's tray of food on the floor and orders him to get on all fours next to it. "Your manners are disgusting," Tom says, "If you're going to eat like a dog you may as well get down on all fours like a dog; get down there and lick the food off the plate till it's clean." Tom later tells you that he did what he did out of frustration and to use a "shock tactic" to change the boy's behavior.

### Queries

What, if anything, should you do in this situation? Did Tom act professionally? Ethically? Should you have intervened on the boy's behalf? What would you do about this incident if you were superintendent of this institution and it was reported to you?

[*Note:* Case Study 13.5 describing the activities of a municipal court judge actually occurred in a Nevada court; the judge was removed from office.]

## Summary

This chapter has examined criminal justice employee behaviors from an ethical standpoint. Ethics forms the foundation for behavior. It is important that administrators and subordinates understand ethics and the role ethics plays in their performance of their duties. Agencies must come to grips with the ethical boundaries of police work to ensure that the boundaries are not violated.

Corruption has few easy remedies. As indicated in the chapter's opening quote by Lord Acton, the bad seek to cloak themselves in secrecy. To avoid rotten apples, criminal justice administrators need to maintain high standards for recruitment and training. And to avoid rotten structures, these kinds of agencies need leaders who will not tolerate corruption, institutional procedures for accountability, and systematic investigation of complaints and of suspicious circumstances.[53]

## Questions for Review

1. How would you define *ethics*? What are examples of relative as well as absolute ethics?
2. Which do you believe are the most difficult ethical dilemmas presented in the case studies? Consider the issues presented in each.

3. Should police accept minor gratuities? Why or why not?
4. How could community policing pose new ethical problems?
5. In what ways can judges, defense attorneys, and prosecutors engage in unethical behaviors?
6. In what substantive ways do the police and corrections subcultures resemble each other?
7. How may corrections officers in prisons be unethical?

# Notes

1. Adapted from John R. Jones and Daniel P. Carlson, *Reputable Conduct: Ethical Issues in Policing and Corrections,* 2nd ed. (Upper Saddle River, N.J.: Prentice Hall, 2001), p. 14.
2. This scenario is loosely based on David Gelman, Susan Miller, and Bob Cohn, "The Strange Case of Judge Wachtler," *Newsweek* (November 23, 1992):34–35. Wachtler was later arraigned on charges of attempting to extort money from the woman and threatening her 14-year-old daughter (it was later determined that the judge had been having an affair with the woman, who had recently ended the relationship). After being placed under house arrest with an electronic monitoring bracelet, the judge resigned from the court, which he had served with distinction for two decades.
3. Adapted from Jones and Carlson, *Reputable Conduct,* pp. 162–163.
4. Richard Kania, "Police Acceptance of Gratuities," *Criminal Justice Ethics* 7 (1988): 37–49.
5. John Kleinig, *The Ethics of Policing* (New York: Cambridge University Press, 1996).
6. T. J. O'Malley, "Managing for Ethics: A Mandate for Administrators," *FBI Law Enforcement Bulletin* (April 1997):20–25.
7. David Carter, "Theoretical Dimensions in the Abuse of Authority," in Thomas Barker and David Carter (eds.), *Police Deviance* (Cincinnati, Ohio: Anderson, 1994), pp. 269–290; also see Thomas Barker and David Carter, "Fluffing Up the Evidence and 'Covering Your Ass': Some Conceptual Notes on Police Lying," *Deviant Behavior* **11** (1990): 61–73.
8. Gary T. Marx, "Who Really Gets Stung? Some Issues Raised by the New Police Undercover Work," *Crime & Delinquency* (1982):165–193.
9. *Illinois v. Perkins,* 110 S.Ct. 2394 (1990).
10. Barker and Carter, *Police Deviance.*
11. Thomas Barker, "An Empirical Study of Police Deviance Other Than Corruption," in Thomas Barker and David Carter (eds.), *Police Deviance,* pp. 123–138.
12. New York City Commission to Investigate Allegations of Police Corruption and the City's Anti-Corruption Procedures, *The Knapp Commission Report on Police Corruption* (New York: George Braziller, 1972), p. 4.
13. Kania, "Police Acceptance of Gratuities," p. 40. For an excellent analysis of how the acceptance of gratuities can become endemic to an organization and pose ethical dilemmas for new officers within, see Jim Ruiz and Christine Bono, "At What Price a 'Freebie'? The Real Cost of Police Gratuities," *Criminal Justice Ethics* (Winter/Spring 2004):44–54. The authors also demonstrate through detailed calculations how the amount of gratuities accepted can reach up to 40 percent of an annual officer's income—and is therefore no minor or inconsequential infraction of rules that can be left ignored or unenforced.

14. Albert A. Seedman and Peter Hellman, *Chief!* (New York: Avon Books, 1974), pp. 43–44.

15. Edwin J. Delattre, *Character and Cops: Ethics in Policing,* 4th ed. (Washington, D.C.: AEI Press, 2002), p. 41.

16. Edward Tully, *"Misconduct,* Corruption, Abuse of Power: What Can the Chief Do?" http://www.neiassociates.org/mis2.htm (Part I) and http://www.neiassociates.org/misconductII.htm (Part II) (accessed September 16, 2005).

17. John P. MacKenzie, *The Appearance of Justice* (New York: Scribner's, 1974).

18. Quoted in Frank Greenberg, "The Task of Judging the Judges," *Judicature* **59** (May 1976):464.

19. Ibid., p. 460; direct quote from the original.

20. For thorough discussions and examples of these areas of potential ethical shortcomings, see Jeffrey M. Shaman, Steven Lubet, and James J. Alfini, *Judicial Conduct and Ethics,* 3rd ed. (San Francisco: Matthew Bender & Co., 2000).

21. Ibid.

22. Ibid., p. vi.

23. Ibid.

24. Ibid., p. vi.

25. Tim Murphy, "Test Your Ethical Acumen," *Judges' Journal* **8** (1998):34.

26. American Judicature Society, *Judicial Conduct Reporter* **16** (1994):2–3.

27. John Adams, "On Government," quoted in Russell Wheeler, *Judicial Administration: Its Relation to Judicial Independence* (Alexandria, Va.: National Center for State Courts, 1988), p. 112.

28. Shaman, Lubet, and Alfini, *Judicial Conduct and Ethics,* p. viii.

29. Deut. 1:16–17.

30. Elliot D. Cohen, "Pure Legal Advocates and Moral Agents: Two Concepts of a Lawyer in an Adversary System," in Michael C. Braswell, Belinda R. McCarthy, and Bernard J. McCarthy (eds.), *Justice, Crime and Ethics,* 2nd ed. (Cincinnati, Ohio: Anderson, 1996), pp. 131–167.

31. *Berger v. United States,* 295 U.S. 78 (1935).

32. See *Dunlop v. United States,* 165 U.S. 486 (1897), involving a prosecutor's inflammatory statements to the jury.

33. 386 U.S. 1 (1967). In this case, the Supreme Court overturned the defendant's conviction after determining that the prosecutor "deliberately misrepresented the truth."

34. Cohen, "Pure Legal Advocates and Moral Agents," p. 168.

35. Ibid.

36. Cynthia Kelly Conlon and Lisa L. Milord, *The Ethics Fieldbook: Tools for Trainers* (Chicago: American Judicature Society, n.d.), pp. 23–25.

37. Ibid., p. 28.

38. Elizabeth L. Grossi and Bruce L. Berg, "Stress and Job Dissatisfaction Among Correctional Officers: An Unexpected Finding," *International Journal of Offender Therapy and Comparative Criminology* **35** (1991):79.

39. Irving L. Janis, "Group Dynamics Under Conditions of External Danger," in Darwin Cartwright and Alvin Zander (eds.), *Group Dynamics: Research and Theory* (New York: Harper & Row, 1968).

40. Ibid.

41. Ibid., p. 85.

42. CBS News, March 30, 1977; see Jones and Carlson, *Reputable Conduct*, p. 76.

43. Jones and Carlson, *Reputable Conduct,* p. 77.

44. F. K. Fair and W. D. Pilcher, "Morality on the Line: The Role of Ethics in Police Decision-Making," *American Journal of Police* **10**(2) (1991):23–38.

45. Tully, "Misconduct, Corruption, Abuse of Power.

46. Stephen J. Vicchio, "Ethics and Police Integrity," *FBI Law Enforcement Bulletin* (July 1997):8–12.

47. Kleinig, *The Ethics of Policing*.

48. Ibid.

49. Sam S. Souryal and Deanna L Diamond, "The Rhetoric of Personal Loyalty to Superiors in Criminal Justice Agencies," *Journal of Criminal Justice* **29**(2001):543–554.

50. Ibid., p. 548.

51. Ibid., p. 549

52. Some of these case studies were adapted from Jones and Carlson, *Reputable Conduct*.

53. Delattre, *Character and Cops,* p. 84.

# Chapter 14

# Rights of Criminal Justice Employees

## Key Terms and Concepts

Americans with Disabilities Act (ADA)

Affirmative action

Bona fide occupational qualifier (BFOQ)

Fair Labor Standards Act (FLSA)

Family and Medical Leave Act (FMLA)

Peace Officers Bill of Rights (POBR)

Reverse discrimination

## Learning Objectives

As a result of reading this chapter, the student will:

- be familiar with laws and rights affecting criminal justice employees
- understand the concept of disparate treatment
- be familiar with effective action plans
- know the elements of a due process claim under U.S. Section 1983
- understand the impact of the Fair Labor Standards Act on criminal justice employees
- understand the impact of sexual harassment in the criminal justice workplace
- know the eligibility requirements for Family and Medical Leave Act benefits
- have an understanding of the Americans with Disabilities Act

> *Uneasy lies the head that wears the crown.*
>
> —William Shakespeare
>
> *Good orders make evil men good and bad orders make good men evil.*
>
> —James Harrington

## Introduction

In the last few decades, the rights and obligations of criminal justice employees, like those of workers in the private sector, have changed dramatically. Changes in values, demographics, law, and technology have blurred the line dividing the manager and those who are managed in enforcement, judicial, and correctional agencies. Today's criminal justice employee is far more sophisticated about employee rights.[1] For that reason, and because of attendant liability considerations (discussed in Chapter 15), contemporary criminal justice managers must be more aware of employees' legal rights.

After an overview of the relevant employment laws, I discuss recruitment and hiring issues, age discrimination, affirmative action, discipline and discharge, pay and benefits, and safe workplace issues. Then I examine constitutional rights of criminal justice employees as determined by the courts regarding free speech, searches and seizures, self-incrimination, religious practices, sexual misconduct, residency requirements, moonlighting, misuse of firearms, alcohol and drugs in the workplace, sexual harassment, and the Americans with Disabilities Act. The chapter concludes with two case studies.

# Overview

Law and litigation affecting criminal justice employees can arise out of federal and state constitutions, statutes, administrative regulations, and judicial interpretations and rulings. Even poorly written employee handbooks or long-standing agency customs or practices may create vested rights. The ripple effect begun by improper or illegal hiring, training, discipline, or discharge can lead not only to poor agency performance and morale, but also to substantial legal and economic liability. It should become apparent in the following overview and the court decisions that follow that utilizing good common sense as well as a sense of fairness will go a long way toward preventing legal problems in the employment relationship.[2]

It should also be noted that the Civil Rights Act of 1991, like its predecessors, may result in further amended versions and changes in public and private sector employment; however, it will take several years for significant decisions to wind their way through the courts for a final determination by the Supreme Court of the intent and reach of the act. Therefore, this section focuses on presenting the issues rather than on attempting to settle the law in these areas.

- *Fair Labor Standards Act* (FLSA; at 29 U.S.C. 203 et seq.). This act provides minimum salary and overtime provisions covering both public and private sector employees. Part 7(a) contains special provisions for firefighters and police officers. I discuss the FLSA more fully later.
- *Title VII of the Civil Rights Act of 1964 and its amendments* (42 U.S.C. 2000e). This broadly based act establishes a federal policy requiring fair employment practices in both the public and private sectors. It prohibits unlawful employment discrimination in the hiring process, discharge, discipline, and working conditions and the unlawful provision of benefits based on race, color, religion, sex, and national origin. Its provisions extend to "hostile work environment" claims based on sexual, racial, or religious harassment.
- *Equal Pay Act* [29 U.S.C. 206(d)]. This legislation provides an alternative remedy to Title VII for sex-based discrimination in wages and benefits when men and women do similar work. It applies the simpler Fair Labor Standards Act procedures to claims. Note that the Equal Pay Act does not mean "comparable worth"—an attempt to determine wages by requiring equal pay for employees whose work is of comparable worth even if the job content is totally different.
- *The Pregnancy Discrimination Act of 1978* [42 U.S.C. Section 2000e(k)]. This act is an amendment to the scope of sexual discrimination under Title

VII. It prohibits unequal treatment of women because of pregnancy or related medical conditions (e.g., nausea). The act requires that employers treat pregnant women like other temporarily disabled employees. The U.S. Supreme Court decided a major case in 1991 that limited employers' ability in excluding women who are pregnant or of childbearing years from certain jobs under a fetal protection policy.[3]

- *Age Discrimination in Employment Act* (29 U.S.C. 623). This act generally prohibits the unequal treatment of applicants or employees based on their age, if they are age 40 years or older, in regard to hiring, firing, receiving benefits, and other conditions of employment.

- *Americans with Disabilities Act of 1990* (ADA) (42 U.S.C. 12112). The goal of this legislation is to remove barriers that might prevent otherwise qualified individuals with disabilities from enjoying the same employment opportunities as persons without disabilities. Before the ADA, the Rehabilitation Act of 1973 (see 29 U.S.C. 701) and its amendments prevented similar disability discrimination among public agencies receiving federal funds. The ADA is discussed more fully later.

- *Section 1983* (codified as Title 42, U.S. Code Section 1983). This major piece of legislation is the instrument by which an employee may sue an employer for civil rights violations based on the deprivation of constitutional rights. It is the most versatile civil rights action and is also the most often used against criminal justice agencies. Section 1983 is discussed more in Chapter 15.

In addition to the those legislative enactments and state statutes that prohibit various acts of discrimination in employment, there are additional remedies that have tremendous impact on public sector employees. Tort actions (a tort is the infliction of a civil injury) may be brought by public sector employees against their employer for a wide variety of claims, ranging from assault and battery to defamation. Contractual claims may grow out of collective bargaining agreements, which may include procedures for assignments, seniority, due process protections (such as in the Peace Officers' Bill of Rights, discussed later), and grievance procedures. Often the source of the right defines the remedy and the procedure for obtaining that remedy. For example, statutes or legal precedents often provide for an aggrieved employee to receive back pay, compensatory damages, injunctive relief, or punitive damages.

# The Employment Relationship

## *Recruitment and Hiring*

Numerous selection methods for hiring police and corrections officers have been tried over the years. Issues in recruitment, selection, and hiring also often involve internal promotions and assignments to special units, such as a special weapons team in a police agency. Requirements concerning age (e.g., the FBI will hire no one older than 37 years of age), height, weight, vision, education, and possession of a valid driver's license have all been utilized over the years in criminal justice. In addition, tests are commonly used to determine intelligence, emotional suitability and stability (using psychological examinations and oral interviews), physical agility, and character (using polygraph examinations and extensive background checks).[4] More recently, drug tests have become frequently used as well (discussed more fully later).

The critical question for such tests is whether they validly test the types of skills needed for the job. A companion concern is whether the tests are used for discriminatory purposes or have an unequal impact on protected groups (e.g., minorities, the physically challenged). As a result of these considerations, a number of private companies provide valid, reliable examinations for use by the public sector.

## Disparate Treatment

It should be emphasized that there is nothing in the law that states that an employer must hire or retain incompetent personnel. In effect, the law does not prohibit discrimination. Thus, it is not unlawful to refuse to hire people who have a record of driving while intoxicated for positions that require driving. What is illegal is to treat people differently because of their age, gender, sex, or other protected status; that is disparate treatment. It is also illegal to deny equal employment opportunities to such persons; that is disparate impact.[5] Federal equal opportunity law prohibits the use of selection procedures for hiring or promotion that have a discriminatory impact on the employment opportunities of women, Hispanics, blacks, or other protected classes. An example of overt discriminatory hiring is reflected in a court decision in 1987 arising out of a situation in a sparsely populated county in Virginia. Four women sued because they were denied positions as courtroom security officer, deputy, and civil process server because of their gender. Sheriffs had refused to hire the women, justifying their decision by contending that being male was a **bona fide occupational qualifier (BFOQ)** for the positions and that because the positions were within the "personal staff" of the sheriff, they were exempt from the coverage of Title VII. The Fourth Circuit overturned a lower court decision, finding that the sheriff did not establish that gender was a BFOQ for the positions and that the positions were not part of the sheriff's personal staff (the positions were not high level, policymaking, or advisory in nature). Thus, the refusal to hire the women violated Title VII.[6] There may, however, be a "business justification" for a hiring policy even though it has a disparate impact. For example, in one case an employer required airline attendants to cease flying immediately on discovering they were pregnant. The court upheld the policy on the ground that pregnancy could affect one's ability to perform routine duties in an aircraft, thereby jeopardizing the safety of passengers.[7]

A classic example of an apparent neutral employment requirement that actually had a disparate impact on gender, race, and ethnicity was the once-prevalent height requirement used by most public safety agencies. Minimum height requirements of 5 feet, 10 inches or above were often advertised and effectively operated to exclude most women and many Asians and Hispanics from employment.[8] Such a requirement has gradually been superseded by a "height in proportion to weight" requirement.

Nonetheless, other existing physical agility tests serve to discriminate against women and small men with less upper-body strength. One wonders how many pushups a police officer must do on the job or be able to do to perform his or her duties adequately, or how m___ ____ ___ walls, ditches, and attics officers must negotiate. (Occasionally, ____ ____ _____ physical abilities testing becomes ludicrous. For example, I or ___ ____ ecruiter from a major western city to recruit students in an up___ ____ l justice course. The recruiter said the city's physical test includ___ ____ ot wall; however, he quickly pointed out that testing staff would ____ ____ applicants over it.)

Litigation is blossomin___ ____ a western city, a woman challenged the police department's ___ ____ test as discriminatory and not job related, prompting the age___ ____ nadian consultant who developed a job-related preemployment ___y test (currently used by the Royal Canadian Mounted Police and other agencies across Canada) based on data provided by officers and later computer analyzed for incorporation into the test. In other words, recruits are now tested on the physical demands placed on police officers in that specific community (no pushups or 6-foot walls are included).[9]

Discrimination may also exist in promotions and job assignments. As an example of the former, a Nebraska female correctional center worker brought suit alleging that her employer violated her Title VII and equal protection rights by denying her a promotion. The woman was qualified for the higher-level position (assistant center manager for programming), and she also alleged that the center treated women inequitably and unprofessionally, that assertiveness in women was viewed negatively, and that women were assigned clerical duties not assigned to men. The court found that she was indeed denied a promotion because of her sex, in violation of Title VII and the equal protection clause of the Fourteenth Amendment; she was awarded back pay ($7,500), front pay ($122 biweekly until a comparable position became available), general damages, and court costs.[10]

With respect to litigation in the area of job assignments, four female jail matrons who were refused assignments to correctional officer positions in Florida even though they had been trained and certified as jail officers were awarded damages. It was ruled that a state regulation prohibiting females in male areas of the jail was discriminatory without proof that gender was a BFOQ.[11] However, a particular assignment may validly exclude one gender. An assignment to work as a decoy female prostitute demonstrates a business necessity for women.[12]

## How Old Is "Too Old" in Criminal Justice?

State and public agencies are not immune from age discrimination suits in which arbitrary age restrictions have been found to violate the law. In Florida, a police lieutenant with the state highway patrol with 29 years of service was forced by statute to retire at age 62. The Equal Employment Opportunity Commission (EEOC) brought suit, alleging that Florida's statute violated the Age Discrimination in Employment Act (ADEA). The court held that age should not be a BFOQ because youthfulness is not a guarantee of public safety. Rather, a physical fitness standard would better serve the purpose of ensuring the ability to perform the tasks of the position.[13]

Indeed, the U.S. Supreme Court rejected mandatory retirement plans for municipal firefighters and police officers.[14] Until 1985, the city of Baltimore had relied on a federal police officer and firefighter statute (5 U.S.C. 8335b), an exemption to the ADEA, to establish age limits for appointing and retiring its fire and police officers; the city also contended that age was a BFOQ for doing so. The U.S. Supreme Court said that although Congress had exempted federal employees from application of the ADEA, another agency cannot just adopt the same standards without showing an agency-specific need. Age is not a BFOQ for nonfederal firefighters (or, by extension, police officers). The Court also established a "reasonable federal standard" in its 1984 decision in *EEOC v. Wyoming*,[15] in which it overturned a state statute providing for the mandatory retirement of state game wardens at age 55; it held that the ADEA did not require employers to retain unfit employees, only to make individualized determinations about fitness.

## Criminal Justice and Affirmative Action

Probably no single employment practice has caused as much controversy as **affirmative action.** The very words bring to mind visions of quotas and of unqualified people being given preferential hiring treatment.[16] Indeed, quotas have been at the center of legal, social, scientific, and political controversy for more than two decades.[17] However, the reality of affirmative action is substantially different from the myth; as a general rule, affirmative action plans give preferred treatment only to affected groups when all other criteria (e.g., education, skills) are equal.[18]

The legal question (and to many persons, a moral one) that arises from affirmative action is, When does preferential hiring become **reverse discrimination?** The leading case here is *Bakke v. Regents of the University of California*[19] in 1978, in which Allan Bakke was passed over for medical school admission at the University of California, Davis, partly because the school annually set aside a number of its 100 medical school admissions slots for "disadvantaged" applicants. The Supreme Court held, among other things, that race could be used as a criterion in selection decisions, but it could not be the only criterion.

In a series of cases beginning in 1986,[20] the Supreme Court considered the development and application of affirmative action plans, establishing a two-step inquiry that must be satisfied before an affirmative action plan can be put in place. A plan must have (1) a remedial purpose, to correct past inequities, and

(2) there must be a manifest imbalance or significant disparity to justify the plan. The Court, however, emphasized that such plans cannot completely foreclose employment opportunities to nonminority or male candidates.

The validity of such plans is generally determined on a case-by-case basis. For example, the District of Columbia Circuit Court held in 1987 that an affirmative action plan covering the promotion of blacks to management positions in the police department was justified because only 174 of the 807 positions (22 percent) above the rank of sergeant were filled by blacks in a city where 60 percent of the labor market was black.[21] Twenty-one past and present nonminority male detectives of the Metropolitan Police Department who were passed over for promotion challenged the department's voluntary affirmative actions plan designed to place "special emphasis" on the hiring and advancement of females and minorities in those employment areas where an "obvious imbalance" in their numbers existed.[22]

The plaintiffs believed that their failure to be promoted was attributable to illegal preferential treatment of blacks and women (reverse discrimination) that violated their rights under Title VII and the due process clause of the Fifth Amendment. The court held that the nonminority and male employees of the department failed to prove that the plan was invalid; a considerable body of evidence showed racial and sexual imbalance at the time the plan was adopted. Also, the plan did not unnecessarily trammel any legitimate interests of the nonminority or male employees because it did not call for displacement or layoff and did not totally exclude them from promotion opportunities.[23]

In summary, then, whenever a criminal justice employer wishes to implement and maintain job requirements, they must be job related. Furthermore, whenever a job requirement discriminates against a protected class, it should have a strong legitimate purpose and be the least restrictive alternative. Finally, attempts to remedy past hiring inequities by such means as affirmative action programs need substantial justification to avoid reverse discrimination.[24]

## *Property Rights in Employment*

The Fourteenth Amendment to the U.S. Constitution provides in part that

> No state shall make or enforce any law which shall abridge the privileges or immunities of citizens of the United States; nor shall any State deprive any person of life, liberty, or property without due process of law; nor deny to any person within its jurisdiction the equal protection of the law.

Furthermore, the Supreme Court has set forth four elements of a due process claim under Section 1983: (1) A person acting under color of state law (2) deprived an individual (3) of constitutionally protected property (4) without due process of law.[25]

A long line of court cases has established the legal view that public employees have a property interest in their employment. This flies in the face of the old view that employees served "at will" or until their employer, for whatever reason, no longer had need of their services. The Supreme Court has provided some general guidance on how the question of a constitutionally protected property interest is to be resolved:

> To have a property interest in a benefit, a person clearly must have more than an abstract need or desire for it. He must have more than a unilateral expectation of it. He must, instead, have a *legitimate claim of entitlement to it.* It is a purpose of the ancient institution of property to protect those claims *upon which people rely in their daily lives, reliance that must not be arbitrarily undermined* [emphasis added].[26]

The Court has also held that employees are entitled to both a pretermination and a posttermination notice,[27] as well as an opportunity to respond, and that state legislators are free to choose not to confer a property interest in public employment.

The development of a property interest in employment has an important ramification: It means that due process must be exercised by a public entity before terminating or interfering with an employee's property right. What has been established, however, is that a probationary employee has little or no property interest in employment. For example, the Ninth Circuit held that a probationary civil service employee ordinarily has no property interest and could be discharged without a hearing or even "good cause." In that same decision, however, the court held that a woman who had passed her 6-month probationary period and who had then been promoted to a new position for which there was a probationary period had the legitimate expectation of continued employment.[28]

On the other hand, an Indiana police captain was deemed to have a property interest in his position even though a state statute allowed the city manager to demote without notice. There, a captain of detectives, a Democrat, was demoted by a newly elected Republican mayor. The court determined that the dismissal of even a policymaking public employee for politically motivated reasons is forbidden unless the position inherently encompasses tasks that render political affiliation an appropriate prerequisite for effective performance.[29]

Normally, however, policymaking employees (often called exempt appointments) possess an automatic exception to the contemporary property interest view. These personnel, often elected agency heads, are generally free to hire and fire those employees who are involved in the making of important decisions and policy. Examples of this area include new sheriffs who appoint undersheriffs and wardens who appoint deputy wardens. These subordinate employees have no property interest in their positions and may be asked at any time to leave the agency or revert back to an earlier rank.

This property interest in employment is, of course, generally implied. An example of this implication is found in a Utah case in which a property interest was found to exist based on an implied contract founded on an employment manual. Due process standards were therefore violated when the police department fired an officer without showing good cause or giving him a chance to respond to the charges against him.[30] In a Pennsylvania case, a patrol officer was suspended for 30 days without pay for alleged violations of personnel policies and was not given an opportunity to file a written response to the charges. The court held that the officer's suspension resulted in a deprivation of property.[31]

The property right in one's employment does not have to involve discipline or discharge to afford an employee protections. The claim of a parole officer that he was harassed, humiliated, and interfered with in a deliberate attempt to remove him from his position established a civil rights action for deprivation of property.[32] This decision, against the Illinois Department of Corrections, resulted from allegations that the department engaged in "a deliberate and calculated effort to remove the plaintiff from his position by forcing him to resign, thereby making the protections of the personnel code unavailable to him." As a result, the plaintiff suffered anxiety and stress and eventually went on disability status at substantially reduced pay.[33]

The key questions, then, once a property right is established, are (1) What constitutes adequate grounds for interference with that right? and (2) what is adequate process to sustain that interference?[34]

## *Pay and Benefits*

The **Fair Labor Standards Act (FLSA)** has had a major impact on criminal justice agencies. One observer referred to the FLSA as the criminal justice administrator's "worst nightmare come true."[35] Enacted in 1938 to establish minimum wages and to require overtime compensation in the private sector, amendments were added in 1974 extending its coverage to state and local governmental employees and including special work period provisions for police and fire employees. In 1976, however, the U.S. Supreme Court ruled that the extension of the act into traditional local and state governmental functions was unconstitutional.[36] In 1985, the Court reversed itself, bringing local police employees under the coverage of the FLSA. In this major (and costly) decision, *Garcia v. San Antonio Transit Authority*,[37] the Court held, 5 to 4, that Congress could impose the requirements of the FLSA on state and local governments.

Criminal justice operations take place 24 hours per day, 7 days per week, and often require overtime and participation in off-duty activities such as court appearances and training sessions. The FLSA comes into play when overtime salaries must be paid. It provides that an employer must pay employees time and a half for all hours worked over 40 per week. Overtime must also be paid to personnel for all work in excess of 43 hours in a 7-day cycle or 171 hours in a 28-day period. Public safety employees may accrue a maximum of 240 hours of compensatory or "comp" time, which, if not utilized as leave, must be paid on separation from employment at the employee's final rate of pay or at the average pay over the last 3 years, whichever is greater.[38] Furthermore, employers usually cannot require employees to take compensatory time in lieu of cash.

A recent decision by the U.S. Supreme Court favored administrators in this regard, however. A county in Texas became concerned that after employees reached their cap on comp time accrued, it would be unable to afford to pay them for overtime worked. So the county sought to reduce accrued comp time and implemented a policy under which the employees' supervisor set a maximum number of compensatory hours that could be accumulated. When an employee's accrued amount of comp time approached that maximum, the employee would be asked to take steps to reduce accumulated comp time. If the employee did not do so voluntarily, the supervisor would order the employee to use his or her comp time at specified times. This policy was challenged in court by 127 deputy sheriffs. The Court held that nothing in the FLSA prohibited employers from instituting such a policy.[39]

An officer who works the night shift must now receive pay for attending training or testifying in court during the day. Furthermore, officers who are ordered to remain at home in anticipation of emergency actions must be compensated. Notably, however, the FLSA's overtime provisions do not apply to persons employed in a bona fide executive, administrative, or professional capacity. In criminal justice, the act has generally been held to apply to detectives and sergeants but not to those of the rank of lieutenant and above.

A companion issue with respect to criminal justice pay and benefits is that of equal pay for equal work. Disparate treatment in pay and benefits can be litigated under Title VII or statutes such as the Equal Pay Act or the equal protection clause. An Ohio case involved matron/dispatchers who performed essentially the same job as jailers but were paid less. This was found to be in violation of the Equal Pay Act and, because discriminatory intent was found, Title VII.[40]

Other criminal justice employee benefits are addressed in Title VII, the ADEA, and the Pregnancy Discrimination Act (PDA). For example, it is illegal to provide less insurance coverage for a female employee who is more likely to use maternity leave or for an older employee who is more liable to use more coverage. In addition, an older person or a woman could not be forced to pay higher pension contributions because he or she might be paying in for a shorter period of time or would be expected to live longer. Regarding pregnancy, the PDA does not require an employer to discriminate in favor of a pregnancy-related condition. It demands only that the employer not treat pregnancy differently from any other temporary medical condition. For example, if an agency has a 6-month leave policy for officers who are injured or ill from off-duty circumstances (on-duty circumstances would probably be covered by workers' compensation), that agency would have to provide 6 months' leave (if needed) for a pregnancy-related condition.[41]

## Criminal Justice and a Safe Workplace

It is unclear what duties are owed by public employers to their employees in providing a safe workplace. Federal, state, and local governments are exempted from the coverage of the Occupational Safety and Health Act (OSHA), in 29 U.S.C. 652. Nonetheless, criminal justice work is often dangerous, involving the use of force and often occurring in locations outside governmental control. Therefore, workplace safety issues in criminal justice are more likely to revolve around adequacy of training and supervision than physical plants.[42]

The Supreme Court has noted the unique nature and danger of public service employment. In one case, the Court specifically stated that an employee could not bring a Section 1983 civil rights action alleging a workplace so unsafe that it violated the Fourteenth Amendment's due process clause. In this matter, a sewer worker was asphyxiated while clearing a sewer line. His widow alleged that the city knew the sewer was dangerous and that the city had failed to train or supervise the decedent properly.[43]

Other federal courts, especially the federal circuits, however, have ruled inconsistently on the safe workplace issue. One federal circuit held that a constitutional violation could be brought if it was proven that the city actively engaged in conduct that was "deliberately indifferent" to the employee's constitutional rights.[44]

However, the Fifth Circuit held differently in a Louisiana case, based on a failure to comply with a court order to have three officers on duty at all times in a prison disciplinary unit.[45] Here, a prison correctional officer in Baton Rouge was the only guard on a dangerous cellblock. While attempting to transfer a handcuffed inmate, the guard got into a scuffle with the inmate and was injured, although not severely. However, he claimed that he received insufficient medical attention and that as a result he became permanently disabled and that the institution "consciously" and with wanton disregard for his personal safety conspired to have him work alone on the cellblock. He invoked 42 U.S.C. 1983 in his charges, claiming that the institution acted in an indifferent, malicious, and reckless manner toward him, and that he suffered "class-based discrimination." The court held that the guard had no cause of action (no federal or constitutional grounds for litigation).

Liability for an employee's injury, disability, or death is a critical concern for criminal justice agencies. In particular, police and correctional officers often work in circumstances involving violent actions. Although state workers' compensation coverage, disability pensions, life insurance, and survivor pensions are designed to cover such tragedies, such coverage is typically limited and only intended to be remedial. On the other hand, civil tort actions in such cases can have a devastating impact on governmental budgets. Clearly, this is a difficult and costly problem to resolve. It is also an area with moral dilemmas as well. For example, what should be done with a prison intelligence unit that has knowledge of an impending disturbance but fails to alert its officers (who are subsequently injured)? And might a police department with knowledge that its new police vehicles have defective brakes fail to take immediate action for fear that its officers will refuse to drive the vehicles, thus reducing available personnel?[46]

# Constitutional Rights of Criminal Justice Employees

## *Freedom of Speech and Association*

Many criminal justice executives have attempted to regulate what their employees say to the public; executives develop and rely on policies and procedures designed to govern employee speech. On occasion those restrictions will be challenged; a number of court decisions have attempted to define the limits of criminal justice employees' exercise of free speech.

Although the right of freedom of speech is one of the most fundamental of all rights of Americans, the Supreme Court has indicated that "the State has interests as an employer in regulating the speech of its employees that differ significantly from those it possesses in connection with regulation of the speech of the citizenry in general."[47] Thus, the state may impose restrictions on its employees that it would not be able to impose on the citizenry at large. However, these restrictions must be reasonable.[48]

There are two basic situations in which a police regulation may be found to be an unreasonable infringement on the free speech interests of officers.[49] The first occurs when the action is overly broad. A Chicago Police Department rule prohibiting "any activity, conversation, deliberation, or discussion which is derogatory to the Department" is a good example, because such a rule obviously prohibits all criticism of the agency by its officers, even in private conversation.[50] A similar situation arose in New Orleans, where the police department had a regulation that prohibited a police officer from making statements that "unjustly criticize or ridicule, or express hatred or contempt toward, or . . . which may be detrimental to, or cast suspicion on the reputation of, or otherwise defame, any person."[51] The regulation was revised and later ruled constitutional.[52]

The second situation in which free speech limitations may be found to be unreasonable is in the way in which the governmental action is applied. Specifically, a police department may be unable to demonstrate that the statements by an officer being disciplined actually adversely affected the operation of the department. A Baltimore regulation prohibiting public criticism of police department action was held to have been unconstitutionally applied to a police officer who was president of the police union and had stated in a television interview that the police commissioner was not leading the department effectively[53] and that "the bottom is going to fall out of this city."[54]

A related area is that of political activity. As with free speech, governmental agencies may restrict the political behavior of their employees. The rationale is that without such restrictions, employees could be pressured by their superiors to support certain political candidates or engage in political activities under threat of loss of employment or other adverse action. At the federal level, various types of political activity by federal employees are controlled by the Hatch Act; its constitutionality has been upheld by the U.S. Supreme Court.[55] Many states have similar statutes, often referred to as "little Hatch Acts."

Although it may appear that Supreme Court decisions have lain to rest all controversy in this area, such has not been the case. Two recent cases show lower courts opting to limit the authority of the state to restrict political activities of their employees. In Pawtucket, Rhode Island, two firefighters ran for public office (mayor and city council member), despite a city charter provision prohibiting all political activity by employees (except voting and privately expressing their opinions). The Rhode Island Supreme Court issued an injunction against enforcing the

charter provision, on the ground that the provision applied only to partisan political activities.[56] In a similar Boston case, however, the court upheld the police
department rule on the basis that whether the partisan–nonpartisan distinction
was crucial was a matter for legislative or administrative determination.[57]

In a Michigan case, a court declared unconstitutional, for being overly broad,
two city charter provisions that prohibited contributions to or solicitations for any
political purpose by city employees.[58] Clearly, although the Supreme Court seems
to be supportive of governmental attempts to limit the political activities of its
employees, lower courts seem just as intent to limit the Supreme Court decisions
to the facts of those cases.

Could a police officer be disciplined, even discharged, because of his or her
political affiliations? The Supreme Court ruled on that question in a case arising
out of the Sheriff's Department in Cook County, Illinois.[59] The newly elected
sheriff, a Democrat, fired the chief deputy of the process division and a bailiff of
the juvenile court because they were Republicans. The Court ruled that it was a
violation of the employees' First Amendment rights to discharge them from non-
policymaking positions solely on the basis of their political party affiliation.[60]

Nonpolitical associations are also protected by the First Amendment; however, it is common for police departments to prohibit officers from associating
with known felons or others of questionable reputation, on the ground that
"such associations may expose an officer to irresistible temptations to yield in
his obligation to impartially enforce the law, and … may give the appearance
that the police are not themselves honest and impartial enforcers of the law."[61]

However, rules against association, as with other First Amendment rights,
must not be overly broad. A Detroit Police Department regulation prohibiting associating with known criminals or persons charged with crimes, except in connection with regular duties, was declared unconstitutional. The court held that
it prohibited some associations that had no bearing on the officers' integrity or
public confidence in the officer (e.g., an association with a fellow church member who had been arrested on one occasion years ago, or the befriending of a
recently convicted person who wanted to become a productive citizen).[62]

Occasionally, a criminal justice employee will be disciplined for improper
association even though it was not demonstrated that the association had a detrimental effect on the employee or the agency. For example, a Maryland court
held that a fully qualified police officer who was a practicing nudist could not be
fired simply on that basis.[63] On the other hand, a court upheld the discharge of
an officer who had had sexual intercourse at a party with a woman he knew to
be a nude model at a local "adult theater of known disrepute."[64]

An individual has a fundamental interest in being free to enter into certain intimate or private relationships; nevertheless, freedom of association is not an
absolute right. For example, a federal district court held that the dismissal of a married police officer for living with another man's wife was a violation of the officer's
privacy and associational rights.[65] Other courts, however, have found that off-duty
sexual activity can affect job performance. When a married city police officer
allegedly had consensual, private, nonduty, heterosexual relations with single

adult women other than his wife in violation of state law criminalizing adultery, the adultery was not a fundamental right. Thus, the officer's extramarital affairs were not protected and the intimate relationship affected the public's perception of the agency.[66]

In another case, a police officer became involved with a city dispatcher who was the wife of a sergeant in the same department. The adulterous officer became eligible for promotion and scored high on the exam. The chief, confirming via an investigation that the officer had in fact been involved in an adulterous relationship with the dispatcher, refused on that basis to promote the officer, as he "would not command respect and trust" from rank-and-file officers and would adversely affect the efficiency and morale of the department. The Texas Supreme Court held that the officer's private, adulterous sexual conduct was not protected by state or federal law; the U.S. Supreme Court denied the appeal.[67]

Finally, the U.S. Court of Appeals for the Sixth Circuit held that a police department could conduct an investigation into the marital sexual relations of a police officer accused of sexual harassment.[68] In this case, there were allegations that the married officer had sexually harassed co-workers and had dated a gang member's mother. The department investigated the accusations, and the officer and his wife brought a Section 1983 action, alleging that the investigation violated their constitutional rights to privacy and freedom of association. The court held that the agency's investigation was reasonable, and, furthermore, that the police department would have been derelict in not investigating the matter.

In summary, police administrators have the constitutional authority to regulate employees' off-duty associational activities, including off-duty sexual conduct that involves a supervisory/subordinate relationship and associations that impact adversely employees' ability to do their jobs or impair the effectiveness and efficiency of the organization.[69]

The First Amendment's reach also includes means of expression other than verbal utterances. The Supreme Court upheld the constitutionality of a regulation of the Suffolk County, New York, Police Department that established several grooming standards (regarding hair, sideburn, and moustache length) for its male officers. In this case, *Kelley v. Johnson*,[70] the Court believed that to make officers easily recognizable to the public and to maintain the esprit de corps within the department, the agency justified the regulations and did not violate any right guaranteed by the First Amendment.

## Searches and Seizures

The Fourth Amendment to the U.S. Constitution protects "the right of the people to be secure in their persons, houses, papers, and effects, against unreasonable searches and seizures." In an important case in 1967, the Supreme Court held that the amendment also protected individuals' reasonable expectations of privacy, not just property interests.[71]

The Fourth Amendment usually applies to police officers when they are at home or off duty in the same manner as it applies to all citizens. Because of the nature of their work, however, police officers can be compelled to cooperate with investigations of their behavior when ordinary citizens would not. Examples include searches of equipment and lockers provided by the department to the officers. There, the officers have no expectation of privacy that affords or merits protection.[72] Lower courts have established limitations on searches of employees themselves. The rights of prison authorities to search their employees arose in a 1985 Iowa case in which employees were forced to sign a consent form for searches as a condition of hire; the court disagreed with such a broad policy, ruling that the consent form did not constitute a blanket waiver of all Fourth Amendment rights.[73]

Police officers may also be forced to appear in a lineup, a clear "seizure" of his or her person. Appearance in a lineup normally requires probable cause, but a federal appeals court upheld a police commissioner's ordering of 62 officers to appear in a lineup during an investigation of police brutality, holding that "the governmental interest in the particular intrusion [should be weighed] against the offense to personal dignity and integrity." Again, the court cited the nature of the work, noting that police officers do "not have the full privacy and liberty from police officials that [they] would otherwise enjoy."[74]

## *Self-Incrimination*

The Supreme Court has also addressed questions concerning the Fifth Amendment as it applies to police officers who are under investigation. In *Garrity v. New Jersey,*[75] a police officer was ordered by the attorney general to answer questions or be discharged. The officer testified that information obtained as a result of his answers was later used to convict him of criminal charges. The Supreme Court held that the information obtained from the officer could not be used against him at his criminal trial because the Fifth Amendment forbids the use of coerced confessions.

In *Gardner v. Broderick,*[76] a police officer refused to answer questions asked by a grand jury investigating police misconduct because he believed his answers might tend to incriminate him. The officer was terminated from his position as the result. The Supreme Court ruled that the officer could not be fired for his refusal to waive his constitutional right to remain silent. The Court added, however, that the grand jury could have forced the officer to answer or be terminated for his refusal provided that the officer was informed that his answers would not be used against him later in a criminal case.

As a result of these decisions, it is proper to fire a police officer who refuses to answer questions that are related directly to the performance of his or her duties provided that the officer has been informed that any answers may not be used later in a criminal proceeding. Although there is some diversity of opinion among lower courts on the question of whether an officer may be compelled to submit to a polygraph examination, the majority of courts that have considered the question have held that an officer can be required to take the examination.[77]

## Religious Practices

Criminal justice work often requires that personnel are available and on duty 24 hours per day, 7 days a week. Although it is not always convenient or pleasant, such shift configurations require that many criminal justice employees work weekends, nights, and holidays. It is generally assumed that one who takes such a position agrees to work such hours and to abide by other such conditions (e.g., carrying a weapon, as in a policing position); it is usually the personnel with the least seniority on the job who must work the most undesirable shifts.

There are occasions when one's religious beliefs are in direct conflict with the requirements of the job. Conflicts can occur between work assignments and attendance at religious services or periods of religious observance. In these situations, the employee may be forced to choose between his or her job and religion. I am acquainted with a midwestern state trooper whose religion posed another related cause of job–religion conflict: His religion (with which he became affiliated after being hired as a trooper) banned the carrying or use of firearms. The officer chose to give up his weapon, and thus his job. A number of people have chosen to litigate the work–religion conflict rather than accept agency demands.

Title VII of the Civil Rights Act of 1964 prohibits religious discrimination in employment. The act defines religion as including "all aspects of religious … practice, as well as belief, unless an employer … is unable to reasonably accommodate to an employee's … religious … practice without undue hardship on the conduct of the employer's business."[78] Thus, Title VII requires reasonable accommodation of religious beliefs, but not to the extent that the employee has complete freedom of religious expression.[79] For example, an Albuquerque firefighter was a Seventh Day Adventist and refused to work Friday or Saturday nights because such shifts interrupted his honoring the Sabbath. He refused to trade shifts or take leave with (as vacation) or without pay, even though existing policy permitted his doing so. Instead, he said that the *department* should make such arrangements for coverage or simply excuse him from his shifts. The department refused to do either, discharging him. The court ruled that the department's accommodations were reasonable and that no further accommodation could be made without causing an undue hardship to the department. His firing was upheld. The court emphasized, however, that future decisions would depend on the facts of the individual case.[80]

A circuit court held that the termination of a Mormon police officer for practicing plural marriage (polygamy) in violation of state law was not a violation of his right to freely exercise his religious beliefs.[81]

## Sexual Misconduct

To be blunt, criminal justice employees have ample opportunity to become engaged in sexual affairs, incidents, trysts, dalliances, or other behavior that is clearly sexual in nature. History and news accounts have shown that wearing a uniform, occupying a high or extremely sensitive position, or being sworn to maintain an unblemished and unsullied lifestyle does not mean that all people will do so for all time. Some people are not bashful about their intentions: Several officers have told me they aspired to police work because they assumed that wearing a uniform made them sexually irresistible. On the civilian side, there are police "groupies" who chase police officers and others in uniform.

Instances of sexual impropriety in criminal justice work can range from casual flirting while on the job to becoming romantically involved with a foreign agent whose principal aim is to learn delicate matters of national security. There have been all manner of incidents between those extremes, including the discipline of female police officers who posed nude in magazines. Some major police departments have even been compelled by their mayors to recruit officers for their sexual preference (i.e., homosexuality).

This is a delicate area, one in which discipline can be and has been meted out as police managers attempt to maintain high standards of officer conduct. It has also resulted in litigation because some officers believe that their right to privacy has been intruded on.

Officers may be disciplined for impropriety involving adultery and homosexuality. Most court decisions of the 1960s and 1970s agreed that adultery, even when involving an off-duty police officer and occurring in private, could result in disciplinary action[82] because such behavior brought debilitating criticism on the agency and undermined public confidence in the police. The views of the courts in this area, however, seem to be moderating with the times. A case involving an Internal Revenue Service agent suggested that to uphold disciplinary action for adultery, the government would have to prove that the employing agency was actually discredited.[83] The U.S. Supreme Court more recently appeared to be divided on the issue of extramarital sexual activity in public employment. In 1984, the Sixth Circuit held that a Michigan police officer could not be fired simply because he was living with a woman to whom he was not married (a felony under Michigan law).[84]

The issue of homosexual activity as a ground for termination of public employees arose in an Oklahoma case in which a state law permitted the discharge of schoolteachers for engaging in "public homosexual activity."[85] A lower court held the law to be unconstitutionally restrictive, and the Supreme Court agreed.[86] Another federal court held that the firing of a bisexual guidance counselor did not deprive the counselor of her First or Fourteenth Amendment rights. The counselor's discussion of her sexual preferences with teachers was not protected by the First Amendment.[87]

## Residency Requirements

In the 1970s and 1980s, interest in residency requirements for governmental employees heightened, especially in communities experiencing economic difficulties.[88] Many governmental agencies now specify that all or certain members in their employ must live within the geographical limits of their employing jurisdiction. In other words, employees must reside within the county or city of employment. Such residency requirements have often been justified by employing agencies, particularly in criminal justice, on the grounds that employees should become familiar with and be visible in the jurisdiction of employment and that they should reside where they are paid by the taxpayers to work. Perhaps the strongest rationale given by employing agencies is that criminal justice employees must live within a certain proximity of their work in order to respond quickly in the event of an emergency.

Prior to 1976, numerous challenges to residency requirements were raised, even after the Michigan Supreme Court ruled that Detroit's residency requirement for police officers was not irrational.[89] In 1976, when the U.S. Supreme Court held that Philadelphia's law requiring firefighters to live in the city did not violate the Constitution, the challenges subsided. The cases now seem to revolve around the question of what constitutes residency. Generally, the police officer must demonstrate that he or she spends a substantial amount of time at the in-city residence.[90] Strong arguments have been made, however, that in areas where housing is unavailable or is exceptionally expensive, a residency requirement is unreasonable.[91]

## Moonlighting

The courts have traditionally supported criminal justice agencies placing limitations on the amount and kind of outside work their employees can perform.[92] For example, police department restrictions on moonlighting range from a complete ban on outside employment to permission to engage in certain forms of work, such as investment counseling, private security, teaching police science courses, and so on. The rationale for agency limitations is that "outside employment seriously interferes with keeping the [police and fire] departments fit and ready for action at all times."[93]

In a Louisiana case, however, firefighters successfully provided evidence that moonlighting had been a common practice for 16 years before the city banned it. No firefighters had ever needed sick leave as a result of injuries acquired while moonlighting, there had never been a problem locating off-duty firefighters to respond to an emergency, and moonlighting had never caused a level of fatigue that was serious enough to impair a firefighter's work. With this evidence, the court invalidated the city ordinance that had sought to prohibit moonlighting.[94]

## Misuse of Firearms

Because of the need to defend themselves or others and be prepared for any exigency, police officers are empowered to use lethal force when justified. Although restricted by the Supreme Court's 1985 decision in *Tennessee v. Garner*[95] (deeming the killing of unarmed, nondangerous suspects as unconstitutional), the possession of, and familiarity with, firearms remains a central aspect of the contemporary officer's role and function. Some officers take this responsibility to the extreme, however, becoming overly reliant on and consumed with their firepower.

## Exhibit 14.1
## Residency Rule Is a Yawner
### New Orleans Residents Don't Seem to Care Where Cops Live

Opponents of a New Orleans residency rule that has been on the books since the 1950's, but largely ignored until now, contend they have proof that a majority of residents do not care if their police officers live outside the city limits.

This month the New Orleans Police Foundation released a study which showed that nearly three-quarters of residents oppose the requirement. The poll of 400 city residents was conducted in September by a political analyst and assistant sociology professor at Xavier University, Silas Lee. His findings showed 73 percent agreeing that "it's OK for police officers to live in other parishes," and 55 percent who somewhat or strongly disagreed with the residency rule.

"I think the study tells us that the people of New Orleans want their city safe and they're willing to have police officers live anywhere as long as they can help achieve that goal," said Bob Stellingworth, the foundation's president. "That's their primary concern, making the city safe to live in," he told the publication New Orleans City Business.

Until 1995, when then-Mayor Marc Morial led the charge to enforce a new and more stringent residency requirement passed by the City Council, New Orleans' domicile rule was not at the top of anyone's agenda, according to local press reports. It requires anyone seeking to work for the municipal government to live within city limits. While a grandfather clause covers those who lived outside of New Orleans at the time it was enacted, they must move to the city if they want to be promoted. ...

Opponents of the residency rule claim that it has made recruitment difficult. The police force is currently 1,600 officers strong, but officials would like to see that figure rise to 2,000. Just 6 percent of the 52 recruits as of Aug. 25, 2004, qualified for employment on the basis of residency. In 2003, that figure was 8 percent, and in 2002, it was 13 percent. ...

Some black supporters, however, believe that the rule will curtail incidents of profiling, harassment and police brutality. ...

According to the findings of the police foundation's poll, 55 percent said they disagreed with the domicile policy, 41 percent said they agreed. A slim majority of 52 percent of blacks agreed with it, but just 1 in 4 white people did so. ...

*Source:* Reprinted with permission from *Law Enforcement News,* November, 2004, p. 5. John Jay College of Criminal Justice (CCNY), 555 West 57th St., New York, NY 10019.

**Author's update:** Obviously this survey was conducted prior to the horrific hurricane, Katrina, which decimated New Orleans in August 2005. On October 28, 2005, 51 members of the New Orleans Police Department—45 sworn officers and 6 civilian employees—were fired for abandoning their posts during the storm. Fifteen other officers resigned when placed under investigation for abandonment.
*Source:* http://www.msnbc.msn.com/id/9855340/print/1/displaymode/1098 (accessed October 28, 2005)

Thus, police agencies typically attempt to restrain the use of firearms through written policies and frequent training in "Shoot/Don't Shoot" scenarios. Still, a broad range of potential and actual problems remains with respect to the use and possible misuse of firearms, as the following shows.

In the face of extremely serious potential and real problems and the omnipresent specter of liability suits, police agencies generally have policies regulating the use of handguns and other firearms by their officers, both on and off duty. The courts have held that such regulations need only be reasonable and that the burden rests with the disciplined police officer to show that the regulation was arbitrary and unreasonable.[96] The courts also grant considerable latitude to administrators in determining when their firearms regulations have been violated.[97] Police firearms regulations tend to address three basic issues: (1) requirements for the safeguarding of the weapon, (2) guidelines for carrying the weapon while off duty, and (3) limitations on when the weapon may be fired.[98]

Courts and juries are becoming increasingly harsher in dealing with police officers who misuse their firearms. The current tendency is to "look behind" police shootings to determine whether the officer acted negligently or the employing agency inadequately trained and supervised the officer/employee. In one case, a federal appeals court approved a $500,000 judgment against the District of Columbia when a police officer who was not in adequate physical shape shot a man in the course of an arrest. The court noted that the District officer had received no fitness training in 4 years and was physically incapable of subduing the victim. The court noted that had the officer been physically fit and adequately trained in disarmament techniques, a gun would not have been necessary. In his condition, however, the officer posed a "foreseeable risk of harm to others."[99]

Courts have awarded damages against police officers and/or their employers for other acts involving misuse of firearms: An officer shot a person while intoxicated and off duty in a bar[100]; an officer accidentally killed an arrestee with a shotgun while handcuffing him[101]; an unstable officer shot his wife five times and then committed suicide with an off-duty weapon the department required him to carry[102]; and an officer accidentally shot and killed an innocent bystander while pursuing another man at night (the officer had had no instruction on shooting at a moving target, night shooting, or shooting in residential areas).[103]

## Alcohol and Drugs in the Workplace

Alcoholism and drug abuse problems have taken on a life of their own in contemporary criminal justice; employees must be increasingly wary of the tendency to succumb to these problems, and administrative personnel must be able to recognize and attempt to counsel and treat these problems.

Indeed, in the aftermath of the early-1990s beating death of Malice Green by a group of Detroit police officers, it was reported that the Detroit Police Department had "high alcoholism rates and pervasive psychological problems connected with the stress of policing a city mired in poverty, drugs, and crime."[104] It was further revealed that although the Detroit Police Department had paid $850,000 to two drug-testing facilities, the department did not have the counseling programs many other cities offer their officers. A psychologist asserted that "There are many, many potential time bombs in that department."[105]

It is obvious, given the extant law of most jurisdictions and the nature of their work, that criminal justice employees must be able to perform their work with a clear head, unaffected by alcohol or drugs.[106] Police departments and prisons will often specify in their manual of policy and procedures that no alcoholic beverages be consumed within a specified period prior to reporting for duty.

Such regulations have been upheld uniformly because of the hazards of the work. A Louisiana court went further, upholding a regulation that prohibited police officers from consuming alcoholic beverages on or off duty to the extent that it caused the officer's behavior to become obnoxious, disruptive, or disorderly.[107] Enforcing such regulations will occasionally result in criminal justice employees being ordered to submit to drug or alcohol tests, discussed next.

### Drug Testing

The courts have had several occasions to review criminal justice agency policies requiring employees to submit to urinalysis to determine the presence of drugs or alcohol. It was held as early as 1969 that a firefighter could be ordered to submit to a blood test when the agency had reasonable grounds to believe he was intoxicated, and that it was appropriate for the firefighter to be terminated from employment if he refused to submit to the test.[108]

In March 1989, the U.S. Supreme Court issued two major decisions on drug testing of public employees in the workplace. *Skinner v. Railway Labor Executives Association*[109] and *National Treasury Employees Union v. Von Raab*[110] dealt with drug-testing plans for railroad and U.S. Customs workers, respectively. Under the Fourth Amendment, governmental workers are protected from unreasonable search and seizure, including how drug testing can be conducted. The Fifth Amendment protects federal, state, and local workers from illegal governmental conduct.

In 1983, the Federal Railway Administration promulgated regulations that required railroads to conduct urine and blood tests on their workers following major train accidents. The regulations were challenged, one side arguing that because railroads were privately owned, governmental action, including applying the Fourth Amendment, could not legally be imposed. The Supreme Court disagreed in *Skinner,* ruling that railroads must be viewed as an instrument or agent of the government.

Three of the most controversial drug-testing issues have been whether testing should be permitted when there is no indication of a drug problem in the workplace, whether the testing methods are reliable, and whether a positive test proves on-the-job impairment.[111] The *Von Raab* case addressed all three issues. The U.S. Customs Service implemented a drug-screening program that required urinalysis for employees desiring transfer or promotion to positions that were directly involved in drug interdiction, where carrying a firearm was necessary, or where classified material was handled. Only 5 of 3,600 employees tested positive. The Treasury Employees Union argued that such an insignificant number of positives created a "suspicionless search" argument; in other words, drug testing was unnecessary and unwarranted. The Supreme Court disagreed, ruling that although only a few employees tested positive, drug use is such a serious problem that the program could continue.

Furthermore, the Court found nothing wrong with the testing protocol. An independent contractor was used. The worker, after discarding outer garments, produced a urine specimen while being observed by a member of the same sex; the sample was signed by the employee, labeled, placed in a plastic bag, sealed and delivered to a lab for testing. The Court found no "grave potential for arbitrary and oppressive interference with the privacy and personal security of the individuals" in this method.

Proving the connection between drug testing and on-the-job impairment has been an ongoing issue. Urinalysis cannot prove when a person testing positive actually used the drug. Therefore, tests may punish and stigmatize a person for extracurricular drug use that may have no effect on the worker's on-the-job performance.[112] In *Von Raab,* the Court indicated that this dilemma is still no impediment to testing. It stated that the Customs Service had a compelling interest in having a "physically fit" employee with "unimpeachable integrity and judgment."

Together, these two cases may set a new standard for determining the reasonableness of drug testing in the criminal justice workplace. They may legalize many testing programs that formerly would have been risky. *Von Raab* presented three compelling governmental interests that could be weighed against the employee's privacy expectations: the integrity of the work force, public safety, and protection of sensitive information. *Skinner* stated that railroad workers also have diminished expectations of privacy because they are in an industry that is widely regulated to ensure safety.[113]

## Rights of Police Officers

Delineated earlier were several areas (e.g., place of residence, religious practice, freedom of speech, search and seizure) in which criminal justice employees, particularly the police, may encounter treatment by their administrators and the federal courts that is quite different from that received by other citizens. One does give up certain constitutional rights and privileges by virtue of wearing a justice system uniform. This section looks at how, for the police at least, the pendulum has swung more in the direction of the rank and file.

In the last decade, police officers have insisted on greater procedural safeguards to protect themselves against what they perceive as arbitrary infringement on their rights. These demands have been reflected in statutes enacted in many states, generally known as the **Peace Officers' Bill of Rights (POBR).**

This legislation mandates due process rights for peace officers who are the subject of internal investigations that could lead to disciplinary action. These statutes identify the type of information that must be provided to the accused officer, the officer's responsibility to cooperate during the investigation, the officer's right to representation during the process, and the rules and procedures concerning the collection of certain types of evidence. Following are some common provisions of state POBR legislation:

*Written notice.* The department must provide the officer with written notice of the nature of the investigation, summary of alleged misconduct, and name of the investigating officer.

*Right to representation.* The officer may have an attorney or a representative of his or her choosing present during any phase of questioning or hearing.

*Polygraph examination.* The officer may refuse to take a polygraph examination unless the complainant submits to an examination and is determined to be telling the truth. In this case, the officer may be ordered to take a polygraph examination or be subject to disciplinary action.

Officers expect to be treated fairly, honestly, and respectfully during the course of an internal investigation. In turn, the public expects that the agency will develop sound disciplinary policies and conduct thorough inquiries into allegations of misconduct.

It is imperative that administrators become thoroughly familiar with statutes, contract provisions, and existing rules between employer and employee so that procedural due process requirements can be met, particularly in disciplinary cases in which an employee's property interest might be affected.

Police officers today are also more likely to file a grievance when they believe their rights have been violated. Grievances may cover a broad range of issues, including salaries, overtime, leave, hours of work, allowances, retirement, opportunity for advancement, performance evaluations, workplace conditions, tenure, disciplinary actions, supervisory methods, and administrative practices. The preferred method for settling officers' grievances is through informal discussion: The employee explains his or her grievance to the immediate supervisor. Most complaints can be handled in this way. Those complaints that cannot be dealt with informally are usually handled through a more formal grievance process, which may involve several different levels of action.

# Sexual Harassment

Sexual harassment became a major workplace problem in the early 1980s and continued to be so through the 1990s and into the new millennium. To borrow a term from early police authors,[114] many "Neanderthals" in the business of police administration simply do not take the necessary steps to understand the breadth and weight of the matter. If these administrators do not learn the law of sexual harassment *in-house* (through training and education), they may eventually learn the law in the *courthouse.* Indeed, in the 1990s, a number of judgments in excess of a million dollars were made against police agencies for sexual harassment.[115]

Sexual harassment involves unwelcome sexual advances; requests for sexual favors; and other similar verbal, visual, or physical conduct that results in sexual submission being expressed or implied as a condition of employment. It can interfere with an individual's work performance or create an intimidating, hostile, or offensive working environment. The unique aspect of sexual harassment is that, generally speaking, the *victim* defines it in terms of what is offensive. Touching is not required.

Since 1986, workers have had the right to sue for sexual harassment. Until 1998, however, the courts remained silent about the precise meaning of the term; during that year, the U.S. Supreme Court clarified the issue with four historic decisions. The Court made it easier for a person who has been harassed to win a lawsuit but gave employers a greater measure of protection from lawsuits if they have a strong program in place to prevent and discipline harassment.[116] Following is an overview of the impact of each of these four decisions.

The old rule was that to prove harassment, a worker had to show that because she resisted sexual advances she was punished in terms of salary, assignments, or promotions. The new rule is that sexual advances count as harassment even if an employee is otherwise treated well. In this case,[117] a supervisor kept making passes at a subordinate but never punished her; in fact, she was promoted once. The Supreme Court ruled that harassment is defined by the behavior of the manager, not by what subsequently happened to the worker.

Another old rule was that if a manager was not informed that an employee was harassing other workers, the supervisor was not normally responsible for the harasser's actions. The new rule is that the administrator can be held responsible for a harasser's actions unless the company has a strong system of dealing with such problems. This decision[118] involved a Florida lifeguard who, for 5 years, endured men requesting sexual favors, groping her person, attempting to break into her shower area, and directing vulgar epithets toward her. The Supreme Court held that it is not enough to have a policy against sexual harassment; it must be disseminated and enforced effectively.

Third, the Court made clear that a worker who is being harassed has a duty to report it, beyond merely telling a friend or co-worker. The victim has to inform the person responsible under the sexual harassment policy.[119]

Finally, the Court unanimously held that sexual harassment at work can be illegal and violates federal antidiscrimination law even when the offender and victim are the same sex. In this case,[120] the harassment claim by a male victim stemmed from four months of work on a Gulf of Mexico oil rig, where he was sexually assaulted, battered, touched, and threatened with rape by his direct male supervisor and a second male supervisor. He quit because he feared the harassment would escalate to rape. The ruling allows victims of homosexual harassment to sue in federal court.[121]

# The Family and Medical Leave Act

The **Family and Medical Leave Act (FMLA),** enacted by Public Law 103-3, became effective in August 1993 and is administered and enforced by the U.S. Department of Labor's Wage and Hour Division. FMLA applies to all public agencies, including state, local, and federal employers; local schools; and private sector employers with 50 or more employees in 20 or more workweeks and who are engaged in commerce. FMLA entitles eligible employees to take up to 12 weeks of unpaid, job-protected leave in a 12-month period for specified family and medical reasons.

To be eligible for FMLA benefits, an employee must:

- Work for a covered employer
- Have worked for a covered employer for at least 12 months (and have worked at least 1,250 hours during that time)

A covered employer must grant an eligible employee unpaid leave for one or more of the following reasons:

- For the birth and care of a newborn child of the employee
- For placement with the employee of a child for adoption or child care
- To care for an immediate family member with a serious health condition
- To take medical leave when the employee is unable to work because of a serious health condition

A serious health condition means an illness, injury, impairment, or physical or mental condition that involves either any period of incapacitation or treatment, or continuing treatment by a health care provider; this can include any period of inability to work, attend school, or perform regular daily activities.

# The Americans with Disabilities Act (ADA)

Much has been written and many monographs and primers are available concerning the **Americans with Disabilities Act (ADA),** which was signed into law in 1990. Therefore, I only briefly cover the law here; however, those in an administrative capacity are strongly urged to become familiar with the literature in order to avoid conflicts with ADA mandates. The law is applicable to background checks; psychological and medical exams; and agility, drug, and polygraph tests.

Although certain agencies in the federal government, such as the Federal Bureau of Investigation, are exempt from the ADA, state and local governments and their agencies are covered by the law. It is critical for administrators to develop written policies and procedures consistent with the ADA and have them in place before a problem arises.[122]

Under the law, criminal justice agencies may not discriminate against qualified individuals with disabilities. A person has a disability under the law if he or she has a mental or physical impairment that substantially limits a major life activity, such as walking, talking, breathing, sitting, standing, or learning.[123] Title I of the ADA makes it illegal to discriminate against persons with disabilities. This mandate applies to the agency's recruitment, hiring, and promotion practices. ADA is not an affirmative action law, so persons with disabilities are not entitled to preference in hiring. However, the law will cause police agencies throughout the United States to adjust and perhaps even completely overhaul their recruitment and selection procedures.

Employers are to provide reasonable accommodation to disabled persons. A reasonable accommodation (80 percent of which have been found to cost less than $100 to effect[124]) can include modifying existing facilities to make them accessible, job restructuring, part-time or modified work schedules, acquiring or modifying equipment, and changing policies. Hiring decisions must be based on whether an applicant meets the established prerequisites of the position (e.g., experience or education) and is able to perform the essential functions of the job. Under the law, blanket exclusions of individuals with a particular disability (such as diabetes) are, in most cases, impermissible.

Corrections agencies—jails, prisons, and detention facilities—are also covered by the ADA; programs offered to inmates must be accessible. For example, if a hearing-impaired inmate wished to attend Alcoholics Anonymous meetings, the corrections facility would need to make reasonable accommodation to allow him or her to do so, through such means as providing a sign language interpreter or writing notes as needed.[125]

# CASE STUDIES

The following case studies will help the reader to consider some of this chapter's materials concerning sexual harassment and ADA issues.

## A Neanderthal Lives!

You are an administrator in a small, minimum-security facility where the day shift is composed of four veteran male officers and one new female officer. The woman is a member of a minority, has a college degree from a reputable out-of-state university, and is married to a member of the armed forces. There have been recent reports from your supervisors of obscene and racially offensive remarks and drawings turning up in the female officer's mailbox, but you have not seen any such materials, nor has the woman complained to you about such occurrences. Today, however, your day shift sergeant storms into your office with a piece of paper he says was just removed from the conference room bulletin board. It shows a "stick figure" woman and contains several racial slurs and comments to the effect that "women don't belong in this man's business, and you should go back where you came from." The woman saw this material, and the sergeant says she is now in the conference room, crying and very distraught.

### Questions for Discussion

1. What would you do about this situation? Do you ignore it? Call the female officer to your office?
2. What if you bring her in and she indicates that you should just leave the matter alone; do you pursue the matter?
3. If you determine which officer is responsible for these materials, what disciplinary action (if any) would you deem warranted? On what grounds?

## At the Heart of the Matter . . .

A police sergeant suffers a heart attack and undergoes a triple heart bypass operation. It is now 4 years later, and he takes and passes the written and oral examinations for lieutenant but is denied promotion solely because of his heart attack. The agency claims that because lieutenants can be assigned as shift commanders, they must be able to apprehend suspects and to engage in high-speed pursuits. In truth, middle managers in the agency are rarely involved in high levels of physical stress. The officer has exercised regularly and has had a strong performance record prior to and after his heart attack. Medical opinion is that his health is normal for someone his age. The agency has adopted community policing, providing the opportunity for a manager to be assigned to one of several lieutenant positions that do not entail physical exertion. The sergeant sues the agency for violating provisions of the ADA.

### Questions for Discussion

1. Is the sergeant "handicapped" within the meaning of the law?
2. Is the sergeant otherwise qualified for the position of lieutenant?
3. Was the sergeant excluded from the position solely on the basis of a handicap? Explain your answer.
4. Should the sergeant prevail in the suit? If so, on what grounds?[126]

## Summary

After providing an overview of related legislation, this chapter examined several areas of criminal justice employee rights, including the issues of drug testing, privacy, hiring and firing, sexual harassment, disabilities, and peace officers' rights. Criminal justice employers' responsibilities were also discussed.

Being an administrator in the field of criminal justice has never been easy. Unfortunately, the issues facing today's justice administrators have probably never been more difficult or complex.

This chapter clearly demonstrated that these are challenging and, occasionally, litigious times for the justice system; one act of negligence can mean financial disaster for an individual or a supervisor.

## Questions for Review

1. What are criminal justice employees' rights in the workplace according to federal statutes?
2. What is the general employee–employer relationship in criminal justice regarding recruitment and hiring and affirmative action?
3. It has been stated that criminal justice employees have a "property interest" in their jobs as well as a right to a safe workplace. What does this mean?
4. What constitutional rights are implicated for criminal justice employees on the job? (In your response, address whether rights are held regarding freedom of speech, searches and seizures, self-incrimination, and religion.)
5. In what regard is a greater standard of conduct expected of criminal justice employees? (In your response, include discussions of sexual behavior, residency, moonlighting, use of firearms, and alcohol/drug abuse.)

# Notes

1. Robert H. Chaires and Susan A. Lentz, "Criminal Justice Employee Rights: An Overview," *American Journal of Criminal Justice* **13** (April 1995):259.
2. Ibid.
3. *United Autoworkers v. Johnson Controls,* 111 S.Ct. 1196 (1991).
4. Kenneth J. Peak, *Policing America: Methods, Issues, Challenges,* 5th ed. (Upper Saddle River, N.J.: Prentice Hall, 2005), Chapter 3.
5. Chaires and Lentz, "Criminal Justice Employee Rights," p. 260.
6. *U.S. v. Gregory,* 818 F.2d 114 (4th Cir. 1987).
7. *Harris v. Pan American,* 649 F.2d 670 (9th Cir. 1988).
8. Chaires and Lentz, "Criminal Justice Employee Rights," p. 267.
9. Ken Peak, Douglas W. Farenholtz, and George Coxey, "Physical Abilities Testing for Police Officers: A Flexible, Job-Related Approach," *The Police Chief* **59** (January 1992): 52–56.
10. *Shaw v. Nebraska Department of Corrections,* 666 F.Supp. 1330 (N.D. Neb. 1987).
11. *Garrett v. Oskaloosa County,* 734 F.2d 621 (11th Cir. 1984).
12. Chaires and Lentz, "Criminal Justice Employee Rights," p. 268.
13. *EEOC v. State Department of Highway Safety,* 660 F.Supp. 1104 (N.D. Fla. 1986).
14. *Johnson v. Mayor and City Council of Baltimore* (105 S.Ct. 2717 1985).
15. 460 U.S. 226, 103 S.Ct. 1054, 75 L.Ed.2d 18 (1983).
16. Chaires and Lentz, "Criminal Justice Employee Rights," p. 269.
17. Paul J. Spiegelman, "Court-Ordered Hiring Quotas after *Stotts:* A Narrative on the Role of the Moralities of the Web and the Ladder in Employment Discrimination Doctrine," *Harvard Civil Rights–Civil Liberties Law Review* 20 (1985):72.
18. Chaires and Lentz, "Criminal Justice Employee Rights," p. 269.
19. *Regents of the University of California v. Bakke,* 98 S.Ct. 2733, 438 U.S. 265, 57 L.Ed.2d (1978).
20. *Wygant v. Jackson Board of Education,* 106 S.Ct. 1842 (1986).
21. Chaires and Lentz, "Criminal Justice Employee Rights," p. 269.
22. *Ledoux v. District of Columbia,* 820 F.2d 1293 (D.C. Cir. 1987), at 1294.
23. Ibid.
24. Chaires and Lentz, "Criminal Justice Employee Rights," p. 270.
25. *Parratt v. Taylor,* 451 U.S. 527, 536–37, 101 S.Ct. 1908, 1913–14, 68 L.Ed.2d 420 (1981).
26. *Board of Regents v. Roth,* 408 U.S. at 577, 92 S.Ct. at 2709.
27. *Cleveland Board of Education v. Loudermill,* 470 U.S. 532, 541 (1985).
28. *McGraw v. City of Huntington Beach,* 882 F.2d 384 (9th Cir. 1989).
29. *Loborn v. Michael,* 913 F.2d 327 (7th Cir. 1990).
30. *Palmer v. City of Monticello,* 731 F.Supp. 1503 (D. Utah 1990).
31. *Young v. Municipality of Bethel Park,* 646 F.Supp. 539 (W.D. Penn. 1986).
32. *McAdoo v. Lane,* 564 F.Supp. 1215 (D.C. Ill. 1983).
33. Ibid., at 1217.
34. Chaires and Lentz, "Criminal Justice Employee Rights," p. 273.
35. Lynn Lund, "The 'Ten Commandments' of Risk Management for Jail Administrators," *Detention Reporter* **4** (June 1991):4.
36. *National League of Cities v. Usery,* 426 U.S. 833 (1976).

37. 105 S.Ct. 1005 (1985).
38. Charles R. Swanson, Leonard Territo, and Robert W. Taylor, *Police Administration: Structures, Processes, and Behavior,* 6th ed. (Upper Saddle River, N.J.: Prentice Hall, 2005), p. 599.
39. *Christiansen v. Harris County,* 529 U.S. 576, 120 S. Ct. 1655, 146 L.Ed.2d 621 (2000).
40. *Jurich v. Mahoning County,* 31 Fair Emp. Prac. 1275 (BNA) (N.D. Ohio 1983).
41. Chaires and Lentz, "Criminal Justice Employee Rights," p. 280.
42. Ibid.
43. *Collins v. City of Harker Heights,* 112 S.Ct. 1061 (1992).
44. *Ruge v. City of Bellevue,* 892 F.2d 738 (1989).
45. *Galloway v. State of Louisiana,* 817 F.2d 1154 (5th Cir. 1987).
46. Chaires and Lentz, "Criminal Justice Employee Rights," pp. 280–283.
47. *Pickering v. Board of Education,* 391 U.S. 563 (1968), p. 568.
48. *Keyishian v. Board of Regents,* 385 U.S. 589 (1967).
49. Swanson, Territo, and Taylor, *Police Administration,* p. 394.
50. *Muller v. Conlisk,* 429 F.2d 901 (7th Cir. 1970).
51. *Flynn v. Giarusso,* 321 F.Supp. 1295 (E.D. La. 1971), at p. 1299.
52. *Magri v. Giarusso,* 379 F.Supp. 353 (E.D. La. 1974).
53. Swanson, Territo, and Taylor, *Police Administration,* p. 395.
54. *Brukiewa v. Police Commissioner of Baltimore,* 263 A.2d 210 (Md. 1970).
55. *United Public Workers v. Mitchell,* 330 U.S. 75 (1947); *U.S. Civil Service Commission v. National Association of Letter Carriers,* 413 U.S. 548 (1973).
56. *Magill v. Lynch,* 400 F.Supp. 84 (R.I. 1975).
57. *Boston Police Patrolmen's Association, Inc. v. City of Boston,* 326 N.E.2d 314 (Mass. 1975).
58. *Phillips v. City of Flint,* 225 N.W.2d 780 (Mich. 1975).
59. *Elrod v. Burns,* 427 U.S. 347 (1976); see also *Ramey v. Harber,* 431 F.Supp 657 (W.D. Va. 1977) and *Branti v. Finkel,* 445 U.S. 507 (1980).
60. *Connick v. Myers,* 461 U.S. 138 (1983); *Jones v. Dodson,* 727 F.2d 1329 (4th Cir. 1984).
61. Swanson, Territo, and Taylor, *Police Administration,* p. 397.
62. *Sponick v. City of Detroit Police Department,* 211 N.W.2d 674 (Mich. 1973), p. 681; but see *Wilson v. Taylor,* 733 F.2d 1539 (11th Cir. 1984).
63. *Bruns v. Pomerleau,* 319 F.Supp. 58 (D. Md. 1970); see also *McMullen v. Carson,* 754 F.2d 936 (11th Cir. 1985), where it was held that a Ku Klux Klansman could not be fired from his position as a records clerk in the sheriff's department simply because he was a Klansman. The court did uphold the dismissal because his active KKK participation threatened to negatively affect the agency's ability to perform its public duties.
64. *Civil Service Commission of Tucson v. Livingston,* 525 P.2d 949 (Ariz. 1974).
65. *Briggs v. North Muskegon Police Department,* 563 F.Supp. 585 (W.D. Mich. 1983), affd. 746 F.2d 1475 (6th Cir. 1984).
66. *Oliverson v. West Valley City,* 875 F.Supp. 1465 (D. Utah 1995).
67. *Henery v. City of Sherman,* 116 S.Ct. 1098 (1997).
68. *Hughes v. City of North Olmsted,* 93 F.3d 238 (6th Cir., 1996).
69. Michael J. Bulzomi, "Constitutional Authority to Regulate Off-Duty Relationships: Recent Court Decisions," *FBI Law Enforcement Bulletin* (April 1999):26–32.
70. 425 U.S. 238 (1976).
71. *Katz v. United States,* 389 U.S. 347 (1967).

72. *People v. Tidwell,* 266 N.E.2d 787 (Ill. 1971).

73. *McDonell v. Hunter,* 611 F.Supp. 1122 (S.D. Iowa, 1985), affd. as mod., 809 F.2d 1302 (8th Cir., 1987).

74. *Biehunik v. Felicetta,* 441 F.2d 228 (1971), p. 230.

75. 385 U.S. 483 (1967).

76. 392 U.S. 273 (1968).

77. *Gabrilowitz v. Newman,* 582 F.2d 100 (1st Cir. 1978). Cases upholding the department's authority to order a polygraph examination for police officers include *Eshelman v. Blubaum,* 560 P.2d 1283 (Ariz. 1977); *Dolan v. Kelly,* 348 N.Y.S.2d 478 (1973); *Richardson v. City of Pasadena,* 500 S.W.2d 175 (Tex. 1973); *Seattle Police Officer's Guild v. City of Seattle,* 494 P.2d 485 (Wash. 1972); *Roux v. New Orleans Police Department,* 223 So.2d 905 (La. 1969); and *Farmer v. City of Fort Lauderdale,* 427 So.2d 187 (Fla. 1983), cert. den., 104 S.Ct. 74 (1984).

78. 42 U.S.C. 200e(j).

79. *United States v. City of Albuquerque,* 12 EPD 11, 244 (10th Cir. 1976); see also *Trans World Airlines v. Hardison,* 97 S.Ct. 2264 (1977).

80. *United States v. Alburquerque,* 545 F.2d 110 (10th Cir. 1977).

81. *Potter v. Murray City,* 760 F.2d 1065 (10th Cir. 1985).

82. *Faust v. Police Civil Service Commission,* 347 A.2d 765 (Pa. 1975); *Stewart v. Leary,* 293 N.Y.S.2d 573 (1968); *Brewer v. City of Ashland,* 86 S.W.2d 669 (Ky. 1935); *Fabio v. Civil Service Commission of Philadelphia,* 373 A.2d 751 (Pa. 1977).

83. *Major v. Hampton,* 413 F.Supp. 66 (1976).

84. *Briggs v. City of North Muskegon Police Department,* 563 F.Supp. 585 (6th Cir. 1984).

85. *National Gay Task Force v. Bd. of Ed. of Oklahoma City,* 729 F.2d 1270 (10th Cir. 1984).

86. *Board of Education v. National Gay Task Force,* 53 U.S.L.W. 4408, No. 83-2030 (1985).

87. *Rowland v. Mad. River Sch. Dist.,* 730 F.2d 444 (6th Cir. 1984).

88. David J. Schall, *An Investigation into the Relationship between Municipal Police Residency Requirements, Professionalism, Economic Conditions, and Equal Employment Goals,* Unpublished dissertation, University of Wisconsin–Milwaukee, 1996.

89. *Detroit Police Officers Association v. City of Detroit,* 190 N.W.2d 97 (1971), appeal denied, 405 U.S. 950 (1972).

90. *Miller v. Police Board of City of Chicago,* 349 N.E.2d 544 (Ill. 1976); *Williamson v. Village of Baskin,* 339 So.2d 474 (La. 1976); *Nigro v. Board of Trustees of Alden,* 395 N.Y.S.2d 544 (1977).

91. *State, County, and Municipal Employees Local 339 v. City of Highland Park,* 108 N.W.2d 898 (1961).

92. See, for example, *Cox v. McNamara,* 493 P.2d 54 (Ore. 1972); *Brenckle v. Township of Shaler,* 281 A.2d 920 (Pa. 1972); *Hopwood v. City of Paducah,* 424 S.W.2d 134 (Ky. 1968); *Flood v. Kennedy,* 239 N.Y.S.2d 665 (1963).

93. Richard N. Williams, *Legal Aspects of Discipline by Police Administrators* (Traffic Institute Publication 2705) (Evanston, Ill.: Northwestern University, 1975), p. 4.

94. *City of Crowley Firemen v. City of Crowley,* 264 So.2d 368 (La. 1972).

95. 471 U.S. 1, 105 S.Ct. 1694, 85 L.Ed.2d 1 (1985).

96. *Lally v. Department of Police,* 306 So.2d 65 (La. 1974).

97. See, for example, *Peters v. Civil Service Commission of Tucson,* 539 P.2d 698 (Ariz. 1977); *Abeyta v. Town of Taos,* 499 F.2d 323 (10th Cir. 1974); *Baumgartner v. Leary,* 311 N.Y.S.2d 468 (1970); *City of Vancouver v. Jarvis,* 455 P.2d 591 (Wash. 1969).

98. Swanson, Territo, and Taylor, *Police Administration,* p. 433.

99.  *Parker v. District of Columbia,* 850 F.2d 708 (1988), at 713, 714.

100.  *Marusa v. District of Columbia,* 484 F.2d 828 (1973).

101.  *Sager v. City of Woodlawn Park,* 543 F.Supp. 282 (D. Colo. 1982).

102.  *Bonsignore v. City of New York,* 521 F.Supp. 394 (1981).

103.  *Popow v. City of Margate,* 476 F.Supp. 1237 (1979).

104.  Eloise Salholz and Frank Washington, "Detroit's Brutal Lessons," *Newsweek* (November 30, 1992):45.

105.  Ibid.

106.  *Krolick v. Lowery,* 302 N.Y.S.2d 109 (1969), p. 115; *Hester v. Milledgeville,* 598 F.Supp. 1456, 1457 (M.D.Ga. 1984).

107.  *McCracken v. Department of Police,* 337 So.2d 595 (La. 1976).

108.  *Krolick v. Lowery.*

109.  489 U.S. 602 (1989).

110.  489 U.S. 656 (1989).

111.  Robert J. Alberts and Harvey W. Rubin, "Court's Rulings on Testing Crack Down on Drug Abuse," *Risk Management* 38 (March 1991):36–41.

112.  Ibid., p. 38.

113.  Ibid., p. 40.

114.  A. C. Germann, Frank D. Day, and Robert R. Gallatti, *Introduction to Law Enforcement and Criminal Justice* (Springfield, Ill.: Charles C Thomas, 1976), p. 224.

115.  See, for example, Ted Gest and Amy Saltzman, "Harassment: Men on Trial," *U.S. News and World Report* (October 21, 1991):39–40, concerning a $3.1 million award to two former Long Beach, California, female police officers.

116.  Marianne Lavelle, "The New Sexual Harassment," *U.S. News and World Report* (July 6, 1998):30–31.

117.  *Burlington Industries v. Ellerth,* 118 S.Ct. 2257, 141 L.Ed.2d 633 (1998).

118.  *Faragher v. City of Boca Raton,* 118 S.Ct. 2275, 141 L.Ed.2d 662 (1998).

119.  *Gebser v. Lago Vista Independent School District,* 118 S.Ct. 1989, 141 L.Ed. 2d 277 (1998).

120.  *Oncale v. Sundowner Offshore Services,* Inc., 523 U.S. 75, 118 S.Ct. 998 (1998).

121.  "Court: Harassment Covers Same-Sex Torment," Associated Press, March 5, 1998.

122.  Paula N. Rubin and Susan W. McCampbell, "The Americans with Disabilities Act and Criminal Justice: Providing Inmate Services," *U.S. Department of Justice, National Institute of Justice Research in Action* (July 1994):2.

123.  Paula N. Rubin, "The Americans with Disabilities Act and Criminal Justice: An Overview," *U.S. Department of Justice, National Institute of Justice Research in Action* (September 1993):1.

124.  "Health and Criminal Justice: Strengthening the Relationship," *U.S. Department of Justice, National Institute of Justice Journal, Research in Action,* (November 1994):40.

125.  Ibid., p. 41.

126.  This case study is based on *Kuntz v. City of New Haven,* No. N-90-480 (JGM), March 3, 1993. Kuntz prevailed, was promoted, and won back pay, demonstrating to the court that his possible assignment to field duties would not be dangerous to him, to other police officers, or to the public.

# Chapter 15

# Special Challenges
## Discipline, Labor Relations, and Liability

## Key Terms and Concepts

| | |
|---|---|
| Appeal | Grievance |
| Arbitration | Job action |
| Automatic records system | Mediation |
| Collective bargaining | Negotiations |
| Early warning system (EWS) | Personnel complaint |
| Esprit de corps | Title 42, U.S. Code, Section 1983 |
| Fact finding | Tort |

## Learning Objectives

As a result of reading this chapter, the student will:

- be familiar with the due process requirements concerning the discharge of public employees
- know the disciplinary actions used by agencies in an investigation of a criminal justice employee
- know the steps taken when a citizen's complaint is filed
- understand the grievance process
- be familiar with collective bargaining and unionization
- know three models used in collective bargaining
- understand the four types of job actions
- know the importance of civil liability and different types of lawsuits filed against criminal justice practitioners
- be familiar with legislation to protect persons who are victims of someone's misuse of authority

*Discipline must be maintained.*

—Charles Dickens

*No man is fit to command another that cannot command himself.*

—William Penn

## Introduction

Several previous chapters have either implied or stated that the major asset and thus the major challenge of any criminal justice agency is its personnel. The ability of such agencies to accomplish their mission ultimately depends on the critically important element of human resources. The expanded labor movement and body of law concerning employees, the increased inclination of citizens to file suit against criminal justice personnel as well as for justice employees to sue their administrators, and the growing willingness of courts and juries to award large cash settlements in such cases all point to the need for great effort and care to be directed to human resource management. Accordingly, this chapter examines three aspects of human resources/personnel administration that loom large among the administrator's challenges: discipline, labor relations, and liability.

Because of their power and authority, criminal justice employees, especially the police, are under greater public scrutiny than most other governmental employees. Therefore, this chapter examines administrators' responsibilities to *discipline* their employees when warranted. Employee misconduct includes those acts that harm the public, including corruption, harassment, brutality, and civil rights violations. Other violations of agency policy, such as substance abuse and insubordination or even minor violations of dress and punctuality, can also lead to disciplinary action.

In the last 50 years, no force has had a greater impact on the administration of criminal justice agencies than *labor relations.* Labor unions represent a major influence that must be reckoned with by criminal justice administrators. This chapter discusses how the unionization movement developed, as well as contemporary elements and practices surrounding collective bargaining by labor and management groups.

Finally, the problem of *liability* is closely related to employee discipline because both can involve misbehavior and harm to others. This chapter discusses laws and legal concepts (such as negligence and torts) that serve to make criminal justice practitioners legally accountable, both civilly and criminally, for acts of misconduct and negligence.

The chapter concludes with two case studies.

# Disciplinary Policies and Practices

## *Maintaining the Public Trust*

The public's trust and respect are precious commodities and can be quickly lost with improper behavior by criminal justice employees and the improper handling of an allegation of misconduct. Serving communities professionally and with integrity should be the goal of every agency and its employees to ensure that trust and respect are maintained. The public expects that criminal justice agencies will make every effort to identify and correct problems and respond to citizens' complaints in a judicious, consistent, fair, and equitable manner.

One of the most important responsibilities of criminal justice agencies is implementing sound disciplinary policies and practices and responding to employee misconduct or performance problems at an early stage.

Employee misconduct and violations of departmental policy are the two principal areas in which discipline is involved.[1] Employee misconduct includes those acts that harm the public, including corruption, harassment, brutality, and civil rights violations. Violations of policy may involve a broad range of issues, including substance abuse and insubordination and minor violations of dress and punctuality.

## Due Process Requirements

The well-established, minimum due process requirements for discharging public employees include that employees must:

1. Be afforded a public hearing
2. Be present during the presentation of evidence against them and have an opportunity to cross-examine their superiors
3. Have an opportunity to present witnesses and other evidence concerning their side of the controversy
4. Be permitted to be represented by counsel
5. Have an impartial referee or hearing officer presiding
6. Have a decision made based on the weight of the evidence introduced during the hearing

Such protections apply to any disciplinary action that can significantly affect a criminal justice employee's reputation and/or future chances for special assignment or promotion. A disciplinary hearing that might result in only a reprimand or short suspension may involve fewer procedural protections than one that could result in more severe sanctions.[2]

When a particular disciplinary action does not include termination or suspension, however, it may still be subject to due process considerations. An example is a Chicago case involving a police officer who was transferred from the Neighborhood Relations Division to less desirable working conditions in the patrol division, with no loss in pay or benefits. The court found that the officer's First Amendment free speech rights were violated because his de facto demotion was in retaliation for his political activities (inviting political opponents of the mayor to a civic function and in retaliation for a speech given there that criticized the police department), and that he was thus entitled to civil damages. The court stated that "Certainly a demotion can be as detrimental to an employee as denial of a promotion."[3]

On the other hand, no due process protection may be required when the property interest (one's job) was fraudulently obtained. Thus, a deputy sheriff was not deprived of due process when he was summarily discharged for lying on his application about a juvenile felony charge, which would have barred him from employment in the first place.[4]

In sum, agency rules and policies should state which due process procedures will be utilized under certain disciplinary situations; the key questions regarding due process are whether the employer follows established agency guidelines and, if not, whether the employer has a compelling reason not to.

At times, the administrator will determine that an employee must be disciplined or terminated. What are adequate grounds for discipline or discharge? Grounds can vary widely from agency to agency. Certainly, the agency's formal policies and procedures should specify and control what constitutes proper and improper behavior. Normally, agency practice and custom enter into these decisions. Sometimes administrators will "wink" at the formal policies and procedures, overlooking or only occasionally enforcing certain provisions contained in them. But the failure of the agency to enforce a rule or policy for a long period of time may provide "implied consent" by the employer that such behavior, although officially prohibited, is permissible. (In other words, don't allow an employee to violate the agency's lateness policy for 3 months and then decide one day to summarily fire him.) Attempts to fire employees for behavior that has been ignored or enforced only infrequently at best may give rise to a defense by the employee.

The hiring of minority employees to meet state hiring goals and then attempting to terminate them as quickly and often as possible violate the employee's Title VII rights. Such a situation occurred in an Indiana case in which it was alleged that black prison correctional officers were hired to fulfill an affirmative action program, only to be fired for disciplinary reasons for which white officers were not discharged.[5]

Generally, violations of an employee's rights in discharge and discipline occur (1) in violation of a protected interest, (2) in retaliation for the exercise of protected conduct, (3) with a discriminatory motive, and (4) with malice.[6]

## A Tradition of Problems in Policing

Throughout its history, policing has experienced problems involving misconduct and corruption. As discussed in Chapter 5, a number of events during the 1990s demonstrated that the problem still exists and requires the attention of police officials. Incidents such as the beating of Rodney King in Los Angeles and Abner Louima in New York by officers and major corruption scandals in several big-city police departments have led many people to believe that police misbehavior is at a higher level today than ever before.

Without question, police administrators need to pay close attention to signs of police misconduct and respond quickly and enact policies to guide supervisors on the handling of disciplinary issues. Such policies should ensure that there is certainty, swiftness, fairness, and consistency of punishment when it is warranted.

## Automated Records Systems

There have been many advances in the use of technology in police discipline. In 1991, the Fresno, California, Police Department automated its disciplinary process in an effort to establish a better system for tracking and sanctioning personnel for various offenses.[7] The principal objectives of this **automatic records system** are to assist the chief of police in administering the department in a more equitable fashion and to improve the department's ability to defend its personnel actions. Within minutes, the database provides supervisors with 5 years of history about standards of discipline for any category of violation. A variety of reports can be produced, showing patterns of incidents for the supervisor.

## Determining the Level and Nature of Action

When an investigation against an employee is sustained, the sanctions and level of discipline must be decided. Management must be careful when recommending and imposing discipline because of its impact on the overall morale of the agency's employees. If the recommended discipline is viewed by employees as too lenient, it may send the wrong message that the misconduct was insignificant. On the other hand, discipline that is viewed as too harsh may have a demoralizing effect on the officer(s) involved and other agency employees and result in allegations that the leadership is unfair. This alone can have significant impact on the **esprit de corps** or morale of the agency.

In addition to having a disciplinary process that is viewed by employees as fair and consistent, it is also important that discipline be progressive and that more serious sanctions are invoked when repeated violations occur. For example, a third substantiated violation of rude behavior may result in a recommendation for a 1-day suspension without pay, but a first offense may be resolved through documented oral counseling or a letter of reprimand. The following list shows disciplinary actions commonly used by agencies in order of their severity.

*Counseling.* This is usually a conversation between the supervisor and employee about a specific aspect of the employee's performance or conduct; it is warranted when an employee has committed a relatively minor infraction or the nature of the offense is such that oral counseling is all that is necessary. For example, an officer who is usually punctual but arrives at briefing 10 minutes late 2 days in a row may require nothing more than a reminder and warning to correct the problem.

*Documented oral counseling.* This is usually the first step in a progressive disciplinary process and is intended to address relatively minor infractions. It occurs when there are no previous reprimands or more severe disciplinary action of the same or similar nature.

*Letter of reprimand.* This is a formal written notice regarding significant misconduct, more serious performance violations, or repeated offenses. It is usually the second step in the formal disciplinary process and is intended to provide the employee and agency with a written record of the violation of behavior; it identifies what specific corrective action must be taken to avoid subsequent, more serious disciplinary steps.

*Suspension.* This is a severe disciplinary action that results in an employee being relieved of duty, often without pay. It is usually administered when an employee commits a serious violation of established rules or after written reprimands have been given and no change in behavior or performance has resulted.

*Demotion.* In this situation, an employee is placed in a position of lower responsibility and pay. It is normally used when an otherwise capable employee is unable to meet the standards required for the higher position, or when the employee has committed a serious act requiring that he or she be removed from a position of management or supervision.

*Transfer.* Many agencies use the disciplinary transfer to deal with problem officers; officers can be transferred to a different location or assignment, and this action is often seen as an effective disciplinary tool.

*Termination.* This is the most severe disciplinary action that can be taken. It usually occurs when previous serious discipline has been imposed and there has been inadequate or no improvement in behavior or performance. It may also occur when an employee commits an offense so serious that continued employment would be inappropriate.

## Positive and Negative Discipline

When policies and procedures are violated, positive or negative disciplinary measures may be imposed. Although different in their philosophy, both seek to accomplish the same purpose: to correct negative behavior and promote the employee's voluntary compliance with departmental policies and procedures.

A positive discipline program (also known as positive counseling) attempts to change employee behavior without invoking punishment. An example of positive discipline or counseling is when an employee ("John") has been nonproductive and nonpunctual, has caused interpersonal problems with co-workers, and/or has other problems on the job. To this point, John has been in control of the situation, on the offensive one might say, whereas the supervisor ("Jane") and his co-workers have been on the defensive. John is jeopardizing the morale and productivity of the workplace, but the preferred approach is to try to salvage him because of the agency's investment in time, funds, and training.

Finally, Jane calls John into her office. She might begin with a compliment to give him (if indeed she can find one), and then proceeds to outline all of his workplace shortcomings; this demonstrates to John that Jane "has his number" and is aware of his various problems. Jane explains to him why it is important that he improve (for reasons related to productivity, morale, and so on), and the benefits he might realize from improvement (promotions, pay raises, bonuses). She also outlines what can happen if he does *not* show adequate improvement (demotion, transfer, termination). Now having gained John's attention, she gives him a certain time period (say, 30, 60, or 90 days) in which to improve; she emphasizes, however, that she will be constantly monitoring his progress. She might even ask John to sign a counseling statement form that sets forth all they have discussed, indicating that John has received counseling and understands the situation.

Note that Jane is now on the offensive, thereby putting John on the defensive and in control of his destiny; if he fails to perform, Jane would probably give him a warning, and if the situation continues, he will be terminated. If he sues or files a grievance, Jane has proof that every effort was made to allow John to salvage his position. This is an effective means of giving subordinates an incentive to improve their behavior while at the same time making the department less vulnerable to successful lawsuits.

Negative discipline is punishment. It is generally used when positive efforts fail or the violation is so serious that punishment is required. Negative discipline

varies in its severity and involves documented oral counseling, letter of reprimand, demotion, days off without pay, or even termination.

## Dealing with Complaints

### Complaint Origin

A **personnel complaint** is an allegation of misconduct or illegal behavior
against an employee by anyone inside or outside the organization. Internal complaints may come from supervisors who observe officer misconduct, officers who
complain about supervisors, supervisors who complain about other supervisors,
civilian personnel who complain about officers, and so on. External complaints
originate from sources outside the organization and usually involve the public.

Complaints may be received from primary, secondary, and anonymous sources.
A victim is a primary source. A secondary source is someone who makes the
complaint on behalf of the victim, such as an attorney, a school counselor, or a parent of a juvenile. An anonymous source complaint derives from an unknown source
and may be delivered to the police station via a telephone call or an unsigned letter.

Every complaint, regardless of the source, must be accepted and investigated in accordance with established policies and procedures. Anonymous complaints are the most difficult to investigate because there is no opportunity to
obtain further information or question the complainant about the allegation.
Such complaints can have a negative impact on employee morale because officers may view such complaints as unjust and frivolous.

### Types and Causes

Complaints may be handled informally or formally, depending on the seriousness of the allegation and preference of the complainant. A formal complaint occurs when a written and signed and/or tape-recorded statement of the allegation
is made and the complainant requests to be informed of the investigation's disposition. Figure 15.1 provides an example of a complaint form used to initiate a
personnel investigation.

An informal complaint is an allegation of minor misconduct made for informational purposes that can usually be resolved without the need for more formal
processes. When a citizen calls the watch commander to complain about the
rude behavior of a dispatcher but does not wish to make a formal complaint, the
supervisor may simply discuss the incident with the dispatcher and resolve it
through informal counseling as long as more serious problems are not discovered and the dispatcher does not have a history of similar complaints.

Few complaints involve acts of physical violence, excessive force, or corruption. Rojek et al.[8] found that complaints against officers also fall under the general
categories of verbal abuse, discourtesy, harassment, improper attitude, and ethnic
slurs.[9] Another study[10] found that 42 percent of complaints involved the "verbal
conduct" of officers; verbal conduct also accounted for 47 percent of all sustained
complaints. The majority of repeated offenses also fell into this category. It is clear
that the officers' verbal actions generate a significant number of complaints.

\*\*\*\*\*\*\*\*\*\*\*\*\*\*\*\*\*\*\*\*\*\*\*\*\*\*\*\*\*\*\*\*\*\*\*\*\*\*\*\*\*\*\*\*\*\*\*\*\*\*\*\*\*\*\*\*\*\*\*\*\*\*\*\*\*\*\*\*\*\*\*\*\*\*\*\*\*\*\*\*\*\*\*\*\*\*\*\*\*\*

Control Number_____

Date & Time Reported     Location of Interview     Interview

_____     _____     _____Verbal   _____Written   _____Taped

Type of Complaint:      ____Force  ____Procedural  ____Conduct
                        ____Other (Specify)

Source of Complaint:    ____In Person  ____Mail  ____Telephone
                        ____Other (Specify)

Complaint originally    ____Supervisor    ____On Duty Watch Commander    ____Chief
Received by:            ____IAU           ____Other (Specify)

Notifications made:     _____Division Commander     _____Chief of Police
Received by:            _____On-Call Command Personnel
                        _____Watch Commander        _____Other (Specify)

Copy of formal personnel complaint given to complainant?   ____Yes ____No

\*\*\*\*\*\*\*\*\*\*\*\*\*\*\*\*\*\*\*\*\*\*\*\*\*\*\*\*\*\*\*\*\*\*\*\*\*\*\*\*\*\*\*\*\*\*\*\*\*\*\*\*\*\*\*\*\*\*\*\*\*\*\*\*\*\*\*\*\*\*\*\*\*\*\*\*\*\*\*\*\*\*\*\*\*\*\*\*\*\*

Complainant's name:                           Address:

_____              _____ Zip_____

Residence Phone:                              Business Phone:

_____              _____  ____

DOB:              Race:              Sex:              Occupation:

_____       _____        _____       _____

\*\*\*\*\*\*\*\*\*\*\*\*\*\*\*\*\*\*\*\*\*\*\*\*\*\*\*\*\*\*\*\*\*\*\*\*\*\*\*\*\*\*\*\*\*\*\*\*\*\*\*\*\*\*\*\*\*\*\*\*\*\*\*\*\*\*\*\*\*\*\*\*\*\*\*\*\*\*\*\*\*\*\*\*\*\*\*\*\*\*

Location of Occurrence:                       Date & Time of Occurrence:

Member(s) Involved:                           Member(s) Involved:
(1) _____          (2)_____
(3) _____          (4)_____

Witness(es) Involved:                         Witness(es) Involved:
(1) _____          (2)_____
(3) _____          (4)_____

\*\*\*\*\*\*\*\*\*\*\*\*\*\*\*\*\*\*\*\*\*\*\*\*\*\*\*\*\*\*\*\*\*\*\*\*\*\*\*\*\*\*\*\*\*\*\*\*\*\*\*\*\*\*\*\*\*\*\*\*\*\*\*\*\*\*\*\*\*\*\*\*\*\*\*\*\*\*\*\*\*\*\*\*\*\*\*\*\*\*

(1) _____  Complainant wishes to make a formal statement and has requested an investigation into the matter with a report back to him/her on the findings and actions.

(2) _____  Complainant wishes to advise the Police Department of a problem, understand that some type of action will be taken, but does not request a report back to him/her on the findings and actions.

\*\*\*\*\*\*\*\*\*\*\*\*\*\*\*\*\*\*\*\*\*\*\*\*\*\*\*\*\*\*\*\*\*\*\*\*\*\*\*\*\*\*\*\*\*\*\*\*\*\*\*\*\*\*\*\*\*\*\*\*\*\*\*\*\*\*\*\*\*\*\*\*\*\*\*\*\*\*\*\*\*\*\*\*\*\*\*\*\*\*

### CITIZEN ADVISEMENTS

(1)   If you have not yet provided the department with a signed written statement or a tape-recorded statement, one may be required in order to pursue the investigation of this matter.

(2)   The complainant(s) and/or witness(es) may be required to take a polygraph examination in order to determine the credibility concerning the allegations made.

(3)   Should the allegations prove to be false, the complainant(s) and/or witness(es) may be liable for criminal and/or civil prosecution.

_____     _____

Signature of Complainant                Date & Time

_____

Signature of Member Receiving Complaint

**Figure 15.1**

Police department formal personnel complaint report form.

Finally, minority citizens and those with less power and fewer resources are more likely than persons with greater power and more resources to file complaints of misconduct and to allege more serious forms of misconduct.[11]

### Receipt and Referral

Administrators should have in place a process for receiving complaints that is clearly delineated by departmental policy and procedures. Generally, a complaint will be made at a police facility and referred to a senior officer in charge to determine its seriousness and need for immediate intervention.

In most cases, the senior officer will determine the nature of the complaint and the employees involved; the matter will be referred to the employee's supervisor to conduct an initial investigation. The supervisor completes the investigation, recommends any discipline, and sends the matter to the Internal Affairs Unit (IAU) and the agency head for finalization of the disciplinary process. This method of review ensures that consistent and fair standards of discipline are applied.

### The Investigative Process

D. W. Perez[12] indicated that all but a small percentage of the 17,000 police agencies in the United States have a process for investigation of police misconduct. Generally, the employee's supervisor will conduct a preliminary inquiry of the complaint, commonly known as fact finding. Once it is determined that further investigation is necessary, the supervisor may conduct additional questioning of employees and witnesses, obtain written statements from those persons immediately involved in the incident, and gather any evidence that may be necessary for the case, including photographs. Care must be exercised that the accused employee's rights are not violated. The initial investigation is sent to an appropriate division commander and forwarded to IAU for review.

## Making a Determination and Disposition

### Categories

Once an investigation is completed, the supervisor or IAU officer must make a determination as to the culpability of the accused employee and report same to the administrator. Each allegation should receive a separate adjudication. Following are the categories of dispositions that are commonly used:

- *Unfounded.* The alleged act(s) did not occur.
- *Exonerated.* The act occurred, but it is lawful, proper, justified, and/or in accordance with departmental policies, procedures, rules, and regulations.
- *Not Sustained.* There is insufficient evidence to prove or disprove the allegations made.
- *Misconduct not based on the complaint.* Sustainable misconduct was determined but is not a part of the original complaint. For example, a supervisor investigating an allegation of excessive force against an officer may find the force used was within departmental policy, but that the officer made an unlawful arrest.

- *Closed.* An investigation may be halted if the complainant fails to cooperate or it is determined that the action does not fall within the administrative jurisdiction of the police agency.
- *Sustained.* The act did occur and it was a violation of departmental rules and procedures. Sustained allegations include misconduct that falls within the broad outlines of the original allegation(s).

Once a determination of culpability has been made, the complainant should be notified of the department's findings. Details of the investigation or recommended punishment will not be included in the correspondence. As shown in Figure 15.2, the complainant will normally receive only information concerning

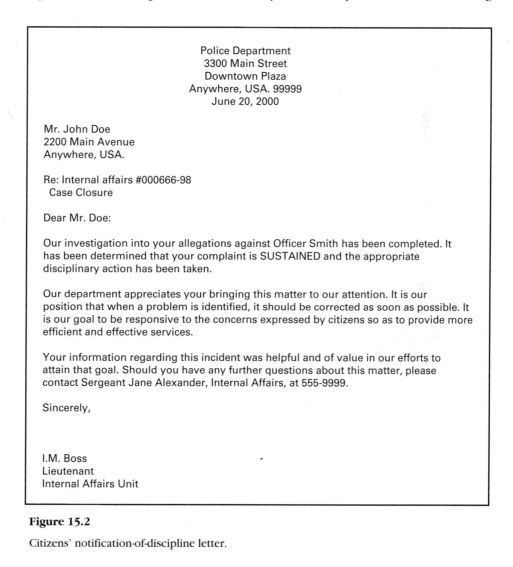

Police Department
3300 Main Street
Downtown Plaza
Anywhere, USA. 99999
June 20, 2000

Mr. John Doe
2200 Main Avenue
Anywhere, USA.

Re: Internal affairs #000666-98
Case Closure

Dear Mr. Doe:

Our investigation into your allegations against Officer Smith has been completed. It has been determined that your complaint is SUSTAINED and the appropriate disciplinary action has been taken.

Our department appreciates your bringing this matter to our attention. It is our position that when a problem is identified, it should be corrected as soon as possible. It is our goal to be responsive to the concerns expressed by citizens so as to provide more efficient and effective services.

Your information regarding this incident was helpful and of value in our efforts to attain that goal. Should you have any further questions about this matter, please contact Sergeant Jane Alexander, Internal Affairs, at 555-9999.

Sincerely,


I.M. Boss
Lieutenant
Internal Affairs Unit

**Figure 15.2**

Citizens' notification-of-discipline letter.

the outcome of the complaint, including a short explanation of the finding along with an invitation to call the agency if further information is needed.

### Grievances

Police officers may complain about contractual or other matters about which they are upset or concerned. Following is an overview of the **grievance** process.

Grievance procedures establish a fair and expeditious process for handling employee disputes that are not disciplinary in nature. Grievance procedures involve collective bargaining issues, conditions of employment, and employer–employee relations. More specifically, grievances may cover a broad range of issues, including salaries, overtime, leave, hours of work, allowances, retirement, opportunity for advancement, performance evaluations, workplace conditions, tenure, disciplinary actions, supervisory methods, and administrative practices. Grievance procedures are often established as a part of the collective bargaining process.

The preferred method for settling officers' grievances is through informal discussion, when the employee explains his or her grievance to the immediate supervisor. Most complaints can be handled through this process. Complaints that cannot be dealt with informally are usually handled through a more formal grievance process, as described next. A formal grievance begins with the employee submitting the grievance in writing to the immediate supervisor, as illustrated in Figure 15.3.

The process for formally handling grievances will vary among agencies and may involve as many as three to six different levels of action. Following is an example of how a grievance may proceed:

*Level I.* A grievance is submitted in writing to a supervisor. The supervisor will be given 5 days to respond to the employee's grievance. If the employee is dissatisfied with the response, the grievance moves to the next level.

*Level II.* At this level, the grievance proceeds to the chief executive who will be given a specified time (usually 5 days) to render a decision.

*Level III.* If the employee is not satisfied with the chief's decision, the grievance may proceed to the city or county manager, as appropriate. The manager will usually meet with the employee and/or representatives from the bargaining association and attempt to resolve the matter. An additional 5 to 10 days is usually allowed for the manager to render a decision.

*Level IV.* If the grievance is still not resolved, either party may request that the matter be submitted to arbitration. Arbitration involves a neutral, outside person, often selected from a list of arbitrators from the Federal Mediation and Conciliation Service. An arbitrator will conduct a hearing, listen to both parties, and usually render a decision within 20 to 30 days. The decision of the arbitrator can be final and binding. This does not prohibit the employee from appealing the decision to a state court.

Failure to act on grievances quickly may result in serious morale problems within an agency.

```
                         Police Department
                       Formal Grievance Form

        Grievance #_____

        Employee Name: _____ Work Phone: _____
        Department Assigned: _____
        Date of Occurrence: _____
        Location of Occurrence: _____

        Name of:   1.   Department Head:_____

                   2.   Division Head:_____

                   3.   Immediate Supervisor:_____

        Statement of Grievance: _____
        _____
        _____
        _____

        Witnesses:_____
        _____
        _____

        What article(s) and or section(s) of the labor agreement of rules and regulations do
        you believe have been violated? _____
        _____
        _____
        _____

        What remedy are you requesting?_____
        _____
        _____



        _____          _____
        Employee signature               Signature of labor representative
```

**Figure 15.3**

Employee grievance form.

### *Appealing Disciplinary Measures*

Appeals processes—frequently outlined in civil service rules and regulations, labor agreements, and departmental policies and procedures—normally follow an officer's chain of command. For example, if an officer disagrees with a supervisor's recommendation for discipline, the first step of an **appeal** may involve a hearing before the division commander, usually of the rank of captain or deputy chief.

The accused employee may be allowed labor representation or an attorney to assist in asking questions of the investigating supervisor, clarifying issues, and presenting new or mitigating evidence. The division commander would have 5 days to review the recommendation and respond in writing to the employee.

If the employee is still not satisfied, an appeal hearing before the chief executive is granted. This is usually the final step in appeals within the agency. The chief or sheriff communicates a decision in writing to the employee within 5 to 10 days. Depending on labor agreements and civil service rules and regulations, some agencies extend their appeals of discipline beyond the department. For example, employees may bring their issue before the civil service commission or city or county manager for a final review. Employees may also have the right to an independent arbitrator's review of the discipline. The arbitrator's decision is usually binding.

### The Early Warning System

Early identification of and intervention in employee misconduct or performance problems are vital to preventing ongoing and repeated incidents. An **early warning system (EWS)** is designed to identify officers whose behavior is problematic (involving citizen complaints or improper use of force) and provide a form of intervention (see Exhibit 15.1). The system alerts the department to

---

### Exhibit 15.1
### A Means of Policing the Police

A lawsuit filed by dozens of plaintiffs alleging they were roughed up by a band of Oakland, California, officers calling themselves "the Riders" was settled for $11 million and resulted in a new Personnel Information Management System (PIMS) being implemented in 2005. PIMS will document use-of-force incidents, citizen complaints, attendance, shootings, and accidents, as well as commendations, awards, and letters of appreciation. Its main purpose is to help supervisors to identify trends that might indicate an officer needs an intervention. Based on a Phoenix, Arizona, model, the system holds supervisors all the way up the chain accountable for doing something and is a tremendous risk management tool; it emphasizes guiding employees, not merely disciplining them. At the extreme, it allows for getting to people before they "crash and burn, and kill somebody in a police pursuit, traffic accident, or whatever." The system refreshes itself nightly by collecting new information added that day. An Oakland police captain emphasized that having many use-of-force incidents or attendance issues does not make one a bad officer; an officer working in a busy area abundant with shootings will be involved in more car chases and fights and have more use-of-force incidents than one working in a less active downtown area.

*Source:* Jim McKay, "Policing the Police: Oakland, Calif., Tackles Police Misconduct Issues with Database," *Government Technology* (October 2004): 48.

these individuals and warns the officers while providing counseling or training to help them change their problematic behavior. Most EWSs require three complaints in a given time frame (normally a 12-month period) before intervention is initiated. The EWS thus helps agencies to respond proactively to patterns of behavior that may lead to more serious problems. The EWS may require that the officer's supervisor intervene with early prevention methods such as counseling or training.

In some cases, repeated incidents of violent behavior may require that officers attend anger training or verbal judo sessions to learn how to deescalate confrontational situations. Some preventive measures, such as counseling, remedial training, or temporary change of assignment, may also be used. A referral to an employee assistance program (EAP) to deal with more serious psychological or substance abuse problems is another possible outcome.

# Labor Relations in Criminal Justice Agencies

As indicated in the Introduction, *labor relations*—a term that includes the related concepts of *unionization* and *collective bargaining*—pose a major challenge to contemporary criminal justice administrators. This section discusses the unionization movement and the processes of **collective bargaining** employed by labor and management.

Probably as a result of their difficult working conditions, as well as traditionally low salary and benefits packages, police and corrections employees have elected to band together within their disciplines to fight for improvement. It is probably also accurate to say that a major force in the development and spread of unionization of these two groups was the authoritarian, unilateral, and "do as I say, not as I do" management style that characterized many police and prison administrators of the past.

## *The Movement Begins: Policing Then and Now*

### *Early Campaigns*

The first campaign to organize the police started shortly after World War I, when the American Federation of Labor (AFL) reversed a long-standing policy and issued charters to police unions in Boston, Washington, D.C., and about 30 other cities. Many police officers were suffering from the rapid inflation following the outbreak of the war and believed that if their chiefs could not get them long-overdue pay raises, then perhaps unions could. Capitalizing on their sentiments, the fledgling unions signed about 60 percent of all officers in Washington, D.C., 75 percent in Boston, and a similar proportion in other cities.[13]

The unions' success was short-lived, however. The Boston police commissioner refused to recognize the union, forbade officers to join it, and filed charges against several union officials. Shortly thereafter, on September 9, 1919, the Boston police initiated their now-famous 3-day strike, leading to major riots and a furor against the police all across the nation; 9 rioters were killed and 23 were seriously injured. During the strike, Massachusetts Governor Calvin Coolidge stated, "There is no right to strike against the public safety by anybody, anywhere, anytime."

During World War II, however, the unionization effort was reignited. Unions issued charters to a few dozen locals all over the country and sent in organizers to help enlist the rank and file. Most police chiefs continued speaking out against unionization, but their subordinates were moved by the thousands to join, sensing the advantage in having unions press for higher wages and benefits.[14] In a series of rulings, however, the courts upheld the right of police authorities to ban police unions.

The unions were survived in the early 1950s by many benevolent and fraternal organizations of police. Some were patrolmen's benevolent associations (PBAs), like those formed in New York, Chicago, and Washington, D.C., whereas others were fraternal orders of police (FOPs). During the late 1950s and early 1960s, a new group of rank-and-file association leaders came into power. They were more vocal in articulating their demands. Soon, a majority of the rank and file vocally supported higher salaries and pensions, free legal aid, low-cost insurance, and other services and benefits. Beginning with the granting of public sector collective bargaining rights in Wisconsin in 1959, rank-and-file organizations were legally able to insist that their administrators sit down at the bargaining table.[15]

### Contemporary Status

Today's police employee organizations are still generally held by administrators as having too much influence; it is argued that these organizations interfere with the management of the agency by taking decision-making power away from the police chief while delving into inappropriate areas of influence, without being accountable, because these organizations have a hand in policy making, but are not elected or appointed by the public.[16]

A survey by Colleen Kadleck of 648 police employee organizations found that typically the organization[17]:

- Is relatively small (median = 60 members; mode = 8; more members means more dues, which can increase the range of activities, e.g., lobbying and lawsuits, that members can take advantage of)
- Was founded after the 1960s (about half being founded in the 1970s and 1980s; those founded after the 1960s tend to be more labor oriented, and 70 percent of them are now involved in collective bargaining)
- Is local in nature (43 percent are affiliated with an organization at the state or national level, which, it is argued, usually results in a more militant organization than one that is locally based)
- Has an elected, sworn officer as leader (96 percent)
- Has a mandatory dues check-off system (73 percent; members' dues are automatically collected through payroll deduction and remitted to the employee

organization by the employer, an effortless means of collecting dues and guaranteeing income for the organization)

- Limits membership, such as patrol officers only (11 percent), patrol and sergeants (26 percent), any sworn member (37 percent), or any police employee (16 percent); 10 percent limit membership to some specific rank

Kadleck also found that the collective bargaining relationship is strong in the Northeast (89 percent of all agencies), West (82 percent), and Midwest (79 percent), but not in the South (35 percent).[18] Furthermore, the leaders of these organizations see their organizations as entitled to an important role in policy development and do not believe that they have too much influence in their departments; they also do not feel that they can trust police management to make good decisions.[19]

## Corrections Follows the Precedent

Correctional officers (COs) were probably the last group of public workers to organize. In the early days after authorization of collective bargaining in the 1960s and 1970s, correctional administrators feared that unionization would diminish management authority and undermine staff discipline and prison security. Over the years that collective bargaining has been in place for correctional agencies, however, the early fears have not materialized, and the benefits of shared governance by line staff and management have led to better decisions and higher morale. As with the police, **negotiations** usually involve pay and benefits for correctional employees, including seniority rights, how staff are selected for overtime, the type of clothing provided to staff by the agency, educational programs, and so forth. After a contract is negotiated, each prison or community corrections office must implement and administer it. When disputes about the true meaning of a contract arise, management can make a decision, and the union can file a grievance to argue it.[20]

Collective bargaining is now well entrenched in prison and other correctional agency operations, and it will continue to have an impact on policy and practice. There remains some disagreement, however, concerning its implications. Some argue that sharing of power in a correctional setting benefits all parties, and that unions are a powerful voice to the legislature for increases in staffing and budgets. Others maintain that collective bargaining has resulted in a clear distinction between line staff and management, with managers no longer looking out for subordinates because union leadership promotes an adversarial relationship. As James Jacobs and Norma Crotty suggested, collective bargaining "has redefined the prison organization in adversary terms so that wardens are bosses and complaints are grievances."[21]

A major issue with corrections unions involves the right to strike. One can only imagine the chaos that would occur if correctional officers strike. Such unlawful strikes have occurred. The most infamous strike action was in New York State in 1979, when 7,000 correctional workers simultaneously struck the state's 33 prisons.

A court found the union in violation of the law, heavily fined the union for the failure of its members to return to work, and jailed union leaders for contempt of court.[22] The strike ended 17 days after it began; the guards gained very few concessions, and salary gains did not offset fines imposed on the strikers.[23]

Finally, another concern regarding collective bargaining is its impact on rehabilitation. Some argue that prison unions, stressing staff safety issues, may impede the institution's efforts toward rehabilitation, while also pointing out that rehabilitative programs that improve inmate morale, reduce idleness, and enhance security result in benefits to the staff who work in prison.[24]

Overall, it is not the existence of collective bargaining that seems to have implications for corrections; rather, perhaps much like the unionization with the police, it is the attitude of agency administrators and union leaders and the relationships that develop that set the direction of the impact. If both parties communicate with and listen to each other, show mutual respect, and are reasonable in their positions, collective bargaining can benefit corrections. If, however, the parties let issues get personal and become overly adversarial, corrections and collective bargaining will experience many negative outcomes.[25]

### Unionization in the Courts

The movement to exercise the right to bargain collectively, especially when compared with law enforcement and corrections, has been rare in the courts, occurring on a random, localized basis; however, unified court systems exist in which court personnel are organized statewide, as in Hawaii. Many states adhere generally to model legislation on public employee relation commissions, which provide mediation and fact-finding services and make determinations of unfair labor practices. On occasion, these commissions make decisions that greatly affect the management authority of the judiciary over its personnel.

When a collective bargaining unit exists in a court system, the process has all the basic elements found in other systems: (1) recognition (the employing court recognizes that henceforth employees will be represented by their chosen agent); (2) negotiation (there are established methods for arriving at a collective bargaining agreements, breaking deadlocks, ratifying contracts, etc.); and (3) contract administration (the day-to-day management of a court is accomplished within the framework of the labor contract).[26]

## Collective Bargaining: Types, Relationships, Negotiation, Job Actions

### Three Models

Each state is free to decide whether and which public sector employees will have collective bargaining rights and under what terms; therefore, there is considerable variety in collective bargaining arrangements across the nation. In states with comprehensive public sector bargaining laws, the administration of the statute is the responsibility of a state agency such as a public employee relations board (PERB) or a public employee relations commission (PERC). There are three basic models used in the states: binding arbitration, meet and confer, and bargaining-not-required.[27] Table 15.1 shows the use of these models in the various states.

The *binding arbitration* model is used in 24 states and the District of Columbia. Public employees are given the right to bargain with their employers.

**TABLE 15.1**   State Collective Bargaining Laws Governing Law Enforcement Officers

| STATE | BINDING ARBITRATION MODEL | MEET-AND-CONFER MODEL | BARGAINING-NOT-REQUIRED MODEL |
|---|---|---|---|
| Alabama | | | X |
| Alaska | X | | |
| Arizona | | | X |
| Arkansas | | | X |
| California | | X | |
| Colorado | | | X |
| Connecticut | X | | |
| Delaware | X | | |
| District of Columbia | X | | |
| Florida | | X | |
| Georgia | | | X |
| Hawaii | X | | |
| Idaho | | | X |
| Illinois | X | | |
| Indiana | | | X |
| Iowa | X | | |
| Kansas | X | | |
| Kentucky | | | X |
| Louisiana | | | X |
| Maine | X | | |
| Maryland | | | X |
| Massachusetts | X | | |
| Michigan | X | | |
| Minnesota | X | | |
| Mississippi | | | X |
| Missouri | | | X |
| Montana | X | | |
| Nebraska | | | X |
| Nevada | X | | |

*(table continues)*

**TABLE 15.1**   State Collective Bargaining Laws Governing Law Enforcement Officers (*continued*)

| STATE | BINDING ARBITRATION MODEL | MEET-AND-CONFER MODEL | BARGAINING-NOT-REQUIRED MODEL |
|---|---|---|---|
| New Hampshire | X | | |
| New Jersey | X | | |
| New Mexico | | X | |
| New York | X | | |
| North Carolina | | | X |
| North Dakota | | | X |
| Ohio | X | | |
| Oklahoma | X | | |
| Oregon | X | | |
| Pennsylvania | X | | |
| Rhode Island | X | | |
| South Carolina | | | X |
| South Dakota | | | X |
| Tennessee | | | X |
| Texas | | | X |
| Utah | | | X |
| Vermont | X | | |
| Virginia | | | X |
| Washington | X | | |
| West Virginia | | | X |
| Wisconsin | X | | |
| Wyoming | | | X |

*Source:* Will Aitchison, *The Rights of Police Officers,* 3rd ed. (Portland, Ore.: Labor Relations Information System, 1996), p. 10.

If the bargaining reaches an impasse, the matter is submitted to a neutral arbitrator, who decides what the terms and conditions of the new collective bargaining agreement will be.[28]

Only three states use the *meet-and-confer* model, which grants very few rights to public employees. As with the binding arbitration model, criminal justice employees in meet-and-confer states have the right to organize and to select their own bargaining representatives.[29] When an impasse is reached, however, employees are at a distinct disadvantage. Their only legal choices are to accept the employer's best offer, try to influence the offer through political tactics (such as appeals for public support), or take some permissible job action.[30]

The 22 states that follow the *bargaining-not-required* model either do not statutorily require or do not allow collective bargaining by public employees.[31] In the majority of these states, laws permitting public employees to engage in collective bargaining have not been passed.

States with collective bargaining must also address the issue of whether an individual employee must be a member of a union that represents his or her class of employees in a particular organization. In a "closed shop," employees must be dues-paying members or they will be terminated by the employer. "Open" shops, conversely, allow employees a choice of whether to join, even though the union has an obligation to represent them.

## *The Bargaining Relationship*

If collective bargaining is legally established, the process of setting up a bargaining relationship is straightforward, although opportunities still exist for disputes. The process for organizing for collective bargaining is as follows: First, a union will begin an organizing drive seeking to get a majority of the class(es) of employees it wants to represent to sign authorization cards. At this point, agency administrators may attempt to convince employees that they are better off without the union. Questions may also arise, such as whether certain employees (e.g., police or prison lieutenants) are part of management and therefore ineligible for union representation.

Once a majority ("50 percent plus one" of the eligible employees) have signed cards, the union notifies the criminal justice agency. If management believes that the union has obtained a majority legitimately, it will recognize the union as the bargaining agent of the employees it has sought to represent. Once recognized by the employer, the union will petition the PERB or other body responsible for administering the legislation for certification.

## *Negotiations*

Figure 15.4 depicts a typical configuration of the union and management bargaining teams. Positions shown in the broken-line boxes typically serve in a support role and may or may not actually partake in the bargaining. The management's labor relations manager (lead negotiator) is often an attorney assigned to the human resources department, reporting to the city manager or assistant city manager and representing the city in grievances and arbitration matters; management's chief negotiator may also be the director of labor relations or human resources director for the unit of government involved or a professional labor relations specialist. Nor is the union's chief negotiator normally a member of the organization involved; rather, he or she will be a specialist brought in to represent the union's position and to provide greater experience, expertise, objectivity, and autonomy. The union's chief negotiator may be accompanied by some people who have conducted surveys on wages and benefits, trends in the consumer price index, and so on.[32]

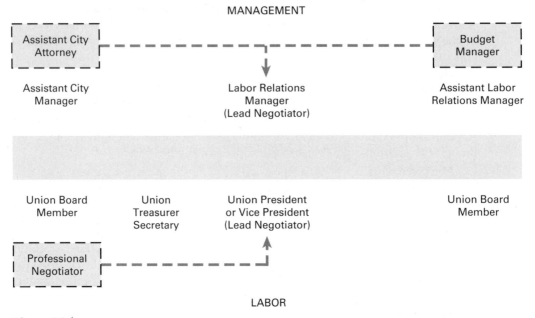

**Figure 15.4**

Union and management collective bargaining teams. *Source:* Jerry Hoover, Chief of Police, Reno, Nevada.

The agency's chief executive should not appear at the table; it is difficult for the chief to represent management one day and then return to work among the employees the next. Rather, management is represented by a key member of the command staff having the executive's confidence.

The issues, and the way in which they are presented, will impact how the negotiations will go. The purpose of bargaining is to produce a bilateral written agreement that will bind both parties during the lifetime of the agreement. Management normally prefers a narrow scope of negotiations because it means less shared power; conversely, the union will opt for the widest possible scope. The number of negotiating sessions may run from one to several dozen, lasting from 30 minutes to 10 or more hours, depending on how close or far apart union and management are when they begin to meet face to face.

In the initial session, the chief negotiator for each party will make an opening statement. Management's representative will often go first, touching on general themes such as the need for patience and the obligation to bargain in good faith. The union's negotiator will generally follow, outlining what the union seeks to achieve under the terms of the new contract. Ground rules for the bargaining may then be reviewed, modified, or developed. The attention then shifts to the terms of the contract that the union is proposing. Both sides need to understand what it is they are attempting to commit each other to. Ultimately, unless a total impasse is reached, agreement will be obtained on the terms of a new contract. The union's membership will vote on the contract as whole. If approved by the membership, the contract then goes before the necessary government officials and bodies for approval.[33]

## *In the Event of an Impasse*

Even parties bargaining in good faith may not be able to resolve their differences by themselves, and an impasse may result. In such cases, a neutral third party may be introduced to facilitate, suggest, or compel an agreement. Three major forms of impasse resolution are mediation, fact finding, and arbitration.

- **Mediation** occurs when a third party, called the mediator, comes in to help the adversaries with the negotiations.[34] This person may be a professional mediator or someone else in whom both parties have confidence. In most states, mediation may be requested by either labor or management. The mediator's task is to build agreement about the issues involved by reopening communications between the two sides. The mediator cannot compel an agreement, so an advantage of the process is that it preserves collective bargaining by maintaining the decision-making power in the hands of the involved parties.[35]

- **Fact finding** primarily involves the interpretation of facts and the determination of what weight to attach to them. Appointed in the same way as mediators, fact finders also do not have the means to impose a settlement of the dispute. Fact finders may sit alone or as part of a panel normally consisting of three people. The fact-finding hearing is quasi-judicial, although less strict rules of evidence are applied. Both labor and management may be represented by legal counsel, and verbatim transcripts are commonly made. In a majority of cases, the fact finder's recommendations will be made public at some point.[36]

- **Arbitration** is similar to fact finding but differs in that the "end product of arbitration is a final and binding decision that sets the terms of the settlement and with which the parties are legally required to comply."[37] Arbitration may be voluntary or compulsory. It is compulsory when mandated by state law and is binding on the parties even if one of them is unwilling to comply. It is voluntary when the parties undertake of their own volition to use the procedure. Even when entered into voluntarily, arbitration is compulsory and binding on the parties who have agreed to it.

The establishment of a working agreement between labor and management does not mean that the possibility for conflict no longer exists; the day-to-day administration of the agreement may also be the basis for strife. Questions can arise concerning the interpretation and application of the document and its various clauses, and grievances (discussed earlier) may arise. The sequence of grievance steps will be spelled out in the collective bargaining agreement and typically include the following five steps: (1) The employee presents the grievance to the immediate supervisor; and, if satisfaction is not achieved, (2) a written grievance is presented to the division commander, then (3) to the chief executive officer, then (4) to the city or county manager, and, finally, (5) to an arbiter, selected according to the rules of the American Arbitration Association.[38]

The burden of proof is on the grieving party, except in disciplinary cases, when it is always on the employer. The parties may be represented by counsel at the hearing, and the format will include opening statements by each side, examination and cross-examination of any witnesses, and closing arguments in the reverse order of which opening arguments were made.[39]

## Job Actions

A **job action** is an activity by employees to express their dissatisfaction with a particular person, event, or condition or to attempt to influence the outcome of some matter pending before decision makers. Employees seek to create pressure that may shift the course of events to a position more favorable or acceptable to them.[40] Job actions are of four types: the vote of confidence, work slowdowns, work speedups, and work stoppages.

- *Vote of confidence.* This job action is used sparingly; a vote of no confidence signals employees' collective displeasure with the chief administrator of the agency. Although such votes have no legal standing, they may have high impact as a result of the resulting publicity.
- *Work slowdowns.* Employees continue to work during a slowdown, but they do so at a leisurely pace, causing productivity to fall. As productivity declines, the unit of government is pressured to resume normal work production; for example, a police department may urge officers to issue more citations so revenues are not lost. Citizens may complain to politicians to "get this thing settled."[41]
- *Work speedups.* These involve accelerated activity in the level of services and can foster considerable public resentment. For example, a police department may conduct a "ticket blizzard" to protest a low pay increase, pressure governmental leaders to make more concessions at the bargaining table, or abandon some policy change that affects their working conditions.
- *Work stoppages.* These constitute the most severe job action. The ultimate work stoppage is the strike, or withholding of all employees' services. This tactic is most often used by labor to force management back to the bargaining table when negotiations have reached an impasse. Criminal justice employee strikes are now rare, however. Short of a strike by all employees are briefer work stoppages, known in policing as "blue flu," that last only a few days.

## Civil Liability

With the exception of physicians, no group of workers is more susceptible to litigation and liability than police and corrections officers. Frequently cast into confrontational situations, and given the complex nature of their work and its requisite training needs, they will from time to time act in a manner that evokes public scrutiny and complaints. The price of failure among public servants can be quite high, in both human and financial terms. Coupled with that is the fact that some police and corrections officers are overzealous and even brutal in their work; they may intentionally or otherwise violate the rights of the citizens they are sworn to protect or the clients they detain or supervise. For these inappropriate actions, the public has become quick to file suit for damages for what are perceived to be egregious actions.

Another trend is for such litigants to cast a wide net in their lawsuits, suing not only the principal actors in the incident, but supervisors and agency administrators as well; this breadth of suing represents the notion of "vicarious liability" or the doctrine of *respondeat superior,* an old legal maxim meaning, "let the master answer." In sum, an employer can be found liable in certain instances for wrongful acts of the employee.[42] Such a case was *McClelland v. Facteau,*[43] in which McClelland was stopped by Officer Facteau for speeding and taken to the city jail; he was not allowed to make any phone calls, was questioned but not advised of his rights, and was beaten and injured by Facteau in the presence of two city police officers who were from different jurisdictions. McClelland sued, claiming that the two police chiefs were directly responsible for his treatment and injuries due to their failure to train and supervise their subordinates properly. Evidence was also produced of prior misbehavior by Facteau. The court ruled that the chiefs could be held liable if they knew of prior misbehavior yet did nothing about it.

Next I examine torts and negligent behaviors that can lead to civil liability and even incarceration for police and corrections personnel in the justice system; following that is a discussion of two major legislative tools that are used to legally attack such activities: Title 42, U.S. Code, Section 1983, and Title 18, U.S. Code, Section 242.

## Torts and Negligence

It is important to have a basic understanding of tort liability. A **tort** is the infliction of some injury on one person by another. Three categories of torts generally cover most of the lawsuits filed against criminal justice practitioners: negligence, intentional torts, and constitutional torts.

*Negligence* can arise when a criminal justice employee's conduct creates a danger to others. In other words, the employee did not conduct his or her affairs in a manner so as to avoid subjecting others to a risk of harm and may be held liable for the injuries caused to others.[44]

*Intentional torts* occur when an employee engages in a voluntary act that has a substantial likelihood of resulting in injury to another; examples are assault and battery, false arrest and imprisonment, malicious prosecution, and abuse of process.

*Constitutional torts* involve employees' duty to recognize and uphold the constitutional rights, privileges, and immunities of others; violations of these guarantees may subject the employee to a civil suit, most frequently brought in federal court under 42 U.S. Code Section 1983, discussed below.[45]

Assault, battery, false imprisonment, false arrest, invasion of privacy, negligence, defamation, and malicious prosecution are examples of torts that are commonly brought against police officers.[46] False arrest is the arrest of a person without probable cause. False imprisonment is the intentional illegal detention of a person, not only in jail, but any confinement to a specified area. For example, the police may fail to release an arrested person after a proper bail or bond has been posted, they can delay the arraignment of an arrested person unreasonably, or authorities can fail to release a prisoner after they no longer have authority to hold him or her.[47]

A single act may also be a crime as well as a tort. If Officer Smith, in an unprovoked attack, injures Jones, the state will attempt to punish Smith in a *criminal* action by sending him to jail or prison, fining him, or both. The state would have the burden of proof at criminal trial, having to prove Smith guilty "beyond a reasonable doubt." Furthermore, Jones may sue Smith for money damages in a *civil* action for the personal injury he suffered. In this civil suit, Jones would have the burden of proving Smith's acts were tortious by a "preponderance of the evidence"—a lower standard than that in a criminal court and thus easier to satisfy.

## Section 1983 Legislation

Following the Civil War and in reaction to the activities of the Ku Klux Klan, Congress enacted the Ku Klux Klan Act of 1871, later codified as **Title 42, U.S. Code, Section 1983.** It states that

> Every person who, under color of any statute, ordinance, regulation, custom, or usage of any State or Territory, subjects, or causes to be subjected, any citizen of the United States or any other person within the jurisdiction thereof to the deprivation of any rights, privileges, or immunities secured by the Constitution and laws, shall be liable to the party injured in an action at law, suit in equity, or other proper proceeding for redress.

This legislation was intended to provide civil rights protection to all "persons" protected under the act when a defendant acted "under color of law" (misused power of office) and provided an avenue to the federal courts for relief of alleged civil rights violations.

Section 1983 also allows for a finding of personal liability on the part of police supervisory personnel for inadequate training or if it is proven that they knew, or should have known, of the misconduct of their officers yet failed to take corrective action and prevent future harm.

Such a case was *Brandon v. Allen*,[48] in which two teenagers parked in a "lovers' lane" were approached by an off-duty police officer, Allen, who showed his police identification and demanded that the male exit from the car. Allen struck the young man with his fist and stabbed him with a knife and then attempted to break into the car where the young woman was seated. The young man was able to reenter the car and manage an escape. As the two teenagers sped off, Allen fired a shot at them with his revolver. The shattered windshield glass severely injured the youths to the point that they required plastic surgery. Allen was convicted of criminal charges, and the police chief was also sued under Section 1983. The plaintiffs charged that the chief and others knew of Allen's reputation as an unstable officer; none of the other police officers wished to ride in a patrol car with him. At least two formal charges of misconduct had been filed previously, yet the chief failed to take any remedial action or even to review the disciplinary records of officers when he became chief. The court called this behavior "unjustified inaction," held the police department liable, and allowed the plaintiffs damages. The U.S. Supreme Court upheld this judgment.[49]

Police supervisors have also been found liable for injuries arising out of an official policy or custom of their department. Injuries resulting from a chief's verbal or written support of heavy-handed behavior resulting in the use of excessive force by officers have resulted in such liability.[50]

Whereas Section 1983 is a civil action, Title 18, U.S. Code, Section 242, makes it a *criminal* offense for any person acting under color of law to violate another's civil rights. Section 242 not only applies to police officers, but also to the misconduct of public officials and to the prosecution of judges, bail bond agents, public defenders, and even prosecutors.

## *New Areas of Potential Liability*

In the 1990s, three areas of potential liability were established that require knowledge on the part of police administrators: vehicle pursuits, handling computer evidence, and providing information to the public via press releases. A considerable amount of controversy has recently been generated regarding so-called "hot" or vehicle pursuits because of the tremendous potential for injury, property damage, and liability involved. Police administrators are revamping their policies and procedures accordingly. As one sheriff stated, "For so long, administrators thought there was really one lethal weapon they gave their officers, and that was the gun, and yet there was another weapon ... their car."[51] As one police procedure manual describes it, "The decision by a police officer to pursue a citizen in a motor vehicle is among the most critical that can be made."[52] In sum, pursuit is justified only when the necessity of apprehension outweighs the degree of danger created by the pursuit. That is there is a nationwide trend by agencies to place more restrictions on pursuits and to have field supervisors (sergeants) call off the chase. It is not uncommon for agency policy to limit the pursuit to two pursuit vehicles: a supervisor and another vehicle authorized by a pursuit monitor.[53]

It is almost impossible today to investigate a fraud, embezzlement, or child pornography case without dealing with some sort of computer evidence. Many police agencies have recruited self-taught experts to fill the role of computer evidence specialists.[54] This increased exposure to computer evidence brings an increase in potential legal liabilities. For example, if a police agency seizes the computer records of an ongoing business, a negative financial impact on the operation of the business may result. Or if it can be shown that the police accidentally destroyed business records through negligence, a criminal investigation might well become the civil suit of the decade.[55] It is crucial that police administrators have personnel trained in the proper procedures for handling computers as well as rules of evidence.[56]

Disseminating public information is another concern. The Louisiana Supreme Court held that police department public information officers (PIOs) can be held liable for unfounded statements they make in news releases. The case involved a defamation suit against the state police in which the PIO told a reporter that the defendant was running a large-scale illegal gambling operation and bilking customers. The court found that the PIO had no reasonable basis for saying the defendant had cheated customers and thus made injurious statements that he had no reason to believe were true. Although the ruling applies only to PIOs in Louisiana, it could grow to have national implications in the future.[57]

## Liability of Corrections Personnel

The liability of corrections workers often centers on their lack of due care for persons in their custody. This responsibility concerns primarily police officers and civilians responsible for inmates in local jails.

When an inmate commits suicide while in custody, police agencies are frequently—and often successfully—sued in state court under negligence and wrongful death claims. The standard used by the courts is whether the agency's act or failure to act created an unusual risk to an inmate. A "special duty" of care exists for police officers to protect inmates suffering from mental disorders and those who are impaired by drugs or alcohol. Foreseeability—the reasonable anticipation that injury or damage may occur—may be found when inmates make statements of intent to commit suicide, have a history of mental illness, are in a vulnerable emotional state, or are at a high level of intoxication or drug dependence.[58]

Suicides are not uncommon among jail inmates; each year, more than 300 jail inmates take their own lives.[59] Inmate suicide rates have also been found to be higher in small jails, and highest in small jails with lower population densities.[60] State courts generally recognize that police officials have a duty of care to persons in their custody.[61] Thus, jail administrators are ultimately responsible for taking reasonable precautions to ensure the health and safety of persons in their custody; they must protect inmates from harm, render medical assistance when necessary, and treat inmates humanely.[62]

Several court decisions have helped to establish the duties and guidelines for jail employees concerning the care of their charges. An intoxicated inmate in possession of cigarettes and matches started a fire that resulted in his death; the court stated that "the prisoner may have been voluntarily drunk, but he was not in the cell voluntarily ... [he] was helpless and the officer knew there was a means of harm on his person." The court concluded the police administration owed a greater duty of care to such an arrestee.[63] Emotionally disturbed arrestees can also create a greater duty for jail personnel. In an Alaskan case, a woman had been arrested for intoxication in a hotel and had trouble talking, standing, and walking; her blood-alcohol content was 0.26 percent. Two and a half hours after her incarceration, officers found her hanging by her sweater from mesh wiring in the cell. The Alaska Supreme Court said the officers knew she was depressed and that in the past few months, one of her sons had been burned to death, another son was stabbed to death, and her mother had died. Thus, the court believed officers should have anticipated her suicide.[64]

In New Mexico, a 17-year-old boy was arrested for armed robbery; he later told his mother he would kill himself before he would go to prison and subsequently tried to cut his wrists with an aluminum can top. The assistant chief ordered the officers to keep watch over him, but he was found dead by hanging the following morning. The state supreme court held that the knowledge officers possess is an important factor in determining liability and negligence in such cases.[65] In a New Jersey case in which a young man arrested for intoxication was put in a holding cell but officers failed to remove the leather belt that he used to take his life, the court found the officers' conduct could have been a "substantial" factor in his death.[66]

Courts have also found the design of detention facilities as a source of negligence. A Detroit holding cell did not permit officers to observe inmates' movements unless the inmates were standing directly in front of the door, and no electronic monitoring devices were in use. A suicide in this facility led the court to hold that these conditions, and the absence of a detoxification cell were proximate causes and constituted a building defect.[67] In another incident, an intoxicated college student was placed in a holding cell at the school's public safety building. Forty minutes after he was placed in the cell, officers found the man hanging from an overhead heating device by a noose fashioned from his socks and belt. The court found the university liable for operating a defective building and awarded the plaintiff $650,000.[68]

The behavior of jail personnel *after* a suicide or attempted suicide may also indicate a breach of duty. Officers are expected to give all possible aid to an inmate who is injured or has attempted suicide. Thus, when officers found an inmate slumped in a chair with his belt around his neck and left him in that position instead of trying to revive him or call for medical assistance, the court ruled this behavior established a causal link between the officer's inaction and the boy's death.[69]

It is clear that correctional administrators must ensure that their organizations are cognizant of their legal responsibilities and expanded custodial role with their detainees.

# CASE STUDIES

The following two case studies will help the reader to apply some of this chapter's materials to real-world issues involving employee rights, law, policy, and decisions concerning whether disciplinary action is warranted.

Consider the following situation, and determine how you, the administrator, would handle it from a disciplinary standpoint.

## Lost Love—and a Lost Laborer?

A police officer, Blake, is dispatched to a domestic violence call; on his arrival, a woman runs out of the house screaming, "Help me! He's going to kill me!" Her right eye is swollen. She also tells the officer, "I've had it with his drinking and womanizing and told him to pack up his things and go. That's when he began beating me."

You, a lieutenant, heard the call go out to Blake from Communications, but at shift's end you cannot find any offense report concerning the matter submitted by Blake. You ask Blake about the report, and he tells you that on entering the home, he observed another officer, Carter, who works in your agency, who commented, "Thanks for coming out here, but things are cool now. She slapped me once, and I dealt with it. I admit I got a little out of hand, but it's under control. She's nothing but a cheating, money-grubbing louse." Blake admits that he purposely avoided completing a report, deciding to consider it "like an offsetting penalty in football" and to overlook the matter.

### Questions for Discussion

1. What would you, as the lieutenant and shift commander, do about this situation?
2. Should you call the female victim, or Officer Carter, into your office for an interview?
3. What if you do bring them both in, separately, and they deny that the incident occurred?
4. What if you bring the woman in and she indicates that she wants to drop the matter, because "it's happened before"; do you pursue it?
5. If you determine that Blake is in fact culpable for not reporting the incident, what actions (if any) would you take? On what grounds?

## Campus Conundrum

You are a new administrator in a medium-sized university police department. The campus normally has about 15,000 students, growing to about 25,000 people for home football games. It is a Saturday afternoon and there is such a game, with all police personnel being deployed in the stadium as is customary. Suddenly a sergeant (one who is popular and prone to dumping a load of trouble in your lap and then walking away) storms into your office. He reports that one of your officers—a younger one who has recently undergone a divorce and, as part of his new lifestyle, purchased a motorcycle—has appeared in the football stadium wearing an earring. You also learn that no formal dress code exists for the department.

## Questions for Discussion

1. Should the sergeant ignore the matter?
2. Do you tell the sergeant to have the officer remove the earring?
3. Do you summon the officer to your office (leaving fewer people for crowd control)?
4. What might be a compromise action until the game is over or until a dress code is enacted?

# Summary

This chapter examined three aspects of administration that pose serious challenges: discipline, liability, and labor relations. It is clear from this triad of issues that administrators need to understand the current and developing laws that serve to make criminal justice practitioners legally accountable; this need cannot be overstated. It is far better to learn the proper means of discipline, areas of liability, and effective collective bargaining methods through education and training than to learn about these issues as a defendant in a lawsuit.

Criminal justice executives need to be proactive and follow appropriate laws and guidelines as they recruit, hire, train, supervise, and negotiate with their subordinates in order to avoid legal difficulties; for administrators not to do so could place them and their jurisdiction at serious financial, legal, and moral risk.

# Questions for Review

1. List and describe the seven forms of disciplinary action that may be taken against police officers.
2. Delineate the minimum due process requirements for discharging public employees.
3. Describe the benefits and functions of an early warning system (EWS) for identifying problem officers.
4. Explain the differences between positive and negative discipline.
5. Describe the categories of dispositions that are commonly used with complaints.

6. Provide an example of how a grievance may proceed through its various levels.

7. Explain how unionization began, its contemporary status in policing, and its influence in the courts and corrections organizations.

8. Describe the three models of collective bargaining and the process that occurs when an impasse is reached.

9. Define tort, Section 1983, and *respondeat superior.*

10. Explain how the following three areas carry the potential for liability: pursuits, computer evidence, and release of public information.

# Notes

1. V. McLaughlin and R. Bing, "Law Enforcement Personnel Selection," *Journal of Police Science and Administration* **15** (1987):271-276.

2. Ibid.

3. *McNamara v. City of Chicago,* 700 F.Supp. 917 (N.D. Ill. 1988), at 919.

4. *White v. Thomas,* 660 F.2d 680 (5th Cir. 1981).

5. *Yarber v. Indiana State Prison,* 713 F.Supp. 271 (N.D. Ind. 1988).

6. Robert H. Chaires and Susan A. Lentz, "Criminal Justice Employee Rights: An Overview," *American Journal of Criminal Justice* **13** (April 1995):273-274.

7. M. Guthrie, "Using Automation to Apply Discipline Fairly," *FBI Law Enforcement Bulletin* **5** (1996):18-21.

8. Jeff Rojek, Allen E. Wagner, and Scott H. Decker, "Evaluating Citizen Complaints Against the Police," in R. G. Dunham and G. P. Alpert (eds.), *Critical Issues in Policing: Contemporary Readings,* 4th ed. (Prospect Heights, Ill.: Waveland, 2001), pp. 317-337.

9. Ibid., p. 318.

10. J. R. Dugan and D. R. Breda, "Complaints About Police Officers: A Comparison Among Types and Agencies," *Journal of Criminal Justice* **19** (1991):165-171.

11. Kim Michelle Lersch, "Police Misconduct and Malpractice: A Critical Analysis of Citizens' Complaints," *Policing* **21** (1998):80-96.

12. D. W. Perez, *Police Review Systems* (Washington, D.C.: Management Information Service, 1992).

13. W. Clinton Terry III, *Policing Society: An Occupational View* (New York: Wiley, 1985), p. 168.

14. Ibid., p. 168.

15. Ibid., pp. 170-171.

16. Colleen Kadleck, "Police Employee Organizations," *Policing: An International Journal of Police Strategies and Management* **26**(2) (2003):344-347.

17. Ibid., pp. 346, 349.

18. Ibid., p. 346.

19. Ibid., p. 349.

20. Richard P. Seiter, *Correctional Administration: Integrating Theory and Practice* (Upper Saddle River, N.J.: Prentice Hall, 2002), pp. 333-334.

21. James B. Jacobs and Norma Meacham Crotty, *Guard Unions and the Future of Prisons* (Ithaca, N.Y.: Institute of Public Employment, 1978), p. 41.

22. James B. Jacobs, *New Perspectives on Prisons and Imprisonment* (Ithaca, N.Y.: Cornell University Press, 1983), p. 153.

23. Ibid., pp. 154–155.

24. Seiter, *Correctional Administration,* p. 337.

25. Ibid.

26. U.S. Department of Justice, National Institute of Law Enforcement and Criminal Justice, *Trial Court Management Series, Personnel Management* (Washington, D.C.: U.S. Government Printing Office, 1979), pp. 42–47.

27. Will Aitchison, *The Rights of Police Officers,* 3rd ed. (Portland, Ore.: Labor Relations Information System, 1996), p. 7.

28. Ibid.

29. Ibid.

30. Ibid., p. 8.

31. Ibid., p. 9.

32. Charles R. Swanson, Leonard Territo, and Robert W. Taylor, *Police Administration: Structures, Processes, and Behavior,* 6th ed. (Upper Saddle River, N.J.: Prentice Hall, 2005), p. 517.

33. Ibid., p. 522.

34. Arnold Zack, *Understanding Fact-Finding and Arbitration in the Public Sector* (Washington, D.C.: U.S. Government Printing Office, 1974), p. 1.

35. Thomas P. Gilroy and Anthony V. Sinicropi, "Impasse Resolution in Public Employment," *Industrial and Labor Relations Review* **25** (July 1971–1972):499.

36. Robert G. Howlett, "Fact Finding: Its Values and Limitations—Comment, Arbitration and the Expanded Role of Neutrals," in *Proceedings of the Twenty-Third Annual Meeting of the National Academy of Arbitrators* (Washington, D.C.: Bureau of National Affairs, 1970), p. 156.

37. Zack, *Understanding Fact-Finding,* p. 1.

38. Swanson, Territo, and Taylor, *Police Administration,* p. 530.

39. Ibid.

40. Ibid., p. 532.

41. Ibid., p. 534.

42. *Monell v. Department of Social Services,* 436 U.S. 658 (1978).

43. 610 F.2d 693 (10th Cir., 1979).

44. H. E. Barrineau III, *Civil Liability in Criminal Justice* (Cincinnati, Ohio: Pilgrimage, 1987), p. 58.

45. Ibid., p. 5.

46. Swanson, Territo, and Taylor, *Police Administration,* p. 549.

47. Ibid.

48. 516 F.Supp. 1355 (W.D. Tenn., 1981).

49. *Brandon v. Holt,* 469 U.S. 464, 105 S.Ct. 873 (1985).

50. See, for example, *Black v. Stephens,* 662 F.2d 181 (1991).

51. Oklahoma County Sheriff John Whetsel, quoted in Nicole Marshall, "Hot Pursuit," *Tulsa World,* June 15, 1998, p. A11.

52. Ronald Palmer, Chief of Police, Tulsa, Oklahoma, *Police Department Procedure Manual,* June 10, 1998, p. 1.

53. Marshall, "Hot Pursuit," p. A11.

54. Michael R. Anderson, "Reducing Computer Evidence Liability," *Government Technology* 10 (February 1997):24, 36.

55. Ibid.

56. Ibid.

57. "Be Careful What You Say," *Law Enforcement News* (December 15, 1997):1.

58. Victor E. Kappeler, *Critical Issues in Police Civil Liability,* 2nd ed. (Prospect Heights, Ill.: Waveland, 1997), pp. 177–178.

59. U.S. Department of Justice, Bureau of Justice Statistics, Jail Suicide Rates 64 Percent Lower than in Early 1980s, http://www.ojp.usdoj.gov/bjs/pub/press/shspljpr.htm (accessed September 28, 2005).

60. Ibid., p. 9.

61. Victor E. Kappeler and Rolando V. delCarmen, "Avoiding Police Liability for Negligent Failure to Prevent Suicide," *The Police Chief* (August 1991):53–59.

62. Ibid., p. 53.

63. *Thomas v. Williams,* 124 S.E.2d 409 (Ga. App. 1962).

64. *Kanayurak v. North Slope Borough,* 677 P.2d 892 (Alaska 1984).

65. *City of Belen v. Harrell,* 603 P.2d 711 (N.M. 1979).

66. *Hake v. Manchester Township,* 486 A.2d 836 (N.J. 1985).

67. *Davis v. City of Detroit,* 386 N.W.2d 169 (Mich. App. 1986).

68. *Hickey v. Zezulka,* 443 N.W.2d 180 (Mich. App. 1989).

69. *Hake v. Manchester Township,* 486 A.2d 836 (N.J. 1985).

# Chapter 16

# Financial Administration

## Key Terms and Concepts

| | |
|---|---|
| Budget | Expenditures |
| Budget audit | Financial accountability |
| Budget cycle | Line-item budgeting |
| Budget execution | Management accountability |
| Budget formulation | Program accountability |
| Corrections reform | Revenue augmentation |

## Learning Objectives

As a result of reading this chapter, the student will:

- be able to define the term *budget*
- understand the concepts of the budget cycle's four steps
- be familiar with the budgeting procedures in the police, courts, and corrections systems
- have examples of different ways in which monies may be acquired
- be able to distinguish among the three different budget formats and the advantages and disadvantages of each
- understand why and how criminal justice policymakers are reforming sentencing laws to reduce corrections expenditures

> *How pleasant it is to have money, heigh ho! How pleasant it is to have money.*
>
> —Arthur Hugh Clough

> *Money is like muck, not good except it be spread.*
>
> —Francis Bacon

## Introduction

The importance of financial administration to organizations in this country is unquestioned. Budgets are the key to financial administration; their development involves planning, organizing, directing, and other administrative functions. If unlimited funds were available, planning would not be needed. As Frederick Mosher observed, "Not least among the qualifications of an administrator is [one's] ability as a tactician and gladiator in the budget process."[1]

Just as individuals need to be responsible with their own finances to avoid legal and personal difficulties, so must governmental administrators be responsible stewards of the public's funds.

This chapter presents some of the fundamental elements of the control of fiscal resources through budgeting. It is not intended to prepare the reader to be an expert on fiscal management, but it provides an overview of some of the basic methods and issues surrounding financial administration.

Of the four component parts of financial administration—budgeting, auditing, accounting, and purchasing—budgeting is the primary focus here. Included are discussions of budget definitions and uses; the influence of politics and fiscal realities in budgeting, which often lead to constricted financial conditions for the organization; the several elements of the budget process, including formulation, approval, execution, and audit; and budget formats. Also presented is an examination of some of the very serious fiscal problems units of government are now experiencing, and what some criminal justice policymakers are doing to reform sentencing laws to reduce corrections expenditures.

The chapter concludes with a case study concerning fiscal exigency.

# The Budget

## *A Working Definition*

The word **budget** is derived from the old French *bougette,* meaning a small leather bag or wallet. Initially, it referred to the leather bag in which the chancellor of the exchequer carried documents stating the government's needs and resources to the English Parliament.[2] Later, it came to mean the documents themselves. More recently, budget has been defined as a plan stated in financial terms, an estimate of future expenditures, an asking price, a policy statement, the translation of financial resources into human purposes, and a contract between those who appropriate the funds and those who spend them.[3] To some extent, all of these definitions are valid.

In addition, the budget is a management tool, a process, and a political instrument. It is a

> comprehensive plan, expressed in financial terms, by which a program is operated for a given period. It includes (1) the services, activities, and projects comprising the program; (2) the resultant expenditure requirements; and (3) the resources available for their support.[4]

It is "a plan or schedule adjusting expenses during a certain period to the estimated income for that period."[5] Lester Bittel added,

> A budget is, literally, a financial standard for a particular operation, activity, program, or department. Its data is presented in numerical form, mainly in dollars ... to be spent for a particular purpose—over a specified period of time. Budgets are derived from planning goals and forecasts.[6]

Although these descriptions are certainly apt, one writer warns that budgets contain an inherently irrational process: "Budgets are based on little more than the past and some guesses."[7]

Financial management of governmental agencies is clearly political. Anything the government does entails the expenditure of public funds.[8] Thus, the most important political statement that any unit of government makes in a given year is its budget. Essentially, the budget causes administrators to follow the gambler's adage and "put your money where your mouth is."[9] When demands placed on government increase while funds are stable or decline, the competition for funds is keener than usual, forcing justice agencies to make the best case for their budgets. The heads of all departments, if they are doing their jobs well, are also vying for appropriations. Special-interest groups, the media, politicians, and the public, with their own views and priorities, often engage in arm twisting during the budgeting process.

# Elements of a Budget

## The Budget Cycle

Administrators must think in terms of a **budget cycle,** which in government (and, therefore, all public criminal justice agencies) is typically on a fiscal year basis. Some states have a biennial budget cycle; their legislatures, such as those in Kentucky and Nevada, budget for a 2-year period. Normally, however, the fiscal year is a 12-month period that may coincide with a calendar year or, more commonly, will run from July 1 through June 30 of the following year. The federal government's fiscal year is October 1 through September 30. The budget cycle is important because it drives the development of the budget and determines when new monies become available.

The budget cycle consists of four sequential steps, repeated every year at about the same point in time: (1) budget formulation, (2) budget approval, (3) budget execution, and (4) budget audit.

## Budget Formulation

Depending on the size and complexity of the organization and the financial condition of the jurisdiction, **budget formulation** can be a relatively simple or an exceedingly difficult task; in either case, it is likely to be the most complicated stage of the budgeting process. The administrator must anticipate all types of **expenditures** (e.g., overtime, gasoline, postage, maintenance contracts) and predict expenses related to major incidents or events that might arise. Certain assumptions based on the previous year's budget can be made, but they are not necessarily accurate. One observer noted that "every expense you budget should be fully supported with the proper and most logical assumptions you can develop. Avoid simply estimating, which is the least supportable form of budgeting."[10] Another criminal justice administrator, discussing budget formulation, added

> The most important ingredient for any budgeting process is planning. [Administrators] should approach the budget process from the planning standpoint of "How can I best reconcile the [criminal justice] needs of the community with the ability of my jurisdiction to finance them, and then relate those plans in a convincing manner

to my governing body for proper financing and execution of programs?" After all, as budget review occurs, the document is taken apart and scrutinized piece by piece or line by line. This fragmentation approach contributes significantly to our inability to defend interrelated programs in an overall budget package.[11]

To illustrate, let us assume that a police department budget is being prepared in a city having a manager form of government. Long before a criminal justice agency (or any other unit of local government) begins to prepare its annual budget, the city manager and/or the staff of the city has made revenue forecasts, considered how much (if any) of the current operating budget will be carried over into the next fiscal year, analyzed how the population of the jurisdiction will grow or shift (affecting demand for public services), and examined other priorities for the coming year. The city manager may also appear before the governing board to obtain information about its fiscal priorities, spending levels, pay raises, new positions, programs, and so on. The city manager may then send all department heads a memorandum outlining the general fiscal guidelines to be followed in preparing their budgets.

On receipt of the city's guidelines for preparing its budget, the heads of functional areas, such as the chief of police, have a planning and research unit (assuming a city large enough to have this level of specialization) prepare an internal budget calendar and an internal fiscal policy memorandum (Table 16.1 shows an internal budget calendar for a large municipal police department). This memo may include input from unions and lower supervisory personnel. Each bureau is then given the responsibility for preparing its individual budget request.

In small police departments with little or no functional specialization, the chief may prepare the budget alone or with input from other officers or the city finance officer. In some small agencies, chiefs and sheriffs may not even see their budget or assist in its preparation. Because of tradition, politics, or even laziness, the administrator may have abdicated control over the budget. This puts the agency in a precarious position indeed; it will have difficulty engaging in long-term planning and spending money productively for personnel and programs when the executive has to get prior approval from the governing body to buy items such as office supplies.

The planning and research unit then reviews the bureau's budget request for compliance with the budgeting instructions and the chief's and city manager's priorities. Eventually, a consolidated budget is developed for the entire police department and submitted to the chief, who may meet with the planning and research unit and bureau commanders to discuss it. Personalities, politics, priorities, personal agendas, and other issues may need to be addressed; the chief may have to mediate disagreements concerning these matters, sometimes rewarding the loyal and sometimes reducing allotments to the disloyal.[12] Requests for programs, equipment, travel expenses, personnel, or anything else in the draft budget may be deleted, reduced, or enhanced.

The budget is then presented to the city manager. At this point, the chief executive's reputation as a budget framer becomes a factor. If the chief is known to pad the budget heavily, the city manager is far more likely to cut the department's request than if the chief is known to be reasonable in making budget requests, engages in innovative planning, and has a flexible approach to budget negotiations.

**TABLE 16.1**   Budget Preparation Calendar for a Large Police Department

| WHAT SHOULD BE DONE | BY WHOM | ON THIS DATE |
|---|---|---|
| Issue budget instructions and applicable forms | City administrator | November 1 |
| Prepare and issue budget message, with instructions and applicable forms, to unit commanders | Chief of police | November 15 |
| Develop unit budgets with appropriate justification and forward recommended budgets to planning and research unit | Unit commanders | February 1 |
| Review unit budget | Planning and research staff with unit commanders | March 1 |
| Consolidate unit budgets for presentation to chief of police | Planning and research unit | March 15 |
| Review consolidated recommended budget | Chief of police, planning and research staff, and unit commanders | March 30 |
| Obtain department approval of budget | Chief of police | April 15 |
| Forward recommended budget to city administrator | Chief of police | April 20 |
| Review recommended budget by administration | City administrator and chief of police | April 30 |
| Approve revised budget | City administrator | May 5 |
| Forward budget document to city council | City administrator | May 10 |
| Review budget | Budget officer of city council | May 20 |
| Present to council | City administrator and chief of police | June 1 |
| Report back to city administrator | City council | June 5 |
| Review and resubmit to city council | City administrator and chief of police | June 10 |
| Take final action on police budget | City council | June 20 |

*Source:* National Advisory Commission on Criminal Justice Standards and Goals, *Police* (Washington, D.C.: U.S. Government Printing Office, 1973), p. 137.

The city manager consolidates the police budget request with those from other municipal department heads and then meets with them individually to discuss their requests further. The city manager directs the city finance officer to make any necessary additions or cuts and then to prepare a budget proposal for presentation to the governing body.

The general steps in budget development are shown in Exhibit 16.1.

The courts have a similar budgetary process. In a large court, the process may include five major procedures: (1) developing an internal budgetary policy,

# Exhibit 16.1
## Steps in Budget Development

Hal Rubin described how the $550 million budget for the California Highway Patrol (CHP) is typically developed. According to the budget section, "It's an all-year and year-on-year process" that begins at the level of the 99 area commands, where budget requests originate. The requests are dealt with in one of three ways: (1) funded within the department's base budget, (2) disapproved, or (3) carried forward for review by CHP personnel.

At the division level, managers review the area requests, make needed adjustments, and submit a consolidated request to the budget section at headquarters. This section passes input from the field to individual section management staff (e.g., planning and analysis, personnel, training, and communications) for review. Budget section staff meet with individual section management staff. Within two or three months, the budget section identifies proposals for new funding that have department-wide impact and passes them on to the executive level.

The commissioner and aides review the figures along with those from other state departments and agree on a budget to submit to the governor. The governor submits this budget to the legislature, which acts on it and returns it to the governor for signature.

*Source:* Hal Rubin, "Working Out a Budget," *Law and Order* (May 1989):27–28. (Budget figure shown is for 2005.)

(2) reviewing budget submissions, (3) developing a financial strategy, (4) presenting the budget, and (5) monitoring the budget. Figure 16.1 illustrates the relationship of the steps in the process.

## Budget Approval

With the city manager's proposed budget request in hand, the governing board begins its deliberations on the citywide budget. The city manager may appear before the board to answer questions concerning the budget; individual department heads also may be asked to appear. Suggestions for getting monies approved and appropriated include the following:

1. Have a carefully justified budget.
2. Anticipate the environment of the budget hearing by reading news reports and understanding the priorities of the council members. Know what types of questions elected officials are likely to ask.
3. Determine which "public" will be at the police department's budget hearing and prepare accordingly. Public issues change from time to time; citizens who were outraged over one issue one year may be incensed by another the next.

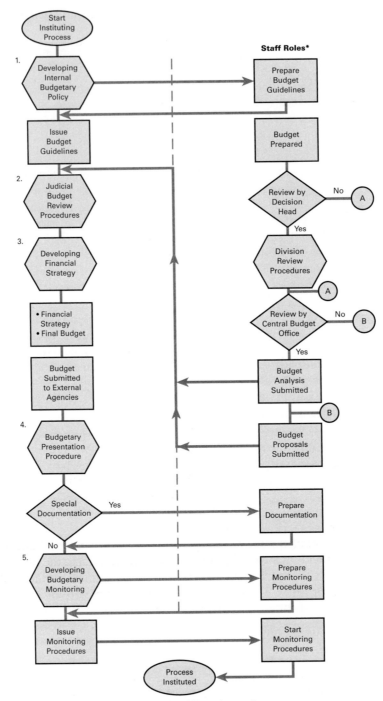

Start
Instituting
Process

1. Developing Internal Budgetary Policy

**Staff Roles***

Prepare Budget Guidelines

Issue Budget Guidelines

Budget Prepared

2. Judicial Budget Review Procedures

Review by Decision Head — No → A

Yes

3. Developing Financial Strategy

Division Review Procedures — A

- Financial Strategy
- Final Budget

Review by Central Budget Office — No → B

Yes

Budget Submitted to External Agencies

Budget Analysis Submitted

B

4. Budgetary Presentation Procedure

Budget Proposals Submitted

Special Documentation — Yes → Prepare Documentation

No

5. Developing Budgetary Monitoring

Prepare Monitoring Procedures

Issue Monitoring Procedures

Start Monitoring Procedures

Process Instituted

* Particularly applicable in a large court, much less so in a small court.

**Figure 16.1**

Steps in a judicial budgetary process.

4. Make good use of graphics in the form of pie charts and histograms but be selective and do not go overboard. Short case studies of successes are normal and add to graphics.
5. Rehearse and critique the presentation many times.
6. Be a political realist.[13]

After everyone scheduled has spoken, the city council gives directions to the city manager to make further cuts in the budget or to reinstate funds or programs cut earlier, and so on. The budget is then approved. It is fair to say that at this stage, budgeting is largely a legislative function that requires some legal action, as a special ordinance or resolution approving the budget is passed each year by the governing board.

The columns in Table 16.2 indicate the budget amount requested by the chief of police, the amount recommended by the city manager, and the amount finally approved by the city council.

## Budget Execution

The third stage of the process, **budget execution,** has several objectives: (1) to carry out the police department's budgeted objectives for the fiscal year in an orderly manner, (2) to ensure that the department undertakes no financial obligations or commitments other than those funded by the city council, and (3) to provide a periodic accounting of the administrator's stewardship over the department's funds.[14]

Supervision of the budget execution phase is an executive function that requires some type of fiscal control system, usually directed by the city or county manager. Periodic reports on accounts are an important element of budget control; they serve to reduce the likelihood of overspending by identifying areas in which deficits are likely to occur as a result of change in gasoline prices, extensive overtime, natural disasters, and unplanned emergencies (such as riots). A periodic budget status report informs the administrator what percentage of the total budget has been expended to date (Table 16.3).

Prudent administrators normally attempt to manage the budget conservatively for the first 8 or 9 months of the budget year, holding the line on spending until most fiscal crises have been averted. Because unplanned incidents and natural disasters can wreak havoc with any budget, this conservatism is normally the best course. Then the administrator can plan the most efficient way to allocate funds if emergency funds have not been spent.

## The Audit

The word *audit* means to verify something independently.[15] The basic rationale for a **budget audit** has been described by the comptroller general of the United States as follows:

> Governments and agencies entrusted with public resources and the authority for applying them have a responsibility to render a full accounting of their activities.

**TABLE 16.2** Police Operating Budget ($) in a Community of 150,000 Population

| DESCRIPTION | FY 2004–2005 EXPENSES | FY 2005–2006 EXPENSES | FY 2006–2007 DEPARTMENT REQUEST | CITY MANAGER | CITY COUNCIL |
|---|---|---|---|---|---|
| **Salaries/wages** | | | | | |
| Regular salaries | 14,315,764 | 14,392,639 | 16,221,148 | 16,221,148 | 16,221,148 |
| Overtime | 988,165 | 782,421 | 951,875 | 951,875 | 711,875 |
| Severence pay | 36,194 | 226,465 | 82,000 | -0- | -0- |
| Holiday pay | 395,952 | 591,158 | 698,958 | 698,958 | 698,958 |
| Callback pay | 45,499 | 49,833 | 49,555 | 49,555 | 49,555 |
| Subtotals | 15,781,574 | 16,042,516 | 18,003,536 | 17,921,536 | 17,681,536 |
| **Employee benefits** | | | | | |
| Retirement | 3,345,566 | 3,485,888 | 4,069,521 | 4,069,521 | 4,069,521 |
| Group insurance | 1,256,663 | 1,467,406 | 1,752,718 | 1,752,718 | 1,752,718 |
| Life insurance | 43,797 | 53,164 | 117,590 | 117,396 | 117,396 |
| Disability insurance | 726,885 | 794,686 | 1,346,909 | 1,346,038 | 1,024,398 |
| Uniform allowance | 188,079 | 193,827 | 196,750 | 196,750 | 196,750 |
| Medicare | 77,730 | 80,868 | 100,058 | 99,739 | 99,739 |
| Long-term disability | 11,583 | 21,974 | 48,517 | 48,517 | 48,517 |
| Subtotals | 5,650,303 | 6,097,813 | 7,583,546 | 7,630,679 | 7,309,039 |
| **Services and supplies** | | | | | |
| Office supplies | 62,357 | 49,292 | 51,485 | 51,485 | 51,485 |
| Operating supplies | 227,563 | 148,569 | 270,661 | 270,661 | 270,661 |
| Repair/maintenance | 248,922 | 195,941 | 233,118 | 233,118 | 233,118 |
| Small tools | 49,508 | 788 | 12,175 | 12,175 | 12,175 |
| Professional services | 337,263 | 290,359 | 334,765 | 334,765 | 334,765 |
| Communications | 287,757 | 223,200 | 392,906 | 392,906 | 392,906 |

**TABLE 16.2** *(continued)*

| DESCRIPTION | FY 2004–2005 EXPENSES | FY 2005–2006 EXPENSES | FY 2006–2007 DEPARTMENT REQUEST | CITY MANAGER | CITY COUNCIL |
|---|---|---|---|---|---|
| Public utilities | 111,935 | 116,773 | 121,008 | 121,008 | 121,008 |
| Rentals | 81,840 | 96,294 | 113,071 | 113,071 | 113,071 |
| Vehicle rentals | 834,416 | 1,193,926 | 1,363,278 | 1,363,278 | 1,169,278 |
| Extradition | 20,955 | 22,411 | 20,000 | 20,000 | 20,000 |
| Other travel | 4,649 | 5,123 | 23,500 | 23,500 | 23,500 |
| Advertising | 2,662 | 2,570 | 4,100 | 4,100 | 4,100 |
| Insurance | 328,360 | 595,257 | 942,921 | 942,921 | 942,921 |
| Books/manuals | 16,285 | 12,813 | 12,404 | 12,404 | 12,404 |
| Employee training | 47,029 | 30,851 | -0- | -0- | -0- |
| Aircraft expenses | -0- | -0- | 15,000 | 15,000 | 15,000 |
| Special inventory | 11,527 | 13,465 | 15,000 | 15,000 | 15,000 |
| Other services and supplies | 1,386,201 | 1,039,651 | 1,386,201 | 1,386,201 | 1,386,201 |
| Subtotals | 4,059,229 | 4,037,283 | 5,311,593 | 5,311,593 | 5,117,593 |
| **Capital outlay** | | | | | |
| Machinery and equipment | 572,301 | 102,964 | -0- | -0- | -0- |
| Totals | 26,063,407 | 26,280,576 | 30,898,675 | 30,863,808 | 30,108,168 |

**TABLE 16.3** A Police Department's Budget Status Report ($)

| LINE ITEM | AMOUNT BUDGETED | EXPENSES TO DATE | AMOUNT ENCUMBERED | BALANCE TO DATE | PERCENTAGE USED |
|---|---|---|---|---|---|
| Salaries | 16,221,148 | 8,427,062.00 | -0- | 7,794,086.00 | 52.0 |
| Professional services | 334,765 | 187,219.61 | 8,014.22 | 139,531.17 | 58.3 |
| Office supplies | 51,485 | 16,942.22 | 3,476.19 | 31,066.59 | 39.7 |
| Repair/maintenance | 49,317 | 20,962.53 | 1,111.13 | 27,243.34 | 44.8 |
| Communications | 392,906 | 212,099.11 | 1,560.03 | 179,246.86 | 54.4 |
| Utilities | 121,008 | 50,006.15 | 10,952.42 | 60,049.43 | 51.4 |
| Vehicle rentals | 1,169,278 | 492,616.22 | 103,066.19 | 573,595.59 | 51.9 |
| Travel | 23,500 | 6,119.22 | 2,044.63 | 15,336.15 | 34.7 |
| Extraditions | 20,000 | 12,042.19 | 262.22 | 7,695.59 | 61.5 |
| Printing/binding | 36,765 | 15,114.14 | 2,662.67 | 18,988.19 | 48.4 |
| Books/manuals | 12,404 | 5,444.11 | 614.11 | 6,345.78 | 48.8 |
| Training/education | 35,695 | 19,661.54 | 119.14 | 15,914.32 | 55.4 |
| Aircraft expenses | 15,000 | 8,112.15 | 579.22 | 6,308.63 | 57.9 |
| Special investigations | 15,000 | 6,115.75 | 960.50 | 7,922.75 | 47.2 |
| Machinery | 1,000 | 275.27 | 27.50 | 697.23 | 30.3 |
| Advertising | 4,100 | 1,119.17 | 142.50 | 2,838.33 | 30.8 |

This accountability is inherent in the governmental process and is not always specifically identified by legislative provision. This governmental accountability should identify not only the object for which the public resources have been devoted but also the manner and effect of their application.[16]

After the close of each budget year, the year's expenditures are audited to ensure that the agency spent its funds properly. Budget audits are designed to investigate three broad areas of accountability: **financial accountability** (focusing on proper fiscal operations and reports of the justice agency), **management accountability** (determining whether funds were utilized efficiently and economically), and **program accountability** (determining whether the city council's goals and objectives were accomplished).[17]

Financial audits determine whether funds were spent legally, the budgeted amount was exceeded, and the financial process proceeded in a legal manner. For example, auditors investigate whether funds transferred between accounts were authorized, grant funds were used properly, computations were made accurately, disbursements were documented, financial transactions followed established procedures, and established competitive bidding procedures were employed.[18]

Justice administrators should welcome auditors' help to identify weaknesses and deficiencies and correct them.

# Budget Formats

The three types of budgets primarily in use today are the line-item (or object-of-expenditure) budget, the performance budget, and the program (or results or outcomes) budget. Two additional types, the planning-programming-budgeting system (PPBS) and the zero-based budget (ZBB), are also discussed in the literature but are used to a lesser extent.

## *The Line-Item Budget*

**Line-item budgeting** (or item budgeting) is the most commonly used budget format. It is the basic system on which all other systems rely because it affords control. It is so named because it breaks down the budget into the major categories commonly used in government (e.g., personnel, equipment, contractual services, commodities, and capital outlay items); every amount of money requested, recommended, appropriated, and expended is associated with a particular item or class of items.[19] In addition, large budget categories are broken down into smaller line-item budgets (in a police department, examples include patrol, investigation, communications, and jail function). The line-item format fosters budgetary control because no item escapes scrutiny.[20] Table 16.2 shows a line-item budget for police, Table 16.4 for a court, Table 16.5 for probation and parole, and Table 16.6 for state prison organizations. Each demonstrates the range of activities and funding needs of each agency. Note in Tables 16.2, 16.5, and 16.6 how a recession affected budgets and requests from year to year in many categories, resulting in severe cuts and even total elimination of items previously

**TABLE 16.4** Operating Budget for a District Court in a County of 300,000 Population

| CATEGORY | AMOUNT ($) |
|---|---|
| **Salaries and wages** | |
| Regular salaries | 2,180,792 |
| Part-time temporary | 9,749 |
| Incentive/longevity | 50,850 |
| Subtotal | 2,241,391 |
| **Employee benefits** | |
| Group insurance | 170,100 |
| Worker compensation | 8,470 |
| Unemployment compensation | 3,220 |
| Retirement | 412,211 |
| Social security | 605 |
| Medicare | 13,503 |
| Subtotal | 608,109 |
| **Services and supplies** | |
| Computers and office equipment | 22,865 |
| Service contracts | 2,000 |
| Minor furniture/equipment | 1,000 |
| Computer supplies | 10,000 |
| Continuous forms | 4,000 |
| Office supplies | 36,066 |
| Advertising | 50 |
| Copy machine expenses | 40,000 |
| Dues and registration | 4,000 |
| Printing | 24,000 |
| Telephone | 16,000 |
| Training | 2,000 |
| Court reporter/transcript | 235,000 |
| Court reporter per diem | 265,000 |
| Law books/supplements | 9,000 |
| Jury trials | 75,000 |
| Medical examinations | 80,000 |
| Computerized legal research | 20,000 |
| Travel | 1,500 |
| Subtotal | 847,481 |
| **Child support** | |
| Attorneys and other personnel | 66,480 |
| Court-appointed attorneys | 656,000 |
| Grand juries | 18,600 |
| Family court services | 762,841 |
| Total | 5,200,902 |

**TABLE 16.5**  Probation and Parole Budget ($) for a State Serving 3 Million Population

| DESCRIPTION | FY 2004–2005 ACTUAL | FY 2005–2006 AGENCY REQUEST | FY 2006–2007 GOVERNOR'S RECOMMENDATION | LEGISLATURE APPROVED |
|---|---|---|---|---|
| Personnel | 13,741,104 | 14,290,523 | 13,620,991 | 13,540,222 |
| Travel | 412,588 | 412,588 | 412,588 | 401,689 |
| Operating expenses | 1,307,020 | 1,395,484 | 1,307,020 | 1,256,787 |
| Equipment | 10,569 | 4,379 | 4,379 | 4,379 |
| Loans to parolees | 4,500 | 4,500 | 4,500 | 4,500 |
| Training | 9,073 | 9,073 | 9,073 | 9,073 |
| Extraditions | 200,000 | 200,000 | 200,000 | 185,000 |
| Client drug tests | 112,962 | 112,962 | 112,962 | 112,962 |
| Home arrest fees | 114,005 | 114,005 | 114,005 | 114,005 |
| Community programs | 50,000 | 50,000 | 50,000 | 47,500 |
| Residential confinement | 496,709 | 500,709 | 496,709 | 487,663 |
| Utilities (paid by building lessors) | | | | |
| Totals | 16,458,530 | 17,094,223 | 16,332,227 | 16,163,780 |

**TABLE 16.6** Operating Budget ($) for a State Medium Security Prison with 1,000 Inmates

| DESCRIPTION | FY 2004–2005 ACTUAL | FY 2005–2006 AGENCY REQUEST | FY 2006–2007 GOVERNOR'S RECOMMENDATION | LEGISLATURE APPROVED |
|---|---|---|---|---|
| **Personnel** | | | | |
| Salaries | 5,051,095 | 5,370,979 | 5,186,421 | 5,105,533 |
| Worker's compensation | 184,362 | 143,462 | 201,198 | 198,016 |
| Retirement | 1,142,010 | 1,174,968 | 1,215,674 | 1,196,028 |
| Recruit tests | 49,447 | 51,528 | 45,692 | 44,972 |
| Insurance | 474,330 | 488,250 | 513,000 | 500,175 |
| Retirement insurance | 30,963 | 31,872 | 35,917 | 35,349 |
| Unemployment compensation | 6,003 | 6,383 | 6,162 | 6,065 |
| Overtime | 165,856 | -0- | -0- | -0- |
| Holiday pay | 150,519 | 158,500 | 154,643 | 151,936 |
| Medicare | 39,965 | 45,140 | 42,225 | 40,948 |
| Shift differential | 95,925 | 101,011 | 98,553 | 96,828 |
| Standby pay | 6,465 | 6,807 | 6,641 | 6,526 |
| Longevity pay | 18,095 | 18,095 | 18,095 | 18,095 |
| Subtotals | 7,415,035 | 7,596,995 | 7,524,221 | 7,400,471 |
| **Services and supplies** | | | | |
| Operating supplies | 180,672 | 277,495 | 180,647 | 214,859 |
| Communications/freight | 4,877 | 5,314 | 5,023 | 5,023 |
| Printing/copying | 20,900 | 47,222 | 19,016 | 21,527 |
| Equipment repair | 14,385 | 13,542 | 14,817 | 14,817 |
| Vehicle operation | 20,405 | 21,601 | 21,016 | 21,016 |
| Uniforms—custody | 118,122 | 105,976 | 103,237 | 113,856 |
| Inmate clothing | 72,436 | 184,790 | 72,430 | 86,167 |
| Equipment issued | 20,403 | 13,236 | 15,451 | 17,086 |
| Inmate wages | 36,645 | 52,815 | 35,572 | 42,309 |

**TABLE 16.6**  (continued)

| DESCRIPTION | FY 2004–2005 ACTUAL | FY 2005–2006 AGENCY REQUEST | FY 2006–2007 GOVERNOR'S RECOMMENDATION | LEGISLATURE APPROVED |
|---|---|---|---|---|
| Food | 895,897 | 1,299,838 | 895,759 | 1,065,403 |
| Postage | 7,738 | 8,793 | 7,036 | 7,738 |
| Telephone | 24,808 | 23,802 | 22,130 | 24,808 |
| Subscriptions | 382 | 401 | 725 | 401 |
| Hand-tools | 110 | 286 | 113 | 113 |
| Subtotals | 1,417,780 | 2,055,111 | 1,392,972 | 1,635,123 |
| **Special equipment** | 116,863 | 34,088 | 12,557 | 13,661 |
| Grounds maintenance | 150,098 | 209,003 | 138,560 | 185,843 |
| Inmate law library | 18,564 | 20,115 | 16,419 | 21,836 |
| Special projects | 53,237 | 8,887 | 8,887 | 8,887 |
| Gas and power | 554,478 | 586,604 | 505,823 | 604,335 |
| Water | 60,390 | 69,377 | 52,266 | 67,171 |
| Garbage | 80,035 | 101,240 | 82,436 | 82,436 |
| Canine unit | 13,936 | 2,521 | 4,260 | 2,543 |
| Total | 9,880,416 | 10,683,941 | 9,738,401 | 10,022,306 |

funded. Also note some of the ways in which administrators deviated from usual practices to save money (e.g., the police budget shows that the department found it to be less expensive to lease patrol vehicles than to buy a huge fleet).

The line-item budget has several strengths and weaknesses. Its strengths include ease of control development, comprehension (especially by elected and other executive branch officials), and administration. Weaknesses are its neglect of long-range planning and its limited ability to evaluate performance. Furthermore, the line-item budget tends to maintain the status quo; ongoing programs are seldom challenged. Line-item budgets are based on history: This year's allocation is based on last year's. Although that allows an inexperienced manager to prepare a budget more easily, it often precludes the reform-minded chief's careful deliberation and planning for the future.

The line-item budget provides ease of control because it clearly indicates the amount budgeted for each item, the amount expended as of a specific date, and the amount still available at that date (see, e.g., Table 16.3).

Virtually all criminal justice agencies are automated to some extent, whether the financial officer prepares his or her budget using a computerized spreadsheet or a clerk enters information onto a database that will be uploaded to a state's mainframe computer. Some justice agencies use an automated budgeting system (ABS) that can store budget figures, make all necessary calculations for generating a budget request, monitor expenditures from budgets (similar to that shown in Table 16.6), and even generate some reports.

## The Performance Budget

The key characteristic of a performance budget is that it relates the volume of work to be done to the amount of money spent.[21] It is input–output oriented, and it increases the responsibility and accountability of the manager for output as opposed to input.[22] This format specifies an organization's activities, using a format similar to that of the line–item budget. It normally measures activities that are easily quantified, such as numbers of traffic citations issued, crimes solved, property recovered, cases heard in the courtroom, and caseloads of probation officers. These activities are then compared to those of the unit that performs the most. This ranking according to activity attempts to allocate funds fairly. Following is an example from a police department: The commander of the traffic accident investigation unit requests an additional three investigators, which the chief approves. Later, the chief might compare the unit's output and costs of the unit to these measures before the three investigators were added to determine how this change affected productivity.[23] An example of a police performance budget is provided in Table 16.7.

The performance budget format could be used in other justice system components as well. The courts could use such performance measures as filing cases, writing opinions, disposing of cases, and accuracy of presentence investigations.

Advantages of the performance budget include a consideration of outputs, the establishment of the costs of various justice agency efforts, improved evaluation

**TABLE 16.7**   Example of a Police Performance Budget

| CATEGORY | | AMOUNT |
|---|---|---|
| **Units/activities** | | |
| Administration (chief) | Subtotal | $ |
| Strategic planning | | $ |
| Normative planning | | $ |
| Policies and procedures formulation | | $ |
| Etc. | | |
| **Patrol** | Subtotal | $ |
| Calls for service | | $ |
| Citizen contacts | | $ |
| Special details | | $ |
| Etc. | | |
| **Criminal investigation** | Subtotal | $ |
| Suspect apprehension | | $ |
| Recovery of stolen property | | $ |
| Transportation of fugitives | | $ |
| Etc. | | |
| **Traffic services** | Subtotal | $ |
| Accident investigation | | $ |
| Issuance of citations | | $ |
| Public safety speeches | | $ |
| Etc. | | |
| **Juvenile services** | Subtotal | $ |
| Locate runaways/missing juveniles | | $ |
| Arrest of offenders | | $ |
| Referrals and liaison | | $ |
| Etc. | | |
| **Research and development** | Subtotal | $ |
| Perform crime analysis | | $ |
| Prepare annual budget | | $ |
| Prepare annual reports | | $ |
| Etc. | | |

of programs and managers, an emphasis on efficiency, increased availability of information for decision making, and the enhancement of budget justification and explanation.[24] The performance budget works best for an assembly line or other organization where work is easily quantifiable, such as paving streets. Its disadvantages include its expense to develop, implement, and operate because

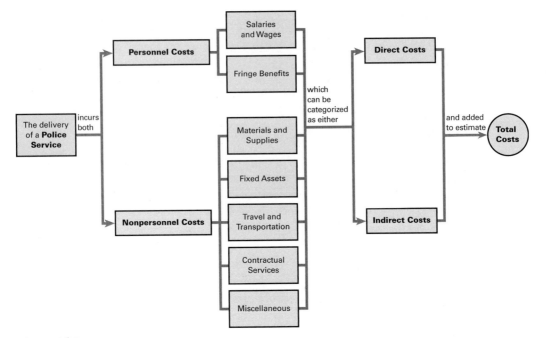

**Figure 16.2**

Elements in the total costs for police services. *Source:* U.S. Department of Justice, National Institute of Justice, *Measuring the Costs of Police Services* (Washington, D.C.: Author, 1982), p. 20.

of the extensive use of cost accounting techniques and the need for additional staff (Figure 16.2 illustrates the elements used to determine the cost of providing police services); the controversy surrounding attempts to determine appropriate workload and unit cost measures (in criminal justice, although many functions are quantifiable, such reduction of duties to numbers often translates into quotas, which are anathema to many people); its emphasis on efficiency rather than effectiveness; and the failure to lend itself to long-range planning.[25]

Determining which functions in criminal justice are more important (and should receive more financial support) is difficult. Therefore, in terms of criminal justice agency budgets, the selection of meaningful work units is difficult and sometimes irrational. How can a justice agency measure its successes? How can it count what does not happen?

## *The Program Budget*

The best-known type of budget for monitoring the activities of an organization is the *program budget,* developed by the RAND Corporation for the U.S. Department of Defense. This format examines cost units as units of activity rather than as units and subunits within the organization. This budget becomes a planning tool; it demands justification for expenditures for new programs and for deleting old ones that have not met their objectives.

A police agency probably has greater opportunities for creating new community-based programs than do the courts or corrections agencies. Some of these include crime prevention and investigation, drug abuse education, home security, selective enforcement (e.g., drunk driving) programs, and career development for personnel. Each of these endeavors requires instructional materials or special equipment, all of which must be budgeted. For example, traffic accident investigation (TAI) may be a cost area. The program budget emphasizes output measures. Outputs for TAI include the number of accidents worked and enforcement measures taken (such as citations issued, DUI and other arrests made, and public safety speeches given). If the budget for these programs were divided by the units of output, the administrator could determine the relative cost for each unit of output or productivity. The cost of TAI, however, entails more than just the TAI unit; patrol and other support units also engage in this program.

Thus, the program budget is an extremely difficult form to execute and administer because it requires tracking the time of all personnel by activity as well as figuring in the cost of all support services and supplies. For this reason, criminal justice agencies rarely use the program budget.[26] Some advantages of the program budget, however, include its emphasis on the social utility of programs conducted by the agency; its clear relationship between policy objectives and expenditures; its ability to provide justification and explanation of the budget; its establishment of a high degree of accountability; and its format and the wide involvement in formulating objectives, which lead employees at all levels of the organization to understand more thoroughly the importance of their roles and actions.[27]

Examples of police and court program budgets are presented in Tables 16.8 and 16.9, respectively.

## PPBS and Zero-Based Budgeting Formats

General Motors used the planning-programming-budgeting system (PPBS) as early as 1924,[28] and the RAND Corporation contributed to its development in a series of studies dating from 1949.[29] By the mid-1950s, several states were using it, and Secretary Robert McNamara introduced PPBS into the Defense Department in the mid-1960s.[30] By 1971, a survey revealed, however, that only 28 percent of the cities and 21 percent of the counties contacted had implemented PPBS or significant elements of it,[31] and in 1971, the federal government announced that it was discontinuing its use.

PPBS treated the three basic budget processes—planning, management, and control—as coequals. It was predicated on the primacy of planning.[32] This future orientation transformed budgeting from an annual ritual to a "formulation of future goals and policies."[33] The PPBS budget featured a program structure, zero-based budgeting, the use of cost-budget analysis to distinguish among alternatives, and a budgetary horizon, often 5 years.[34]

**TABLE 16.8** Example of a Police Program Budget

| PROGRAM AREA | | AMOUNT |
|---|---|---|
| Crime prevention | Subtotal | $ |
| Salaries and benefits | | $ |
| Operating expenses | | $ |
| Capital outlay | | $ |
| Miscellaneous | | $ |
| Traffic accident investigation | Subtotal | $ |
| Salaries and benefits | | $ |
| Operating expenses | | $ |
| Capital outlay | | $ |
| Miscellaneous | | $ |
| Traffic accident prevention | Subtotal | $ |
| Salaries and benefits | | $ |
| Operating expenses | | $ |
| Capital outlay | | $ |
| Miscellaneous | | $ |
| Criminal investigation | Subtotal | $ |
| Salaries and benefits | | $ |
| Operating expenses | | $ |
| Capital outlay | | $ |
| Miscellaneous | | $ |
| Juvenile delinquency prevention | Subtotal | $ |
| Salaries and benefits | | $ |
| Operating expenses | | $ |
| Capital outlay | | $ |
| Miscellaneous | | $ |
| Special investigations | Subtotal | $ |
| Salaries and benefits | | $ |
| Operating expenses | | $ |
| Capital outlay | | $ |
| Miscellaneous | | $ |
| Etc. | | |

Associated with PPBS, the zero-based planning and budgeting process re-quires managers to justify their entire budget request in detail rather than simply to refer to budget amounts established in previous years.[35] That is, each year all budgets begin at zero and must justify any funding. Following Peter Phyrr's use of zero-based budgeting at Texas Instruments, Governor Jimmy Carter adopted it in Georgia in the early 1970s and then as president implemented it in the federal

**TABLE 16.9**   Example of a Court's Program Budget

| PROGRAM AREA | | AMOUNT |
|---|---|---|
| Adjudicate criminal cases | Subtotal | $ |
| Adjudicate felony cases | Total | $ |
| Adjudicate misdemeanor appeals | Total | $ |
| Adjudicate civil cases | Subtotal | $ |
| Adjudicate major civil cases | Total | $ |
| Adjudicate minor civil cases | Total | $ |
| Adjudicate domestic relations cases | Total | $ |
| Adjudicate juvenile cases | Subtotal | $ |
| Adjudicate delinquency and dependent and neglect cases | Total | $ |
| Adjudicate crimes against juveniles | Total | $ |
| Provide alternatives to adjudication | Subtotal | $ |
| Divert adult offenders | Total | $ |
| Divert juvenile offenders | Total | $ |
| Provide security | Subtotal | $ |
| Handle prisoner transport | Total | $ |
| Provide courtroom security | Total | $ |
| Etc. | | |

*Source:* U.S. Department of Justice, National Institute of Law Enforcement and Criminal Justice, *Financial Management* (Washington, D.C.: The American University, 1979), p. 41.1.

government for fiscal year 1979. An analysis of this experience at the Department of Agriculture indicates that although its use saved $200,000 in the department's budget, it cost at least 180,000 labor-hours of effort to develop.[36]

It is important to note that few organizations have budgets that are purely one format or another; therefore, it is not unusual to find that because of time, tradition, and personal preferences, a combination of several formats is used.

# Potential Pitfalls in Budgeting

## *The Need for Budgeting Flexibility*

Ancient Greek mythology tells of a highwayman named Procrustes who had an iron bedstead. He measured all who fell into his hands on the bed. If they were too long, their legs were lopped off to fit it. If they were too short, they were stretched to fit the bed. Few criminal justice administrators have not seen their monies and programs laid out on the Procrustean bed of a state or municipal budget officer and lopped off.

It therefore becomes imperative to build as much flexibility into the planned program and budget as possible. One technique is to make up three budgets: an optimistic one, reflecting the ideal level of service to the jurisdiction and organization; an expected one, giving the most likely level of service that will be funded; and finally, budget plan that will provide a minimum level of service.[37]

To maximize the benefits of using budgets, managers must be able to avoid major pitfalls, which, according to Samuel Certo,[38] include the following:

1. Placing too much emphasis on relatively insignificant organizational expenses. In preparing and implementing a budget, managers should allocate more time to deal with significant organizational expenses and less time for relatively insignificant ones. For example, the amount of time spent on developing and implementing a budget for labor costs typically should be more than the amount of time managers spend on developing and implementing a budget for office supplies.

2. Increasing budgeted expenses year after year without adequate information. Perhaps the best-known method developed to overcome this potential pitfall is zero-based budgeting.[39]

3. Ignoring the fact that budgets must be changed periodically. Administrators must recognize that factors such as the cost of materials, newly developed technology, and demands for services are constantly changing and that budgets should reflect that by being reviewed and modified periodically. The performance budget (discussed earlier) is designed to assist in determining the level of resources to be allocated for each organizational activity.

## Common Cost and Waste Problems

To manage costs, administrators must be able to identify areas where waste and costs might be controlled. Louise Tagliaferri[40] identified 14 common cost factors that can be found in most organizations. Note that some costs are simply uncontrollable, but others are within the scope of the manager to reduce or at least maintain within a reasonable range:

Absenteeism and turnover
Accident loss
Direct and indirect labor
Energy
Maintenance
Materials and supplies
Overtime
Paperwork
Planning and scheduling
Product quality

Productivity

Tools and equipment

Transportation

Waste

Tagliaferri also noted that "literally billions of dollars are lost to industry (and criminal justice!) each year through carelessness, inattention, inefficiency, and other cost problems."[41]

# Should Criminal Justice Policies— and Budgets—Be Reformed?

It is impossible to watch a newscast or read a newspaper without seeing some mention of a myriad of problems that affect our nation's cities. Virtually every state, county, and country faces the dilemma of what to do about crime, the homeless, and the growing substance-abusing population (who are also frequently mentally ill), and other social problems—with limited financial resources. This is the challenge for all governing boards and administrators, and several states have convened economic summits to seek ways to deal with these fiscal problems.

## *States Grapple with Large Deficits*

As the new millennium began, and particularly after 9/11, many states experienced large budget shortfalls; in 30 states where shortfalls have been identified, the amounts reached levels of $35 to $40 billion, or about 7 to 8 percent of those states' expenditures. The main cause of this state fiscal crisis is flagging state revenues; state taxes now make up a smaller share of the economy than at any time in the last 30 years. Other reasons for the states' financial woes are actions by the federal government, particularly in the following areas[42]:

- *Restrictions on state taxation.* For example, the federal Internet Tax Freedom Act bars states from taxing the access fees that people pay for Internet service; in addition, two Supreme Court decisions prevent state and local governments from collecting sales taxes on most catalog or Internet purchases.

- *Unfunded mandates.* In several policy areas, such as special education and the No Child Left Behind education initiative, the federal government has placed requirements on state and local governments without adequately funding them.

- *Shifting health care costs.* The cost of health care for low-income elderly and disabled people has been shifting from Medicare to Medicaid. Because Medicare is fully federally funded, whereas states pay nearly half of all Medicaid costs, this shift in costs from Medicare to Medicaid has increased the financial pressure on states.

States must seek new ways of **revenue augmentation;** in 2005 some even began levying taxes on elective cosmetic procedures, such as breast implants, liposuction, and face lifts (Americans now spend about $8.4 billion per year on such surgeries).[43]

## *Strategies for Policymakers to Consider*

Clearly something must be done with the burgeoning cost of criminal justice activities. One of the areas of criminal justice that has been given a lot of attention with regard to cost cutting is **corrections reform,** particularly prisons, inmates, and systems of offender sentencing. A report by the Justice Policy Institute outlined a series of issues that policymakers can consider as they make budget decisions[44]:

A. *Reform sentencing and drug laws.* Many people feel that the budget woes discussed previously will force lawmakers to consider revising some of the tough mandatory criminal penalties that are packing states' overburdened prisons. The engine behind the commitment of so many nonviolent offenders was the mandatory sentencing reforms of the 1990s. These policies took away discretion in sentencing from judges. If convicted, an individual was required to serve a set sentence, without regard for mitigating factors. These sentencing laws are the driving force behind the exponential growth of the prison system and largely affect nonviolent drug offenders, many of them women. Many states have enacted reforms to these laws and others are considering reducing sentences for some drug and nonviolent offenses and eliminating mandatory minimums for nonviolent crimes. Such reforms can literally save millions of dollars.

---

**EXHIBIT 16.2**
**Recruit Screening Hurt by Budget Shrinkage**

Without a psychologist at the South Carolina Criminal Justice Academy to screen new police recruits, many of the state's smaller departments are going to have to come up with a way of screening applicants themselves, police chiefs say.

The psychologist was one of several positions cut by the academy due to budgetary constraints, according to Sid Gaulden, a spokesman for the South Carolina Department of Public Safety.

The academy, he told Law Enforcement News, is funded entirely through a portion of the fees and fines collected around the state. In the past three years, such funding has dwindled.

"The decision was made," said Gaulden. "Most of the folks—there were 18 who were let go—were basically maintenance staff. There was one instructor who was brand new, and the psychologist."

While larger agencies, such as Charleston's, have their own staff to conduct the psychological testing, many of South Carolina's law enforcement agencies relied on the service provided by the academy.

"It was a mistake," Manning Police Chief Randy Garrett said of the retrenchment. "Having that individual there to screen these applicants before we send them to the academy has been nothing but a plus for the state of South Carolina."

"I understand budget and stuff like that," Garrett told LEN, "but when you sit down and you need to see where you want to cut fat, you need to look at some of the most important positions, and that is an important position. That will affect this entire state." . . .

At least some of the departments are making arrangements to contract privately with counselors, said J.C. Rowe, executive director of the South Carolina Association of Chiefs of Police. But it will come at a high cost.

Both the Irmo and Manning agencies have roughly 20 sworn officers. Neither jurisdiction can afford to pay for private services.

Garrett said his agency will have to come up with its own screening mechanism—a procedure he concedes he knows nothing about developing.

"I've been lucky in my 30 year career," he said, "and don't get me wrong, in the last 12 years I've had a lot to do with hiring and firing and I've made one or two mistakes. But I would have had a lot more mistakes on hand if it had not been for the psychologist saying, 'This guy doesn't need to carry a gun and a badge.'"

Dorothy McCoy, a Columbia psychologist, said she was shocked to learn of the position being cut. She and a colleague, Ron Frier, have formed a partnership to provide evaluations, stress tests and counseling for the law-enforcement agencies. They put up a Web site, police-stress.com, in October.

"Everybody is having a real rough time," said Rowe of the state chiefs' association. "I'm sure probably the academy must know what it's doing, but it did create a hardship, especially for small departments. It's just something we'll have to live with until we can do better."

*Source:* Reprinted with permission from *Law Enforcement News,* March 2004, pp. 1, 14. John Jay College of Criminal Justice (CCNY), 555 West 57th St., New York, N.Y. 10019.

Given that the majority of mandatory minimums are applied to drug offenses, if nonviolent drug offenders were instead diverted into intensive outpatient drug treatment programs, the savings could be tremendous. Some states have enacted laws to ease the burden of low-level drug offenders on the system. For example, Arizona voters passed Proposition 200, which diverts drug offenders into treatment rather than prison. Such programs save the state millions of dollars per year.

Another possible approach is to establish a sentencing commission to review the state's existing sentencing structure, laws, policies, and practices and recommend to the state supreme court and legislature changes regarding the criminal code, rules of criminal procedure, and other appropriate policies and procedures.

B. *Look at nonviolent prisoners and special populations.* There are large numbers of people serving time in prisons for nonviolent and first-time offenses. In addition, there are specific populations that pose little risk to the public and cost the state enormous amounts of money to house and care for, such as elderly prisoners, chronically ill or dying prisoners, and women. The costs of incarcerating women are considerable. They often require more extensive health care services and have children, and many of these are thrown into the child welfare system when their mothers are imprisoned. In addition, research has shown that children of incarcerated parents are at high risk for becoming incarcerated themselves. In effect, in continuing to rely on incarceration for these women, we are ensuring future increased prison costs.

Elderly prisoners represent another population that poses little risk to the public, yet costs a great deal to incarcerate. Due to higher health care costs, these inmates cost three times more to incarcerate than younger prisoners. Truth in Sentencing laws and the abolishment of parole will ensure that more and more people will be growing old behind bars. Virginia has passed legislation allowing early release of inmates older than the age of 65 years who have served a minimum of 5 years or those older than 60 years who have served at least 10 years. Similarly, Texas has passed a bill to ease overcrowding by allowing supervised release for chronically ill prisoners to more appropriate facilities. The cost of care for chronically and terminally ill inmates is staggering, whereas such individuals pose a negligible risk to public safety.

C. *Consider parole reforms.* Research has shown that the public supports prevention and rehabilitation efforts as responses to crime. Parole and "good-time" have been shown to be effective ways to control prison population levels. Confronted with the costs associated with more prison construction, some states have made a decision to use their release powers more effectively by identifying more potential candidates for parole. In addition, parole officers have used more alternatives to revocation for minor violations of conditions of parole.

## Exhibit 16.3
## Defeat of Budget Measures Has Some Agencies Scrambling for Funds

The rejection by voters on Nov. 2 of a ballot measure that would have raised Los Angeles County's sales tax by half a cent has forced Los Angeles City Council members to come up with a new way to pay for the hiring of thousands of additional police officers.

The city was one of numerous municipalities nationwide that tried on Election Day to persuade voters to say yes to tax increases and bond issues that would benefit public safety. The results of those efforts were mixed. . . .

But the measure failed to garner the two-thirds majority it needed to pass. City voters backed Measure A by 64 percent; county voters by only 59.6 percent.

The initiative was supported by both Los Angeles Police Chief William Bratton and county Sheriff Lee Baca. Revenue from the increase would have rebuilt the county's public safety budget, Baca told The Copley News Service, and helped the Los Angeles Police Department realize its goal of having a force of 10,000 or more officers.

But it was difficult to persuade voters to pay for more police and sheriff's deputies, said the two law enforcement officials. . . .

But while Los Angeles struggled in vain to win voter support for a tax increase for public safety, almost 70 percent of voters in Oakland approved Measure Y, an initiative that will bring in roughly $20 million a year through increases on property and parking taxes. . . .

With the revenues from Measure Y, the city will be able to expand the police force by 63 officers. Money will also be provided for prevention programs and social services programs aimed at helping parolees find work and keeping teenagers out of trouble.

In San Diego County, meanwhile, voters in El Cajon approved a sales-tax increase, from 7.75 percent to 8.25 percent, that will provide $62 million for new police and fire stations and an animal shelter. . . .

- In Clark County, Nev., voters passed a ballot proposal that will leave it to state legislators to decide whether the county's 7.5-percent sales tax should be increased to help fund public safety agencies.

  The nonbinding measure called Question 9 narrowly won, with 51.5 percent of the vote. Under the proposal, the tax would be raised by a quarter-cent in 2005 and by another quarter-cent in 2009. But before that can happen, legislators said they wanted assurances that county and Las Vegas officials will not use the funds to cover police staffing while giving the agencies smaller budget increases each year. . . .

- The East Cleveland, Ohio, Police Department was dealt a blow when a measure that would have allowed the City Council to raise property taxes without having to go to voters was soundly rejected.

A five-year, 10-mill operating levy, Issue 30's passage would have halted layoffs in the department. The East Cleveland force has already withstood two rounds of layoffs. The first, in May, wiped out all of the agency's support staff, including corrections officers, clerks and dispatchers. On Oct. 31, it laid off nine officers and four other employees.

- Voters in St. Peters, Mo., also voted no to a charter amendment that would have placed a 1.6 percent tax on all out-of-state purchases over $2,000.

The ballot failed by a 2-to-1 margin. It was the third time in the past seven years that St. Peters officials were turned down by the electorate.

The anticipated revenue, which was estimated to be roughly $1 million a year, would have gone into a general fund that pays for the municipality's essential services, including police protection.

*Source:* Reprinted with permission from *Law Enforcement News,* November 2004, pp. 1, 8. John Jay College of Criminal Justice (CCNY), 555 West 57th St., New York, N.Y. 10019.

# CASE STUDY

The following case study challenges the reader to consider what he or she would do as an administrator in a city that is experiencing severe financial times, and to confront the question of what kinds of services both inside and outside the agency might be cut or eliminated in order to maintain public safety. This scenario also points out the kinds of "crisis management" that require so much of an administrator's time and preclude the kinds of strategic planning efforts that should be done.

## The Emptying Horn of Plenty

The chief of police in a small (20,000 population) city has seen nearly one third of the agency's officers leave in the last year. Budget cuts, attrition, and better salaries in other regional agencies have been the impetus for the departures. Furthermore, the city council is proposing a 15 percent cut in the police budget for the coming year. Citizens are already complaining about delays in police responses and about having to drive to the police department to make complaints or to file reports. The county sheriff has offered in the local newspaper to provide backup for the city when needed, but the chief of police believes the sheriff to be power hungry and primarily motivated by a desire to absorb the city's police force into his agency. Severe cutbacks have already been made in the DARE and gang prevention programs, and other nonessential services have been terminated. A number of concerts, political rallies, and outdoor events—all of which are normally peaceful—will be held soon during the summer months, requiring considerable amounts of overtime; the chief's view is that "It's better to have us there and not be needed than vice versa." Federal grants have run out.

One of the chief's staff suggests that the chief propose to the city council a drastic reduction in the city's parks, streets, or fire department budget, those monies being transferred to the police budget. The council, in turn, already wants to explore the possibility of hiring private security services for some events. Exacerbating the situation is the fact that violent crimes are increasing in the jurisdiction.

### Questions for Discussion

1. What measures could the chief implement or propose to the council to slow or eliminate the resignations of sworn personnel?
2. How might the chief obtain more revenues or, alternatively, realize some savings for the department?
3. Should the chief go public with the idea of reducing budgets in the parks or other city departments?
4. How should the chief deal with the local sheriff's offer?

# Summary

This chapter focused on a singularly important area of financial administration, budgeting, and included its elements, formats, and potential pitfalls. Emphasis was placed on the need for administrators to develop skill in budget formulation and execution.

This chapter also discussed the budget process and different types of budgets. No single budgeting format is best; through tradition and personal preference, a hybrid format normally evolves in an organization. Nor should an administrator, under normal circumstances, surrender control of the organization's budget to another individual or body; the budget is too integral to planning, organizing, and directing programs and operations.

Finally, it was shown that particularly hard times have befallen state and local units of government since 9/11. In these extremely difficult times of fiscal exigency, the justice administrator should attempt to become knowledgeable about, and recommend, sound means for reducing expenditures through changes in policy.

# Questions for Review

1. What is a budget? How is it used?
2. What is a budget cycle? What is its importance in budgeting?
3. What is involved in formulating a budget? Its approval and its execution?
4. List four types of budget formats used in the past. Which type is used most frequently? What are its major advantages and component parts?
5. What are some of the very serious fiscal problems units of government are now experiencing, and what are some criminal justice policymakers doing to reform sentencing laws to reduce corrections expenditures?

# Notes

1. Quoted in Charles R. Swanson, Leonard Territo, and Robert W. Taylor, *Police Administration: Structures, Processes, and Behavior,* 6th ed. (Upper Saddle River, N.J.: Prentice Hall, 2005), p. 682.
2. James C. Snyder, "Financial Management and Planning in Local Government," *Atlanta Economic Review* (November/December 1973):43–47.
3. Aaron Wildavsky, *The Politics of the Budgetary Process,* 2nd ed. (Boston: Little, Brown, 1974), pp. 1–4.
4. Orin K. Cope, "Operation Analysis—The Basis for Performance Budgeting," in *Performance Budgeting and Unit Cost Accounting for Governmental Units* (Chicago: Municipal Finance Officers Association, 1954), p. 8.

5. Lester R. Bittel, *The McGraw-Hill 36-Hour Management Course* (New York: McGraw-Hill, 1989).

6. Ibid., p. 187.

7. Robert Townsend, *Further Up the Organization: How to Stop Management from Stifling People and Strangling Productivity* (New York: Alfred A. Knopf, 1984), p. 2.

8. Roland N. McKean, *Public Spending* (New York: McGraw-Hill, 1968), p. 1.

9. S. Kenneth Howard, *Changing State Budgeting* (Lexington, Ky.: Council of State Governments, 1973), p. 13.

10. Michael C. Thomsett, *The Little Black Book of Budgets and Forecasts* (New York: AMACOM, American Management Association, 1988), p. 38.

11. Quoted in V. A. Leonard and Harry W. More, *Police Organization and Management,* 7th ed. (Mineola, N.Y.: Foundation Press, 1987), p. 212.

12. Swanson, Territo, and Taylor, *Police Administration,* p. 693.

13. Adapted, with some changes, from Wildavsky, *Politics of the Budgetary Process,* pp. 63–123.

14. Lennox L. Moak and Kathryn W. Killian, *A Manual of Techniques for the Preparation, Consideration, Adoption, and Administration of Operating Budgets* (Chicago: Municipal Finance Officers Association, 1973), p. 5, with changes.

15. Lennis M. Knighton, "Four Keys to Audit Effectiveness," *Governmental Finance* **8** (September 1979):3.

16. The Comptroller General of the United States, *Standards for Audit of Governmental Organizations, Programs, Activities, and Functions* (Washington, D.C.: General Accounting Office, 1972), p. 1.

17. Ibid.

18. Peter F. Rousmaniere, ed., *Local Government Auditing* (New York: Council on Municipal Performance, 1979), Tables 1 and 2, pp. 10, 14.

19. Swanson, Territo, and Taylor, *Police Administration,* p. 707.

20. Allen Schick, *Budget Innovation in the States* (Washington, D.C.: Brookings Institution, 1971), pp. 14–15. Schick offers 10 ways in which the line-item budget fosters control.

21. Malchus L. Watlington and Susan G. Dankel, "New Approaches to Budgeting: Are They Worth the Cost?" *Popular Government* **43** (Spring 1978):1.

22. Jesse Burkhead, *Government Budgeting* (New York: Wiley, 1956), p. 11.

23. Larry K. Gaines, John L. Worrall, Mittie D. Southerland, and John E. Angell, *Police Administration,* 2nd ed. (New York: McGraw-Hill, 2003), p. 519.

24. Swanson, Territo, and Taylor, *Police Administration,* p. 710.

25. Ibid, p. 711.

26. Gaines, Southerland, and Angell, *Police Administration,* p. 519.

27. Ibid.

28. David Novick, ed., *Program Budgeting* (New York: Holt, Rinehart and Winston, 1969), p. xxvi.

29. Ibid., p. xxiv.

30. Council of State Governments, *State Reports on Five-Five-Five* (Chicago: Author, 1968).

31. International City Management Association, *Local Government Budgeting, Program Planning and Evaluation* (Washington, D.C.: Author, 1972):7.

32. Allen Schick, "The Road to PPBS: The Stages of Budget Reform," *Public Administration Review* **26** (December 1966):244.

33. Ibid.

34. Swanson, Territo, and Taylor, *Police Administration,* p. 712.

35. Peter A. Phyrr, "Zero-Base Budgeting," *Harvard Business Review* (November/December 1970):111–121; see also E. A. Kurbis, "The Case for Zero-Base Budgeting," *CA Magazine* (April 1986):104–105.

36. Joseph S. Wholey, *Zero-Base Budgeting and Program Evaluation* (Lexington, Mass.: Lexington Books, 1978), p. 8.

37. Donald F. Facteau and Joseph E. Gillespie, *Modern Police Administration* (Upper Saddle River, N.J.: Prentice Hall, 1978), p. 204.

38. Samuel C. Certo, *Principles of Modern Management: Functions and Systems,* 4th ed. (Boston: Allyn & Bacon, 1989):484–485.

39. George S. Minmier, "Zero-Base Budgeting: A New Budgeting Technique for Discretionary Costs," *Mid-South Quarterly Business Review* **14** (October 1976):2–8.

40. Louise E. Tagliaferri, *Creative Cost Improvement for Managers* (New York: Wiley, 1981), p. 7.

41. Ibid., p. 8.

42. Center on Budget and Policy Priorities, "A Brief Overview of State Fiscal Conditions and the Effects of Federal Policies on State Budgets," http://www.cbpp.org/10-22-03sfp4.htm, May 12, 2004 (accessed February 15, 2005).

43. Karen Springen, "A Taxing Procedure," *Newsweek* (February 21, 2005):10.

44. American Friends Service Committee, "Alternative Budget Suggestions for the State of Arizona Relative to Criminal Justice," March 2002, http://www.afsc.org/az/altbudg.htm (accessed February 15, 2005).

45. Hal Rubin, "Working Out a Budget," *Law and Order* (May 1989): 27–28.

# Chapter 17

# Technologies Now and for the Future

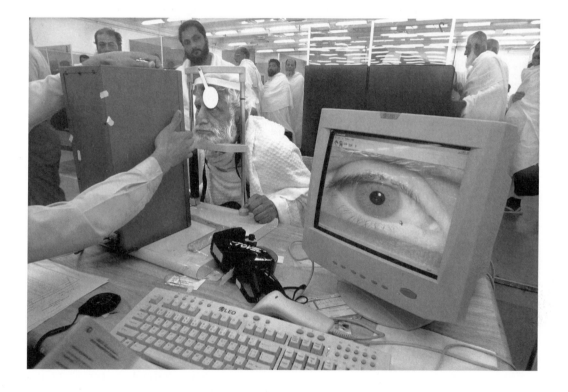

## Key Terms and Concepts

Augmented reality (AR)

Biometrics

Courtroom 21 Project

Crime mapping

Gang intelligence system

Less-than-lethal weapons

Offender management

Pursuit management

Reverse 911

Unmanned aerial vehicles (UAVs)

## Learning Objectives

As a result of reading this chapter, the student will:

- know how technologies can address the challenges of combatting terrorism
- be familiar with new and less-than-lethal weapons used by law enforcement
- understand the kinds of hardware and Web-based tools that are assisting law enforcement, as well as those that are in development
- have an understanding of the benefits of crime mapping and gang intelligence systems
- know what applications augmented reality (AR) and unmanned aerial vehicles (UAVs) promise for the future
- be able to distinguish among the six types of court technologies
- be familiar with the features of the Courtroom 21 Project
- be aware of technologies used in correctional facilities for inmate riots and for inmate management
- understand how probation and parole officers are partnering with police and using technologies to track violators
- know what the field of biometrics promises for the future

> *Everything that can be invented has been invented.*
> —Charles H. Duell,
> Commissioner of Patents, 1899

> *There is no reason for any individual to have a computer in their home.*
> —Kenneth Olsen, president and
> founder of Digital Equipment Corp., 1977

## Introduction

Technology consists primarily of tools for making people more productive. These tools provide administrators with opportunities to reshape the future with increased effectiveness and productivity.[1] Many of today's challenges for administrators involve these technologies. Communications systems that allow criminal justice agencies to share information, a more credible means of identification ensuring that a person is really who he says he is, a less-than-lethal weapon that is highly effective, security for the Internet—all these issues existed *before* September 11, 2001.[2]

Leadership is crucial to the development of new technologies. Without a leader championing these innovations, it is unlikely that the impetus needed for the cultural changes that technology requires will exist. These technologies and the accompanying policy must be consistent with the agency's overall goals and philosophy. The way in which administrators prepare for and address these administrative issues will largely determine the level of success enjoyed by any new technology project.[3] Other related challenges involve acquiring the necessary revenue for funding these technologies, as well as the slowness with which government moves because of the constraints in purchasing.

Because the police component is where the bulk of technological research and development—and use—has occurred in criminal justice, I begin by examining many developments in this field. Included is a discussion of technologies for combatting terrorism; then I present a variety of less-than-lethal tools, as well as several Web-based technologies and methods and some fascinating tools that are in development. Here two technologies are described that warrant being followed closely and are still in the early stages of development: augmented reality and unmanned aerial vehicles.

Following that, I review six major types of court technologies that exist, with emphasis on the Courtroom 21 Project, which is at the center of research and development in this field. Finally, I examine corrections, including what is being done technologically in institutions (prisons and jails) to manage inmates, as well as in probation and parole to identify violators. The chapter concludes with a brief discussion of the rapidly expanding field of biometrics.

# Law Enforcement Tools and Methods

As will be seen, police officers of the future will, and must, function in very different ways from officers of the past, especially with the specter of terrorism now at the forefront.

## *Technologies versus Terrorists*

The terrorist attacks on September 11, 2001, not only changed the way federal, state, and local law enforcement agencies approach their mission (they now must also protect citizens against attack from the outside, rather than only from within), but also set in motion research and development of new technologies for protecting against terrorist acts. Following are some technologies that are being or have been developed to assist in detecting and foiling terrorists:

- A low-dose X-ray imager sees through garments to detect hidden weapons, drugs, or other contraband (the September 11 terrorists slipped through checkpoints with box cutters).
- Surveillance cameras can scan faces and feed the images to a computer that scours a database of digital mug shots for a match (these devices were used during the Super Bowl in early 2001 in Tampa, Florida).[4]
- Better bomb-detecting technology is also being developed, including machines that perform a cross-sectional X-ray scan of checked baggage. Ion-sniffing swabs can find bomb residue on hand luggage.
- Also being considered for limited use are "smart cards"—IDs equipped with memory chips that store personal data and can track movements and transactions.[5]
- In the future we should also begin "connecting the dots with the data"—linking information from various arms of the criminal justice system about the people who commit crimes, based on "integrated justice" information systems. Just as search engines on the Web allow instantaneous access to vast sources of information, we must create a system in which secure facilities (like airports) can access resources like the terrorist "watch list" in the FBI's National Crime Information Center.
- It is also important to connect everyone with 211 and 311 because during times of perceived emergency, people call 911, which can be potentially catastrophic if the 911 system becomes inundated with nonemergency calls that clog out emergency calls; citizens with true emergencies or critical information for the police must have a means of communicating.
- A sport utility vehicle developed by Raytheon is a four-wheel-drive, self-contained, computer-controlled command and control center with wireless, cell and satellite communications that permit emergency workers at a "ground zero" to talk to one another, even with incompatible radios.[6]

Also in development are facial and fingerprint recognition technologies that are combined with an information engine. This system could snoop through public and private databases to establish behavior patterns of an individual as a way to flag deviations that could indicate links to terrorism; it could also be used to evaluate behavior of cargo container shippers, adding a layer of protection in a transportation segment that receives little scrutiny.[7]

## Recent Developments in Less-Than-Lethal Weapons

Police departments nationwide continue to look to new techniques of offender that offer **less-than-lethal weapons** as an alternative, "intermediate" weapon between the voice and the gun. Many less-than-lethal alternatives are relatively inexpensive for agencies to adopt and can significantly reduce a department's liability.[8]

The Taser enjoys increasing popularity among police agencies; by late 2004, more than 100,000 police officers at 5,500 police agencies were armed with Tasers. Critics including the American Civil Liberties Union, however, contend that, with more than 70 suspects nationwide having died after being shocked by the Taser from 1999 to 2004, greater controls need to be placed on its use. They argue that it should only be used in life-threatening situations, and that more study needs to be done on the Taser's effects on suspects who are agitated, intoxicated, mentally unstable, or who have preexisting heart ailments.[9]

Also introduced of late are two types of foam that may hold promise. One is supersticky: Intruders are drenched in a substance that, when exposed to the air, turns into taffylike glue. The other creates an avalanche of dense soap bubbles that leaves offenders unable to see or move but still able to breathe. Other chemical compounds, known as "slick'ems" and "stick'ems" make pavements either too sticky or too slippery for vehicles to move.[10]

There is also strong interest in beanbag rounds (sometimes called kinetic batons) and capture nets. Beanbag rounds (a pellet-loaded bag that unfurls into a spinning pancake) have become extremely popular. They have been adopted by police agencies across the country and have been successfully used to help end a number of standoffs.[11] A Spiderman-style net gun known as the WebShot is designed to wrap up and immobilize a suspect. The WebShot gun has been on the market since 1999 and is in trial use with the Los Angeles and San Diego Police Departments. WebShot is ideally used against an unarmed person who is being combative.[12]

The Less Than Lethal program of the National Institute of Justice coordinates research on such weapons, ensuring that they are technically feasible and also practical for police officers. In addition to the WebShot gun, the program recently provided funding for research into the following technologies[13]:

- The Laser Dazzler, a flashlight device designed to disorient or distract suspects with a green laser light
- The Sticky Shocker, a wireless projectile fired from a gas gun that sticks to the subject with glue or a barb, attaches to clothing, and delivers an electric shock
- The Ring Airfoil Projectile, a doughnut-shaped, hard-rubber weapon that is under redesign to also disperse a cloud of pepper powder on impact

Pepper spray, or oleoresin capsicumoc (OC), is now used by an estimated 90 percent of police agencies, according to the National Institute of Justice.[14] This spray inflames the mucus membranes of the eyes, nose, and mouth, causing a severe burning sensation for 20 minutes or less.[15] The spray is highly effective in subduing suspects without causing undue harm or long-term effects.[16] Another relatively new less-lethal tool is a compressed-air gun that fires small pellets filled with OC or other gases.[17]

## Crime Mapping

Computerized **crime mapping** has been termed "policing's latest hot topic."[18] For officers on the street, mapping puts street crime into an entirely new perspective; for administrators, it provides a way to involve the community in

# Exhibit 17.1
# Shocking Developments in Police Weaponry

They are called nonlethal weapons, but after the death of a college student who was shot with a pepper-ball gun and concerns that Tasers may have played a role in some in-custody fatalities, that once-useful designation no longer seems to fit.

Victoria Snelgrove, 21, died of a head injury on Oct. 21 when a projectile filled with pepper gas struck her in the eye. Boston police had been using the nonlethal device to control a hostile crowd.

Boston Police Commissioner Kathleen O'Toole temporarily suspended use of the weapon, an FN 303 pellet-spray gun, and within days appointed an independent panel headed by a former federal prosecutor to investigate Snelgrove's death.

Fatalities of the sort that occurred in Boston are unusual, experts say, but serious injuries are not. In July, 19-year-old Matthew Goldsich of Avon, Gonn., was hit in the eye with a rubber bullet during an altercation. Police responded to the rock-and-bottle-throwing melee by firing rubber bullets, pepper spray, and bean bag projectiles. The rubber bullet that hit Goldsich shattered his eye socket.

The electric stun gun has been a welcome addition to the nonlethal arsenal of more than 5,400 law-enforcement agencies nationwide, and has been used roughly 50,000 times in police situations, according to Taser International, the Scottsdale, Ariz-based company that manufactures the device.

Since 2001, however, 70 people have died after being shocked, including six who died in June—the most in any single month, The *New York Times* reported. Another newspaper, *The Arizona Republic,* published the results of a survey which found that in eight of 71 deaths following a Taser shock since 1999, the stun gun could not be ruled out as a contributing factor or cause of death by medical examiners.

Taser International contends that such deaths are due to drug overdoses or other factors that would have led to the same result anyway. Drug use was a common factor in 71 deaths cited by *The Republic.*

The type of shocks administered as part of training and those given to suspects in the field are quite different, The Times reported. Volunteers will often receive the 50,000-volt shock for a half-second or less; suspects are often hit repeatedly with the Taser and shocked for as long as five seconds. It can be even longer if police hold the trigger down.

Moreover, critics charge that using the Taser has become routine in cases where before its deployment, no force would have been used at all.

Miami officers shocked a first-grader this year, then in November jolted a 12-year-old girl. While Police Director Bobby Parker defended the decision to Taser the 6-year-old boy because he had threatened to injure himself with a piece of glass, he could not defend the use of the weapon on the girl. She had apparently been drunk and skipping school when she was shocked.

In another incident, a 9-year-old girl handcuffed by a South Tucson, Ariz., officer was shocked. In Kansas City, police zapped a 66-year-old woman while citing her for improper use of her car horn.

*Source:* Reprinted with permission from *Law Enforcement News,* December 2004, p. 11. John Jay College of Criminal Justice (CCNY), 555 West 57th St., New York, N.Y. 10019.

addressing its own problems by observing trends in neighborhood criminal activity. Crime mapping also offers crime analysts graphic representations of crime-related issues. Furthermore, detectives can use maps to better understand the hunting patterns of serial offenders and to hypothesize where these offenders might live.[19]

Computerized crime mapping combines geographic information from global positioning satellites with crime statistics gathered by a department's computer-aided dispatching (CAD) system and demographic data provided by private companies or the U.S. Census Bureau (some agencies acquire information from the Census Bureau's Internet home page). The result is a picture that combines disparate sets of data for a new perspective on crime. For example, a map of crimes can be overlaid with maps or layers of causative data: unemployment rates in the areas of high crime, locations of abandoned houses, population density, reports of drug activity, or geographical features (such as alleys, canals, or open fields) that might be contributing factors.[20] The hardware and software are available to nearly all police agencies, costing just a few thousand dollars.

Following are instances of successful outcomes using crime mapping:

- When an armored car was robbed in Toronto, dispatchers helped officers chase the suspects through a sprawling golf course using the mapping feature of the CAD system.
- The Illinois State Police map fatal accidents throughout the state and show which districts have specific problems. It can correlate those data with citations written, seatbelt use, and other types of enforcement information.
- The Salinas, California, Police Department maps gang territories and correlates socioeconomic factors with crime-related incidents. Murders are down 61 percent, drive-by shootings 31 percent, and gang-related assaults, 23 percent.[21]

The NIJ's Crime Mapping Research Center, established in 1997, provides information concerning research, evaluation, and training programs through its Web site.[21a]

Exhibit 17.2 discusses the use of interactive crime mapping on the Internet, in San Diego, California, and Figure 17.1 is the initial screen that appears when the user chooses "vehicle and traffic incidents" from the San Diego County Web site, providing information about auto thefts and burglaries as well as traffic accidents.

---

### EXHIBIT 17.2
### Interactive Crime Mapping on the Internet

Recently, San Diego County's Automated Regional Justice Information System (ARJIS) developed the first multiagency interactive crime mapping Web site in the nation, making interactive crime maps available to the public on the Internet. These systems not only enable citizens to obtain much more information than was previously available, but also preclude their having to make formal requests for information while freeing crime analysts to devote more time to analyzing crime instead of providing reports to the public. Now, anyone in the world can query and view certain crime, arrest, call, and traffic data for the county. Searches can be geographical (by street, neighborhood, police beat, or city), as well as by time of day or day of week. People access ARJIS for a variety of purposes, including wanting to learn about crime in their area, for a grant proposal, to support a debate on an issue, for citizen patrol, and even for real estate agent information.

*Source:* Adapted from *Crime Mapping News* [a Police Foundation newsletter] **3** (Summer 2001):1–6.

---

## Accident Investigation

Related to the aforementioned computerized crime mapping in law enforcement is the added use of global positioning satellites for accident investigation.

A multicar accident can turn a street or highway into a parking lot for many hours, sometimes days. There is the necessity for the police to collect evidence relating to the accident, including measurement and sketches of the scene and vehicle and body positions, skid marks, street or highway elevations, intersections, and curves. These tasks typically involve a measuring wheel, steel tape, pad, and pencil. The cost of traffic delays—especially for commercial truck operators—is substantial for each hour that traffic is stalled.

Some police agencies have begun using a global positioning system to determine such details as vehicle location and damage, elevation, grade, radii of curves, and critical speed. A transmitter takes a series of "shots" to gain the exact location and measurements of accident details such as skid marks, area of impact, and debris. That information is then downloaded into the system and the coordinates plotted onto an aerial shot of the intersection or roadway. With the aid of computer technology, the details are then superimposed onto the aerial shot, thus recreating the accident scene to scale. Finally, digital photos of the accident are incorporated into the final product, resulting in a highly accurate depiction of the accident. With a fatal or major injury accident, what once required several officers up to 18 hours' time is reduced to mere minutes.[22]

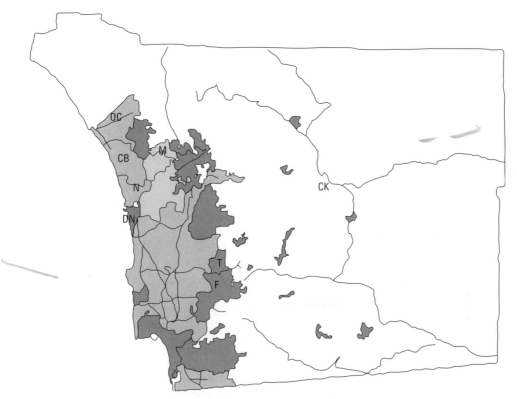

**Figure 17.1**

San Diego County's Automated Regional Justice Information System (ARJIS) map of
vehicle thefts, burglaries, and traffic accidents and citations; available at: http://www.
arjis.org/mapping/help/disclaimer.html. *Source:* City of El Cajon Police Department.

Geographic profiling is most effective when used in conjunction with other
information. For example, the Washington State Attorney General's office uses a
homicide investigation and tracking system (HITS) that includes crime-related
databases and links to vice and gang files, sex offender registries, corrections
and parole records, and Department of Motor Vehicle databases. HITS can simultaneously scan these databases. When an agency in the state has a major crime
in its jurisdiction, the case is loaded into a central system, which scans every
database and linking file for connections by comparing eyewitness descriptions
of a suspect and vehicle. It then builds a dataset containing profiles of the offender, the victims, and the incidents. The dataset then goes into a geographic
information system (GIS), which is described later.[23]

## *Ending High-Speed Pursuits*

Tremendous potential exists for injury, property damage, and liability resulting
from high-speed chases by police; indeed, this is such a concern that some

agency administrators have developed **pursuit management** policies that completely prohibit such activities by officers.

Tire spikes can be deployed when a fleeing vehicle is approaching and then retracted so that other vehicles and police cars can pass safely. Tire spikes often do not work, however, or result in the suspect losing control of the vehicle (although some spike devices are designed to prevent this by breaking off in the tires and thus deflating them slowly).[24] One device has been developed using a short pulse of electrical current to disrupt electronic devices that are critical to the continued operation of the vehicle ignition system. Once pulsed, the vehicle rolls to a controlled stop similar to the effect of running out of fuel and will not restart until the affected parts are replaced.[25]

## Crime Scenes

Several technologies exist or are being developed relating to crime scene investigations. Three-dimensional computer-aided drafting (3D CAD) software is available for a few hundred dollars. By working in 3D, CAD users can create scenes that can be viewed from any angle. Technical evidence can be visualized by nontechnical observers. Juries can "view" crime scenes and see the location of evidence; they can view just what the witness says he or she saw. Police input the exact dimensions and get a scaled drawing. A 5-day, 40-hour course in 3D CAD is available for police investigators, traffic accident reconstructionists, and evidence technicians.[26]

Crime scene evidence is often too sketchy to yield an obvious explanation of what happened. New software called Maya has been developed for this field, called forensic animation; this software helps experts to determine what probably occurred. Maya is so packed with scientific calculations that it can create a virtual house from old police photos and replicate the effects of several types of forces, including gravity: how a fall could or could not have produced massive injuries, how flames spread in a house fire, and the way smoke cuts a pilot's visibility in a plane crash.[27]

The Federal Department of Energy is also testing a prototype laptop computer equipped with digital video and still cameras, laser range finders, and a global positioning system. A detective using it can beam information from a crime scene back to a laboratory to get input from experts. Researchers are also working on a chip that would give police the ability to process more evidence, including DNA samples, at the crime scene, eliminating the risk of contamination en route to the lab.[28]

## Gang Intelligence Systems

The escalating problem of street gangs has prompted many police departments to search for a tool that could help them to deal with the problem. Several agencies now use a **gang intelligence system** to collect information in a database, allowing officers to enter and access key pieces of data such as gang names, vehicles, weapons, suspect associates, and incident dates. Even if an

EXHIBIT 17.3
## Cops Get an Extra Set of Eyes

It's a device to make a film student jealous.

"The Detective" is a video system that can analyze crime-scene tapes taken from several different angles. It can slow them down, splice and clarify images, magnify them, put the same camera angles together, and basically watch an incident unfold from beginning to end as if it were a movie.

That's just what police detectives in Roanoke, Va:, did when a bank was robbed just one day after the department received the product on Jan. 20. Investigators spent half the night teaching themselves how to use the equipment.

"The Detective" accounts for about half of the $70,000 spent on equipment upgrades in creating the department's new Criminal Intelligence and Technology Unit. Other elements will include thermal imaging and night vision equipment.

"We're just putting it all under one roof, so to speak," Detective Mark Chandler told The Roanoke Times & World News.

Trying to piece together the bank-robbery tape was like putting together a puzzle. Like many businesses, the bank had tried to get the most out of its video-surveillance system. That meant six different camera angles, all flashing by at high speed.

"It's just the fact that we're now able to slow it down to the point where we're able to pick out details," said Chandler, one of the seven investigators assigned to the CITU.

Another new program called "3D Eyewitness" will allow the user to create a three-dimensional crime scene drawn to the measurements taken by detectives.

*Source:* Reprinted with permission from *Law Enforcement News,* July 2004, p. 1. John Jay College of Criminal Justice (CCNY), 555 West 57th St., New York, NY 10019.

officer has a small piece of information to work with, such as a nickname or partial license plate number of a suspect's car, the system's cross-referencing function connects that information to additional information in the database about gang members, their activities, addresses, descriptions, and photos. Officers can even access the database in their patrol cars by using laptops. The system also allows photographs to be stored and linked with other information about suspects. A statewide gang intelligence system, California's CAL/GANG, is a relational database that holds and categorizes everything from nicknames to tattoos on suspected or known gang members. This system, which has been credited for solving a number of high-visibility gang crimes, is now being considered by other states, including Florida, that have a significant gang problem.[29]

## *Other Technologies*

Even a small agency can afford a laptop and a modem to send encrypted data to officers in the field.[30] A growing number of U.S. police departments, including small agencies, are using laptop computers with wireless connections to crime and motor vehicle databases. Officers can access court documents, in-house police department records, and a computer-aided dispatch system, as well as enter license numbers into their laptop computers. Through various databases, the police can locate drivers with outstanding warrants, expired or suspended licenses, and criminal backgrounds.[31]

Chapter 3 discussed community-oriented policing and problem solving (COPPS). Technology can certainly assist in this endeavor. Some cities now employ a sophisticated system that uses an integrated CAD system, mobile data terminals (or MDTs, in-car computers), and message switching and routing tools to collect, store, monitor, and retrieve information needed for COPPS. They can sort data to present information to citizens in an easy-to-understand format at neighborhood meetings.[32]

Some cities are also developing a geographical information system that enables officers to plot criminal activity on an electronic map. Layers of information can then be added to the map to create a picture of crime trends.[33]

Some police agencies have begun using a version of a surveying instrument that electronically measures and records distances, angles, elevations, and the names and features of objects. With this system, officers can spend an hour or so getting measurements at major traffic accidents, push a button, and have the system draw lines pertinent to the accident to scale; this process enables officers to get 40 percent more measurements in about 40 percent of the time, thus allowing the traffic flow to resume much more quickly. This system is also being used at major crime scenes. Its only drawback is that it cannot be used in heavy rain or snow.[34]

One tool used routinely during a drunk-driving stop is a small, portable machine that resembles a video-game cartridge used as a breath-screening device. The DUI suspect blows into it, and the officer takes the reading of the amount of alcohol in the suspect's system. Law enforcement officials hope that this device can be adapted so that the test can be used in court. If so, it would save time in transporting DUI suspects, testing them, and finding that their blood level was below the legal limit because of the elapsed time.[35]

Following are brief descriptions of other newly developed technologies for use by the police:

- *VINE (Victim Information and Notification Everyday)* is an automated notification system allows registered users to know almost immediately of any change in the status of a particular offender. This information can be sent via telephone, e-mail, or pager to crime victims, usually within 15 minutes of a change in an offender's status. Users can also be notified of release, escape, transfer, sentence expiration date, or death of an inmate.[36]
- Police reports often require 45 minutes to an hour of writing. With a *voice recognition* system, a software program uses a police knowledge base

EXHIBIT 17.4
Car 54, Where Are You?

Along with the ability to file reports, look up criminal histories and watch live dispatch entries from their cars, police officers in Sandy, Utah, can now see the locations of their own cruisers and those of other active duty personnel on their vehicles' computer screens.

The Auto Vehicle Locator (AVL), a global positioning system, was installed last year as part of a $70,000 technology upgrade of the department's fleet that was paid for with a federal grant. It allows officers at command posts and in vehicles to track the location of any patrol vehicle.

According to the agency, the innovation will drastically reduce response times by sending the officer closest to the scene, and will ensure that neighborhoods are being watched by logging all patrol activity. Moreover, its ability to track officers to a location could prove a life-saving feature. . . .

While concerns about loss of privacy had been raised when the technology was considered several years ago, those appear to have fallen by the wayside. There have been no complaints lately, said Capt. Gary Cox of South Jordan, which also uses the AVL system.

"The whole technology package is being received very well," Chapman told The Salt Lake Tribune. "We just want to reassure [officers] that we're not out there to be Big Brother."

*Source:* Reprinted with permission from *Law Enforcement News,* June 2004, p. 8. John Jay College of Criminal Justice (CCNY), 555 West 57th St., New York, N.Y. 10019.

combined with report-form templates that prompt with on-screen questions to which the officer responds verbally. This technology helps police officers to input information without having to type it all in.[37]

- A new *video camera* has been developed that is so small it can be hidden in a police badge, allowing officers to discreetly videotape every field interrogation, routine traffic stop, and domestic disturbance they encounter. The device, sure to stir a personal liberty debate, could also put a new twist on police brutality litigation.[38]

- *Global positioning system (GPS) technology* is being used around the world for finding drowning victims in deep oceans, rivers, and lakes with zero visibility.[39]

- More than 125 police agencies in the United States are using *electric bicycles.* They look like normal mountain bikes, but the flip of a switch provides a turbo power boost of electric power enabling the bike to attain a speed of up to 20 miles per hour, allowing for faster acceleration for climbing hills.[40]

### *Reverse 911*

**Reverse 911** systems give public safety and police agencies a viable option for alerting the public in times of impending danger, such as escaped or dangerous individuals, missing persons, a string of crimes, or chemical spills. Citizens and businesses can be warned quickly by phone by the system. An operator records a message, brings up a map on a computer screen, designates a target area or chooses a preloaded map area, and the system dials all the numbers in the database within that targeted area and sends the recorded message.[41]

## Future Attractions: Augmented Reality and Unmanned Aerial Vehicles

Two technologies that warrant being followed closely and are still in the early stages of development are **augmented reality (AR)** and **unmanned aerial vehicles (UAVs)**.

AR combines the real and the virtual, displaying information in real time.[42] AR is already here: In television broadcasts, yellow first-down lines are superimposed on a football field, and driver and speed information is tagged to race cars as they speed around a track. At a more advanced level, today's military fighter pilots can observe critical information superimposed on the cockpit canopy.[43]

Fundamentally, an AR system consists of a wearable computer, a head-mounted display, and tracking and sensing devices along with advanced software and virtual three-dimensional applications. AR has many possible uses in the future of policing, such as the following:

- Real-time language translation, along with data on cultural customs and traditions
- Real-time intelligence about crimes and criminals in the patrol area
- Facial, voiceprint, and other biometric recognition data of known criminals
- Integration of chemical, biological, and explosives sensors that detect local contamination
- Accessibility of scalable, three-dimensional maps (with building floor plans, utilities systems, and so forth),[44] including the ability for police SWAT officers to use advanced optics to zoom and use thermal and infrared imaging to locate fleeing criminals, as well as distinguish "friend-or-foe" and reduce or eliminate friendly-fire casualties.
- Speaker-recognition technology for investigative personnel to accurately match voices against those of known criminals and lip-read from a distance
- Thermal imaging to improve interrogations by indicating truthfulness of suspects' statements police and corrections

- Video feeds for supervisors from personnel on the street or prison so they could determine what their personnel are seeing in real time and monitor the physical status of their personnel during critical incidents.[45]

Certainly a number of issues would accompany the planned adoption of AR. Would AR bring us dangerously close to a real-life "Robo-Cop" scenario in the future? The answer to that question is in the eye of the beholder. It cannot be questioned, however, that AR technology and the aforementioned uses will soon be available and could provide the criminal justice system with a degree of efficiency and effectiveness never seen before.

Another technology that warrants being followed closely is that of unmanned aerial vehicles (UAVs)—powered aerial vehicles that do not carry human operators. They use aerodynamic forces to provide air vehicle lift, and are designed to carry nonlethal payloads for missions such as reconnaissance, command and control, and deception. UAVs are directed by a ground or airborne controller, and come in a variety of designs from those that could fit into a backpack to one with a longer wingspan than a Boeing 747. There are more than two dozen companies in the United States involved in production or prototype UAV products.[46]

Although UAV research and development is now almost totally in the military domain, their potential uses for law enforcement are limitless. As examples, a low-flying UAV could patrol a given stretch of road, on vigil for high-speed offenders; images could be sent to a monitor in a patrol car along with rate of speed, direction of travel, and GPS coordinates, which can be map overlaid for the officer on the ground.[47] UAVs could also provide real-time reconnaissance, surveillance, and target spotting in a variety of situations.[48]

Other technologies that are being explored by the military and private research laboratories in certain situations include the following:

- A portable, battery-powered sonic rifle that fires "bullets" of earsplitting noise, as high as 140 decibels, creating the equivalent of an instant migraine headache.
- A sprayable slime that makes walkways and other surfaces as slippery as ice.
- The world's foulest odor, termed a "souped-up version of human waste."

Each of these projects focuses on exploiting the body's senses.[49]

# Court Technologies

"Courts are their records." This adage captures the essence of the important role played by the courts in serving as the primary repository for the records of the community's arrests, convictions, births, deaths, marriages, divorces, and so on. In so doing, lawyers, judges, and society generally create a blizzard of paper documents daily, all of which require sorting, filing, and indexing for later retrieval. Many courthouses have file cabinets occupying every inch of wall space, as well as basements filled with boxes of decaying records.

This section reviews the six fundamental types of technology that assist the courts in accomplishing their mission as a repository of information, resolving their paper burden, and improving their overall functioning. I also view a futuristic court that has been created to showcase technological products.

## Six Types

Court technologies can be categorized into six areas: data systems, office automation, court records, testimony, evidence, and legal information.

1. Data systems are computer-based tools used to organize information and assist work processes. The court case management system is the most important data system used by the judicial branch. It consists of five essential components: key case information in a highly structured format, computer instructions or programs, computer and telecommunications hardware, people to use and manage the system, and operations procedures to link the work of people with the work of the machines. In addition, courts may use data systems for jury, budget, personnel, and similar functions. Technologies allow remote access to court information and electronic transactions with the court through dial-up lines, kiosks, and the Internet.

2. Office automation technology involves tools that improve personnel effectiveness and productivity, including document production, organization of information, communication, financial and statistical analysis, education and planning, and managing work.

3. Court records technologies manage the documents filed with the court and include imaging, fax filing, workflow, document management systems, and electronic filing. These technologies improve the efficiency of court staff. Costs are reduced for courts, litigants, and the public because documents can be processed more quickly, and access to information is enhanced dramatically. Electronic filing has the potential to become an exciting advance for courts that wish to streamline their expanding caseloads.[50] Courts are realizing that computer filing and retrieval of documents can be faster, less expensive, and more accurate and secure than the traditional method; furthermore, computerized documents require far less space to store than paper. Another growing solution to the courts' record-keeping problem is document imaging. Courts enter information into case-processing systems from numerous sources. Some documents submitted directly to the administrator's or clerk's office could be scanned into the imaging system locally. Other documents come from external sources such as attorneys, police and probation agencies, and community services. These documents could be scanned into the system remotely or faxed directly into the system.[51] Figure 17.2 shows a sample page of document imaging.

4. Testimony technologies are used to facilitate, capture, store, and reproduce testimony offered in a courtroom. They include audio and video recording, videoconferencing, language translation, and computer-aided transcription. Videoconferencing is becoming one of the most demanded systems in

**Figure 17.2**

A sample document imaging screen. *Source:* National Center for State Courts, *Court Technology Reports, Vol. 4* (Williamsburg, Va.: Author 1992), p. 15. Copyright 1992. Used with permission.

---

### EXHIBIT 17.5
### Technology at the Trial

An excellent example of technologies in the courtroom is testing that is now occurring in the Courtroom 21 Project. There, in a mock trial involving a federal manslaughter case (where a company is charged with using a stent that was not approved, by the Food and Drug Administration, resulting in a patient's death), instead of telling jurors what happened, the Courtroom 21 project attempts to use new technologies involving holographic evidence and "immersive virtual reality" to *show* jurors what happened, actually putting them in the environment where the alleged crime occurred. Jurors viewed holographic images of the human circulatory system; the image appears three dimensional when a juror moves his or her head. With immersive virtual reality, jurors don special goggles and view the operating room as if they were actually there—some even become dizzy. Data from the operating room are entered into a computer, which forms the images seen through sophisticated goggles.

*Source:* Jim McKay, "Technology on Trial," *Government Technology* (December 2002): 82.

today's courts. The primary components of a simple videoconferencing system are television cameras, monitors, microphones, speakers, and a communications network.[52] Courts in at least 30 states use video arraignments for first-appearance felonies and misdemeanors,[53] which represent about three fourths of new criminal cases each year. Approximately 200 video arraignment sites exist in state court systems. Video arraignment provides several benefits, including reduced security risks associated with transporting and handling inmates, reduced overcrowding of courthouse holding facilities, improved custody conditions for defendants while they await arraignment, improvements in the overall efficiency of court proceedings, reduced tension levels among guards and prisoners, minimized delays, and reduced or eliminated commingling of first-time offenders with hardened offenders.[54]

5.  Evidence technologies assist lawyers in presenting evidence in the courtroom. They allow attorneys to offer clearer and more convincing illustrations of the points they are trying to make to a judge or jury. Tools include sound and visual reinforcement devices, document cameras, computers, and projectors.

6.  Legal information technologies aid access to case law, statutes, rules, and other legal materials. Large mainframe-based depositories of legal materials have been supplemented by CD-ROM–based legal collections and legal databases accessed through the Internet.[55]

This list demonstrates that technologies are changing the way the courts work. Clearly, members of the judicial branch—especially chief judges and court administrators—must be knowledgeable about their application, cost, and policy implications while understanding that some traditional ways of doing things must become obsolete. The electronic filing of information is especially critical for the future of courts as they attempt to become less laden with, and dependent on, their mountains of paper.

## *The Courtroom 21 Project*

The College of William and Mary and the National Center for State Courts unveiled the **Courtroom 21 Project** in 1993 in Williamsburg, Virginia; at that time, it was the most technologically advanced courtroom in the United States, although some of its original features are not in use today. Nonetheless, this project demonstrates how technology can enrich the legal process by assisting court actors.[56]

Now termed the "dream technology court" and the "world's center for experimental work,"[57] Courtroom 21 has approximately 25 affiliates worldwide, each using Courtroom 21 technologies in actual court proceedings.[58] The hub of the project, and its experimental center, is the McGlothlin Courtroom at William and Mary University.[59] A retrofitted courtroom into which the latest in modern technology has been installed, it is the most technologically advanced trial and appellate courtroom in the world. The facility is capable of carrying out almost anything that needs to be done in a courtroom, including electronic filing; Internet-based case docketing; sophisticated electronic case management; electronic motions, briefs, and arguments; multiple concurrent appearances by judges, lawyers, parties, and

---

⚖️ **EXHIBIT 17.6**
**Instant Access for All, and a Speedier Court**

A new electronic imaging system is greatly assisting circuit courts in Martin County, Florida, and could lead to a near-paperless court in the future. The new imaging system links the three county sheriff's offices, the state attorney general's office, the public defender, and judges. Judges who rotate within a four-county circuit now have access to all cases. When an arrest is made, an arrest affidavit is scanned and goes into a queue at the clerk's office. It is then assigned a court case number and is available for judges to peruse for first appearances, which by law must occur within the first 24 hours after arrest. With the arrest

information, such as criminal history or results of a Breathalyzer test, on an electronic filing system and with video conferencing, judges can expedite first appearances without transporting suspects from the jail to the courthouse and without asking clerks to hustle paperwork from county to county. Local public defenders can keep up on all the new information that is added to each case rather than make trips to the courthouse; the system also speeds case processing for the state attorney general, who has 21 days to file charges in a case.

*Source:* Jim McKay, "Swifter Justice," *Government Technology* (June 2002): 32.

---

witnesses; technology-based evidence presentation; immediate Web-published court records; connectivity at the counsel table for lawyers; technology-aided foreign language interpretation; jury box computers for information display (for documents, real evidence, live or recorded video, transcription, and the usual graphics—charts, diagrams, pictures); and LEXIS legal research. Judges and counsel are provided immediate access to legal resources through the LEXIS online legal database. If an unanticipated legal question arises during trial, judges and counsel can use the computers to consult the database, and much more.

The best-known element of Courtroom 21 is its annual laboratory trial—a 1-day simulated case, traditionally presided over by a federal judge and decided by a community jury (one such case is described in Exhibit 17.5).

# Institutional Corrections

## *Putting down a Riot*

With America's prison population growing (see Chapter 10), the need for corrections officers to develop tactics and equipment to handle outbreaks of violence has also risen. Although full-scale riots are rare in American prisons, potentially violent situations (such as inmates' refusing to leave their cells) can occur almost daily.

*...e* are wall-climbing reconnaissance robots and futuristic *...s"* designed to sweep rioters into a corner or stun them with a *...* There is a Hydro-Force fogger (a cross between a fire extin- *...can* of Mace). A rolling barrier with wheels and side shields pre- *...s* from being struck by thrown objects.[60] A "stinger" grenade that *...d* emits dozens of hard rubber pellets is particularly useful in a *...* yard riot.

*...tions* officers often train with such devices in full view of the inmates *...* he kinds of tools that can be employed. According to one prison ad- ministrator, what separates prison professionals from inmates is constant train- ing and measured, unflappable control.[61]

## Offender Management

Technology is changing methods of **offender management** as administrators increasingly adopt Web-based systems to manage the flow of information. New Web-based technology is now used to educate prisoners, treat prisoners who are addicted to drugs or are sex offenders, and provide vocational training. Prison administrators now keep accurate records of inmates' purchases for items in the prison store, payments to victims and their families, and other reasons for which money flows in and out of prisoners' bank accounts.[62] Automated systems con- trol access gates and doors, individual cell doors, and the climate in cells and other areas of the prison. Corrections agencies have also used computers to con- duct presentence investigations, supervise offenders in the community, and train correctional personnel. With computer assistance, jail administrators receive daily reports on court schedules, inmate rosters, time served, statistical reports, maintenance costs, and other data.

## Automated Direct-Supervision in Jails

Direct-supervision jails are springing up across the country, eschewing typical jail cells with steel bars. Some of these facilities are replacing the bars with bar- coded wristbands and state-of-the-art computerized information management systems. As one data communications engineer stated, "Everything from the toi- lets to the telephones is fully computerized" in these facilities.[63]

The information technology package used in these kinds of facilities in- cludes live-scan fingerprinting, an automated fingerprint identification system, digitized mugshots, and computerized inmate and records management. Each inmate's wristband is keyed into the central computer system, which contains his or her name, physical description, picture, and prisoner number; the system is used to track each inmate's location, visitors, library use, medical treatment, and court appointments. The system is expected to reduce costs, provide a new level of records integrity, and increase the safety of both officers and inmates by allowing the administrators to develop a completely cashless inmate society. Without cash and with limits set on how much an inmate can spend each week, correctional officers hope to curtail contraband problems. This cashless system virtually eliminates the illicit transactions that once were common because the administration can now regulate and monitor the flow of goods and services.[64]

## *"Virtual Visits" to Hospitals and Courtrooms*

Prison and jail inmates make frequent visits to hospitals and courtrooms, which poses public safety concerns. In Ohio alone, 40,000 inmate trips to and from medical facilities were eliminated because videoconferencing technology made medical consultations available from within the institution. An onsite prison physician or nurse assists with the physical part of the examination, taking cues from the offsite specialist via video and relaying information such as electrocardiogram and blood pressure data.[65]

Increasingly, prisons are using video not only for medical visits, but also for arraignments, parole violation hearings, and distance learning.

# Probation and Parole

## *Corrections–Police Interface: Sharing Information*

An excellent example of how two subsystems can work toward the common goal of getting offenders off the streets is given by the system in effect in Portland, Oregon. There, the county's probation and parole agencies rely on the Portland Police Bureau (PPB) as its eyes and ears in keeping track of their clients.

When an officer runs a check on a subject with his or her in-car computer, the system searches through the PPB's modified CAD dispatching system and searches the state's data system for information on the subject. If he or she is on probation or parole, a screen is generated and sent to the officer to fill in. The screen contains queries on the subject's circumstances, such as whether drugs, alcohol, or weapons are involved, or other situations that might constitute a violation of the subject's probation or parole conditions. The screen also solicits the officer's remarks on, for example, the subject's being in proximity to a known drug house, the persons he or she is associated with, and so on.[66] If a probationer or parolee is found to be in violation of his or her conditions, in a matter of minutes the officer will receive a request to detain the individual.

Exhibit 17.7 shows another good example of partnering between the police and corrections personnel, in this case in tracking sexual predators.

## *Kiosk Check-in for Probationers*

A relatively new computer system allows probationers who pose little or no public risk and need little personal supervision to check in from a remote location rather than make a trip to the probation officer's office. The probationer simply pushes a few buttons at an electronic kiosk to show he or she has not left town and perhaps breathes into a Breathalyzer if abstention from alcohol is a condition of probation. The system is user-friendly, accessible, and works without invading privacy.[67]

---

## Exhibit 17.7
## Technology on the Trail of Sexual Predators

All 50 states have now enacted some means for tracking sex offenders. Pinellas County, Florida, is one jurisdiction that goes beyond mere tracking, proactively using technology to track sex offenders and to enforce restrictions on where they can live. Florida law prohibits sex offenders from living within 1,000 feet of sensitive facilities or places where children congregate, such as schools, day care centers, beaches, or parks. Therefore, before an offender can move from city to city, the state department of corrections or a county sheriff's office must verify that the intended address is outside the 1,000-foot buffer. To accomplish this task, a Web-based, GIS crime-analysis system was developed that is capable of accessing and integrating data in a central repository. A sex predator/offender-tracking (SPOT) unit within the sheriff's office develops maps and reports that are sent to probation offices in the field via the county's intranet. When the SPOT unit receives notice of a proposed destination address for an offender or predator on parole, the officer pulls up a map of the area, accesses a list of sensitive facilities and their addresses, and draws a 1,000-foot buffer around the address in question. If any facilities are within the buffer, the move is denied.

*Source:* Bill McGarigle, "Picking Up the Trail," *Government Technology* (October 2001): 56.

---

The kiosks are strategically located and linked to a network of personal computers in the probation department. During the initial meeting with a probation officer, a probationer's biometric keys (fingerprints, voice, retina scan, signature, hand structure) and a digital photo of the face are captured electronically. They are entered, along with case-specific information, into the database. The system's server can be programmed to expect check-ins from several times a day to weekly, monthly, or longer intervals. Specific questions can be written for each client. A probationer may stop at any kiosk, where a biometric sample is taken via scanner and compared to the one collected during enrollment. Once identification is established, the probationer may check in. The kiosk operates every day, serving a maximum of 180 people per day.[68]

## A Body of Evidence: Biometrics

A technology that was growing rapidly even before the September 11 terrorist attacks involves **biometrics:** a system that converts the patterns of the iris, fingertip, hand, or face into a badge of identity. U.S. sales of biometric devices nearly doubled from 2000 to 2001, from $76.8 million to $160.3 million.[69] Employees at some businesses punch in and out by placing their hand on a reader, as do schoolchildren, who have their finger-scan verified for enrollment in lunch programs.[70] Although such systems are far from perfect and still contain glitches, they have widespread potential to boost security and convenience, this country. These technologies also have their detractors, who worry about issues of privacy, prompting calls for laws that would regulate how biometric data could be collected and used.[71]

## For More Information

Those wishing to learn more about the new developments in technology may find the Web address http://www.govtech.net helpful. This resource provides information about new products, solutions to problems, jobs, training resources, and conferences. For Internet access to the National Criminal Justice Reference Service Online, use Telnet to access ncjrsbbs.aspensys.com or Gopher to access ncjrs.aspensys.com. The United Nations Crime and Justice Information Network can be reached at http://uncjin.org/. Many more relevant Web sites are provided in Appendix I.

## Summary

This chapter reviewed several exciting technological advances that are in use by, or are being developed for, law enforcement, courts, and corrections organizations. Readers, especially administrators, managers, and supervisors, are encouraged to keep abreast of advances in this area because in this age of computer technology—and terrorism—almost anything is possible.

## Questions for Review

1. What are some of the latest developments in less-than-lethal weapons for the police?
2. How are technologies assisting with the fight against terrorism and in crime mapping? Tracking sexual predators and accident investigation? Gang problems and high-speed pursuits?
3. Explain how augmented reality (AR) and unmanned aerial vehicles (UAVs) function and the kinds of uses they may provide when deployed in law enforcement.
4. What are the six major technological capabilities now in use in the nation's courts? What are some of the futuristic technological items or methods found in a Courtroom 21 Project setting?

5. What can technologies offer to correctional institutions for putting down a riot? Managing inmates?

6. Explain what is meant by biometrics, as well as its potential advantages and problems.

7. What advances in probation and parole are being used to help to identify violators?

# Notes

1. Lawrence P. Webster, "How Technology Can Help Court Leaders Address the Justice Needs of a Multicultural Society in the Twenty-first Century," *The Court Manager* **15**(3) (2000):48.

2. Jim McKay, "When the Dust Settles," *Government Technology* (*Supplement: Crime and the Tech Effect*) (April 2002):5.

3. Gerald W. Schoenle, "Mobile Computing Policy Perspectives: The Buffalo Experience," *The Police Chief* (September 2001):38.

4. "Surveillance Cameras Stir Up Static," *Law Enforcement News* ( July/August 2001):13.

5. Dana Hawkins and David LaGesse, "Tech vs. Terrorists," *U.S. News and World Report* (October 8, 2001):16–17.

6. Ibid.

7. John Croft, "Aerospace Giants Repackage Military Technology for Home," *Aviation Week & Space Technology* (October 21, 2002):67–68.

8. "Rethinking Stopping Power," *Law Enforcement News* (November 15, 1999):1, 9.

9. "Civil Rights Advocates Calling for Restrictions on Stun Guns," *Reno Gazette Journal* (Associated Press), September 27, 2004, p. 4B.

10. John Barry and Tom Morganthau, "Soon, 'Phasers on Stun'," *Newsweek* (February 7, 1994):24–25.

11. Ibid.

12. Luis Cabrera, "Police Explore 'Less-Than-Lethal' Weapons," Associated Press ( June 19, 2000).

13. Ibid.

14. "Rethinking Stopping Power," *Law Enforcement News* (November 15, 1999):5.

15. "Effectiveness Times Three," *Law Enforcement News* (May 15, 1993):1.

16. Ibid., p. 6.

17. "Rethinking Stopping Power," p. 5.

18. Lois Pilant, "Computerized Crime Mapping," *The Police Chief* (December 1997):58.

19. Dan Sadler, *Exploring Crime Mapping* (Washington, D.C.: U.S. Department of Justice, National Institute of Justice, Crime Mapping Research Center, 1999), p. 1.

20. Pilant, "Computerized Crime Mapping," p. 58.

21. Ibid., pp. 66–67.

21a. National Institute of Justice, Crime Mapping Research Center, http://www.ojp.usdoj.gov/cmrc (accessed September 19, 2005).

22. Alison Bath, "Accident scene investigation is high tech," *Reno Gazette Journal* [Sparks Today section], November 18, 2003, p. 4.

23. Bill McGarigle, "Crime Profilers Gain New Weapons," *Government Technology,* **10** (December 1997):28–29.

24. Ibid.

25. http://www.jaycor.com/jaycor_main/web-content/eme_ltl_auto.html (accessed September 20, 2005).

26. Tod Newcombe, "Adding a New Dimension to Crime Reconstruction," *Government Technology* 9 (August 1996):32.

27. John McCormick, "Scene of the Crime," *Newsweek* (February 28, 2000):60.

28. Joan Raymond, "Forget the Pipe, Sherlock: Gear for Tomorrow's Detectives," *Newsweek* (June 22, 1998):12.

29. Raymond Dussault, "CAL/GANG Brings Dividends," *Government Technology* (December 1998):124.

30. Tod Newcombe, "Bandwidth Blues," *Government Technology* 9 (August 1996):1, 52.

31. Kaveh Ghaemian, "Small-Town Cops Wield Big-City Data," *Government Technology* 9 (September 1996):38.

32. Justine Kavanaugh, "Community Oriented Policing and Technology," *Government Technology* 9 (March 1996):14.

33. Ibid.

34. Bill McGarigle, "Electronic Mapping Speeds Crime and Traffic Investigations," *Government Technology* 9 (February 1996):20–21.

35. Justine Kavanaugh, "Drunk Drivers Get a Shot of Technology," *Government Technology* 9 (March 1996):26.

36. Richard Ehisen, "One Step Ahead," *Government Technology* (April 2002):42.

37. Keith W. Strandberg, "Law Enforcement Computers and Software," *Law Enforcement Technology* (May 1998):40.

38. Douglas Page, "Picture This: Oak Ridge National Laboratory (ORNL) Has Developed a Police Shield That Doubles as a Video Camera," *Law Enforcement Technology* (June 1998):70.

39. "The Vanishing," *Government Technology* (July 1998):50.

40. "Utah Offers First Electric Bike School," *Law Enforcement Technology* (December 1998):36.

41. Jim McKay, "Emergency Contact," *Government Technology* (March 2002):38.

42. Thomas Cowper, "Improving the View of the World: Law Enforcement and Augmented Reality Technology," *FBI Law Enforcement Bulletin* (January 2004):13.

43. Ibid., p. 15.

44. Ibid., p. 16.

45. Chris Forsythe, "The Future of Simulation Technology for Law Enforcement: Diverse Experience with Realistic Simulated Humans," *FBI Law Enforcement Bulletin* (January 2004):19–21.

46. Brian P. Tice, "Unmanned Aerial Vehicles: The Force Multiplier of the 1990s," http://www.airpower.maxwell.af.mil/airchronicles/apj/4spr91.html (accessed January 17, 2004).

47. "UAV One—The Unmanned Aerial Vehicle Source," http://www.uav1.com/ (accessed January 17, 2004).

48. Tice, "Unmanned Aerial Vehicles."

49. Seth Hettena, "Military Developing Non-Lethal Weapons," Associated Press (March 24, 2002).

50. David J. Egar, *Electronic Filing*. Paper presented at the Fourth National Court Technology Conference, National Center for State Courts, Nashville, Tennessee, October 1994, p. 3.

51. Carter C. Cowles, "Document Imaging," *Court Technology Reports* 5 (1992):26–27.

52. National Center for State Courts, Knowledge and Information Services, "Videoconferencing Court Technology Briefing Paper," (1995), www.ncsonline.org/WC/Education/VidConGuide.htm 1995 (accessed September 20, 2005), p. 1.

53. Ibid.

54. Ibid., pp. 24–25.

55. Adapted from Webster, "How Technology Can Help Court Leaders," pp. 48–50.

56. Fredric I. Lederer, "Courtroom 21: A Model Courtroom of the 21st Century," *Court Technology Bulletin* **6**(1) (January/February 1994):1, 5.

57. Jim McKay, "Technology on Trial," *Government Technology* (December 2002):83.

58. Ibid.

59. Fredric I. Lederer, "The Courtroom 21 Project: Creating the Courtroom of the Twenty-First Century," *Judges' Journal* **43**(1)(Winter 2004):39–40.

60. Thomas Hayden, "Putting Down a Riot," *U.S. News and World Report* (June 14, 2004): 72–73.

61. Ibid.

62. Shane Peterson, "The Internet Moves behind Bars," *Government Technology* (Supplement: *Crime and the Tech Effect*) (April 2001):18.

63. Raymond Dussault, "Direct Supervision and Records Automation," *Government Technology*, **8** (August 1995):36.

64. Ibid., p. 37.

65. Jim McKay, "Virtual Visits," *Government Technology* (October 2001):46.

66. Jim McKay, "The Portland Connection," *Government Technology* (February 2004): 46, 48.

67. James Evans, "Kiosk Check In for Probationers," *Government Technology* **8** (May 1995):42.

68. Ibid., pp. 42, 44.

69. Drew Robb, "Spotlight on Biometrics," *Government Technology* (Supplement: *Crime and the Tech Effect*) (April 2002):10.

70. Dana Hawkins, "Body of Evidence," *U.S. News and World Report* (February 18, 2002):58.

71. Ibid.

# Appendix I

# Relevant Web Sites and Listservs

*360 Degrees: Perspectives on the Criminal Justice System*
http://www.360degrees.org
A collection of stories from inmates, correctional officers, lawyers, judges, parole officers, parents, victims, and others whose lives have been affected by the criminal justice system.

*The Administrative Office of the United States Courts*
http://www.uscourts.gov/adminoff.html
The administrative arm of the federal judiciary provides service to the federal courts in three essential areas: administrative support, program management, and policy development.

*American Bar Association (ABA)*
http://www.abanet.org
With more than 400,000 members, the ABA provides law school accreditation, continuing legal education, information about the law, programs to assist lawyers and judges in their work, and initiatives to improve the legal system for the public.

*American Correctional Association*
http://www.aca.org
The American Correctional Association is the oldest and largest correctional association in the world; it provides professional development, accreditation, consulting, publications, conferences, technology, and testing services

*American Judicature Society*
http://www.ajs.org
Primary areas of focus are judicial independence, ethics in the courts, judicial selection, the jury, court administration, and public understanding of the justice system.

*American Probation and Parole Association (APPA)*
http://www.appa-net.org

APPA is an international association composed of individuals from the United States and Canada actively involved with probation, parole, and community-based corrections in both adult and juvenile sectors.

*American Society for Industrial Security (ASIS)*
http://www.asisonline.org
ASIS is an international organization for professionals responsible for security, such as corporate managers, directors of security, consultants, and federal, state, and local law enforcement officials. ASIS publishes related articles and monographs.

*Bureau of Justice Statistics*
http://www.ojp.usdoj.gov/bjs
This agency is the primary U.S. source for criminal justice statistics. BJS collects, analyzes, publishes, and disseminates information on crime, offenders, crime victims, and the operation of justice systems. Numerous publications are available.

*Center for Law and Social Policy*
http://www.clasp.org
This site serves a nonprofit organization with expertise in both law and policy affecting the poor. The site has publications and an audio conferencing capability.

*Commission on Accreditation for Law Enforcement Agencies*
http://www.calea.org/
Its purpose is to improve the delivery of law enforcement service by offering a body of standards, developed by law enforcement practitioners, covering a wide range of up-to-date law enforcement topics.

*Community Policing Consortium*
http://www.communitypolicing.org
A partnership of five of the leading police organizations in the United States, it plays a principal role in the development of community policing research, training, and technical assistance.

*Computer and Internet Security Resources*
http://virtuallibrarian.com/legal
Collection of links to Web sites focusing on Internet security and privacy.

*Computer Security Institute*
http://www.gocsi.com
Computer Security Institute is a leading membership organization specifically dedicated to serving and training information, computer, and network security professionals.

*CopSeek.com*
http://www.copseek.com
Many links to law enforcement sites with a good search feature. Another excellent list of law enforcement agencies can be found at Just4Cops.

*Corrections Connection*
http://www.corrections.com
Voted a Microsoft "Outstanding Criminal Justice Site," the Corrections Connections provides links to almost every correctional organization in the country and to all kinds of corrections information. It contains more than 10,000 links to corrections-related sites and literature.

*Counterterrorist Organization Profiles*
http://www.terrorism.com/modules.php?op=modload&name=CTGroups&file=index
Information about those who combat terrorism worldwide.

*Court TV*

http://www.courttv.com

Court TV is a 24-hour-a-day, 7-day-a-week cable legal news network and cable programmer dedicated to reporting on the U.S. legal and judicial systems. This site provides information about their coverage, some with full text concerning the trials they cover.

*Courts.Net*

http://www.courts.net

This site has links to courts in all 50 states as well as federal courts.

*Crime Spider—A Crime and Justice Search Engine*

http://crimespider.com

A crime and justice Internet search engine offering information on a wide range of sites, including cybercrime, industrial espionage, detectives, domestic violence, private investigations, and criminalistics.

*Crime Theory.Com*

http://www.crimetheory.com

An educational resource for the learning and teaching of theoretical criminology.

*CrimeLynx—The Criminal Defense Practitioner's Guide through the Internet*

http://www.crimelynx.com

This site has a legal resource center with research links, links to experts, investigation links, and crime policy links. A criminal justice center with media links, shopping, and chat is also available on the site.

*Criminal Law Links*

http://www.findlaw.com/01topics/09criminal/

The Criminal Defense and Criminal Justice section of this leading legal portal site.

*Death Penalty Information Center (DPIC)*

http://www.deathpenaltyinfo.org

This site contains a wealth of information on the death penalty.

*Dumb Laws*

http://www.dumblaws.com

Dumb laws from all states and a wide variety of foreign jurisdictions are included. The site has the full text of many of the laws cited.

*Exploring Forensics. Evidence: The Silent Witness*

http://library.thinkquest.org/TQ0312020

An award-winning, student-created site about forensics.

*Federal Bureau of Prisons (BOP)*

http://www.bop.gov

The BOP oversees the federal prison system and endeavors to ensure that inmates are well prepared for a productive and crime-free return to society.

*Find Law*

http://www.findlaw.com

One of the leading law reference sites online.

*Global Bibliography of Prison Systems*

http://www.uncjin.org/country/GBOPS/gbops.html

Provides practitioners, scholars, and students with a comprehensive source for identifying written information on the prison system from as many countries of the world as possible.

*The Institute for Criminal Justice Ethics*

http://www.lib.jjay.cuny.edu/cje/html/policeethics.html

The only nonprofit, university-based center of its kind in the United States; established to foster greater concern for ethical issues among practitioners and scholars in the criminal justice field

*International Association of Chiefs of Police (IACP)*

http://www.theiacp.org

Established in 1893, the IACP is the world's oldest and largest organization of police executives, with 16,000 members; it launches programs, conducts research and training, and promulgates standards. Publishes *The Police Chief* monthly.

*JUSTINFO: The Newsletter of the National Criminal Justice Reference Service*

http://virlib.ncjrs.org/JUSTINFO.asp

Updates new publications, grants and funding opportunities, and other news and announcements; available by free subscription, e-mailed on the 1st and 15th of every month.

*Juvenile Justice Magazine Online*

http://www.juvenilejustice.com

Current issues of this bimonthly magazine are available.

*Law Enforcement Jobs*

http://www.lawenforcementjobs.com

Arguably the best site on the Web for anyone looking for employment in the law enforcement field, the site lists jobs with local, state, and federal agencies; the U.S. military; private security; associations; and schools. The site is free to job seekers, and allows one to post a resume and cover letter online and manage one's search online with a Job Seeker Account.

*Law Guru*

http://www.lawguru.com

An excellent legal search engine.

*Law Links*

http://www.counsel.com/lawlinks

This site assists with locating and contacting criminal defense and specialized attorneys.

*Law News Network*

http://www.law.com

A national daily newspaper for and about the legal profession. A service of American Lawyer Media, it describes itself as the most current and comprehensive legal news source anywhere.

*Law.com*

http://www.law.com

An excellent site for lawyers, students, and business and government officials to learn more about the law. Many legal resources, a legal dictionary, a careers service, and state-specific databases are available.

*LawCrawler*

http://lawcrawler.findlaw.com

One can search by keywords or relevant Web sites.

*'Lectric Law Library (The 'Lectric Law Library)*

http://www.lectlaw.com

An excellent collection of online legal materials and resources.

*Lexis ONE*
http://www.lexisone.com
An excellent free legal research site providing searchable case law, free legal forms, a statutory law guide, a legal Internet guide, and much more. The site is part of the Lexis-Nexis family of products.

*MegaLinks in Criminal Justice*
http://faculty.ncwc.edu/toconnor
A very comprehensive site with just about everything related to crime and law enforcement.

*National Association of Police Organizations (NAPO)*
http://www.napo.org
NAPO is a nationwide coalition of police unions and associations that serves to advance the interests of U.S. law enforcement officers through legislative and legal advocacy, political action, and education.

*National Center for Missing & Exploited Children*
http://www.missingkids.com
Contains information about missing children and children who have been abused or exploited.

*National Center for Policy Analysis*
http://www.ncpa.org/pi/crime/crime71.html
A site dedicated to probation, parole, sentencing, prison, and court issues.

*National Center for State Courts*
http://www.ncsconline.org
Organization providing support and assistance to state courts and their operation.

*National Center for Victims of Crime (formerly the National Victim Center)*
http://www.ncvc.org
Extensive online resource for victim information and advocacy. Contains many links and information about the organization's advocacy efforts.

*National Center for Women and Policing*
http://www.womenandpolicing.org/aboutus.asp
Promotes increasing the numbers of women at all ranks of law enforcement as a strategy for improving police response to violence against women, reducing police brutality and excessive force, and strengthening community policing reforms.

*National Clearinghouse for Alcohol and Drug Information (NCADI)*
http://www.health.org
The NCADI acts as an information services facility (English, Spanish, TDD capability) equipped to respond to the public's alcohol, tobacco, and drug (ATD) inquiries. It has publications and research material.

*National Council on Crime and Delinquency (NCCD)*
http://www.nccd-crc.org
Focus is on children as victims and perpetrators of crime and the needs of dependent children.

*National Crime Prevention Council*
http://www.ncpc.org
The mission is to enable people to create safer and more caring communities by addressing the causes of crime and violence and reducing the opportunities for crime to occur.

*National Criminal Justice Reference Service (NCJRS)*
http://www.ncjrs.org
A U.S. Department of Justice's site, which focuses on international, juvenile, and drug crimes. There is a database search engine and catalogs.

*National District Attorneys Association (NDAA)*
http://www.ndaa-apri.org
The goal of the NDAA is to be the voice of America's prosecutors and to support their efforts to protect the rights and safety of the public.

*National Institute of Justice (NIJ)*
http://www.ojp.usdoj.gov/nij
A component of the Office of Justice Programs, NIJ is the research agency of the Department of Justice. NIJ supports research, evaluation, and demonstration programs as well as the development of technology. Programs and publications are numerous.

*National Institute of Justice International Center*
http://www.ojp.usdoj.gov/nij/international
The Center seeks to facilitate, evaluate, and disseminate national and international criminal justice research and information. The Center's Virtual Library—a repository of information related to transnational crime and justice issues—is a key feature.

*National Judicial College (NJC)*
http://www.judges.org
NJC offers many different kinds of short courses for trial court and administrative law judges and court personnel, and cosponsors a Master's of Judicial Studies degree program.

*National Law Enforcement and Corrections Technology Center*
http://www.nlectc.org
This site publishes and distributes many free publications concerning computers and software, equipment of all types, weapons and ammunition, and communications.

*National Organization of Black Law Enforcement Executives (NOBLE)*
http://www.noblentl.org
NOBLE's mission is to ensure equity in the administration of justice in the provision of public service to all communities and to serve as the conscience of law enforcement by being committed to justice by action.

*National Security Institute—Computer Security Resources*
http://nsi.org/compsec.html
Many links to resources on computer and Internet security.

*National Sheriffs' Association*
http://www.sheriffs.org
Serving more than 20,000 sheriffs, deputies, jail administrators, corrections officials, court security officers, chiefs of police, and federal law enforcement agents, NSA provides training, information, and other services. Publishes *Sheriff* magazine monthly and other bulletins.

*National Youth Gang Center (NYGC)*
http://www.iir.com/nygc
Information on youth gangs including statistics and probable solutions.

*Office for Victims of Crime (OVC)*
http://www.ojp.usdoj.gov/ovc

U.S. Department of Justice site with information about crime victims and resources for crime victims. Contains an extensive collection of links to other relevant information.

*Office of Community-Oriented Policing Services (COPS)*
http://www.cops.usdoj.gov
Established by Congress with passage of the 1994 Violent Crime Control and Law Enforcement Act, this organization was authorized to spend $8.8 billion over 6 years for grants to add community policing officers to the streets and to advance community policing. COPS has a wide range of publications and related activities and programs.

*Office of Juvenile Justice and Delinquency Prevention (OJJDP)*
http://ojjdp.ncjrs.org
Provides information on grants, news, conferences, and publications.

*Office of National Drug Control Policy (ONDCP)*
http://www.whitehousedrugpolicy.gov
This agency serves as the central research and development organization in the U.S. government for counterdrug enforcement and drug abuse education, prevention, and treatment.

*Parents of Murdered Children (POMC)*
http://www.pomc.com
POMC is the only national organization that is specifically for the survivors of homicide victims; provides supportive family services after the murder of a family member or friend.

*Partnerships Against Violence (PAVNET)*
http://www.pavnet.org
PAVNET offers a library of information about violence and youth at risk, with data from seven federal agencies. Resources are shared through the Pavnet mailgroup.

*Patterns of Global Terrorism*
http://www.state.gov/s/ct/rls/pgtrpt
Annual reports since 1994 on the nature of terrorism and of U.S. response.

*Police Executive Research Forum (PERF)*
http://www.policeforum.org
PERF is an organization dedicated to improving policing and advancing professionalism through research, public policy debate, provision of management services and executive development training, and publishing.

*Police Foundation*
http://www.policefoundation.org
Conducts research in police behavior, policy, and procedure; defines, designs, conducts, and evaluates controlled experiments testing ways to improve the delivery of police services.

*Police Guide*
http://www.policeguide.com
One of the largest police sites on the Internet. The site consists of 238 separate Web pages, and is growing.

*Policy Action Network*
http://movingideas.org
A site dedicated to economic, political, domestic, health, and education issues.

*Preventing Crime, What Works, What Doesn't, What's Promising*
http://cjcentral.com/sherman/sherman.htm

Online copy of a report sponsored by the National Institute of Justice dealing with a review of crime prevention efforts in the United States. A "must read" for those with an interest in crime prevention programs.

*RAND Drug Policy Research Center*
http://www.rand.org/multi/dprc
RAND's goal is to conduct the empirical research, policy analysis, and outreach needed to help community leaders and public officials to develop more effective strategies for dealing with drug problems.

*Reintegrative Shaming Experiments*
http://www.aic.gov.au/rjustice/rise/index.html
Reports examine and present evidence from reintegrative shaming experiments (RISE) about the effects of diversionary restorative justice conferences on repeat offending.

*Royal Canadian Mounted Police (RCMP)*
http://www.rcmp-grc.gc.ca
This extensive site provides information on many of the facets of the RCMP organization.

*Sourcebook of Criminal Justice Statistics*
http://www.albany.edu/sourcebook
Home of the online version of the Sourcebook of Criminal Justice Statistics—the largest compilation of criminal justice statistics available anywhere. The Sourcebook site is updated continuously.

*Stop Prisoner Rape*
http://www.spr.org/index.html
A small but growing national nonprofit organization dedicated to combating the rape of male and female prisoners and to helping survivors of jailhouse rape.

*Supreme Court Opinions from the Legal Information Institute*
http://www.law.cornell.edu/focus/bulletins.html
Provides a free current awareness service via e-mail, distributing the syllabi of U.S. Supreme Court decisions in bulletin format within hours after their release.

*Talk Justice*
http://talkjustice.com
The nation's premier criminal justice discussion forum, offering a number of message boards; it is available to students, professors, professionals, and interested citizens.

*Technology and Privacy (Home Page of Gary T. Marx)*
http://web.mit.edu/gtmarx/www/garyhome.html
Professor Marx posts numerous articles on technology and privacy.

*Terrorism Documents*
http://www.terrorism.com/modules.php?op=modload&name=Downloads&file=index
Links to documents maintained by the Terrorism Research Center.

*Terrorist Group Profiles*
http://www.terrorism.com/modules.php?op=modload&name=TGroups&file=index
Profiles of terrorist groups maintained by the Terrorism Research Center.

*Terrorism Research Center*
http://www.terrorism.com
Many online resources dealing with terrorism, terrorist organizations, and antiterrorism efforts.

*U.S. Department of Justice*
http://www.usdoj.gov
A good starting point for research about federal law enforcement and crime data.

*U.S. Department of State: Patterns of Global Terrorism Reports (1994-2000)*
http://www.state.gov/www/global/terrorism/annual_reports.html
Text of the State Department's analysis of global terrorism. Brief discussion of terrorist acts and organizations and discussion of antiterrorist initiatives.

*U.S. Supreme Court*
http://supct.law.cornell.edu/supct
Provides full texts of cases.

*U.S. Supreme Court*
http://www.supremecourtus.gov
A round-the-clock access to the U.S. Supreme Court, this site provides public access to the Court's decisions, argument calendar, schedules, rules, visitors' guides, building photos, and bar admission forms.

*Uniform Crime Reports (UCR)*
http://www.fbi.gov/ucr/ucr.htm
The most recent crime reports collected by the FBI and made available to the public.

*United Nations Human Rights Web Site*
http://www.ohchr.org/english
This site focuses on the functioning of the United Nations system in the field of human rights. They have publications and press releases.

*University of Phoenix*
http://online.uophx.edu/onlinebiz/index.html
Offers a comprehensive and fully accredited distance-learning Bachelor of Science degree in Criminal Justice Administration. Designed for the working professional, courses can be designed to fit students' schedules.

*Vera Institute of Justice*
http://www.vera.org
Working in collaboration with government, the Vera Institute of Justice designs and implements innovative programs that encourage just practices in public services and improve the quality of urban life.

*Versus Law*
http://www.versuslaw.com
Subscription-based service allowing search of federal and state case law.

*Victims' Information*
http://virlib.ncjrs.org/VictimsOfCrime.asp
Extensive collection of information about victims of crime.

*White House's Social Statistics Briefing Room on Crime Data*
http://www.whitehouse.gov/fsbr/crime.html
Collection of selected data concerning crime in the United States.

*World Wide Web Security FAQ*
http://www.w3.org/Security/Faq/www-security-faq.html
Very useful resource for anyone with, or considering, a Web site.

Listservs

*Amnesty International*
Global views on human rights, government, child abuse, and criminal statistics. To subscribe, send a message "AMNESTY" to listserv@suvm.syr.edu.

*Center for Disease Control and Prevention (CDC)*
MMWR-toc (Morbidity Mortality Weekly Report Statistical Bulletin). To subscribe, send a message "subscribe mmwr-toc" to lists@list.cdc.gov.

*Criminal Justice Discussion List (CJUST-L)*
A forum for the free and open discussion of criminal justice issues and problems, theoretical or real. To subscribe, send a message "subscribe cjust-l firstname lastname" to listserv@cunyvm.cuny.edu.

*Domestic Preparedness Support Listserv*
http://odp.ncjrs.org/content/subscribe.asp.

*Future Law Discussion (FUTUREL)*
To subscribe, send a message "subscribe futurel firstname lastname" to listserv@vm.temple.edu. If there are problems, e-mail Richard Klein at rklein@vm.temple.edu.

*Journal of Criminal Justice and Popular Culture (CJMOVIES)*
Publishes reviews of all types of popular culture artifacts and original essays pertaining to the intersection of popular culture and criminal justice. To subscribe, send a message "subscribe cjmovies firstname lastname" to listserv@albany.edu.

*JUSTINFO electronic newsletter (National Criminal Justice Reference Service)*
http://www.ncjrs.gov/justinfo/dates.html

*National American Indian Court Judges Association (NAICJA) Listserv*
This listserv was established exclusively for active tribal judges to facilitate electronic announcements by NAICJA and confidential interchanges among tribal judges about pending matters or other sensitive subjects. To subscribe, send a message to NAICJA@TribalResourceCenter.org. In the subject line enter SUBSCRIBE.

*National Association of Blacks in Criminal Justice (e-newsletter)*
http://www.nabcj.org/listserve.html
The National Association of Blacks in Criminal Justice seeks to focus attention on relevant legislation, law enforcement, prosecution, and defense-related needs and practices, with emphasis on the courts, corrections, and the prevention of crime. Among its chief concerns is the general welfare and increased influence of African Americans and people of color as it relates to the administration of justice.

*Research Methods Discussion List*
To subscribe, send a message "subscribe METHODS" to comserv@vm.its.rpi.edu.

*Tribal Court Clearinghouse—Tribal Children's Justice Act*
General discussion on topics pertaining to Tribal Children's Justice Act programs. To subscribe, send a message "subscribe CJAlistserve firstname_lastname" to imailsrv@tribal-institute.org.

*Tribal Court Clearinghouse—Tribal Healing to Wellness Court Listserv*
To subscribe, send a message "subscribe RFPlistserve your_name" to TLPIWellness-crts@tribal-institute.org.

*Victims of Trafficking and Violence Protection Act of 2000; Trafficking in Persons Report, U.S. Department of State, 2005*
http://www.ncjrs.org/spotlight/trafficking/summary.html

*Weekly United Nations News (UN-NEWS)*
To subscribe, send a message "subscribe un-news firstname lastname" to listserv@ unmvma.unm.edu.

*White House Summaries (WH-SUMMARY)*
To subscribe, send a message "subscribe wh-summary e-mail-address" to majordomo@reeusda.gov.

# Appendix II

# Writings of Confucius, Machiavelli, and Lao-Tzu

The writings of certain major figures have stood the test of time. The analects of Confucius (551–479 BCE) and the teachings of Machiavelli (1469–1527) are still quite popular today. Many graduate and undergraduate students in a variety of academic disciplines analyze the writings of both, especially Machiavelli's *The Prince*. Both men tend to agree on many points regarding the means of governance, as the following will demonstrate. After presenting some comments from each philosopher, I will consider their application to justice administration.

Confucius often emphasized the connection between morality and leadership, saying, for example,

> He who rules by moral force is like the pole-star, which remains in its place while all the lesser stars do homage to it. Govern the people by regulations, keep order among them by chastisements, and they will flee from you, and lose all self-respect. Govern them by moral force, keep order among them ... and they will ... come to you of their own accord. If the ruler is upright, all will go well even though he does not give orders. But if he himself is not upright, even though he gives orders, they will not be obeyed.[1]

Confucius also commented on the leader's treatment of subordinates: "Promote those who are worthy, train those who are incompetent; that is the best form of encouragement."[2] He also felt that leaders should learn from and emulate good administrators:

> In the presence of a good man, think all the time how you may learn to equal him. In the presence of a bad man, turn your gaze within! Even when I am walking in a party of no more than three I can always be certain of learning from those I am with.

> There will be good qualities that I can select for imitation and bad ones that will
> teach me what requires correction in myself.[3]

Unlike Confucius, Machiavelli is often maligned for being cruel; the "ends justifies the means" philosophy imputed to him has cast a pall over his writings.
However, although he often seems as biting as the "point of a stiletto"[4] and at
times ruthless ("Men ought either to be caressed or destroyed, since they will
seek revenge for minor hurts but will not be able to revenge major ones,"[5] and
"If you have to make a choice, to be feared is much safer than to be loved"[6]) he,
like Confucius, often spoke of the leader's need to possess character and compassion. For all of his blunt, management-oriented notions of administration,
Machiavelli was prudent and pragmatic.

Like Confucius, Machiavelli felt that administrators would do well to follow
examples set by other great leaders:

> Men almost always prefer to walk in paths marked out by others and pattern their
> actions through imitation. A prudent man should always follow the footsteps of the
> great and imitate those who have been supreme. A prince should read history and
> reflect on the actions of great men.[7]

Machiavelli's counsel also agreed with that of Confucius with regard to the need
for leaders to surround themselves with persons both knowledgeable and devoted: "The first notion one gets of a prince's intelligence comes from the men
around him."[8]

But, again, like Confucius, Machiavelli believed that administrators should be
careful of their subordinates' ambition and greed:

> A new prince must always harm those over whom he assumes authority. You cannot
> stay friends with those who put you in power, because you can never satisfy them as
> they expected. The man who makes another powerful ruins himself. The reason is
> that he gets power either by shrewdness or by strength, and both qualities are sus-
> pect to the man who has been given the power.[9]

On the need for developing and maintaining good relations with subordinates,
he wrote:

> If ... a prince ... puts his trust in the people, knows how to command, is a man of
> courage and doesn't lose his head in adversity, and can rouse his people to action by
> his own example and orders, he will never find himself betrayed, and his founda-
> tions will prove to have been well laid. The best fortress of all consists in not being
> hated by your people. Every prince should prefer to be considered merciful rather
> than cruel. The prince must have people well disposed toward him; otherwise in
> times of adversity there's no hope.[10]

In this era of collective bargaining and a rapidly changing workforce, contemporary criminal justice administrators might do well to heed the comments of Confucius and Machiavelli.

Perhaps a leader, in the purest sense, also influences others by example.
This characteristic of leadership was recognized in the sixth century BCE by Lao-
Tzu, who wrote,

The superior leader gets things done
With very little motion.
He imparts instruction not through many words
But through a few deeds.
He keeps informed about everything
But interferes hardly at all.
He is a catalyst.
And although things wouldn't get done as well
If he weren't there.
When they succeed he takes no credit.
And because he takes no credit
Credit never leaves him.[11]

## Notes

1. Confucius, *The Analects of Confucius,* Arthur Waley (trans.) (London: George Allen and Unwin, 1938), pp. 88, 173.
2. Ibid., p. 92.
3. Ibid., pp. 105, 127.
4. Niccolo Machiavelli, *The Prince,* Robert M. Adams (trans.) (New York: W.W. Norton, 1992), p. xvii.
5. Ibid., p. 7.
6. Ibid., p. 46.
7. Ibid., pp. 15, 41.
8. Ibid., p. 63.
9. Ibid., pp. 5, 11.
10. Ibid., pp. 29, 60.
11. Quoted in Wayne W. Bennett and Karen M. Hess, *Management and Supervision in Law Enforcement,* 3rd ed. (Belmont, Calif.: Wadsworth, 2001), p. 63.

# INDEX